GREAT
LITERATURE
OF THE
EASTERN WORLD

GREAT LITERATURE OF THE EASTERN WORLD

The major works of prose, poetry and drama
from China, India, Japan, Korea and the Middle East

EDITED BY IAN P. MCGREAL

HarperCollins *Publishers*

HarperCollins books may be purchased for educational, business, or sales promotional use. For information,
please write to: Special Markets Department, HarperCollins Publishers, Inc., 10 East 53rd Street,
New York, New York 10022.

FIRST EDITION
Designed by Irving Perkins Associates

Library of Congress Cataloging-in-Publication Data

Great literature of the Eastern World / Ian McGreal, editor.

p.   cm.

Includes bibliographical references.

ISBN 0-06-270104-5

1. Oriental literature—History and criticism.   I. McGreal, Ian P., 1919–

PJ307.G74   1996

895—dc20   95-26313

CIP

97 98 99 00 PS/RRD 10 9 8 7 6 5 4 3 2

CONTENTS

India

Japan

Korea

Middle East

PREFACE

Great Literature of the Eastern World is composed of descriptive essays on over 100 of the most noteworthy literary works of China, India, Japan, Korea, and the Middle East. The book serves as a guide to works essential to an understanding and appreciation of Eastern culture.

The novels, short stories, poetry, essays, and drama of the great nations of the Middle and Far East express a distinctive perspective on the human condition and experience in a part of the world that remains an entrancing enigma to most of the Western world.

In this great body of literature we find an acknowledgment of the vulnerability of human life in a universe of physical, moral, and spiritual forces that operates according to an organic system of principles and laws. At the same time those who have achieved some degree of enlightenment through reflections on the meaning and quality of human experience emphasize the power of the individual person to control the will, to discipline the self, and to open the spirit to the beauty of the world.

But despite an intellectual and spiritual sophistication that is pervasive in the Eastern world, there are individual differences in both experience and perspective that reflect the creative richness of the human species. These differences are discernible in the philosophies of the East (previously explored in *Great Thinkers of the Eastern World*) but perhaps even more clearly and vividly in the poetry, fiction, and drama of Asia. It is as if the great Eastern writers were attempting to say that whatever may be true of us all, each person is unique in the universe and this uniqueness shows itself in the imagery of literature, and in the enduring portraits of precise moments of sensitivity, passion, and expectation.

For the majority of Western readers, the striking imagery, illuminating insights, and human drama of Eastern literature can be grasped and appreciated only as if through a glass darkly—that is, by way of translations. Some are tempted on that account to turn away from the great literature of Asia on the ground that it is forever inaccessible to those who do not know Chinese, Sanskrit, Pali, Japanese, Korean, Arabic, or Persian. And then, of course, there are those who are satisfied to know a few of the tales from *The Arabian Nights*—it doesn't especially matter if they are in translation—and a few of the verses from Fitzgerald's *Rubaiyat of Omar Khayyam*. The poetry may not be entirely faithful to the original but at least the lines awaken a romantic dream in the Westerner: to live a life removed from the trials of daily life by making do with a glass of wine, a loaf of bread, and an attractive and compliant companion.

But the liberating truth is that there are excellent translations of most of the Eastern classics and modern works, translations composed by persons who know the original languages and accordingly grasp the associations that give depth and breadth to lines of poetry, scenes of drama, the characters in a novel, and the persuasive utterances of literary essays. By turning to the translations, one is given the gift of entrance into a world that is not only exotic but rewarding, not only pervaded by a wisdom that has worldwide relevance but made vital by the passions of persons like oneself.

Accordingly, *Great Literature of the Eastern World* not only provides descriptions of the content and meaning of the most famous works of Asian literature—through essays written by scholars who have specialized in studying the literature they write about, many of whom are themselves translators—but also calls attention to translations and related works that are accessible to Western

readers and make possible through their own reading the enjoyment of the literature as sensitively
and intelligently translated.

Some of the Eastern classics that one might expect to find in *Great Literature of the Eastern World*
are not here but only because they are philosoph-
ical/religious works prominently featured in this
book's predecessor, *Great Thinkers of the Eastern
World* (also edited by Ian P. McGreal and published
in Fall, 1992, by HarperCollins). *Great Thinkers of
the Eastern World* emphasizes *ideas* and their place
in philosophical and religious perspectives; the
present volume concerns itself with the *expression
of human experience* through literature—through
the use of images, recitals of significant events or
moments, and reflection on what has happened in
life.

Some works, of course, are borderline or, perhaps one should say, of two literary worlds: the
world of ideas, and the world of experience (as, to
some degree, all literary works are). Accordingly,
in *Great Thinkers of the Eastern World*, for example, there is an essay on *Yi Jing* (*I Ching*), or the
Book of Changes, that emphasizes the philosophical ideas of that masterpiece, while in the present
volume, the *Book of Changes* is treated as a literary
expression of experiences leading to philosophical
insights.

There are a few other cases of classic works dealt
with in both books—but there are no duplications
of essays or even of scholars discussing a particular
work. We decided that it is better to have a work
like the *Bhagavad Gita* discussed in both books, but
by different scholars and from different perspectives, than to force a complete division that falsifies
the range of values exemplified by certain classic
works.

A few words about the presentation of material
in this book:

The Chinese terms and names used in this book
are in the Pinyin form of romanization, with the
Wade-Giles version given in parentheses after the
Pinyin. This will be helpful for those using indexes

and catalogs that were written before the Pinyin
came into common use.

An attempt has been made to minimize the use of
diacritical marks in articles in the Indian, Japanese,
Korean, and Middle East sections; sometimes the
diacritical marks are used when a name or term is
first used, but not afterwards; sometimes the diacritical marks (as with Japanese names employing
the bar over certain letters) are used throughout
articles because of a strong convention; sometimes,
as with names that have become familiar without
the diacritical marks, the marks are omitted. For
the most part, however, the editor has attempted to
follow the preferences shown by the contributors of
articles.

Perhaps it is common knowledge by now that
Chinese and Japanese names (unless transposed for
use in English-speaking contexts) have the family
name first; the given name, second: for example, Li
Bo (Li Po), where Li is the family name. The *zi*
(*tzu*) element in some Chinese names, as in Laozi
(Lao Tzu) is neither a family nor a given name; it is
an honorific term, roughly translatable as "master." A sometimes confusing practice is that of
referring to Japanese writers by their given names
alone; this is a scholarly tradition that continues to
be practiced although it is not universal.

The selection of literary works to be included as
subjects of discussion in this book was made by the
editor after consulting extensively with contributors to this book and with other scholars and by
reviewing a number of bibliographies and tables of
contents of anthologies and studies of Asian literature. We have done our best, both in the selection of
works to be discussed and in the essays written
about them, but there will be differences of opinion
about the final contents; this is to be expected,
perhaps even to be welcomed. What is important is
that serious attention has been given here to a body
of great literature that deserves to become part of
everyone's experience.

Ian P. McGreal

ACKNOWLEDGMENTS

Great Literature of the Eastern World would not have been possible without the availability and use of hundreds of excellent source books, reference works, and critical commentaries, including specifically those that are cited in the "Further Reading" sections of the articles written expressly for this book. We acknowledge with respectful appreciation the use of these works.

Among the works that have been especially helpful to the editor in the preparation of this volume, in addition to the source books and reference works cited at the ends of the articles, are the following:

A Guide to Oriental Classics, 3rd edition. Edited by Wm. Theodore de Bary, Ainslie Embree, and Amy Vladeck Heinrich. New York: Columbia University Press, 1989.

Sources of Chinese Tradition. Introduction to Oriental Civilizations, Wm. Theodore de Bary, series editor. Compiled by Wm. Theodore de Bary, Wing-tsit Chan, and Burton Watson. With contributions by Yi-pao Mei, Leon Hurvitz, T'ung-tsu Ch'u, Chester Tan, and John Meskill. New York: Columbia University Press, 1960.

Sources of Indian Tradition. Introduction to Oriental Civilizations, Wm. Theodore de Bary, series editor. Volume 1: *From the Beginning to 1800,* edited and revised by Ainslie T. Embree. Volume 2: *Modern India and Pakistan,* edited and revised by Stephen Hay. New York: Columbia University Press, 1988.

Sources of Japanese Tradition. Introduction to Oriental Civilizations. Wm. Theodore de Bary, series editor. Volume 1. Compiled by Ryusaku Tsunoda, Wm. Theodore de Bary, and Donald Keene. New York: Columbia University Press, 1985.

The Cambridge Encyclopedia of China. Brian Hook, editor; Denis Twitchett, Consultant Editor. Second edition. Cambridge: Cambridge University Press, 1991.

We wish also to acknowledge with our appreciation and thanks the granting of permission from the following publishers for the reprinting of material from copyrighted books:

In the article "The *Book of Poetry,*" material from *A Source Book in Chinese Philosophy,* translated and compiled by Wing-tsit Chan. Copyright © 1963, Princeton University Press.

In the article "The Poetry of Tao Yuanming," material from *T'ao Yüan-ming: His Works and Their Meaning,* Vol. 1, by A. R. Davis. Copyright © 1983, Hong Kong University Press. Reprinted with the permission of Cambridge University Press.

In the article "The Poetry of Wang Wei," material from *Poems of Wang Wei* by G. W. Robinson. Harmondsworth, Middlesex, England: Penguin Books, 1973. Copyright © 1973 by G. W. Robinson. Reproduced by permission of Frederick Warne & Co.

In the article "The Poetry of Li Bo (Li Po)," material from *Li Po and Tu Fu* by Arthur Cooper. Harmondsworth, Middlesex, England: Penguin Books, 1973. Copyright © 1973 by Arthur Cooper. Reproduced by permission of Frederick Warne & Co.

In the article "The Poetry of Hanshan," material from *The Poetry of Han-shan* by Robert G. Henricks. Copyright © 1990, State University of New York Press. Reprinted by permission of the State University of New York Press.

In the article "*Treasury of Well-Turned Verses,*" material from *An Anthology of Sanskrit Court Poetry* by Daniel H. H. Ingalls. Cambridge: Harvard University Press, 1965. Copyright © 1965 by the President and Fellows of Harvard College.

In the article "The Poetry of Ghalib," material from *The Ghazals of Ghalib* by Aijaz Ahmad. Copyright © 1972 by Columbia University Press. Reprinted with permission of the publisher. And material from *The Golden Tradition* by Ali Ahmed. Copyright © 1973 by Columbia University Press. Reprinted with permission of the publisher.

In the article "*Gita Govinda*," material from *Love Song of the Dark Lord: Jayadeva's Gitagovinda* by Barbara Stoler Miller. Copyright © 1977 by Columbia University Press. Reprinted with permission of the publisher.

CONTRIBUTORS

Sonja Arntzen (*Ph.D., University of British Columbia*). Associate Professor, East Asian Studies, University of Alberta, Edmonton, Canada.

William G. Boltz (*Ph.D., University of California, Berkeley*). Associate Professor, Department of Asian Languages and Literatures, University of Washington, Seattle, Washington.

Robert Alan Burns (*Ph.D., University of New Brunswick, Canada*). Associate Professor, Division of English and Applied Linguistics, University of Guam, Mangilao, Guam.

Pierre Cachia (*Ph.D. University of Edinburgh*). Professor Emeritus of Middle East and Asian Languages and Literatures, Columbia University.

Michael F. Carson (*Ph.D., University of Washington*). Professor, Department of English and Biblical Languages, Taiwan Adventist College, Nantou County, Taiwan.

Narayan Champawat (*Ph.D., University of California, Los Angeles*). Professor of Philosophy Emeritus, California State University, Northridge, California.

Linda H. Chance (*Ph.D., University of California, Los Angeles*). Assistant Professor, Department of Asian and Middle Eastern Studies, University of Pennsylvania, Philadelphia, Pennsylvania.

Rececca L. Copeland (*Ph.D., Columbia University*). Assistant Professor, Department of Asian and Near Eastern Languages and Literatures, Washington University, St. Louis, Missouri.

Nina Cornyetz (*Ph.D., Columbia University*). Assistant Professor, Department of East Asian Languages and Cultures, Rutgers University, New Brunswick, New Jersey.

Dick Davis (*Ph.D., University of Manchester, U.K.*). Associate Professor of Persian, University of Ohio, Columbus, Ohio.

David Earhart (*Master of Comparative Culture, Sophia University*). Staff, Rissho Kosei-kai, Tokyo, Japan.

Jeannette L. Faurot (*Ph.D., University of California, Berkeley*). Professor of Chinese, Department of Oriental and African Languages and Literatures, University of Texas, Austin, Texas.

Stephen L. Field (*Ph.D., University of Texas at Austin*). Associate Professor, Department of Modern Languages and Literatures, Trinity University, San Antonio, Texas.

Ferial J. Ghazoul (*Ph.D., Columbia University*). Professor, Department of English and Comparative Literature, American University in Cairo, Cairo, Egypt.

Bina Gupta (*Ph.D., Southern Illinois University*). Professor of Philosophy; Director, South Asia Language and Area Center, University of Missouri, Columbia, Missouri.

James M. Hargett (*Ph.D., Indiana University*). Associate Professor and Chair, Department of East Asian Studies, State University of New York, Albany, New York.

Barbara Harlow (*Ph.D., State University of New York, Buffalo*). Professor, Department of English, University of Texas, Austin, Texas.

Dennis Hirota Author and editor. Head Translator, Shin Buddhism Translation Series, Kyoto; Adjunct Professor, Institute of Buddhist Studies, Berkeley, California.

Lawrence F. Hundersmarck (*Ph.D., Fordham University*). Professor, Department of Philosophy and Religious Studies, Pace University, White Plains, New York.

Kichung Kim (*Ph.D., University of California, Berkeley*). Professor, Department of English, San Jose State University, San Jose, California.

Russell Kirkland (*Ph.D., Indiana University*). Associate Professor, Department of Religion, University of Georgia, Athens, Georgia.

Faye Yuan Kleeman (*Ph.D., University of California, Berkeley*). Assistant Professor, Department of Literatures and Language, University of California, Riverside, California.

David R. Knechtges (*Ph.D., University of Washington*). Professor of Chinese, Department of Asian Languages and Literatures, University of Washington, Seattle, Washington.

Ko Won (Sung-Won Ko) (*Ph.D., New York University*). Instructor, Department of English and Foreign Languages, University of La Verne, La Verne, California.

Kenneth G. Koziol (*M.A., Indiana University*). Editor, Institute for Nonprofit Organization Management, University of San Francisco, San Francisco, California.

Jon LaCure (*Ph.D., Indiana University*). Assistant Professor, Department of Romance and Asian Languages and Literatures, University of Tennessee, Knoxville, Tennessee.

Krishna Lahiri (*Ph.D., University of Pennsylvania*). Language Minority Program, School District of Philadelphia, Pennsylvania.

Peter H. Lee (*Ph.D., University of Munich*). Professor and Chair, Department of East Asian Languages and Cultures, University of California, Los Angeles, California.

Philip Lutgendorf (*Ph.D., University of Chicago*). Associate Professor, Department of Asian Languages and Literature, University of Iowa, Iowa City, Iowa.

Aminah Beverly McCloud (*Ph.D., Temple University*). Assistant Professor of Islamic Studies, Department of Religious Studies, De Paul University, Chicago, Illinois.

Ian P. McGreal (*Ph.D., Brown University*). Professor of Philosophy Emeritus, California State University, Sacramento, California.

Marvin Marcus (*Ph.D., University of Michigan*). Associate Professor of Japanese, Department of Asian and Near Eastern Languages and Literatures, Washington University, St. Louis, Missouri.

Stephen D. Miller (*Ph.D., University of California, Los Angeles*). Assistant Professor, Department of Oriental Languages and Literatures, University of Colorado, Boulder, Colorado.

Carol Anne Morley (*Ph.D., Columbia University*). Associate Professor of Japanese, Japanese Program, Wellesley College, Wellesley, Massachusetts.

Katsuyo Motoyoshi (*M.A., Columbia University*). Independent scholar.

Wenchin Ouyang (*Ph.D., University of Virginia*). Assistant Professor, Department of Asian and Middle Eastern Languages, University of Virginia.

Prabhjot Parmar (*M.A., Panjab University, Chandigarh, India*). Independent Scholar.

Laurel Rasplica Rodd (*Ph.D., University of Michigan*). Professor of Japanese, Chair, Department of East Asian Languages and Literatures, University of Colorado, Boulder, Colorado.

Pargol Saati (*M.A., Columbia University*). Independent scholar.

Richard Salomon (*Ph.D., University of Pennsylvania*). Professor, Department of Asian Languages and Literatures, University of Washington, Seattle, Washington.

James D. Sellmann (*Ph.D., University of Hawaii*). Assistant Professor, Department of Philosophy, University of Guam, Mangilao, Guam.

Michael A. Sells (*Ph.D., University of Chicago*). Associate Professor, Department of Religion, Haverford College, Haverford, Pennsylvania.

Richard H. Shek (*Ph.D., University of California, Berkeley*). Professor, Department of Humanities, California State University, Sacramento, California.

Kim Skoog (*Ph.D., University of Hawaii*). Associate Professor, Division of Humanistic Studies, University of Guam, Mangilao, Guam.

Frederick M. Smith (*Ph.D., University of Pennsylvania*). Assistant Professor, Department of Asian Languages and Literatures, University of Iowa, Iowa City, Iowa.

Richard J. Smith (*Ph.D., University of California, Davis*). Professor, Department of History, Rice University, Houston, Texas.

S. E. Solberg (*Ph.D., University of Washington*). American Ethnic Studies, Comparative Literature, University of Washington.

Virginia Skord Waters (*Ph.D., Cornell University*). Assistant Professor, Department of Asian Studies, Manhattanville College, Purchase, New York.

Fatima Wu (*Ph.D., University of Southern California*). Assistant Professor, Department of Asian and Pacific Studies, Loyola Marymount University, Los Angeles, California.

CHINA

THE *BOOK OF POETRY*

Title in Chinese: *Shijing* (*Shih Ching*) (Sometimes translated as the *Book of Songs* or the *Book of Odes*)
Authors: Unknown.
Literary Form: Anthology of China's earliest poems and songs
Dates of Composition: Poems date from tenth to sixth centuries B.C.; believed to have been edited by Confucius (d. 479 B.C.)

Major Themes

Virtuous wives and husbands are happier than those who are faithless.
The life of the soldier involves suffering for both the soldier and his family; but if he is heroic all are served.
Human beings live in a moral universe; the universe is morally indifferent.
We must praise the ancestors through ritual sacrifice.
Earthly rulers should obey the Emperor on High and hold fast to Heaven's mandate.
The elderly should be respected and honored.

In the *Analects*, it is related that Confucius likened life without a study of the *Book of Poetry* to facing a brick wall. Of all the world's ancient civilizations, the Chinese produced more historical and poetic literature than any other culture. The focus of the ancient Chinese literary mind was on the historical moral lessons concerning the sage kings and tyrants, lessons that were often recited in the highest cultural forms of poetic verse. But poetry was also occupied with expressing the values of daily life, usually through the use of significant imagery.

The poems of the *Book of Poetry* are employed not as an escape from reality but as a record and celebration of historical, seasonal, and daily events. The fantastic and escapist elements of poetry are not represented in the *Book of Poetry*, but develop later in the Zhou (Chou) dynasty (c. 1122–221 B.C.), as in the *Li Sao* of Qu Yuan (Ch'ü Yüan) (343–278 B.C.).

Tradition has it that originally there were over 3,000 poems, which Confucius, according to legend, edited down to the 310 he regarded as most noteworthy. (The collection has traditionally been referred to as the "Three Hundred.")

The *Book of Poetry* (or *Songs*, or *Odes*) is one of the five Confucian classics, along with the *Book of History*, the *Book of Changes*, and the *Book of Ritual*, and *The Spring and Autumn Annals* (which records the history of Confucius's home state of Lu). These five classics served as the basis of a "Confucian" education, and the state civil service examination system until the Song (Sung) dynasty (A.D. 960–1279). The philosophy of Zhu Xi (Chu Hsi) (1130–1200) won influence among the literati, who turned the exam's focus to the "Four Books": the *Analects*, the *Mencius*, the *Great Learning*, and the *Doctrine of the Mean*. Originally there were six classics, but the *Book of Music* was lost in antiquity—some lists supplant it with the *Rites of Zhou* (*Chou*).

The classics other than the *Book of Poetry* pertain to practical matters and political affairs of state. Why, then, would a book of poetry be included in the Confucian classics? This question is actually posed in the *Analects*, and Confucius replies that a study of the poems will give one a good grasp of language and make one aware of the names of the flora and fauna. An important part of education, according to the Confucian theory, is to become a person of letters, to become educated. As a man of letters, the Confucian gentleman was supposed to be not only the moral exemplar of the Confucian virtues, but also one who never tires of teaching and learning. As such, the Confucian gentleman was expected to be an accomplished calligrapher, painter, and poet.

In the *Analects*, Confucius praises the *Book of Poetry* for its educational value:

The Master said, "Why is it none of you, my young friends, study the *Odes*? An apt quotation from the *Odes* may serve to stimulate the imagination, to show one's breeding, to smooth over difficulties in a group and to give expression to complaints.

"[The *Odes* teach us that:] Inside the family there is the serving of one's father; outside, there is the serving of one's lord; there is also the acquiring of a wide knowledge of the names of birds and beasts, plants and trees."

(LAU, 1986)

Of all the long standing literate cultures, the Chinese certainly take first place in preserving the traditional poetic literature, which especially flourished in the Tang dynasty (618–907) and is rooted in the classics of poetry. In *Sunflower Splendor* (see Further Reading), W.C. Liu and I.Y. Lo note five differences between Chinese and European poetry. First, the Chinese tradition, beginning with the *Book of Poetry*, is a 3,000-year-old tradition. Second, Chinese poetry, from its inception, is closely linked with music; the *Book of Poetry* is made up of ballads, folk songs, songs for court banquets, ritual hymns, poems in praise of wise rulers, love songs, and war songs. The third relates to poetry's musical nature and the monosyllabic character of classical Chinese: ". . . the rhythmic quality of Chinese verse is based . . . (except for ancient poetry) on a patterned alteration of words of different tone or pitch." Fourth, Chinese poetry is very compact and often omits the subject of the sentence. Finally, Chinese poetry knows no social classes; traditionally, it has been written by people from all walks of life. Generally speaking, the poems of the *Book of Poetry* predominately consist of four characters per line with an end rhyme; they also contain internal rhymes, alliteration, assonance, and onomatopoeia.

The *Book of Poetry* was spared the fires of the infamous "Burning of the Books" during the Qin (Ch'in) Dynasty in 213 B.C. Because it was classified as poetry, it was not perceived as an explicit threat to political and philosophical doctrine.

Realities of the Human Condition

The contents of the *Book of Poetry* are varied. The ballads, folk songs, and ritual ceremonial hymns comprise a wide array of material: love poems, and poems of daily pleasures, hardships, and anxieties. When the poems take on political topics, they praise proper government or direct satires against misrule. The poems also describe a variety of human affairs; there are poems of war and the soldier's life, peasant folk songs, harvest songs, love poems and wedding songs, and poems about official court sacrificial ritual. And, of course, a number of poems deal with ancestor veneration.

The *Book of Poetry* has inspired the Chinese spirit for nearly 3,000 years because it depicts the perennial realities of the human condition. "A Simple Rustic You Seemed," for example, expresses a woman's lament over the double standard by which men and women are judged:

> Before shedding from the mulberry tree,
> How glossy green the leaves are!
> Alas, you turtledove,
> Eat not the mulberries!
> Alas, you women
> Do not dally with men!
> When a man dallies,
> He will still be pardoned;
> But when a woman dallies,
> No pardon will she have.

A few lines later the poem continues, relating the hardships experienced by women in all ages:

> Three years I was your wife,
> I never tired of household chores.
> Early I rose and late I went to bed;
> Not a morning was I without work.
> First you found fault with me,
> Then treated me with violence.
> My brothers, not knowing this,
> Jeered and laughed at me.
> Quietly I brood over it
> And myself I pity.

(WU-CHI LIU, TR., LIU AND LO, 1975)

Although nearly 3,000 years old, this poem captures the plight of women oppressed by a double standard where excuses can be made for men, but women are discarded in divorce.

The Moral and Indifferent Universe

The poems are diverse in nature and some present contradictory world views. Many poems declare that humans live in a moral universe, and ring true to the later teachings of Confucius and Mencius; but the text is not consistent. Some poems propose that the universe is morally indifferent to human concerns and human behavior. Such poems reflect a non-anthropocentric, non-moral, naturalistic universe consistent with the later teachings of Laozi (Lao Tzu) or Xunzi (Hsün Tzu).

Many of the poems celebrate ideas and activities that would later become important elements of the Confucian tradition; they encourage moral training by developing one's self-cultivation through veneration of the ancestors, the Emperor on High, and the natural cycles of heaven:

Abundant is the year, with much millet and much
    rice,
And we have tall granaries,
With hundreds of thousands and millions of units.
We make wine and sweet spirits
And offer them to our ancestors, male and female,
Thus to fulfill all the rites,
And bring down blessings to all.

                    (CHAN, 1969)

Respect for the ancestors, and especially for the Emperor on High, was tied to the concern of maintaining political power by securing the mandate of Heaven. The king's exercise of virtue in ruling was a sign that he held the mandate of Heaven and the blessings of the ancestors, as expressed in the following poem:

    The mandate of Heaven,
    How beautiful and unceasing!
    Oh, how glorious

Was the purity of King Wen's virtue!
With blessings he overwhelms us.
We will receive the blessings.
They are a great favor from our King Wen.
May his descendants hold fast to them.

                    (CHAN, 1969)

From the seventeenth to the mid-twentieth century, most Western interpreters saw the image of an anthropomorphic god in the concepts of the "Lord on High" and "Heaven's mandate." But the traditional Chinese interpretation, especially as it was expressed by such commentators as Zheng Xuan (Cheng Hsüan) (A.D. 127–200) and Zhu Xi (Chu Hsi) (A.D. 1130–1200), was to read these concepts as evidence of a natural moral universe without any connotations of a personal anthropomorphic god.

"Don't you mind your ancestors!"

The following poem contains the perplexing line "Don't you mind your ancestors," but it should not be misconstrued as an attempt to discredit the importance of ancestor veneration. The context of the poem makes it clear that if one's ancestors have behaved without virtue and acted against the natural harmony and the mandate of Heaven, then, and only then, should one avoid following their example. The filial descendants are still expected to honor the position and title of the ancestor:

They (descendants of Yin) became subjects of the
    Chou.
Heaven's mandate is not constant.
The officers of Yin were fine and alert.
They assist at the libation in our capital.
In their assisting in the libation,
They always wear skirted robes and close caps.
Oh, you promoted servants of the king,
Don't you mind your ancestors!

Don't you mind your ancestors!
Cultivate your virtue.
Always strive to be in harmony with Heaven's Man-
    date.
Seek for yourselves the many blessings.

Before Yin lost its army,
Its kings were able to be counterparts to the Lord on
*   High.*
In Yin you should see as in a mirror
That the great mandate is not easy [to keep].

(CHAN, 1969)

The poetic style, form, and content of the *Book of Poetry* speak to the human condition and stimulate the human spirit so profoundly that, after 3,000 years the *Shijing* is not only a Chinese classic but also one of world literature.

JAMES D. SELLMANN

Further Reading

Translations

Chan, Wing-tsit, trans. and comp. *A Source Book in Chinese Philosophy*. Princeton, N.J.: Princeton University Press, 1963. An excellent sourcebook and commentary. Chan shows the independence and sensitivity of his judgment in his discussion of the *Book of Poetry*, especially in his translation and interpretation of the line, "Don't you mind your ancestors!"

Lau, D. C., trans. *Confucius, The Analects*. London: Penguin Books, 1986. A useful translation.

Legge, James, trans. and ed. *The Chinese Classics*. 5 vols. (Hong Kong, 1861–72), New York: Ox-

ford University Press, 1961. Contains Legge's translation of the *Book of Poetry*.

————. *The She King or the Book of Ancient Poetry*. London: Trubner, 1871. (Reprinted as *The Book of Poetry*, New York: Paragon Book Reprint Corporation, 1967.)

Liu, Wu-chi, and Irving Yucheng Lo, trans. and eds. *Sunflower Splendor: Three Thousand Years of Chinese Poetry*. Bloomington IN: Indiana University Press, 1975. This work offers a fresh translation of 12 poems from the *Shijing*.

Waley, Arthur, trans. *The Book of Songs*. London: Allen & Unwin, 1937. This work is often praised as the most lucid translation.

Related Studies

Chow, Tse-tsung, ed. "The Early History of the Chinese Word *Shih* (Poetry)," in *Wen-lin: Studies in the Chinese Humanities*. Chow Tse-tsung, ed. 151–209. Madison WI: The University of Wisconsin Press, 1968.

Dobson, W. A. C. H. *The Language of the Book of Songs*. Toronto, Canada: University of Toronto Press, 1968. An illuminating study of the creative use of language in *The Book of Songs*.

Wang, Ching-hsien. *The Bell and Drum: Shih Ching as Formalistic Poetry in an Oral Tradition*. Berkeley CA: University of California Press, 1974.

THE *BOOK OF CHANGES*

Title in Chinese: *Yijing* (*I-ching*)
Authors: Unknown: Composite work.
Literary Form: Contains elements of poetry, prose, and folklore.
Date of Composition: Origins unclear; probably not put together as a coherent text until the ninth century
B.C. (The so-called "Ten Wings" were added in the early Han Dynasty [206 B.C.–A.D. 222])

Major Themes

Hexagrams, made up of yin-yang lines, represent the basic kinds of change in the universe.

The relationships and processes of Heaven and Earth are knowable, since the mind of Heaven and the mind of Man are one.

As a reflection of the cosmic way, the Dao (Tao), the Yijing provides guidance for proper conduct in the present and the future.

The *Book of Changes (Yijing)*, also known as the *Zhouyi (Changes of Zhou/Chou)* originated over 3,000 years ago as a book of divination. The basic text, which underwent considerable evolution in the pre-imperial era (up to 221 B.C.), consists of a series of 64 six-line symbols known as hexagrams (*gua/kua*). The theory of the Yijing is that these hexagrams represent the basic circumstances of change in the universe; and by consulting the *Yijing* with a reverent spirit, one can select a hexagram that will provide guidance for the present and the future.

Each hexagram has a name (*guaming/kuaming*) that refers to a physical object, an activity, a state, a situation, a quality, an emotion, or a relationship; thus: *Ding (Ting)* (Cauldron), *Dun (Tun)* (Retreat), *Meng* (Youthful Ignorance), *Yu (Yü)* (Enthusiasm), *Song (Sung)* (Conflict), *Tongren (Tung jen)* (Human Fellowship), and so forth. In addition, each hexagram possesses a short, cryptic description of several words, called a "judgment" (*tuan/t'uan* or *guaci/kua-tz'u*), and a brief written interpretation for each line of each hexagram (*yaoci/yao-tz'u*). These descriptions and interpretations are drawn from a wide variety of sources: peasant omens, rhymed proverbs, riddles, paradoxes, and fragments of story and song drawn from popular lore (oral history), as well as elite literary traditions.

The basic text of the *Yijing* reveals a number of early and long-standing Chinese cultural preoc-

cupations. It tells of the need to use language properly, to refine one's nature, and to strive to become a "superior man" (*junzi/chün-tzu*); it emphasizes the importance of family relationships (including ties with one's ancestors), ritual, and music; it speaks of the value of the past as well as the inevitability of change; it deals with the regulation of time and space; and it displays an acute awareness of status distinctions. Virtually all levels of Chinese society are represented in the line readings: men, women, children, royalty and other elites, merchants, servants, priests and magicians (even robbers). Central social values include truthfulness, loyalty, and sincerity. The early strata of the text are noteworthy, however, for their lack of a systematic moral vision or framework. Military affairs and the administration of justice receive substantial attention in the line readings, indicating attitudes somewhat at odds with most later conceptions of Confucianism.

Nature Symbolism

Much of the symbolism of the basic text is related to nature: heavenly objects, thunder and lightning, wind, rain, earth and fire, and mountains, lakes, rocks, and trees. There are animals of every description in the work, from supernatural beasts, such as dragons, to both wild and domestic animals (even hamsters). Color and directional symbolism is quite common, as are references to various parts of the human body. Other frequently encountered symbols include precious objects (gold, silk, and jade), food of various sorts, eating utensils, sacrificial vessels, vehicles (such as wagons and carts), weapons, and mundane household items. Among the more esoteric references in the *Yijing* are those that refer to "a husband and wife rolling their eyes," "dried gristly meat," the "tusk of a gelded boar."

The significance of many of these symbols has been debated for centuries. It is not hard to see why. In the first place, the early hexagram and line references are often obscure and incomplete. The details of divinations, myths, and anecdotes that once helped to explain or amplify the original text of the *Yijing* were often lost or became distorted. Also, the meanings of certain words and phrases changed over time. For these reasons, among others, a great many commentaries came to be written on the *Book of Changes* from the Han period (206 B.C.– A.D. 222) onward. Until the twentieth century, however, most of these works did not provide reliable information on the most ancient forms of *Yi* usage.

The "Ten Wings"

During the early Han, a set of poetic appendices known as the "Ten Wings" (*shiyi/shih-i*) became permanently attached to the *Yijing*, and the work received imperial sanction as one of the five major Confucian classics (*wujing/wu ching*). The Ten Wings—particularly the so-called "Great Commentary" (*Dazhuan/Ta-chuan* or *Xici zhuan/Hsi-chuan*)—articulated the *Yijing*'s implicit cosmology and invested the classic with a new literary flavor and style. The world view of this amplified version of the *Changes*, influenced heavily by the thought of the early Han philosopher Dong Zhongshu (Tung Chung-shu), emphasized correlative thinking, a humane cosmological outlook, and a fundamental unity and resonance between Heaven, Earth, and Man. It also stressed the pervasive notion of *yin-yang*: complementary and cyclical movement.

Virtually all of the post-Han commentaries on the *Yijing* were based on the recension of the text in the third century A.D. by Wang Bi (Wang Pi). Wang's own exegesis, for which Richard John Lynn has recently provided an excellent English-language translation, exerted an enormous influence on Chinese thought for the next 1,000 years or so. It did not, however, preclude substantial scholarly disagreement, nor did the equally influential work of Cheng Yi (Ch'eng I) and Zhu Xi (Chu Hsi) in the Song dynasty (960–1279 B.C.). Thus we find Ni Yuanlu (Ni Yüan-lu) lamenting in the fourteenth century that after more than "ten thousand generations" of written commentaries there was still no standard interpretation of the *Changes*. In an attempt to be both comprehensive and fair-minded, many scholars simply accumulated different commentaries and appended them to the Wang Bi text. In 1715, for instance, more than 200 such works were incorporated into the Kangxi (K'ang-hsi) emperor's officially sanctioned edition of the classic.

The Measure of Heaven and Earth

Despite deep scholarly disagreement, or perhaps because of it, for some 2,000 years the *Yijing* had an importance in Chinese culture comparable to that of the Bible in Western culture. Like the Bible, it was a work of virtually unchallenged scriptural authority—an inspiration to the elite, and a comfort to commoners as well. In the words of the "Great Commentary": "The *Yijing* contains the measure of Heaven and Earth; thus it enables us to comprehend the Way." But unlike the Bible, the *Yijing* was the product of natural observation by the ancient Chinese sages, not the holy word of a transcendant God. Furthermore, the Way, or *Dao (Tao)*, upon which the *Yijing* was based, had no Creator or Supreme Ordainer, nor did it promote the idea of "original sin" and evil as an active personal force.

The *Yijing* gives no hint of a purposeful beginning, nor an apocalyptic end: whereas the Bible takes the view that human beings are answerable only to God and not their own culture, the *Yijing* assumes something of the reverse. Western thought held that the mind of God is beyond complete understanding; but in traditional Chinese thought, the basic assumption was that the mind of Heaven could be known, and that the ways of fate could thus be discerned. The huge and unbridgeable gulf between God and his creatures in the Western tradition had no counterpart in the Chinese intellectual tradition.

One might say, however, that, like that of the Bible in the West, the *Yijing* had a profound effect on various realms of Chinese culture—notably the development of classical discourse, the evolution of formal philosophy, the analysis of art and literature, and the reinforcement of certain social values and customs. It shaped the contours of Chinese mythology in several respects, and even came to play a significant role in Chinese science.

The Language and Style of the Yijing

From a linguistic standpoint, the *Yijing*'s basic text displays a special sensitivity to rhymes and homophones, which encouraged puns and double entendres in Chinese speech and writing. In the "Ten Wings" there is a marked tendency to pair words and concepts with opposite or complementary meanings—a prominent feature of Chinese poetry and prose throughout the imperial era. The *Yijing* also displays a highly refined system of symbolic logic that relies not only on the analysis of various hexagrams and their broken (*yin*) and/or solid (*yang*) lines, but also on different configurations of three-line "trigrams" contained within each hexagram. The complex numerological and metaphorical symbolism of the *Yijing*, together with its *yin-yang*-oriented "logic" of correlative duality, contributed to a powerful Chinese preference for allegory, analogy, and the use of numerical and other relational symbolism for making an argument.

The "Great Commentary" describes the discursive style of the *Changes* as one of using "words that are indirect but which hit the mark." Thus we read that, although the names connected to the hexagrams and lines may appear trivial, "they embrace many categories and are far reaching and refined. Things are openly set forth, but they also contain a deeper secret." Guided by this sort of an

intellectual outlook, most Chinese scholars lacked a Western-style concern with separate qualities or "laws" of identity. They saw no need to rely on anything like the Aristotelian syllogism as a form of "higher" logic, nor did they consider it desireable to elaborate in a systematic way the symbolic connections that inhered in a given text. In other words, the aphoristic and highly metaphorical nature of the *Changes* encouraged an intuitive and intellectual approach to understanding.

The *Yijing* not only provided several of the most basic terms of traditional Chinese cosmology, but also served as a conceptual point of departure for most philosophical discussions of space and time. Not only did the classic inspire a great many derivative works, but also provided a virtually indispensible philosophical vocabulary for an extremely wide range of Chinese thinkers. It served as the locus classicus for such fundamental concepts as *yin* and *yang* and *Taiji (T'ai-chi)* (the Supreme Ultimate), as well as for such time-honored ontological distinctions as between "what exists before physical form" (*xing er shang/hsing erh shang*) and "what exists after physical form" (*xing er xia/hsing erh hsia*). Moreover, because so many provocative concepts in the *Yijing* were not well-defined in the text itself, they could be used in many different ways. As a result of both the prestige and the ambiguity of the *Book of Changes*, Confucians, Daoists, and Buddhists alike called upon it to bolster their arguments concerning cosmology, epistemology, ontology, and ethics.

The Literary Influence of the Yijing

The *Yijing* influenced literary developments in China, but in ways quite unlike those of the Bible in the West. For example, the Changes avoids elaborate myth as a way of dealing with questions of time and change, while the Bible revels in its narrative structure. Whereas the Bible presents us with the image of a self-conscious alienation from civilization and a certain "liberation" from redundant historical patterns, the *Yijing* places special emphasis on the *yin-yang* cycles of waxing and waning and of predictable patterns of alternation and displacement. These cycles and patterns, in turn, became the foundation of traditional Chinese aesthetics. As Andrew Plaks has noted, the *Yijing*'s principles of bipolarity, ceaseless alternation, presence within absence, and infinite overlapping, are basic to a major portion of the Chinese literary tradition.

Chinese scholars wrote thousands of essays on the *Yijing* from the Han period to the Qing (Ch'ing) (A.D. 1644–1912). Many of these, along with various inscriptions, memorials, eulogies, poems, and works of rhyme-prose (*fu*) focusing on the classic, are contained in the great Qing encyclopedia known as the *Gujin tushu jicheng (Ku-chin t'u-shu chi-ch'eng: Synthesis of Illustrations and Writings, Ancient and Recent)*. But the *Yijing*'s paucity of both parables and anecdotes diminished its value as a direct source of representational art in China. It is true, of course, that trigrams became a common decorative motif on craft productions, and that certain animal symbols discussed in the *Yijing*, such as flying dragons, were depicted in various types of Chinese representative art. One can even find paintings that show scholars intently contemplating the *Changes*. But the *Yijing* did not provoke an artistic outpouring of the sort that the Bible's innumerable stories and parables did in the West.

What the *Yijing* did provide was an analytical vocabulary, based on both trigram and hexagram symbolism, which proved extraordinarily serviceable in a wide range of creative activities. The renowned scholar Zhang Xuecheng (Chang Hsüeh-ch'eng) (A.D. 1738–1801), for example, employed the symbolism of *Qian (Ch'ien)* ("Heaven," "Creative," *yang*, and so forth) and *Kun (K'un)* ("Earth," "Receptive," *yin*, and so forth) in comparing the "round and spiritual" (*yang*) writing of the early Han-period historian Sima Qian (Ssu-ma Ch'ien) (c. 145 B.C.–c. 90 B.C.) to the "square and sagacious" (*yin*) writing of his successor Ban Gu (Pan Ku) (A.D. 32–A.D. 92). Similarly, the author of the famous painting guide entitled the *Jiezi yuan huazhuan (Chieh-tzu yüan hua-chuan) (Mustard Seed Garden Manual)* used the vocabulary and numerical symbolism of the *Yijing* in describing techniques such as the composition of plum trees. A number of Chinese scholars also used the *Yijing* to interpret the characters in China's greatest novels, including *Xiyou ji (Hsi yu chi) (Journey to the West), Shuihu zhuan (Shui hu chuan) (Water Margin)*, and *Honglou meng (Hung lou meng) (Dream of the Red Chamber)*.

The Scientific, Social, and Political Significance of the Hexagrams

Chinese scientists even used *Yijing* symbolism to explain natural phenomena. We should not be surprised at this, for if, as the "Great Commentary" claimed, the trigrams and hexagrams of the *Yijing* truly express the principles and patterns of all phenomena in Heaven and on Earth through images and numbers, then all things are equally susceptible to interpretation and classification in terms of the *Changes*—not only art and literature, but also science, technology, and mathematics. As the index to the monumental Qing literary compendium, known as the *Siku quanshu (Ssu-k'u ch'üan-shu) (Complete Collection of the Four Treasuries)*, put the matter: "The way of the *Yijing* is broad and great. It encompasses everything, including astronomy, geography, music, military methods, the study of rhymes, numerical calculations, and even esoteric alchemy."

Hexagrams thus had explanatory value as scientific symbols. For instance, the hexagram *Xun (Hsün)* (signifying "the gentle," "the penetrating," and "the wind") came to be identified with the phenomenon of human respiration. Similarly, *Yi (I)* (the corners of the mouth, nourishment) referred to eating. *Guan (Kuan)* (contemplation, view) pertained to vision. The Ming scholar Wang Kui (Wang K'uei) tells us, "The upper eyelid of human beings moves, and the lower one keeps still. This is because the symbolism of the hexagram Guan embodies the idea of vision. Windy Xun [a trigram] is moving above, and earthly Kun [also a trigram] is immobile below." His explanation of *Yi* as a symbol for the process of chewing is similar: the lower trigram (*Zhen/Chen*: Thunder) represents the movement of the lower jaw in eating, while the upper one (*Gen/Ken*: Mountain) indicates immobility.

The influence of the *Yijing* was no less substantial in the realm of Chinese social and political life. In the first place, we should remember that emperors, officials, and other elites used it regularly to make important decisions as did commoners through the medium of fortune-tellers. Secondly, the Changes provided a cosmologically grounded justification for the political and social hierarchies of imperial China from Han times through the Qing. The hexagram *Guimei (Kuei-mei)* (Marrying Maiden), for instance, casts the role of Chinese women solely in terms of their subordination to men in marriage, concubinage, or slavery. Likewise, *Jiaren (Chia-jen)* (Household Member) stipulates that a wife must submit totally to her husband's authority.

All hexagrams had potential applicability to human affairs, but some were more commonly employed as symbolic referents than others. Among the most frequently used, in addition to *Guimei* and *Jiaren*, were: *Qian (Ch'ien)* (signifying male control); *Kun (K'un)* (female compliance); *Song (Sung)* (litigation); *Shi (Shih)* (military affairs); *Bi (Pi)* (union and accord); *Li* (circumspect behavior); *Yu (Yü)* (comfort or satisfaction); *Shihe (Shih-ho)* (criminal law); *Fu* (return); *Wuwang (Wu-wang)* (absence of falsehood); *Daguo (Ta-kuo)* (excess); *Heng* (perseverence); *Tun (T'un)* (retreat); *Jin (Chin)* (advance in rank); *Mingyi (Ming-i)* (failure to be appreciated); *Kui (K'uei)* (separation or alienation); *Kuai (K'uai)* (breakthrough); *Gou (Kou)* (social intercourse); *Cui (Ts'ui)* (people gathered around a good ruler); *Sheng* (the career of a good official); *Ding (Ting)* (nourishment of talents); *Jian (Ch'ien)* (slow and steady advance); *Feng* (prosperity); *Lü* (travel and strangers); *Huan* (dispersion); *Jie (Chieh)* (restraint); *Zhongfu (Chung-fu)* (kingly sway); *Jiji (Chi-chi)* (accomplishment); and *Weiji (Wei-chi)* (something not yet completed).

The neo-Confucian compilation known as the *Jinsi lu (Chin-ssu lu) (Reflections on Things at Hand)*, one of the most influential books in late imperial times, employs about 50 different hexagrams, including most of the above-mentioned, to illustrate various social and political themes. In the chapter on governing, for example, we find:

> It is difficult to govern a family whereas it is easy to govern the world, for the family is near while the world is distant. If members of the family are separated, the cause surely lies with women. This is why the hexagram *Kui (K'uei)* ["To Part"] follows the hexagram *Jiaren (Chia-jen)* ["Family"], for "When two women live together, their wills move in different directions." This is why [the sage emperor] Yao, having put the empire in order, gave his two daughters in marriage to Shun in order to test him and see whether the throne should be given to him. Thus it is that, in order to see how he governs his empire, we observe the government of his family.

During the Qing dynasty, a number of iconoclastic scholars identified with the so-called School of Han Learning or *kaozheng (k'ao-cheng)* (evidential research) questioned the authenticity of certain post-Han accretions to the *Yijing*, including the so-called River Chart *(Hetu/Ho-t'u)* and Luo Writing *(Luoshu/Lo-shu)*. But the *Yijing* managed to retain its "scriptural" authority despite such attacks. Even Wang Fuzhi (Wang Fu Tzu) (A.D. 1619–1692), one of the most skeptical of all Qing scholars, wrote that the *Book of Changes* was "the manifestation of the Heavenly Way, the unexpressed form of nature, and the showcase for sagely achievement. Yin and yang, movement and stillness, darkness and lightness, contraction and expansion" all are inherent in it. Spirit operates within it; the refined subtlety of ritual and music is stored in it; the great utility of humaneness and right behavior issues forth from it; and the calculation of order and disorder, good and bad fortune, life and death is in accordance with it."

Western imperialism in the latter half of the nineteenth century brought with it a host of new ideas concerning the structure and function of the universe, but many Chinese still claimed, as they had done since the time of the Jesuits in the seventeenth century, that all foreign science and mathematics were derived from the *Yijing*. In fact, it was not until radical change finally came to China in the aftermath of the devastating Sino-Japanese War (A.D. 1894–1895) that the *Yijing*, as a classic of now-discredited Confucianism, lost most of its institutionalized political and social authority.

The Contemporary View of the Yijing

Despite its loss of authority, the *Yijing* remains a vital document that is studied, consulted, and often revered by many people in China and abroad. Japan, Hong Kong, and Taiwan have long been havens for devotees of the *Book of Changes* as a source of much valuable and stimulating scholarship. Even in China itself, where investigation and especially use of the *Yijing* has been stigmatized as a reflection of "feudal" superstition, there is evidence of revived interest in the one-time classic.

How do we account for the *Yijing*'s continued appeal? The main reason, of course, is that the work still has something important to say. But what is it? In part, the attraction of the *Changes* is simply aesthetic: the language and imagery are undeniably entrancing. The classic also retains its fascination as a book of divination, although it has often been naively misunderstood and misapplied, particularly in the West. Further, as in times past, the *Yijing* remains useful as a means of promoting introspection and self-knowledge by challenging the reader to make unanticipated connections between events and conditions, whether spirtual assistance is explicitly acknowledged as playing a role in establishing the link or not. Certainly Chinese scholars employed the document for this purpose, even if unconsciously, as they attempted to "resolve doubts" (*jueyi/chüeh*).

A number of contemporary Chinese and foreign scholars have found in the *Yijing* elements of modern mathematics and science that seem to transcend the boundaries of culture. Some maintain, for instance, that the *Book of Changes* contains an incipient "algebra of the universe." Others have gone so far as to claim that the hexagrams of the classic were originally designed as a high-efficiency information transfer system analogous to contemporary computer coding based on the optimal units of two (the number of basic trigrams in each hexagram) and three (the number of lines in each trigram). Tang Mingbang, for his part, asserts that the forms of atomic structure in nuclear physics, the genetic code in molecular biology, and the eight-tier matrix in linear algebra are all related to the logic of the *Yijing*. Such attempts to link the *Changes* with modern scientific thought are not likely to yield many useful insights, but the effort is probably worth making anyway. After all, the basic challenge of the *Yijing* has always been to make creative connections and to establish meaningful relationships.

RICHARD J. SMITH

Further Reading

Translations

Legge, James, trans. *The Yi King; or Book of Changes.* Oxford: Clarendon Press, 1882. A standard but somewhat dated translation that includes no Chinese characters. An edition of this work by Z. D. Sung, entitled *The Text of Yi King* (1935), uses the basic Legge translation but modifies the original organization and supplies Chinese characters for the English text.

Lynn, Richard John, trans. *The Classic of Changes: A New Translation of the I Ching as Interpreted by Wang Bi.* New York: Columbia University Press, 1994. An excellent annotated translation of both *The Book of Changes* and one of its most important commentaries.

Wilhelm, Richard and Cary F. Baynes, trans. *The I Ching or Book of Changes.* Princeton, N. J.: Princeton University Press, 1967. A basically reliable but somewhat loose translation of the *Book of Changes*, based primarily on an "orthodox" Qing dynasty edition of the classic. Wilhelm's translation into German has itself been translated into English by Baynes.

Related Studies

Cheng, Chung-ying, and Elton Johnson. "A Bibliography of the *I Ching* in Western Languages." *Journal of Chinese Philosophy*, 14 (1987).

Ho, Peng Yoke (He Bingyu). "The System of *The Book of Changes* and Chinese Science," *Japanese Studies in the History of Science*, 11 (1972).

Liu, Zheng. "The Dilemma Facing Contemporary Research in the *Yijing*," *Chinese Studies in Philosophy*, 24.4 (Summer, 1993). Argues that most present-day studies of *Yijing* in China suffer from old-fashioned methods of research, inadequate theory, and a certain "narrowness of vision."

Loewe, Michael, ed. *Early Chinese Texts: A Bibliographical Guide*. Berkeley, CA: The Society for the Study of Early China and the Institute of East Asian Studies, University of California, Berkeley, 1993. Contains an illuminating article on the textual evolution of the *Yijing*.

Peterson, Willard. "Making Connections: Commentary on the 'Attached Verbalizations' of the *Book of Changes*," *Harvard Journal of Asiatic Studies*, 42.1 (June, 1982). A sophisticated analysis of the four main arguments of the "Great Commentary."

Plaks, Andrew. *Archetype and Allegory in the Dream of the Red Chamber*. Princeton, N.J.: Princeton University Press, 1976. A brilliant study of one of China's greatest novels, placing considerable emphasis on the *Yijing* as providing the conceptual and structural underpinning of the book.

Shchutskii, Iulian. *Researches on the I Ching*. Trans. William MacDonald and Tsuyoshi Hasegawa. London: Routledge and Kegan Paul, 1980. An excellent translation of a pioneering Russian study of the *Yijing*.

Smith, Kidder, et al. *Sung Dynasty Uses of the I Ching*. Princeton, N. J.: Princeton University Press, 1967. An analysis of four different scholarly approaches to the *Yijing* during the Song period.

Smith, Richard J. *Fortune-tellers and Philosophers: Divination in Traditional Chinese Society*. Boulder, CO.: Westview Press, 1991. Devotes considerable attention to the *Yijing* as a seminal work in the Chinese mantic tradition.

Tang, Mingbang. "Recent Developments in Studies of the *Book of Changes*," *Chinese Studies in Philosophy* (Fall, 1987). An overview of different scholarly approaches to the *Yijing* in the People's Republic of China.

Wilhelm, Helmut. "The Book of Changes in the Western Tradition," *Parerga*, 2 (1975). An overview of the way the *Yijing* has been evaluated and employed by Western scholars.

THE *BOOK OF HISTORY*

Title in Chinese: *Shujing* (*Shu Ching*), *Shang Shu*, or *Shu*
Author: Unknown. Contains imperial court documents (some believed to be later forgeries) from the earliest rulers down to the Zhou dynasty.
Literary Form: Historical essays
Date of Composition: Oldest material was written between the tenth and sixth centuries B.C.

Major Themes

The study of history is required for self-cultivation.

If self-realization and moral development are to occur, then one must venerate and understand the ancestors.

The ruler must respect and obey the Emperor on High (shang di/shang ti) *to maintain political control.*

The mandate of Heaven (tian ming/t'ien ming) *justifies the dynastic cycle.*

The moral example of the ancient sage kings should be used as the guideline for successful rulership.

The lessons of history show that the sages ruled by virtue, and only appealed to a "rule of law" to maintain order when the people or tribes had lost all sense of shame.

Viewing it from an analytic frame of reference, one might question why a history book is introduced as a literary work. Aside from the influence of the *Book of History (Shujing)* on later works of literature, there are at least three reasons why historical documents classify as a literary genre. First, historical documents, like any literature, are an art form: they draw feeling, emotion, and idea from the audience. Second, history as literature guides one through a rational process of explanation and decision making. Finally, and most important for the Chinese context, history provides moral instruction.

The traditional Chinese mind as reflected in its literary achievements was dominated by two styles—the poetic and the historic. Because the Chinese by far have produced more poetry and history texts than any other traditional peoples, it is not surprising that among the five Confucian classics there are two texts dealing with historical material.

The Confucian Classics

The *Book of History* is one of the five Confucian classics, along with the *Book of Changes* (divination), the *Book of Poetry*, the *Book of Rites*, and the *Spring and Autumn Annals*, which served as the basis of a Confucian education for well over the past 2,000 years. Originally there were six classics—the *Book of Music* (*Yue jing/yüeh ching*) was lost in antiquity; some lists replace it with the *Rites of Zhou* (*Zhouli/Chou li*). Before the *Book of History* was edited, some historical records were inscribed on bamboo slats and on bronze works, and, of course, the famous oracle bones from the Shang period. It is now believed that some parts of the *Book of History* are forgeries of a later period probably from the Han dynasty (206 B.C.–A.D. 220) when the extant redactions were compiled.

Classics of Chinese History

There are three significant texts of ancient Chinese history. The first is the *Book of History*, which contains documents and speeches relating the events of the traditional Confucian ministers and rulers, for example, Emperors Yao, Shun, Yu (Yü), and Tang (T'ang), founder of the Shang dynasty (1766–1040 B.C.), and Kings Wen and Wu, founders of the early or Western Zhou (Chou) dynasty (1040–770 B.C.). The *Spring and Autumn Annals* is the second major historical text of Chinese antiquity; it records the major events in the state of Lu from 722 to 481 B.C.. There was a text called the *History of the Chou* (*Zhou Shu*), but it was lost after the "burning of the books" in 213 B.C. The third major historical text is the *Records of the Grand Historian, (Shiji/Shih chi)*, which is the first of the 24 dynastic histories.

Traditionally, Confucius is attributed with authoring some of the classics: it has been proposed that he compiled the *Spring and Autumn Annals*, and edited some or all of the classics. Most contemporary scholars doubt these claims. When one studies any pre-Qin (Ch'in) literature, it is important to keep in mind that Li Su, prime minister to the first emperor of Qin, ordered the burning of private libraries in 213 B.C., and that the Confucian classics had to be reconstructed from memory in the Early Han dynasty (206 B.C.–A.D. 8). Because these reconstructed texts were written in the new script style, they are referred to as the "new texts" (*jinwen/chin wen*). In the Later Han dynasty (A.D. 25–220), during the construction of a palace, texts were discovered, according to legend, in the walls of what was Confucius's house. These texts, written in the pre-Han "old script" (*guwen/ku wen*) style, are referred to as the "old texts" even though they were found after the "new texts."

One should not be confused by the labels, "new," "old," because they refer to the written script style of the characters, not to the historical sequence in which the text were written or discovered. The supernatural nonrational approach of the new text school dominated from the Later Han (A.D. 25–220) to the Tang (A.D. 618–905). The natural and rational old-text-school approach won out during the Tang and Song (Sung) (A.D. 960–1278) revivals of Confucianism. It is important to keep in mind that the classics were reconstructed during the Han dynasty, and thus, contain material from that later period. Many scholars especially doubt the authenticity of the *Tang shi (T'ang Shih)* section of the Shang documents and the "Grand Plan" or *Hung fan* section of the Zhou documents. Despite the interpolation of later material, philologists and linguists have identified core passages in each of the classics that are believed to pre-date the Han period.

The *Book of History* made an indelible mark on Chinese literature, especially that of the Later Zhou dynasty. It is often quoted in later works; and these quotes serve three purposes simultaneously. First, they display the literary adroitness of authors who quote it—the assumption was that authors wise enough to quote the *Book of History* must have something important to say. Second, the quotations enhance the artistic beauty of the work. Third, they give a voice of historic authority to the writer's argument. The quotations from the *Book of History* are usually quite obscure, and it is not readily apparent how they are intended to support the author's position. Since the quoted material is written in arachic Chinese, it forces the reader to slow down to decipher the passage. The reader is expected to meditate on the classical meaning of the passage, and to project his or her feeling and emotion into the quoted material, thereby drawing inspiration from it. In other words, the *Book of History* and its particular quoted passages are looked upon as highly cultured works of art meant to inspire the readers' creative participation in culture. Thus, the study of the historical documents, reading the text and reference to it, was deemed crucial for one's enculturation and personal cultivation as a learned, cultured person.

Mythology and History

It is important to acknowledge that, whereas the earliest literature of many ancient cultures begins with a mythology of the gods and semi-divine heroes, mythology is lacking in archaic Shang and Zhou culture. The *Book of History* represents the earliest compilation of ancient documents consisting of announcements, counsels, speeches, and oral reports supposedly made by ancient rulers and ministers. The "characters" in these documents are not gods or divine beings. From the ancient Chinese perspective, these "characters" were understood to have been actual historic people. Some scholars have argued that the ancient Chinese myths about the gods were humanized and historicized by later writers, but there is in fact no evidence that such myths ever existed. Since the ancient Chinese were a down-to-earth, this-worldly, practical-minded people, their literary tradition does not begin with supernatural myths about the gods, but rather with the *Book of History* or similar documents relating the events and actions of ancient rulers and culture heroes.

Granted, some of the documents relate fantastic descriptions, like the material describing Yu (Yü)—the great draining off the flood waters by dredging out the river beds and piling up the earth to construct the high plains and mountains. As fantastic as this may sound, the ancient Chinese took the deed to be an historic fact. The story reveals an important character of the Chinese mind. In the flood stories from Western literature, human beings are helpless, and at best, able to build an ark and ride out the deluge. In the Chinese story, they undertake a grand engineering project, re-shape the earth, and drain off the flood. It is impor-tant to keep in mind that the actual engineering projects of the ancient Chinese—the Great Wall diversion of rivers to irrigate the dry plateau of Sezchuan, and the grand imperial canal system connecting the southern rivers with the Yellow River in the north—actually did reshape the ter-rain. Was the seminal idea for such projects laid down in the document concerning Yu the Great? What the ancient Chinese historic literature teaches is that the ancient rulers, ministers, and culture heroes solved the problems of their day by applying rational problem solving techniques rather than su-pernatural powers or magical formulae. In later times when the documents were used for educa-tional purposes, the message is very clear—one should follow the down-to-earth rational problem-solving approach of the ancients, that is, one should do things the old fashioned way, the practical way.

History Used for Moral Instruction

In addition to being used as an artistic device and as an heuristic tool for teaching rational understand-ing—the most significant and common use of *The Book of History*, according to the Chinese mind—was for moral instruction and self- cultivation. One cannot overstate the importance to the Chinese of the study of history for self-cultivation. Without an understanding of the cultural past, without learning from both the positive and negative role models of antiquity, one cannot make headway in self-realization. The classical Chinese approach to his-tory is unlike modern academic history, which studies history to make projections on future social, political, and economic relations. The ancient Chi-nese studied history for moral insight, especially for their own personal self-understanding. The Confucian method in moral education is to teach by example.

The documents in *The Book of History* are a disjointed collection of reports and court speeches from which one can glean insight into both proper and improper forms of behavior. For example, after relating the significant events of the reigns of the first three emperors, Yao, Shun, and Yu, the fourth chapter of *The Book of History* presents "The Counsels of Kao Yao." Kao Yao was a chief minis-ter who served under both Shun and Yu. In the following passage he advises Emperor Yu on the role of moral cultivation in proper government:

> Do not neglect the various officials. The work of Heaven is performed by men taking its place. Heaven establishes the duties, charging us with the five duties and five courses of proper conduct. Heaven establishes the rit-uals, charging us with the five ritual relation-ships to be instituted. . . . The mandate of Heaven establishes the virtuous, and there are the five forms of proper clothing and the five decorations. Heaven establishes the punish-ment for the guilty, and there are the five punishments and the five applications.

> (FUNG [MODIFIED], 1952)

Ancestor veneration plays and important role in Confucian self-cultivation. If one is to understand oneself, then one must first understand one's ances-tors, especially the way of the ancient sage rulers. The sage rulers are the moral exemplars, although the tyrants set a negative example. In the *Lu Xing (Lü Hsing)* chapter of the *Book of History*, one finds that the following passage illustrates the significance of following the positive role model:

> Consider the commissioning of three different ministers who each labored with compassionate anxiety on behalf of the masses. Po Yi presented laws to prevent the masses from being punished. Yu pacified the waters and land, presiding over the naming of the rivers and hills. Ji [Hou Chi] expanded the knowledge of agriculture for the extensive cultivation of the various grains. When these three ministers accomplished their respective work, the masses were well off.
>
> (FUNG [MODIFIED], 1952)

This passage is used to justify the dominate literary theme of governing by virtue. Respect for the ancestors is intimately tied to veneration of the ancestral father and the founding emperor of the dynasty, that is, the Emperor on High, and the mandate of Heaven, which can be secured only by the king's virtue and the rule of law.

> Yin (Shang) having lost the mandate of Heaven, we, the Zhou, have received it. But I dare not say with certainty that our heritage will forever truly remain on the side of fortune. If Heaven renders sincere help, I do not dare say with certainty that the final end will result in misfortune. Oh! You have said, Prince, "It depends on ourselves." I also dare not rest in the mandate of the Lord on High, forever refraining from thinking of the awe-inspiring power of Heaven.
>
> The mandate of Heaven is not easily preserved. Heaven is hard to depend on. Those who have lost the mandate did so because they could not practice and carry on the reverence and the brilliant virtue of their forefathers. As for the present, it is not that I, a little one, have a way of correcting our king. My way of leading him would be merely to make it possible to apply the glory of the forefathers to our young king.
>
> (CHAN, 1963)

The educational program is evident. One studies the moral examples of history to learn and put into practice the brilliant virtue that made the ancient sages worthy of our veneration. By performing the rites of reverence, or ancestor veneration, the ruler and ministers hope to display a rule of virtue and thereby maintain the mandate of Heaven.

Consider the significant passage from "The Announcement of Duke Shao," which lays stress on virtue and establishes the literary context to pose important questions concerning human nature:

> Let the king first bring under his influence the administrators of the affairs of Yin and place them in the midst of the administrators of our Zhou. Their natures will thus be regulated, and they will improve daily.
>
> Let the king be serious in what he does. He should not neglect to be serious with virtue.
>
> (CHAN, 1963)

This passage is one of the earliest to direct the Chinese mind to examine human nature, its relationship with virtue, and the means of educating and developing human nature to maintain social harmony. These themes would subsequently occupy a good deal of attention in Chinese literature and philosophy.

JAMES D. SELLMANN

Further Reading

Translations

Legge, James, trans. *The Chinese Classics.* 5 volumes. New York: Oxford University Press, 1961. Legge's translations were first published in Hong Kong, 1861–72.

Waltham, Clae, trans. and ed. *Shu ching, Book of History: A Modernized Edition of the Translations of James Legge.* Chicago: H. Regnery Co., 1971. A useful edition, faithful to the Legge translations, but updates (for the time) the romanization and fuses the two original translations.

Related Studies

Allan, Sarah, and Alvin P. Cohen, eds. *Legend, Lore, and Religion in China.* San Francisco: Chinese Materials Center, 1979. See Allan's essay, "Shang Foundations of Modern Chinese Folk Religion."

De Bary, William D., Wing-tsit Chan, and Burton Watson, comps. *Sources of Chinese Tradition.* New York: Columbia University Press, 1960. An excellent source of important passages from the Chinese classics, with an informative text providing both historical background and essential explanations. The book begins with an overview of the five Confucian classics.

Bodde, Derk. "Myths of Ancient China," in *Mythologies of the Ancient World.* Ed. S. N. Kramer. New York: Anchor Books, 1961. Bodde argues that there is a lost Chinese mythology which the Confucians supposedly humanized.

Chan, Wing-tsit. *A Source Book in Chinese Philosophy.* Princeton N.J.: Princeton University Press, 1963. An excellent source of key passages from the classics of Chinese philosophy and historical literature.

Fung, Yu-lan. *History of Chinese Philosophy.* vol. I, Derk Bodde, trans. Princeton N. J.: Princeton University Press, 1952. A standard history that puts the classics into context in an illuminating way. Begins with the five classics.

Giles, H. A. *A History of Chinese Literature.* New York: Grove Press Inc., 1928. Originally published in 1901, this is both a useful and entertaining review of the highlights of Chinese literature.

Hirth, Friedrich. *The Ancient History of China.* New York: Columbia University Press, 1908. A history of ancient China based on the historical classics.

Hsiao, Kung-chuan. *A History of Chinese Political Thought.* Trans. F. Mote. Princeton N. J.: Princeton University Press, 1979. Discusses some of the modern scholarship on the *Book of History.*

THE *COMMENTARIES OF ZUO (TSO)* ON THE *SPRING AND AUTUMN ANNALS*

Title in Chinese: *Zuo zhuan (Tso chuan)*
Author (by tradition): Zuo Qiu-ming (Tso Ch'iu-ming)
Born: Unknown
Died: Unknown
Literary Form: Historical chronicle
Date of Composition: Transmitted orally for generations, written down in the late fourth century B.C.

Major Themes

High officials who were skillful statesmen advised the princes of the various states and enabled them to prosper.
Ability in the art of persuasion was a great asset to a ruler.
If powerful families became dissatisfied with a ruler, they became a threat to the ruling house.
Music reveals the inner moral constitution of individuals or of the state.

The earliest work in a genre that became one of the most important in Chinese literature is the long and influential historical chronicle, *Zuo zhuan (Tso chuan)*. The title means literally "the tradition of Zuo," but because the book is understood to be commentary on the Confucian history of the state of Lu 722–481 B.C., the *Chun-qiu (Ch'un-ch'iu: (The Spring and Autumn Annals)*, it is usually called "Zuo's Commentaries."

Scholars have debated the author, date, and nature of the *Zho zhuan* from ancient times to the present. According to tradition, a man named Zuo Qiu-ming (Tso Ch'iu-ming) was the author or compiler, but no one has been able to show when or where he lived. Today, most scholars are agreed that *Zuo zhuan* is a chronicle of events from 722 to about 450 B.C., probably transmitted orally for several generations. It was then written down, perhaps in the late fourth century B.C. This consensus has not come easily: the facts of the case having been thoroughly confused by the vicissitudes of handing down a manuscript through many centuries filled with wars and revolutions, including the famous book burning of 213 B.C., when it was apparently proscribed. A legend believed by many in Han time (206 B.C.–221 A.D.) was that the *Zuo zhuan* was found in a wall of Confucius's house when it was torn down to make way for some improvements in the duke's palace in the mid-second century B.C.

In spite of its uncertain provenance, *Zuo's Commentaries* is viewed as one of the most important works in Classical Chinese and one of the great accomplishments of all Chinese literature. Already an influential book in the Han period, it was officially recognized as one of the classics in the Tang (T'ang) Dynasty (A.D. 618–907), and in the Song (Sung) Dynasty (A.D. 960–1279). It was included in the collection of 13 classics.

The events chronicled in *Zuo's Commentaries* took place between 722 and 450 B.C., covering much of the "Spring and Autumn" period of the *Chun-qiu* (although the last year specifically covered in the *Zho chuan* is 424 B.C.). But the language of the book, as we have it, is not from that early time: it is the language of the so-called "Warring States" time (403–222 B.C.). Another difference between the original text and the one we have now, as scholars have determined, is that at some point in its history someone cut it up according to the entries in the *Chun-qiu*. Who did this, and why, are questions that have not satisfactorily been resolved. Often, while reading other ancient books, we may read short sections of text that are found in and are thought to be quotations of the *Zho chuan*. The *Zuo chuan* is the most important, and often, the only source of information on the Spring and Autumn period in China.

The Spring and Autumn Period

The Spring and Autumn period is one of 272 years in the middle of the Zhou Dynasty. Although there was technically a member of the House of Zhou on the throne and ruling the empire throughout the period, the dynasty was in trouble by the Ninth century B.C., and its real influence declined drastically during the eighth century B.C., when the Zhou capital was moved to the east to escape pressure from "barbarians." The period before removal of the capital (769 B.C.) is sometimes called "Western Zhou," and the period after it, "Eastern Zhou" (to 256 B.C., including the Spring and Autumn and Warring States periods). The original fiefs of Zhou gradually assumed the role of independent states in a political system that had some similarities to feudalism in Western Europe and Japan. This situation was regarded as temporary, and one state was expected to eventually dominate the others, and ultimately succeed the Zhou.

The princes of the various states were commonly called "dukes," and as time went on, some were even able to use the title "king" in their own states. High officials who were skillful statesmen were valued advisors to the rulers. Every Chinese schoolchild knows the stories of the most famous of those advisors. The size and power of the various states of Spring and Autumn waxed or waned, each according to their ability to take advantage of their political situation. Some states flourished and grew, absorbing smaller states and gaining influence through military adventures. Others disappeared, were diminished, or held their own by alliances and deft diplomacy.

The elements of an exciting story were present in the Spring and Autumn period. The *Zho chuan* chronicles these events in a vast collection of anecdotes, annals, and episodes—a loosely connected history of the political, social, and cultural changes of the time. As the large states Qin (Ch'in), Jin (Chin), Qi (Ch'i), and Chu (Ch'u) jockeyed for

position and the smaller states maneuvered desperately to stay alive, the political landscape took on the familiar cast of power politics, while the echoes of earlier traditions became weaker and weaker. Statesmen who under such circumstances could advise their princes on how to steer their states rose to honor and high emolument.

The Zho Chuan Chronicle

Zho chuan is a long chronicle, the longest work before the Han Dynasty, and has provided a great supply of some of the best known heroes, rogues, sages, and fools in Chinese history. It covers the period in which the great sages Laozi (Lao Tzu) and Confucius lived, providing a noble antecedent for the great Han history *Shiji (Shih chi)* "Historical Records" and the dynastic histories of the following ages.

If one wants to follow the fortunes of a particular state or a certain person, one is obliged in many cases to skip around to find the relevant entries because the events in the *Zho chuan* are chronological. Some entries are long and cover many years, because the book frequently gives a thorough account of any background necessary to understanding the event. Other entries are quite short, depending on how much the author expects the readers to know about the background.

An example of the longer account opens the *Zho chuan*. The time is 722 B.C., and the account describes the events that led to an older brother's coming to battle with his younger brother in the city of Yan. The story begins with the marriage of their parents and the breech birth of the first brother. Because of the painful birth, the mother hates the older brother and subsequently tries to persuade the duke, her husband, to displace the older brother with the younger as his heir. The duke steadfastly refuses. When the older brother accedes to the throne of the state (the state of Zheng, one of the smaller states; surrounded by Qin, Jin, and Chu), his mother begs him to give his younger brother a large and wealthy city to rule, which the new duke dutifully does. The new duke's advisors warn him that his younger brother will use the city as a power base and try to take over the state. The duke acknowledges the danger, and promises to watch his brother carefully. The younger brother does indeed try to win the allegiance of border areas near him. The duke's advisors are quite nervous and advise that he move on the brother and "put him out of the way." The duke continues to watch, sees that his brother will go too far, and plans to take action at the right moment. The younger brother begins to collect taxes and consolidate his power. The duke's advisors tell him that immediate action is imperative, but the duke is unwilling to act, predicting the collapse of the whole plot.

The younger brother raises an army and conspires with his mother to open the gates of the capital to admit the rebel army. When the duke gets word of this development, he sends his own troops to attack the younger brother in his stronghold. The rebel brother flees to Yen, where he is crushed by the duke's forces.

The *Zuo* is not finished yet. A short commentary has been inserted here in the narrative to explain why the *Chun-qiu* entry concerning the above events calls the younger brother by his name, Duan, and does not mention that he was the duke's brother. It was, says Zuo, because he did not act as a younger brother should: he was not submissive to his older brother. And the duke is cited only by his title because he did not properly instruct his younger brother on the proper role of a younger brother.

Then the *Zuo* continues the story by relating the result of the mother's plot against her oldest son, the duke. He takes an oath never to see his mother again until death—the Chinese expression is "until I have reached the yellow spring (under the yellow earth)." The oath becomes generally known, and the duke receives a visit from one of his high officers. They eat together, and the officer takes a piece of meat from his bowl and puts it aside. The duke asks why. The officer explains that he and his mother share everything, and begs to be allowed to give her this meat. "You're lucky to have a mother to share with," says the duke. "I alas, have none." Because the officer asks about his comment, the duke explains the oath he has taken and now regrets, but feels he cannot break. The

officer suggests a plan for the duke to dig a tunnel underground and meet with his mother there. The duke is overjoyed, as is his mother, and they meet according to this plan. Afterwards, the *Zuo* records, they are mother and son again.

The Art of Persuasion

Ability in the art of persuasion was a talent valued by rulers in the Spring and Autumn times. Now and then, this art occasioned some spectacular reversals of fortune among the states of this period, and its sequel, the Warring States. If an advisor could show a prince where his true interest lay, a state could be won or lost. One of best known of such situations recorded in the *Zuo* is usually called "Zhu Zhiwu brings about the withdrawal of Qin's army." In 638 B.C., Zheng, a minor state, is besieged by the large states Jin and Qin: Zheng had not treated the ruler of Jin with respect seven years earlier, when he was an outcast forced to live in neighboring states waiting for his chance to return. Perhaps more important, Zheng is inclined to side with its powerful neighbor to the south, Chu, in disputes with the other great states. Zheng's future looks dim until a gifted citizen of Zheng, Zhu Zhiwu, is smuggled out of the besieged city and makes his way to the Qin encampment. He persuades the ruler of Ch'in that his interest would be better served by not cooperating with the powerful and expansionist state of Jin. Qin withdraws, then Jin withdraws.

Zhu had saved Zheng with his tongue. Zheng lasted for another two and a half centuries, in fact.

Powerful families, if they became dissatisfied, were a threat to the ruling house of a state. The ruling house sometimes produced heirs that were not suited for the responsibilities of the head of a state. Therefore, ministers who were faithful to the ruler and still commanded the respect of the people might become legends. These three ingredients are found in one of the best known episodes in Spring and Autumn times. The story is told in the entry for the year 547 B.C. about Cui Shu, a grandee of the state of Qi, Duke Zhuang, a somewhat insensitive ruler, and Yan Ying, advisor to the ducal house of the state of Qi. The story begins when Cui meets a beautiful widow, the sister of his household steward, and wants to marry her. This won't do, the steward explains, because she is a relative (she has the same surname). This answer does not satisfy Cui who turns to divination.

There is then some discussion about the negative force of the hexagram thrown from the *Yijing (The Book of Changes)*, but Cui thinks that the first husband took any bad luck on himself. He marries the widow anyway. The duke, however, takes a fancy to her too, and openly has an affair with her. Cui employs an ally of the duke, and they trap him in Cui's house visiting Cui's wife. After the assassination, Yen Ying comes to Ts'ui's house to pay his respects to the dead duke, whose corpse is still there. He takes the same oath that the other nobles make to Cui, but reverses the words so that the effect is support for the ducal house. Cui is unwilling to put him to death because the people respect him.

If the intrigues and plots of the Spring and Autumn period in China remind one of Medieval Europe in some ways, there is also much that is distinctively Chinese. In 605, the powerful southern state of Chu quells some barbarians along its northern border with Zhou, the state left to the (nominal) ruling dynasty of the empire. The king of Zhou sends one of his wisest counselors, Wangsun Man, to meet the commander of the Chu army, the Viscount of Wu, with congratulations and presents. During their meeting, the viscount asks about the size and weight of the Zhou's tripods. These tripods, nine in all, one for each of the ancient provinces of the empire, represent the authority conferred on the Zhou to rule. This seems to be a thinly disguised suggestion that perhaps it is time for new leadership in the empire. In reply, Wangsun makes the famous statement, "It [authority] lies in moral integrity, not in the tripods themselves." He then discourses on the legend of the tripods: how their origin in the Xia dynasty was part of the tribute paid to the ruler from the nine provinces; how there were representations of them on the strange and remarkable things from each province; how these representations were used to instruct the people that encountered these strange objects, so they would not think of them as monsters or evil spirits and act superstitiously; and how this act promoted harmony between heaven and earth and secured blessings for the people. The envoy explains that, because the last ruler of Xia blotted out the dynasty's previous virtue, the tripods were transferred to the Shang dynasty, where they remained for 600 years. Because the Shang became cruel and oppressive, he explains, the tripods have now come to the House of Zhou. If the virtue is not there, the envoy continues, then no matter how big the tripods might be, they would weigh light. If it is there, then no matter how small they might be, they would weigh heavy. Heaven favors moral integrity, Wangsun concludes, and the tripods are in the right place for the time being. They were forecasted to remain with Zhou for thirty generations (by the first Zhou king), and although the virtue of Zhou has declined, Heaven has not changed its mandate. It is too early to ask about the weight of the tripods.

The Power of Music

Confucius is supposed to have written a "Book of Music" (the *Yue jing*), but the book was lost, probably during the Warring States time. We know from other sources, however, that Confucius considered music very important.

The *Zuo zhuan* tells us something about how music was viewed when Confucius was only seven or eight years old. This was in 543 B.C., when an envoy from the state of Wu made a tour of the other courts to open communications with Wu's new ruler. His visit to Lu (Confucius's home state) is especially interesting: during it, the envoy asks to hear the music of Zhou. Lu was well known for maintaining the tradition of the early music. This music consisted, in large part, of the words of the odes from the *Book of Poetry* (or *Odes*) with their instrumental and dance accompaniment. The idea that music reveals the inner moral condition of the individual or the state that produced it became a standard Confucian idea, but obviously existed long before the sage adopted it.

The envoy is presented with an exhibition of the odes grouped by region, much as we have them today; and after each group is played, he makes comments, thereby becoming one of the earliest literary critics in Chinese history. About the odes of Zheng (the state besieged by Jin and Qin), he remarks, "They are beautiful! But so detailed that the people may not be able to bear them. In that case, perhaps Zheng will be among the first states to be destroyed." Actually, Zheng lasted more than twice as long as his own state of Wu, which was taken over 70 years later by its neighbor.

The envoy also finds the odes of the powerful state of Qi to be beautiful: "One cannot know how far this state will go," he remarks. Of Qin, the state that eventually succeeds in subduing all the other states, he says, "Its music has the sound of a cultivated state. Perhaps it has become great because it occupies the former seat of Zhou [before it moved the capital]." Chen's music, however, "shows a state without proper rulers, can it last very long?" (Chen was taken over by Chu five years before Wu was lost.)

As the musicians and dancers work their way through the rest of the odes, the envoy becomes more and more enthusiastic, even putting some of his comments into verse. Finally, after finishing the music of Zhou and Shang, which is also in the *Shi jing*, they come to the music of Xia (the earliest dynasty); and the envoy exclaims, "Stop the exhibition! Even if it were filled with the most abundant virtue, no music could add to this. If there is more, I dare not ask for it."

Brilliant histories were to be written later but, in certain respects, the *Zuo zhuan* would never be surpassed. Contemporary critics say that if we read it today, then we are immediately removed to an arena where we can almost participate in the events of 2,500 years ago. In both literature and historical prose, its position is secure.

MICHAEL F. CARSON

Further Reading

Translation

Translations in this article are by Michael F. Carson.

Legge, James, trans. and ed. *The Chinese Classics*, vol. V *(The Ch'un Ts'ew with The Tso Chuen)*. London: Henry Frowde, 1872. This is the only English translation of the *Zuo zhuan*. Although a lot has happened in the study of Old Chinese since Legge's work, this translation is still very useful. It has been reprinted in Hong Kong (1961), and Taipei (1965). Legge's foreword may be the single best introduction to the *Zuo zhuan* in English.

Related Studies

Ch'en, Shou-Yi. *Chinese Literature: A Historical Introduction.* New York: Ronald Press. 1961. A long chronological account of literary developments in China from the beginning, with short sketches of authors, and some sample translations from various works.

Creel, Herrlee G. *The Origins of Statecraft in China.* vol. 1. Chicago: University of Chicago Press, 1970. See the many references in the index, but especially pages 475–478. One of the best known Western historians of China comments on the various sources for ancient Chinese history.

Karlgren, Bernard. "On the Authenticity and Nature of the *Tso Chuan*." *Goteborgs Hogskolas Arsskrift*, XXXII (1926), 3–65. Technical and scholarly, by the foremost Western authority on Old Chinese, this article is hard going, but worth the effort.

THE *BOOK OF THE WAY*

Title in Chinese: *Daode jing (Tao-te ching)* or *Laozi (Lao-tzu)*
Author: Traditionally attributed to Laozi, but authorship unknown
Literary Form: Poetry and prose
Date of Composition: c. 300 B.C.

Major Themes

There is an enduring natural reality known as the Tao*, which gives life to all things.*

The Tao exemplifies wuwei *(wu-wei: "non-action"), a behavior characterizable as benign non-involvement, illustrated through images of unassuming life-giving forces like water and mother.*

Human beings have digressed from the Tao*, and need to return to it, thereby attaining individual success and socio-cosmic harmony.*

One returns to the Tao by foregoing foolish interventional schemes (like those of the Confucians), practicing instead the behaviors exemplified by the Tao.

The *Daode jing (Tao-te ching) (Book of the Way)* is an ancient Chinese example of wisdom literature. It is the most well-known work of Chinese literature, and possibly the most well-known work of any non-Western civilization. It is known throughout the world, for it has been translated into every major language on earth, and into many minor ones. There are over a hundred versions in English alone. In fact, the *Daode jing* has been translated more often into more languages than any other work in history except the Bible. And like the Bible, it was the product of a complex compositional process, the unravelling of which is still ongoing among scholars.

The Nature of the Daode jing

The *Daode jing* is a relatively brief text, just over 5,000 characters long. Its form is part poetry, part prose. At the opening of the Han dynasty at the end of the third century B.C., the text was commonly circulated in two sections, one labeled *Dao (Tao)* and the other labeled *De (Te)*; some scholars believe that those divisions were just a matter of convenience of storage. In the *Mawangdui (Mawangtui)* manuscripts (discovered by archaeologists in the 1970s), the *De* chapters precede the *Dao* chapters; in the more familiar edition of Wang Bi (a commentator of the third century A.D.), the

two sections are reversed (chapters 1–37 being *Dao* and 38–81 being *De*). Since the first century B.C., the text has generally been divided into 81 chapters. Today's readers should bear in mind that these divisions may not have been present in the "original" text; and it is by no means clear that any real meaning should be read into them.

At first glance, the *Daode jing* is a jumble of unrelated sayings. Some have concluded that the unknown person(s) who collected the sayings imposed no structure upon the resulting text. Others have argued that no one would have been likely to have composed so formless a text. So we should conclude that it did in fact once possess a coherent structure that was subsequently lost. A few scholars have speculated that the text became deranged when the strings binding the ancient bamboo strips came undone, but such imaginings do not withstand critical analysis. A number of twentieth-century scholars, Chinese and Western alike, have taken the peculiar liberty of reorganizing the text itself. Such rearrangements are often little more than an arbitrary imposition of the interpreter's own perspective onto the text, which sometimes destroy the subtle vestiges of meaningful order already present within it. Much more misleading to readers, however, is the unending flow of pseudo-translations by fatuous dilettantes, who delude themselves and the public into a false belief that they have a true understanding of the text.

The "Authorship" of the Daode jing

Until recent centuries, the *Daode jing* was almost universally accepted as the creation of an ancient Chinese wise man known as Laozi (hence the other name by which it is commonly known), an attribution that gradually came to be challenged by Chinese scholars, and in the twentieth century, subjected to increasing criticism by Chinese, Japanese, and Western scholars alike. The traditional attribution rests ultimately on the reports of historian Sima Qian (Ssu-ma Ch'ien) in his *Shiji (Shih-chi)*, composed c. 100 B.C.. By ancient standards, Sima was a conscientious historian; and his annals are generally trustworthy. But when he attempted to sketch the lives of the great thinkers of ancient China, he ran across a problem: there was no trustworthy data in his day regarding the identity of the author of the *Daode jing*. Consequently, he provided several conflicting identifications, admitting ultimately that he had no way to decide among them. According to the most famous account, "Laozi" had been a man named Lao Dan (Lao Tan), an archivist for the Zhou (Chou) ruling house from whom Confucius had sought advice about propriety (*li*). Other sources indicate that Confucius may indeed have met someone named Lao Dan; but evidence suggests that this person had nothing to do with "Taoist thought," much less with the *Daode jing* itself. The most recent scholarship suggests that someone of the third century concocted the fiction of Lao Dan as the *Daode jing*'s "author" in an effort to lend it the lustre of a learned man in royal service, whom even Confucius had respected and sought to learn from. Yet, the mistaken belief that the *Daode jing* was written by a wise man named "Laozi" endures. Readers should bear firmly in mind that, in reality, such notions rank with the attribution of the Pentateuch to Moses or the book of *Proverbs* to Solomon.

It is possible that some of the ideas found in the *Daode jing* may have begun to take form sometime during the general period in which Confucius lived. But scholars today, in the West and in Asia alike, generally agree that the actual text of the *Daode jing* is a much later product. In actuality, the *Daode jing* first appeared sometime during the early third century B.C. In fact, it was certainly later than the writings of Zhuang Zhou (Chuang Chou), the fourth-century author of the earliest sections of the "Daoist" work named for him, the *Zhuangzi (Chuang-tzu)*.

The Teachings of the Daode jing

The focus of the *Daode jing* is something called the "Dao" ("Tao"), a term that cannot adequately be translated. The text says that the Dao is "vague and subtle," and it never provides definitions. Instead, it employs metaphors to suggest the nature of the Tao, and to describe behaviors that are similar to its way of working. Most basically, the term Tao seems to denote a natural force that runs through all things and guides them through their natural course of development. It is an inexhaustible source of life and power, and is constantly at work in the world in subtle and imperceptible ways. Both its reality and its nature can be perceived by observing the world around us. However, most people have lost sight of the Tao, and have given way to unnatural behaviors that go contrary to it. The goal of the *Daode jing* is to persuade the reader to abandon those behaviors, and to learn once again how to live in accord with the true course of life. One can achieve those goals by appreciating the true nature of life, and modifying one's behavior to be more like that of the Tao.

Specifically, the Tao is humble, yielding, and non-assertive. Like a mother, it benefits others selflessly: it gives us all life and guides us safely through it, asking nothing in return. This altruistic emphasis of the *Daode jing* has seldom been noticed, but is one of the most important lessons that it draws from the observation of the natural world. Water, for instance, is the gentlest and most yielding of all things, yet it can overcome the strongest substances and cannot itself be destroyed. More importantly, however, water lives for others: it provides the basis of life for all things, and asks nothing in return. If we learn to live like water does, we will be living in accord with the Tao, and its Power (*De*) will carry us safely through life. Such a way of life is called *wuwei*, usually translated as "non-action." *Wuwei* means foregoing all activity intended to effect desired ends. Instead, one should follow one's natural course and allow all other things to do likewise, lest our willful interference disrupt things' proper flow. Few modern readers have ever grasped the full radicality of the ideal of *wuwei*. Many of us today (like the ancient Chinese Confucians and Mohists—followers of Mozi [Mo Tzu]) look at the world and see things that we think need correcting. The *Daode jing* would actually have us do *nothing whatsoever* about them. The repeated phrase "do nothing, and nothing will be undone" admonishes us to trust the Tao—the natural working of things—and never to do anything about anything. Actually, such is the most that anyone can do, because the Tao, as imperceptible as it is, is the most powerful force in existence, and nothing can thwart its unceasing operation.

The Origins of the **Daode jing**

Probably the most common mistake people make when trying to understand the *Daode jing* is that of assuming it represents a uniform system of thought that evolved in the mind of a single person. In reality, the *Daode jing* is unquestionably the result of a long process of development, the contours of which can be reasonably deduced by combining analysis of the work's form and contents with a knowledge of the social and intellectual history of ancient China. Only by understanding how the *Daode jing* evolved can one truly understand its contents. The *Daode jing* can best be compared to works of "wisdom literature" like the Biblical *Book of Proverbs*. In other words, its primary purpose is to provide the reader with profound advice on how to live his life. Oddly, this simple fact is seldom appreciated. Many have misinterpreted the *Daode jing* as a philosophical treatise, or as just another manifestation of a universal mystical wisdom. Such interpretations misconstrue the fundamental nature of the work. The key to understanding the *Daode jing* is that it had a unique

textual history: current research suggests that it originated in the real-life oral wisdom teachings of a local community, and was then transformed by anonymous editors into an expression of socio-political principles designed to compete with those of the Confucians and Legalists.

Some scholars today continue to read the *Daode jing* as the product of ancient Chinese intellectuals, members of the same social elite that produced the Confucians and many of the leading spokesmen for other schools of thought. Just as texts like the *Mozi*, for instance, show dissatisfaction with the Confucian perspective, so does the *Daode jing*. So, some scholars reason that, it too must have been the work of "alienated idealists" trying to critique existing social and political conditions. But such socio-political positions, though clearly present in the *Daode jing*, really seem to have little to do with its most basic themes, such as the reality of the force called "the Tao." Nor does the text's sociopolitical slant seem to harmonize well with its most emphasized lesson for human life—that one should emulate the Tao by playing no active role in human affairs. If one were really to practice *wuwei*, as the *Daode jing* says a true sage does, wouldn't one just live one's own life, in accord with the natural order, completely ignoring the social and political "issues" of the day? Yet, the *Daode jing* contains many chapters dedicated to demonstrating how a Sage can rule a nation or even fight a war. The irony actually gives us clear indication of the *Daode jing*'s textual history: while once a collection of teachings for personal life in accord with the deepest order of reality, it was transformed into a tract designed to have a sociopolitical relevance.

The best explanation for those facts seems to be as follows. At some point prior to 300 B.C., there was a community somewhere in ancient China (quite possibly in the southern state of Zhu (Chu) that passed down a tradition of homespun wisdom. Originally, that wisdom consisted of such "real-life" advice as parents and other elders in any culture normally provide orally to young people: Behave in a wise and healthy way, and you will have a full and comfortable life free from conflict or unexpected suffering. Here we can appreciate why neither Sima Qian nor anyone else in third to second century China could identify the wise man supposedly designated by the term *laozi*. Far from having been a personal name, the term *lao* has its everyday meaning of "aged." It was a Japanese scholar, Kimura Eiichi, who first argued that *laozi* was not originally a title for some wise "Master Lao," but rather a generic reference to "the old ones" from whom anyone in any culture receives one's earliest and most important lessons in life. What sets this particular tradition apart from the normal wisdom of any other community is that some of its participants had evidently meditated upon the world's workings to the point of perceiving a universal force that could be experienced by deep introspection. Thus, the key to the oral tradition that constituted the wisdom of "the old ones" (*laozi*) is the concept that we should learn to perceive its reality and, by focusing on it, return to our "natural" behaviors—living a quiet life of humble beneficence, and giving selflessly to others, as a mother does. This tradition, one should note, was *not* the product of any social or intellectual elite: it was the accumulated wisdom of generations of old folk (probably women and men alike), passed down to each generation in a small-scale rural community. For convenience, we may refer to that tradition as the teachings of the "Laoist community."

Ancient China had been undergoing radical sociocultural changes since the seventh century B.C., and by the fourth century those changes were accelerating ever more rapidly: political disintegration was accompanied by rapid economic change and the decay of certain social values and traditions. In certain locales, especially around political centers in the north, members of the emerging *shi (shih)* class began formulating new analyses of what was going wrong with society and recommendations for rectifying the wretched state of affairs. That class included such fifth-century B.C. teachers as Confucius and his critic Mozi (*Mo-tzu*), and Confucius's fourth-century defender Mencius (*Mengzi/Meng Tzu*). Each of these men argued that the state of the world could be rectified by the activity of a self-selecting elite of wise and dedicated individuals who would learn to exemplify a proper set of

virtues and to lead the world back to the sociopolitical harmony that it had supposedly enjoyed in the days of the ancient sage-kings.

Circumstantial evidence suggests that toward the end of the fourth century young people from the Laoist community arrived in one of the newly emerging political centers, and became interested in the debates that were raging among the *shi* intellectuals around the rulers' courts. They compared the intellectuals' sociopolitical arguments with the teachings of their own traditional heritage, and developed the radical idea that the "old folks" teachings about *wuwei* and the natural order could be applied to the problems with which the intellectuals were so concerned. They then wrote down the memorable lessons of the "old ones" and added passages to explain how *wuwei* could enable a ruler to bring peace and order to his land. Other passages were added to address other issues current among the "intellectual elite" of the day, such as warfare. The resulting text—a combination of traditional oral wisdom and unprecedented sociopolitical doctrines—was then promulgated among intellectuals, identified only as the teachings of *laozi*—"the venerable elders." The intellectuals failed to understand that term, and assumed that the text must have been the name of some thinker, just like *Mozi*, or *Mengzi*. By the middle of the third century, the ideas found in it came to fascinate a large segment of the intelligentsia, and thinkers of every stripe, including Confucians and even Legalists, began to incorporate them into their own teachings.

Later, in Han times, librarians who faced the need to catalogue the multifarious pre-Han texts grouped together certain works that seemed to share similar themes. Thus the text called *Laozi* came to be classed together with writings like those of Zhuang Zhou and his followers under the rubric of *daojia (tao-chia)*. Later generations reified that library classification into a school of thought, now familiar to Asians and Westerners alike as the Daoists. Admiring Han emperors dignified the text then known as *Laozi* with the honorific title *jing*, "classic," which in earlier times had been reserved for the early Zhou texts that the Confucians promoted. Since the text in those days was kept in two sections, *Dao* and *De*, the resulting classic was denominated *Daode jing* (in the Mawangdui versions, *Dedao jing*).

The Relationship of Form and Contents in the Daode jing

The *Daode jing*, as we have it today, is not like any of the classical Chinese works with which people are generally familiar. It is not a collection of dialogues and pronouncements, like *Mencius* or the *Analects* of Confucius. Nor is it a set of reasoned arguments, like portions of the *Mozi* or *Xunzi*. The text that it most resembles is a little-known work of the same period called the *Neiye (Nei-yeh)*, a text of some 1,600 characters. The *Neiye* teaches the individual how to attract and internalize spiritual forces, including forces called *dao* and *de*, by means of a meditative process of quiescence and purification. The *Neiye* was influential in early Han times, but lost its prominence when it was incorporated into a collection called the *Guanzi (Kuan-tzu)* and ceased to circulate independently. The similarities of form and content between the *Neiye* and the *Daode jing* have led scholars today to believe that the editors of the *Daode jing* drew inspiration from the *Neiye*.

A notable feature of both texts is the absence of proper names and references to specific locations or events, whether historic or fictitious. Most other classical Chinese texts contain at least some traces of the compilers' own lives and the milieux in which they lived. Even the *Zhuangzi*, which shares a similar understanding of life, is radically different in style and structure: it records the profound and whimsical reflections of a brilliant mind upon problems of human life, but it also tells stories, in which real or fictive characters wrestle with life's mysteries. The *Daode jing* tells no stories and mentions no characters. It contains only vague references to "the Sage," "the ancients," or "the lord of ten thousand chariots." It thus seems that its editors deliberately constructed a text that could never be connected to any specific place or person, or to any identifiable intellectual tradition. One could infer that they intended to obscure the origins

of the collected material. But more likely, the editors were employing a literary device for a specific effect upon the reader: because one is confronted directly and immediately with provocative and cryptic sayings, and never distracted by references to what anyone else has ever thought or done, one's focus is always upon oneself, and upon the world in general. This focus induces the reader not only to cultivate the desired values and behaviors, but to perceive his or her true reality to be grounded in the natural order and in the cosmos as a whole, rather than in any historical particularities.

Clearly, part of the final editor's goal was very much like that of Zhuang Zhou's school—to force the reader to come to terms with a startling new perception of his own reality. For instance, ancient proverbs (from the Laoist tradition, and possibly elsewhere) were cast in an unexpected new context, twisting the reader's frame of reference in order to stimulate a radically new perspective upon reality. In part, this device was a deliberate exploitation of the fact that the reader of the text was ignorant of the oral tradition of the ancient Laoist community: aphorisms the meaning of which may have once been explained in person by local elders were now context-free. The editor sometimes provided a new context by "explaining" the adage. But he often left meaningful gaps, juxtaposing passages that had no readily apparent connection. He thus requires the reader to make leaps of comprehension. The result is a text whose "meaning" was designed to be a *process*: coming to understand it takes many re-readings, through which one comes to perceive entire new levels of meaning. The *Daode jing's* method of teaching thus parallels and reinforces its content, and understanding one sheds light upon the other. In addition, by leaving the reader to make his or her own connection, the *Daode jing* appeals to readers on different levels: regardless of one's level of sensitivity or understanding, one is drawn in, receiving a challenge that is not only suited to one's present state of awareness, but also leading one ever further into new levels of understanding. It is these qualities as much as *Daode jing's* ideas about life that enthralled centuries of Chinese readers, and continues to have the same effect on readers throughout the world today.

RUSSELL KIRKLAND

Further Reading

Translations

Chan, Wing-tsit, trans. *The Way of Lao Tzu*. Indianapolis: Bobbs-Merrill, 1963. A substantial presentation of the text, with copious notes from both traditional commentaries and modern studies by Asian and Western scholars. The translation is occasionally skewed by Chan's Neo-Confucian bent, but his examination of the text's traditional attribution is of lasting value.

Henricks, Robert G., trans. *Lao-tzu Te-Tao Ching*. New York: Ballantine Books, 1989. The new standard by one of the West's foremost authorities on the Mawangdui editions of the text.

Related Studies

Boltz, Judith Magee. "Lao-tzu." In *The Encyclopedia of Religion*. New York: Macmillan, 1987, 8:454–59. A thorough critical exploration of the figure "Laozi" throughout Chinese history, by a reliable, well-informed specialist.

Graham, A. C. "The Origins of the Legend of Lao Tan." In Graham's *Studies in Chinese Philosophy and Philosophical Literature*. Albany: State University of New York Press, 1990, 111–24.

LaFargue, Michael. *The Tao of the Tao te ching: A Translation and Commentary*. Albany N.Y.: State University of New York Press, 1992. An intriguing analysis by a non-sinologist who specializes in hermeneutic theory. While some of LaFargue's provocative ideas (like his rearrangement of the text) are debatable, his interpretive models are a significant contribution to our understanding of the text.

Lau, D. C., trans. *Chinese Classics: Tao Te Ching*. Hong Kong: Chinese University Press, 1982. A revised edition of the most sober and substantial study of the *Daode jing* in the English language.

Waley, Arthur, trans. *The Way and Its Power: A Study of the Tao Te Ching and Its Place in Chinese Thought*. London: George Allen and Unwin, 1934. An influential study that served as the standard for 30 years.

THE ART OF WAR

Title in Chinese: *Sunzi bingfa (Sun-tzu ping fa)*, also known simply as *Sunzi (Sun-tzu*, sometimes *Sun Tzu)*.
Author: Unknown. The traditionally recognized author is *Sun Wu*, usually known as *Sunzi (Sun-tzu)*, *Sun* being the surname, *Wu* the given name, and *zi (tzu)* a suffix indicating aristocratic lineage.
Born: fl. c. 500 B.C. (traditional date)
Literary Form: Essays
Date of Composition: Traditional: c. 500 B.C. Probable actual date of composition: c. 300 B.C.

Major Themes

Warfare is the art of deception.
The most important targets are the opponent's strategies and alliances; least important are his troops and fortifications.
Battles are sustained and won through the use of head-on attacks and peripheral strikes, and through exploitation of given circumstances.
The most effective strategic position is to appear to have no position.
War must be fought dispassionately.

The Art of War is a slim but very highly regarded and influential treatise on warfare in ancient China, written in a straightforward narrative prose style, in 13 chapters, each only a page or two long. As is the case for many ancient Chinese texts, authorship is traditionally attributed to an early, somewhat idealized, culture figure about whom little, if anything, is factually known. The name of the text in its simplest form *(Sunzi/Sun Tzu)* is simply the name of this presumed author, in the present case Sunzi, who is reputed to have lived around 500 B.C.

The first-century B.C. biography of Sunzi implies, but does not expressly state, that Sunzi authored a 13-chapter work on the art of war. Apart from that, the biography consists of no more than a single anecdote recounting a demonstration of Sunzi's military skills. To show a skeptical king how he can instill a sense of absolute respect for a military commander's authority, Sunzi is described as undertaking the training of two platoons of palace ladies in the techniques of uniform drill-field movements. When the ladies repeatedly giggle instead of following his commands, Sunzi orders their two leaders, the king's favorite consorts, to be beheaded. The king, watching from a palace balcony, is greatly dismayed by this sudden action and directly countermands the order. Yet the behead-

ings proceed apace, with Sunzi explaining that certain prerogatives are reserved for a military commander and are therefore beyond the reach even of a king. The two platoons of palace ladies are then seen to respond to Sunzi's commands with utmost obedience and to perform the drills in exemplary fashion.

The language and content of *The Art of War* suggest that it is a composition of the third or late fourth century B.C., rather than of the fifth or late sixth, as tradition would have it. The actual author is unknown. Archaeologists working in China in the 1970s and 1980s discovered manuscript fragments of another military text, very similar in content and style to the *Sunzi*, that seems to correspond to a lost work known traditionally as the *Sun Bin bing fa (Sun Pin ping fa)*, compiled by a certain Sun Bin. The same first-century B.C. biography of Sunzi, which was referred to above, identifies Sun Bin as a late fourth-century B.C. descendant of Sunzi, a period entirely compatible with the language and content not only of the *Sun Bin bing fa* fragments, but of the transmitted *Sunzi* itself.

The content of both the *Sun Bin bing fa* and the *Sunzi* reflects what is known in Chinese history as the Warring States period (481–221 B.C.). While war had always been a natural state of affairs among the loosely federated states that made up pre-imperial China, it took on a heightened importance from the fifth century B.C. on—when individual states were increasingly under the exclusive control of single rulers, each exercising authority from a single capital. This replaced an earlier system of diffuse authority associated with a hereditary nobility scattered across the state in an extended kinship network. The centralization of power in hands often at odds with the former hereditary ruling houses made war an ever more crucial aspect of state policy, and compelled the rulers to expand and strengthen their armies. This in turn gave rise to a class of military specialists, experts in the art of warfare, who were independent of the old ruling houses and unrelated to traditional hereditary lines. Sunzi is the premier, if only eponymous, representative of this class.

The Basic Principles of Warfare

The major themes of the work are expressed in their most general form in the first seven chapters. Discussions of specific points of military strategy and tactics are found in the second half.

Warfare is the art of deception. For Sunzi, to deceive means no more than purposely to mislead and dissemble, or to befuddle and confuse. One can deceive by what one does or says on the battlefield or at court. Sunzi makes this general point explicit in Chapter 1: "When you are well able to handle the conflict, give your opponent the impression that you are unable. When you are prepared, give him the impression of being unprepared. When you are near, give him the impression of being at a distance; when at a distance, give the impression of being nearby."

The most important targets are the opponent's strategies and alliances; least important are his troops and fortifications. This principle is an indirect reflection of the premise, fundamental throughout *The Art of War* and reminiscent of the Marshal de Saxe—the best victory is that won by effective and thorough preparations and foreknowledge, open intimidation and secret negotiation, without ever having actually to raise a pike on the field of battle. Sunzi says in Chapter 3: "To win a hundred victories in a hundred battles . . . is not as good as to force the opponent to submit without having to go to battle at all."

Battles are sustained and won through the use of "head-on" attacks and "peripheral" strikes and through exploitation of the given circumstances. It is with this principle that Sunzi introduces the only genuinely technical strategic concepts in the work. The terms "head-on" and "peripheral," in Sunzi's terminology *zheng (cheng)* and *qi (ch'i)*, might equally be translated as "direct" and "indirect." The word *qi* literally means "off-center, eccentric." In the simplest sense, a *zheng* attack constitutes the main thrust of an army, the act of direct confrontation with the opponent, whereas the *qi* is a secondary, or flanking, strike from an unexpected direction—a surprise attack that catches the opponent off-guard at a vulnerable spot.

The *zheng* and *qi* types of action are not seen as distinct and unrelated to each other, but as two fluctuating parts of a single overall method of battlefield tactics. Each becomes the other repeatedly and inevitably as the battle unfolds: when a peripheral strike is first felt, the main confrontation is underway elsewhere on the battlefield; but as the peripheral strike attracts full response from the opponent, it becomes the locus of the main confrontation and then is, by definition, no longer peripheral but direct; at that point, a subsequent, unexpected and peripheral strike at a different spot reshapes the battle again; and so on indefinitely. A successful commander turns the battle from the direct and "head-on" to the peripheral and back repeatedly, acting each time before the opponent realizes how the engagement is evolving. By maintaining this kind of momentum he keeps the opponent constantly off balance. The opponent is able to undertake no initiatives of his own because his energies are completely engaged in reacting to these shifting *zheng* and *qi* maneuvers.

The third word that Sunzi uses as a technical military concept is *shi (shih)*, meaning "the force of circumstances." Its definition includes everything from the lay of the land and anticipated weather conditions, to the prevailing omen-lore and reputation of the contending parties: forces that a commander cannot alter, but can turn to his own advantage. In the simplest sense, using *shi* to one's own advantage means nothing more than what Sunzi says in chapter 9: "In getting through mountains, rely on the valleys, . . . after crossing rivers, get as far beyond them as possible, . . . never engage an opponent with your back to the water." The circumstances at issue in these examples are the features of the terrain.

In other instances the circumstances can be psychological. Sun Bin, the fourth-century B.C. military expert and putative descendant of Sunzi, once advised a general of the state of Qi (Ch'i): "The Qi troops have a reputation for reticence and desertion. The first evening after you have invaded the state of Wei, have your troops build 100,000 campfires, the second evening build 50,000, the third 20,000. This will make the Wei defenders think more than half of your army has deserted. . . ." This is what is meant by turning the force of circumstances, in this case Qi's reputation for desertion, to one's own advantage.

The most effective strategic position is to appear to have no position. This principle in some ways recapitulates aspects of the three preceding it: appearing to have no position is a form of deception; its effect is intended to confound the opponent's strategies, it does not bear on his fortifications; and it may easily entail an attempt to manipulate the given circumstances to one's own advantage. All the same, Sunzi identifies it explicitly because he sees it as underlying every victory in battle. In this sense he means that one must never be able to discern, after the fact, what action a victorious commander took that gained him his victory.

War must be fought dispassionately. Sunzi never uses the Chinese word *chou* (ch'ou), which corresponds to English "enemy" and carries an emotionally tinged meaning of "inimical" and "hated/ hateful," but always uses the more objective and neutral term *di* (ti) "opponent," that is, "someone against whom you find yourself set or matched." The avoidance of emotionally charged terminology in the *Sunzi* is undoubtedly deliberate and goes hand in hand with the explicit admonition that wars

must be fought dispassionately. Anytime a commander allows himself to take action based on anger, fear, hope, hate, or any other emotional extreme that might jeopardize his otherwise coldly reasoned judgment, he risks disaster. Thus, in chapter 8, Sunzi says: "If a commander is prone to rage and volatility he is vulnerable to provocation; if he is concerned too much with remaining personally unsullied he is vulnerable to insult; if he cares too much for the welfare of his people he opens himself to trouble." And in Chapter 12: "A ruler cannot raise an army solely out of anger; a commander cannot take to the battlefield solely based on the heat of the moment."

The Philosophical Concept of War in Ancient China

Implicit throughout the work, but never openly discussed, is the assumption that war is a natural aspect of the political and social environment of man, and an intrinsic part of the state's matrix of responsibilities. It was an expected, if unwelcome, mark of human behavior. Unlike in the West, war in China was never conceived of as reflecting an eternal and irreconcilable battle between the forces of Good and Evil, or indeed between absolute opposites of any character: "right and wrong," "us and them," and "believer and infidel." The ancient Chinese were as able as anybody, of course, to distinguish "good" from "bad," and "this" from "that." But when they did, the "this's" and "that's" were matters of degree, not absolutes. Absent as well, consequently, are portrayals intended to justify, not to mention glorify, war based on such an aggrandized conception. For Sunzi, and for the more than two millennia of Chinese generals and statesmen who followed, war was a necessary bother, gravely serious as a practical matter, but never elevated to the status of a philosophically or morally inspired crusade. It was never seen as a life-and-death struggle for survival between antithetical national, cultural, or religious ideals of the kind consecrated for all time in the West on the field of Marathon.

The counterpart to war was called in Chinese, *an*,

a word conventionally translated as "peace," but that actually means "stability." The balance between war and stability varied over time, along a "social orderliness" scale with "good order" at one end and "chaos" at the other. War was simply a degree of strife approaching, if not actually reaching, open battle, which shifted state and society toward the "chaotic" end of the scale. As war was resolved, whether through negotiation or battlefield victory, social conditions moved back toward the "orderly" end of the same scale.

The pair of complementary terms "war" and "stability" must be distinguished from the parallel notions of "martial" and "civil" as aspects of early Chinese society. The former were looked upon as transient manifestations of changing social or political circumstances, the latter as inherent features of the social order. An ideal and stable society presumed an equilibrium between its civil and martial strengths; too much of one and too little of the other, irrespective of which was predominant, led to instability and potentially to war. While war itself might be undesirable and should be avoided whenever possible, the underlying martial aspect of society was always taken as intrinsic and natural, and as a necessary counterweight to the civil.

The principles, strategies, and tactics explicitly prescribed in the *Sunzi* form themselves around the practical goal of victory over an opponent in an immediate setting; the underlying implicit goal is the restoration of the proper balance between the twin virtues of the martial and the civil in human society, nothing grander.

WILLIAM G. BOLTZ

Further Reading

Translations

Ames, Roger T., trans. *Sun-tzu: the Art of Warfare*. New York: Ballantine Books, 1993. A rather free, philosophically intrepretive translation. Strengths include an extended discussion of the work from a philosophical rather than historical perspective, and translation of the recently discovered bamboo-strip manuscript fragments of the *Sun Pin bing fa* and other similar fragments.

Giles, Lionel, trans. *Sun-tzu on the Art of War*. London: Luzac & Co., 1910. The classic, standard translation; still the best overall. Especially useful for its analytic presentation of the text and inclusion of principal commentaries in the discussion.

Griffith, Samuel B., trans. *Sun Tzu, the Art of War*. Oxford: Clarendon Press, 1963. Characterized by very good extended introductory essays on the date and composition of the text, the Warring States background and the nature of war in ancient China, and on the influence of the *Sunzi* on Mao Tse-tung.

Sawyer, Ralph D., trans. and ed. *The Seven Military Classics of Ancient China*. Boulder, CO. Westview Press, 1993. Includes a translation of the *Sunzi*, and has an excellent introduction and an extensive bibliography.

THE POETRY OF QU YUAN (CH'Ü YÜAN)

Author: Qu Yuan (Ch'ü Yüan), also known as Qu Ping (Ch'ü Ping)
Born: c. 343 B.C.
Died: The death of Qu Yuan is traditionally dated to 278 B.C., 18 years after the death of King Huai of the state of Chu. However, some modern scholars speculate that Qu Yuan died just after his banishment, around 315 B.C..
Major Poems: "Encountering Sorrow," "Nine Songs," "Heaven Questions"

Major Themes

The "Encountering Sorrow" records the confessions of a wronged minister, who remains virtuous to his king even in the face of death.

The "Nine Songs" records the pleas of the forlorn shaman-priest who is thwarted in his quest of a goddess.

The "Heaven Questions" records the queries of an inquisitive poet who is skeptical about the role of Heaven in contemporary society.

Qu Yuan is first mentioned in a second-century B.C. lament by the Han dynasty statesman, Jia Yi (Chia I). Banished to Changsha in the far south by an unjust king, Jia Yi wrote a poem praising a certain Qu Yuan who had met a similar fate. About a century later, Sima Qian (Ssu-ma Ch'ien) in his *Shi ji (Shih chi) Records of the Grand Historian* [early first century B.C.]), compiled a biography of Qu Yuan. Here the poet is also referred to as Qu Ping. Qu Yuan lived in the chaotic Zhan Guo (Chan Kuo), or Warring States period (403–221 B.C.) of China, when the three states of Chu (Ch'u) in the south, Qin (Ch'in) in the west, and Qi (Ch'i) in the northeast dominated the political scene. Qu Ping was a high official involved in a court intrigue during the reign of King Huai of the state of Chu (reigned 328–296 B.C.). As a result of slander from rival officials, Qu Ping, the loyal and accomplished high minister, was dismissed from office. While Qu was out of favor, King Huai was duped by an eloquent Qin diplomat, was betrayed by his younger son, and eventually died imprisoned in the state of Qin. Sima Qian's biography relates that Qu Ping wrote his masterpiece, *"Li Sao"* ("Encountering Sorrow"), just after being dismissed from office (c. 315 B.C.). According to the biography, he then lived to see King Huai die in Qin. Much later, he threw himself into the Miluo River (near present-day Changsha) and drowned.

The collection of literature that contains the three poems listed under "Major Poems" above, dates from the second century A.D. An imperial librarian named Wang Yi (Wang I) edited and annotated an existing collection probably compiled two and a half centuries earlier by Liu An, Prince of Huainan (c. 135 B.C.). Wang Yi named his anthology *Chu Ci (Ch'u Tz'u)*: literally the *Songs of Chu*. As it is understood by modern scholars, the anthology includes the one poem that is unquestionably attributable to Qu Yuan, the "*Li Sao*," plus seven works by the school of Qu Yuan in the late Warring States period, as well as nine imitative works dating from the Han dynasty (206 B.C.–A.D. 221).

"Encountering Sorrow"

"*Li Sao*" ("Encountering Sorrow") leads off the anthology; it has the distinction of being the first poem in Chinese history that is not anonymous. Arguably the best known poem in the entire Chinese tradition, its author is hailed as the father of Chinese poetry. In a personalized style unprecedented in classical China, Qu Yuan pleaded his individual case of injustice, all the while making use of exotic imagery with origins in the sacrificial rites of the local religions of southern China. The rites will be discussed in the next section.

Ever since the third century, the poem has been

called an allegory. The poet had good reason to hide his objectives in writing the poem. Banished to Jiangnan (the Chu district south of the Yangzi River) by the court of King Huai, Qu Yuan could not directly criticize a sitting government for fear of reprisal. On one level of the allegory, the persona is the banished minister lamenting the separation from his wayward king. But he calls his king the "Fair One" or the "Fragrant One," the same name used by the shaman of the "Nine Songs" to refer to his goddess. Indeed, the king first appears to be the persona's lover:

And I thought how the trees and flowers were fading and falling,
And feared that my Fairest's beauty would fade too.

(LINES 19–20: HAWKES, 1985)

Later, conversely, the persona appears to be the king's lover:

All your ladies were jealous of my delicate beauty;
Gossiping, slandering, they say I love wicked ways.

(LINE 87: HAWKES, 1985; LINE 88, WATSON, 1984)

This mixture of the romantic role with the official role of the poet-persona is just one facet of the complex allegory.

Weary from making his futile plaint, the persona eventually turns his gaze to Heaven. In pursuit of Heaven, he must become a shaman, and to reach this state he must cultivate, ingest, and clothe himself in fragrant flowers such as chrysanthemum, heliotrope, and angelica. Representing another level of allegory, these flowers are the symbols of virtue. Once enough virtue has been cultivated, the persona is capable of harnessing the power of natural deities in order to mount to heaven:

I yoked a team of jade dragons to a phoenix-figured car
And waited for the wind to come, to soar up on my journey.

(LINES 183–84: HAWKES, 1985)

But, as with the palace of the king, the gatekeeper of Heaven refuses to open, and the persona must return to earth in dejection.

Denied twice, not only by his sovereign, but also by the High God, the persona shifts his quest back to the romantic mode. Now he seeks betrothal with a "fair lady":

I gazed on a jade tower's glittering splendour
And spied the lovely daughter of the Lord of Song.
I sent off the magpie to pay my court to her,
But the magpie told me that my suit had gone amiss.

(LINES 235–38: HAWKES, 1985)

The woman referred to here is Jian Di (Chien Ti), virgin mother of Xie (Hsieh), the first ancestor of the Shang dynasty kings. Along with Fu Fei and the Lord of Yu's daughters each of the ladies sought is a goddess or spirit. Each of them in turn refuses to be romanced, as do the gods and goddesses of the "Nine Songs" (to be discussed below).

Still undaunted, the persona consults a shaman who divines by the *Yijing (I Ching)*. The advice is auspicious, and he begins one last quest "in search of a mate." He heads west toward the mythical Kunlun mountains but is unable to locate a "fair lady," so he ascends once again up to Heaven. On the way he looks back, catches a glimpse of his old home, and cannot go further. This is the end of the poem; the final stanza hints at the poet's fate:

Enough! There are no true men in the state; no one understands me.
Why should I cleave to the city of my birth?
Since none is worthy to work with in making good government,
I shall go and join Peng Xian in the place where he abides.

(LINES 369–72: HAWKES, 1985)

Peng Xian (P'eng Hsien) was a Shang dynasty (1766–1122 B.C.) shaman who drowned himself, which is what Qu Yuan is presumed to have done. "The Fisherman," another poem in the *Chu Ci*, depicts Qu Yuan as a dejected exile contemplating suicide: "I would rather cast myself into the waters of the river and be buried in the bowels of fishes, than hide my shining light in the dark and dust of the world." The dragon boat festival is held every summer in his honor, when offerings of rice are thrown into the river to keep the fish from eating the poet's corpse.

The ultimate in personalized writing, *"Li Sao"* might be considered a literary suicide note. Such desperate actions were justifiable when one's honor could not otherwise be proven. Nothing like the poem's highly emotional language existed previously in the Chinese tradition, but it was imitated frequently in the centuries following its popularization. Other aspects of its imagery were also borrowed, in particular the images of exotic vegetation and the motif of shamanistic journeys. These are the legacy of the sacrificial rituals that persisted in the local cults of southern China during the Warring States period.

"Nine Songs"

The second work in the *Chu Ci* anthology is the *"Jiu Ge"* [*"Chiu Ko"*] "Nine Songs"). Each of these, while subjective in mode like "Encountering Sorrow," speaks from the point of view of a *wu* (shaman)—a professional spirit medium that dominated the religious practices of southern Chu. According to Wang Yi, Qu Yuan composed the poems after observing authentic rites that celebrated these gods and goddesses. Modern scholars speculate that the songs stem from an oral tradition that predated Qu Yuan, who, at most, merely collected or edited them.

The collection of poems actually consists of eleven works: nine individual songs addressed to gods or goddesses, one eulogy to the spirits of fallen soldiers, and the fragment of a hymn. Excluding these last two, the remaining nine can be analyzed as follows. Two songs are mainly objective descriptions of sacrificial rites addressed to two major gods: **Donghuang Taiyi (Tung-huang T'ai-i)**, the Great One, Monarch of the East (possibly an eastern Chinese name for the High God Shangdi [Shang-ti]); and **Dong Jun (Tung Chün)**,

the Lord of the East (a name for the Sun). In addition to the shaman who invokes the spirit, and the god who answers the summons, there are musicians, dancers, and a choir to give the religious pageant of these two songs its proper majesty. The first song is pure ritual, a rich ceremony of sacrificial feasts, singing and dancing. The Great One is not observed until the last line of the poem.

The five notes chime in thick array;
The Lord is pleased and happy, his heart is at rest.

(LINES 14–15: WALEY, 1973)

In the second song, the sun appears in the east and slowly soars across the sky. Meanwhile the pageant continues below him. Finally, as the sun is about to set the Lord of the East speaks:

I gather my reins and my chariot sweeps aloft.
I take up my long arrow and shoot at the Heavenly Wolf.

(LINES 20–21: WALEY, 1973)

The element of ritual pageantry diminishes as the status of the god decreases.

The remaining songs are mainly subjective interactions between the shaman and individual gods or goddesses, namely: **Yunzhong Jun (Yün-chung Chün)**, The Lord Within the Clouds (probably a Thunder God); **Xiang Jun (Hsiang Chün)**, Princess of the Xiang River, and **Xiang Furen (Xiang Fu-jen)**, Lady of the Xiang River (said to be the wives of Sage-king Shun, who threw themselves into the river when their husband died); **Da Siming (Ta Ssu-ming)** and **Shao Siming (Shao Ssu-ming)** (two manifestations of the God of Fate, who determined the length of human lives); **He Bo (Ho Po)**, the River Earl (a dragon god that controlled the Yellow River); **Shan Gui (Shan Kuei)**, the Spirit of the Mountain (thought to be the Lady of Gaotang (Kao-t—ang), goddess of Shaman Mountain).

Each of these poems opens with the shaman seeking a goddess or god in an imaginary landscape of luxurious vegetation. When the union is imminent, the spirit suddenly departs, rejecting the shaman, who thereafter wanders forlorn about the wilderness:

The wind soughs and soughs, the trees rustle;
My love of my Lord has brought me only sorrow.

("*SHAN GUI*," LINES 27–28: WALEY, 1973)

Scholars know very little about the religious cults that existed in those days, but sexual interaction between the shaman and the spirit was evidently powerful "medicine." This is the motif that lends the greatest imaginative force to the "Encountering Sorrow," when its persona transforms into a shaman in order to pursue his quest for the goddess.

"Heaven Questions"

The third work in the *Songs of Chu* is the "*Tian Wen*" ("*T'ien Wen*"): "Heaven Questions." It is a long poem of 95 quatrains, each of which poses one to four questions about heaven, earth, and human society. Since the Tang dynasty (A.D. 618–907) the poem has been divided into three sections. Part I, called "The Patterns of Heaven," is an ancient Chinese cosmogony. It begins as follows:

> *In the beginning of old,*
> *All is yet formless, no up or down.*
> *Dark and light are a blur,*
> *The image is only a whir.*
> *Bright gets brighter, dark gets darker,*
> *The* yin *mingles with the* yang—
> *Then was the round pattern manifold.*
> *What an achievement that was!*

(FIELD, 1992)

Part II, the "Patterns of Earth," to a great extent follows the journey taken by the Great Yu (Yü), founder of the Xia (Hsia) dynasty, who quelled the floods and demarcated the nine regions of China.

> *Flood waters deep,*
> *How were they filled?*

> *The Nine Regions of the earth,*
> *How were they arranged?*

(FIELD, 1986)

Part III, "Human Affairs," which makes up over two-thirds of the poem, is a rambling query ranging across the Xia (Hsia), Shang, and Zhou (Chou) dynasties (1122–249 B.C.). It is concerned mainly with the rise and fall of dynasties and the role Heaven takes in choosing successive dynastic founders:

> *Tang came down to tour the realm.*
> *There he found Yi Zhi [I Chih].*
> *When Jie [Chieh] was banished for his crimes,*
> *Why were lords and black hairs glad?*

(FIELD, 1986)

Tang was the first ruler of Shang, and Jie was last ruler of Xia.

The "Heaven Questions" is commonly attributed to Qu Yuan, thanks to a fanciful story appended by Wang Yi explaining the circumstances of its origin. In his preface to the poem Wang claims that Qu Yuan wrote these questions on murals he observed in the shrines of the Chu ancestors. Such an explanation for the poem's origin is no longer entertained. Scholars now speculate that it was compiled at the Jixia (Chi-hsia) Institute in the state of Qi, which was a sort of "think tank" for King Xuan (Hsüan) (reigned 319–301 B.C.). This institute is the origin of the *Guanzi*, much of the *Huainanzi*, and possibly the *Daode Jing (Tao Te Ching)*. Since it is known that Qu Yuan made several journeys to Qi as envoy of Chu, it is possible that he learned of the compilation and collected fragments then in circulation. While there are certainly similarities between "*Tian Wen*" and "*Li Sao*"—the same legends are referred to in both poems—however, the poetic phrasing is rarely the same. And the meter of "*Tian Wen*" is unlike anything else in the *Chu Ci*. While we may never know who authored the poem, it has remained one of the most important works from *The Songs of Chu*.

Some four or five other pieces in the *Chu Ci* are

traditionally attributed to Qu Yuan. There is the *"Jiu Zhang" ("Nine Declarations"),* which includes the important work, *"Huai Sha" ("Embracing Sand"),* a poem that treats the suicide of Qu Yuan. Sima Qian included this poem in his biography. *"Yuan You" ("Far-off Journey")* is a Daoist poem describing a journey to Heaven that ends not in dejection, but in pure ecstasy. *"Bu Ju," ("Divination")* and *"Yu Fu" ("The Fisherman")* are imaginary accounts of episodes in Qu Yuan's life, and are reminiscent of stories in *Zhuangzi (Chuang Tzu),* a contemporary work of Daoist philosophy.

STEPHEN L. FIELD

Further Reading

Translations

Field, Stephen, trans. *Tian Wen: A Chinese Book of Origins.* New York: New Directions, 1986. A translation with notes on "Heaven Questions."

———. "Cosmos, Cosmograph, and the Inquiring Poet: New Answers to the 'Heaven Questions.' " *Early China* 17 (1992): pp. 83–110. Includes a translation of "Heaven Questions."

Hawkes, David, trans. *The Songs of the South: An Anthology of Ancient Poems by Qu Yuan and Other Poets.* London: Penguin Books, 1985 (1959). The standard English translation of the entire *Chu Ci.* Excellently researched, very reliable study of the tradition that produced the poems. Originally published in 1959, the translation was substantially revised in 1985.

Waley, Arthur, trans. *The Nine Songs: A Study of Shamanism in Ancient China.* San Francisco: City Lights, 1973 (1955). A translation with short commentary of the nine songs that are addressed to gods and goddesses.

Watson, Burton, trans. and ed. *The Columbia Book of Chinese Poetry: From Early Times to the Thirteenth Century.* New York: Columbia University Press, 1984.

THE BOOK OF RITES

Title in Chinese: *Liji (Li-chi)* (Also translated as *Record of Ritual*)
Authors: Composite work of ancient texts
Date of Compilation: Compiled during Han dynasty (206 B.C.–A.D. 222)
Literary Form: Prose essays

Major Themes

The observance of proper ritual preserves status distinctions and harmonizes social relationships.
Ritual is more important than law in maintaining social order.
Proper ritual reflects the structure of the universe, just as appropriate music reflects cosmic harmony.

The *Liji (The Book of Rites)*, sometimes entitled in translation *Record of Ritual*, a work which became one of the hallowed "Five Classics" of Confucianism during the Han dynasty (206 B.C.–A.D. 222), bears abundant testimony—offered, one might say, in several different literary voices—to the central role of ritual *(li)* in traditional Chinese culture. By Han times the term *li* had come to signify all forms of sacred and secular ceremony, as well as the entire body of social institutions, rules, regulations, conventions, and norms that governed human relations in China. *Li* has been variously translated as rites, ritual, standards of social usage, mores, politeness, propriety, and etiquette, but no single term does full justice to the wide range of its meanings and manifestations.

The Land of Ritual and Righteousness

The *Liji*, combined with two other ancient ritual texts—the *Zhouli (Chou-li) (Rites of Zhou)* and the *Yili (I-li) (Etiquette and Ritual)*—exerted a profound influence on Chinese society from Han times into the twentieth century. These works, particularly the Liji and *Yili*, provided hundreds of general principles and guidelines, as well as literally thousands of specific prescriptions, for proper conduct in nearly every realm of traditional Chinese life. Furthermore, these works inspired a huge number of supplementary ceremonial handbooks, which left few questions of ritual or etiquette to chance. From the Han period onward, the Chinese commonly referred to their country as "the land of

ritual and righteousness" *(liyi zhi bang/li-i chih pang)*, equating these virtues with civilization itself.

China's earliest written records, inscribed on so-called oracle bones and bronze vessels during the Shang dynasty (c. 1800–c. 1045 B.C.), indicate a preoccupation with *li*. In Shang usage, the term *li* referred primarily to a set of religious sacrifices that both expressed and undergirded the king's authority; but by Zhou (Chou) times (c. 1045–256 B.C.), the notion of *li* had expanded considerably to embrace not only official sacrifices and secular ceremonies, but also day-to-day community rituals, domestic observances, and various forms of polite behavior. This broader application of the term defined the scope of the *Liji*, which began to take shape in the Zhou period.

Ritual occupied an especially important position in the thought of Confucius (c. 551–479 B.C.), which helps account for its endurance in traditional times. In fact, a common term for Confucianism throughout the imperial era (221 B.C.–A.D. 1912) was *lijiao (li-chiao)*, or "the teachings of ritual." Confucian regard for ritual made possible the elevation of the *Liji* to the status of a classic in the Han period, for, as the *Hanshu* (History of the [Former] Han) tells us pointedly, the *Liji* was written by "the pupils of the original seventy disciples [of Confucius]."

The *Analects* of Confucius is replete with aphorisms relating to *li*. "To conquer the self and return to the rites is humaneness [*ren/jen*]," Confucius once said. When asked how a person could achieve

this object, the sage replied, "Do not look at what is contrary to *li*; do not listen to what is contrary to *li*; do not say what is contrary to *li*; and do not make any movement contrary to *li*." Confucius considered the dictates of propriety to be far more important than law in encouraging correct behavior: "For managing the world and pacifying the people there is nothing greater than ritual," he once said; and again, "If the people are led by laws, and an attempt made to give them uniformity by means of punishments, they will try to avoid the punishment, but have no sense of shame. If [however] they are led by virtue, and an attempt is made to give them uniformity by means of ritual, they will have a sense of shame and become good."

Ritual as an Ordering Principle

Of the many famous followers of Confucius, Xunzi (Hsün Tzu) (c. 310–220 B.C.) placed the greatest emphasis on ritual as an ordering principle. He maintained that "Through *li*, Heaven and Earth join in harmony, the sun and moon shine, the four seasons proceed in order, the stars and constellations march, the rivers flow, and all things flourish; men's likes and dislikes are regulated and their joys and hates made appropriate. Those below are obedient, those above are enlightened; all things change but do not become disordered; only he who turns his back on the rites will be destroyed." Such views inform the entire world view articulated in the *Liji*.

Xunzi believed, as did Confucius, that music, like ritual, was a useful tool for teaching people "how to behave." "Music," he wrote, "embodies an unchanging harmony, while ritual represents unalterable order. Music unites that which is the same; ritual distinguishes that which is different. Through the combination of rites and music the human heart is governed. To seek out the beginning and exhaust all change—this is the emotional nature of music; to illumine the truth and do away with what is false—this is the essence of ritual." Similarly, the *Liji* states: "Music is the harmony of Heaven and Earth; ritual is the order of Heaven and Earth. Through harmony all things are trans-

formed; through order all things are distinguished. Music arises from Heaven; ritual is patterned after Earth. . . . Only when one understands the functions of Heaven and Earth can one institute ritual and music."

The views of Xunzi predominate in the "orthodox" edition of the *Liji*, which dates from the early Han period (see below). In fact, this particular version includes numerous lengthy sections and shorter passages that have been drawn almost verbatim from the book that bears Xunzi's name. At the same time, however, certain portions of the *Liji* bear the unmistakable imprint of Xunzi's idealistic rival Mencius (c. 370–290 B.C.)—notably the short philosophical chapters known as the *Daxue (Ta hsüeh) (Great Learning)* and the *Zhongyong (Chung yung) (Doctrine of the Mean)*. So revered were these two texts that they eventually came to be grouped together with the *Analects* and the *Mencius (Mengzi)* as the "Four Books"—the succinct embodiment of all Confucian wisdom for many Chinese scholars.

The Liji as an Anthology

Unlike the *Zhouli* and *Yili*, the *Liji* has no unified structure. Rather, it is a somewhat unwieldy anthology of ancient usages, prescriptions, definitions, and anecdotes interwoven with some much higher-quality literary texts. According to a standard account in the *Suishu (Official History of the Sui Dynasty)*, the formation of the *Liji* can be traced to King Xian of Hejian (d. 131 B.C.), who initially collected about 130 remnants of various Zhou dynasty ritual texts (known generically as records, *ji*). Subsequently, Liu Xiang (Liu hsiang) (79–8 B.C.) "set these texts in order, epitomized them, and added . . . [new materials]." Then two individuals who lived at about the same time—Dai De (Tai Te) and his nephew, Dai Sheng (Tai Sheng)—used Liu Xiang's materials to compile their own respective versions of the *Liji*. Further additions were reportedly made by the late Han scholar Ma Rong (Ma Jung) (A.D. 79–166), but the standard text seems to be close to, if not identical with, Dai Sheng's original version. The edition by Dai De, of which ap-

proximately one-half has been preserved for posterity as the *Da Dai Liji (Senior Dai's Record of Ritual)*, came to be viewed by many later scholars as "a blatant forgery." But in subject matter it has much in common with Dai Sheng's canonical *Xiao Dai Liji (Junior Dai's Record of Ritual)*.

Despite its decidedly Confucian moral orientation, the *Liji* reflects other philosophical influences as well. For instance, a large portion of the *Lüshi chunqiu (Lü-shih ch'un ch'iu) (Spring and Autumn of Master Lü)*, a cosmological tract written under Legalist sponsorship during the Qin dynasty (221–206 B.C.), appears in the *Record of Ritual* as the *Yueling (Yüeh-ling) (Monthly Commands)*. Moreover, certain parts of the Liji have a decidedly Daoist flavor. Thus, when a passage from the *Liji* begins with a statement such as "The Master says," we cannot always assume that the reference is to Confucius himself. Nonetheless, most commentators, including the influential Han commentator Zheng Xuan (Cheng Hsüan) and the later Tang exegete Kong Yingda (Kung Ying-ta), considered the *Liji* to be an integral part of the Confucian corpus.

From a literary standpoint, the 49 chapters of the *Liji* vary substantially in length, contents, and style. On the whole, Chinese commentators have considered the *Daxue* and *Zhongyong*, together with the *Wangzhi (Wang-chih) (Royal Institutions)*, *Liyun (Li-yün) (Evolution of Ritual)*, *Xueji (Hsüeh-chi) (Record of Study)*, and *Yueji (Yüeh-chi) (Record of Music)*, to be the most beautifully written parts of the book. Ranked second are another six chapters—the *Jingjie (Ching-chieh) (Explications of the Classics)*, the *Fangji (Fang-chi) (Records of Preventive Measures)*, the *Biaoji (Piao-chi) (Manifest Records)*, the *Ziyi (Tzu-i) (Black Robe)*, the *Ruxing (Ju-hsing) (Confucian Behavior)* and the *Dazhuan (Ta-chuan) (Great Commentary)*—not to be confused with the famous *Yijing (I Ching)* commentary of the same name. In the third category are certain portions of a few other random chapters—notably the *Liqi (Li-ch'i) (Ceremonial Vessels)*, the *Jiyi (Chi-i) (Meaning of Sacrifices)*, the *Juli (Chü-li) (Minor Rites)*, and the *Yueling*.

Despite its heterogeneous content, its lack of a systematic structure, and its relatively recent origins, the *Liji* contributed to the formation and perpetuation of traditional Chinese culture in two important ways. First, it provided an enduring metaphysical rationale for Chinese ritual practices, thus undergirding various social assumptions and types of social behavior with a powerful philosophical sanction. Second, it provided basic guidelines for proper behavior that remained valid for most Chinese subjects into the first decade of the twentieth century.

The Liji *and Proper Conduct*

The metaphysics of the *Liji* can be summarized briefly in the following passage:

> The rules of ceremony [*li*] originate in the great unity, which differentiated into Heaven and Earth, turned into *yin* and *yang*, changed to become the four seasons, and then became embodied in spirits. . . . These rules have their origin in Heaven and their movement extends to Earth. They extend to all the affairs of life. They change with the seasons and accord with various allotments and conditions. . . . Thus ritual and righteousness enable us to understand the way of Heaven and act in accordance with human feelings.
>
> (LEGGE, 1885, 1967)

Viewed from this perspective, ritual is nothing more (but certainly nothing less) than the successful imitation of natural processes by human beings. Or, to cite the *Liji* again: "The sages created music in response to Heaven and they instituted *li* to match Earth. When *li* and music are distinct and complete, Heaven and Earth function in perfect order."

Li, like music, had transformative power in the traditional Chinese view—the capacity, in fact, to prevent distress and "to make mutual respect prevail within the four seas." Employed by the ruler and other "superior men," it encouraged right behavior at all levels of society; and followed as a standard of proper conduct, it imposed restraints on individuals and preserved social distinctions. As the *Liji* states:

> The rules of propriety [*li*] furnish the means of determining the observances toward relatives, as near and remote; of settling points which may cause suspicion or doubt; of distinguishing where there should be agreement, and where difference; and of making clear what is right and what is wrong. . . . To cultivate one's person and fulfill one's words is called good conduct. When conduct is ordered and words are in accordance with the *dao*, we have the substance of the rules of propriety.
>
> (LEGGE, 1885, 1967)

Ceremonies were thus "a great instrument in the hands of the ruler," providing "the means by which to resolve what is doubtful, clarify what is abstruse, receive the spirits, examine regulations, and distinguish humaneness [*ren*] from righteousness [*yi*]. . . . To govern a state without ritual would be like plowing a field without a plowshare."

As a reading of the *Liji* indicates clearly, the Chinese considered ritual and propriety essential to the performance of filial duties and to the overall harmony of the household. The *Neize (Nei-tse) (Inner Regulations)* chapter of the *Liji* provides a great number of detailed guidelines for all kinds of domestic duties and actions. The following excerpt suggests the kind of behavior expected of men and women, including husbands and wives:

> Men should not speak of what belongs to the inside [of the house], and women should not speak of external matters. Except at sacrifices and funeral rites, they should not hand vessels to one another. If they have occasion to give or receive anything, the women should accept it in a basket. . . . . . . They should not go to the same well, nor to the same bathing house. They should not share the same mat . . . or wear similar upper or lower garments. . . . On

the road, a man should take the right side, and a woman the left.

(LEGGE, 1885, 1967)

The remarkable feature of these and many other such stipulations in the *Liji* is that they continued to be honored, at least within elite society, for more than 2,000 years.

Similarly, throughout the imperial era certain group rituals—notably the so-called "community drinking ceremony" (*xiangyin jiu/hsiang-yin chiu*)—followed the guidlines laid down in the *Liji*. It is true, of course, that Chinese ritual forms never remained static; they changed with the times, as Patricia Ebrey's admirable research on Zhu Xi's *Jiali (Chia-li) (Family Rituals)* amply demonstrates. Nonetheless, the continuities in Chinese ritual practice over long periods of time appear more striking than the departures.

During the early Qing dynasty (A.D. 1644–1912), scholars of evidential research (*kaozheng xue/k'ao-cheng hsüeh*) began to subject the *Liji*, and in fact all of the classics, to close philological scrutiny as part of a general campaign designed to "purify" Confucianism. Their goal was to call into question what they considered to be the pernicious exegetical influence of Buddhist-inspired neo-Confucianism. They therefore emphasized pre-Buddhist sources of authority dating from the Han dynasty and sought to place ritual at the center of their "fundamentalist" vision in order to provide an absolute and "objective" standard of behavior for all people to follow. Yet despite their careful and conscientious scholarship, the ideological zeal of the *kaozheng* advocates occasionally caused them to ignore philological evidence or to go well beyond it. Thus, for example, the great *Qing (Ch'ing)* scholar *Dai Zhen (Tai Chen)* used the Han dynasty commentaries of Zheng Xuan (Cheng Hsüan) in a surprisingly selective way, and the highly respected Ruan Yuan (Juan Yüan) went so far as to embrace Senior Dai's questionable version of the *Liji* simply because it contained more material attributed to Zengzi (Tseng Tsu), a direct disciple of Confucius.

After the fall of the Qing dynasty in 1912, traditional ritual practices and traditional texts, including the *Liji*, came under fierce attack, especially during the New Culture Movement (c. 1915–1925). In response to increasingly shrill demands by nationalistically inspired Chinese to "destroy the old and establish the new" (*pojiu lixin/p'o-chiu li-hsin*), "modern" ritual texts and practices began to appear in China. As a consequence, the *Liji* as a whole never recovered its former respectability. Thus, while questions of ritual and propriety continue to occupy the minds of the Chinese in such diverse areas as Taiwan, China itself, and Hong Kong, the only parts of the *Liji* that are still read with real interest are the *Daxue* and the *Zhongyong*.

RICHARD J. SMITH

Further Reading

Translations

Legge, James, trans. *The Li Ki, Book of Rites.* Oxford: Oxford University Press, 1885. Reprinted with a useful introduction by Ch'u Chai and Winberg Chai, eds., *Li Chi, Book of Rites.* New Hyde Park, N.Y.: University Books, 1967. The translation is basically reliable but somewhat dated.

Related Studies

Biot, Édouard. *Le tcheou-li ou Rites des Tcheou.* Paris: Imprimerie Nationale, 1851. An early study of one of the three major Chinese ritual classics.

Chow, Kai-wing. *The Rise of Confucian Ritualism in Late Imperial China: Ethics, Classics, and Lineage Discourse.* Stanford, CA: Stanford University Press, 1994. An outstanding study of both the theory and practice of Chinese ritual in the Ming and Qing periods.

Ebrey, Patricia. *Confucianism and Family Rituals in Imperial China: A Social History of Writing about Rites.* Princeton, N.J.: Princeton University Press, 1991. A fascinating analysis of the various transformations in Chinese ritual texts over time.

———, trans. *Chu Hsi's Family Rituals: A Twelfth-Century Chinese Manual for the Performance of Cappings, Weddings, Funerals, and Ancestral Rites.* Princeton, N.J.: Princeton University Press, 1991. An excellent, throughly annotated translation of Zhu Xi's paradigmatic *Jiali.*

Fingarette, Herbert. *Confucius: The Secular as Sacred.* New York: Harper and Row, 1972. A pioneering study, controversial but also stimulating.

Loewe, Michael, ed. *Early Chinese Texts: A Bibliographical Guide.* Berkeley, CA: The Society for the Study of Early China and the Institute of East Asian Studies, University of California, Berkeley, 1993. Contains individual discussions of all three major Chinese ritual texts: *Liji, Zhouli,* and *Yili.*

Smith, Richard J. "Ritual in Ch'ing Culture," in Kwang-Ching Liu, ed., *Orthodoxy in Late Imperial China.* Berkeley, CA: University of California Press, 1990. An analysis of the integrative role of ritual in Qing dynasty China.

Steele, John, trans. *The I-li or Book of Etiquette and Ceremonial.* London: Probsthain and Co., 1917. An early study of one of the three major Chinese ritual classics.

THE *BOOK OF HUAINANZI (HUAI-NAN TZU)*

Title in Chinese: *Huainanzi (Huai-nan Tzu)*.
Authors: King Liu An, King of Huainan (and Su Fei, Li Shang, Zuo Wu [Tso Wu], Tian You [T'ien Yu], Lei Bei [Lei Pei], Mao Bei [Mao Pei], Wu Bei [Wu Pei], Jin Chan [Chin Ch'ang], and other unnamed literati)
Born: 180 or 179 B.C. (King Liu An)
Died: 122 B.C. (King Liu An)
Literary Form: Prose, poetry
Date of Composition: Completed 139 B.C.

Major Themes

To govern properly, the ruler must understand cosmology.
The Daoist sage or true person practicing non-purposeful action is the consummate ruler.
To realize the self is to realize the dao.
There is a cosmogonic origin of the universe.
The ruler must understand astronomy, geography, and agriculture in addition to the more traditional military arts, and court ritual-music to be an effective commander.
Among the many arts of rulership, it is most important for the ruler to practice non-purposeful action.
The successful administration develops and maintains political purchase or strategic advantage.
Law and clan morality must be artfully blended to institute a practicable form of government.
The reigning administration must ensure that the people obtain meaningful employment.
The social and political order must benefit the masses.

The *Huainanzi*, originally called the "Inner Book," is the sole survivor of a trilogy, consisting of an "Outer Book" and "Central Chapters," written at the court of the second king of Huainan, Liu An. The *Huainanzi* is composed of 21 chapters, dealing with a wide range of topics such as cosmology, cosmogony, taxonomy, physiology, astronomy, geography, forestry, culture and custom, the art of rulership, military strategy, and court ritual. It systematizes all of the philosophy and science known in its day, which it primarily presents in a syncretic fashion, attempting to utilize all the "schools" of thought, past and present. It must be noted, however, that some scholars debate the syncretic interpretation, arguing that the text is merely an eclectic conglomeration. However, a careful reading of the text shows that not only do the writers and editor of the *Huainanzi* draw from various literary sources, but they also artfully weave that eclectic material into a new synthesis within each chapter and the text as a whole.

The 21 chapter titles are: 1, Tracing the Source of the Way; 2, Original Reality; 3, Patterns of the Heavens; 4, The Lay of the Land (Shapes of the Terrain); 5, Seasonal Rites; 6, Examining Mysteries; 7, Essence and Spirit; 8, Fundamental Standards; 9, Arts of Rulership; 10, Errors in Designations; 11, Leveling Customs; 12, Responses of the Way; 13, Far-reaching Discussion; 14, Inquiring Words; 15, Military Strategy; 16, Discussing Mountains; 17, Discussing Forests; 18, The Human Realm; 19, Necessity of Cultivation; 20, The Grand Category; and 21, Essential Summary.

The *Huainanzi* was written during a period of political strife. In fact, the political struggle may have provided the impetus for Liu An to compile the text to serve not only as his literary pastime but also an escape from the conflicts that surrounded him in its attempt to resolve those issues at least in writing.

Liu Chang (Liu Ch'ang), Liu An's father, was the seventh son of the founder of the Han dynasty, Liu Bang (Liu Pang). Liu Chang became embroiled in court intrigue, and died on the way to his banishment. Emperor Wen divided the fief of Huainan among Liu Chang's three sons, and Liu An was enfeoffed with the section retaining the original name, Huainan.

Liu An developed a love of learning and literature at an early age. He was interested in all kinds of philosophy and literature, but he was especially drawn toward Daoism (Taoism), especially the philosophy of the *Zhuangzi* (*Chuang tzu*), and the meditative and alchemical practices of the *fang shi* (*fang shih*) (esoteric masters). By 154 B.C. Liu An was the patron of a large number of scholars and esoteric masters. Under Liu An's leadership, these scholars carried on the cultural traditions of the ancient state of Chu (Ch'u), which contained elements of shamanism and mysticism reflected in the *Chu ci* (*Ch'u tz'u*) (*Poems of Chu*), the *Zhuangzi*, and the *Huainanzi*. While the Northern scholars, like Dung Zhongshu, focused on Confucian studies, the Southern scholars at Liu An's court emphasized Daoism and a variety of other pre-Han literature.

In 139 B.C., Liu An presented a copy of the "Inner Book" to his nephew, Emperor Wu, who was delighted with the work and placed it in the imperial library, a move that most likely accounts for its survival.

Historians are not exactly sure how Liu An became implicated in a plot against the Emperor, but in 122 B.C. imperial troops attacked Huainan. According to one account, Liu An committed suicide; according to another, he became an immortal and ascended into the heavens. Whatever happened, we are sure that Liu An, his family, many of his guest scholars, and much of his library perished.

Liu An was a literary master, and a total of 12 works, mostly lost now, are attributed to him or his court. In addition to the trilogy, of which the *Huainanzi* is the sole survivor, Liu An authored a collection of poems, a commentary on the *Li-sao* poem, and two essays on the *Zhuangzi*. His court produced a collection of poems, a collection of songs and poems, a work on astronomy, a commentary on the *Book of Changes*, and at least one, possibly two, treaties on alchemy. It is surely a great loss that only fragments of these works are now extant.

It has been argued that the *Huainanzi* exhibits elements of Liu An's self-image: the recurring term for the Daoist "true person" (*zhen ren/chen jen*) is taken to be a description of Liu An. The major theme of Chapter 14 concerns the manner in which a sage ruler conducts oneself in an age of decay and decadence wherein one's art of rulership goes unrecognized. Chapter 15 presents a justification of the "just war" to be waged by the sage ruler. The "just war" argument, coupled with actual or perceived armaments build-up and court intrigue, may have led to Liu An's demise.

Classical Chinese literature typically ties together advice and techniques for self-cultivation, especially for the ruler and ministers, with the arts of rulership. The *Huainanzi* is no exception. Usually the dominant theme of a book, especially in classical Chinese literature, appears in the opening sections or chapters. The *Huainanzi* opens with two chapters on Daoist philosophy, but it approaches them with extremely different perspectives. The first chapter is written in the aesthetic and creative genre of the *Laozi (Lao Tzu)* and *Zhuangzi*; it is very poetic in form and content. The second chapter is written in the style of Huang-Lao (Yellow Emperor) and Laozi Daoism; opening with a structured and analytical interpretation of the *Zhuangzi* passage, it is less poetic in form and content, and employs analytic prose.

Although the first two opening chapters of the *Huainanzi* are predominately Daoist in tone and content, they also exhibit the syncretic approach of incorporating ideas from other philosophies to make Daoism as practical as possible. The subsequent chapters integrate and synthesize the various ancient teachings and contemporary knowledge of the world to assist the ministers and ruler in self-cultivation and the arts of rulership.

The style of the text is written in a blending of poetry, that is, rhymed verse and prose. The authors or editor worked hard to develop as many parallel structures and rhymes as possible because this style was considered to be the highest form of literature. The authors wrote the text by blending prose and poetry, and integrating the various ancient teachings into a coherent work and practical political philosophy. Thus, the *Huainanzi* represents the highest form of thought and literature in the syncretic approach.

One of the predominant Daoist themes in the *Huainanzi* is that self-realization or self-integration—*zi de (tzu te:* literally "self-obtaining") is to realize the way (*dao/tao*). The true persons are those who make the way real in their lives, and they are the ones who should be considered the true rulers, whether or not they reside on the throne. Toward the end of the first chapter, there is an interesting passage that proposes that "to possess the empire" does not mean to monopolize political power, but rather to practice self-integration and becoming one with the way. To realize the self is to realize the *dao*, and in doing so one gains a piercing insight into the interactions among the myriad things of nature, especially the arts of rulership. Such insight makes clear that the interaction of things is one of natural spontaneity (*ziran/tzu-jan*) and non-purposeful action (*wuwei/wu-wei*).

The *Huainanzi* echoes *Master Lu's Spring and Autumn Annals* (*Lüshi chunqiu/Lü-shih ch'un-ch'iu*) in proposing that the Daoist sage, or true person practicing non-purposeful action, becomes the consummate ruler. Among the many arts of rulership, it is most important for the ruler to practice non-purposeful action. Most of Chapter 9 of the *Huainanzi* develops this idea. In both texts, the ruler must take no personal action in governing the state and allow the various ministers to be actively engaged in administration. Just as the way takes no particular action, so too the ruler does not get involved in the details of governing.

The Daoists do not have a monopoly on the concept of non-purposeful action. The Confucians and Legalists have their own respective interpretations. For the Daoist, it is the operative processes of nature. For the Confucians, it is a moral concept, and for the Legalists a political one. The syncretic approach of the *Huainanzi* blends disparate approaches of these three philosophies by naturalizing the Confucian morality and softening the Legalist hard line of punishments.

The second chapter of the *Huainanzi* begins with a passage from Chapter 2 of the *Zhuangzi* concerning the cosmogonic origin of the universe. In the *Zhuangzi* this passage is used to uncover the limits of language. In the *Huainanzi*, the passage is taken to be a literal description of the origin of the universe. The theme of this chapter is that to govern properly the ruler must understand cosmogony and cosmology.

After explaining the origin of the universe, the text relates stories to establish that human history has continued to devolve, to lose the way, which has resulted in a period of decay and decadence. The chapter clearly argues that one's ability to embody the way does not lie with the person alone, but also depends on the spirit of the times and one's strategic position. The writing style and form of argumentation in this chapter stand in marked contrast to that of the first chapter.

The third chapter of the *Huainanzi* also opens with a cosmogonic and cosmological focus. The authors attempt to justify their interpretations by appealing to their comprehensive historic knowledge and detailed understanding of the nature and structure of the world. A recurring theme is that the ruler must understand astronomy, geography, and agriculture in addition to the more traditional military arts and court ritual music to be an effective commander.

The *Huainanzi* offers instruction on all these topics, presenting itself as the indispensable guide to the arts of rulership. According to the *Huainanzi*, the need for a leader and the arts of rulership came into existence because of the loss of the way. Where the Confucians, Mohists, and Legalists each in their own unique fashion propose that the institution of the ruler was an evolved benefit for mankind, the *Huainanzi* depicts the golden age of mankind as one of pristine simplicity without a ruler. After the natural pure simplicity was lost, then the need for law and order arose in the age of decay and degeneration. In this age of decadence, law and clan morality must be artfully blended to institute a practicable form of government. With this proposal to meld law and custom, the eclectic philosophy of the *Huainanzi* skillfully unites the major breach between the Confucians, who advocate rule by clan morality, and the Legalists, who espouse rule of law.

The *Huainanzi* places a good deal of emphasis on the concept of political purchase or strategic advantage (*shi/shih*) especially in Chapter 9 on the arts of rulership. Time and again the text advocates that the successful administration develops and maintains strategic advantage. Strategic advantage is not limited to knowing the lay of the terrain and the movement of enemy troops. It also entails an understanding of one's own people, their customs and the desires of one's own ministers, in addition to the customs and desires of the people and ministers of other states. Political purchase is promoted as a key method for maintaining order. It also assists the ruler in developing symbiotic relationships with his ministers; in this regard *Huainanzi* differs from the Legalist's use of the concept *shi*. The ruler's loss of political purchase is evidence of his decline. Finally, Chapter 9 of *Huainanzi* emphasizes that the ruler employ *shi* rather than attempt to rely on his own personal skill or moral persuasion.

The *Huainanzi* develops two ideas implicit in pre-Qin humanism which are explicitly stated in the *Lüshi chunqiu*, namely, that, one, the masses must be utilized with meaningful work, and two, the social and political order must benefit them. These ideas conflict with the Legalist ideas that government primarily benefits the ruler who maintains power by intimidating the people with rewards and punishments.

The *Huainanzi* adopts the basic tenet of humanistic political theory that the reigning administration must ensure that the people obtain meaningful employment, but it also develops a hybrid concept of properly utilizing the masses. It softens the Legalist notion of utilizing the people to the ruler's advantage by adopting the Daoist idea that each particular character, in fulfilling its nature, gives expression to the organismic harmony. The principle of properly employing the masses represents an important aspect of a government for the people.

Another important aspect of government for the people is disclosed in the principle of benefiting the masses. The *Huainanzi* develops the idea that the social and political order must benefit the masses. It establishes this point on the Legalist principle of everyone's promotion of one's own self-interests and blends it with the Confucian and Mohist idea that the condition of the people is reflected in the condition of the ruler. The benefit of the masses is the necessary condition: only after it has been fulfilled can the ruler gain benefit from the political order. Utilizing the people and benefiting the masses are political expressions of the Daoist notion of harmony.

The *Huainanzi*'s recurring theme of realization through self-integration—the co-dependent unity of self and other, and of ruler and the masses—is a complex form of Daoist nature mysticism wherein the human seeks and finds a mystical union with the here now world, rather than a transcendent God or absolute reality. In Chapter 14, the "true man" is described as one who lives as if he were not separated from the primal great one (*tai yi/t'ai i*). The cosmogonic, cosmological and mystical elements of the text certainly left a mark on the subsequent development of Neo-Daoism and the Daoist liturgy.

The concluding chapter of the *Huainanzi* gives a brief summary of prior intellectual history to establish how the earlier schools of thought were limited by their respective circumstances. It relates how the authors of the *Huainanzi* observed the forms of heaven above and earth below, took into account all the past and present affairs of humans, carefully weighed all circumstances, systems, and forms of measure to establish what is correct, thereby penetrating the essentials of the Way and the customs of the Three Kings, and capturing the minute details of the subtlest mystery. With this comprehensive approach, it is proposed that the text contains the solution to all problems; it can show one the way to unify the empire, bring order to all things, and understand the various classes and categories. It does not advocate the teachings of any one school, and thus it can be used to respond to any situation, anywhere, anytime.

JAMES D. SELLMANN

Further Reading

Translations

Ames, Roger T. *The Art of Rulership*. Honolulu: University of Hawaii Press, 1983. Gives a translation and analysis of Chapter 9 of the *Huainanzi*.

Major, John S. *Heaven and Earth in Early Han Thought: Chapters Three, Four and Five of the Huainanzi*. Albany, N.Y.: State University of New York Press, 1992.

Wallacker, Benjamin. *The Huai-nan Tzu, Book Eleven: Behavior, Culture, and Cosmos*. New Haven, CT: American Oriental Society, 1962. Although the translation is dated now, it does provide useful insights on the nature of the text.

Related Studies

Hsiao, Kung-chuan. *A History of Chinese Political Thought*. Trans. F. Mote. Princeton, N.J.: Princeton University Press, 1979. Provides a very readable analysis, but one must be cautious of his generalizations.

LeBlanc, Charles. *Huai-nan tzu: Philosophical Synthesis in Early Han Thought*. Hong Kong: Hong Kong University Press, 1985.

Roth, Harold D. *The Textual History of the Huai-nan Tzu*. Ann Arbor, MI: AAS Monograph Series, 1992. This work gives a complete historical analysis of the various editions of the text.

Sellmann, James D. "Three Models of Self-Integration (*tzu te*) in Early China," *Philosophy East and West*, 37/4, October, 1987. This article analyzes self-realization in the "schools" of thought which affect the *Huainanzi*'s conception.

Wallacker, Benjamin. "Liu An, Second King of Huai-nan (180?–122 B.C.)." *Journal of the American Oriental Society*, 92, 1972, 36–42.

RECORDS OF THE GRAND HISTORIAN

Title in Chinese: *Shiji* (*Shih-chi*)
Author: Sima Qian (Ssu-ma Ch'ien)
Born: c. 145 B.C., Longmen
Died: c. 90 B.C., Changan (?)
Literary Form: A series of historical accounts

Major Themes

True understanding of events comes only through a comprehensive view of history.
Both man and his environment have an impact on history, but the will of the individual is still paramount. History usually vindicates the good.

The *Shiji* is a comprehensive history of China, far surpassing anything that had been previously attempted. It covers the period from the reign of the mythical Yellow Emperor (traditionally, 2697–2599 B.C.), which is the perceived beginning of Chinese civilization, to the reign of the Emperor Wu of the Han (140–87 B.C.), whom the author served. The scope of the history is vast by any standard, and deals with the important events, institutions, and personages of a 2,500 year period of history, not only of China itself but of all the peoples and regions known to the Chinese of his time.

Author on a Personal Mission

Sima Qian was China's greatest historian; he was also one of China's most influential prose stylists. His lifetime parallels that of the Emperor Wu (140–87 B.C.), the strong-willed ruler who brought the Han dynasty to its peak of power and at whose court Sima Qian spent most of his life. What little is known of Sima Qian's personal life comes from the autobiographical section at the end of his great work, the *Shiji*, and from a long letter written around 91 B.C. to Ren An (Jen An), a friend who was in prison. Sima Qian came from a family of Han dynasty court astrologers or historians, whose primary duties concerned astronomy, portents, the calendar, and maintenance of the imperial archives. Sima Qian's father, Sima Tan (T'an), was appointed Grand Astrologer shortly after that Emperor Wu's accession in 141 B.C. Sima Tan, perhaps

on his own initiative, planned to write a work of history and began to collect material for it. After the death of his father, Sima Qian succeeded to the post in 108 B.C. and, in accordance with his father's dying request, took up the task of writing the history. Although certain portions of the text itself may have been started by Sima Tan, credit for the completed work is given to Sima Qian.

Sima Qian traveled all over China in the imperial service, using his travels to aid his research of past and contemporary events. In 99 B.C. he offended the emperor by defending a general who had failed in a campaign against the Xiongnu (Hsiungnu), a people who lived to the north of the empire. As a result, Sima Qian was condemned to undergo castration, the severest penalty next to death. He chose castration over suicide in order to finish the *Shiji*, a work he hoped would redeem his name.

Scope and Structure of the Shiji

To present such a wealth of material, Sima Qian rejected the strictly chronological presentation of earlier historical works and instead arranged his 130 chapters into five large subject sections. The first section, "Basic Annals," consists of 12 chapters devoted to the histories of the earlier dynastic houses or, in the case of the reigning Han dynasty, to the lives of individual emperors. As this structure implies, the detail increases as the time period draws nearer to Sima Qian's lifetime. The Annals section is followed by 10 "Tables" that organize chronologically the sequence of rulers, feudal lords, famous ministers, generals, and other noteworthies. These tables are useful both for their clear presentation of temporal relationships and for their proposed solutions to various problems of chronology. Next comes eight "Treatises" that discuss rites, music, pitch-pipes (tied to military technology), the calendar, astronomy, state sacrifices, levees and canals, and economics. In this section, Sima Qian explores the influence of nonhuman factors on history and traces the changes in these various topics from age to age. The treatises are followed by 30 chapters, called "Hereditary Houses," that narrate the history of the feudal states of Zhou (Chou) and the more important fiefs of the Han. The last section, "Biographies" or "Accounts," is by far the largest (seventy chapters) of the *Shiji* and, in terms of literary influence, the most important. This section presents a picturesque gallery of humanity—political figures, generals, philosophers, poets, reasonable and harsh officials, assassins, male favorites of the emperors, diviners, and money-makers—and includes accounts not just of individuals but also of groups such as the northern Xiongnu and the tribes of the southwest. One of the chapters is devoted to the history of medicine. The section closes with an autobiography of Sima Qian himself.

The *Shiji* is not a continuous narrative, but a series of accounts that supplement one another. Within each section of the *Shiji*, the chapters are usually arranged in a clear and consistent chronological order, but the grouping of the material into sections and the essentially biographical approach of most of the chapters necessitated Sima Qian's scattering of information pertaining to any given period into many chapters. Hence, if one is tracing the history of a particular period, it is best to approach it through a system of cross-referencing rather than by reading the chapters in sequence.

Most of the sections end with a brief comment, usually starting with the phrase, "The Grand Astrologer remarks . . . ," in which Sima Qian adds his personal observations on the section. These comments follow no fixed pattern. They include moral generalizations, notes on sources, personal reactions, additional information, analyses of historical causes, speculative questions, and justifications of Sima Qian's own life.

While the authenticity of most of the present version of the *Shiji* is generally accepted, some problems exist. Up to as many as 10 of the original chapters may have been reworked, and several others appear to be fragmentary or incomplete. The present text also includes a number of minor passages inserted by interpolators, particularly by Chu Shaosun (fl. after 50 B.C.), and systematic commentaries added from the fifth century onwards.

Sources of the **Shiji**

It is probable that some of the preliminary work for the creation of the *Shiji* was started by Sima Qian's father, Sima Tan. When Sima Qian succeeded his father as Grand Astrologer, Sima Qian had ready access to the imperial archives and probably read extensively. In the *Shiji* he directly refers to more than 88 other documents and includes quotations from numerous inscriptions and memorials. While he rarely identifies the precise source for any particular part of his history, his comments reveal an acute awareness of the importance and difficulties of textual evidence and show his pioneering efforts toward a critical and objective use of sources.

To fill out the genealogical accounts of ancient times, Sima Qian compiled the chapters of the Basic Annals section by including large portions of the *Shujing (Shu Ching) (Book of History)*. While Sima Qian seems to have accepted rather uncritically the accounts and genealogies developed by earlier writers, he distances himself a bit from this material by warning that the age of the sage rulers is too far away to be described in detail.

In his account of pre-Qin history, Sima Qian relied heavily on three well-known sources, the *Zuozhuan (Tso chuan) (Tso Commentary)*, the *Guoyu (Kuo yü) (Conversations of the States)*, and the *Zhanguoce (Chan-guo ts'e) (Intrigues of the Warring States)*, weaving together material selected from these sources with other material. He probably utilized the *Chu Han chunqiu (Ch'u Han ch'un-ch'iu) (Spring and Autumn of Chu and Han)* by the early Han statesman Lu Jia (Lu Chia), as well as imperial inscriptions for information on the early Han period. For the rest of the Han period until his own time, Sima Qian probably relied on his own research of official documents preserved at court, speeches and writings of his contemporaries, and the accounts of men who witnessed the events described. Because the style of some of the earlier works was considered difficult by his time, Sima Qian made what changes were necessary to render the passages easily comprehensible to Han readers.

Sima Qian's Contribution to Historiography

Early histories created in chronicle form had existed before the time of Sima Qian, most notably the *Spring and Autumn Annals* and the *Tso Commentary*. But the form of the *Shiji*, with its division of material into "Annals," "Treatises," "Biographies," etc., seems to have been Sima Qian's own creation. By creating such a unique form, Sima Qian was able to impose a hierarchical order on his material, suggesting by the place in which he presents a certain account something of its importance and reliability. The form allows him to focus upon the flow of events, the origin and development of institutions, and the lives of individuals without the necessity of frequent digressions.

Sima Qian tries to maintain accuracy and objectivity by quoting extensively from original sources; supplanting the contents of the official documents with his own travels, personal observations, and interviewing of eyewitnesses (for the account of his own age); and reserving his personal judgments for the brief comments sections. He also expands the domain of historical evidence when he suggests that examining physical artifacts (such as the clothes and sacrificial vessels he saw at historical sites) can also help in understanding the past. Moreover, as he traveled from place to place, he gained an appreciation for different regional characteristics and occasionally tried to tie these regional distinctions to the events of his work.

However, accuracy is not his sole goal. What we read in the *Shiji* is not pure, objective history, but rather history as seen and understood by one partic-

ularly astute observer and editor. Instead of the simple nuances of wording or special instances of inclusion or exclusion, which the commentaries ascribe to Confucius in the *Chunqiu*, Sima Qian carefully selects and positions the material to make his interpretive points and build interest, employing a wide array of literary techniques to shape his readers' perceptions unobtrusively: direct speech, comments, anecdote (used to establish a character), juxtaposition, flashback, impersonal narration, and categorization among others. His goal is to achieve moral instruction by various means, including the use of humor and the introduction of sex. He uses these techniques to break the temporal flow and allow the reader to examine these events and individual actions atemporally so that his message gets through. Furthermore, Sima Qian's commentary reinforces the interplay between the action and the interpretation. It provides Sima Qian greater freedom to synthesize and explicate, and serves as a division between chapter and theme. This innovative method of writing history, accurate yet interpretive and thorough, is his major contribution to historiography.

Sima Qian was probably the first writer to put such information in the form of chapters devoted to the lives of single individuals or groups of individuals. In the biographical section, he was clearly influenced by the idea of types, for often he groups together in a single chapter the lives of several men with common interests or personalities (wise minister, decadent king, buffoon, loyal scholar, *femme fatale*). Each character's image is usually constructed with selected deeds and speeches related only to public affairs. We get to know who they are and how they act, but there is little sense of how they became the individuals they are shown to be. There is a sense, however, that while the character is the moving force behind events, the events have also made clear imprints on his life. Sima Qian gives far more attention than his predecessors to the influence of geography, climate, economic factors, customs, and institutions upon the course of history. But when all other factors have been taken into account, it is still primarily the will of the individual that directs the course of history.

Sima Qian's World View

Sima Qian appears to have believed in a moral universe characterized by the "Way of Heaven." However, there may not be one absolutely correct interpretation of Heaven's will; the same event may have different, equally valid meanings in different contexts. In this universe, which lacks any strong element of the supernatural, the good should generally prosper while the wicked are punished. He was of course perplexed by situations that seem to subvert that idea. Rewards, for example, are not always immediate, nor are punishments. For him, instances that run counter to the ideal were often due to our incomplete knowledge of the situation. A generous person may not receive recognition in his or her lifetime; or a person who seems virtuous may some day be found a devious scoundrel. The same is true for the seemingly wicked ruler. Accordingly, history was not a game for Sima Qian: it is an activity of high moral seriousness. For him, as for Confucius (if one accepts the traditional interpretation of the *Annals*), the function of history was still to teach moral lessons, to "censure evil and encourage good." But to really acquire the complete picture, according to Sima Qian, the history must be comprehensive. Sima Qian gave validity to his interpretive judgments by grounding them in objective facts. But even his history was not totally adequate, for Sima Qian also realized that there were limits on his ability to find justice in history.

Influence of the Shiji

Since its composition over 2,000 years ago, the *Shiji* has been widely and affectionately read not only by educated Chinese but also by students and scholars in the rest of Eastern Asia. The reason for its continued popularity lies undoubtedly in its succinct and penetrating biographies of great figures of the past with their dramatic episodes and deft anecdotes. The form and style of the *Shiji* were so striking that it became the model, with few modifications, for all subsequent dynastic histories.

Sima Qian tells his long and complex story with an economy of expression that is extremely valued

in classical Chinese. His narration is direct and concrete, with few adverbs or adjectives. In addition, his frequent use of direct discourse and his concise arrangement of historical events allow him to capture the drama and passion of the past. His legacy is a prose with a vigorous, regular cadence, sometimes incorporating parallel structure but not bound by it, that became the standard for all later biographical writing, both historical and fictional. One can easily see the interplay of its episodic structure, the linear narration of individual chapters, and the flat or stereotypical characterization in almost every long traditional piece of fiction, such as *Sanguozhi yanyi (San kuo chih yen-i) (Romance of the Three Kingdoms), Shuihuzhuan (Shui hu chuan) (Water Margin),* and *Honglou meng (Hunglou meng) (Dream of the Red Chamber).*

Finally, his autobiographical postface to the *Shiji* and his "Bao Ren An shu" ("Pao Jen An shu") (Letter in Reply to Ren An), in which Sima Qian lays bare his feelings about the great disappointment and tragedy in his own life, established the autobiography and personal letter as models for the "literature of frustration." Indeed, Sima Qian felt that all great literature was a product of suffering and frustration and he employed his unique editing style to demonstrate this view.

KENNETH G. KOZIAL

Further Reading

Translations

Bodde, Derk. *Statesman, Patriot, and General in Ancient China.* New Haven, CT: American Oriental Society, 1940. Contains three biographies of the Qin dynasty (255–206 B.C.).

Dolby, William, and John Scott. *Warlords.* Edinburgh: Southside, 1974. Includes 13 chapters of the *Shiji* translated.

Kierman, Frank A., Jr. *Ssu-ma Ch'ien's Historiographical Attitude.* Wiesbaden: Otto Harrossowitz, 1962. Includes translation of four late Warring States biographies.

Watson, Burton. *Records of the Grand Historian.* 2 vols. New York: Columbia University Press,

1961. Contains translation of 40 chapters of the *Shiji*.

Yang, Hsien-yi, and Gladys Yang. *Records of the Historian*. Hong Kong: Commercial Press, 1974. Contains translation of 40 chapters of the *Shiji*.

Related Studies

Allen, Joseph R. "An Introductory Study of Narrative Structure in the *Shiji*." In *Chinese Literature, Essays, Articles, and Reviews* 3 (1981): 31–66. Examines the structure of the *Shiji*.

Beasley, W. G., and E. G. Pulleybank, ed. *Historians of China and Japan*. London: Oxford University Press, 1961. Contains several essays on early Chinese historiography, including that of Sima Qian.

Gardner, Charles. S. *Chinese Traditional Historiography*. Cambridge, MA: Harvard University, 1938; 1970 reprint. Provides an overview of the premodern Chinese historiography.

Watson, Burton. *Early Chinese Literature*. New York: Columbia University Press, 1962. Surveys the development of early classical Chinese literature.

INTRIGUES OF THE WARRING STATES

Title in Chinese: *Zhanguoce (Chan-kuo ts'e)*
Author: Unknown
Literary Form: Dialogues, discourses, and anecdotes
Date of Composition: No later than 8 B.C.

Major Themes

Why fight when one can gain what one wants by diplomacy?
It is important to understand the inevitability of change and to take advantage of it.
Human beings, especially if they are reasonable, can change destiny.
By listening to good advisors, rulers will learn to moderate their desires.

The *Zhanguoce* is the largest collection of short dialogues, discourses, and anecdotes dealing with historical and political situations of the Warring States period (403–221 B.C.), and some events dating as early as 475 B.C.. Traditionally considered a work of history, the *Zhanguoce*, or at least part of it, has come to be viewed by a growing number of scholars in the East and West less as a book of history in the strict sense and more as a book of literary and rhetorical value. The work portrays the intense struggle of several Chinese states for hegemony, the complex diplomatic maneuvering, and the eventual rise of the state of Qin (Ch'in) to unify the empire. As seen in this work, the rulers of these states employ personal advisors to aid them in getting the better of their opponents. Noblemen and commoners, professional court counselors and itinerant amateurs, all vie with one another, often unscrupulously, to reach the ears of these rulers and other important leaders of the day in order to offer timely and perhaps wise advice.

Sources of the Zhanguoce

There is much controversy about the origin of the material in the *Zhanguoce* as well as the status of its two extant versions. The Han historian, Sima Qian (Ssu-ma Ch'ien) (c. 145–c. 90 B.C.), without citing the actual source, utilized a great deal of material similar to what is found in the present-day *Zhanguoce* for parts of his famous history, *Shiji*

(Records of the Grand Historian [Astrologer]), that relate to the Warring States period. It is therefore probable that much of the material contained in the modern editions of the *Zhanguoce* was composed by the early part of the second century B.C.

Liu Xiang (Liu Hsiang) (c. 79–c. 6 B.C.), one of the great scholars and imperial librarian of the Han dynasty, writes in his preface to the *Zhanguoce* that the basic text, as he found it in the imperial archives, which may have been the one used as a source by Sima Qian, had fallen into disarray. He then incorporated fragmented collections of other texts with this original and called them the *Zhanguoce*. Much of this material was quite probably derived from historical materials as well as that of romances or legends, written or oral, based upon the lives of its major protagonists. The sections dealing with Su Qin (Su Ch'in) possibly came from a lost book or a collection of anecdotes about the itinerant persuader. One of the original texts Liu Xiang used was arranged according to Chinese states with events happening in a rough chronological order. Liu then ordered his larger edited work in a similar fashion. The resulting work had 33 chapters, which is the same number as found in present-day editions. Possibly, there has been significant alteration, addition and deletion of material in the text through the centuries. The two most common editions of the work, the *Bao biao (Pao piao)* (standard) version, and the *Yao Hong (Yao hung)* version, came together only during the Song (Sung) dynasty. Generally the contents of these versions are the same; but there are some wording differences, and the material is arranged differently under the names of prominent states of the period.

The Zhanguoce *as History*

As reported in his preface, much of Liu Xiang's interest in compiling the *Zhanguoce* was historical. The *Zhanguoce* does, for example, contain many historical elements including accounts of battles, strategic conferences, and other important events that actually took place—such as the fall of Yiyang, the first great walled city to fall when Qin broke through to China proper via the Hangu pass; the long siege of Handan, the capital of the state of Zhao (Chao) and the most sophisticated metropolis of its time; and the attempted assassination of the Qin emperor by Jing Ke (Ching K'o). In addition, the situations revolving around the myriad of persuasions and anecdotes in the work are often historical in nature.

While speeches seem to have been important state documents in the Warring States period and were treated by historiographers as key events, the speeches or arguments to be found in the *Zhanguoce* have only a limited historical value because of the contradictions and anachronisms many of them contain. Still, the persuasions and much of the remaining narration probably give a truer reflection of the times than any subsequent Confucian-oriented history, shedding some light on Chinese military strategy and warfare, logistics, and economics.

The Art of Persuasion

The material now found in the *Zhanguoce* was probably not intended to be solely historical. More than in most other early works of Chinese literature, the great majority of the historical events in the *Zhanguoce* are presented through rhetorical situations. The *Zhanguoce* exhibits hundreds of examples of artful rhetoric and different rhetorical structures, most purportedly given by wandering persuaders. The persuasions demonstrate a high level of finesse and sophistication. As such, they are the culmination of a genre that developed from the intense political competition of the Warring States period, which includes the serious and moralistic collections of persuasive speeches found in the *Guoyu (Kuo-yü) (Conversations of the States)* and the *Yanzi chunqiu (Yen Tzu ch'un-ch'iu) (Spring and Autumn of Master Yan)*, and reflects a fusion of the emergent realpolitik of the times with literary form. It is also possible that at least some of the persuasions were originally collected as examples of fine rhetorical exercises or to make a manual on rhetoric.

Generally, the persuasions in the *Zhanguoce* portray one-to-one conversations between an itinerant advisor and a ruler of one of the states of the period, a minister, or a military leader. Most follow a similar pattern. Usually a speech begins with a problem, often narrated in a brief introductory sentence or sentences. Frequently the subject is the formation of an alliance, most often the Vertical and Horizontal Alliances (supposedly authored by Su Qin and Zhang Yi [Chang I] respectively), or an impending attack by a neighboring state. Someone, sometimes a minister or an roving persuader, then offers advice to the leader involved. The speaker will often start his speech with a generalization or a principle. Sometimes the speaker simply uses a paradoxical introductory remark to arouse the listener's interest or curiosity. For example, "I ask to speak three words. If I speak one word more, I ask to be boiled alive!" More often though, the persuader starts out with a rather matter-of-fact statement of the situation before either developing an elaborate argument or making an immediate, astute, or clever point. Several of the *Zhanguoce* persuaders seem to revel in rudeness. Many of their opening remarks are more shocking than polite.

The arguments of the *Zhanguoce* persuaders exude expediency. The persuader's words, however, are not pure sophistry, that is, the persuader is not intending to trick his listener into some imprudent action. Most of the situations—for example, the news of an attack—require immediate action; and the persuader, through his presentation of the "facts" turns the situation to the advantage of the listener by manifesting a practical, commonsense approach to the problem at hand. One main type of argument often employed is recalling past great kings, a technique frequently used in other texts of the Warring States period. The persuader usually tells of the successes or failures of these great rulers in order to move the listener, usually a ruler himself, to admiration or fear. Occasionally exaggeration plays a part in magnifying the deeds or misdeeds. The *Zhanguoce* persuaders also show a great concern for the geopolitical situation of a state and occasionally put forth a line of reasoning based on a long-range outlook, but again it is usually only as a result of immediate action derived from a more pressing issue.

The persuasion may end with a restatement of the original principle or a statement of a new principle and thereby repeat the process. Very often the persuasive passage ends with a short bit of narration, similar to the introductory statement, that tells whether or not the listener followed the advice. Sometimes even the historical results of the decision are then narrated. The listener in the *Zhanguoce* almost always obediently follows the persuader's words, and the results are just as the advisor predicted.

The rhetoric encountered in persuasions of the *Zhanguoce* is generally exhortatory and dissuasive, though mainly the latter with a decided anti-Qin flavor. It is not, however, overtly logical and systematic as might be expected. Instead it relies on a rich variety of indirect rhetorical effects and devices common to both Chinese and Western rhetoric. The persuaders of the *Zhanguoce*, for instance, rely heavily on parallel structure (juxtaposition, comparison, and contrast), rhythm, repetition, and hyperbole for effect. Their rhetoric is anecdotal, allegorical, and illustrative, though sometimes obscure, perhaps owing to our inability to understand fully the allusions of a bygone era. The imagery of both the persuasions and the general narration is vivid, with an economical and clear prose throughout. Now and then, a fable will be employed to great rhetorical effect.

The Politics and Philosophy of the *Zhanguoce*

The *Zhanguoce* depicts what was traditionally considered to be an evil era in Chinese political history. Orthodox critics, accordingly, condemned the work because it presents an amoral view of life and politics. Even though the actual words of its persuasions are probably fictitious, they give a picture of the thought processes that went into political and strategic planning of the middle and late Warring States period. Over the centuries the *Zhanguoce* has often been classified as a work of the *conghengjia (ts'ung-heng chia)* (School of the Vertical and Horizontal Alliances), a school or a classification of itinerant advisors or diplomats of various philosophical tendencies who wrote on generally anti-Qin themes. The persuasions featuring advisors like Su Qin and Zhang Yi are said to represent the writings of this school. Portions of the *Zhanguoce* reflect elements of Mohism and Legalism, other parts resemble the fragments of works attributed to Nominalist School, but not enough to classify the work as part of these schools.

The *Zhanguoce* reveals much about the psychology of the late Warring States period, particularly as it pertains to human interaction. The work, on the one hand, is infused with a basic cynicism. The speeches tell the listener that old rules are too old, and that no scheme is too devious if it can achieve its goal. On the other hand, the *Zhanguoce* conveys a certain force—the power of the individual to change destiny. Men, not spirits, make the world what it is. If one can come to understand the flow and possibilities of change, perhaps one can manoeuvre through reasoned argument into other courses of action—the power of the word over the force of action.

The *Zhanguoce* persuasions are a product of the transition from the feudal Zhou period to the bureaucratic unification in the Qin and Han empires, with the persuader standing in direct line between the *shi* (*shih*: diviner/astrologer) of the Zhou dynasty and the Han dynasty bureaucrat. Persuasive and bureaucratic skills came to be more important in the Late Warring States period than ties to the royal family. The art of persuasion, as seen in the *Zhanguoce*, was probably the individual's only outlet in an authoritarian world. The work shows a confidence that eloquence will be rewarded with power, fame, and wealth. One must use the political system: rulers are generally not well advised. By listening to good advisors who use realistic arguments, rulers will learn to moderate their desires and either win the day, or at least come through crisis without much harm. Linked to the political, this-worldly character of the persuasions is a conscious, earthy sense of wit that highlights the impacts of the rhetoric.

Influence of the Zhanguoce

The *Zhanguoce* has been both admired and condemned. Representatives of the orthodoxy have considered it an immoral work based upon a period of evil political scheming. Nevertheless, the intriguing rhetoric, practical philosophy, and lively history found in the work have fascinated Chinese readers throughout the centuries.

It is quite clear that the *Zhanguoce* contains some elements of fiction—for example, the extended passage on Jing Ke's failed attempt to assassinate the Qin emperor—and may thus have influenced subsequent historical narratives, such as the *Sanguozhi yanyi (San kuo chih yen-i) (Romance of the Three Kingdoms)* and quite clearly the *Dong Zhou lieguo zhi (Tung Chou lieh-kuo chih) (A History of the States of Eastern Zhou)*, with many stories in the latter work being based upon figures found in the *Zhanguoce*.

The persuasions in the *Zhanguoce* are often written in the finest, most polished prose and thus have left an indelible mark on the Chinese language.

Sima Qian, whose own writing was considered a model for the development of the literary language, was probably the first person to be influenced by the work's prose style when he used the material found in the *Zhanguoce* to form much of his history of the Warring States period and his biographies of period personages. Phrases from the *Zhanguoce* have now become common sayings used to this day both in the spoken and written language.

KENNETH G. KOZIOL

Further Reading

Translation

Crump, James I., trans. *Chan-kuo Ts'e*. Oxford: Clarendon Press, 1970. An accurate and complete translation of the *Zhanguoce*.

Related Studies

Crump, James I. "The *Chan-kuo ts'e* and Its Fiction." *T'oung Pao*, 48.4–5 (1960), 305–75. Examines fictional elements in the anecdotes found in the *Zhanguoce*.

———. *Intrigues: Studies of the Chan-kuo ts'e.* Ann Arbor, MI: University of Michigan Press, 1964. Studies the nature of the *Zhanguoce* and the role of rhetoric within the work.

Prusek, Jaroslav. "A New Exegesis of the *Chan-kuo ts'e*." *Archiv Orientalni*, 34 (1966) 587–92. A study of the nature and origin of the *Zhanguoce*.

Watson, Burton. *Early Chinese Literature*. New York: Columbia University Press, 1962. Surveys the development of early classical Chinese literature including the *Zhanguoce*.

THE POETRY OF TAO YUANMING (T'AO YÜAN-MING)

Author: Tao Yuanming (T'ao Yüan-ming), also known as Tao Qian (T'ao Ch'ien)
Born: A.D. 365
Died: A.D. 427
Major Poems: "Returning to My Old Home," "At the Beginning of Spring in the Year *Kuei-Mao (Guimao)*," "Returning to Live in the Country," "Return Home!," "Peach Blossom Font"

Major Themes

To live a reclusive life far from the life of politics and the court is to enjoy a life of simplicity and honesty.
As time passes, places and people change, but there are enduring values.
There is satisfaction, even for a poet, in hard work in the fields.
A farming community that managed to cut itself off from the world could be an ideal realm.

By the time Tao Yuanming was born, his family's fortunes were at low ebb. His father died when Tao Yuanming was twelve years old, and the same year a barbarian strongman swept down from the North, nearly capturing the Eastern Jin dynasty (A.D. 317–420) capital at Jiankang (modern Nanjing). Tao Yuanming, who was managing the family's landholdings, married and fathered his first son by his late teens. Approaching thirty years of age, when his and his nation's fortunes were declining, Tao finally took an official position as Libationer in the provincial capital of Xunyang (modern Jiujiang). But he resigned after a short while and returned home. Eventually he took other positions, and after several years of absence Tao went home again, where he wrote "Returning to My Old Home":

Formerly I was living in the capital,
But after six years I left for home.
Although today is my first day back,
Yet I am sad and have many griefs.
The field paths are unchanged from before,
But sometimes village houses are missing.
When I make the round of my old home,
Of older neighbours few still remain. . . .

(DAVIS, VOL. 1, 1983, P. 88)

This return may have been on the occasion of his mother's death in the winter of 401. According to the poetry written in this period, Tao now worked the land with his own hands, probably for the first time in his life. Lines from the poem "At the Beginning of Spring" capture the contentment of his reclusive life:

I grasp the plough, glad at the season's tasks;
With smiling face I encourage the farm folk. . . .

When the sun sets, we return home together;
With a jug of wine I cheer my near neighbours. . . .

(DAVIS, VOL. 1, 1983, P. 85)

"Returning to Live in the Country"

"Returning to Live in the Country," one of Tao's best known works, is a series of five poems, also probably written at this time. Commonly regarded as his best example of realistic description, these poems evoke an emotional spectrum from reserved happiness to deep sadness. An abridgement of the poems follows:

I

I have opened up waste land at the edge of the south wild;
I have kept rusticity, returned to garden and fields.
. . . .
Faint are the villages of distant men;
Thick is the smoke from their houses.
. . . .
Dogs bark in the depths of the lanes;
Cocks crow at the tops of the mulberries. . . .

II

. . . .

At times again in the waste ground and byways
Parting the grasses, I share men's comings and
* goings.*
When we meet, there is no discursive talk;
We speak of the growth of mulberry and hemp. . . .

III

. . . .

I have planted beans under the southern hill;
The weeds grow thick, the bean shoots are thin.
Rising at dawn, I attend to the weeds;
Moon-girt, hoe on shoulder, I return. . . .

IV

. . . .

We linger among the mounds and banks,
Where I brood on the one-time dwellings.
Of wells and hearths, the places remain;
Of mulberry and bamboo, rotted stumps are left.

V

. . . .

When the sun sets, it is dark in the house.
But a thorn fire serves for a bright candle.
Joy comes and we grieve that the night is short;
Already once again we have come to sunrise!

(DAVIS, VOL. 1, (1983), PP. 45–7)

Images such as the clearing of land and planting of beans, conversation with neighbors, and sunrise to sunset work, all strike the reader as genuine. Yet the lines hide certain images that embody some of Tao Yuanming's most idealistic visions. For example, the last two couplets of poem 1 are an allusion to chapter 80 of the *Daode jing (Tao-te ching)* This chapter describes a utopia where the barking of dogs and crowing of cocks could be heard from neighboring "kingdoms," but the citizens of one kingdom were content never to visit the citizens of another. Here the four lines not only capture the ambience of a pristine village scene, but also portray the Daoist (Taoist) image of simplicity and self-sufficiency. Yet the idealism does not detract from the perceived realism of the images. Tao is perfectly capable of creating a paradise that he does not simultaneously inhabit.

"Return Home!"

In autumn of the year 405, still in straightened circumstances, Tao accepted a post as magistrate in the neighboring community of Pengze. It was to be his last official position. At the end of the year when the Inspector came on his rounds, rather than bow to someone he considered contemptible, Tao Yuanming resigned his post a mere 80 days after accepting it and returned to his farm. The following excerpts are from "Return Home!," the "manifesto" he wrote on the occasion of that final return:

Return home!
My fields and garden will be covered with weeds;
Why not return? . . .
My boat lightly tosses on the broad waters;
The wind, whirling, blows my robe about. . . .
Then I espy my humble house;
So I am glad, so I run.
The servants welcome me;
The children wait at the gate. . . .
Return home!
Let there be an end to intercourse, a break from
* society!*
The world and I shall be estranged from one an-
* other;*
If I harnessed my carriage again, what should I
* seek? . . .*
Riches and honour are not my desire;
The Heavenly Village I may not hope for.
I desire a fair morning to go out alone;
Sometimes to plant my staff and weed or hoe;
Or climb the eastern hill and let out long whistles;
Or looking on the clear stream, compose a poem.
So following change, I shall go to my end;
Happy in my destiny, why should I doubt any more?

(DAVIS, VOL. 1, 1983, PP. 192–4)

This idealistic vision of the official returning to a farm grown up in weeds, with the purpose of singlehandedly restoring it to its productive capability, is still free of the sobering facts of reality. Yet the poet specifically denies that he seeks the unreal world of immortals (the "Heavenly Village"), which had occupied the minds of poets for centuries. Without toil and hardship—the pejorative aspects of self-sufficient living—the scene of the return is idyllic, with plenty of leisure time for the poet to pursue his romantic interests.

After Tao had been farming in earnest for five years, his tone began to change. Written in the year 410, his poem "Harvesting the Dry Rice in the Western Field" speaks of the "usual jobs" and the "tasks" and the bitterness of the farmer's life; gone are all references to leisure. Instead, Tao describes the workaday regimen of sunup to sundown toil. In order to increase his fortitude against this harsh existence, he invokes the names of two famous hermits, Chü (Ju) and Ni, who had once chastised Confucius. The age-old aristocratic code prescribed "concealment" when the Dao did not prevail in the kingdom. Confucius acted to change the system rather than retreat from it, and was rebuked by the hermits. Tao side with Ju and Ni, and chooses the farmer's life, but in Tao's day such a choice was not necessarily a safe one. This was the life he would continue to live uninterrupted for the next two decades as he wrote the greater portion of his poetic corpus.

"Peach Blossom Font"

The most famous of Tao Yuanming's works of poetry is "Peach Blossom Font," a fictionalized account of an ideal realm hidden away from the world. His record documents the flight of a group of Qin (Ch'in) dynasty (255–206 B.C.) refugees to a hidden retreat in the mountains of Wuling (in modern day Hunan Province). The premise of his fiction is quite believable—history records similar flights from the tyranny of the first emperor. In fact, until the modern period many readers of this poem accepted its story as historical fact. The following introduction is gleaned from a prose version of the poem.

A fisherman was ascending a stream in his boat when he came upon a grove of peach trees in full bloom. He followed the grove which ended at the stream's source at the bottom of a hill. In the hill he found a cave with a light at the other end. Squeezing through the entrance he walked for a short while until the cave emerged out into the open. Before him lay a pristine farming community, the inhabitants of which were all very surprised to see him. They asked him many questions about life on the outside, and then feasted him in their homes. After several days as he prepared to leave, his hosts advised him not to reveal their location to the outside world. But he promptly told everyone of his great discovery as soon as he had returned home. However, try as he may, he could not find his way back to the peach blossom font.

When the Ying upset the heavenly order,
Worthy men fled from their age.
Huang and Ch'i went to Mount Shang,
And these men also went away.
The traces of their going were gradually hidden;
The paths they came by became weedy and abandoned.

(DAVIS, VOL. 1, 1983, P. 196)

Ying is the surname of the First Emperor of Qin, while Huang and Qi (Ch'i) are hermits who fled when Ying proclaimed himself "first universal emperor" in 221 B.C. The poem goes on to describe farming scenes which, not surprisingly, are similar to the poet's descriptions of his own farming community. The barnyard animals from the *Daode Jing* reappear. However, one factor clearly marks the society of Peach Blossom Font as utopian. The poem reveals that these farmers paid no tax, which could happen only in an ideal world. The poem celebrates the simplicity of the reclusive life, with its attendant harmony. "Although there is no calendar's record, / The four seasons themselves complete the year," the poem declares: harmony can exist without the contrivance of a calendar only in Peach Blossom Font, for the calendar is one of the most important manifestations of dynastic power. The poem concludes with the lines:

May I ask the gentlemen who wander within the
*   world,*
How they measure what is beyond the dust and
*   noise?*
My desire is to tread the light air
And soar high, seeking my fellows.

(DAVIS, VOL. 1, 1983, P. 197)

Thus the poet enters subjectively into the poem, asks the reader to evaluate such places, and then expresses his own desire to travel there. Later poets such as Wang Wei (701–761), when they imitated this poem, transformed the inhabitants of Peach Blossom Font into immortals.

As a tale, "Peach Blossom Font" utilizes several motifs that do not occur in the poet's other works, such as peach blossoms and the fisherman's journey through the cave. These are obviously characteristics of a dreamland or golden world, representing here the boundary line between the real and ideal worlds. The hidden valley and its camouflaged "font" or "grotto" served to enclose and thus seal off a timeless paradise. Tao's name for this world, *taohua yuan* (peach blossom font) eventually came to denote the very essence of paradise in China. As a result, the existence of this poem has tended to blur the distinction between real and ideal in all of Tao Yuanming's works. Realistic scenes are too fantastic to believe, while the fictional tale is a purported historical event.

Tao Yuanming's experiment in country living was one of the most admirable attempts by any scholar in Chinese literary history to break the back of stifling tradition. His groundbreaking in the field of poetry assured him a place in the upper ranks of great Chinese poets. Although he was not a widely popular poet in his lifetime, and his works were neglected by the court for a century after his death in 427, still his images became the model for centuries of succeeding poets. The term he used to refer to his farm became the name of the genre he popularized. The term *tianyuan* (field and garden) eventually was adopted as the designation for a literary tradition that developed in imitation of Tao Yuanming. Many poets were to take his lead in seeking inspiration and solace from country life, yet seldom again was there to be a poet of his stature willing to take up the plow in earnest.

STEPHEN L. FIELD

Further Reading

Translations

Davis, A. R., trans. *T'ao Yüan-ming (A.D. 365–427): His Works and Their Meaning.* 2 vols. London: Cambridge University Press, 1983. A meticulous translation and study of the complete poetic works of Tao Yuanming. Volume two contains the original Chinese text. Quotations from this book are reprinted with the permission of Cambridge University Press, © Hong Kong University Press, 1983.

Fang, Roland C., trans. *Gleanings from Tao Yuanming.* Taipei: Lailai Publishing Corp., 1980. A bilingual translation by a translator of Chaucer and Shakespeare.

Hightower, James R., trans. *The Poetry of T'ao Ch'ien.* London: Oxford University Press, 1970. A scholarly translation, perhaps less accurate in places than the more recent translation, but with more natural-sounding English.

THE POETRY OF XIE LINGYUN (HSIEH LING-YÜN)

Author: Xie Lingyun (Hsieh Ling-yün); also known as Xie Kangle (Hsieh K'ang-lo), Duke of Kangle (Duke of K'ang-lo).
Born: A.D. 385 (in Guiji, modern Shaoxing, Zhejiang province)
Died: A.D. 433 (in Nanhai, or modern Canton, Guangdong province)
Major Poems: "Passing Through My Shining [Shih-ning] Estate," "Leaving West Archery Hall at Dusk," "On My Way from South Mountain to North Mountain, I Glance at the Scenery from the Lake," "Journeying the Stream: Following the Jinzhu Torrent I Cross the Mountain"

Major Themes

The world of nature—its mountains, rivers, and other features—should be celebrated in poetry.
With the passage of time come sorrows and memories, but there is satisfaction to be found in observing the transformations of nature.
One sometimes longs to communicate one's ideas and experiences to others.
Through the contemplation of nature one senses an enduring reality and attains enlightenment.
A simple life free from the trials of success and failure is the best.

A new style of poetry emerged in early fifth-century China that put a premium on accurate, realistic description of landscape. No longer regarded as a mere "supporter" of lyrical expression, scenic description was now becoming the primary element in Chinese poetry. At least two reasons account for this new trend. First, as a result of the wars in the early fourth century, many northern aristocrats and their families fled south, where they found mild climates and beautiful landscapes. Second, many of these aristocrats had the leisure time to take pleasure tours through the scenic southern countryside. Their reactions to these attractive environs found expression in their verses. The underlying premise of their new approach to composing landscape poetry was really quite simple: much pleasure and joy can be derived from observing and appreciating the physical details of handsome natural environments. The most famous practitioner of these new poetics was Xie Lingyun. He has even been touted by some critics as the "father" of landscape poetry (*shanshui shi/shan-shui shih*: literally, "mountain and river verse") in China, although the appropriateness of this attribution is debatable: he certainly was not the first Chinese poet to use natural scenes to express feelings and emotions. There is no denying, however, that Xie

crafted his "mountain and river" poems in ways that were new in Chinese literary history. At the same time, historians and critics have devoted much attention to Xie Lingyun's role as a Buddhist thinker and to the considerable influence he exerted on that religion in its Chinese setting.

Xie Lingyun was born in 385 into one of the most powerful aristocratic families of the entire Six Dynasties period (A.D. 220–589). The Xie family originally came from what is now Henan (or Honan) province in north-central China, but had moved to southeast China sometime during the fourth century to avoid the wars raging in the north. By the end of that century, they were probably the most influential family in the southeast. The Xie's power and influence derived in large part from the accomplishments and fame of several family members who had won reputation before Xie Lingyun's time. Prominent among Xie Lingyun's ancestors was his great-great uncle, Xie An (A.D. 320–385). Although historians have praised Xie An's skills as a statesman, he is perhaps equally famous as a man of letters. In fact, before taking up office at the age of 40 and embarking on a political career, Xie An spent many years living in comfortable retirement in the scenic hills of Guiji (modern Shaoxing, Zhejiang province). During this period, Xie An was often in the company of the celebrated calligrapher Wang Xizhi (Wang Hsi-chih, (A.D. 321–379) and others, with whom he would often roam in the mountains and compose poetry.

By all accounts, Xie Lingyun was a precocious child. His talent for calligraphy became apparent early on, while he was living under the "magical protection" of a Daoist (Taoist) master in Hangzhou (apparently, Xie has been sent there for Daoist training). Later, while was living in the capital Jiankang (modern Nanjing, Jiangsu province), he came under the sway of his uncle Xie Hun, one of the best poets of the period. Xie Hun had founded his own exclusive literary salon, to which he invited only the most talented younger members of the Xie family. This group, run personally by Xie Hun in the role of tutor and critic, served as a training academy for young litterateurs. It was in this setting that Xie Lingyun received his basic training as a poet. It should perhaps also be mentioned that Xie Lingyun now possessed considerable wealth, for apparently, while still a young man he had inherited his grandfather's title—Duke of Kangle—as well as his fortune. To say the least, with his literary talent, substantial wealth, and strong family connections, Xie Lingyun's future looked extremely bright.

When he was about 20 years old (sometime around 405), Xie Lingyun took up his first official post as an aide on the staff of the grand marshal Sima Dewen. Thereafter he served in a number of official posts. At this point in his life, Xie seemed destined for a brilliant and distinguished future in government. In 422, however, Xie Lingyun's career took a negative turn when he supported his friend Liu Yizhen's bid for the throne. Liu failed, was exiled and eventually murdered for his role in the power struggle. For his part, Xie Lingyun was demoted to the post of prefect of Yongjia commandery (a seaport on the coast of Zhejiang). Many of Xie's most famous verses were composed during his year of exile in Yongjia, a time when he took less interest in government, as his political career was now essentially over, and greater aesthetic interest in landscape. Following his exile year in Yongjia, Xie was able to return to his family estate

at Shining. Thereafter, he intermittently held other government posts, but became increasingly arrogant and bitter, especially towards men who held political power at court. In 433, because of alleged maladministration, Xie was banished to the south (modern Guangdong), where he was charged with plotting a rebellion and executed publicly.

Fewer than 100 of Xie Lingyun's verses survive, most of which date after 421. These works are customarily divided into three groups: the first was written while serving in Yongjia (A.D. 422–423); the second was written while he was convalescing (perhaps from pulmonary tuberculosis) at his family estate (called Shining) outside Guiji (A.D. 423–430); the third was written while combining enjoyment of nature's physical splendor along with a religious quest for enlightenment (A.D. 431–433). Among these works, the most famous and influential are those poems that describe—often in vivid detail—the landscapes Xie Lingyun observed in Shining, as well as those encountered during his various travels. Traditional and modern critics praise these works as China's earliest "true" landscape verse. Specifically, these poems are lauded for their artistic and realistic representation of landscape (in Chinese literary criticism, this quality is sometimes called *xingsi / hsing-ssu*, or "verisimilitude"). As an example, consider the following lines from the poem "Passing Through My Shining Estate," written during a brief visit to Shining while on his way to exile in Yongjia:

Trekking these hills, I comb their heights and depths,
Crossing rivers, I exhaust their courses upstream and down—
Cliffs sheer down from the closely layered ranges,
Islets weave round the endless line of shoals;
White clouds enfold dark boulders,
Green bamboos bewitch clear ripples.

(WESTBROOK, TR., LIU AND LO, 1975)

Note how Xie's lines in this poem alternate between mountain and water/river scenes. The modern scholar Kang-i Sun Chang has argued convincingly that this descriptive technique, together with a mix of comprehensive and close-up scenic views, constitutes the essence of the poet's versimilitude in *shanshui* poetry. That is not to say, however, that Xie's landscape poetry is lacking in lyrical expression. The following lines, selected from "Leaving West Archery Hall at Dusk" (West Archery Hall was situated neat Yongjia), weigh heavy with thoughts about the passage of time and events of the past:

Under morning frosts the maple leaves turn scarlet,
In the evening dusk mists grow shadowy.
As the season passes one's grief is not slight;
Sorrows come and memories weigh down.

(WESTBROOK, TR., LIU AND LO, 1975)

The poet's persona and emotions emerge even more forcefully in the closing lines of "On My Way from South Mountain to North Mountain, I Glance at the Scenery from the Lake":

A heart that embraces natural transformations is
*   never bored,*
Yet the more I contemplate nature, the more my
*   concerns deepen.*
I do not lament that the departed is remote,
I only regret that I have no friend as companion.
Traveling alone is not what makes me sigh,
But to whom can I convey the reasons of my appre-
*   ciation and dissatisfaction?*

(CHANG, 1986)

On some occasions in his landscape poetry Xie Lingyun seeks and seems to achieve some sort of mystical vision of nature. That is to say, his observation and contemplation of a landscape somehow allow him to merge with, or become one with, the natural environment to the point that all distinctions are lost, even those between the scene observed and the poet himself. At the same time, this visionary experience frees Xie from worldly cares such as political office. As an example, consider the closing couplet of "Journeying by Stream: Following the Jinzhu Torrent I Cross the Mountain":

Viewing this scenery I discard worldly cares;
Awakened once and for all, I'll gain total abandon-
*   ment.*

(WESTBROOK, LIU AND LO, 1975)

Some critics and literary historians have suggested that Xie's visionary experience here is related to the Buddhist ideal of "sudden illumination" or "sudden inspiration" (*dunwu/tun-wu*), a concept developed by the monk Zhu Daosheng (Chu Tao-sheng, c. A.D. 360–434). This argument is convincing, for we know that Xie Lingyun was a strong supporter of this ideal.

Xie Lingyun's greatest achievement as a writer was his undeniable skill at composing landscape verse that reflects intense intimacy between himself and scenes around him. Critics such as Tao Hongjing (Dao Hung-ching, A.D. 452–536), writing only about a century after Xie's death, were already beginning to notice his significant role in literary history: "Men have always spoken and will always speak of the beauty of mountains and streams. . . . Yet, since the time of [Xie] Kangle, no one has been able to feel at one with these wonders, as he did." (*Murmuring Stream*) No traditional critic, however, more succinctly and accurately captures the essence of Xie Lingyun's talent and role in the development of *shanshui* poetry in China than the famous Tang dynasty poet Bai Ju-yi (Pai Chü-i, A.D. 772–846):

Master Xie's talents were broad,
But he was at odds with his times.
His lofty ambitions, sadly were of no use,
He needed to vent his feelings,
Once expressed, they became landscape poetry,
In which excellent taste harmonized with extraordi-
*   nary imagination.*

(CHANG, 1986)

Bai Juyi's argument seems right on the mark: the adversity and suffering that Xie Lingyun experienced in the final decade of his life inspired him to produce his greatest literary masterpieces. This "formula," if we may call it that, is not uncommon at all in China. In fact, most of China's greatest poets—Qu Yuan (Ch'ü Yüan), Du Fu (Tu Fu), and many others—produced their greatest poetic expression during periods of intense personal hardship.

JAMES M. HARGETT

Further Reading

Chang, Kang-i Sun. *Six Dynasties Poetry*. Princeton, N.J.: Princeton University Press, 1986. The second chapter of this work is devoted to Xie Lingyun.

Frodsham, J. D. *The Murmuring Stream: The Life and Works of Hsieh Ling-yün*. 2 vols. Kuala Lumpur: University of Malaya Press, 1967.

Liu, Wu-chi, and Lo, Irving Yucheng, eds. *Sunflower Splendor: Three Thousand Years of Chinese Poetry*. New York: Doubleday, Anchor Books, 1975. Also, Bloomington, IN: Indiana University Press, 1975. The quotations used in this article of translations by Francis Westbrook come from this volume. A very interesting and helpful resource.

Mather, Richard B. "The Landscape Buddhism of the Fifth Century Poet Hsieh Ling-yün." *Journal of Asian Studies* 18 (1958–1959): 67–79.

———. "Hsieh Ling-yün." In *The Indiana Companion to Traditional Chinese Literature*. Ed. William H. Nienhauser Jr. Bloomington, IN: Indiana University Press, 1986, 428–430.

SELECTIONS OF REFINED LITERATURE

Title in Chinese: *Wen xuan (Wen hsüan)*
Compiler: Xiao Tong (Hsiao T'ung), Crown Prince Zhaoming (Chao-ming) of the Liang
Born: A.D. 501, Xiangyang (Hsien-yang), China
Died: A.D. 531, Jiankang (modern Nanjing), China
Form: Anthology of prose and poetry
Date of Compilation: C. A.D. 526

Major Themes

Rhapsodies on famous Chinese cities and palaces, imperial hunts, and rituals: the grandeur and glory of the Chinese empire.

Poetic accounts of travels to scenic and historical sites: what the lessons of the past can teach the present.

Rhapsodies and poems on the natural world: the wonders of mountains and rivers, nature as a refuge for the recluse, descriptions of natural phenomena such as snow, wind, and the moon.

The frustrations of official life and complaints by failed scholar-officials.

Laments for the deceased in prose and verse.

Feast, farewell, and ceremonial poems.

Prose genres: disquisitions on philosophy and politics, petitions and memorials to the emperor, imperial pronouncements, letters and prefaces, inscriptions and admonitions.

The *Wen xuan* was compiled at the court of the Xiao Tong, crown prince of the Liang dynasty. Xiao Tong was the oldest son of Xiao Yan (A.D. 464–549), founder of the Liang dynasty. From an early age Xiao Tong was surrounded by eminent literary men, and his residence, the Eastern Palace, was the major center of literary activity in the capital. The prince and his literary companions spent many hours strolling the palace grounds discussing literature and composing extemporaneous poems. Xiao Tong also was an avid book collector; and largely through his efforts, the Eastern Palace library grew to some 30,000 volumes. Xiao Tong sponsored the compilation of several literary collections, of which the most famous is the *Wen xuan*. He died in April 531 at the age of 29, presumably as the result of shock after being injured in a boating accident on a palace lake.

Originally in 30 chapters, but rearranged by a seventh-century editor into 60 chapters, the *Wen xuan* contains 761 works of prose and poetry by over 130 writers from the third century B.C. to the sixth century A.D. The criteria of selection, delineation of genres, thematic categories, and chronologi-

cal divisions greatly influenced later Chinese anthologies. In addition, the works included in the *Wen xuan* became an important part of the classical Chinese literary canon. Of the works of the pre-Tang period the *Wen xuan* still represents the best selection of rhapsodies, lyric poetry, and prose.

Wen xuan *and the Literary Canon*

The elevation of the *Wen xuan* to canonical status occurred very rapidly. Almost immediately after its compilation, it became the text from which most literary men obtained their literary education. This was particularly true during the Tang dynasty, when the *Wen xuan* was one of the primary texts studied by those preparing for the civil service examination, which required candidates to compose poetry to set themes. The *Wen xuan* was regarded as the storehouse of literary knowledge that, if committed to memory, would enable one to write elegant prose and verse.

During the Tang dynasty, which is the golden age of Chinese poetry, poets were intimately familiar with the *Wen xuan*. It was primarily through the

Wen xuan that educated men of the Tang gained their knowledge of the classical literary tradition, and many of them could recite lines from the *Wen xuan* as easily as educated Englishmen could quote Homer and Virgil. Even as late as the Song dynasty, after the elimination of the poetry requirement from the examinations, the *Wen xuan* still was venerated as a model for literature. The *Wen xuan* was also transmitted to Korea and Japan, where it long has been held in great esteem.

The Concept of Literature

The *Wen xuan* reflects a view of literature that may properly be called moderate. It is a good example of the venerable Chinese idea of attaining a mean—a compromise between extreme positions. At the time of its compilation, literature was defined in one of two ways. On the one hand, there was the view that upheld the old Han dynasty idea of literature as a didactic instrument to promote political, social, and moral ends. According to this school, literature was not an independent art, but one subordinate to the values of the Confucian scriptures. The other view, a more recent one current especially in the literary salons of the Liang period, including a salon centered around Xiao Tong's younger brother, Xiao Gang (Hsiao Kang, A.D. 503–551), essentially repudiated Confucian literary values, and divorced literature from any pragmatic or didactic function. Literature, in fact, should be liberated from social, political, or moral constraints, and instead be the "unbridled expression of feelings" (*fangdang/fang tang*). The new poetry that emanated from the Liang literary salons thus was basically a poetry of craft distinguished for its careful attention to prosody, dainty and delicate style, mild eroticism, restrained emotion, writing for entertainment and the display of wit, and lack of seriousness and moral purpose.

Xiao Tong's concept of literature lies somewhere between the pragmatic views of the Confucian conservatives and the technical concepts of the poetic innovators. In his preface to the *Wen xuan*, which is one of the principal documents of medieval Chinese literary thought, Xiao Tong presents his views on literature, and in particular, what should and should not be included in anthologies. The title of his collection is significant—"Selections of Refined Literature"—with the emphasis on selections. In his preface to the *Wen xuan*, Xiao Tong indicates that he was concerned with the lack of order in the literary tradition, and especially in the collections that had been compiled up to his time. Thus, he took great care to establish the ordering criteria for his collection. Xiao Tong groups his selections by genre. Although the *Wen xuan* was not the first genre anthology, it probably was the first collection that was a well-ordered selection based on a clear concept of what properly belongs in an anthology.

The term that Xiao Tong uses for literature, *wen*, is a very complex term in the Chinese tradition. The earliest sense of this word is "marking" or "pattern." In early texts, *wen* can refer to the markings on birds and beasts, the patterns of clothing and embroidery, the veins of stones and shells, or a tattooed body. Even the heavens had *wen*; *tianwen* (heaven's markings) is the Chinese term for the astral bodies: the stars, planets, and constellations all arranged in patterns parallel to the human world. Thus, *wen* had the meaning of cosmic pattern.

Wen also was the basic pattern of human civilization, and in early texts it was the principal word used to designate "culture" and the virtues of peace and civilization, as opposed to the values of war. As a particular form of culture and marking— that etched by humans on shells or ox bones, carved on stone or bronze, written on bamboo strips, silk, or paper—*wen* means "writing." Related senses of the word are "ornament," "form" (as opposed to "substance"), and of course "literature."

In his preface, Xiao Tong uses *wen* in several of its multiple senses. He conceives of it first in the broad sense of "pattern," whether it be the inscribed markings on stone and wood, or the "patterns of the sky." However, his primary emphasis is not on *wen* in its broader sense, but in the narrower meaning of *belles lettres*. For example, he refers to the poems of an ancient southern poetic tradition as *wen.* Elsewhere, he designates certain prosodic forms as *wen.*

In addition to *wen,* Xiao Tong uses other virtually synonymous terms to designate the types of works he selected for inclusion in the *Wen xuan.* All of these bisyllabic compounds contain one element in common—the word *pian,* which literally means "individual piece" of writing. According to Xiao Tong, his anthology is a collection of pieces of poetry and prose that exist independent of a larger work. They are relatively short pieces that can be inserted into the anthology without damaging their integrity.

Xiao Tong's concern with the integrity of a literary work led him to confine his anthology to works that could stand alone. Thus, the *Wen xuan* does not contain any excerpts from the Confucian classics, primarily because, in Xiao Tong's view, such hallowed works should not be "weeded and mowed, cut or trimmed."

In addition to excluding excerpts from the Confucian classics, Xiao Tong also deliberately excluded texts of ancient speeches and oratory, the works of the philosophers, and histories. Xiao Tong states that he was not interested in works that were solely concerned with "setting forth doctrines" or "praising right and wrong." In this respect, Xiao's views coincide with the literary innovators of his time.

The *Wen xuan* also played an important role in establishing many of the norms by which genres were later defined throughout the Chinese literary tradition. The 37 genres of the *Wen xuan* can actually be reduced to three general categories: one, the *fu,* rhapsody; two, *shi (shih)* or lyric poetry; and three, miscellaneous prose. Although this tripartite scheme was never applied in the Chinese tradition, it is a useful way of identifying the basic kinds of literary writing that prevailed before the Tang dynasty.

One could divide the *Wen xuan* into two basic types of literature, poetry and prose, for the *fu* is basically a type of poetry. The *fu* is a form of rhyme-prose that has no exact Western equivalent. The Han form of the *fu* has the following features: an ornate style, lines of unequal length, mixtures of rhymed and unrhymed passages, elaborate descriptions, hyperbole, extensive catalogues, and often a moral conclusion. For much of the Han dynasty, the *fu* was primarily a form of court literature. All of the major *fu* poets served at the imperial court, where they presented their rhapsodies to the emperor. The *fu* in fact was the poetic form most suited to celebrate the power and glory of the Han empire. Thus, the most famous Han rhapsodies are long poems on the imperial capitals, palaces, and hunting parks. Written in a grand, ornate style, these poems invariably enumerate the material riches and praise the magnificent achievement of the Han imperium. Although some poets in good Confucian fashion tempered their praise with mild cautions to the emperor on the folly of extravagance and ostentation—the complaints mostly are about hunts and excursions draining the resources of the state—the poems are filled with a spirit of confidence and enthusiasm for the unity and prosperity that the Han empire achieved. Because the *fu* loomed so large in the pre-Tang literary tradition, and was always treated as a genre independent from lyric, much as the epic was in Western literature, it would be doing the genre a disservice to obscure it under the general rubric of poetry.

The *shi* was an ancient form that goes back to the *Book of Songs.* In the Han dynasty it was transformed from a predominantly four-syllable line pattern to a five-syllable line form. After the Han, pentasyllabic verse was the prevailing form of poetic expression. Poets expanded the range of *shi* composition to include landscape, reclusion, philosophy, travel, and friendship, and descriptions of objects.

Genres and Themes

The ordering of the genres in the *Wen xuan* tells us much about Xiao Tong's literary values. First, the sequence of the genres provides a clear indication of Xiao Tong's order of preferences among the vast array of literary forms that existed in his time. The first genre in the anthology is the *fu,* and thus Xiao Tong attached the most importance to this literary form. Not only does Xiao Tong place the *fu* at the head of the anthology, but he also discusses it first in his preface. Within the *fu* category, Xiao Tong places primary emphasis on the *fu* pieces of the Han, and his selection is dominated by the imperial rhapsodies of the Han. The *fu* section contains 15 subject categories, the ordering of which is significant. The first four subjects are all on imperial themes: capitals, sacrifices, the ceremonial plowing of the sacred field, and hunting. By giving first place to these subjects Xiao Tong reflects the old Han dynasty view that the ultimate concern of literature was the state. The capital, for example, was more than just a city: it was the center of imperial power. It also was a symbol of the cosmos, and thus poems on the great cosmic and imperial center naturally occupied the first place in the anthology.

Although the state of Xiao Tong's time was a pale imitation of the great Han empire, the ideological basis of empire still persisted. Perhaps as a member of the Liang ruling house, especially in light of his position as heir to the imperial throne, Xiao Tong viewed the Han as a golden age of unity and prosperity. Poems that praised the glories of the magnificent empire of the past might have been inspiring at a time when the Chinese state was constantly harassed and humiliated by the Central Asian kingdoms of the north. Thus, it should not be too surprising that the old Han dynasty values were an important influence on the formation of Xiao Tong's literary thought, which as far as the ordering of the *Wen xuan* genres was concerned, was very conservative and traditional. The next thematic group consists of two closely related subject categories, "recounting journeys" and "sightseeing." Since these categories are concerned with travel and movement, they naturally follow from the last of the imperial themes, hunting. Hunting, in fact, is traditionally associated with travel and excursion in ancient China, and thus the progression from the imperial themes to travel is remarkably smooth. However, unlike the poems in the imperial themes section, these pieces are more personal travel narratives that recount tours to historical sites, ascents to high places (a tower and a mountain), and a visit to a ruined city.

The next group is what the Chinese called *yongwu* (*yung wu*) (poems on things). The *yongwu* theme was favored in the court salons of Xiao Tong's time. The range of subjects is very large and encompasses poems on celestial phenomena (the sun, moon, weather, seasons), geographical features (such as mountains, rivers, lakes, and ponds), buildings, plants and animals, and manmade implements (musical instruments, jewelry, fans, carved stones). Most of the *yongwu* pieces of Xiao Tong's time are in the *shi*, or lyric poetry, form. Xiao Tong seems to have deliberately excluded these pieces in favor of *fu* on *yongwu* themes. This is another example of Xiao Tong's ability to compromise between contemporary and traditional literary values.

The first of the *yongwu* categories is called "palaces and halls," which includes rhapsodies on the palaces of princes. From the palaces and halls, one moves outdoors to the natural world, first with rhapsodies on rivers and seas, then with natural phenomena such as the wind, snow, and moon, and concluding with poems on birds and animals. The last rhapsody in the birds and animals group, which is a piece on a wild crane trained to dance to music, has been interpreted as an allegorical poem in which the captive bird represents the poor scholar whose rise in the bureaucracy has been hampered by the rigid social and political barriers of the time. It thus provides a good transition to the next general grouping, which we may call "frustration and sorrow." These are all rhapsodies in which the poet pours out his personal feelings, either to express frustration at the unfairness of the political system, or to lament the passing of a dear friend or relative.

The last two general categories do not follow so easily from the preceding themes. The next category is the loose grouping of literature and music. Literature (especially poetry, which is the main concern of the one rhapsody that is included in the section on literature) and music were strongly linked with feelings, especially sorrow, and perhaps that is why Xiao Tong placed them after the "frustration and sorrow" group.

The final category, which rests by itself, is what Xiao Tong labelled "passion." It is a rather curious section that contains four mildly erotic rhapsodies, three of which recount sexual liaisons between a mortal and a goddess. This is the one category in which Xiao Tong accords with the tastes of contemporary court salons, where erotic poetry was the rage.

The lyric poetry section of the *Wen xuan* represents a rather conservative selection. Although Xiao Tong selected *fu* on erotic themes, he did not include any *shi* pieces on this theme. Nor did he select any lyric poems on *yongwu* themes, which were also very popular at the court salons of his time. The lyric poems in the *Wen xuan* consist primarily of pieces of the well-established poets of the third through the fifth centuries. These poets wrote well-crafted poems on such subjects as the quest for immortality, escape from the travails of the human world, the delights of nature, and the hardships of war. One of the more controversial features of the lyric poetry selection is the small amount of space devoted to the poetry of Tao Qian (Tao Ch'ien / Tao Yuanming, (A.D. 365–427), who is generally acknowledged to be the foremost Chinese poet prior to the Tang dynasty. Although Xiao Tong personally admired Tao Qian's poetry, he was probably following the contemporary opinion, which did not regard Tao Qian as a major poet.

The prose section of the *Wen xuan* is dominated by works in the parallel prose style. The identifying features of parallel prose include the extensive use of parallel lines, numerous allusions, ornate language, euphony (including in some cases rhyme), and set rhythmic patterns (usually four-syllable or six-syllable lines). Parallel-style pieces are found throughout the prose section in a variety of forms. The last five chapters, which contain examples of dirges, laments, epitaphs, grave memoirs, condolences, and offerings, are almost exclusively parallel-style compositions. In the Chinese tradition, *Wen xuan* is generally considered the earliest collection of parallel prose. It is possible that one reason Xiao Tong excluded the classics, philosophical writing, and history from *Wen xuan* is because parallelism is less common in such works.

The term *wen* in the title *Wen xuan* literally means "literature." However, the kind of *wen* that Xiao Tong and his co-editors chose to include in the anthology is a special kind of literature. It is literature in an elegant and refined style. There is no room in the collection for works written in vulgar language, humorous writings, or works derived from the popular tradition, such as the Han dynasty popular songs and ballads. The emphasis is on the orthodox Confucian tradition. There are few Buddhist works and no religious Daoist (Taoist) pieces. The Daoist tradition represented in the *Wen xuan* is that of classical Daoism (*Laozi / Lao Tzu, Zhuangzi / Chuang Tzu*). Even the Buddhist works it contains are not doctrinal essays, but writings that make minimal use of Buddhist terminology. Because of the dominance of works in an elegant, often parallel style, the *Wen xuan* is more than "Selections of Literature," as a literal translation of the title would have one believe, but rather "Selections of Refined Literature," or even "Choice Examples of Elegant Writing."

DAVID R. KNECHTGES

Further Reading

Translation

Knechtges, David R. *Wen-xuan or Selections of Refined Literature*. vol. 1: *Rhapsodies on Metropolises and Capitals*. Princeton, N.J.: Princeton University Press, 1982. vol. 2: *Rhapsodies on Sacrifices, Hunts, Travel, Palaces and Halls, Rivers and Seas*. Princeton, N.J.: Princeton University Press, 1987.

Related Study

Hightower, James Robert. "The *Wen Hsüan* and Genre Theory," *Harvard Journal of Asiatic Studies* 20 (1957): 512–33.

THE POETRY OF WANG WEI

Author: Wang Wei
Born: 699 or 701, Qi (Ch'i), Shanxi (Shan-hsi) province
Died: 760 or 761, Lantian (Lan-t'ien)
Major Poems: The Wang River poems, poems of Cloud Valley, "Morning Audience," "The Emperor Commands a Poem Be Written and Sent to My Friend, Prefect Wei Xi," "From Puti Monastery," "Living in the Hills," "Hibiscus Hill," "Bamboo Lodge," "Deer Park," "Goodbye to Tsu the Third at Chichou"

Major Themes

There is a grandeur about the court, but when one is alone in a state of nature one realizes the truths and values of a reality beyond perception.

Friendship is one of life's rewards and a continuing source of inner strength.

The simple life, especially when one lives close to nature, is the most rewarding.

Poetry is the only way to express what is otherwise inexpressible.

Wang Wei, the "quiet poet," regarded by many critics as one of China's greatest poets, ranking with Li Bo (Li Po) (701–762) and Du Fu (Tu Fu) (712–770), was born in Shanxi (Shansi) Province to a distinguished family of government officials. From a very early age—some say at the age of nine—he wrote poetry and practiced other arts, including calligraphy, music, and painting. (Although none of his paintings remains, he was regarded as a painter of rare genius, and his work was very much imitated in the schools and by later artists.) He left home at the age of 15 and traveled for a brief period before resuming his studies. He earned honors as a student, and after passing the *jinshi (chin-shih)* ("presented scholar") examination he was given the first of a long list of government positions, which he left from time to time for travel, contemplation, and the creation of poems and paintings.

Early in his government career, after having been appointed Director of Imperial Music, he was relieved of his position—probably because of court politics—and assigned a minor position as keeper of the granary in a small town. He wrote a poem about his disappointment and then used the time afforded by his undemanding position to lead a contemplative life of quiet study and the writing of more poetry.

Wang Wei married early, but his wife died around 730, and he never remarried. He began a 10-year study of Buddhism with the Chan master Daoguang (Tao-kuang). After his mother died in 750 he stayed at the family estate of Wangchuan (Wang-ch'uan) for a period of mourning and returned there periodically for spiritual refreshment and the writing of poetry.

During a period of rebellion by the Mongol An Lu-shan, who forced Emperor Hsüan Tsung to flee to Chengtu, Wang Wei was captured by the enemy forces. He attempted suicide, pretended he was dumb, and was finally forced to accept a position in the new government. When the rebels were overthrown Wang Wei managed to become part of the imperial court again, perhaps because of a poem written during the rebellion that was critical of the rebels.

He held a number of positions of growing importance as grand secretary and reached his highest political peak when he was appointed assistant secretary of state. When he died in 760 or 761 he was buried at the Wangchuan estate.

The Distinctive Features of Wang Wei's Poetry

After Wang Wei's death, his brother Wang Jin (Wang Chin) at imperial order turned over the collection of Wang Wei's poems that had survived the accidents of time, frequent moves, and insurrection. There are over 400 poems remaining of an original number that may have been 2,000 or more.

Wang Wei's poems are frequently divided into convenient classes of poetry—sometimes by reference to formal features (such as numbers of lines and numbers of characters in the lines) and perhaps more often by subject matter: court poems, nature poems, Buddhist poems, and poems of friendship. We will employ the subject matter classification for the making of summary statements and the presentation of striking examples.

Whatever the form and whatever the subject matter, Wang Wei's poems have features that can be recognized as uniquely characteristic. They are *quiet* in imagery, atmosphere, and sentiment; they are the products of a contemplative mind that could see the implications of natural scenes that to others have no meanings either by association or by relationship to human contemplators, or by the respectful recognition of cosmic forces and directions that become clear only to those who respond to and accept them as significant.

The poems are *imagistic*: they build sharply defined images (as one would expect of a painter-poet)—sometimes static, sometimes fluid, often colorful, and sometimes pervaded by sound. All the senses are appealed to. The images may have traditional meanings from classical sources, but those meanings are not necessary to the expression of a human experience that appeals to the reader as universal; it is not so much that the classical allusions enhance the images as that the images enhance the classical associations.

Wang Wei's poems are for the most part *economical*; that is, they say enough; no more is needed. The art shown in the poetry is like that of the photographer or painter who turns to the world as it is, only to abstract from it and construct an image, hence, an experience that is profoundly moving and significant.

Despite their imagistic character and their economy of style, Wang's poems are *multi-dimensional*; that is, the poems are the emotive expressions of a unique human individual while at the same time they both portray nature as seen by that individual and relate the experience to the human experience generally and to the cosmic implications of what is seen and felt. All this is accomplished without intellectual posturing or metaphysical jargon: what Wang sees, even when he sees what is beyond perception, he sees through a glass brightly.

Of course, there are other poetic virtues that cannot be identified by those confined to translations—the appropriate and often surprising use of sound and rhythm, the multi-layered connotations of the Chinese characters in context, and even (as we shall show by reference to a critic's analysis) a reliance on the appearance and structure of the characters themselves.

The Court Poems

The court poems were sometimes written in response to an imperial request; sometimes they were written in celebration of, or in recognition of, a significant event occurring at court, and sometimes, although written at court, the poems were a personal expression of the poet's own perceptions and emotions.

The moment one turns to the court poems of Wang Wei, it becomes apparent that although the poems were written at court, or about the court, or about matters in some way related to the court (otherwise the poems would not be classified by scholars—not by Wang—as "court" poems), they are not the contrivances of someone simply celebrating events at court, responding in kind to imperial poetry, or seeking favor. They are from the same artist, and expressive of the same range of sentiments and ideals, as are the poems classified under other titles. Consider, for example, "Morning Audience":

White and pure, the bright stars are high.
The distant sky dawns on a vast expanse.
Darkness of sophora mist does not disperse;
Cries of citywall crows gradually cease.
Just now I hear the sounds from the tall pavilion
But cannot yet distinguish the wardrobe room.

Rows of silver candles have already formed:
Through the Golden Gate chariots solemnly drive.

(YU, 1980, P. 87)

The grand setting of the court—as seen in the mists of early morning, the sounds of birds and of interior activity, and, finally, the arrival of the day's first chariots as they pass through the palace's Golden Horse Gate—is shown quietly, with appropriate imagery, economics, and with a growing sense of imperial drama.

Wang Wei's life may have been spared because of the following poem written to protest a forced concert in the palace by court musicians after the conquest by the rebel forces of An Lushan and the expulsion of the emperor. The poem was written while Wang Wei was imprisoned in Puti Monastery and was given secretly to his friend P'ei Ti, who was himself a poet and had told Wang Wei of the concert and of the tears of the musicians:

Its ten thousand doorways pain the heart: wild
* smoke rises;*
The hundred officials: when will they again attend
* the emperor's court?*
Autumn sophora leaves fall in the empty palace;
Beside Frozen Jade Pool, music from pipes and
* strings.*

(WAGNER, 1981, P. 50)

Nature Poems

The only way to appreciate fully the nature poetry of Wang Wei is by reading it. Even in translation the poems have a quality that is striking and unique: they are understated but evocative, brief but telling, clear but suggestive. Consider the poem "Living in the Hills":

In calm loneliness I shut my door
Against the whole afterglowing sky
Cranes are nesting in all the pines
No visitors at my wicket gate
Tender bamboos with the new bloom on them
Red lotuses shed of their old garments

A lamp shines out at the ford
Water-chestnut pickers come home.

(ROBINSON, 1973, P. 84)

Of special interest is the poem "Hibiscus Hill," not only because of the quiet eloquence of the imagery but because of a remarkable feature of the Chinese characters that make up the first line of the poem (to be shown and discussed afterwards):

The blossoms on high hibiscus boughs
Fling crimson through the mountains.
Families no longer live in this deserted valley,
Yet season after season the hibiscus still blooms
* in profusion.*

(CHANG AND WALMSLEY, 1958)

As the magnolia trees blossom, they resemble lotuses; all over the mountain side the red calyxes open and fall; there is no sound anywhere. Here is an image of nature where no one is present, but only the absent poet can catch the silence and the color.

The first line of the poem as written with Chinese characters is:

木末芙蓉花

(YU, 1980, P. 235)

In *Chinese Poetic Writing*, François Cheng comments on this first line as written in Chinese characters:

The line is translated "At the end of the branches, the hibiscus flowers." Even the reader who does not know Chinese can easily become sensitive to the visual aspect of these characters. . . . Viewing these characters in order gives the visual impression . . . of a tree blossoming into flower. . . .

(CHENG, 1982, P. 9)

Since Wang Wei was a great painter and calligrapher, it is indeed credible that he would have taken advantage of the pictorial quality of the line of characters: if these characters were put on cards fastened together and then flipped (as with booklets that present "moving pictures"), one would see the blossoming of the hibiscus and its coming to full flower.

Buddhist Poems

As one might expect, Wang Wei's "Buddhist" poems are nature poems, and they possess the distinctive virtues of all his poetry. The following famous poem, "Bamboo Lodge," is generally admired for its atmosphere, its meaning, and its closing line:

> *Alone I sit amid the dark bamboo,*
> *Play the zither and whistle loud again.*
> *In the deep wood men do not know*
> *The bright moon comes to shine on me.*

> (YU, 1980, P. 204)

A problem for the translator is the use of the Chinese character *xiao (hsiao),* meaning "to whistle." If the poem portrays a meditative person alone in a dark bamboo grove, isolated from others and having no companion save the moon, why is this solitary person whistling, rather than humming, or praying, or contemplating? It is because the "whistling" is a meditative whistle, a breathing out that makes a sound, part of the meditative practice. A note by Pauline Yu (see Yu, 1980, p. 191) offers an explanation: "A 'whistle' (*xiao*) was probably a combination of Taoist breathing techniques and whistling [that] was said to express feelings and was associated with harmonizing with nature and achieving immortality. . . ."

For readers unacquainted with the *xiao*, the reference to whistling is jarring: someone is strumming away and whistling; the whole atmosphere appears to be too lighthearted to be associated with Buddhist meditation. In the attempt to resolve the problem, various alternative phrases have been

used: "sit and croon," "sing and sing," "give a loud whistle," "whistle song," "whistle a tune," and so forth.

There is perhaps no satisfactory resolution: unless the reader knows there is a meditative way of whistling, the meaning is lost. One also may fail to appreciate the poet's sense of communion with the moon, a kind of reciprocal "shining" or "looking" that is implicit in the poem. The difficulties of translation may be resolved by the translator's commitment to expressions that do much, if not all, of the work, but they cannot ever be overcome.

A poem that is in some ways similar to "Bamboo Lodge" is "Deer Park":

> *Empty mountain, no one is seen.*
> *Only the echo of human voices is heard.*
> *Returning light enters the deep grove,*
> *And again shines on the green moss.*

> (WAGNER, 1981, P. 148)

As Marsha L. Wagner points out in a comment following her translation, this poem, despite its simplicity, is "filled with Buddhist overtones." Deer Park, she tells us: is "the place near Benares where the Buddha preached his first sermon after after his enlightenment"; a deer that escapes entrapment is a conventional Buddhist symbol for a recluse; and the image of the empty mountain "suggests a transcendent vision of the illusory material world."

Poems of Friendship

There are many poems of friendship among Wang's works; they usually relate friendship to the satisfactions to be found in nature and in isolating oneself from the busy world; they emphasize the sorrows of parting and the joys of reunion; above all, they call attention to the sympathy between persons of like temperament and faith.

A characteristic friendship poem is the following, "Good-bye to Tsu the Third at Chichou":

> *Smiles of meeting turned to parting tears*
> *Sad house, and town impenetrably dead*

Far mountains sharp on the cold sky
Long river racing in the dusk
Boat cast off and you sailed away
Beyond my gaze, while I still stand.

(ROBINSON, 1973, P. 54)

A descriptive essay, especially with only a few examples of the poetry, can only hint at the charms and incisiveness of the hundreds of poems composed by Wang Wei.

IAN P. MCGREAL

Further Reading

Translations and Related Studies

Chang, Yin-nan, and Lewis C. Walmsley, trans. *Poems by Wang Wei*. Rutland, VT: Charles E. Tuttle, Co., 1960. Contains a helpful introduction, translations of 136 poems. A small, attractive volume, with illustrations.

Cheng, François. *Chinese Poetic Writing*. Bloomington, IN: Indiana University Press, 1982. A sensitive and revealing study of the uses of the Chinese language in the writing of poetry.

Barnstone, Tony, and Willis Barnstone, and Xu Haixin, trans. *Laughing Lost in the Mountains: Poems of Wang Wei*. Hanover, N.H.: University Press of New England, 1991. An excellent introduction by the Barnstones, "The Ecstasy of Stillness," prepares the way for an outstanding collection of 171 creatively translated poems.

Robinson, G. W. *Poems of Wang Wei*. Harmondsworth, Middlesex, England: Penguin Books, 1973. A solid and sensitively rendered collection, with a helpful introduction by Robinson.

Wagner, Marsha L. *Wang Wei*. Boston: Twayne Publishers, G. K. Hall & Co., 1981. An excellent critical commentary and review of Wang Wei's poetry, with many striking translations. Covers the poet's life and his accomplishments as court poet, nature poet, Buddhist poet, and painter.

Yu, Pauline. *The Poetry of Wang Wei: New Translations and Commentary*. Bloomington, IN: Indiana University Press, 1980. An intensive and insightful commentary, with excellent translations of 150 poems. Also includes the Chinese texts of the poems and a useful glossary.

THE POETRY OF LI BO (LI PO)

Author: Li Bo (Li Po); also known as Li Bai (Li Pai)
Born: 701, Central Asia(?)
Died: 762, Dangtu, Sichuan province
Major Poems: "Quiet Night Thoughts," "Ancient Airs" [59 poems], "The Road to Shu Is Hard," "Drinking Alone Beneath the Moon"

Major Themes

When one is alone, one can know real peace.
Sometimes one regrets being away from home and the chores of daily life there.
The world changes, wealth and honor come to nothing: what is to be gained by constant striving?
Drinking wine alone under the moon, I know the companionship of moon, my shadow, and myself.

If one were to page through just about any anthology of traditional Chinese verse, it is virtually certain that the section devoted to Tang dynasty (618–908) poetry would be longer than any other represented period in Chinese literary history. Verses by China's best-known poets—Li Bo (701–762), Du Fu (Tu Fu) (712–770), Wang Wei (701–761), Han Yu (Han Yü) (768–824), Bo Juyi (P'o Chü-i) (772–846), Li He (Li Ho) (790–816), and many others—would probably dominate these pages. Among them, Li Bo and his contemporary and friend Du Fu share the honor of being the most famous of all.

Many reasons account for Li Bo's fame. For one thing, much of his poetry is stylistically simple. At the same time, he is fond of using hyperbole and irony in his verses and on occasion even departs on wild flights of fantasy. Such qualities are immediately appealing to most readers. A second reason for Li Bo's fame is that he was one of only a very few Chinese poets to be immediately and widely recognized as a "poet genius" by his contemporaries. That is to say, he could dash off outstanding lines of verse spontaneously without any forethought or crafting whatsoever, so the legend goes. Some traditional critics tell us that Du Fu and other contemporaries admired Li Bo's "genius" because it was "supernaturally inspired." It might also be mentioned that some literary historians attempt to link Li's seemingly effortless literary style to the "mysterious" Central Asian origin of his family. While it seems likely that Li Bo's family originally came from somewhere in Central Asia, it is unclear how "romantic" origins or "foreign blood" might relate to his character or genius as a poet.

Despite Li Bo's exalted status as China's "greatest poet," there is little serious scholarship on him or his poetry available in any language. Part of this is due to the elusive qualities of Li's verse (the precise qualities of his poems are extremely difficult, if not impossible, to pinpoint and dissect); part of this is due to the fact that his biography and career are characterized more by innuendo and anecdotes than facts and dates.

Li Bo was probably born somewhere in Central Asia in 701, where his family (traders?) had been living in some sort of exile for about a century. His family returned to China when he was about five years old, and settled in a place called Changming (in modern Sichuan province). Li Bo spent his boyhood there. In the mid-720s he left home and traveled eastward down the Yangzi Valley, sightseeing and trying to make the necessary connections to gain public attention and thereby win appointment to government office. By 742 or 743 he managed to get a position in the Hanlin Academy in Chang'an (the capital, now Xian). While serving in the capital Li Bo apparently managed to build quite a reputation as a drunk, which inspired numerous stories and anecdotes. After two years in Chang'an, however, Li Bo fell victim to Court intrigues and was expelled from the capital. He thereupon wandered throughout east and southeast China, often proclaiming himself an "unappreciated man of talent" who was slandered and driven away from Court by jealous enemies. In the 750s, after the outbreak of the An Lushan Rebellion, Li Bo became implicated in a secondary revolt. He was arrested for treason, but later managed to win release. The final years of his life were spent wandering through the Yangzi Valley, again trying to find a patron who might help him win a favorable position with the central government in Chang'an. In 762 Li Bo was finally appointed to office by the emperor. Unfortunately, by the time his appointment orders reached him in Sichuan, Li was already dead.

Li Bo's Poetry

Approximately 1,100 poems attributed to Li Bo survive, though no doubt a good number of these are spurious: Li Bo's *general* style is easily imitated; moreover, many poems of unknown authorship seem to have been attributed to his hand. Although Li Bo composed verse in numerous forms, he preferred the older, less restricted meters that were ungoverned by the recently developed rules, as they were reflected in the *lüshi (lü-shih)*, or "regulated verse," form. Thus, most of Li Bo's poems are written in one of three styles: the brief, four-line quatrain *(jueju/chüeh-chü)*; the longer "ancient poems" *(gushi/ku-shih)*; and the Music Bureau (folksong) and *gexing (ko-hsing)* (ballad) forms.

As for the quatrains, the following is Li Bo's best-known verse and just might be the most famous poem ever written in the Chinese language. Simplicity and accessibility—two hallmark qualities of Li Bo's poetry in general—are immediately apparent in this famous *jueju*. It is titled "Quiet Night Thoughts":

Before my bed there is bright moonlight
So that it seems like frost on the ground:
Lifting my head I watch the bright moon,
Lowering my head I dream that I'm home.

(COOPER, 1973, P. 109)

Li Bo wrote a famous series of 59 poems simply titled "Ancient Airs" *(Gufeng/Ku-feng)*, all of which concern ancient stories and sayings. The following verse, representative of Li Bo's ancient-style poems, concerns the famous story of Zhuangzi's (Chuang Tzu's) (also known as Zhuang Zhou/ Chuang Chou) "butterfly dream." Lines 5–6 refer to a famous fairytale: the Marquis of Dongling (Tung-ling), once a high official in the Qin (Ch'in) (221–207 B.C.) government, resignedly turned to growing melons outside the Green Gate of Chang'an after the Qin was overthrown by the Han dynasty:

Did Chuang Chou dream
he was a butterfly,
   Or the butterfly
that it was Chuang Chou?

   In one body's
metamorphoses,
   All is present,
infinite virtue!

   You surely know
Fairyland's oceans
   Were made again
a limpid brooklet,

   Down at Green Gate
the melon gardener
   Once used to be
Marquis of Tung-ling?

   Wealth and honour
were always like this:
   You strive and strive,
but what do you seek?

(COOPER, 1973, P. 141)

Here Li Bo assumes the voice of the moralist: the entire world is constantly undergoing change and metamorphosis—Zhuangzi and his butterfly, the massive ocean around Fairyland *(Penglai/P'eng-lai)* has dwindled to a stream, the melon seller at Green Gate was once the powerful Marquis of Dongling, and so on. If wealth and honor are so ephemeral, he asks, then exactly what is it that we really seek in our struggle and striving?

As for the "Music Bureau" folksongs and the *gexing*, or ballad forms, the former derives its name from the ancient Music Bureau (or *yuefu/ yü-fu*), established in 90 B.C. to collect folksongs from the common people in order to gauge their needs, desires, and feelings about the government. Many later poets, including Li Bo, consciously imitated the styles used in these ancient folksongs. The greatest appeal of these works is their simplicity and use of folk motifs such as fantastic journeys, ancient legends, and mythic figures, which are combined to create extremely dramatic situations. The *gexing* form is similar to the *yuefu* folk ballad. One difference, however, is that whereas poets often speak through their own voice in the *gexing*, they tend to adopt various stock *yuefu* voices or personae in the Music Bureau folksongs.

Li Bo was best known to his contemporaries for his folksongs. His masterpiece in this genre is "The Road to Shu Is Hard" (*"Shudao nan"/"Shu-tao nan"*), a long work that describes the great difficulties of traveling from the Tang capital in Chang'an to Chengdu (in Shu, which is now known as Sichuan province).

Several common features of *yuefu* ballads are present in "The Road to Shu Is Hard." For instance, the poem is comprised of lines in irregular meter ranging from four to eleven syllables each. Moreover, long subordinate clauses form many of these lines: such clauses are generally more common in Chinese prose than poetry. What distinguishes Li Bo as a master of the *yuefu* form, however, is his graphic description and urgent tone and especially his extravagant use of hyperbole and unrestrained expression. Without a doubt, the *yuefu* form was ideally suited to serve as literary outlet for Li Bo's tremendous power of imagination.

A self-portrait of Li Bo is found in his "Drinking Alone Beneath the Moon" (the following are excerpts):

With a jar of wine I sit by the flowering trees,
I drink alone, and where are my friends?
Ah, the moon above looks down on me;
I call and lift my cup to his brightness....

We're all friends to-night,
The drinker, the moon and the shadow.
Let our revelry be meet for the spring time!

(OBATA, 1935, P. 85)

Tradition has it that Li Bo drowned one night because he leaned too far over the edge of a boat in a drunken effort to embrace the reflection of the moonlight. The story is most certainly false, as are most of the legends associated with our poet. And yet these fictions have continued to circulate for more than a thousand years. Indeed, it would seem that the historical Li Bo and the legendary Li Bo—a happy union that fuels imaginations—will forever remain inseparable.

JAMES M. HARGETT

Further Reading

Translations

Cooper, Arthur, trans. *Li Po and Tu Fu*. Harmondsworth, Middlesex, England: Penguin Books, 1973.

Obata, Shigeyoshi, trans. *The Works of Li Po, The Chinese Poet*. New York: Paragon Books, 1965 (reprint of 1935 edition).

Waley, Arthur. *The Poetry and Career of Li Po*. London: George Allen & Unwin Ltd., 1950.

Related Studies

Eide, Elling. "On Li Po," in *Perspectives on the T'ang*, Arthur Wright and Denis Twitchett, eds. New Haven, CT: Yale University Press, 1973, pp. 367–403.

Hargett, James M. "Li Bo (710–762) and Mount Emei" in *Cahiers d'Extrême-Asie* 8 (1995), pp. 101–18.

THE POETRY OF DU FU (TU FU)

Author: Du Fu (Tu Fu)
Born: 712, Gong prefecture (modern Gong county, Henan), China
Died: 770, near Tanzhou (modern Changsha, Hunan)
Major Poems: "Ballad of Pengya," "Northward Journey," "Expressing My Feelings on Going from the Capital to Fengxian Prefecture," "Ballad of the Army Carts," "The Recruiting Officer of Shihao," "Lament for the Prince," "The Separation of an Old Man," "Twenty Miscellaneous Poems from Qinzhou," "Autumn Inspirations," "Autumn Wastes," "Yangtze and Han Rivers"

Major Themes

The most important duties of the scholar are to show compassion for the people and provide loyal service to the state.

Although a scholar-official encounters misfortune, the suffering of the common people is greater; those who suffer most from the effects of war and insurrection are the commoners.

In old age, one may find contentment in family and nature.

To many Chinese, Du Fu is the greatest Chinese poet. He is admired for his poetic craft, his compassion for the plight of the common people, and his strong sense of public duty. He was born near the capital of Chang'an (now Xi'an). His grandfather was Du Shenyan (Tu Shen-yen) (d. 705), a famous poet-official of the Empress Wu era. Little is known of Du Fu's early years. He began writing poetry at the age of seven. In 735 he went to the capital to take the *jinshi (chin-shih)* examination. As a candidate from the capital district, Du Fu had great confidence that he would easily pass the exam. However, Du Fu failed the examination that was held in 736. After failing the exam, Du Fu traveled to the northeast to visit his father, who was serving in a provincial post. According to Du Fu's own account, he spent much of his time enjoying the pleasures of hunting, riding horses, archery, and falconry.

After the death of his father in 740, Du Fu became responsible for his family. Official employment was impossible for him to find. He spent 743–44 in Luoyang earning a meager income as a secretary hired to draft documents for dignitaries. In midsummer of 744 he went to Chenliu (east of Luoyang) to attend the funeral of his step-grandmother. Here he met the great Tang (T'ang) poet Li Bo (Li Po) for the first time. Li Bo already was a celebrity, and Du Fu had yet to achieve a reputation. In a poem addressed to Li Bo, Du Fu gently chides him for his wine-drinking.

Du Fu journeyed to the capital in 745, during which time he saw many of his friends executed, banished, or driven to suicide by the members of a political clique led by the prime minister Li Linfu. In 747, Du Fu sat for a special examination to discover hidden talent. He did not pass the exam, but was encouraged to present samples of his writing to Emperor Xuanzong (Hsüan-tsung). The emperor was sufficiently impressed and ordered Du Fu be given a special examination. Although Du Fu did not pass, he was allowed to proceed to the Bureau of Selection to wait for a position to open up for him. A long three years later he finally received an appointment. In the meantime, he and his family suffered bitterly waiting for the slow-moving bureacracy to act. The autumn of 754, in which there was unceasing rain for a period of 60 days in the capital area, was particularly hard to endure.

Du Fu finally had to move his family out of the capital. He moved them to Fengxian about 80 miles northeast of Chang'an. In 755, Du Fu returned to Chang'an alone. In autumn of that year, he was given an appointment as police commissioner of Hexi (modern Heyang, Shaanxi), not far from Fengxian. Du Fu was not pleased with this extremely low position, which primarily was charged with punishing draft dodgers and tax evaders, and he declined the appointment. He was then given another position on the staff of the heir designate.

Du Fu did not get a chance to serve in office, for the An Lushan Rebellion had just broken out. He immediately went to Fengxian to care for his wife and children. Fearing for their safety, he moved them to Fuzhou (modern Fu county, Shaanxi). He describes the journey to Fuzhou in his famous poem "Ballad of Pengya." After assuring his family's safety, Du Fu, dressed as a peasant, set off to join the court of the new emperor, Suzong (Sutsung) (reigned 756–762). On the way, he was captured by a rebel band and taken to Chang'an, where he was released.

About a year later Du Fu fled Chang'an and made his way to Fengxiang (100 miles west of Chang'an), where Emperor Suzong had established a provisional government. Suzong gave Du Fu an appointment as Reminder of the Left. Du Fu immediately offended the emperor with his much too frank admonitions. In autumn of 757, Suzong gave Du Fu special leave to return to Fuzhou to visit his family. Du Fu wrote his famous long narrative poem, "Northward Journey," about his trip to Fuzhou and his arrival home.

In November of 757, the An Lushan rebels were defeated near Chang'an. Emperor Suzong then was able to return to the capital. Du Fu probably was in the entourage that accompanied the emperor when he triumphantly entered Chang'an on December 8, 757. Du Fu continued in his post as Reminder. However, in June of 758, several of Du Fu's associates were dismissed from the court and banished to remote regions. Du Fu himself was soon dismissed as well and banished to Huazhou (60 miles east of Chang'an) where he assumed the post of administrator in the bureau of merit.

Toward the end of January 759 Du Fu went to Luoyang on business. On his return journey to Huazhou, he saw many people still suffering from the effects of the rebellion. By autumn of 759, Du Fu had become utterly disillusioned with official life. Deciding that he could no longer serve in of-

fice, he resigned his post. He then traveled together with his family to Qinzhou (modern Tianshui, Gansu).

Du Fu arrived in Qinzhou in September of 759. Qinzhou was a frontier city where he had relatives and friends. In December 759, Du Fu left Qinzhou for Tonggu (modern Cheng county, Gansu), where he stayed only briefly before departing for Chengdu on December 24. Du Fu arrived in Chengdu in early 760. He took up residence in the Caotang (Ts'ao T'ang) Monastery, which was an old Buddhist temple on the bank of the Huanhua Stream, a tributary of the Jin River in the western suburbs of Chengdu. Near this monastery Du Fu built a house, commonly referred to as Caotang (Thatched Hut), in which he lived during the time he spent in Chengdu. During this time, Du Fu relied on his friend Yan Wu (d. 765), the military governor of Chengdu, for financial support. Except for brief trips to neighboring areas, Du Fu remained in Chengdu until 765. Sometime in the summer of 764, upon Yan Wu's recommendation, Du Fu received an appointment as consultant auxiliary secretary of the ministry of public works. This was the highest position Du Fu ever held, and is thus often referred to as Minister of Public Works Du.

Yan Wu died in May 765 and Du Fu left Chengdu with his family for Kuizhou (modern Fengjie, Sichuan), located near the scenic gorges of the Yangtze River. Du Fu arrived in Kuizhou in the spring of 766. He took up residence in Nangdong, a small village several miles northeast of Kuizhou. He lived in the Western Tower, a tall wooden structure located on a rock that rose steeply from the Yangtze. He remained here until the spring of 767. This was a very productive period for Du Fu. He wrote about 400 poems in the two years he spent in Kuizhou.

Early in 768, Du Fu left Kuizhou and continued his journey down the Yangtze to Jiangling. Du Fu remained in Jiangling until the autumn of 768. He was quite ill at the time. He wished to return to Chang'an, but incursions by Tibetan raiders prevented him from doing so. In early 769, he traveled throughout the area of Dongting Lake. In February 769, Du Fu sailed down Dongting Lake to the mouth of the Xiang River. Then he journeyed down to Tanzhou (modern Changsha). After traveling in the Hunan area, Du Fu died near Tanzhou in November or December of 770.

From Self-Confidence to Frustration

In his poetry written before the An Lushan rebellion, Du Fu's most common subject is the expression of his ideals and aspirations. In "Twenty-two Rhymes to Assistant Director Wei," written to seek patronage from a high official, Du Fu immodestly compares himself with such great writers as Cao Zhi (Ts'ao Chih) and Yang Xiong (Yang Hsiung). He also complains that despite his many attempts to find a patron, he has been utterly frustrated in his attempt to obtain even a menial position. After the death of his father in 740, Du Fu's life was indeed hard. By 755, he was deeply tormented. In his long "Expressing My Feelings on Going from the Capital to Fengxian Prefecture: Five Hundred Characters," Du Fu presents himself as full of internal conflict. He declares that he had long contemplated becoming a recluse who hides away "on river and sea," but his concern for the plight of the people and his desire to be of service to emperor Xuanzong are stronger. Yet, despite his yearning to fulfill his Confucian duty to serve, Du Fu shows that he is aware of the emperor's dissipation. As he recounts his journey past the Huaqing (Hua Ch'ing) Palace where Emperor Xuanzong dallied with his favorite consort Yang Guifei (Yang Kuei-fei), Du Fu contrasts the extravagance of the nobles, who dine on camel-hoof stew and eat tangerines imported at great expense from the tropics, with the plight of the those who froze to death on the roadside. Du Fu wrote this poem just on the eve of the An Lushan rebellion, and he personally saw many people who were victims of government abuse and neglect. Du Fu, too, was a victim, for his young son died of starvation before he arrived in Fengxian. However, rather than bemoan his own fate, he expresses indignation at the plight of ordinary people who, unlike him, were unable to be excused from taxes or military service.

Social and Political Themes

Du Fu is the only poet of his time who wrote directly about the events of the An Lushan rebellion. Many of his poems deal with the situation around the capital during and immediately after the rebellion. In these pieces he shows a strong social conscience, and he often overtly condemns the government for its lack of sympathy with the plight of the commoners who suffered most during the rebellion. Du Fu has several excellent poems describing what he saw in the capital while it was occupied by the rebels. One of them, "Lament for the Prince," is about a young Tang noble who had been abandoned in the capital when the rest of the imperial family fled. In some of his shorter poems, Du Fu combines an expression of grief at his personal and family tragedy with outrage at the bitter suffering of the common people. Already in one of his early poems, "Ballad of the Army Carts," Du Fu had dramatically exposed the horrors of war. After the rebellion, when he was touring the area of Huazhou, he wrote six poems ("The Three Recruiting Officers" and "Three Separations") from the point of view of those who were most affected by the rebellion, the conscripts and their families. In "The Recruiting Officer of Shihao" Du Fu tells of calling upon a family whose three sons were conscripted into the army. Two of the sons already have died, and the third is still on a military campaign. When the recruiting officer comes to the house to press the old grandfather into service, the grandmother offers herself instead. "The Separation of an Old Man" describes the dramatic parting scene between an old woman and her husband who is forced to join the army. The old man bitterly complains that the entire land is covered with military expeditions and beacon fires.

Family and Personal Feelings

Du Fu is the first poet of the Chinese literary tradition to write extensively about his wife and children. In his poems about his travels, Du Fu often includes details about his family members. In "Ballad of Pengya," written in 757 to recall the events of the An Lushan rebellion, he says that his infant daughter "was so hungry she gnawed at me." Fearing that wild beasts would hear her cries, he hugged her to him, and "covered her mouth." Meanwhile his young son runs off to pick sour plums to eat.

The most vivid depiction of family is in "Northward Journey," which Du Fu wrote in 757 when he travelled to Fuzhou to rejoin his family after being separated from them during the An Lushan rebellion. He arrives home to see his wife and children dressed in patched clothing. His son, whose "face is whiter than snow," runs barefoot to his father, while his two daughters appear before him clad in dresses made from an old brocade in which the designs are topsy-turvy. He then gives them presents: powder and kohl, quilts and curtains. The daughters comb their hair and smear makeup all over their faces. Such scenes of domestic life were unknown in Chinese literature before Du Fu, but became more common after him. The order and disorder that he describes in his family life often serves as a microcosm of the larger situation of the state and society of his time.

The Later Poems

When Du Fu abandoned his official career and took up residence first in Qinzhou, and then in Chengdu, he had more time to devote to writing poetry. Du Fu composed over half of his 1,450 poems during the last 10 years of his life. During this period we see distinct changes in his poetry. His style becomes more complex, his syntax is often crabbed and awkward, he makes extensive use of allusion, and instead of the ballad form that he had used earlier, he writes in the regulated forms of the octave and quatrain. Although he writes on conventional themes, especially landscape and historical sites, his treatment of them is uniquely Du Fu. For example, in his "Twenty Miscellaneous Poems from Qinzhou," the dark autumn rains of Qinzhou become virtual symbols of the northwestern landscape, and represent for him the bleak isolation that he felt in this desolate area. On the other hand, the

landscape poems he wrote in Chengdu show him more satisfied with his surroundings. He often portrays himself as an eccentric hermit much like Tao Yuanming (T'ao Yuan-ming) of the Six Dynasties period. Even when the wind blows the roof off his house, he declares himself content.

During the four years that Du Fu traveled down the Yangtze River he wrote more than 600 poems. While he was in Kuizhou, Du Fu wrote his most complicated poems. They include two important series: the eight "Autumn Inspirations" and the five "Autumn Wastes." In these poems, Du Fu writes about the autumn scenes of the Kuizhou area: the dew that withers the maple trees, the mallow going to seed, pine cones blown from the trees by the breeze, white autumn sands. Although he is about as far from the capital as he can be, he cannot forget what he deems his life's failure—his inability to become a high minister who might have saved the state from disaster. Indeed, this is the persistent theme of much of Du Fu's poetry. In one of his latest poems, "Yangtze and Han Rivers," he portrays himself as a "decayed scholar," and a "stranger" who long been away from his home in the north. Although the sun is setting, "his heart is still strong," and even though the autumn wind blows about him, he has recovered from sickness. In the final couplet of the poem, Du Fu compares himself to an old horse, who though no longer able to run long distances, still is useful, if only for his good sense of direction.

Although Du Fu was not considered an important poet in his own time, his influence on later Chinese poetry was great. By the mid-Tang period, poets such as Bo Juyi (Po Chü-i and Li He (Li Ho) were inspired to write protest poems in his style. In the Song (Sung) dynasty, he became the most admired Tang poet, and in the eleventh and twelfth centuries poets began assiduously to imitate his diction, syntax, and intricate use of allusion. Du Fu eventually became known as the "poet historian," for his poems were regarded as records of the history of his time. For some, Du Fu was even the "sage of poetry." Thus, he became the equivalent of Confucius in the realm of poetry. His poetry was viewed as without flaw and, above all, impossible for other poets to surpass.

DAVID R. KNECHTGES

Further Reading

Translations

Alley, Rewi, trans. *Selected Poems of Tu Fu*. Peking: Foreign Languages Press, 1962. Free translation of Du Fu's best-known poems.

Cooper, Arthur, trans. *Li Po and Tu Fu*. New York: Penguin Books, 1973. Translation of selected poems.

Von Zach, Erwin, trans. *Tu Fu's Gedichte*. 2 vols. Cambridge, MA: Harvard University Press, 1952. Translation into German of all of Du Fu's poetry.

Related Studies

Davis, A. R. *Tu Fu*. New York: Twayne Publishers, 1971. The best general literary and biographical treatment.

Hung, William. *Tu Fu, China's Greatest Poet*. Cambridge, MA: Harvard University Press, 1952. The most authoritative English-language biography.

Owen, Stephen. "Tu Fu," in *The Great Age of Chinese Poetry*. New Haven, CT: Yale University Press, 1981, 183–224. An excellent literary-historical treatment.

THE POETRY OF HANSHAN (HAN SHAN)

Author: Hanshan (Han Shan); Kanzan (in Japanese); also known as Cold Mountain.
Born: Seventh century?
Died: Seventh century?
Major Poems: The "Cold Mountain" poems

Major Themes

The poet's ascent of Cold Mountain (Hanshan) is a spiritual or religious effort.
Anyone who casts off worldly concerns and seeks spiritual inspiration may sit with Hanshan among the white clouds.
Everyone needs to realize the self, to be free from authority and social convention.
One can learn more from reading the poems of Hanshan (the poet) than from reading the sūtras.

Hanshan was a seventh- or eighth-century Chinese Buddhist recluse who wrote many poems about his life alone in the mountains. The word *han* in Chinese is an adjective meaning "cold" or "chilly"; *shan* is a noun meaning "mountain(s)" or "hill(s)." Thus, Hanshan has come to be known in English as "Cold Mountain."

At first glance, his verses are not unlike those of other eremitic "mountain poets" in China with an interest in Chan (Ch'an) (or Zen) Buddhism: Hanshan describes his home in the Tiantai (T'ien-t'ai) Mountains of southeast China in dramatic but appealing language; at the same time, he constantly reminds us of his quest for enlightenment, or finding the proper "road" or "way" (*dao/tao*). On these accounts, at least, Cold Mountain is not different from other reclusive Chinese poets with an interest in Chan Buddhism. This is one reason why his poetry has received so little attention in Chinese literary history. On the other hand, outside of China, Cold Mountain has become a cult figure in the Chan/Zen tradition. Moreover, in the West—especially in the United States—he is undoubtedly one of China's most widely read and most popular poets. His verses have been rendered into English by eminent translators such as Arthur Waley and Burton Watson. Hanshan has also been translated by the American poet Gary Snyder. Currently there are at least a dozen different translations of Hanshan's poems available in Western languages. Why

has Cold Mountain received so much attention, especially outside of China? The answer to this question becomes all the more fascinating when we consider that next to nothing is known about this shadowy figure from China's distant past.

The Mystery of "Cold Mountain"

It would be an understatement to say little is known about Hanshan. To begin with, his real name is a mystery. "Cold Mountain" is a nickname (some say a religious appellation) presumably taken from the place where he lived, but it is not a specific, identifiable place name. Nor do we even know the century in which he lived. Estimates range from the Sui dynasty (581–618) to the late Tang (T'ang) (618–907). The research of E. G. Pulleyblank, based on the rhyme schemes used in Hanshan's extant verses, dates some of Cold Mountain's poems in the early seventh century. Other verses in the collection, however, are dated by Pulleyblank to the late Tang (tenth century).

The only source of information available on Hanshan is a preface to his *Works* written by an obscure official named Lüqiu Yin (Lüch'iu). The preface relates that Lüqiu, after taking up the post of prefect in Tai county, Zhejiang, once paid a visit to two eccentric Buddhists named Hanshan and Shide (Shih-te) in the nearby Tiantai Mountains. Here is the essence of Lüqiu Yin's report:

As for Master Han-shan, we don't know where he came from. . . . From time to time he would go back and forth between his retreat and the Kuo-ch'ing Temple, wearing birchbark as his hat, dressed in a cotton-fur robe and worn-out shoes. Sometimes he would chant and recite in the long corridors; sometimes he'd whistle and sing through country homes. No one really understood him. . . . [Later] they left the temple and went back to Cold Cliffs [this is an alternate name for Cold Mountain's retreat], where Master Han-shan entered a cave and was gone, the cave closing up on its own.

He used to write down poems on bamboo trees and stone walls. Altogether, the poems he wrote on house walls in country homes come to over three hundred. I have edited them together into one volume.

(HENRICKS, 1990, P. 29)

Although Lüqiu Yin's preface offers a neat explanation of how Hanshan's poems were gathered together and edited into a single anthology, there are a number of problems with his account. The biggest mystery of all is Lüqiu Yin himself. No historical evidence can be found to corroborate the existence of such a person. Nor does the preface provide any factual information about Hanshan's life. The fact is, we cannot prove that a single poet named Hanshan ever existed. To put it another way, we have absolutely no idea who wrote the body of poems traditionally associated with "Cold Mountain." As for Lüqiu Yin's preface, it has served the singular purpose of providing rich fuel to feed and cultivate the legend of Hanshan.

Stories about Cold Mountain (the person and the place) abound. In Buddhist biographical sources, for instance, we find conversations between Hanshan, his sidekick Shide, and their common master—a person named Fenggan (Feng-kan). These conversations portray our trio of recluses as zany, ebullient figures who blurt out nonsense phrases while singing, dancing, and guffawing

about. As for Cold Mountain's verses, they also provide scattered hints and references about the poet. For instance, mention of books left to him by his parents suggest that he was raised in an educated family. He also mentions that he was married and had a son. Other references in the poems indicate that he prepared, and perhaps even passed, the civil service examinations, but for one reason or another never received an appointment to office. But here—as with the Lüqiu Yin preface—we must be careful, because no corroborating evidence exists to prove *anything* about Hanshan's life and career. We need to be especially wary when using the poems to glean biographical data. This is because Pulleyblank's research has shown that it is quite possible, even likely, that the collected poems of Hanshan in circulation today came from *at least* two hands. The net result of all this uncertainty (myth?) about Hanshan—fueled by the preface, various "recorded conversations" and stories, and the poems themselves—has been continuous growth of the Cold Mountain legend. We should also note that his legend has also been perpetuated in art, for numerous "portraits" of Hanshan and Shide, usually having a big laugh about something, continue to circulate.

The Buddhist Poet and the Image of Cold Mountain

Hanshan is identified as a "Buddhist" poet not only because he used Buddhist technical terms in his verses but, more importantly, because he has a general outlook on life that reveals belief in *karma* and reincarnation (to mention two examples); it is this orientation that makes him a "Buddhist." As far as we know, he never took monastic vows. It should also be mentioned that Hanshan's Buddhist orientation did not prevent him from occasionally expressing Daoist ideas or engaging in Daoist activities such as yoga, breathing exercises, and ingesting life-extending herbs. Thus, although Hanshan's primary outlook on life was Buddhist, but he was hardly a purist. At times he even mutters a Confucian idea or two.

Although the poetry of Hanshan is not generally regarded as ranking with the work of such renowned poets as Li Bo (Li Po), Du Fu (Tu Fu), and Su Shi (Su Shih), it is remarkable in the care with which the *image* of Cold Mountain (the mountain locality) is vividly drawn and given significance in his verses. There is an intriguing aura about the mountain and the poet that must be credited for the effectiveness of the poetry. All legends, commentaries, and even visual representations of Hanshan are tied in one way or another to this unique image.

In the introduction (p. 3) to his Hanshan translations published in *Encounter* in 1954, Arthur Waley perceptively remarks that "In his poems Cold Mountain is often the name of a state of mind rather than of a locality." No verse among Hanshan's verses perhaps better illustrates this point than the following:

Climb up! Ascend! The way to Han-shan;
But on Han-shan the roads never end.

The valleys are long, with boulders in heaps and
  piles;
The streams are wide, with grasses both wet and
  damp.

The moss is slippery—it has nothing to do with the
  rain;
The pines sigh and moan, but they don't rely on the
  wind.

Who can transcend the cares of the world,
And sit with me in the white clouds?

                    (HENRICKS, 1990)

The language of the poem is simple and direct—hallmark qualities of Hanshan's verse. Its accessibility is one reason for his poetry's great appeal, especially among Western readers. Note that the images used by the poet are drawn entirely from his Cold Mountain world: a road, valleys, streams, pine trees, and a white cloud. Despite the simplicity of the language and imagery, even first-time readers of Cold Mountain would probably realize instinctively that "there is something else going on" in his poetry. Indeed, the first couplet of the above poem

immediately attracts one's attention: how could any mountain road "never end"? Aren't most mountain roads designed to reach some destination? At this point (or, after reading a few more choice selections from Hanshan's poetry) it becomes apparent that the poet's ascent of Cold Mountain is a spiritual or religious quest, the purpose of which is to "transcend the cares of the world." But it is a difficult and perilous road, blocked with "boulders in heaps and piles" and made dangerous by "grasses both wet and damp." If, however, readers are able to cast off worldly concerns and follow the "Cold Mountain road," then one day they may sit with Hanshan among the "white clouds."

More than anything else, Hanshan's poetry is about self-realization and freedom. This, one could argue, is the root of his appeal, especially to Western readers. He is an individual spirit totally unsuited for the family/group orientation of Confucianism. Instead, he prefers to defy authority, flout social convention, and sing about his independence and freedom among the white clouds of Hanshan.

Buddhist and Daoist Themes

Hanshan is certainly best known for his poems that describe Cold Mountain and the difficulties encountered while traveling the road to its summit. Such works, however, represent only a portion of his surviving corpus of 311 poems. Many of his didactic verses deal with Buddhist themes, such as the evils of eating fish and meat, rebirth and reincarnation, "phony" Buddhists, and so on, while others concern more mundane themes such as love and marriage, the plight of the poor, and separation from family and friends. A good number of verses also deal with Daoist themes, such as the pursuit of long life and immortality and various issues raised in Daoist classics such as *Laozi (Lao Tzu)* and *Zhuangzi (Chuang Tzu)*. The point here is that when viewed collectively, Hanshan's surviving works concern numerous topics and themes and any general assessment of his poetry must consider all of these poems.

Translators and commentators have pointed to

distinguishing features in addition to that of thematic variety in Hanshan's poetry, such as his use of colloquial expressions and phrases, his clever transformation of Buddhist parables or aphorisms into poems, his use of graphic, striking images, and his wit and humor. One verse that seems to illustrate many of these qualities is the following:

Pigs eat the flesh of dead men,
And men eat the guts of dead pigs.

Pigs don't seem to mind human stench,
And men—to the contrary—say pig meat smells
*   sweet.*

When pigs die, throw them into the water;
When men die, dig them a hole in the ground.

If they never ate one another,
Lotus blossoms would sprout in water that bubbles
*   and boils.*

(NO. 70, HENRICKS, 1990, P. 118)

The didactic import of this verse presented in very graphic terms (uncommon in Chinese poetry) is unmistakable. Yet, at the same time, Hanshan is able to temper his serious tone with a touch of humor and irony (lines 4 and 8). This dual approach is not unusual in Cold Mountain's verse. To be sure, the heavy religious content of his poetry requires a serious tone. But Hanshan seems never to take anything or anyone (especially himself!) too seriously, and it is precisely this quality that makes his verses so much fun to read.

Finally, from time to time Hanshan gives advice to his readers. This is the final poem in his collection:

If your house has the poems of Han-shan in it,
They're better off for you than reading sūtras!

Write them down on your screen,
And from time to time take a look.

(NO. 311, HENRICKS, 1990, P. 415)
JAMES M. HARGETT

Further Reading

Translations

Henricks, Robert G., trans. *The Poetry of Hanshan*: *A Complete, Annotated Translation of Cold Mountain*. Albany, N.Y.: State University of New York Press, 1990. Includes translations and commentaries of Hanshan's 311 extant poems. (Quotations so cited are from Henricks, *Poetry of Hanshan*, and are reprinted by permission of the State University of New York Press © 1990.)

Snyder, Gary. "Cold Mountain Poems." *Evergreen Review* 2.6 (Autumn 1958): 68–80; reprinted in Snyder's *Riprap and Cold Mountain Poems*. San Francisco: Four Seasons Foundation, 1965. Snyder's English renditions are extremely readable and succeed in capturing the freedom and tone of Hanshan's trip up the "Cold Mountain road."

Waley, Arthur, trans. "27 Poems by Hanshan." *Encounter* 3.3 (September 1954): pp. 3–8.

Watson, Burton, trans. *Cold Mountain: 100 Poems by the T'ang Poet Han-shan*. New York: Columbia University Press, 1970.

Related Studies

Kahn, Paul. *Han Shan in English*. Buffalo, N.Y.: White Pine Press, 1989. Addresses the fascinating question of how an obscure poet-monk from ancient China has become one of the best-known poets in America.

Pulleyblank, E. G. "Linguistic Evidence for the Date of Hanshan." In Ronald C. Miao, ed., *Studies in Chinese Poetry and Poetics*, Vol. 1, 163–95. San Francisco: Chinese Materials Center, 1978.

THE PROSE WORKS OF HAN YU (HAN YÜ)

Author: Han Yu (Han Yü)
Born: 768, Chang'an (modern Xi'an), China
Died: December 25, 824, Chang'an
Major Works: "Tracing the Origins of the Way," "Offering to the Crocodiles," "Disquisition on Teachers," "Preface Sending Off Meng Jiao [Meng Chiao]," "Memorial on the Buddha Bone," "Biography of Mao Ying [Tipp O'Hair]"

Major Themes

Buddhism, Taoism, and heterodox ideas have done great harm to orthodox Confucian values, and they must be opposed.

Writing and moral cultivation are one, and just as a person cultivates his moral character he must cultivate his writing style.

The model for literary style is the literature of the Han and pre-Han periods.

When a person does not attain his "equilibrium" he "sounds forth" to express his feelings.

Han Yu is one of the greatest Chinese prose writers. He was the leader of an important reform movement that sought to revive ancient literary values and style. A strong proponent of traditional Confucian values, he wrote vituperative denunciations of Buddhism and Taoism.

Han Yu was born into a family of distinguished scholars and writers. Although his ancestral home was Heyang (modern Meng county, Henan), the more prestigious members of the Han clan came from Changli (modern Lulung, Hebei). Thus, he is often referred to as Han Changli. His mother and father died when he was a baby, and he was raised by his brother Han Hui (c. 740–c. 781), who was an associate of the prominent literary reformers of the time. In 777, Han Hui was sent into exile to remote southern city of Shaozhou (modern Shaoguan City Guangdong), where he died in 780 or 781. His sister-in-law, née Zheng, then took responsibility for caring for him. Between 786 and 791, Han Yu attempted and failed the metropolitan examinations three times. Finally, in 792 in the exam presided over by an eminent literary reformer, he passed. In the following three years (793–95), Han Yu thrice attempted and failed the placement examination. Between 796 to 800 the only employment that Han Yu could obtain was on the staff of military governors in the Henan area.

In 801, Han Yu received his first capital appointment—professor in the Four Gates Academy. He was one of six professors who had charge of educating the sons of nobility, officials of seventh rank or higher, and talented commoners. In winter of 803, Han Yu was transferred to the post of investigating censor. Han Yu took his job as censor seriously, and on one occasion (the end of 803) he and two other censors submitted a strongly worded memorial protesting the heavy corvée and taxes imposed upon the people of the capital area in a time of severe drought. Shortly after submitting this memorial, Han Yu was dismissed from office and ordered to be sent into exile as prefect of Yangshan (modern Yangshan, Guangdong). Han Yu arrived in Yangshan in spring of 804. He was appalled by this uncivilized place, which he described in most unflattering terms in his "Preface Sending Off Ou Ce [Ou Ts'e]." In September 805 he received an appointment as administrator of the judicial service in Jiangling. It was after his Yangshan exile that Han Yu wrote his most famous statement of his philosophical ideals, "Tracing the Origins of the Way."

Han Yu served almost two years in Jiangling. In late summer 807 he was recalled to serve as professor in the Academy of the Sons of the State. Han held various offices until 819, when he was dismissed from office and banished to Chaozhou (modern Chaozhou, Guangdong). The cause of his dismissal was a memorial he submitted to the emperor protesting the display of a so-called finger bone of the Buddha in the imperial palace. He delivered a vituperative attack on Buddhism, not only for encouraging the people to engage in unseemly practices, but also because it was a foreign importation. The most offensive part of Han Yu's memorial was his claim that honoring the Buddha bone would shorten the emperor's life.

Although Han Yu spent only six months in Chaozhou, he figures prominently in the lore of the region. It was here that he wrote his famous essay, "Offering to the Crocodiles," a piece that ostensibly was intended as an exorcism to expel crocodiles from the Chaozhou area. As a result of a general amnesty issued by the emperor in August of 819, Han Yu was able to leave Chaozhou. In November 820, he received a summons to return to the capital as rector of the Imperial University. After his return to the capital, Han Yu served in a series of high central government positions, including vice-president of the ministry of personnel, a post he assumed in September 822. In July 823 Han Yu was named metropolitan prefect of Chang'an. He returned to the ministry of personnel in November of the same year. By this time he was old and frail. In February 824 he requested and was granted sick leave. He retired to a villa near Qinling, the site of the tomb of the first Qin emperor. Han Yu died on December 25, 824. He was buried on April 21, 825 in the Han family cemetery in Heyang.

Writing Is a Moral Act

Han Yu considered that one of his most important roles was that of teacher. In an essay entitled "Disquisition on Teachers," written in 802 during the first year he served at the Imperial Academy, Han Yu argued that all men of learning have an obligation not only to serve as a teacher, but even to seek out instruction from others. Han Yu claimed that "a sage has no constant teacher," and even Confucius had many teachers. Han Yu took his role as teacher very seriously, and many young men sought him

out for advice and instruction. One young man sent a letter to Han Yu requesting advice on writing. Han Yu replied to him in a letter ("Response to Li Yi") in which he clearly formulates his ideas on literature and the way in which a writer must develop his craft. Han Yu believed that the cultivation of the proper style is a long and arduous task to which Han Yu himself already has devoted over 20 years. His prescription for literary cultivation included reading only those books written from the Han and before, thinking only the ideas of the ancient sages, eliminating stale expressions and heterodox (that is, Taoist and Buddhist) ideas, cultivating writing as one cultivates character, and being ever alert for impurities contaminating what one writes. Han Yu further claimed that writing is a purely moral act, and only the man who has properly cultivated the Way of morality and goodness, as exemplified in the classics, can write properly.

Another of Han Yu's important statements on literature is his "Preface Sending Off Meng Jiao." Meng Jiao was a leading poet, who despite his great literary skill had failed the civil service examination numerous times. In 803 he was very depressed at the prospect of taking up a low level position in the local administration. Han Yu sent him this farewell preface to console him. In this piece Han Yu proposes that whenever things of nature or human beings fail to attain a state of equilibrium, they sound forth. Human beings have many ways to sound forth, including crying, music, speech, and literature. Han Yu is particularly concerned with the way in which men throughout history have used literature to "sound forth" when they lost their "inner equilibrium." He concludes that all great literature is the product of some loss of equilibrium, usually extreme despondency over some failure in life, but also excessive joy. According to Han Yu, it is Heaven that determines how one expresses oneself: Heaven can mute the voice of poets and cause them to sing in praise of the state, or it can starve them and disturb their spirits so that they sing of their misfortunes. Han Yu's theory of literary expression has been very influential in the Chinese tradition, and even in modern times, it is cited by Chinese intellectuals as a justification for using literature for social protest.

Origins of the Way

"Tracing the Origins of the Way," which is Han Yu's most important statement of his philosophical views, is a spirited defense of Confucian orthodoxy. Han Yu fervently believed that orthodox teachings had been corrupted by Taoism and Buddhism. Han Yu begins his essay discussing the cardinal ethical principles of Confucianism, benevolence and propriety, which he believed had been distorted by the Taoists. Next, Han Yu traces the decline of civilization, which began after the death of Confucius. Schools that espoused ideas inimical to Confucius's teachings did great harm to the transmission of the orthodox ethical teachings. The only thinker who upheld the orthodox tradition was Mencius. Han Yu also denounces Buddhists and Taoists for their rejection of the political and social order. The main duty of the ruler is to govern, the principal function of the official is to implement the ruler's commands, and the primary obligation of the people is to raise crops, make tools and vessels, and exchange goods and commodities. However, Buddhists and Taoists in their effort to seek "stillness and quietude, silence and extinction," wish to do away with these functions, and thus the social order has been harmed. They also have complicated society by adding two social classes to the traditional fourfold division of scholar, farmer, merchant, and artisan. Han Yu's primary concern here was with the growing economic power of the Buddhist monastic estates, which had become extremely wealthy in this period. Han Yu's remedy for the degeneration of society that was caused by adherence to Buddhism and Taoism is to turn their monks into lay people, burn their books, and secularize their temples. In short, he demanded that Buddhism and Taoism be curtailed, if not banned entirely.

Han Yu was particularly opposed to Buddhism. In his "Memorial on the Buddha Bone" he protests the display in the palace of a what was claimed to

be finger-bone from the corpse of Buddha. Han Yu vehemently attacks Buddhism not only for encouraging people to engage in unseemly practices such as burning their heads and fingers, but also because it was a foreign religion. According to Han Yu, Buddha was a barbarian who did not dress in Chinese fashion and did not speak Chinese; if he were to appear at court today, the emperor would receive him politely and then escort him out of the country under armed guard. Han Yu argued, if the living Buddha would not be allowed to remain in China "to delude the people," how can the emperor permit the worship of his "decayed and rotten bones." Han Yu urged the emperor to have the relic destroyed. Han Yu was quite daring in this essay, for he argued that emperors who zealously worshiped Buddhism all had short lives. Emperor Xianzong (Hsien-tsung), to whom Han Yu addressed this memorial, was offended at the suggestion that he too would be short-lived. Thus, Han Yu received the severe punishment of banishment to Chaozhou.

Ancient Prose Style

Han Yu was the most forceful advocate in the Tang dynasty for a return to the style of antiquity. His literary ideal was what he called *guwen* or "ancient style literature," which to him meant the literature of the pre-Han and Han periods. This style was opposed to "contemporary style," which was dominated by a highly ornate and mannered style known as "parallel prose." Although Han Yu believed that a writer should model his prose upon the prose of the pre-Han and Han masters, he was not a slavish imitator of classical prose. He in fact was a great innovator, both in his style and content. Han Yu is thus known primarily for his originality and creativity in the writing of conventional genres. Han Yu transformed such genres as the grave inscription, preface, letter, and biography in significant ways. In many of his grave inscriptions, especially those written for friends and men he admired, he uses the opportunity of memorializing the deceased to draw a moral or make a philosophical point. For example, in his "Epitaph for Liu Zongyuan [Liu Tsung- yüan]," he concludes that if Liu Zongyuan had not been sent into exile for such a long period, he would not have composed great literature.

Han Yu also expanded the use of the preface and letter. He is well known for his numerous farewell prefaces, of which his "Preface Sending Off Meng Jiao" is a good example. As in his grave inscriptions, Han Yu often uses the farewell preface to express a personal philosophy or viewpoint. Han Yu also was a prolific letter writer, and he expanded the range of topics to include advice to students, political protest, and expressions of personal complaint. In his "Letter to Cui Qun," for example, he puts forth the shocking proposition that Heaven is inimical to men of integrity and talent, and seems to side with petty-minded and mediocre people.

Han Yu also demonstrates his creative genius in the writing of short biographies. Many of his biographies are allegories. "Biography of Mao Ying [Tipp O' Hair]," which is a parody of the traditional dynastic history biography, is a fictional account of the writing brush. The writing brush, which is personified as a figure named Mao Ying (Tipp O' Hair), provides diligent service assisting the emperor in recording important state events. As soon as its hair begins to fall out, and is no longer fit for writing, it is discarded. It is possible that this piece was intended as an allegory of the loyal official who is cast aside when his service is no longer required. "Biography of Wang Chengfu the Mason" tells of a wall plasterer who survives longer than the wealthy and powerful because he understands how to perform the work for which he is most suited.

DAVID R. KNECHTGES

Further Reading

Eide, Elling O. "Another Go at the *Mao Ying chuan*," *T'ang Studies* 8–9 (1990–91): 105–11. A highly skillful translation of "The Biography of Tipp O'Hair."

Hartman, Charles. *Han Yü and the T'ang Search for Unity*. Princeton, N.J.: Princeton University Press, 1986. The most detailed and comprehensive study of Han Yu in English.

Hightower, James Robert. "Han Yü as Humorist," *Harvard Journal of Asiatic Studies* 44.1 (1984): 5–27. Translation and discussion of Han Yu's humorous prose writings.

Mei, Diana Yu-shih Chen. "Han Yü as a Ku-wen Stylist." In *Tsing Hua Journal of Chinese Studies* 7.1 (1968): 143–208. A good introduction to Han Yu's "ancient literature" style.

Nienhauser, William H., Jr. "An Allegorical Reading of Han Yü's "Mao-Ying Chuan" (Biography of Fur Point)," *Oriens Extremus* 23.2 (1976): 153–74. Argues that the "Biography of Tipp O'Hair" is a political allegory.

Shih Shun Liu, trans. *Chinese Classical Prose: The Eight Masters of the T'ang-Sung Period*. Hong Kong: The Chinese University Press, 1979, 23–97. Translation of 16 of Han Yu's prose pieces.

Yang, Xianyi, and Gladys Yang, trans. *Poetry and Prose of the Tang and Song*. Beijing: Panda Books, 1984, 63–98. Translation of 14 of Han Yu's prose pieces.

THE POETRY OF BO JUYI (PO CHÜ-YI)

Author: Bo Juyi (Po Chü-Yi)
Born: 772, Xinzheng (Hsin-cheng: (modern Xinzheng, Henan Province), China
Died: 846, Longmen
Major Poems: Boshi Changqing ji (Master Bo's Changqing Era Collection); "Song of Everlasting Regret," "Songs of Qin [Ch'in]," "New Ballads"

Major Themes

The function of poetry is to expose and comment on social and political abuses.
Conscription and harsh taxation result in extreme suffering for the common people.
A Tang emperor, captivated by a beautiful concubine, loses his throne, and puts her to death; after mourning for her, the emperor meets a Taoist priest who is able to summon her soul.

Bo Juyi was born in Xinzheng prefecture of Zhengzhou (modern Xinzheng, Henan). In his later years he lived on the outskirts of Luoyang. In 832 he moved into an unoccupied portion of the Xiangshan (Hsiang-shan) Monastery east of the Longmen (Lung-men) cave area located south of Luoyang. Bo took the name *Xiangshan jushi* (Recluse of the Xiang Hills). Thus, Bo Juyi is also known as Bo Xiangshan.

Bo Juyi passed the *jinshi* (*chin-shih*) examination in 800. In 802 he was one of eight candidates who passed the placement examination. His friend Yuan Zhen (Yüan Chen; 799–831), a prominent poet and official, also passed at the same time. In 806 both Yuan Zhen and Bo Juyi passed a special palace examination that finally won them positions. Bo Juyi had an illustrious official career. From 807–811 he served in the capital. He was a member of the Hanlin Academy and served as Reminder of the Left. The latter position was that of a remonstrance official who was responsible for pointing out errors in state documents. Bo Juyi understood his duty not only to correct documents, but also to comment on policy matters mentioned in the documents. Thus, during the three years he served in this post he submitted numerous proposals for reducing government expenditures, eliminating corruption, and exposing eunuch abuses of authority. Bo Juyi also wrote a number of protest poems that address many social and political issues of the day.

In early summer 811 Bo Juyi's mother died, and he had to resign office to observe mourning for her. He remained out of office until 814, when he was recalled to the capital to serve as assistant secretary to the heir designate. In 815 the minister Wu Yuanheng (Wu Yüan-heng) had the military governor Li Shidao (Li Shih-tao) assassinated. When Bo Juyi demanded that the criminal be arrested, members of the Wu Yuanheng faction had him banished to Jiangzhou (modern Jiangxi). Bo Juyi was able to spend time in the area of the scenic Mount Lu. He built a thatched hut below Incense Burner Peak. In 818 Bo Juyi was transferred to the remote outpost of Zhongzhou (modern Zhong county, Sichuan).

In 820 Emperor Xianzong (Hsien-tsung) suddenly died, and he was succeeded by Li Heng (Emperor Muzong/Mu-tsung, reigned 820–824). In 821 the new emperor changed the reign-period title to Changqing (Ch'ang-ch'ing) (Prolonged Felicitation) and recalled Yuan Zhen and Bo Juyi to the capital. Yuan Zhen served in the highest ministerial positions. Bo Juyi held a much lower position as superior secretary in the bureau of visitors. In 822 Yuan Zhen was ousted from power in a factional struggle, and Bo Juyi was reassigned to the provinces, this time to Hangzhou, where he held the position of governor. In 824, Bo Juyi returned to the capital to serve as chief gentleman-in-waiting to the heir designate, which was a sinecure because no heir had yet been designated. He much of his time in the countryside. He also took a great interest in music and dancing, especially the courtesan songs that were now popular among the literati.

In 825 Bo Juyi again was sent to the provinces, this time to Suzhou, where he was appointed governor. He served here until 827, when he resigned because of illness. After recovering from his illness Bo Juyi returned to the capital and held a series of appointments. In 829 he moved to Luoyang where he held the post of Governor of Henan. In 832 he moved into an unoccupied part of the Xiangshan Monastery in Longmen, which is famous for its rock sculptures. It was at this time he began calling himself *Xiangshan jushi*.

For the next 13 years, Bo Juyi remained in semi-retirement, spending much time with Buddhist monks. He also devoted his remaining years to collecting and arranging his complete works. In 844 he presented copies of his collection to the principal monasteries of the towns where he had served. Bo Juyi died in 846. He was buried in the Longmen Hills.

Bo Juyi's Poetry Collection

In the fourth year of the Changqing period (824), Yuan Zhen edited Bo Juyi's writings into a 50-chapter collection, the *Boshi Changqing ji* (Master Bo's Changqing Era Collection). He also wrote a preface to the collection, which is dated 825. This preface gives a detailed account of Bo Juyi's career. Two years before his death, Bo Juyi edited his own collection, adding 25 more chapters. Bo Juyi's collection of over 2,800 poems is the largest among Tang dynasty poets. His poetry long has been admired in China, Japan, and Korea for its simplicity and direct manner of expression. His "Song of Everlasting Regret" is one of the best known Tang dynasty poems.

Poetry Remedies Social Ills

From the time he served as Reminder, Bo Juyi displayed a strong interest in using poetry as a means of exposing social ills. In an model examination essay from this period, he proposed that the Tang court revive the ancient "song collecting office," the function of which was to collect popular songs. The songs served as a kind of barometer of popular feeling—songs of praise meant that imperial rule was benevolent and effective, while satires and complaints meant that government was oppressive and incompetent. Bo Juyi wrote a long letter to Yuan Zhen in which he stated his views about the proper function of poetry. In the letter he tells Yuan that while he was serving as Reminder, he was requested by the emperor to report on the sufferings of the people. In some cases he found it is impossible to discuss the matter directly in a petition or memorial, and thus he wrote poems for the purpose of "relieving the ills of the people, and repairing the defects of the time." To expose the abuses of the eunuchs, Bo wrote "Spending the Night in a Village North of Zigo Mountain." The poem tells of a band of eunuch rowdies who come into a village, help themselves to food and drink, and cut down a precious tree that an old man had tended for 30 years.

Bo Juyi wrote over 170 poems of social protest and political criticism which he placed in his collection in a section labelled *fengyu* (*Feng-yü*) (criticisms and moral lessons). They include 2 important sets, the 10 "Songs of Qin" and his 50 "New Ballads." The "Songs of Qin" are short pieces that comment on political and social problems of the day. "The Double Tax" exposes the hardship inflicted on farmers who must sell their crops at a discount to unscrupulous landlords and merchants in order to pay their taxes in cash. "Light Chariots and Fat Horses" mocks eunuch military officers, who feast on rare delicacies imported from distant places, while people in a drought-stricken area are reduced to cannibalism. In "Buying Flowers" Bo Juyi satirizes the conspicuous consumption of the residents of Chang'an, who flock to the markets to buy peonies when they are blooming in the spring. An old peasant comments that the price they pay—5 bolts of silk for 500 blossoms—would pay the taxes of ten peasant families.

The "New Ballads" are poems in a form of poetry known as *yuefu* (*yüeh-fu*). The *yuefu*, which literally means "music bureau poetry," originally were folksongs and ballads that were collected by the imperial bureau of music. Most of the early *yuefu* are anonymous narrative poems that express complaints against the hardships of conscription, an unfaithful husband or lover, corruption in high places, the tragedies of war, or burdensome taxation. Before Bo Juyi, except for a few pieces by Du Fu (Tu Fu) and Li Bo (Li Po), the *yuefu* was a highly conventionalized and lifeless genre. It was Bo Juyi's goal to revitalize the *yuefu*, and he and his friend, Yuan Zhen, led a movement to use the *yuefu* ballad form as a vehicle for writing protest poetry. This movement is called the "New *yuefu* Movement."

In his preface to the "New Ballads," Bo Juyi declares that these poems have no set length, and their main purpose is to convey "ideas" rather than display literary style. Bo deliberately wrote in a language that was "simply and direct" that could be easily read or understood when recited. The themes concern social and political abuses. Among the most moving pieces are those that expose the evils of conscription. "The Old Man of Xinfeng with a Broken Arm" tells of a man who escaped the draft by crushing his arm with a stone. Although he was unable to use his arm, unlike most of his contemporaries, he was able to live to the age of 88. In "Tibetan Prisoners of War" Bo tells the story of a Han Chinese born in the northwest, who was captured by the Tibetans. After living in captivity for 40 years, he was taken prisoner by a Tang army. Mistaken for a Tibetan, he was to be sent to the southeast, presumably to do conscript labor. The poem is a narrative piece that relates the unfortunate man's plight. Other pieces in the "New Ballads" are complaints about the hardships of taxation ("The Old Man of Duling"), the abuse of government authority to confiscate property without due compensation ("The Old Charcoal Seller"), and the mistreatment of palace ladies ("The Lady of Shangyang Palace").

"Song of Everlasting Regret"

Bo Juyi's best known poem is a long romantic ballad, "Song of Everlasting Regret." Bo Juyi wrote this poem in 807 while he was visiting the Xianyou Monastery about 50 miles west of Chang'an (now Xi'an). He and two other scholars began talking about the tragedy of Emperor Xuanzong and his beautiful concubine, Yang Guifei (Yang Kuei-fei) (Precious Consort Yang). When the An Lushan rebellion broke out in 756, the emperor and his immediate entourage had to flee the capital. Their destination was Shu (modern Sichuan) in the southwest, but after traveling only 30 miles, soldiers in the imperial bodyguard refused to move on unless the emperor had Lady Yang put to death. Xuanzong reluctantly consented, and continued on to Shu, where he abdicated the throne to his son. Later, after the rebels were defeated, he returned to the capital, reputedly haunted by the memory of his beloved consort. Bo Juyi's "Song of Everlasting Regret" is a poetic account of Xuanzong's affair with Lady Yang. In the first part of the poem, Bo Juyi tells of Yang Guifei's captivation of the emperor, who is so enthralled with her beauty, he neglects his official duties. Although Bo Juyi overtly displays his disapproval of such imperial dissipation, he also shows sympathy for the lady. One of the most dramatic scenes in all of Chinese poetry are the lines he devotes to describing Lady Yang's death; without referring to her directly, Bo simply says "lovely curved moth-eyebrows died before the horses." (Yang Guifei actually was strangled, not trampled to death.) Bo Juyi goes on to recount the retired emperor's return to his old palace, where every place and thing stirs memories of the deceased Lady Yang. Finally, he meets a Taoist adept who is able to summon the lady's spirit from a Taoist paradise. She gives him keepsakes to take back to Xuanzong as tokens of her love. The poem ends with Bo Juyi's trenchant comment that even though heaven and earth are long-lasting, "this regret, stretches on and on, with no time to end."

Poems of Leisure and Sorrow

The poems in Bo Juyi's collection are organized into four groups. The first of these are the "New Ballads." The other categories are "poems of leisure," "poems of sorrow," and "regulated poems."

The latter are poems written to strict prosodic rules, and although Bo has more poems in this category than any other, he valued these pieces the least. They consist mainly of pieces written for formal occasions or in his capacity as an official.

The poems of leisure are pieces that express personal moods and feelings. In "Early Morning Escorting the Doctors of Art to the Examination," written in 805, Bo gently pokes fun at men who must rise early to take the capital examination while he is able to lie late in bed. "Singing Alone in the Mountain," which Arthur Waley has translated under the title "Madly Singing in the Mountains," is Bo Juyi's passionate statement of his love for composing and reciting poetry in a remote mountain retreat. Other pieces tell of visits to pleasant scenic spots and temples. One of the best known of these is "Traveling to Wuzhen Monastery," a long poem translated by Arthur Waley under the title "The Temple."

The poems of sorrow are pieces expressing personal sadness and grief. Included in this group is "Song of Everlasting Regret." Among the more personal pieces are laments for the death of friends and relatives, and complaints about banishment and hardship.

DAVID R. KNECHTGES

Further Reading

Translations

Alley, Rewi, trans. *200 Selected Poems. Bai Juyi.* Beijing: New World Press, 1983. Free translations of selected poems.

Levy, Howard S., trans. *Translations from Po Chü-i's Collected Works.* 2 vols. New York: Paragon, 1971.

———, and Henry Wells. *Translations from Po Chü-i's Collected Works.* Vols 3–4. Taipei: Chinese Materials Center, 1976, 1978.

Waley, Arthur, trans. *Translations from the Chinese.* New York: Alfred A. Knopf, 1941. Contains translations of 110 poems. These two volumes contain rather literal renderings of selected poems.

Related Studies

Feifel, Eugen. *Po Chü-i as Censor.* The Hague: Mouton, 1961. A study of an important period of Bo Juyi's official career.

Waley, Arthur. *The Life and Times of Po Chü-i.* London: Allen and Unwin, 1949. The standard English-language biography.

THE POETRY OF LI HE (LI HO)

Author: Li He (Li Ho)
Born: 790, Changgu, Fuchang prefecture (modern Yiyang, Henan), China
Died: 816, Changgu
Major Poems: "Divine Strings," "Matters Sealed in Green Writings," "Ballad of a Pained Heart," "Thirteen Poems from My Southern Garden," "Song of General Lü," "Changgu"

Major Themes

The spirit realm is a world of wonder and mystery.
The official world is corrupt and dangerous.
Nature is full of delight and beauty.

Li He is one of the leading poets of the early ninth century. His extant collection contains 242 poems. Like several of his contemporaries, Li He favored writing in the *yuefu (yüehfu)* or "folk ballad" form. Over half of his collection consists of *yuefu*. Li He is best known for his social protest verse and supernatural poems full of strange images mostly drawn from the mystical realm.

Li He was born in Changgu, which was located about 50 miles west of the Tang eastern capital of Luoyang. His father, Li Jinsu (Li Chin-su), was a minor official who died when Li He was quite young. Li He's mother came from a more prominent family, the Zheng (Cheng) clan of Henan. Li He was a child prodigy and reputedly composed verse at the age of seven. According to the *New Tang History*, he was thin and delicate, and he had bushy eyebrows and unusually long fingernails. Li He wrote poetry at great speed. He often would go out riding accompanied by a servant. Whenever he was inspired by something, he would write it down on a piece of silk and throw it in a bag. As soon as he had finished a piece, he did not much care what happened to it. His mother would send a maid to search in his bag, and when she saw how much he had written, she would angrily exclaim, "This boy simply will vomit out his heart!"

Li He had hoped to take the *jinshi* (presented scholar) examination, and given his considerable poetic skill, he had a good chance of passing. In addition, one of his patrons was Han Yu, who was holding high office in Luoyang at the time. Li He easily passed the local Luoyang district examination in 809, but when he arrived in Chang'an (now Xi'an) in late 810 the authorities would not permit him to sit for the exam. The examiners claimed that since Li He's deceased father's name was Jinsu, the word *jin* in *jinshi* violated the taboo on his deceased father's name. Han Yu was outraged by the examiners' decision, and wrote an essay in Li He's defense, "Discussion of Taboos."

Being barred from the examinations had a traumatic effect on Li He, and from this time on much of his poetry is filled with extreme bitterness and frustration. Although Li He could not sit for the examination, he did receive in 812 an appointment as grand master of ceremonies in the bureau of ritual. Li found the duties of this post, which he described as the work of a servant "holding dustpan and broom," as boring and stultifying. Li He did find enjoyment in the pleasure quarters of the capital. Li often composed songs for parties attended by rich young dandies and beautiful courtesans.

In 814 Li He resigned his post in the Bureau of Rites and returned to his home in Changgu. Li He wrote a long poem entitled "Chang gu" in which he describes the beauty of the area. At this time he was only 23 years of age and considered himself an utter failure.

Having been frustrated in his pursuit of a civilian career, Li He then decided to enter military service. In the autumn of 814 he joined the staff of a general stationed in Lu-zhou (modern Changzhi, Shanxi). He wrote a number of frontier poems that express his revulsion at the misery, death, and hardship that he saw in the border region. Li He was not physically suited for the rugged frontier life, and he was often ill, probably from tuberculosis. He returned to Changgu in 817, where he died at the age of 26.

Supernatural Themes

The themes of Li He's poetry cover a broad range. He wrote complaints about corrupt and rapacious officials, and the hardships of conscript soldiers and poor peasants. He also wrote descriptions of beautiful women and landscape scenes. However, he is best known for his poems on supernatural themes. These pieces are full of such images as ghosts, demons, spirits, bones, blood, tombs, and corpses. He has screeching and wailing phoenixes, gaunt dragons dancing, aged hares and cold toads crying, weeping mole-crickets, blue raccoon-dogs weeping blood, shivering foxes dying, nine-headed serpents devouring men's souls, poisonous dragons, and drooling lions. Li He even attributes animate qualities to inanimate objects: his describes swords that roar and fly, statues that weep, and painted dragons that are ridden by rain goblins.

In one of his most dramatic poems on the supernatural, "Divine Strings," Li He presents an imaginary account of a shamanistic rite in which a female shaman invites gods to enjoy the ceremony. The shamaness offers libations to welcome the spirits, and in response, clouds in which spirits descend to earth darken the sky. Incense from a jade brazier lit by the shamaness to attract the spirits spurts out like the sound of drums. As sea spirits and mountain demons take their places, paper money crackles in the whining whirlwind. The shamaness takes up a magic lute gilt with dancing simurghs, and knitting her brow, she alternately strums a note and utters an incantation. Shouting to the spirits in the stars and summoning demons, she invites them to partake of the offerings in cups and plates. The human observers of the rite feel a cold chill as they observe the mountain goblins devouring the food from the dishes. As the sun sets over the nearby mountain, the poet is unsure whether the spirits are real or not, but he does see the medium's

changing expressions, which presumably reflects the pleasure or displeasure of the gods. As the rite ends, the shamaness bids farewell to the gods who gallop back on their steeds to the green hills.

Li He has two other pieces with similar titles, "Song of the Divine Strings" and "Parting Song of the Divine Strings" that also recount shamanistic rites. The former piece portrays a shamaness" exorcism of malevolent creatures including a blue raccoon-dog, a fox spirit, and a 100-year-old owl. Although some scholars have argued that Li He did not really believe in the existence of the supernatural, these poems show that he was strongly interested in the subject, and that he took a sensual delight in portraying the spirit world.

Li He also wrote poems on Taoist religious themes. In "Matters Sealed in Green Writings" he describes the Taoist rite of composing prayers written in vermilion ink on green paper. This particular prayer was addressed to the Primal Father, who was the supreme deity of Heaven. At the end of his poem Li He tries to summon up the ghost of the Han scholar-poet Yang Xiong (Yang Hsiung) (53 B.C.–A.D. 18) by holding up a halberd, a weapon that Yang Xiong once wielded as a palace guard.

The Suffering Poet

Li He often presents himself as a figure of the suffering poet. He compares himself to the ancient poet Qu Yuan (Ch'u Yüan), who having been rejected by his ruler, composed melancholy songs complaining about his miserable fate:

> Moaning, I imitate the songs of Chu;
> Sick bones wounded by deep emotion.
> On an autumn form white hair grows,
> Tree leaves weep in the wind and rain.
>
> ("BALLAD OF THE PAINED
> HEART": KNECHTGES, TRANS.)

Although Li He believed good poetry was the product of suffering, he had no illusions about its efficacy to save the world. In the sixth of his "Thirteen Poems from My Southern Garden," he writes about sitting up through the night "searching for lines, picking phrases, growing old carving insects" ("carving insects" is a pejorative expression for trivial writing). Given the fact that military men are those who are most needed in this time of incessant warfare, "what place is there for writings that weep at the autumn wind?"

Li He also uses color, especially white, to symbolize emotion. In ancient Chinese thought, white is associated with west and autumn, and thus can symbolize old age and death. Li He uses white to describe scenes that are desolate, gloomy, and even foreboding. In Li He's poems, the sky, the fields, the grass, and even the autumn wind are white. In one poem he depicts a garden in a deserted courtyard on a cold, moonlight night as a "placid white void" ("Song Lyrics on the Twelve Months Written While Taking the Examination in Luoyang"). In another poem, he describes the setting sun as the "white effulgence returning to the western mountains" ("Ballad of Unending Time").

Satires

Li He wrote many satires. In "Joys of the Honorable Princess on Military Campaign" he pokes fun at a Tang princess who is on an outing accompanied by ladies-in-waiting clad in military costumes. "Song of the Old Jade Gatherer" is a social protest poem on the perils encountered by those who risk their lives quarrying jade. Li He tells of one elderly jade hunter who rappels down a steep cliff into a ravine and upon seeing a creeper-vine called "heart-break" recalls his wife and children in his home village.

Because his official career was thwarted by political enemies, Li He viewed the pursuit of a government career as dangerous for a man of talent and integrity. In "Do Not Go out of the Gate, Sir" he portrays the official world as filled with vicious men whom he describes as "nine-headed serpents that devour men's souls," or snapping dogs that pursue a virtuous man in order to "eat his flesh." As a result, good men either starve to death or die young from worry and melancholy. In another piece entitled "Ballad of the Ferocious Tiger," Li

He uses the image of a fierce tiger, which no one, even fabled animal tamers, could control, to represent oppressive government officials.

In one of his most biting satires, "Song of General Lü," Li He attacks eunuchs and female favorites who so dominated the imperial court that brave and able generals were not put in charge of the army, even in times of insurrection. Although the general wishes to raise his sword and quell the uprising, the imperial army is led by a "powdered lady-commander." This commander undoubtedly was a notorious eunuch official of the time. Li He mocks him by sarcastically contrasting his perfumed arrows with the metal lances that the urgent situation really requires.

Li He may even have been bold enough to criticize the emperor himself. Several of his poems have been interpreted as satires on his emperor's quest for immortality. In "Regretting the Shortness of the Day" he mocks the most famous seeker of the elixir of immortality among Chinese emperors, Liu Che (Liu Ch'e) (Emperor Wu) of the Han, by referring to his many bones that have "stagnated" in his tomb since his death centuries ago. The implication is that the contemporary Tang Emperor Xianzong's quest for immortality is just as futile as was Liu Che's.

Landscape

Li He loved the scenery of his home area of Changgu, and thus most of the poems he wrote here are descriptions of the gardens, rivers, and mountains on or near his family estate. Li He wrote a long poem, titled simply "Changgu," in which he describes the area in great detail. This is not the usual bland Tang landscape poem, but one filled with vivid and sensual descriptions of nature: the fragrance of bamboo fills the still silence; their "powdered nodes" are a fresh halcyon blue; the grass grows like tresses of hair; the glistening dew weeps dark tears; on scented paths "aged reds" (flowers) are tipsy; swarms of insects "engrave" ancient willows and a waterfall cascades down like a cape made of Chu silk. Li He views this place as an escape from the travails of the world, where prefectural magistrates do not bother him and tax collectors do not call. Yet, he does not wish to retire here yet, for he must first attain a high official post.

DAVID R. KNECHTGES

Further Reading

Translations

Frodsham, J. D., trans. *Goddesses, Ghosts, & Demons.* The Collected Poems of Li He (790–816). San Francisco: North Point Press, 1983. A revised version of Frodsham 1970.

———. *The Poems of Li Ho.* Oxford: The Clarendon Press, 1970. A translation of all of Li He's poems.

Related Studies

South, Margaret T. *Li Ho: A Scholar-Official of the Yüan-ho Period (806–821).* Adelaide, Australia: Library Board of South Australia, 1967. A detailed biography.
Tu Kuo-ch'ing. *Li Ho.* Boston: G. K. Hall, 1979. A general biographical and literary study.

THE PROSE WORKS OF OUYANG XIU (OU-YANG HSIU)

Author: Ouyang Xiu (Ou-yang Hsiu)
Born: 1007, Mianzhou (modern Mianyang, Sichuan province)
Died: 1072, Yingzhou (modern Fuyang, Anhui province)
Major Works: Various memorials submitted to the Court, expository essays on political matters), obituaries, *New Tang History*, *New History of the Five Dynasties*, *Postscripts to Collected Ancient Inscriptions*, "Record of The Old Drunkard's Pavilion," "The Autumn Sound"

Major Themes

The serious purpose of all literature is to transmit and teach Confucian orthodoxy.
All written works should bear the author's distinctive individual style.
The rich, profound, and forceful ancient-style prose practiced by the great Tang dynasty writer Han Yu (768–824) is especially worthy of emulation.
The manifold matters and things of the phenomenal world, including such mundane items as musical instruments, rocks, and fish ponds, are perfectly acceptable topics for treatment in literary works.

From a cultural standpoint, the Song (Sung) dynasty (960–1279) represents a "golden era" in Chinese history. The exquisite paintings, tapestries, and porcelains of the period—all well known to Western connoisseurs—richly convey the refinement and sophistication of Song life in general, while other developments, such as the appearance of the compass, gunpowder, and moveable type, reveal a society strikingly modern in character. Several major changes took place in Chinese civilization during the Song. None of these, however, had a more profound and lasting impact than the growth of private and public education and the expansion of the civil service examination system. The numbers of young scholars who were able to matriculate through this system and win positions in the state bureacracy expanded tremendously during the Song, and it was these men who, as "scholar-officials" in China's government administration, held a monopoly on political power. While most of them actively pursued careers in the civil service system, all sought to perfect the arts of the *wenren (wen jen)*, or "cultured man." These arts include literature, painting, calligraphy, history, philosophy, and classical studies. Perhaps no other figure of the period better represents the realized ideal of the Song dynasty *wenren* than Ouyang Xiu. A man of many talents and abilities, he is unquestionably one of China's greatest and most influential writers of classical Chinese prose (*guwen*).

Ouyang Xiu was born in a remote corner of the Song empire called Mian county (Mianzhou; situated near what is now Mianyang City in north-central Sichuan province), where his father, Ouyang Guan, was serving as an official. Ouyang Xiu's father died when he was just four years old. His mother then took the boy to join the household of an uncle, Ouyang Ye, who lived faraway in Sui county (on the Han River in modern Hubei). Ouyang Xiu remained there until he was 21 years old. Reliable details of his education are lacking, but we do know that he took the provincial examinations in Sui county when he was 16 and failed because he violated a rhyme convention in an answer. In 1027 he sat for same the examination, only to fail a second time. Ouyang Xiu then tried a different approach common in the Song: he presented samples of his writing to a Court official serving in nearby Hanyang. Impressed with Ouyang's writing talents, the official retained him, and the next year took the young protégé to the capital in Kaifeng (modern Henan). There Ouyang Xiu placed first in a qualifying exam for one of the imperial colleges. In 1030 he took and passed with distinction two of the highest level examinations in the capital. Having now succeeded in the exams, he embarked on a career as a scholar-official. That journey lasted a lifetime.

Ouyang Xiu's first appointment was to a minor government post in Luoyang. Three years later, however, he found himself working in the Imperial Library in Kaifeng. While in the capital, Ouyang became closely associated with Fan Zhongyan (Fan Chung-yen) (989–1052), a leading statesman of the day. When Fan's outspoken criticism of Court policies got him demoted and removed from the capital, other officials who supported his criticisms also found themselves exiled from the political scene in Kaifeng. Ouyang Xiu was among them. Soon he was on his way to a place called Yiling, situated at the mouth of the Yangzi Gorges in Western Hubei. The pristine beauty of the area is referred to frequently in Ouyang's literary works of this period.

In the early 1040s, the political fortunes of Fan Zhongyan, Ouyang Xiu, and other "reformers" changed, and they were recalled to the capital to resume office. For his part, Ouyang Xiu served as a Drafting Official. In effect, he was now drafting edicts on the Emperor's behalf. Only scholar-officials with superior writing talents and literary reputation served in such posts. Soon, however, the political tides changed once again, and Fan Zhongyan and other reformers were banished from the capital. At first, Ouyang Xiu was spared exile, but soon a much more damaging development took place: Ouyang Xiu was publicly charged with having committed incest with a distant family relative and was thrown into prison. Although he was acquitted of the charge in no less than three separate trials, on the pretext of a technicality involving the woman's purchase of some land under the Ouyang name, Ouyang Xiu was exiled to isolated Chu county (Chuzhou; modern Chu county, Anhui province). The leisurely relaxation he enjoyed in Chu county is reflected in many of the poems and prose pieces written during this exile phase. One of his most famous writings, "Record of the Old Drunkard's Pavilion" ("Cuiweng ting ji"/"Ts'ui-weng chi"), was composed at this time. Although still in the early stages of his career as an official, by the time of his exile to Chu county Ouyang Xiu

had already grown tired of Court politics. He even had thoughts of abandoning his career as a scholar-official and pursuing a life of leisure and writing.

After leaving Chu county, Ouyang Xiu successively held two similar posts in different counties away from Kaifeng. In 1054, after having just completed the obligatory two-and-a-half-year mourning period for his deceased mother, Ouyang Xiu again returned to the capital, where he would remain for the next 13 years. Shortly after his return to Kaifeng, Ouyang Xiu was commissioned to direct the compilation of a new official history of the Tang dynasty entitled Xin Tangshu (New Tang History). He was also appointed to the Bureau of Academicians, and later became an assistant chief minister. Ouyang Xiu's political power and influence reached a pinnacle during this period. But, as is often the case in the Song dynasty politics, he became embroiled in court controversies. The dispute on this occasion concerned imperial succession. To make matters worse, one of Ouyang Xiu's former protégés formally accused Ouyang of having committed incest with his own daughter-in-law. As with the accusation 20 years earlier concerning his supposed niece, the charges were dropped due to insufficient evidence. Ouyang Xiu's honor and reputation, however, were damaged severely. A year later, in 1068, he requested permission to retire permanently from government, but his plea was rejected. After holding two more posts in the provinces, his request to withdraw from public service was finally granted in 1071. The following summer, he died at the age of 65.

The Prose Reformers

In order to understand and appreciate Ouyang Xiu's talents as a master prose writer, one needs to know something about the major shift in the standards for writing prose that occurred in the eleventh century. Up until that time candidates who took the civil service examinations were required to compose their answers in couplets of semantically parallel lines (noun matching noun, verb matching verb, and so on) containing flowery, ornate diction, and literary allusions. This "parallel prose" (*piantiwen/p'ien-t'i wen*) style dominated prose writing during Tang dynasty as well. A few voices of that period, most notably Han Yu (Han Yü, 768–824), protested against the excesses and artificiality of parallel prose and advocated a return to the terse and straightforward type of prose used by the ancients, which they called *guwen* (*ku-wen*), or "ancient-style prose." Despite these voices of dissent, *piantiwen* remained the prevailing standard until the eleventh century. It was at that time that Ouyang Xiu and others questioned the requirement that examination answers be written in parallel prose. This form, they argued, put emphasis on style over content. These priorities, according to Ouyang Xiu and other "prose reformers," should be reversed. The result was a revival of the *guwen* ideals advocated earlier by Han Yu.

Ouyang Xiu's greatest personal contribution to the so-called Ancient-Style Prose Movement in the eleventh century took place in 1057, when he served as administrator of the examinations. Holding this powerful position meant that Ouyang had control over the content and grading of the exam papers. In a bold move, Ouyang Xiu not only formulated questions that addressed real political problems, but moreover failed all the candidates who wrote their answers in parallel prose and similar styles. These innovative moves angered many candidates and officials in the bureaucracy; but eventually Ouyang Xiu's new standards prevailed. In examinations given after 1057, candidates could employ the more straightforward "ancient prose style." This is Ouyang Xiu's crowning achievement to the *guwen* cause.

The Formal and Informal Writings

Ouyang Xiu's oeuvre, entitled *Master Ouyang Wenzhong's Collected Works* (*Ouyang Wenzhonggong ji/Ou-yang Wen-chung Kung chi*), contains many different types of prose. For the sake of convenience, they may be classified into two general categories: *formal* writings and *informal* writings. For the most part, Ouyang's formal writings include memorials to throne (*zouyi/tsou-i*), expository essays (*lun*), and obituaries (*muzhiming/mu-*

chih ming), that is, texts to be inscribed on a large steles or gravestones). Memorials to the emperor and obituaries might seem, at least to the unsuspecting Western reader, more "functional" than literary. In traditional China, however, formal writings of this sort (like virtually all writings) were judged by strict literary standards.

Two other points are worth noting here. First, Ouyang Xiu's reputation as a great prose writer is built on his skill at composing memorials, essays, and obituaries. The reason for this is simple: in Ouyang Xiu's time, these were the most prestigious types of writing. A second and equally significant point is this: the straightforward "ancient prose" style promoted by Ouyang Xiu and others during the eleventh century was mainly concerned with formal prose writings, that is, the kind of prose used in examination essays and later in the bureaucracy.

The second category of Ouyang Xiu's prose—the informal or occasional pieces—include letters (*shu*), prefaces (*xu/hsü*), colophons (*ba/pa*), farewell accounts (*songxu/sung-hsü*) and records or dedication inscriptions (*ji/chi*). It is ironic that whereas Ouyang's literary reputation during the Song was built on his formal prose writings, his renown in literary history is based almost totally on his informal pieces, especially his *ji*, or records. The main reason for this shift is not difficult to pinpoint. Ouyang Xiu's formal writings are "restricted" in the sense that they are intimately tied to eleventh-century politics or figures of that period. His informal pieces, on the other hand, are more personal, subjective, and (at times) even lyrical, and thus are more appealing to a wider audience over time. This explains why virtually every anthology of traditional Chinese prose includes works such as Ouyang Xiu's "Record of the Old Drunkard's Pavilion" (*"Cuiweng ting ji"/"Ts'uiweng t'ing chi"*) and "The Autumn Sound" (*"Qiu sheng"/"Ch'iu sheng"*), which is a mixture of prose passages and rhymed and metered lines, to name just two examples. But what particular features of these works and their analogues qualify Ouyang Xiu as a *great* prose writer?

The one quality that most distinguishes Ouyang

Xiu's prose style is its originality. His acknowledged indebtedness to literary paragons of the past, especially Han Yu, and his leadership role in the Ancient Prose Movement notwithstanding, Ouyang Xiu created an unprecedented prose style. The hallmark of this style is its highly personal tone. That is to say, Ouyang Xiu's writings all bear the distinctive imprint of his personality. Among his prose pieces, the less structurally "restrictive" informal prose genres offered Ouyang more opportunity to reveal his subjective, personal side, and he took full advantage of the opportunity. A good example is the *ji*, or record/inscription form. Although *ji* were usually written at the request of a friend or acquaintance (often to commemorate the construction of a pavilion or studio), Ouyang Xiu generated many *ji* on his own. Take, for instance, his famous "Record of [Inscription for] the Old Drunkard's Pavilion," written in 1046 during his exile in Chu county. Although the title suggests an account of the pavilion, its builder, history, and so on, the piece actually describes—in vivid, congenial, and almost "friendly" language—Ouyang Xiu himself (the "Old Drunkard"), and the wine parties that he often hosted at the pavilion. Perhaps no other prose piece in Ouyang Xiu's *Works* more vividly reveals his genial personality.

Finally, we must also keep in mind that Ouyang Xiu was a wordsmith. Despite the informal, personal, and even sentimental tone of his writings, Ouyang Xiu was above all else a literary craftsman. Every word, line, and paragraph of everything he ever wrote is carefully constructed for public con-

sumption and for posterity. This careful attention to language, combined with the author's masterful control of rhetorical devices such as irony, allegory, and humor, often creates multiple layers of meaning in his writings. It is precisely Ouyang Xiu's technical skill as a writer, his unique prose style, and his role as leader of the "Ancient Prose" movement during the Song dynasty that account for his deserved reputation as one of China's greatest prose writers.

JAMES M. HARGETT

Further Reading

Related Studies

Chen, Yu-shih. "The Literary Theory and Practice of Ou-yang Hsiu," in *Chinese Approaches to Literature*. Ed. Adele Austin Rickett. 67–96. Princeton, N.J.: Princeton University Press, 1978. Contains a useful discussion of the structural elements used in the "Record of the Old Drunkard's Pavilion."

Egan, Ronald C.. *The Literary Works of Ou-yang Hsiu (1007–1072)*. Cambridge, MA: Cambridge University Press, 1984. This is the most informative study of Ouyang Xiu's various types of literary works (prose, poetry, rhapsodies [*fu*], and songs [*ci*]) available in any language.

Liu, James T.C.. *Ou-yang Hsiu: An Eleventh Century Neo-Confucianist*. Stanford, CA: Stanford University Press, 1967.

THE POETRY OF SU SHI (SU SHIH)

Author: Su Shi (Su Shih); also known as Su Dongpo (Su Tung-p'o)
Born: 1037, Meishan (modern Meishan, in southwestern Sichuan province)
Died: 1101, Changzhou (modern Changzhou City, Jiangsu)
Major Poems: *Southern Travels Collection,* "On the Yangzi Watching the Hills," "Written on the Wall at West Forest Temple," "Prose Poems on the Red Cliff"

Major Themes

Any topic—a toad, the lament of a farm wife, bad wine, a mosquito, the carefree days of a fisherman—is suitable for poetry.

Poets should merge themselves with the world around them, and not content themselves with simply polishing their literary creations.

States of spiritual transcendence and life in the mundane world can each offer fulfillment and delight. (The problem is—can one balance the two? If so, how?)

The life and literary output of Su Shi (also known by his literary name, Su Dongpo, or "Su of Eastern Slope") is probably more heavily documented and studied that any other figure of the Song (Sung) dynasty (960–1279). In addition to the numerous biographies produced in traditional and modern times, his many volumes of formal and informal prose writings have received continuous critical attention for almost a millennium. As for the author's verse, no fewer than seven copiously annotated editions of Su Shi's 2,400 extant poems still circulate today. And, within the United States alone, major monographs on the life and literary works of Su Shi continue to appear (three of them were published between 1990 and 1994). Why has so much attention focused for so long on this particular figure from China's distant past? Although Su was a major eleventh-century political personality, and, like Ouyang Xiu (Ou-yang Hsiu) and other contemporaries, was highly skilled in calligraphy and painting, he was above all else a master of arts and letters. The genius shown in his literary productions—especially his poetry—makes him one of the most extraordinary figures ever to grace the pages of Chinese literary history.

Su Shi was born in early 1037 in Meishan, Sichuan (Shu, as it was then called), not far from foothills of famous Mount Emei. Although his remote family background is uncertain, we know that his grandfather, Su Xu (Su Hsü) (973–1047), was a landowner whose wealth allowed his sons, Su Xun (Su Hsün) (1009–1066) and Su Huan (1000–1062), to study and prepare for the Song civil service examinations. The older of the two brothers, Su Huan, passed the exams and pursued a generally lackluster career as a government official. His younger brother Su Xun, however, failed the exams and thereafter spent much of his time either at home or traveling about the empire. One of Su Xun's chief activities in Meishan was overseeing the education of his two sons. Su Shi was the older of the two boys. His younger brother was named Su Che (Su Ch'e) (1039–1112). Also involved in the education of the two boys was their mother, née Cheng (Ch'eng)—an educated woman who was from a prominent family, and was a devout Buddhist.

In 1056 Su Xun took his sons to the capital in Kaifeng for the purpose of participating in the civil service examinations, scheduled for the beginning of the new year (1057). Quite by chance, Su Shi and Su Che arrived in Kaifeng in the very same year that Ouyang Xiu, the presiding official for the 1057 exams, changed the answer format. Instead of calling for the customary parallel prose form, Ouyang Xiu required candidates to use a more straightforward and direct "ancient prose style." This move created a scandal in the capital, for the changes in examination format were not announced ahead of time. In any case, Su Shi placed second in this exam and Su Che also earned a high passing grade. Both became instant celebrities. But just a few months after his sons' success in the capital, Su Xun received word from home that his wife had died. He immediately returned to Shu with Su Shi and Su Che in order to observe the obligatory 27 months of mourning.

Return to Kaifeng

Su Xun and his sons returned to the capital in 1059. This trip, which followed the southern river route from Shu to Kaifeng, produced the famous volume of 100 verses titled *Southern Travels Collection* (*Nanxing ji/Nan-hsing chi*). After their arrival in the capital, Ouyang Xiu sponsored Su Shi to take a special examination (called the *xianliang/hsien-liang*, or "worthy and virtuous," examination) designed to discover and promote scholars of extraordinary ability, regardless of background or previous experience. Su Che was also sponsored by a major political figure—Sima Guang (Ssu-ma Kuang) (1019–1086). Su Shi and Su Che both passed this special exam (only 39 candidates managed to pass this test throughout all the years of the Northern Song, 960–1127) and immediately received appointments to provincial posts. At the same time, Su Xun also managed to have himself appointed to a official position, though he never passed the government examinations. In 1061, then, all three Sus embarked upon careers that would earn them fame in Chinese literary and political history.

The details of Su Shi's long political career are complex, tedious, and at times confusing. It will suffice here to present only a brief outline of his activities as a government official. From early 1062 until early 1065, he served as an assistant prefect in a place called Fengxiang (in modern Shaanxi province), near the border of the non-Chinese Xixia state. Su's tour in Fengxiang was largely uneventful. He returned to Kaifeng in 1065, where he was appointed to a position in the History Institute. In the following year, tragedy struck the family a

second time: Su Xun died in the capital. His sons immediately left their posts and accompanied their father's body home for burial and observation of the required period of mourning. Almost three years passed before the Su brothers could return to the capital in 1068.

Criticism of the "Reformers"

The decade of the 1070s was an especially difficult time for Su Shi. Put simply, he found himself out of favor with the ruling political clique in Kaifeng. These "reformers" in the capital had initiated a number of policies to overhaul the dynasty's faltering administrative and fiscal system. Unfortunately, many of their "reforms" brought severe hardship to people in the provinces. Su Shi knew this because he had served in a number of provincial posts throughout the 1070s. Unable to repress his strong feelings on this issue, Su Shi leveled harsh criticisms against the reformers in the capital. These attacks earned him many enemies. In 1079 matters came to a head: Su was arrested on charges of slandering the emperor, imprisoned in Kaifeng, released, and finally exiled to a place in central China (on the banks of the Yangzi River) called Huang county (Huangzhou). Su spent four years there.

The major events in Su Shi's political career over the next 15 years essentially repeat the cycle just outlined. That is to say, Su returned to the capital in 1085 after the downfall of the "Reformers Party." Between 1086 and 1093 he held a variety of posts in Kaifeng and the provinces. In 1094, however, the Reformers made a political comeback, and Su Shi once again received exile orders. This time he was to proceed to Hui county (Huizhou) in remote Guangdong province in the south. And, in 1097, he was ordered to an even more distant and downright dangerous region—Hainan Island. But then, in 1100, Su was allowed to return to the mainland and was restored to office. He died the next year.

Su Shi's Poetry

It is evident from this brief biographical sketch that Su Shi spent much of his adult life moving from place to place, and shifting from office to office. Most scholar-officials in traditional China had similar experiences, for they were routinely dispatched to a new post once every three years. It is for this reason that much of Su Shi's literary output—especially his poetry—concerns his experiences traveling around the Chinese empire. But this is just one aspect of his work. The numerous styles and themes that characterize his 2,400 surviving poems make it impossible to arrange his verse into neat topical categories for discussion. For this reason, what follows merely touches upon some of the more salient characteristics and concerns of Su Shi's poetry.

Despite the failure of Su Shi's political ambitions, the humiliation he suffered during periods of exile, the disgrace resulting from his arrest and imprisonment for slandering the emperor, and the physical hardships suffered during extensive traveling, Su Shi expresses little bitterness in his poems. With the exception of the disappointment Su often felt (and wrote about) over the infrequency of meetings with his younger brother, a deep affection for his fellow man underlies much of Su Shi's writing. He even developed and openly expressed respect for his rival Wang Anshi (1021–1086), who led the very political group that was responsible for sending Su into exile no less than 12 times. Su Shi's affection for his fellow man reflects his strong interest in life itself. He seems fascinated with everyone and everything around him, and his keen power of observation is manifest in his poems. As an example, consider the last two couplets of "On the Yangzi Watching the Hills," a verse penned on the deck of a boat while passing through the scenic Three-Gorges portion of the river:

I look up; a narrow trail angles back and forth,
a man walking it, high in the distance.
I wave from the deck, trying to call,
but the sail takes us south like a soaring bird.

(WATSON, 1975, P. 17)

As for Su Shi's knack for observation, notice how, as told in "Written on the Wall at West Forest Temple," his painter's eye brilliantly "fails" to capture the essence of scenic Mount Lu (Lushan):

From the side, a whole range; from the end, a single
*   peak;*
far, near, high, low, no two parts alike.
Why can't I tell the true shape of Lushan?
Because I myself am in the mountain.

(WATSON, 1975, P. 108)

Critics and literary historians have praised this quatrain as the quintessential expression of Mount Lu, not only because Su Shi captures the vastness and variety of Lushan in just a few lines, but also because of the poet's simple yet brilliant observation about the impossibility of discerning the "true shape" (or essential nature) of the mountain. The general technique used to craft the two verses cited here is evident in many Su Shi poems: they are spontaneous, straightforward, and unrestrained. At the same time, they are often unconventional. Most Chinese poets would never call out to a stranger in the distance. Fewer still would take the time to chronicle their "failure" to capture the essence of a famous mountain.

As in the two samples of verses just considered, most of Su Shi's poems are descriptions of actual occurrences in his life (the one exception to this observation is verse he composed to be inscribed on paintings). Paging through his *Collected Works*, a Western reader would probably be surprised at the especially large number of poems he wrote for social occasions, such as drinking parties, farewell banquets, holiday gatherings, and so on, as well as the large number of verses written as correspondence with friends and relatives. Oftentimes, Su and his friends would use the same rhyme scheme when exchanging such social poems. Su Shi and his younger brother Su Che routinely echoed rhyme sequences in their poetic correspondence.

Another pervasive quality of Su Shi's literary works is philosophical or meditative reflection. As one would perhaps expect, Confucian ideals are present in Su's verse. We also find Buddhist ideas and Daoist (Taoist) musings. Su seems to have been interested in philosophical Daoism since the days of his youth, especially in the works of Laozi (Lao Tzu) and Zhuangzi (Chuang Tzu). His fascination with these teachings is perhaps most apparent in his sensitivity to the natural world in general, and to landscapes in particular. Tales about Daoist transcendents (*xian/hsien*) riding cranes through the heavens also fascinated him, as did the idea of the Creator (*zaohuazhe/tsao-hua che*)—a force ever-present in the natural world capable of influencing the destinies of all beings in the universe.

Su Shi's first contacts with Buddhism came from his parents. While his mother taught him about Pure Land piety and devotion, his father introduced him to Chan monks, who had won reputations based on literary achievements as well as their spiritual attainments. Su included among his circle of friends some of the most celebrated Buddhist monks of day. After his exile to Huangzhou in 1080, Su Shi's interest in Buddhism deepened. He turned inward in search of some release or accommodation from a life and career that was increasingly unpleasant. He immersed himself in Buddhist texts and meditation, and it was about this time that he adopted the sobriquet "Su of East Slope," after the plot of land he farmed in Huangzhou. During and after his exile there, Su's writings—including his poetry—display a renewed strength and increased vitality. A strong spirit of detachment also informs many of his best Huangzhou verses.

Although Su Shi's fame as a poet rests primarily on his masterpieces written in the traditional *shi* form, he achieved preeminence as a writer of other verse forms, including *ci* (lyrics for songs with lines of varying length, often arranged in two stanzas) and *wenfu* (a mix of prose and parallel, rhyming passages; sometimes translated as "prose poems" or "belletristic prose"). His experiments in the *ci* (song-lyric) form expanded the thematic scope of that genre. Essentially, Su Shi took a song form and molded it into a literary creation suitable for just about any subject. At the same time he infused his *ci* with wit and humor, a quality not often seen in earlier song-lyrics.

Su Shi's two "Prose Poems on the Red Cliff," written in 1082 during the Huangzhou exile, have also won him fame as a master of the *wenfu* (prose poem) form. In the Song dynasty, the prose-poem—an ancient literary genre that by the Tang (T'ang) dynasty (618–960) had become rigid, imitative, and elaborate displays of pedantry—found new life and vitality first from Ouyang Xiu and then from Su Shi. Su's prose poems are characterized by an easy, free-flowing, and buoyant style that is immediately accessible and appealing. Here are the closing lines of the first of the "Prose Poems on the Red Cliff," written after an all-night drinking party on a boat cruising the waters near the famous Red Cliff (site of a famous ancient naval battle):

> *My friend . . . washed the wine cups and filled them again. But the fruit and other things we had brought to eat were all gone and so, among the litter of cups and bowls, we lay down in a heap in the bottom of the boat, unaware that the east was already growing light.*

(WATSON, 1975, P. 96)

Su Shi's zest for life is indeed intoxicating. And it is precisely this quality that has most endeared him to readers for the last thousand years.

JAMES M. HARGETT

Further Reading

Translation

Watson, Burton, trans. *Selected Poems of Su Tung-p'o*. Revision of 1975 edition Port Townsend, WA: Copper Canyon Press, 1994.

Related Studies

Eagan, Ronald C.. *Word, Image, and Deed in the Life of Su Shi*. Cambridge, MA: Harvard University Press, 1994.

Fuller, Michael A.. *The Road to East Slope: The Development of Su Shi's Poetic Voice*. Stanford, CA: Stanford University Press, 1990.

Grant, Beata. *Mount Lu Revisited: Buddhism in the*

Life and Writings of Su Shih. Honolulu: University of Hawaii Press, 1994.

Hatch, George C. "Su Shih," in *Sung Biographies*, Ed. Herbert Franke. vol. 2: 900–68. Wiesbaden: Franz Steiner, 1976. This is one of the most insightful biographies of Su Shi available in English.

Lin, Yutang. The Gay Genius: *The Life and Times of Su Tungpo*. New York: The John Day Company, 1947.

ROMANCE OF THE WESTERN CHAMBER

Title in Chinese: *Xixiang ji (Hsi-hsiang chi)*
Author: Wang Shifu (Wang Shih-fu)
Born: c. 1230, Dadu (Ta-tu; modern Beijing)
Died: c. 1300
Literary Form: Romantic drama
Date of Composition: Second half of the thirteenth century

Major Themes

The union of a talented young scholar and a gifted young beauty represents the ideal of romantic love.
The most sensual and erotic of all Chinese worlds is dominated by images of water, moonlight, and shadowy monastery chambers, where yin, *or female, forces (represented by the lead female character Ying-ying) reign supreme over* yang, *or male forces (represented by the lead male character Student Zhang).*
All talented young scholars/gifted young beauty romances end happily, but the couple must first overcome a series of formidable obstacles before they are united.

Romance of the Western Chamber (also translated as *Story of the Western Wing*) has been praised by traditional and modern critics as China's greatest northern-style (*zaju*) drama. Since its appearance in the early decades of the Yuan (Yüan) dynasty (1260–1368), the play has enjoyed tremendous popularity, and through various adaptations in regional theater today remains a favorite among theatergoers in China. The great appeal and wide circulation of *Romance of the Western Chamber* has not only inspired numerous sequels and adaptations, and not only influenced untold numbers of later dramas, novels, and short stories, but also played a major role in the development of drama criticism in China.

Authorship of the Yuan dynasty *zaju* version of the *Xixiang ji* is usually attributed to Wang Shifu. As is the case with most Yuan playwrights, practically nothing is known about Wang's life and career. An entry in *The Ghost Register* (*Lugui bu*), a fourteenth-century source that provides some limited biographical information on Yuan dramatists, mentions only that Wang Shifu was a native of Dadu (modern Beijing) and that he composed a total of 14 plays. Three of these works survive in complete form: *Romance of the Western Chamber* (Xixiang ji), *Hall of Beautiful Spring (Lichun tang/Li-ch'un t'ang)*, and *Tale of the Dilapidated Kiln*

(Poyao ji/P'o-yao chi). The last two mentioned works are mediocre in quality and have not attracted much attention. A few critics have even questioned the attribution of these plays to Wang Shifu. As for the authorship of the *Xixiang ji*, some traditional scholars, most notably the influential critic Jin Shengtan (Chin Sheng-t'an) (1610–1661), have argued that *Romance of the Western Chamber* is actually the collaborative work of Wang Shifu and Guan Hanqing (Kuan Han-ch'ing). Jin and others contend that Wang composed the first four parts of the play, and Guan the fifth and final one. Modern critics, however, have convincingly discounted Jin Shengtan's dual-authorship theory.

The Basic Plot

The story line in the *Xixiang ji* can be summarized as follows: Student Zhang (Chang), a brilliant young scholar with a bright future, while on his way to the capital to continue his preparations for the civil service examinations, stops and takes lodging in a local monastery in order to visit an old friend who lives in the area. By chance, Widow Cui (Ts'ui), the widow of the late prime minister and coincidentally a distant relative of Zhang's, also stops at the same monastery while returning home with her two children to bury her husband. The very instant he first spies Madame Cui's beautiful young daughter, Ying-ying (sometimes her name is translated literally as "Oriole"), Zhang falls deeply in love with her. Ying-ying, however, has already been betrothed to the hideous Zheng Heng (Cheng Heng). After hearing this news, Student Zhang falls into a deep melancholic stupor. When a local military commander stages a mutiny, surrounds the monastery, and demands that Ying-ying be handed over to him, Madame Cui promises her daughter's hand to anyone who can protect her and her daughter. Student Zhang seizes this opportunity to call on his friend in the area, the powerful general Du Jue (Tu Chüeh), who immediately suppresses the rebellion. With Ying-ying and her family now saved from the bandits, Student Zhang thinks he can now look forward to marrying the love of his life. But then Madame Cui breaks her promise, and our love-struck hero—confused, desperate, and out of control—attempts to seduce the young girl; but she scolds him for his improper behavior and lascivious designs. The dispirited Zhang once again falls into deep depression and this time becomes seriously ill. Eventually, Ying-ying is brought by her maidservant Hongniang (Hung-niang; sometimes translated "Crimson") to spend the night with Zhang, and their relationship is consummated. Soon, however, their affair is discovered. Madame Cui promises Ying-ying to Zhang, but only if he succeeds in the civil service examinations. After Student Zhang travels to the capital, passes the exams, and returns to the monastery to claim his bride, he discovers that Ying-ying's original fiancé, Zheng Heng, has also shown up and that Madame Cui has once again reneged on her promise and has offered her daughter to Zheng. Finally, through a second intervention of Du Jue, the lovers are united in marriage and live happily ever after.

Sources of the Story

The story line in Wang Shifu's Yuan-dynasty play has two sources. The earliest of these is the Tang (T'ang) dynasty (618–907) short story "Story of Ying-ying" ("Ying-ying zhuan"/"Ying-ying chuan"), written by Yuan Zhen (Yuan Chen, 779–831), one of the most celebrated poets and statesmen of the period. The main source and immediate predecessor of the Yuan dynasty play, however, is Dong Jieyuan's (Tung Chieh-yüan's) (fl. 1190–1208) *Master Dong's Romance of the Western Chamber* (*Xixiang ji zhugongdiao*/*Hsi-hsiang chi chu-kung-tiao*). Dong's *zhugongdiao* (sometimes translated as "medley" or "chantefable") differs from Yuan Zhen's story, which is written in classical Chinese prose, in two significant ways. First, Dong's *Medley* consists of alternating verse sections (for singing) and prose passages (for narration); second, in "The Story of Ying-ying," Student Zhang abandons the prime minister's daughter after seducing her. In Dong's rendition, however, instead of rejecting Ying-ying, Zhang marries her in the end. The length of *Master Dong's Romance of the Western Chamber* (5,263 lines of verse and 184 prose passages, some of which are lengthy) may help to explain the extraordinary length of Wang Shifu's play—a pentalogy of five connected plays with a continuous story line throughout, each with four acts. This means that Wang's play is approximately five times longer than most other dramas of the Yuan period, which usually have only four acts.

Although Wang Shifu generously borrowed from Yuan Zhen's story and Master Dong's medley (like many Elizabethan dramatists, Yuan playwrights relied heavily on past stories, poems, and plays and made little attempt to invent completely original plot lines), his contribution and innovations in plot construction, characterization, and superb lyric poetry combine to make the *Xixiang ji* an outstanding work of dramatic literature in its own right. The central theme in the story, which pits the natural inclinations of a talented young scholar (*caizi*/*ts'ai-tzu*) and gifted young beauty (*jiaren*/*chia-jen*) against the barriers of conventional morality (represented in the play by the stern, double-dealing mother) and evil (represented by Zheng Heng, the original fiancée, and by Sun the Flying Tiger, leader of the mutiny) is a common theme in Yuan drama.

Wang Shifu's Creative Contributions

What makes Wang Shifu's story line outstanding, however, is the way in which he varies and alternates totally different scenes. For instance, we find moments of great tension, action, and suspense—such as the scene where the monastery is surrounded by bandits attempting to kidnap Ying-ying—as well as moments of hilarious comedy—such as the sacrificial scene in the temple when Ying-ying's extraordinary beauty disrupts what should have been a most solemn ceremony. On the other hand, we also find many extremely romantic and delicate moonlit scenes laden with the lovers' sighs and tears, the soothing notes of a Chinese zither, and the sweet fragrance of incense, flowery shadows, and gentle breezes—all simultaneously heightening the anticipation and eventual fulfillment of romantic love.

Student Zhang and Ying-ying's appeal as characters stems from the sometimes unpredictable way in which they diverge from the standard rules of behavior that governed every aspect of a young person's life in traditional China. Although cast in the stock roles of "talented scholar" and "gifted beauty," they are hardly "type" or conventional characters. Ying-ying at first appears as a quiet and modest young woman, dignified in her bearing and manner, and always mindful of the rules of propriety. Student Zhang also comes from a distinguished family. He initially presents himself as an upright, talented scholar whose one ambition in life is to pass the civil service examinations and win honor for himself and his family. In the end, however, Wang Shifu's paragons of beauty, talent, and decorum—Ying-ying and Zhang—are both overcome by their strong, uncontrollable desire for the physical fulfillment of love.

Perhaps the most fascinating character in *Romance of the Western Chamber* is Hongniang (Hung-niang), Ying-ying's trusted maidservant. Throughout the play she serves as a catalyst for the actions of the other major characters. At first, Hongniang acknowledges the rules of conventional morality. For instance, early on she reprimands Zhang for making improper inquiries about her mistress. But later, when Madame Cui reneges on her promise of Ying-ying's hand to Scholar Zhang, Hongniang becomes sympathetic to the young lovers. Unlike the typical maidservant character in Yuan dramas, who play nothing more than a stock, supporting role, Hongniang ingeniously lies, persuades, and manipulates Zhang and Ying-ying into action, and even openly reprimands Madame Cui for her double-dealing, all for the purpose of uniting the two young lovers.

Wang Shifu also excelled at composing *qu* (*ch'ü*), or song-poems (that is, the arias in the plays). In fact, the skill with which he composed the countless number of song-poems throughout *Xixiang ji* has been praised by virtually all critics, both traditional and modern, and perhaps more than any other reason, accounts for the greatness of his *Romance of the Western Chamber*. Whether depicting an evocative landscape, a humorous occasion in a temple, or an intimate love scene, Wang's song-poems blend scene, mood, and emotion in a way that evokes an almost overpowering depth of feeling. Take, for instance, the majestic lines sung by Student Zhang in the opening scene of the play, in which, on his way to the capital and away from home for the first time, he draws an analogy between a scene observed on the Yellow River and his own life:

East and west, it breaches into the nine regions,
North and south it threads together a hundred
* streams.*
A homing vessel: is it fast or not? How does one see
* it?*
Like a crossbow bolt's sudden leaving of the string.

(WEST AND IDEMA, 1991, P. 174)

Now consider Wang Shifu's delicate description of Ying-ying, also sung by Zhang in the early scenes of the play:

If it weren't for the softness of that fragrant path
* padded with tattered red,*

How could it betray the light imprint of her foot as it
*   treads the perfumed dust?*

(WEST AND IDEMA, 1991, P. 179)

Or the following, sung by Ying-ying at a feast given
in Zhang's honor as he is about to depart for the
capital:

I see him stop his welling tears, daring not let them
*   fall*
Lest others know.
Suddenly seeing each other, we bow our heads,
Heave heavy sighs,
Rearrange our garments of plain silk.

(WEST AND IDEMA, 1991 PP. 350–51)
JAMES M. HARGETT

Further Reading

Translation

West, Stephen H., and Wilt L. Idema, trans. *The
    Moon and the Zither: The Story of the Western
Wing.* Berkeley, CA: University of California
Press, 1991. This translation supplants all previous English renditions of the play. The translators also provide a study of the authorship, background, and major themes of the play.

Related Studies

Chen Lili, trans. *Master Tung's Western Chamber
    Romance (Tung Hsi-hsiang chi chu-kung-tiao).*
    Cambridge, MA: Cambridge University Press,
    1976. This work includes a study and translation
    of the text that served as the direct source of
    Wang Shifu's *Romance of the Western Chamber.*
Crump, J. I. Chinese *Theater in the Days of Kublai
    Khan.* Tucson, AZ: University of Arizona Press,
    1980. Crump's study offers an informative and
    entertaining introduction to Yuan dynasty
    theater.
Hightower, James R. "Yüan Chen and the Story of
    Ying-ying" in *Harvard Journal of Asiatic
    Studies* 33 (1973): 90–123. A study and transla-
    tion of the Tang dynasty tale that was the source
    of Wang Shifu's *Xixiang ji.*

THE PLAYS OF GUAN HANQING (KUAN HAN-CH'ING)

Author: Guan Hanqing (Kuan Han-ch'ing)
Born: c. 1220s
Died: c. 1300
Major Plays: *Lord Guan Goes to the Feast with a Single Sword, Crying for Cunxiao* (or *Death of the Winged Tiger General*), *Rescued by a Coquette, The Riverside Pavilion, The Jade Mirror Stand, The Butterfly Dream,* and *Injustice to Dou E* (or *Snow in Midsummer*).

Major Themes

A courageous and confident military hero will prevail over the enemy unless evil doers interfere (but those who do evil will eventually be punished).

Marriages based on love and mutual respect are more likely to lead to happiness than those that are not. It is better for a woman to marry an older man who loves her than a younger man who does not.

Women from various walks of life can possess intelligence, resourcefulness, and even fearlessness.

Although those who hold power in society often oppress the common people, if one vigorously remains true to a set of moral principles based on truth and fairness, there is always hope that justice will eventually prevail.

Guan Hanqing is China's best known and most prolific playwright. He lived during the Yuan (Yüan) dynasty (1260–1368), a time when China was invaded and occupied by foreign conquerors—the Mongols. This was the same period in which Marco Polo (c. 1254–1324) visited the Middle Kingdom. Despite the presence of alien rulers, the theater flourished in China under Mongol rule. The spectacular growth of cities at this time provided a fitting environment for all sorts of entertainment, especially dramatic performances. These urban centers in Yuan dynasty China were directly responsible the rise of the *zaju (tsa-chü)* drama, a theatrical form in four acts that consists mainly of dialogue and arias. Although this "golden age of Chinese drama," as it is so often called, produced a host of outstanding playwrights, none occupies a more preeminent position than Guan Hanqing. More than 60 plays are attributed to his authorship, some 21 of which are extant today. Fifteen of these works are complete and include several comedies and melodramas, one farce, and at least two works that might be called tragedies. The remainder survive only in partial or fragmented form.

Guan Hanqing's productivity and exalted status as the "father of Chinese drama" notwithstanding, few facts are known about his life. Scholars agree on only a few minor details of his biography: Guan was a native of Yanjing (later known as Dadu) in north China (modern Beijing); he once visited Lin'an, the capital of the Southern Song (Sung) dynasty, sometime after its fall to the Mongols in 1276; and he lived to an old age. Virtually every other surviving account or anecdote related to his life and career is controversial and thus unreliable. His extant plays, however, provide ample material to describe and define Guan's skill as a dramatic artist.

Guan's Artistic Priorities

The most distinguishing feature of Guan Hanqing's plays is the vivid picture they reveal of Chinese society under Mongol rule in the thirteenth century. A close reading of his extant works strongly suggests that Guan had two artistic priorities. First, he was most interested in portraying characters who are convincingly real and believable on stage. Guan Hanqing loathed one-dimensional, stereotypical characters such as women bound by rituals and behaviors designed by men (examples include the obedient young maidservant, the dutiful wife, the loyal widow, and so on). He also avoided common plot lines such as that of the young scholar, bound for the capital to take the civil service examinations, who encounters obstacle(s) on the road, eventually overcomes these impediments, and wins first-place in the examinations. Instead, Guan sought to achieve an atmosphere of realistic portrayal that mirrors the complexities of life in Yuan dynasty China, which helps to explain the general lack of supernatural miracles common to the works of many of his contemporary Yuan playwrights. Moreover, Guan generously mixes seriousness and humor to illustrate "positive" (filial piety) and "negative" (overblown vanity and pride are among his favorite targets modes of behavior in his characters.

As for his second artistic priority, although Guan Hanqing undoubtedly wrote dramatic works that were designed for performance and entertainment, like virtually all Chinese authors, he also created characters and story lines intended to instruct his audience. This didactic purpose of his plays always features the diametrically opposed forces of "good" (a paragon of moral virtue) and "evil" (an oppressor of the common people) in conflict with one another. Without exception, the forces of good eventually overcome those of evil.

Dramatic Themes

Although one could discuss Guan Hanqing's plays in a number of ways, a convenient and useful approach is by theme. This is because most plays written in China during the Yuan period fall into easily identifiable thematic categories, two or more of which often overlap in the same play. The most popular of these concern the following: love and marriage, religion and supernatural happenings, history/military and pseudo-historical/military figures and episodes, family and social situations, murder and courtroom drama, and bandit-hero adventures.

Guan's plots touch on all of these subjects; but he seems to have favored three types of works. One of these was the historical/military play, two repre-

sentative examples of which are *Lord Guan Goes to the Feast with a Single Sword (Dandao hui/Tan-tao hui)* and *Crying for Cunxiao (Ku Cunxiao/K'u ts'un-hsiao)*.

Lord Guan Goes to the Feast with a Single Sword is a historical drama set in the Three Kingdoms period (220–265) that celebrates the heroism of Lord Guan, a general of the state of Shu who loyally defends his ruler's territory against the kingdom of Wu. Throughout the play, Guan Hanqing focuses on Lord Guan's strength, courage, confidence, and invincibility. In the final scene, when asked to surrender, the general instead valiantly confronts and disposes of his enemy, then walks away unharmed.

Crying for Cunxiao is also a historical play, set in early tenth century. The story line centers around the brave and loyal general Li Cunxiao, who is slandered by his stepbrothers and rivals and eventually executed (he is torn to pieces by five carts). The emphasis in the fourth and final act is the guilt and remorse of Li Cunxiao's adopted father, the general Li Keyong (Li K'o-yung). As in all Yuan plays, the guilty evildoers (in this case, the two stepsons) are executed and the hero's unjust death is avenged.

Although Guan Hanqing's historical plays are not among his most powerful works, he penned *Lord Guan Goes to the Feast with a Single Sword, Crying for Cunxiao*, and similar plays because Yuan audiences demanded action and violence in dramatic performances. Plays featuring heroic/ military figures were an ideal vehicle to meet such audience demands. It might also be mentioned that these are the only plays in which Guan's male characters play "hero" roles.

The Drama of Love and Marriage

A second general theme in Guan's *Works* is love and marriage. This is common topic in Chinese literature, and is usually portrayed in a sterile and highly stylized manner. For example, in many (if not most) Yuan plays, young unmarried women are portrayed as "prizes" won by successful examination candidates. Rarely do we find a serious and complex character portrait of a woman. In Guan Hanqing's works, however, there is no shortage of such characters.

In *Rescued by a Coquette (Jiufeng chen/Chiu-feng ch'en)*, a play considered by many to be one of the best Yuan dynasty *zaju* comedies, Guan brilliantly portrays a battle of wits between a sing-song girl (that is, a prostitute-entertainer) and the powerful, evil son of an official. The playwright's ultimate purpose is to reveal the innermost thoughts and desires of the sing-song girl, who, as it turns out, is not lascivious and greedy but, like many women, interested in love, marriage, and security. Not only does the sing-song girl Zhao Paner (Chao P'an-erh) emerge as a crafty and worthy opponent to the profligate young official, but her wit, intelligence, and courage make her a genuine heroine.

Another female lead, Tan Qier (T'an Ch'i-erh), appears in *The Riverside Pavilion (Wangjiang ting/Wang-chiang t'ing)*. In this work we again encounter an intelligent and courageous heroine pitted against a worthless but mighty male rival—Lord Yang. After having Tan Qier prevail over her opponent, Guan Hanqing addresses the question of her widowhood. Although widows were strongly discouraged from remarrying in ancient China, Guan Hanqing allows Tan Qier to take a second husband. The playwright's description of their romantic love is unmatched in Chinese literature.

A third and final example of a love-and-marriage play is the *The Jade Mirror Stand (Yujing tai/Yü-ching t'ai)*. This work is based on a traditional story about a May-December marriage. Although such unions appeared "unnatural" to many in traditional China, Guan Hanqing apparently approved of such marriages. His message is very simple: it is better for a woman to marry an older man who loves her than a younger man who does not. At the same time, Guan portrays the serious and comic aspects of lust for physical love (at first, the old scholar is completely debased by his lechery) but the playwright masterfully does so in way that reveals physical desire as a natural rather than a sinful inclination.

Courtroom Dramas

Among Guan Hanqing's plays dealing with justice and trials, *Injustice to Dou E (Dou E yuan/Tou O yüan)* undoubtedly provides the most drama and greatest emotional appeal. The plot line of this and other "courtroom" dramas is similar: early on in the play the protagonist is wrongly accused of a crime and unjustly punished (execution is the usual form of punishment). The remaining acts focus upon retribution and the redress of wrongs, which is usually brought about in a courtroom scene by a wise judge, a bandit-outlaw, or supernatural intervention.

In the case of *Injustice to Dou E*, Dou E is a young widow who dutifully lives with and serves her mother in law. Their tranquil and uneventful world is suddenly shattered, however, with the arrival of two evil suitors, to whom the mother-in-law is indebted for saving her life earlier. The mother-in-law is willing to marry the older suitor, but Dou E—still faithful to her husband's memory and filial duty to her mother-in-law—steadfastly refuses. The younger suitor then decides to get rid of the mother-in-law (to "free" Dou E), but his plot goes awry and his accomplice is poisoned instead. Dou E is thereupon dragged off to court where she is forced to confess to killing the suitor, is sentenced to death, and then executed. Later, with the assistance of some timely divine intervention, the case is reopened, Dou E is exonerated posthumously of her guilt, and the villain is duly punished.

Throughout the play, but especially in the arias, Guan Hanqing elevates Dou E as a person of tremendous moral courage who, despite pain, torture, and even death, remains true to the virtues of chastity and filial duty. Her character is also appealing because she is a "mere" commoner who is unrelenting in her fight against oppression in a morally corrupt society. In the end, justice is won, but only after the innocent are forced to endure much suffering. Ultimately, Guan Hanqing's emphasis is on the moral lesson: though the good and innocent are often crushed by evil oppressors, all villains—

regardless of their social station—are eventually held accountable for their crimes.

JAMES M. HARGETT

Further Reading

Translations

Dolby, William, trans. *Kuan Han-ch'ing's San-ch'ü Poems*. Edinburgh: W. Dolby, 1990.

Shih, Chung-wen, trans. *Injustice to Tou O (Tou O Yüan): A Study and Translation*. Cambridge, MA: Cambridge University Press, 1972.

Yang, Hsien yi, and Gladys Yang, trans. *Selected Plays of Guan Hanqing*. 2nd. ed. Beijing: Foreign Languages Press, 1979. Contains a preface by Wang Jisi and translations of eight plays: three concerning justice and trials, three on love and marriage, and two works with historical themes. This is the only anthology of Guan Hanqing's plays in English. The quality of the translations, however, is poor.

Related Studies

Oberstenfeld, Werner. *Chinas bedeutendster Dramatiker der Mongolenzeit (1280–1368) Kuan Han-ch'ing*. Frankfurt am Main: Peter Lang, 1983.

Seaton, Jerome P. "A Critical Study of Kuan Han-ch'ing: The Man and His Works." Ph.D. dissertation, Indiana University, 1968. Still the only full-length study in a Western language on Guan Hanqing and his works. Includes extensive discussion and analysis of the plays.

Shih, Chung-wen. *The Golden Age of Chinese Drama: Yüan Tsa-chü*. Princeton, N.J.: Princeton University Press, 1976. This is probably the best general introduction to Yuan dynasty theater available in English.

THE WATER MARGIN

Title in Chinese: *Shuihu zhuan (Shui-hu chuan)*
Other Titles of English Translations: *Outlaws of the Marsh, All Men Are Brothers*
Author: Shi Nai'an (Shih Nai-an) and/or Luo Guanzhong (Lo Kuan-chung)
Born: c. fourteenth century
Died: Date unknown
Literary Form: Novel in colloquial language
Date of Composition: Composed c. middle of fourteenth century, with numerous subsequent recensions

Major Themes

Loyalty to the state and righteousness among friends are of utmost importance.
The integrity and survival of the heroic community must be preserved at all cost.
The government is run by corrupt officials, and ordinary people are powerless to resist their oppression.
The only way to fight a corrupt government is to band together and uphold a gang morality.
Women are creatures of lust and when they betray their men they deserve to be tortured and killed.
People who are not part of the gang are fair game to be plundered and slaughtered.

In February 1121, a band of 36 outlaws under the leadership of a man named Song Jiang (Sung Chiang) wreaked havoc in the province of Shandong (Shantung) in northern China. This small contingent of troublemakers was but a minor irritant when compared with the whole range of threats (both domestic and external) that the hapless Emperor Huizong (Hui-tsung, r. 1101–1125) of the Song (Sung) dynasty (960–1278) had to confront as his reign declined precipitously due to official malfeasance and the resulting widespread discontent and resentment among his subjects. Fortunately for the emperor, Song Jiang's group soon surrendered to the government forces dispatched against it. Indeed, in an unexpected twist of events, Song and his cohorts joined the government in the suppression of other larger-scaled rebellions, including the one led by the infamous Fang La in the south.

The above are the bare facts that formed the core of *Shuihu zhuan*, China's most celebrated classic novel on the shadowy world of bandits, ruffians, and vagabonds. Song Jiang, China's version of Robin Hood, became a fascinating figure for storytellers, dramatists, and writers within a century after his death. During the succeeding centuries and under different dynastic reigns, the story of Song and his comrades was told and enacted with increasing embellishment and complexity. The prompt books and scripts used by the storytellers and village actors to make each episode of the band's exploits more exciting than the previous one helped to create a special aura for this group of outlaws.

As the stories evolved, Song Jiang's gang of heroes also expanded in size. Now numbering 108—with 36 portrayed as major figures who were believed to be incarnations of celestial stars and the remaining 72 as minor supporting characters born of terrestrial but equally divine origins—members of the *shuihu* (marsh) band are depicted as driven by corrupt officials and a rapacious government to congregate at Liangshanbo, a mountainous stronghold surrounded by a reed marsh hundreds of acres in area and dissected by innumerable waterways and secret hideouts. There they form a brotherhood to register their protest against the unjust government and exemplify a justice that often contravenes the legal code.

The first full-length novel on the Liangshanbo band was based on the prompt books, popular song narratives, dramas, and even antecedent prose works that covered much of the storylines in rudimentary form. Completed most probably during the transitional decades from the Yuan to the Ming dynasties (mid-1300's), this version was traditionally attributed to either Shi Nai'an (Shih Nai-an) or Luo Guanzhong (Lo Kuan-chung), or to both. Both Shi and Luo were literary talents of considerable renown who hailed from the Lower Yangzi (Yangtze) River region in the fourteenth century. As a matter of fact, Luo has also been associated with another classic Chinese novel, the *Sanguozhi yanyi (San-kuo chih yen-i) (Romance of the Three Kingdoms)*. Yet neither's authorship of *The Water Margin* has been irrefutably established. At the same time, no other plausible name has been identified either.

The Shi-Luo edition, if it ever existed at all, is no longer extant. However, most students of Chinese literature agree that it most likely contained a unified account of all 108 heroes, provided many details in the full character portrayal of all the important figures, and offered a closure to the stories of these men (and a few women) whose colorful lives had captivated the imagination of the Chinese people. This Shi-Luo prototype version apparently went untouched for the next two centuries. Beginning in the middle of the sixteenth century, however, various recensions of the novel appeared. These versions represented different redactions, emphases, and interpretations, ranging in length from 70 to 124 chapters.

The most popular and influential version of the *Shuihu zhuan* is the 70-chapter recension which first appeared in the middle of the seventeenth century. For nearly 200 years it overshadowed and eclipsed all other versions. Edited and commented upon by the scholar Jin Shengtan (Chin Sheng-t'an) (1608–1661), this edition has the story of the Liangshan heroes end abruptly. After all 108 of them have, due to various personal circumstances, found their way to Mt. Liang and assembled together into a sworn brotherhood, the entire band is executed by order of the government in a dream by one of the main characters. In the longer and earlier versions, the Liangshanbo group surrenders to the government out of a sense of loyalty, and even helps it suppress several rebellions. In the course of doing so, however, many of the members die off. In the end, even Song Jiang is martyred when he is ordered to drink a poisonous wine sent to him by his persecutors in the name of the Emperor. His other trusted lieutenants commit suicide. The tragic deaths of the Liangshan heroes only help to enhance their mystique and popularity. Their poignant and colorful lives have become legendary.

The Historical Context and the Major Characters of the Novel

The last years of the Northern Song dynasty, presided over by Emperor Huizong, an artistically and romantically inclined individual with no political or administrative savvy, were very bad times for the Chinese people. Externally, the country was threatened by restless border tribes such as the Khitans and the Jurchens, who saw the weakness of China as a golden opportunity for them to take over the reins of government. Domestically, there was widespread disaffection among the people as the rich enjoyed official patronage and succeeded in fattening themselves further, while the vast majority of the populace was left vulnerable to exorbitant taxation, rapacious extortions, and brazen persecutions. Otherwise law-abiding citizens were often driven to criminality and outright rebellion because of the unreasonable demands of the government and the insatiable avarice of the officials.

The principal characters of *The Water Margin* come from precisely this lower stratum of Northern Song society—good people in bad times forced by various circumstances to "climb Mt. Liang" and become outlaws in the eyes of the government. Though the novel identifies 108 men and women as leaders of the Liangshanbo lair, only a few stand out as true presences who deserve detailed artistic description. Its success in portraying the personalities of these individual heroes is what earns the novel its lasting place in Chinese literature and folklore. Included among the figures that receive the most focused depiction are the band leader Song Jiang, his axe-wielding and impulsive sworn brother Li Kui (Li K'uei), the wild and gluttonous monk Lu Zhishen (Lu Chih-shen), the tiger-killing hunter Wu Song (Wu Sung), and the upright but luckless military instructor Lin Chong (Lin

Ch'ung). All of them, and many others in the novel, have checkered lives filled with strong emotions and vitality. They are flesh-and-blood characters who inhabit the vibrant world of low-ranking clerks, military officers, merchants, hunters, thieves, monks, and innkeepers. Their diverse background provides an authentic and lively depiction of China's real populace.

The Water Margin is most captivating when it traces the career of these major characters before they become outlaws. The stories of how Song Jiang is forced to kill his mistress who threatens to expose him to the authorities for serving as an informant for some criminal elements, how Li Kui kills a tigress and her cubs for their having devoured his aging mother, how Lu Zhishen wreaks havoc in a Buddhist temple after a wild bout of gluttonous eating and excessive drinking, how Wu Song murders his adulterous sister-in-law and her lover to avenge the death of his older brother, and how Lin Chong is driven into total desperation by unscrupulous officials who covet his beautiful wife, have all become the most well-known and memorable episodes of *The Water Margin*. They are part of the collective experience of the Chinese people.

After the heroes have assembled at Liangshanbo, their attention turns to survival and aggression. Numerous military campaigns are launched against neighboring communities and resistance is offered to the government forces sent to suppress them. There is much bloodshed and carnage, brought about by ingenious stratagem and heroic disregard for danger. More fighting occurs even after the band surrenders to the government, as it now dedicates itself to the defeat of the state's other more threatening enemies. The ranks of the Liangshan brotherhood become thinner as the campaigns progress, ending in total destruction with the deaths of Song Jiang and the other characters.

Loyalty and Righteousness

As pseudo-history *The Water Margin* provides a vivid picture of the decadence and corruption of the final years of the Northern Song court. Surrounded by sycophantic ministers whose greed has resulted in the disaffection of the people toward his reign, the Huizong Emperor is portrayed by the novel as an ineffectual monarch who hardly qualifies to sit on the throne. The entire empire is allowed to disintegrate because the people are exorbitantly taxed and the border defense is lax, thereby inviting the "barbarians" to develop designs on China. The society is rife with tension, as the displaced peasants become roving bandits and as the border tribes threaten invasion. The loyalty *(zhong/chung)* of the Liangshan heroes is thus made inexplicable, in light of such an undeserving recipient. Yet somehow the emperor is left unscathed, while the Liangshan gang directs its wrath mainly at the ministers. This is how the novel upholds loyalty to the state, yet maintains a populist hostility towards the government. The state, symbolized by the emperor, and the government, represented by the ministers, are conveniently divorced. Just at the point when the combined strength of the heroes has proved to be invincible, as evidenced by the repeated defeat of the imperial forces sent against them, the Liangshan band decides to surrender and to ask for the emperor's pardon. This is all the more remarkable in light of the fact that Song Jiang and his comrades are actually in an uncontested position to take over the empire and to receive the Mandate of Heaven. Ironically, of course, their loyalty is repaid with treachery and persecution— not by the emperor, but by his sinister ministers— that result in the dispersal of the band and the death of all the major leaders.

Of far more significance to the Liangshan heroes is the cardinal Confucian virtue of righteousness *(yi/i)*, here better understood as fidelity to one's comrades. It is this sense of abiding friendship and commitment among the heroes that informs many of the most memorable scenes in the novel. Because of Lin Chong's appreciation of his martial arts, the monk Lu Zhishen dedicates himself to Lin's protection by killing the guards as the latter is framed by Minister Gao (Kao) and is targeted to be murdered on his way to the destination of his exile. Also, because of his indebtedness to a comrade, Wu Song slaughters a local bully and his entire family without hesitation. Likewise, another hero named Yang Xiong (Yang Hsiung) is perfectly willing to torture and sadistically kill his wife who dares to slander his sworn brother Shi Xiu (Shih Hsiu). All these are examples of a gang mentality that conflicts with other normative values such as benevolence, altruism, and commiseration for the suffering of others.

Pearl Buck's rendering of the title of the novel as *All Men Are Brothers* is misleading precisely because the members of the gang are extremely sparing in their bestowal of friendship. They are an exclusive and tightly-knit group, generous and loyal to one another, but callous and cruel to all outsiders. It may be more appropriate to regard the theme of the novel as "some men are brothers, but the rest are enemies of the brotherhood."

The narrative is replete with episodes of wanton violence perpetrated by the heroes against all others who either actively oppose them or who simply have the misfortune of standing in the path of their destructive outbursts.

Violence and Aggression

All too frequently, the Liangshan members take justice into their own hands, unflinchingly inflicting mayhem and murder even on innocent bystanders. The sadistic cruelty with which the gang attacks the Zhu (Chu) family village and the Zeng (Tseng) market town is a glaring example of this callousness toward bloodshed and suffering. This apparent absence of compassion is sometimes curiously exhibited toward fellow band members as well, particularly during recruitment attempts or maneuvers to preserve unity. In these cases, deceit and cunning are practiced with justification. One example of the former is the tactics used by the band to persuade the military commander Qin Ming (Ch'in Ming) to join, which involves a stratagem whereby the hapless Qin will be denounced by the government as a traitor and his entire family punished with death, thus driving him to seek shelter with the gang. An incident exemplifying the latter is Song Jiang's tricking his sworn brother Li Kui into drinking the poisonous wine which he himself has been ordered to consume by the corrupt officials in the name of the emperor, for the rather twisted reason that it will prevent Li from rebelling after Song's death, thereby preserving the loyalist fame of the Liangshan heroes.

Misogyny and the Mistreatment of Women

Another noteworthy feature of the novel is its portrayal of, as well as attitude toward, women. To the modern reader, the streak of misogyny in *The Water Margin* is very apparent. Women are generally scorned by the heroes variously as ignorant nonentities, burdensome weaklings who invariably cause trouble for their mates, and outright adulteresses whose insatiable sexual appetite often results in death for themselves and for their partners. In short, the heroes generally hold women in contempt for being helpless creatures, objects of lust, and aggressive pursuants of sexual fulfillment. Women are therefore treated with callousness and brazen cruelty. They are viewed as enemies of all good men who, by definition, have to resist the temptation offered by their very existence. The female gender is associated with a flood-like destructive power that has to be combatted in order to protect the honor and integrity of the heroes, most of whom are bachelors. The few women among the gang are veritable amazons who have completely lost their femininity and are counted as warriors in their own right.

Thus the Liangshan members harbor a misogyny that, when combined with the wanton violence they commit, makes them most sadistic in their punishment of women who have wronged them. The utter abandon and wild savagery with which the *femme fatale* characters, such as Pan Jinlian (P'an Chin-lien) and Pan Qiaoyun (P'an Ch'iao-yun), are tortured and killed by the heroes produce some of the most hair-raising and blood-curdling scenes of the novel.

Shuihu zhuan occupies a lasting place in Chinese literature. It depicts a fascinating world of diverse characters and real emotions. It has been interpreted as a work upholding the normative values of loyalty and righteousness, and as a proto-revolutionary narrative glorifying anti-government protests. The central figures are *déclassé* members of Chinese society, whose trials and tribulations have become part of Chinese folklore. Yet the novel's endorsement of violent savagery and deceitful trickery makes it a rather unsettling work for the cultural historian of China. The blind rage and the dark destructive power with which many of the heroes strike out at their opponents are truly frightening. The misogynist attitude of the Liangshan band, expressed blatantly with sadistic cruelty, is equally disturbing. Perhaps it is this successful combination of both the bright and the dark sides of the Chinese mentality that makes the novel so captivating.

RICHARD SHEK

Further Reading

Translations

Buck, Pearl S., trans. *All Men Are Brothers.* New York: The John Day Company, 1933. Based on the 70-chapter edition.

Jackson, J. H., trans. *Water Margin.* Shanghai: The Commercial Press, 1937. Based on the 70-chapter edition.

Shapiro, Sidney, trans. *Outlaws of the Marsh.* Beijing: Foreign Language Press, 1988. Based on a combination of the 70- and 100-chapter editions.

Related Studies

Hsia, C. T. *The Classic Chinese Novel.* New York: Columbia University Press, 1968. Chapter 3 of this highly authoritative analysis is focussed on this novel. Very suggestive approaches to the understanding of its major themes.

Irwin, Richard G. *The Evolution of a Chinese Novel: Shui-hu-chuan.* Cambridge, MA: Harvard University Press, 1966. The only full-length monographic study of the novel in English. It examines the antecedents to the prose novel and provides a useful synopsis of each of the 100 chapters of the novel as an appendix.

Plaks, Andrew H. *The Four Masterworks of the Ming Novel.* Princeton, N.J.: Princeton University Press, 1987. Chapter 4 of this monumental work is devoted to a careful structural and textual analysis of this novel. It is a good source for the voluminous secondary scholarship on the novel written by Chinese, Japanese, and European scholars.

ROMANCE OF THE THREE KINGDOMS

Title in Chinese: *Sanguo zhi yanyi (San-kuo chih yen-i)*
Author: Attributed to Luo Guanzhong (Lo Kuan-chung)
Born: c. 1330 in Taiyuan, Shanxi Province, China
Died: c. 1400
Literary Form: Novel in the vernacular, with poetry and rhymed prose
Date of Publication: 1522

Major Themes

Loyalty and righteousness make a hero.
Human beings must act in harmony with heaven, earth, and other persons to arrive at success and power.
History provides lessons for all posterity.
Disunity invites conquest.
The legitimate succeeding emperor calls for lineage, courage, and virtue.

The history of the collapse of the Han dynasty and the following period of the Three Kingdoms (A.D. 220–265) was first recorded by the historian Chen Shou (Ch'en Shou) (died A.D. 297), who served in court. This record was written in 65 chapters which consist of biographies of some of the important figures of that age. The novel *Romance of Three Kingdoms* (sometimes called *Story of Three Kingdoms*), with a preface dated 1494, was not published until 1522.

The presumed author of this novel is Luo Guanzhong, a writer who did not leave much information about himself behind for posterity. With the sobriquet "Huhai sanren"/"Hu-hai san-jen" ("Wanderer by Lake and Sea"), Luo was a loner. A man who was keenly interested in Chinese history, Luo in his lifetime was famous for editing and revising works by previous writers. *Three Kingdoms* is one of them, to cite an example. Another well-known Chinese novel, *The Water Margin (Shuihu zhuan)*, is also sometimes attributed to Luo.

Luo was not the magician who changed the historical record of the Three Kingdoms into novel form. During the time gap between the Three Kingdoms period to the Ming dynasty (1368–1643) when Luo lived, there appeared various additions and changes to the historical record by Chen Shou. For example, Pei Songzhi (P'ei Sung-chih) (373–451), a scholar-official who lived in the Jin dynasty

(265–419) after Chen, added to his predecessor's records a vast amount of materials from over 200 sources. Pei may have been the first person to insert certain fictional elements into the records. When it came to the Northern Song period (1066–1084), Sima Guang (Ssu-ma Kuang), another court historian, wrote a new history of China, beginning with 403 B.C. to A.D. 959. His record of Late Han to the Three Kingdoms period again finds its way into the novel *Three Kingdoms*. The earliest printed version of the novel appeared around 1321–1323, entitled *The Three Kingdoms, a Popular Tale (Sanguo Zhi Pinghua)*, during the Yuan dynasty (1277–1367). This version is a conglomeration of episodes and stories from Yuan drama, prompt books by professional storytellers, and records from various historical documents. When these altered materials accumulated over the centuries came to Luo's hands, he had to administer a major revision in order to make it an interesting and coherent piece of literature.

A major drawback to the *Pinghua* version is its use of stories involving the supernatural and superstitions. In this book, the historical upheaval of the Three Kingdoms is enveloped in a retribution/karma thematic frame. The story begins with the first emperor of Han wrongly executing his three generals in court. When their souls finally go down to Hades for judgment, the three generals are given a chance to avenge themselves in their next life. They are reborn as the three leaders of the Three Kingdoms, overthrowing the last Han emperor, while the judge from Hades himself is reborn as the one who finally overcomes all three and unites China once again as Jin. With such a preternatural setting, the *Pinghua* version was never considered a worthy book for the serious Confucian reader. It was pure entertainment for those who read or listened to it.

Luo's version of *Three Kingdoms* has 24 volumes, with two sections to each volume. He not only created China's first novel but was also a renowned author of popular fiction in his time. By taking the crude and unsophisticated *Pinghua* version and changing it into a novel with accurate names and places, Luo embellished the book with vivid descriptions and lively characterizations. Historical facts were reinstalled, while supernatural events, such as the reincarnation incidents, were eliminated. Luo's version was not published until 1522, over 100 years after his death, a time when publishing had become a more widespread and cheaper practice than handcopying.

Yet, interestingly enough, the version of *Three Kingdoms* we are reading today is not exclusively Luo's but is also the work of a seventeenth-century writer named Mao Zonggang (Mao Tsung-kang). Just as Luo has revised his predecessors' works, his own were also rewritten by his successors. In the Qing dynasty (1644–1910), Mao, following his father Mao Lun's directorship, took up the pen to revise Luo's *Three Kingdoms*. The format of the novel was changed so that it contained 120 chapters, with many stylistic changes that brought the work even closer to history and reality. It was the Jiangsu native, Mao, who actually increased the readability of the book with his talents for revision—deleting cumbersome verses and putting more emphasis on rhetoric and syntax.

The Historical Background

Romance of the Three Kingdoms is an historically-based work presented in fictional form. The time period covered begins with the end of the Han dynasty, A.D. 168 to the year of the first emperor of Jin in A.D. 280. The Three Kingdoms refers to the three regions of Shu Han, Wei, and Wu that fought against one another to vie for power after the fall of the Han empire.

The region of Shu Han, which occupies the upper Yangzi Valley in the southwest, was led by Liu Bei (Liu Pei; also known as Xuande/Hsüan-te), Guan Yu (Kuan Yü, also known as Yunchang/Yünch'ang) and Zhang Fei (Chang Fei; also known as Yide/I-te). Wei, in the Yellow River plains, was under the command of Cao Cao (Ts'ao Ts'ao; also known as Cao Mengde/Ts'ao Meng-te). Wu, controlling the lower Yangzi Valley in the central east, was the territory of Sun Quan (Sun Chüan; also known as Zhongmou/Chung-mou).

Out of the wars among these three forces, there emerge political strife and court intrigues. The first 80 chapters of the book deal with the reign of the last emperor of Han, Xian (Hsien). The next 40 chapters concentrate on the kingdom's split into the hands of three powers, Liu, Cao, and Sun. Chapter 120 depicts the founding of Jin (Chin). The total number of characters portrayed in the book comes to nearly a thousand.

Because of the storytelling tradition in the Song (Sung) period, and the aid of the dramatists" collaboration during the Yuan (Yüan) dynasty, the heroes from *Three Kingdoms* are not strangers to the common people. There might be some who have never read the book, but most Chinese know about Liu Bei, Guan Yu, and Cao Cao. Children, too, are familiar with the particular episodes that contain lessons for the young. For example, in chapters 37 and 38, the Shu Han leader Liu Bei attempts three times in extremely bad weather to meet a renowned hermit-scholar and seek his advice. When Liu finally finds the hermit, Zhuge Liang (Chu-ko Liang) (also known as Kong Ming/K'ung Ming), he is given extensive and wise advice by the sage. Liu begs Zhuge Liang to leave his hermitage and join Liu's company so that he will be available for advice. Zhuge at first refuses, but he recognizes Liu's need and appreciates his sincerity, and he finally agrees to leave his hermitage. This episode is a lesson in humility. The great general disdains the use of his power to force Zhuge to join him; he makes his need known and moves the sage by his persistence. Zhuge becomes his prime minister and a great military stategist.

The Peach Garden Vow

One of the most famous scenes in the book is the taking of a vow by Liu, Guan, and Zhang in a peach orchard, where they swear to stay together, help one another, and persevere in their alliance until death:

> We three, Liu Pei, Kuan Yü and Chang Fei, though of different families, swear brotherhood, and promise mutual help to one end. We will rescue each other in difficulty, we will aid each other in danger. We swear to serve the state and save the people. We ask not the same day of birth but we seek to die together. May Heaven, the all-ruling, and Earth, the all-producing, read our hearts, and if we turn aside from righteousness or forget kindliness, may Heaven and man smite us!

(BREWITT-TAYLOR, TR., 1925, 1985)

This pledge of mutual support and loyalty remains as an example of exemplary friendship and love. The three "brothers" have become popular heroes and appear in embroidery, paintings, and drama.

Cao Cao, the Image of Evil

Cao Cao, the villain of the novel, is the very embodiment of hypocrisy, treachery, and evil. Serving as the prime minister of Han, Cao utilizes his power to usurp the kingdom. His ruthlessness shows itself when his father and his family are robbed and killed by a rebel group. He brings his forces to invade the city and proceeds to kill the city's commander, as well as all the commoners he comes across (chapter 10).

Another case of Cao's cruelty appears in chapter 4. Before he comes to power, Cao tries to assassinate the then-incumbent prime minister, Dong

Zhuo (Tung Cho), but fails. Dong orders immediate pursuit of Cao, who has fled into his father's sworn brother, Lu's, household. There the host plans to slaughter a pig to serve a feast for the guest. As soon as Cao sees the family sharpening a knife, he takes it as a sign of Lu's betrayal. Without looking into the facts, Cao kills Lu's family of eight. When Cao meets Lu on his way back from purchasing wine for the occasion, Cao does not spare Lu either, thus killing the whole family.

Cao's philosophy in life is that he need not be grateful to anyone, and he will not let anyone take advantage of him. For his selfish and vicious acts, as portrayed in *Romance of the Three Kingdoms,* Cao has become the image of ultimate evil in Chinese history.

Zhuge Liang, Military Strategist

There are more than 100 big and small battles described in the novel. The opposing forces require many military advisers and war strategists. The most well-known adviser of all undoubtedly is the prime minister of Shu Han, Zhuge Liang, the hermit who agreed to assist Liu Bei in the attempt to conquer Cao Cao. Zhuge is not only a learned man but also a sorcerer with magic powers. By looking at heaven and reading the stars, the sage is able to foretell the weather, predict life and death, as well as other important future events. Yet his best talents stem from his wisdom in strategic planning. As soon as the enemy hear his name, they shake with fear. Even after his death, his name affects people far and near. In chapter 104, after Zhuge has died, his army follows his idea of putting up a wooden image of him to frighten the enemy away.

Zhuge Liang's shrewdness is manifested in chapter 46 when he is given three days by his ally to make 10,000 arrows, preparing for combat with Cao Cao. Instead of asking for the necessary raw materials to accomplish this major project, Zhuge asks for 20 ships each equipped with 30 men and 1,000 bundles of straw. The bundles of straw were lashed against the sides of the ships. For two days, Zhuge relaxes in his camp. On the evening of the third day, in the midst of a thick fog that Zhuge predicts, Zhuge orders his ships to close in on Cao's anchored fleet and army by the river, beating the drums and shouting out loud at the same time. Cao, suspecting a surprise attack by Zhuge, hidden by the fog, orders his soldiers to shoot arrows out as quickly as possible. When Zhuge's ships return by daybreak, they bring back with them more than 10,000 arrows caught in the straw bundles. This incident proves Zhuge's cleverness and his ingenious ability to predict the weather conditions.

Another resourceful military strategist in the novel is Zhou Yu (Chou Yü), an ally of Han. In the battle of Three Rivers as recounted in chapter 45, Zhou, without losing a single man, tricks Cao into killing two of his most capable generals, Cai and Zhang. It begins with Cao's sending forth a spy named Jiang (Chiang) to recruit Zhou, hoping to weaken Liu Bei's military force. Jiang, being a childhood friend of Zhou's, guarantees that he will be able to persuade Zhou to surrender. When Jiang arrives at Zhou's camp, he is greeted with warmth and enthusiasm. Zhou orders his men to relax, saying that he will take the night off and enjoy it with his longtime friend. Both men drink and talk, while the name Cao never crosses their lips. During the night, Zhou becomes drunk and invites Jiang to stay for the night in the host's tent. During his sleep Zhou mumbles about having Cao's head in a matter of days. On the desk, Jiang finds a confidential letter presumably written by Cao's two generals, Cai and Zhang, stating that they are forced to work under him, and they swear to decapitate Cao as soon as the chance arises. Immediately, Jiang hides this letter on his person and pretends to be asleep.

Zhou wakes up, and having forgotten what happened the night before, asks who is the man sleeping next to him. The host also inquires of the guards outside the tent whether they have heard him talking in his sleep. Then a guard comes announcing the arrival of a secret messenger from the Cao force. The message is: Generals Cai and Zhang report that nothing can be done soon. At this, Zhou returns to his tent and finding Jiang still in bed, falls asleep again himself. Jiang now thinks of leaving Zhou before he discovers the loss of the confidential letter. He steals out of camp and rushes back to Cao with the important news of Cai and Zhang's betrayal. When Cao sees the letter, in his fury he orders the two generals to be executed. It is only afterwards that Cao realize that both he and Jiang have fallen into Zhou's trap.

Courage, Bravery, and Righteousness

Romance of the Three Kingdoms is a book of heroes and heroic feats. Zhuge is a hero because he is a capable statesman and a shrewd strategist. Liu Bei is a hero because he respects the learned and the wise like Zhuge. Zhang Fei, his sworn brother, although an impulsive man, is a mighty warrior. He is described as a strong man with a thunderous voice. There is a time in the novel when Zhang succeeds in driving off an army with his roar. He is a man of excellent character: he admires and supports whoever is a person of integrity, and he is dedicated to defeating the wicked.

Most readers would agree that Guan Yu, one of the sworn brothers of Liu Bei, is the hero of the novel. In his character, we find both courage and bravery. Described as a strong man with a deep, ruddy face, Guan is wounded during one of his military exploits by an arrow dipped with poison (chapter 75). The renowned doctor Huatuo (Hua-t'o) comes and offers his service to cure him. Huatuo proposes an operation and suggests the use of a pole, on which a ring hangs, to hold Guan's afflicted arm in place. Covering Guan's face, he would be able to cut open his arm, reach to the bone to remove the poison. Yet Guan turns this ghastly surgery into a chess game with meat and wine. Discarding the use of the pole, the general sits calmly at a chess game with his colleague, Ma, drinking wine and enjoying his meat. While the doctor is doing his cutting, scratching, and sewing, Guan is talking, eating, and drinking. All present are amazed at the general's courage. In chapter 50, when Cao is about to lose the war and be captured, Guan sets him free at the last moment, paying Cao back for his favors in the past. For what he has done, Guan is prepared to face death by court martial.

Another physician, Ji Ping (Chi P'ing), shows

both courage and loyalty as a subject of Han (chapter 23). In order to get rid of the rebellious prime minister, Cao Cao, Ji Ping vows to sacrifice himself and his family if need be. He signs a secret pact with a loyal group at court, waiting for the chance to take Cao's life. In pledging his oath, to show his determination he bites off one of his fingers. Ji Ping's chance comes when Cao summons him to cure his chronic headache. Carefully Ji prepares a poisoned bowl of herbs. Cao, who has been forewarned by a runaway servant from one of the men in the loyal group, asks Ji to taste it first. When Ji tries to force it down Cao's throat, the latter pushes the bowl to the ground where the tiles are cracked by the poison. Cao immediately orders torture on Ji and asks for the names of the loyal group. The doctor is under such severe physical torture that no spot on his body is not bruised or bleeding. Then Cao orders that Ji's other nine fingers be cut. When Ji claims that he still has lips and a tongue to curse Cao, the latter orders Ji's tongue to be pulled. At this point, the pain-stricken Ji kills himself by crushing his head against the steps. This episode reveals a determined and pure soul. Ji Ping is now another word for loyalty in Chinese history.

Not only are men devoted and patriotic in saving their country, but women are too. The few female characters in the *Three Kingdoms*, such as Empress Fu (chapter 66) and Madam Sun (chapter 55) are women of courage and intelligence. Under house arrest, Empress Fu tries to save the emperor by inciting a rebellion against the vicious power of Cao, who later discovers the truth and beats her to death, killing at the same time, her two sons and her father's family. Madam Sun, a woman used by her brother Sun Quan to appease Liu Bei, helps Liu to escape her brother's capture. She is described as a martial arts master with an army of trained maidservants.

The one woman who succeeds in initiating the downfall of a wicked and obnoxious ruler is Diao Chan (Tiao Ch'an) (chapters 8–9). This is during the time before Cao rises to power. The Han prime minister, Dong Zhuo (Tung Cho), usurps power from the emperor and plans to rule the country. A faithful courtier named Wang devises a plan to create conflict between the two most fearsome powers in the country, Dong and his adopted son, Lu. Wang bids Diao Chan, the most beautiful of his domestic entertainers whom he treats as his own daughter, to lure both Lu and Dong so that there will be dissension between them. Wang arranges matters so that Diao is promised to both Lu and Dong. When Wang sends Diao to Dong, he tells Lu that he is forced to do it because of his fear of Dong. Diao, with tears, encourages Lu to kill his father so that they can be together for the rest of their lives. Under Lu's sword, Dong dies; his head is cut off and exhibited in a public square.

The Preternatural and Retribution

Although Mao and Luo, the two main editors of the *Three Kingdoms*, vowed to delete supernatural, superstitious, and unreliable elements from earlier versions, some still can be found in the novel. This is because the idea of karma and retribution have been deeply imbedded in Chinese culture for hundreds of years. According to Confucianism, the mandate of heaven is not easily to be ignored. Buddhism teaches that one reaps what one sows.

Before the deaths of Dong Zhuo and Cao Cao, there are many heavenly signs of their inevitable fate, but they are ignored or misinterpreted. While Lu plots to kill Dong, his mother is strangely restless and distraught, but he ignores the sign. His carriage breaks down on the way to the capital where the rebels led by Lu are waiting to attack him, and his horse rips its headgear; when Dong asks his companions the meanings of these signs, he is told that because he will be emperor soon, he should discard his old carriage and horses. There is a wind storm, and Dong hears children singing an ominous verse about the withering of grass in the meadow, but again Dong is given a positive interpretation of these signs. When a Daoist priest appears carrying a staff with a white cloth on which a mouth is drawn, Dong is told that the priest is a madman. It is not long afterwards that Dong is killed and beheaded.

Cao Cao, plotting to seize power, orders the execution of Empress Fu and Concubine Dong, and he places the emperor under house arrest. Cao then suffers a severe headache and hallucinations. In his dreams he sees his bloodstained victims coming before him and seeking his death. He dreams of three horses eating from one manger (indicating the succession of the Ma [horse] family). He attempts to cut down an ancient pear tree that he had been told is inhabited by a spirit; and the tree groans and spatters him with blood. That night the spirit of the pear tree appears and proclaims that Cao's days are numbered and strikes him with a sword. He suffers a blinding headache and lies in agony for days until he finally dies.

For many readers over the centuries, these supernatural elements have added to the exotic charm of the story; the suffering of evil men has both interested and satisfied those who read *The Romance of the Three Kingdoms*. History, although altered by invention and superstition, comes alive in the recounting of many strange events and triumphs of good over evil. As Herbert A. Giles has written in *A History of Chinese Literature*, "If a vote were taken among the people of China as to the greatest among its countless novels, the *Romance of the Three Kingdoms* would indubitably come out first."

FATIMA WU

Further Reading

Translations

Brewitt-Taylor, C. H., trans. *Romance of the Three Kingdoms* [by] Lo Kuan-chung. 2 vols. Rutland, VT: Charles E. Tuttle, 1959. This is a complete translation done in 1925 (by Kelly & Walsh, Shanghai) of 120 chapters of the novel. Roy Andrew Miller from International Christian University in Tokyo wrote an eight-page introduction for the book.

———. *Romance of the Three Kingdoms* [by] Luo Guan Zhong. 2 vols. Singapore: Graham Brash, 1985. Another edition of the Brewitt-Taylor translation.

Pan, Qinmeng. *A Gathering of Heroes (Qun ying hui)*. Beijing: Zhaohua Publishing House, 1983. This is a juvenile book with selected picture stories from chapters 45 and 46 in the *Three Kingdoms*. The illustrations are done by Ling

Tao while the stories are edited by the Shanghai People's Fine Arts Publishing House.

———. *The Battle of Red Cliff (Chibi dazhan)*. Beijing: Zhaohua Publishing House, 1983. This is again a juvenile book translating a major battle in the novel resulting the split of the three powers. The illustrations are done by Liu Xiyong and editing is by the Shanghai People's Fine Art Publishing House.

Roberts, Moss, trans. *Three Kingdoms, A Historical Novel by Luo Guanzhong*. Berkeley, CA: University of California Press, 1991. This is a complete translation in one big volume in hardback. There is also a Foreword by John S. Service, and an Afterword by the translator. The sections on notes, principal characters, chronology of main events, titles, terms and offices in *Three Kingdoms*, abbreviations, and maps make this translation valuable. The Afterword, in particular, is very useful in understanding the sources, background and structure of the novel.

———. *Three Kingdoms: A Historical Novel by Luo Guanzhong*. 3 vols. Beijing: Foreign Language Press, 1994. This is the Roberts translation in three volumes in paperback, filled with black and white illustrations of the main characters and events.

———, trans. and ed. *Three Kingdoms: China's Epic Drama*, New York: Pantheon Books, 1976. This abridged translation has 65 chapters out of the 120. Many of these are only partially translated with many bridges, condensations, and splices. This version concentrates on chapters 20–85. What is valuable about this book is its inclusion of maps, an index and some black and white illustrations from the 1644, 1829, and 1894 editions of the novel.

Yang, Xianyi, and Gladys Yang, trans. *Excerpts from Three Classical Chinese Novels*, Beijing: Panda Books, 1981. This book carries excerpts from three Chinese novels. *Flowers in the Mirror, Pilgrimage to the West*, and *Three Kingdoms*. The chapters translated are 43–50, on "The Battle of Red Cliff" (page 7–122). There is also a commentary on the novel written by Chen Minsheng on page 123–132.

JOURNEY TO THE WEST

Title in Chinese: *Xiyou ji (Hsi-yu Chi)*
Author: Wu Chengen (Wu Cheng-en)
Born: c. 1500 in Waian, Jiangsu Province, China
Died: c. 1582 in Waian, Jiangsu Province, China
Literary Form: Episodic novel in 100 chapters written in colloquial Chinese
Dates of Composition and Publication: Composed between the late 1560's and the year of the author's death; first published c. 1592

Major Themes

All religions are valid, provided that one is sincere and devoted.
The way to the understanding of life is to suffer, endure, and learn.
Human frailties have their comic aspects.

Wu Chengen's father, although just a vendor selling frills and laces in his shop, was a man of letters. His daily avid reading influenced his son Chengen's life to a great extent. Young Wu was described as quick and brilliant by his contemporaries. Though he failed continuously in the government recruiting examinations, he wrote several books in his lifetime.

At the age of 51, Wu left his hometown for Nanjing. It was not clear whether he was urged to go because of financial problems in the family, or by his mother's orders to try one more time to excel. The result was that he became a lost soul there, living on the money he got from writing and copying essays for others. In his 60s, he managed to attain the position of a provincial governor in Changxin only for a short while. A cynical scholar, who called himself Master Sheyang, Wu never established a congenial relationship with his superiors. The same happened in his next position working for a duke. For the next decade or so, until his death, he returned to his native town enjoying himself with poetry and essays. It is believed that *Journey to the West* was written during his retirement years.

If one is asked to name a Chinese book that is known to all ages and all social levels, one has to nominate *Journey to the West*. An illiterate in China might not have read it, but he or she must have heard about it or seen it performed on stage. The

main characters, especially Monkey, have appeared in operas, cartoons, movies, juvenile books, and colloquial tales. In other words, it is a story that everyone knows about.

The Basic Story and Its Origins

Journey to the West depicts a seventh-century Buddhist monk called Tripitaka (based on the historical figure Xuanzang/Hsüan-tsang) undertaking an arduous journey from China to India for the purpose of obtaining Buddhist scriptures. With him on his journey are three disciples: Monkey, Pigsy, and Sandy. The journey on foot takes a long time to cover during which the party comes upon fierce animals, spirits, monsters, ghosts, and other man-made and natural barriers. Only with faith, confidence, and hard work can they overcome these hurdles to arrive in India. Many times they all come close to losing their lives or giving up hope of seeing India, but with perseverence and determination they succeed in the end. And, of course, all four are satirically canonized as Buddhist saints as a result.

It is important to note that Wu Chengen did not create the story of *Journey to the West*. The trip made by the Buddhist monk is an actual event that happened during the Tang dynasty (618–907). From historical records, we know that the monk undertook a journey of thousands of miles on foot from China to India for the purpose of obtaining the Buddhist scriptures. He was gone for 17 years during which he went through thick and thin risking his life. This almost impossible journey was later dramatized in operas and colloquial fiction; and other characters, such as Monkey, Pigsy, and Sandy, slowly made their debut as part of the story of the trip.

When he began his novel, Wu had knowledge of pre-existing works about the pilgrimage to the west. Some of these works are not available to us now. Yet we know that the materials used by Wu to create his 100-chapter novel were episodic and incomplete, written in primitive, straightforward narrative styles. In other words, Wu, with his power of imagination and his talents in writing, turned whatever incongruous and fragmented writings he came across into an interesting, lively, and satirical work. The greatness of his creation stems from his ability to come up with 81 different calamities for the journey, his great sense of humor, his resourcefulness in portraying the four main characters with uniqueness and consistency, and his genius in writing a book that is both didactic and entertaining.

The 100 chapters can be divided into three parts: chapters 1 through 7 talk about Monkey's background and his rhapsody in heaven; chapters 8 through 12 concentrate on the origin and reasons for Tripitaka to take up this long journey; and, lastly, chapters 13 through 100, comprising the principal narrative portion of the novel, take the readers along on this journey with tears, laughter, and excitement. Almost every chapter can be read independently, although the storyline is connected and enlivened by the four main characters.

The Historical and Religious Background

The two most obvious interpretations of *Journey to the West* rest on its historical and religious aspects. The historical outlines of the journey have been mentioned above: a 26-year-old monk, Xuanzang, sets out on a journey to the west to find and bring back the Buddhist sutras. Once he arrives, he obtains the Buddhist books, which he is himself unable to read. Therefore, he stays to learn the language and afterwards he returns to his homeland, where he begins to translate the scriptures for the benefit of his people. Of his hard work and devotion, there are many records and historical texts on this unique and generous event, *Journey to the West* being one of them.

As a Buddhist tale in origin, if not in execution, the novel serves as a witness to the faith. Tripitaka and his three disciples, moved by with faith and devotion, are aided by the Goddess of Mercy (the Bodhisattva, Kuan-yin) during their trip. Almost all the good characters in the book, such as Buddha, Goddess of Mercy, and Manjusri, belong to the Buddhist canon, while minor roles such as the evil characters, monsters, and spirits come from Taoist and other spheres. The basic theme of the book dwells on the Buddhist ideas of karma, reincarnation, and retribution. In many places, we see that Buddhist personnel are given priorities and favors: for example, when Monkey creates a disturbance in the celestial world, all the heavenly saints fail to subdue him except Buddha himself, whose unlimited power entraps Monkey in his palm. (Monkey makes a great leap from Buddha's palm and presumes himself to have traveled thousands of miles; in fact, he has gone only to the base of one of Buddha's fingers.) Kuan-yin saves the traveling group from their calamities in at least five incidents; and, when the four finally arrive at the Temple of Thunder Clap in India where Buddha resides, they are rewarded with immortality and official titles in heaven.

Throughout the novel, Buddhist moral injunctions against killing, drinking, and the involvement of monks in sexual matters are stated repeatedly in numerous places. Tripitaka, a young man with a stronghold in the Buddhist faith, is the target partner of matrimony by female rulers of Amazon-like countries during the journey. Monsters and spirits understand that if they get a chance to eat Tripitaka's meat, they will attain immortality. So they turn themselves into attractive females or sometimes pitiful old hags to lure the monk. Very often, Tripitaka depends on his spiritual and religious strength to fight off these monsters while waiting for his disciples to come and deliver him.

Chapters 44 to 47 portray the four travelers—Tripitaka, Monkey, Pigsy, and Sandy—coming upon three Daoist (Taoist) priests in Cart-slow Kingdom: Tiger-strength, Deer-strength, and Ram-strength. Under the command of the emperor of Cart-slow, Tripitaka, Monkey, Pigsy, and Sandy are pitched against the "three Immortals"—Tiger Strength, Deer Strength, and Ram Strength—to compete in their magical powers. They defeat the Daoists in meditating on the top of a tower of tables, the "Cloud Ladder," when Monkey changes himself into a centipede and crawls into the nostril on a Daoists's head, at which point the Daoist falls from the top of the Cloud Ladder; Monkey and his companions win again when the contest is to identify an object inside a closed box—but they succeed only because Monkey changes himself into a gnat and makes changes in what the King had put into the box. Monkey then triumphs in contests to survive being immersed in boiling oil, the severing of his head, the cutting open of his torso, and in other tasks, so that he wins the emperor's favor. Since Monkey and his group triumph over the Daoists, Buddhist power has conquered all. Yet in chapter 47, Wu Chengen shows his generous religious perspective when, through Monkey's mouth, he calls for giving respect to all three religions: "Never again follow false doctrines nor follow foolish courses, but know that the Three Religions are one. Reverence priests, reverence Taoists too, and cultivate the faculties of man" (Waley, 1943).

The Novel as Allegory

Great literature is usually subject to a number of interpretations. *Journey to the West* can be read allegorically as a psychological novel, with Tripitaka as the protagonist, that excludes any religious implications. The novel will then be viewed as a portrait of the human being's spiritual quest as psychologically understood: the novel (one might say) deals with the ego, the id, and the libido, and it shows how a questing person can come to self-understanding.

Tripitaka, a monk as well as a young man, takes up this journey to India. The spirits, monsters, and elves that block his way can be seen as seductions and distractions from his own mind. They present barriers and problems in the progress of his journey or life. It is only by overcoming them that he can be his own master. Just before he leaves for the trip, Tripitaka tells his colleagues about his fears for the trip ahead: "It is the heart alone that can destroy them" (Waley). The "them" here are enemies of the heart, of the self. As an honest upright monk, Tripitaka is bound by morals and obligations. He is supposed to be void of human desires for sex, money, fame, and power. His behavior conforms to whatever society has prescribed for a Buddhist monk.

Symbolically, Monkey, Pigsy, and Sandy represent basic aspects of Tripitaka's character that have to be brought under control and harmonized.

Monkey, born out of a rock, goes for power and fame in the beginning of the story. He wants to take the place of the Jade Emperor in heaven, so that he can be the ruler of the universe. Money has no effect on Monkey (as it does on Pigsy, who would risk his life for food, drink, and treasures). During the trip, Monkey always volunteers to confront monsters and spirits just for the sake of showing off his martial skills and power. He kills, he is able to transform himself into 72 various forms and shapes, and he can fly (one somersault of his takes him 108,000 miles). The only way he can be controlled is to tighten the metal ring on his head by incantations. This is to say, Monkey's actions can be dictated only by the mind.

Pigsy is the only main character who is married, although he does not have a good relationship with his wife or his in-laws. His unpleasant countenance is a symbol of the sensuous behavior that dominates his life. Bodily desires, such as food, drink, women and money, are his goals in life. The trip to India has never been attractive to him. In many instances, he declares that he would rather go home to his wife than continue the effort to attain the scriptures. In some ways, he is the total opposite of Monkey, who is egoistic and ambitious.

Sandy is a minor character compared to Monkey

and Pigsy; he is a symbol of the dark forces within us that aim to destroy and to kill. When Tripitaka, Monkey, and Pigsy first come across Sandy, he is a merciless killer by the river, with skulls of human victims eaten by him hanging on his neck.

Close to the end of the journey, all three characters change. Monkey now sees freedom as something more valuable than power or fame. He feels certain calmness and peace when he sees snow-bound scenes. Fame has no effect on him and he now finds no need to show off his martial skills. Pigsy too, requires less food and he does not talk nonsense anymore. The shedding of the old self is symbolized in chapter 98 when the party of four arrive at the foot of the hill where Buddha lives. By the river bank, the four try to go across on a bottomless boat. The frightened Tripitaka falls into the river and is later saved by Monkey. Yet, in the water there floats a dead body at which they all scream: "it's you, it's you" (Waley). This is a spiritual rebirth for all four, especially Tripitaka; they realize that the old self is dead and is now replaced by a new one. Metaphorically, all four arrive at their destination, where they are spiritually saved and elevated.

Is the Novel Just an Entertaining Story?

Many critics reject the religious and psychological interpretations that have been popular over the centuries. Especially concerning the religious approach, many critics blame scholars for creating something Wu never intended to convey. According to these critics, Wu was just writing a book of humor and satire—to give his readers, who are common people, some happiness to color their ordinary lives. Wu wrote the *Journey to the West* by using materials he had in hand and by adding more by his imagination. The use of urine in place of miracle water in chapter 45 is vulgar but funny; Pigsy's bathing with the spider-spirits in Cobweb Cave is hilarious; Monkey's attempts to attain the magic fan from Princess Jade Countenance in order to cross the Mountain of Flames are both ingenious and interesting. Neither themes nor teachings were planned (the critical argument continues). In order

to enable the common people to understand and enjoy his story, Wu chose to use as background the Buddhist religion, its stories, and its tradition—all of which were deeply engraved in the people's minds at that time.

Whether the interpretation of *Journey to the West* is religious, psychological, spiritual, or moral, the novel is remarkable as an entertaining portrait not only of Chinese society and manners but also of the human condition itself.

Perhaps some understanding of the intent of the novel can be attained by considering the following incident: The four main characters return to the temple to see Buddha because they want to complain about having been given blank scriptures. Monkey believes that they were given blank scriptures in response to the meager commission they had given the arhats. In a fit of anger, they reveal the situation to Buddha who replies: "[A]s a matter of fact, it is such blank scrolls as these that are the true scriptures. But I quite see that the people of China are too foolish and ignorant to believe this, so there is nothing for it but to give them copies with some writings on" (Waley, 1943).

Whether they are blank scriptures or scriptures with writings is not important. What was important to Wu Chengen, one would suppose, is that readers grasp his ideas about life and humanity and that they appreciate his humor and imagination.

FATIMA WU

Further Reading

Translations

Jenner, W. J. F., trans. *Journey to the West* by Wu Chengen. 3 vols. Beijing: Foreign Language Press, 1984. This is a full translation of the novel with prose and verse. Volume one covers chapters 1 to 31; volume two, chapters 32 to 66; and the last volume, chapters 67 to 100. The three volumes carry illustrations and portraits of the main characters from a lithographic edition dated 1888.

Waley, Arthur, trans. *Monkey* by Wu Ch'eng-en. New York: John Day Co. 1943. This abridged translation gives a full version of the beginning and ending of Wu's work, with most of the 81 calamities missing to give a feeling of completeness to the story. The four calamities included are: "The Lion Demon in the Kingdom of Crow Cock," "The Cart-slow Kingdom," "The River that Leads to Heaven and the Great King of Miracles," and "The Eighty-first Calamity."

Yu, Anthony C., trans. and ed. *Journey to the West* by Wu Chengen. Chicago: University of Chicago Press, 1980. This is a complete translation of Wu's novel, in four volumes each consisting of 25 chapters. Yu not only gives a full footnote coverage, but he also provides the reader with a detailed index section and a 62-page introduction.

GOLDEN LOTUS

Title in Chinese: *Jin Ping Mei (Chin P'ing Mei)*
Author: Unknown
Literary Form: Novel in 100 chapters in colloquial Shandong dialect
Dates of Composition and Publication: Composed 1590's; first complete version printed in 1610

Major Themes

Those who overindulge in sexual activities and illicit behavior will bring suffering and death to themselves.
The way of life that encourages moderation and self-control is Buddhism.
Wealth and noble status do not bring happiness.
Women may resort to craft, deception, and sexual lures in order to triumph over others, but their fall can in part be related to the corrosive effects of male domination.

The author of *Golden Lotus* remains a mystery despite scholars' and critics' persistent investigation over the centuries. "Xiao Xiao Sheng [Hsiao Hsiao Sheng] from Lanling" or the "Laughing Laughing Scholar from Lanling" leaves us no clues as to who he was or where he was from. There are a number of places called Lanling in China. From the content of the book itself, as well as the prefaces by contemporaries who read the work, scholars today come up with several names of who might be the possible author or who have had a close relationship to the birth of the book. These literary men were once all actively involved with the copying or reprinting of the book; they include Shen Defu (Shen Te-fu) (c. 1609), Yuan Xiaoshou (Yüan Hsiao-shou) (c. 1609), and Wang Shicheng (Wang Shih-ch'eng) (c. 1695).

To complicate the matter further, there are two versions of *Golden Lotus*. One is simply called *Golden Lotus*; the other is *Golden Lotus with Zi Songs (Jin Ping Mei zihua/Chin P'ing Mei tzuhua)*. The main difference between these two versions is that the former one is written mainly in prose, while the latter contains pornographic scenes and is heavily interspersed with unrhymed verses called the *zi (tzu)*, which was a popular poetic style during the Sung (Song) dynasty (960–1279). There are also two theories surrounding these two books. One is that an incomplete *Golden Lotus* first appeared around 1596. It was circulated only within a small group of people. No one knows exactly to what extent it was incomplete. Today, the oldest version available to us is *Golden Lotus with Zi Songs*, which was printed in 1617. Some scholars agree that this is the product of a group effort during the Ming dynasty (1369–1644), aimed at rewriting the incomplete *Golden Lotus*. With fragments of the *Golden Lotus* in their hands, these Ming scholars rewrote the *Golden Lotus with Zi Songs* in 100 chapters, putting in at the same time the licentious parts.

Another theory deals with the ethical elements of the story. When *Golden Lotus with Zi Songs* first appeared (1573–1619), its bold pornographic content shocked those who read it. Especially for the Confucianists and the puritans, this piece of licentious fiction was considered immoral and harmful to its readers. Very soon, it was banned and ostracized. The few who recognized the value of the book tried to salvage the work by cutting out the pornographic passages. Hence, a new version of *Golden Lotus* suitable for all ages and both sexes emerged (1628–1643).

With or without the licentious parts, *Golden Lotus*, one of the four great novels of the Ming period besides *Romance of the Three Kingdoms (Sanguozhi yanyi/San kuo chih yen-i)*, *Journey to the West (Xiyouji/Hsi yu chi)* and *The Water Margin (Shuihuzhuan/Shui-hu chuan)*, remains a coherent, touching and interesting story of the Sung dynasty.

The Structure of the Novel

The novel can roughly be divided into three parts. Chapters 1 through 8 concentrate on the main character Ximen Qing (Hsimen Ch'ing) and his paramour Lotus (Jinlian/Chin-lian), who later becomes his fifth wife. Chapters 9 through 79 depict Ximen's love for Vase (Li Pinger/Li P'ing-erh), who becomes his sixth concubine and gives him his first son. This is the longest section of the novel for it not only reveals the relationship among the wives, but it also gives an account of Ximen's gradual success as a local official of eminence until his death. The last part of *Golden Lotus* contains the story of Moon Lady, Ximen's first wife, who tries to manage the household and bring up their son after the demise of the head of the family. It is this very last section of the novel that arouses the critics' suspicion. Somehow, its style, as well as its content, which seems, to most, superfluous after the death of Ximen, do not appear to have been written by the same author who wrote the previous parts.

These 100 chapters portray the private and social life of Ximen Qing. The duration of time covered in this tale is 16 years (1112–1127) in the Sung dynasty, and most actions and events take place in the City of Qinghe, Dongping Prefecture in Shandong Province. The Chinese title of the book, *Jin Ping Mei*, is derived from the three main female characters: Jin from Jinlian (Lotus), Ping from Lipinger (Vase) and Mei from Chunmei (Ch'un-mei; Spring Plum), Lotus's maid.

A "Pornographic" and Didactic Novel

Ximen Qing, the protagonist of the tale, is a man of voracious sexual appetite and ambition. With six wives at home serving him, he still goes for maids, young male servants, his servants' wives, wet nurses, prostitutes, and other people's wives. Originally an owner of an apothecary shop in Qinghe City, through bribery Ximen gradually builds up connections with the local officials, who in turn connect him to the authority in the Eastern Capital. The richer and more powerful he becomes, the more women he covets. Lotus, his fifth wife, is acquired through a conspiracy in which her former husband is murdered. Then, in order to marry Ximen, Vase first has to rush her husband to his end, and then lure Ximen with her sumptuous dowry. When Ximen's secret liaison with a servant's wife is discovered, she is subjected to the mercy of his jealous wife, Lotus, who finally drives the poor woman to suicide. While Ximen indulges himself in brothels, some of his wives at home make him a cuckold by sexual meetings with servants and relatives. Ximen is not aware of his wives' intense jealousy, especially that of Lotus, who is responsible for ending the life of his first son by Vase. Finally Ximen, a man who possesses charm, charisma, and a mind for success, at the age of 33 dies in Lotus's arms.

Why does the author spend his time on detailed descriptions of sexual scenes? Is he driven to show the reader how much he knows about sexual equipment and positions, or is he a sex maniac himself? Critics all admit that the sensual parts of the book are technically just as good as the nonsensual ones. Obviously, the author has enjoyed writing these parts as much as showing off his knowledge or experience in these matters. What is more important here is the author's attitude penetrating his words. Sex is human, it is gratifying, yet it is also the origin of vice. If Xiao Xiao Sheng were interested in presenting Ximen as a happy and satisfied libertine, he surely would not have arranged for his early and unwelcomed death. If the women have married the man they want and feel free to act on passionate impulse, why are they so lonely?

There is a strong moral statement implicit in the portrayal of these characters: be good and faithful, or you will be punished. If punishment does not come in this life, it will in the next. The purpose of the sex scenes, then, is to entertain and to teach. In other words, the author has a moral purpose in writing this tale. Accordingly, some critics would say that, considered as a whole, the book is not pornographic despite its preoccupation with sexual activity.

The theme of the novel lies in the last chapter in which Moon Lady, Ximen's first wife, travels with her son Xiaoge (Hsiao-ko) and several trustworthy servants to find refuge with Xiaoge's future in-laws in order to escape the war. On the way, she comes across a monk who asks for her son to be his follower. The idea is of course rejected because Xiaoge is the only heir in the family. That evening, the company spends the night in a Buddhist temple, where Moon Lady's maid, Little Jade, witnesses the reincarnation of Ximen, Lotus, Vase, Spring Plum, and others. Also, Moon Lady's dream, in which Xiaoge is eventually decapitated, prompts her to give him up to the monk. In order to comfort and assure her that she has made the right decision, the monk points his staff at the sleeping Xiaoge, who suddenly turns into the image of the suffering Ximen in heavy shackles. At this point, Moon Lady is suddenly illuminated about reincarnation and rebirth, crime and punishment. Xiaoge is actually the reincarnation of the sinful Ximen, who now re-enters the family just to destroy it in the future. By joining the Buddhist order, Ximen's sins are purged, and he is now free for reincarnation.

Xiaoge's presence in the novel is to give a didactic message to the reader: lasciviousness is the worst sin of all, for it inevitably leads to others— jealousy, greed, and murder. The main characters of the novel, Ximen, Lotus, Vase and Spring Plum, all die young because of their over-indulgence in sex and illicit behavior. The creed is clear: Buddhism is the only way.

First Naturalistic and Realist Novel

Even when *Golden Lotus* is stripped of its "pornographic" passages, it remains complete in its themes and development. The author has used real historical personnel such as Caijing (Ts'ai Ching), the prime minister, and other court officials in the Sung dynasty to give the background and the setting for his work. With the invading wars of the barbarians and the rebels, the author purposely uses history to reflect the society at his own time, the Ming period. For example, scenes of the corruption at court, the grand birthday present for Cai, and Cai's obsequious role in offering the emperor his favorite precious stones at the cost of the lives of the common people, are satirical comments on

the political life of the author's own time: the poor have no means of feeding themselves, while the rich and the powerful oppress and exploit them.

A well-known critic of *Golden Lotus with Zi Songs*, Mr. Wei Ziyun, claims that the novel is not just the first pornographic novel, but also the first novel of naturalism and realism in China. Very often, its pornographic content distracts and bars truth-seeking readers and serious scholars from looking further into the book and its themes. Yet, Wei's comment on the sexual content of the book is a positive one: he sees it as the author's means to maintain the novel on a realistic level rather than allow it to become simply a didactic or religious story.

Besides fostering a moral tone, this piece of "licentious" fiction affords the reader a humanistic approach. Whether portrayals of the love act between husband and wives, or of coition between two sex-hungry individuals, or of the secretive relationships of adulterous couples, or of sexual intercourse as a physical favor bestowed by the master on a serving maid, or of the scheming and intrigues among concubines to curry their man's attention, or of the yearning for love and sexual satisfaction by the concubines who are doomed to be passive in this respect, these passages tell us a lot about the times: how women and maids were treated by their husbands and masters, and how corruption and self-destruction could rob love, sex, and human relationships of their positive values. For this reason, the novel should be viewed as a work on the relationships between men and women, husbands and wives, morality and debauchery, self-control and total dissipation, universal laws and human ones, religion and life.

The Feminist Critique of the Novel

New criticism on *Golden Lotus with Zi Songs* centers on feminist studies that emphasis on the characters of Lotus, Vase, Spring Plum, and Moon Lady. For centuries, the first three women named above have been labelled as tramps for their blatant sexual behavior and appetite. Lotus tries to seduce her brother-in-law, Wu Song (Wu Sung), in the first chapter; in the second chapter, she is already falling for Ximen. Even after her marriage to the latter as his fifth wife, she initiates sexual liaisons with a family member named Chen (Ch'en) and with other young male domestic servants around her. Lotus's tricks on and traps for the other wives make her the most vile and vicious women in the book.

Yet the critical argument in her defense is this: does an ambitious and aggressive woman like her have a choice? She is sold at the age of nine after her father's death. At 15, she is again sold to a man over 60 who takes her virginity. Then this senior man gets rid of her under his wife's pressure by arranging her marriage to the elderly Wuda (Wu-ta). When the wealthy and handsome Ximen appears in her life, the beautiful Lotus of course prefers him over her husband (Ximen poisons Wuda and frees Lotus for his own uses.). Although life in the Ximen household is one of luxury and leisure, Lotus is lonely. She desperately tries to keep her pride and survive among the other concubines. It is a big blow to her when Ximen's sixth wife, Vase, manages to produce a son.

Ximen, the head of the household, is a totalitarian. It is "reasonable" for him to have as many as six wives at home, plus numerous sexual laisons within the family and outside. But if any of his wives goes against his will or provokes his temper, he uses physical punishment on them, such as whipping them naked. At the least, Lotus and Vase have tasted his whips. One can imagine the kind of life a woman lives in such a household. Rather than living happily and peacefully, a woman in such circumstances is always under the pressure to produce sons, is exploited by others, and is caught up with intrigues and conspiracy against the others. At the end, the concupiscent Lotus kills the sexually-encumbered Ximen during the process of attaining sexual satisfaction, something she is entitled to enjoy as a woman. At the age of 32, she is avenged by Wu Song, Wuda's brother, for becoming Ximen's concubine after Ximen had murdered Wuda.

Although Vase joins the Ximen family as the sixth mistress with very attractive dowry, she is at first ignored and beaten. She finally manages to win her husband's favor and become his first wife to have a son. For this reason, Vase unknowingly provokes Lotus's jealousy, whose machinations lead to her son's death and finally her own. Our heroine, Vase, the foil of Lotus, is a generous, kind, and gentle woman who becomes a victim in the complicated concubinary system. The pursuit of happiness and love with Ximen brings Vase nothing but suffering and despair. She dies at 27 under much pressure, and having suffered pain and an unbearable feeling of loss for her dear baby boy. Ximen mourns her death without knowing that it is he himself who has brought her to an immature end.

Lotus's personal maid, Spring Plum, the third heroine of the story, also dies young at the age of 29. As a female from a poor family, she is first sold as a maid. After Ximen dies and her mistress Lotus leaves the family, she is put up for sale as a piece of merchandise until another man, an official named Chou (Ch'ou), picks her up as a concubine. Of course, Spring Plum's life, like those of the other women in the novel, goes from happiness to despair with her husband's fortune. But Spring Plum, perhaps, is the luckiest of the three, for she finally manages to become the principal wife with an heir. It is only debauchery on her part, involving a deceitful affair with, among others, Chou's son, that destroys her in the end.

These three women—Lotus, Vase, and Spring Plum—just like Ximen himself, are all brought to a premature death due to their immoral behavior and illicit relationships with men. Critics ask: could they have done otherwise? What was life like for them back then? Was that kind of life enough to satisfy these active and ambitious ladies? Why must one be like Moon Lady, a monotonous, malleable, and unimaginative being? Is there space and possible acceptance in society for a bold, creative, and natural woman? Even with Moon Lady, the all-compromising woman, is life fair to her when she ends up living a lonesome life without her only son? Longevity is her sole reward in the novel for being moral and religious. The story of these women is a realistic condemnation of the low state of morality among the ruling classes and of the exploitation of women by their husbands, lovers, and masters.

If *Golden Lotus* is read seriously, it is found to be a striking and realistic portrait of the decadence of the Ming period, and although it is sometimes absorbing as a novel of manners, it succeeds in showing that depravity leads to suffering and death and that, despite its inhibiting features, a life of virtue is to be preferred to a life of vice.

FATIMA WU

Further Reading

Anonymous. *Chin P'ing Mei: The Adventurous History of Hsi Men and his Six Wives*. New York: G. P. Putnam's Sons, 1947. This abridged translation follows the events surrounding the main characters, cutting out those concerning the minor ones as well as the sexual scenes. The introduction and notes cover 14 pages.

Roy, David T., trans. *The Plum in the Golden Vase* or *Chin P'ing Mei*, Princeton, N.J.: Princeton University Press, 1993. This translation may still be in progress, because, as of now, only volume one is available. This volume covers chapters 1 to 20, with a 32-page introduction, a 36-page index, bibliography on both primary and secondary sources, two appendixes, and classical illustrations throughout the book. This complete translation offers both the *zi* songs and the pornographic parts. By far, this translation offers the most detailed scholarship for the study of *Golden Lotus*.

Egerton, Clement, trans. *The Golden Lotus*. London: Routledge and Kegan Paul, 1972. Four volumes. This is a translation of the novel complete except for the *zi* songs. Volume one covers chapters 1 to 27; volume two, chapters 28 to 53; volume three, chapters 54 to 75; and volume four, chapters 76 to 100. Egerton also provides us with a list of characters and a short introduction for reference.

STRANGE STORIES FROM A CHINESE STUDIO

Title in Chinese: *Liaozhai Zhiyi (Liao-chai Chih-i)*
Author: Pu Songling (P'u Sung-ling)
Born: 1640, Liuchuan, Shandong Province, China
Died: 1715, Liuchuan, Shandong Province, China
Literary Form: 494 short stories in classical Chinese language
Dates of Composition and Publication: Composed between c. 1670–1707; published c. 1766

Major Themes

The world of the preternatural is a replica of the real world in ethical, social, and political terms.
Religious ethics and humanitarian behavior are necessary for survival, success, and happiness.
Women, too, deserve respect and freedom for their contributions to the family and their strength in upholding moral ideals.

Near the end of the Ming dynasty (1368–1644), Pu Songling was born the fourth son to his father, a scholar-turned-merchant, as the family finances dwindled. The senior Pu was quite successful in trade only in the beginning, after which the whole family suffered for his failure. For this reason, Pu Songling's childhood was not a pleasant one. Yet he grew up under his father's influence as a talented scholar. The old man took special pride in recommending his fourth son out of five as the brightest in the family.

At the age of 19, Pu fulfilled his father's wish by passing all three local examinations as preliminary steps in attaining a government position, and he acquired quite a respectable reputation among local literary circles. Yet for the next 40 years or so, he never succeeded in passing any provincial examinations. To support his family, he had no choice but to teach. After his mother died, Pu, at the age of 40, left his family and taught at his friend Bi Jiyou's (Pi Chi-yu's) residence. The latter was a governor who admired Pu's literary talents. Pu spent 30 years in his friend's house teaching the minors, as well as writing official documents when the need arose. During the years he was teaching, Pu never gave up his wish to take examinations to become an official.

In his spare time, Pu wrote quite a number of books. *Liaozhai Zhiyi* is a monumental work collected in 12 volumes. His other works include: four volumes of essays; six of poetry; five on miscellaneous subjects, such as a calendar and a comprehensive dictionary for peasants; sixteen popular musical narratives; one musical play; and a novel, *A Marriage to Awaken the World*.

Pu Songling, living in China, a country deeply affected by Confucian and Buddhist mores and ruled by a foreign power (the Manchurians), and a man who had failed in his examinations and career, suffered from mixed emotions of frustration and ambition. It was the conglomeration of all these influencing factors that affected the author in his composition of the *Liaozhai Zhiyi*.

The Confucian and Buddhist ethics, emphasizing moral behavior, filial piety, and self-discipline, seemed like invisible fetters impeding his free will. Confucian scholars and educated men especially, had to adhere to these ethical codes in order to set good examples for others. Often in doing so, they had to ignore their own wishes. The Confucianists also denied the freedom to love, for marriage was to be decided and arranged by one's parents only. This was particularly so in the case of women, whose lives were often controlled by others. By writing supernatural tales in which the impossible can become possible, Pu gave women the poetic justice to fulfill their dreams and he gave himself an imaginary world in which he could act freely according to his own inclinations.

The political situation at Pu's time was extremely unstable. The Ming dynasty fell when Pu was only five years old and the Manchurians invaded and undertook the rule of China. Local resistance was overwhelming and the foreign regime had to suppress these rebellions in order to consolidate its rule. At the same time, the Manchu government saw that controlling scholars and restricting what they wrote would strengthen the government's control over the commoners. Under such pressure, it was necessary for Pu to write symbolic tales of supernatural fiction rather than realistic and critical essays that would bring him into conflict with the new rulers.

As Pu never passed another examination after he was 19, he harbored complaints and discontentment concerning the examination system. His *Strange Stories from a Chinese Studio* thus became a convenient outlet for launching an attack against examiners, the academic system itself, and incompetent scholars who had somehow managed to succeed.

Pu did not want to write merely traditional supernatural tales; he wanted to write his own. Although he claimed in the preface that he had collected these tales from his friends and relatives, it is more likely that he used materials he had heard and manipulated them creatively to serve his own ends.

Strange Stories is an important work in Chinese literary history because of its scope, which covers religion, history, philosophy, and art. In these massive volumes of stories, one finds tales on fox fairies, ghosts, flowers, and stone spirits. In many instances, the lives of human beings and gods intertwine, so much so that their identities become interchangeable.

Hell and Morals

Unlike the western novel, in which Gothic devices (the representation of the fearsome and supernatural) are used to represent and symbolize the unknown and the fantastic, Pu uses the novel to explicate the already known, the world in front of our very eyes. In the west, hell is entirely removed from the human world; it is the unfathomable depths to which sinners are consigned for eternal suffering. Hell and the world of the living exist in a dichotomous relationship in which each excludes the other. But hell in the *Strange Stories* is not only a unique place of punishment and suffering, as depicted in the west; it is also a replica of the living world with similar social structures and moral values. Symbolically, Pu was writing about the living world by disguising it as the lower one. There is corruption, bribery, and darkness in hell as in reality. In Pu's hell, justice is upheld.

A good example can be found in the story "Xi Fengping" ("Hsi Fang-p'ing") ("In the Infernal Regions" [Giles]). Xi travels to the lower world in order to save his father from suffering for a crime he never committed. The judges in hell call for severe physical torture of Xi Fengping because he gives them no bribes. Fengping undergoes many tortures, including having to lie on a red-hot iron couch "until the fire ate into his bones" and being cut in half vertically (starting with his head and brain), but because of his persistence and strength of character he is miraculously put together again and eventually succeeds in clearing his father of the false charges. After the beleaguered father and son finally come upon an upright judge who straightens things out for them, both the father and son—after having died and, in the case of Fengping, being born again as a little girl and dying of starvation in three days—are reborn in their own home. Their enemies have been tortured in the infernal regions, and the Xi family enjoys prosperity and long life.

This story serves as a typical satire directed against the bureaucratic system, which is inundated by corruption and injustice at that time. Writing stories about hell was a convenient and safe way of attacking the Manchurian bureaucracy, which was protected by a system of censorship.

Many of Pu's hell stories are meant to be morally didactic. It is important to know that Pu's ethical world is derived from Buddhism and Confucianism. As a Confucianist scholar, Pu lived up to his name by living an honest life in poverty, at the same time expounding the Confucian ideas of filial piety—loyalty to the country and benevolence in his writings. The Buddhist ideas of reincarnation and karma also find their way into Pu's fictional world.

In the story "Yenwang" ("King of Hell"), Li has the opportunity to visit the lower world because of his respect for and humility before the gods. There he sees his sister-in-law being nailed to the door by her limbs. According to the lords of hell, her behavior toward her husband's concubine has been so cruel that she deserves utmost punishment before death. Having seen for himself the kind of suffering his sister will have to endure in the nether world if she does not reform, Li is given the mission to correct her morally once he returns to earth. When Li's sister-in-law, who is ill in bed, hears from Li what she had done in secret to the concubine, she is terrified. Immediately, she changes her attitude toward the concubine and very soon becomes well.

In writing this story of hell, Pu expresses the Confucian ideal of benevolence, as well as the Buddhist law of karma. Stories like these were meant to be deterents of crime and misdemeanor. There are quite a few more tales on the subject of hell. Some examples for further reading are: "An Inspector of Misdeeds," "Three Lives," and "A Feast of Yama Raja."

"The Fighting Cricket"

Pu understood the plight of poor peasants who worked hard not only to support themselves but also to pay annual tariffs. His compassion for this diligent group is shown in his poetry and other works. He cared for them enough to edit a dictionary of daily-use words, a medical guide for common illnesses, and a calendar for agricultural purposes, all of which were written in a simple style for better understanding by this uneducated group.

A good portion of the tales in *Strange Stories* deal with peasants and simple folks from the countryside. The story "Cuzhi" ("The Fighting Cricket") is one of Pu's tales written out of sympathy for the peasant class. Because the emperor has taken pleasure in cricket games, his subjects order various provincial and local officials to provide a number of fighting crickets to court to be used for the majesty's enjoyment. Cheng, a local magistrate, is given the task of collecting crickets. He searches about for crickets but can find only weak specimens that would be unable to fight. After he is given a hundred blows with bamboo by the bailiff, he is finally directed by a fortune teller to a place where, with much difficulty (and various mysterious events), he finds a splendid cricket that he feeds generously with crab meat and chestnuts. His only son, who is nine years old, plays with the insect while Cheng is out and the cricket escapes; in his frantic effort to recapture the cricket, the boy breaks the cricket's leg and the cricket dies. The child is so frightened at the thought of what his father will do to him that he jumps into the well before his father returns. The parents think that the child is dead, but as they prepared to bury him they find that he is still breathing but out of his mind and desirous of sleep. The parents are despairing, but they also have to worry about finding a fighting cricket for the bailiff. During the period when Cheng's son is in a coma, a small but sturdy cricket hops onto Cheng's sleeve. Cheng tests its skill and it proves to be a smarter and better fighter than a cock. He turns it over to the bailiff, who also is surprised at its talents. In the court, the emperor, too, is amazed by its dancing and fighting abilities. Finally Cheng is rewarded with beautiful furs, carriages, and houses. Not only that, his son wakes up one day saying that, in his sleep, he had dreamed that he was a cricket that had won many fights.

This story is a dream-come-true for the poor and the oppressed. Pu first shows how ridiculous it is that an honest man can be oppressed by his superiors, in this case, the emperor's whims for cricket fighting. The game is just a pasttime for the emperor, while it turns into a matter of life and death for others. This tale also shows how officials use their power to oppress and to exploit the people below them. The pressure of the government extends to the nine-year-old who kills himself because of fear and guilt (although he later miraculously revives). Pu does not want to relate a meaningless tragedy; he romanticizes the situation by providing a happy ending. At the end, justice is secured; Cheng's son revives, and Cheng is rewarded with riches and comforts. This is a poor man's dream: miracles happen when all hopes fail. During his coma, the boy becomes a cricket to save his father, to fulfill his obligation of filial piety, and to redress the wrong he had done in injuring and bringing about the death of the first cricket. Obviously, Pu's romanticism includes Confucian and ethical elements.

There are many more examples of stories involving dreams and miracles. To cite a few, *"Huabi"* *("Hua-pi")* ("The Wall Painting") is a romantic story about a scholar's escape into the fantasy world. He enters the heavenly world inside a wall painting in a temple where he and his friend are visiting. In heaven, he is married to a beautiful fairy and leading a happy life until the heavenly king discovers their secret union. The monk from the temple comes to his rescue when he calls him back to the world. This tale reflects the dream of the scholar in his spiriitual escape from the mundane world.

"A Bao" ("A Pao"), a story of a miracle that happens to a man looked down upon by others, and *"Xu Huangliang" ("Hsü huangliang")* ("Another Evanescent Dream"), in which a man comes to a philosophical understanding of life, are stories of wishfulfillment and escape. These escape stories served as the lid of a tea kettle letting out steam building up in lives of poverty, injustice, and suffering.

Female Foxes and Spirits

One will find that many of the tales in *Strange Stories* are about foxes and spirits. Fox tales are a tradition not only in China but also in Japan and other Asian countries. In ancient Chinese folktales, foxes are portrayed as versatile animals. In order to attain its purpose, an old fox can turn itself into the image of a beautiful young woman, a learned and handsome scholar, an old respectable man, the member of a human family, or even Buddha himself. The fox's ability for transformation depends on its age and its power of sorcery. Compared to other animals, the fox, because of its versatility in transformation, is able to be closer to and more involved with human beings. The animal takes part in almost all of human social activities, including love, education, and religion.

Pu's bad fox spirits are traditional. These spirits usually bewitch and possess their victims, ruining their health and causing their families' concern. In most of the fox spirit tales, the fox spirits are exorcised by a Taoist priest or a helper who drives away or kills the spirit. Many of these bad spirits die of lasciviousness.

The most touching of Pu's fox characters are those who possess human virtues and values. The female fox in the story *"Yatou" ("Ya t'ou")* is a perfect model of a chaste and virtuous wife. Coming from a brothel, Yatou differs from her fox sisters in that she is not promiscuous in the practice of her profession. Once she devotes herself to Wang, she swears fidelity to him. Despite physical torture inflicted by her fox mother, Yatou remains faithful. She suffers under her mother's hands for years until her son grows up to be a young man and rescues her from agony. Yet she does not want her mother to be hurt. She is heartbroken when she finds out that her half-human son has killed both her mother and sister. Yatou is a woman who dares to love and is willing to die in order to keep her chastity. She is defeated only by her own kindness toward her family. She is very human, as she values chastity and family ties and is willing to sacrifice herself for both.

There are water ghosts, female ghosts, wandering and hungry ones from hell in the *Strange Stories*. Like the fox spirits, none of these ghosts possesses superhuman powers. The most they have is the foreknowledge of future events that they lack the power to control. "Wang Liulang" is a very good example of a virtuous ghost. As fishermen Xu and Wang have been friends for a year without Xu's knowing that Wang is a water ghost. Every evening, Xu drinks with Wang, who in return gives advice to Xu where to drop his net. As a result, Xu never fails to catch what he needs. One day, Wang reveals his identity and claims that his reincarnation is at hand. There will be a woman drowned the next day and she will be his substitute. The next day, everything happens as Wang has predicted, except that the woman is miraculously rescued just before she is drowned. Wang comes to Xu again and admits that he has saved the woman because she has a young child. He does not want to ruin two lives to save his own.

From then on, Wang and Xu are friends again, with Wang having no definite hope of finding another substitute in the near future. Then a message comes from heaven commending Wang on his magnanimity and self-sacrifice. He is given an official position in heaven without going through the process of reincarnation.

There are many more tales on virtuous and moral ghosts and spirits. Pu used these tales to teach, to commend and to uphold morality. Yet critics agree that the prolific author is more of a humanist than a religious advocate. To Pu, religion and philosophy were not bad; they were there to pose guidelines and social standards. But to be human is the most important of all. To achieve his goal of emphasizing the importance of a virtuous humanity, Pu used romanticism and fantasy in creating his characters and tales. The master of supernatural tales in Chinese literature, Pu Songling, believed that humanity is what gives life to hope, happiness, and immortality.

FATIMA WU

Further Reading

Translations

Giles, Herbert A., trans. *Strange Stories from a Chinese Studio*. New York: Dover Publication, Inc., 1969. Giles was the first person to translate the *Liaozhai Zhiyi*. His work began in 1877 and the first edition came out 1880. It has 165 stories, some of which deviate from the original depending on Giles's personal preference. Those that he deemed tedious and uninteresting, he would abridge. No special theme is involved in this collection.

Lu, Yunzhong, and Chen Tifang, Yang Liyi, and Yang Zhihong, trans. *Strange Tales of Liaozhai*. Hong Kong: Commercial Press, 1988. This is probably one of the most recent translations available. It includes 85 stories, and notes the original Chinese titles. Beautiful illustrations adorn this edition.

Mair, Denis C., and Victor H. Mair. *Strange Tales from Make-do Studio*. Beijing: Foreign Language Press, 1989. These 48 tales come with illustrations and a 13-page introduction.

Quong, Rose, trans. *Chinese Ghost and Love Stories*. New York: Pantheon Books Inc., 1946. This translation includes 40 stories from the *Liaozhai zhiyi*. It is not divided into volumes and there is no reference to the original text. The book is augmented by pictorial illustrations.

THE SCHOLARS

Title in Chinese: *Rulin waishi (Ju-lin wai-shih)* (Unofficial History of the Literati)
Author: Wu Jingzi (Wu Ching-tzu)
Born: 1701, Quanjiao
Died: 1754, Yangzhou
Literary Form: Novel, satirical
Date of Composition: 1739–1750

Major Themes

Fame, riches, and rank may vanish without a trace, so aspire not to these.
To live quietly and contentedly in a green plot is as good as being immortal!
To be ignorant is far less blameworthy than to be immoral.
It is the very taste of success that corrupts.

The *Rulin waishi (The Scholars)* is one of the six great traditional Chinese novels and is a landmark in satirical realism. The novel consists of 55 chapters loosely strung together by a narrative in the style of a picaresque romance. It describes the machinations of a large number of persons, mainly scholars and pseudoscholars, who make their appearances one after the other, interact in a series of incidents, and then disappear. The work can be roughly divided into three parts flanked by a prologue and an epilogue. The prologue and epilogue present idealized portraits of hermetic sages against whom the counterfeit scholars in the main body of the novel are to be judged.

Part I (chs. 2–30) consists of satirical stories about individuals seeking official position, fame, and wealth. Part II (chs. 31–36) tells the story of the quixotic Du Shaojing (Shao Ching) and his fellow scholars of Nanjing who eventually perform a commemorative ceremony at a local temple. Part III (chs. 37–54) is a miscellaneous group of episodes, some of which revert to the satiric modes of parts I and II, while others are romances about men and women of extraordinary Confucian conduct. Most of the characters are based on real people who lived at the time of the author, but the author placed them in the previous dynasty, the Ming.

Wu Jingzi

Wu Jingzi wrote during the reign of the Emperor Jianlong (Chien-lung; 1736–1795), at the height of Qing dynasty prosperity. He was born into an Anhui province gentry family of declining fortunes. Wu's future at first seemed promising when he succeeded at the lowest level government examination (*xiucai/hsiu-ts'ai*) in 1720. However, the focus of his life changed after his father's death as he squandered most of his personal inheritance in pursuit of wine and women. Wu became uncomfortable with the criticism he received from family and acquaintances concerning his lifestyle and decided to move to Nanjing where he continued to live beyond his means. Still acknowledged for his scholarly potential, he was invited to take a special imperial examination in 1736. However, because of health or other reasons he did not attend the session. His main public achievement, one for which he was apparently most proud, was that he gave what remained of his fortune to complete the renovation of a temple in honor of former sages. Wu's extant poetry indicates that he continued to be sensitive to criticism and that his decision to give up seeking an official position caused him some anguish. Wu probably started work on *The Scholars* in 1739 and completed it around 1750. He remained for the rest of his life in the Nanjing area barely getting along by taking on various kinds of literary employment.

A Satirical Novel

The Scholars is the first satirical novel of China to be written from a Confucian point of view and to achieve an almost complete disassociation from religious beliefs. Its principal target is the typical Chinese scholar of the time who was totally preoccupied with winning honors and rising in the official bureaucracy to the neglect of both moral character and technical training. A second major target is the imperial examination system, which had a sterilizing effect on scholarship, and, as seen by Wu, a detrimental influence on the moral values of the intellectuals who participated in the system. Wu's exposure of the ignorance and shamelessness of his contemporaries indicates a belief that there is nothing inherently honorable about career success—leading an ordinary, good life is more valuable than being a high official, and solid learning is to be more cherished than ability to write an artificially styled, eight-legged essay.

To highlight his point of view, Wu presents characters who lead ordinary, but exemplary lives—painters, tailors, widows, and military officers—to illustrate how mean and miserly some of the successful scholars had become. A number of Wu's satiric victims are young opportunists who compromise their moral integrity whenever opportunity knocks—for example, the young scholar, Kuang Chaoren (K'uang Ch'ao-jen), who at first exhibits two worthy virtues (filial piety and studiousness) but later accepts the patronage of a local magistrate to forward his career. Wu was equally ardent in attacking the by-products of orthodox Confucian conventions, such as the practice of encouraging widows to follow their deceased husbands to the grave.

Some critics see Wu's satirical efforts as anti-Manchu, and claim that as the reason why the novel is set during the Ming dynasty, a native Chinese dynasty. However, Wu appears to be quite impartial, being critical not only of service to the Manchu government, but of service to all governments that compromise adherence to Confucian principles. For instance, although the Ming emperor is generally portrayed in a favorable light in the novel, Wu derides the Ming decision to change the examination system and thus allow the rise of young opportunists who are not grounded in real learning.

For about two-thirds of the work, Wu's satire is sharp and effective. The author is, on the whole, unbiased and open-minded. He has no apparent personal axes to grind, nor does he appear to be using himself as the yardstick of moral perfection. His criticism is not biting and is usually tempered with a touch of sympathy for even the worst of the human foibles. As the author rambles on from episode to episode, his satire, however, gradually loses its sense of perspective and lapses into spells of the absurd. This is especially true in the last third of the work, where Wu's satirical control flags precipitously as his art becomes more personal and less urbane. Because the particular social conditions Wu criticizes have faded into history, certain elements of his satirical art are difficult to decipher fully.

The Eremitic Ideal

Wu Jingzi's satire is founded on his perceptions of idealistic Confucianism, and the eremitic standards with which it measures Chinese society. The stories of the recluse painter Wang Mian in the prologue and of the four eccentrics at the end argue for a life of uncompromising self-cultivation, possible only to those unfettered by the search for rank and wealth. In this world view, which draws on a sense of resignation and nostalgia for the lost paradise of a great culture, the only persons who are naturally ethical are the social outsiders—hermit-types to whom the fate of the world is a matter of indifference. Moreover, there is little that can be taken seriously, particularly the artificial constructs of the government bureaucracy and its entry path, the examination system.

With his illustrious family background, Wu maintains a clearly elitist attitude throughout the work toward all pretenders to learning and bureaucratic office. Rank and wealth were things that he probably took for granted, and he thought that they were extremely unworthy to covet them. Wu's eventual impoverishment seems to have further confirmed his prejudice against all upstarts. This pride is expressed most clearly by Du Shaojing (Tu Shao-ching), the character in the novel whose life reflects that of the author in major ways. Du's decision to preserve his integrity and give up most of his fortune to perform commemorative rituals at a temple parallels the temple-building episode in the author's own life—both leaving a sense of futile accomplishment. Wu was not a complete nihilist; however, his pessimism concerning the efficacy of institutional reform and his belief in the futility of government social action surface over and over again throughout the work. What Wu attacks are the Confucian conventions that have been emptied of their meaning and have led to hypocrisy and even cruelty.

A Keen Observer of His Time

Wu Jingzi further strengthens his satire through an acute awareness of the social conditions of his time, something not seen much in earlier fiction, and by his skillful characterization of different human and social types. His work portrays not only the life of the Confucian elite, but also that of a rich assemblage of ordinary men and women in everyday commoner, bourgeois, and official surroundings. In *The Scholars*, a mere tailor or actor is recognized as a highly respectable person, even a model, while a military officer is seen as inherently lovable. In Wu's world, moral propriety is not always rewarded: a good man does not necessarily get his just deserts, while a corrupt man may prosper precisely because he is morally unscrupulous. Wu seems to have had little notion of systematic societal reform, but he does present an enlightened view of the integrity of the individual.

Wu displays a marked ambivalence towards the possibility of predestination in human affairs. Through the actions and reactions of his characters, the author not only reveals his skepticism regarding the beliefs and practices of the Confucian elite, but he also targets such practices as fortune-telling, astrology, and geomancy, which are merely means for the unscrupulous to extract money from the gullible.

A New View of Women

The Scholars contains a diversified gallery of women, something again unprecedented up to that time in Chinese fiction. Throughout the novel, Wu presents a number of women who are neither submissive nor inferior to men, and he highlights the inequities between men and women in Chinese society—especially the plight of prostitutes—and he makes clear his opposition to concubinage. Wu's sensitive treatment of women and insights into relations between men and women are much in advance of his time.

Breakthroughs in Narration

The Scholars represents several other major milestones in the development of Chinese fiction, marking a prominent transition from folk literature to modern belles lettres. It is the first major fictional work to be written by one hand, and the first to be wholly independent of historical or legendary cycles. It is also the first major novel to consciously use the colloquial vernacular, an early form of the Chinese national language called *guoyu (kuo-yü)*.

While Wu retains a minimal number of storytellers' formulas in his language and style, he makes no use of songs or of stock poetic vocabulary and relies on his own description of people and places of the Jiangnan region of China (near Nanjing). Descriptive passages in earlier fictional works were often written as verse interludes; however, in *The Scholars* these passages are integral parts of the narration. In fact, only two poems appear in the work at all, one at the beginning and one at the end. Furthermore, no other major Chinese novel starts by placing the reader directly into the dramatic action—from the very beginning of the first chapter—with the characters going about their business, conversing on day-to-day matters, and gradually revealing themselves.

The narrative form of this novel reflects elements used effectively in historical prose, particularly that of Sima Qian (Ssu-ma Ch'ien) (c. 143– c. 90 B.C.). For example, just as Sima Qian did in the biographies of his *Shiji* (Records of the Grand Historian [Astrologer]), Wu juxtaposes stories of heroes and nonheroes, offering points of comparison. Furthermore, like a good historian or story-

teller, Wu's narrator, operates with a very low profile, bringing the reader directly into contact with
the story and making the characters come alive
through their actions rather than by a recitation of
their characteristics by the narrator.

Influence of the Novel

Following Wu Jingzi's *The Scholars,* there was a
marked rise in both the volume and intensity of
writing about the positive role of women in Chinese society. However, *Rulin waishi* had its greatest
impact on the development of social criticism in
fiction. The tradition of social concern it spawned
was developed in the fiction of late Qing (Ch'ing)
authors such as Li Baojia (Li Pao-chia) (1867–
1906), Liu E (Liu O) (1857–1909), and Wu Woyao
(1866–1910). It had a particularly profound influence on Lu Xun (Lu Hsün) who examined it in his
Brief History of Chinese Fiction and also wrote
some of modern China's most powerful and artful
satire and social criticism. Under the political
stresses of more recent times, this satirical tradition
took on great vitality and dominates much of the
twentieth-century literary scene.

KENNETH G. KOZIAL

Further Reading

Translation

Yang, Hsien-yi, and Gladys Yang, trans. *The
Scholars.* Peking: Foreign Languages Press,
1957. A generally accurate and nearly complete
translation. Leaves out chapter 56 and various
passages.

Related Studies

Brandauer, F. R. "Realism, Satire, and the *Ju-lin
wai-shih.*" *Tamkang Review* 20(1), 1–21. Argues
that Wu Jingzi's technique balances the opposing forces of satire and realism.

Hsia, C. T. *The Classic Chinese Novel: A Critical
Introduction.* Bloomington, IN: Indiana University Press, 1968. Covers the major works of Chinese traditional fiction.

Lu, Hsün. *A Brief History of Chinese Fiction.*
Trans. Yang Hsien-yi and Gladys Yang. Peking:
Foreign Language Press, 1954. Surveys the development of fiction in China from the Tang
dynasty to the late Qing.

Ralston, David L., ed. *How to Read the Chinese
Novel.* Princeton, N.J.: Princeton University
Press, 1990. Makes available English translations of Chinese comments on traditional fiction,
including *Rulin waishi.*

Ropp, Paul S. *Dissent in Early Modern China: Ju-
lin wai-shih and Ch'ing Social Criticism.* Ann
Arbor, MI: University of Michigan Press, 1981.
Examines the place of *Rulin waishi* in the context of Chinese social criticism.

Wong, C. Timothy. *Wu Ching-tzu.* Boston: Twayne
Publishers, 1978. Recounts the biography of Wu
Jingzi and examines Wu Jingzi's satirical art and
the eremitic ideal as seen in the work.

DREAM OF THE RED CHAMBER

Title in Chinese: *Honglou meng (Hung-lou meng)*
Author: Cao Xueqin (Ts'ao Hsüeh-ch'in)
Born: c. 1715
Died: 1763
Literary Form: Novel
Date of Publication: First printed edition, 1792

Major Themes

Nothing in life is permanent.
Life is characterized by passion for the things, people, and experiences of this world, all of which are illusory.
It is difficult to distinguish between dreams and waking, illusion and reality, the false and the true.
Being faithful to one's inner nature often conflicts with social obligations, causing suffering.
Fate or karma determines to a great extent how our lives will be played out.

Dream of the Red Chamber is widely acknowledged to be China's greatest novel. This panorama of life in a large, aristocratic Chinese household has fascinated readers of all ages and backgrounds since it was first circulated in manuscript form in the late eighteenth century. The genius of the novel lies in its amazing complexity presented with a seemingly simple directness. Teenage boys and girls are enthralled by the psychological realism of the love stories, while mature scholars marvel at the intricacy of the various strands and levels of the plot. Widely appealing as the novel is, questions about its interpretation abound, and a whole school of scholarship called "Redology" *(hongxue/hunghsüeh)* has arisen to study the work.

The history of the text itself is complex and uncertain. One group of scholars believes that the present 120-chapter edition consists of 80 chapters written by Cao Xueqin and 40 chapters written by Gao E (Kao Ngoh), the editor of the first printed edition, that follow plot lines sketched out by Cao. Another group of scholars holds that all 120 chapters were written by Cao himself.

Most scholars believe that the novel is to some extent autobiographical. There is little doubt that the vivid descriptions of the family compound, of the food, clothing, furniture, games, and daily activities of its inhabitants, stem from Cao's memo-

ries of his own childhood and youth in his wealthy family's compounds in Nanjing and Beijing. The gradual decay and downfall of the family in the novel also reflects the Cao family's decline, which left Cao Xueqin himself in poverty in his adulthood. What is in dispute is the extent to which the individual characters in the novel resemble Cao Xueqin and his own family and friends, which of the events described in the novel actually took place, and which are purely fictional.

Scope of the Novel

Dream of the Red Chamber can be viewed as a portrait of two branches of the aristocratic Jia (Chia) family (the surname "Jia" is a homophone for the Chinese word for "false"), living in Beijing during the mid-eighteenth century. Though the main characters are the teenage boy Baoyu (Pao-yu) and two of his female cousins, the novel is really about the household as a whole, with its scores of family members and servants all living in two vast adjoining compounds. Love affairs, games and amusements, power struggles, sibling rivalries, parent-child conflicts, master-servant relations, financial difficulties, political intrigues, betrayals, jealousy, illness, murder, suicide—all kinds of activities and permutations of personal relations are described with a clarity and directness seldom seen in Chinese fiction.

The work is too complex to be summarized in a few sentences; but two broad plot lines can be singled out. First, the inexorable decline of the Jia family from wealth and prominence to poverty and disgrace; and second, Baoyu's ill-fated love for his cousin Daiyu (Tai-yu) that results in his leaving the worldly life to become a monk. Intertwined with the second theme is the story of a mysterious jade pendant which was found in Baoyu's mouth when he was born (his name, Baoyu, means "precious jade"), which seems in some way to contain his life spirit. This motif is the source of the novel's alternate title, The *Story of the Stone (Shitou ji)*.

The novel begins in heaven, where an unusual stone had sheltered a tender plant from the withering rays of the sun; dew condensed on the stone had watered the plant, and because of this the plant owed the stone a "debt of tears." The stone was born into the world as Baoyu, and the plant as his beloved Daiyu; and thus their love was fated from before their birth to be unhappy. The author's periodic reminders of the connection between the world above, where fates are determined, and this earthly world, where we have the illusion of making choices, provide a weighty Buddhist grounding for the work as a whole.

Characters and Characterization

The central figure, Jia Baoyu, is the son of a strict Confucian scholar, Jia Zheng (Chia Cheng), and grandson of Grandmother Jia, the wise and kindly head of the Rongguo (Jung-kuo) branch of the Jia clan. Baoyu has a sensitive, artistic nature, and much prefers associating with his female cousins and his maids to studying Confucian classics. One of the major tensions of the novel is the relationship between Baoyu and his father, between following his own inclinations and performing his filial duties. The author clearly sympathizes with Baoyu in this conflict, and in so doing distinguishes this novel from the countless morality tales that are standard fare in Chinese fiction. This is probably one reason why the book was considered unsuitable

reading for young people until well into the present century.

Baoyu has two female cousins who come to live in the Rongguo compound, Daiyu and Baochai (Pao-ch'ai). Daiyu is slender, ethereal, and ultra-sensitive, and is Baoyu's true love; Baochai is more robust and cheerful, and is the Jia family's choice as a bride for Baoyu. The relations among Baoyu, Daiyu, and Baochai are another center of tension in the work.

Baoyu's lecherous cousin Jia Lian (Chia Lien) is married to a fiery-tempered and capable young woman Xifeng (Hsi-feng), who in the course of the novel assumes more and more responsibilities in the family until finally she is put in charge of managing the affairs of the Ningguo (Ning-kuo) branch of the clan, whose compound adjoins the Rongguo compound. Jia Lian's escapades and Xifeng's manipulative activities provide some of the most colorful and horrifying episodes in the novel.

Two other peripheral but key characters are the Daoist monk and Buddhist priest who appear in the first and last chapters and at various times during the story. They serve to remind the readers of the connection between this earthly life and the world above, and they are associated with Baoyu's getting and losing his jade pendant.

In addition to these major characters there are several maids, actors, princes, nuns, country-bumpkin relatives, and others too numerous to mention, who play significant minor roles in the novel.

One of the great accomplishments of the novelist is the way he has been able to depict vividly individualized characters, true to life, and memorable. Women are portrayed with particular sensitivity.

Reflections on Society

Confucian ethics dictates that the individual subordinate his or her personal wishes to the family's welfare, as defined by the eldest males in the family. In practical terms this means that children should always obey their fathers and wives should obey their husbands. The tacit assumption is that the head of the household will make decisions based on moral wisdom and compassion, and that everyone will benefit. But what happens when the eldest males abuse their authority, or when they are not competent to make wise decisions for their family? *Dream of the Red Chamber* implicitly questions the Confucian values that permeate Chinese society by showing that suffering results from the rigid application of empty Confucian forms.

Baoyu's ongoing conflict with his father is the main focus of this theme. His father's greatest wish is that Baoyu will study hard to pass the imperial examinations so that he can become a government official; his second wish is that Baoyu will marry a cheerful, healthy girl and produce one or more sons to carry on the family line. Both of these wishes represent positive and reasonable Confucian ideals, but both conflict with Baoyu's inner nature: he much prefers reading poetry or helping his maids put on their lipstick to studying the Confucian classics; and he wants to marry the frail, neurotic Daiyu rather than his parents' choice, Baochai (Pao Ch'ai).

Most heroes in traditional Chinese fiction are either good scholars or capable warriors. A character like Baoyu normally would be dismissed as a spoiled child who needs some discipline; he would be judged by both author and reader from within the Confucian value system held by Baoyu's father. *Dream of the Red Chamber* is unique in its questioning of the dominant value system and in its examination of life from the point of view of characters who feel trapped and unfulfilled in the system.

Cao Xueqin suggests that one of the underlying problems of the dominant social system is its "sham" quality, its "falseness" and "emptiness." He attacks not only sham Confucian values, but also sham Buddhist and Daoist beliefs and practices, and false and empty values of any kind. False feelings of superiority based on wealth and status come under attack many times.

Allegorical, Symbolic, and Religious Dimensions

Most readers recognize an allegorical dimension to *Dream of the Red Chamber*, but there is much

disagreement as to the nature and significance of the allegory. The jade found in Baoyu's mouth at his birth, for example, surely has a special meaning in the story, but the meaning is not clear. We know the jade's history: originally it was a magical stone that could change size at will, but was rejected by the goddess Nu-wa when she chose stones to repair a hole in the heavens. A Daoist priest and Buddhist monk found the despondent stone in heaven, carved a few words on it, and sent it to earth in Baoyu's mouth. Eons later another Daoist returned to heaven and found the stone with the whole story of Baoyu's life on earth written on it; he copied and published it, and that is how we now have this novel.

According to the Daoist who discovered the text carved on the stone, the theme of the work is Passion. The narrator tells us in the first chapter that the Daoist read the work starting from Emptiness, from whence he saw Forms; Forms gave rise to Passion; through Passion he entered the world of Forms; and from Forms he returned to a true understanding of Emptiness. This hint from the author gives the readers a perspective from which to approach this enormously complex work. It is a Buddhist perspective that while recognizing the overwhelming power exhibited by the fascinating variety of worldly objects and experiences, believes that all the sensations and passions they evoke are but empty illusions. True enlightenment comes when one sees the emptiness of worldly concerns and renounces the world, as Baoyu does at the end of the novel.

Another allegory is associated with the magnificent Grandview Garden that the Jia family built between the two family compounds to house the Jia's eldest daughter, now an imperial concubine, on her brief visit to see her family. After her departure, Baoyu and the unmarried girls of the family move into the garden and live blissfully for a time in this secluded paradise. Gradually a series of events occur that brings the impurities of the outside world into the garden, signaling the beginning of the downfall, not only of the inhabitants of the garden, but of the entire Jia household.

Dreams play an important part in the novel.

While not strictly allegorical or symbolic, they foretell events in the story or describe experiences in a realm other than that of the earthly plane. For example, a dream sequence occurs early in the novel in which Baoyu learns the secrets of love-making and also glimpses an album of pictures that suggests the fate of several of the women in the story. Later in the novel the nun Miaoyu dreams of her future abduction, and Daiyu has a horrifying dream in which she realizes that she will not be able to marry Baoyu. The dreams contain truths belonging to a realm that, if not more real than waking life, participate in a different kind of reality.

JEANNETTE L. FAUROT

Further Reading

Translations

Cao, Xueqin. *The Story of the Stone [Dream of the Red Chamber].* Vols. 1–3, trans. David Hawkes; Cao Xueqin and Gao E, vols. 4–5, trans. John Minford. Middlesex, England: Penguin Books, 1973–1986. These five volumes taken together are the definitive English translation of *Dream of the Red Chamber.*

————. *A Dream of Red Mansions.* trans. Yang Hsien-yi and Gladys Yang. 3 vols. Beijing: Foreign Language Press, 1978–80. Another excellent translation, by China's leading translation team.

Related Studies

Knoerle, Jeanne. *The Dream of the Red Chamber: A Critical Study.* Bloomington, IN: Indiana University Press, 1972. A good introduction to the text.

Plaks, Andrew H. *Archetype and Allegory in The Dream of the Red Chamber.* Princeton, NJ: Princeton University Press, 1976. A thorough examination of the allegorical aspects of the novel.

THE WORKS OF LU XUN (LU HSÜN)

Author: Lu Xun (Lu Hsün): pseudonym of Zhou Shuren (Chou Shu-jen)
Born: 1881, Shaoxing, China
Died: 1936, Shanghai, China
Major Works: *Call to Arms* [stories] (1923), *Wandering* [stories] (1926), *Wild Grass* [prose poems] (1927), *The Grave* [essays] (1927), *And That's That* [essays] (1928)

Major Themes

The Chinese people of the twentieth century suffer from a spiritual sickness that infects and weakens the entire society.

Manifestations of this sickness include greed, self-deception, passivity, lack of compassion for others, and delight in oppressing the weak.

Literature, especially fiction, is a means to awaken the people to their plight, if not to cure them.

None of the major political movements—Nationalist, Anarchist, or Communist—addresses the root causes of China's problems.

Though it is hard to see how China can be saved, it is better to cling to a possibly false hope and to work for change than to give in to despair.

Lu Xun is generally acknowledged to be the father of modern Chinese literature. He wrote his most famous works during the turbulent period between the fall of the Qing Dynasty (1911) and the establishment of the Nationalist government in Nanjing (1927), and his writing reflects the social turmoil and moral uncertainty of that era.

Born into a literati family that had fallen on hard times, Lu Xun read voraciously as a child and became thoroughly familiar with traditional Chinese literature. He spent his late teens and early twenties studying first at the Naval Academy and then at the School of Railways and Mines, both in Nanjing, where he was exposed to Western ideas for the first time. A Chinese translation of Huxley's *Evolution and Ethics* impressed him deeply, and he decided to contribute to China's progressive evolution by studying science, specifically modern medicine, in Japan.

While in Japan he had a revelation that changed the course of his career. His microbiology professor customarily showed slides of current events at the end of his lectures. It was the time of the Russo-Japanese War in northeastern China, and one day the professor showed a picture of a Chinese man who was about to be beheaded by the Japanese for spying for the Russians. Surrounding the spy stood a crowd of Chinese people who were waiting eagerly to see the beheading. Lu Xun realized at that moment that there was a deeper sickness among the Chinese than the sicknesses of the body, namely, a sickness of the spirit, manifested in callous, cowardly, and passive behavior. What use was it, he asked himself, to cure the bodies of his countrymen if they remained infected with debilitating spiritual ills?

The best way to address the nation's spiritual ills, he thought, would be through literature. Together with a group of like-minded Chinese friends in Japan he decided to start a magazine; but to his disappointment, the enterprise folded before publication of the first issue. Lu Xun returned to China where he held various teaching posts and eventually was appointed to the Ministry of Education in Beijing. He arrived in Beijing in 1912, the first year after the overthrow of the Qing empire, harboring great hopes for China's future. But the corruption and ineffectiveness of the new government and the apparent futility of his own efforts sent him into a period of depression and soul-searching from which he was not to emerge for six years.

A second major turning point in his life occurred

when a friend came to visit him and ask him to write a piece for a progressive journal, *New Youth*. Lu Xun declined, arguing that there really was no point in trying to awaken the nation to its ills. In a famous analogy, Lu Xun likened China to an iron room with no windows or doors. The people inside were about to suffocate, he said, and it would be kinder to let them die in ignorance in their sleep than to wake them up only to alert them to their inevitable doom. His friend disagreed, pointing out that if enough people were awakened it might be possible for them to break out of the iron room. Lu Xun was convinced by his friend's plea, and wrote a story, "Diary of a Madman," which was published in *New Youth* in May, 1918.

During the years 1919–1927 Lu Xun wrote many stories and essays, and taught in colleges in Beijing, Xiamen (Amoy), and Guangzhou (Canton). He was active in social and cultural movements, supported women's rights, and encouraged numerous young writers. Targeted as a left-wing revolutionary by the Nationalist government then in power, he moved to Shanghai late in 1927 to seek safety in the international settlement there. In Shanghai he was one of the leading progressive writers in the country's most active literary community. He had stopped writing short stories, but continued writing satirical essays, and translated numerous works, mainly Russian fiction and literary criticism, from Japanese to Chinese. He died of tuberculosis in Shanghai in 1936.

Lu Xun's collected works contain two volumes of short stories (*Call to Arms* and *Wandering*), a volume of classical stories retold, one volume each of prose poems and reminiscences, a history of Chinese fiction, and sixteen volumes of essays. The remainder of this article will briefly examine some of his short stories, prose poems, and essays.

"Diary of a Madman"

"Diary of a Madman" ("*Kuangren riji*"/"*K'uang-jen jih-chi*") (1918), the story with which Lu Xun broke his silence, is written in the form of a series of diary entries made by a man suffering from acute paranoia. The man believes that his brother and his

brother's friend are trying to fatten him up in order to eat him. Indeed, the "madman" is convinced that all of China is caught up in a vast conspiracy to eat people. When he reads Chinese history books he sees the words "Eat People" written between the rows of characters. He recalls stories of how people in the past ate human flesh, sometimes with public approval, and he suspects that he himself may have eaten slivers of his own sister's flesh in a soup. Perhaps there are children who have not yet eaten human flesh, he muses at the end. The story concludes with a famous appeal, "save the children."

A preface within the story notes that the madman did recover and eventually take up a bureaucratic post, and that his incoherent ravings are preserved here for future medical research. Some critics have noted that the madman's sentiments are quite similar to Lu Xun's: both are terrified by the crass inhumanity of the people around them and by the kinds of barbaric behavior that Chinese history seems to have accepted as normal and sometimes even glorified. Both fear that they too have been infected with the disease of cannibalism, but both cling to a slim hope that perhaps the next generation can break out of these destructive patterns.

"Medicine"

"Medicine" ("*Yao*") (1919) continues the theme of physical and spiritual sickness. In this story the father of a boy dying of tuberculosis goes out to buy a "guaranteed cure," a steamed roll dipped in the fresh blood of an executed criminal (revolutionary). He manages to obtain a blood-soaked roll and feed it to his son, but the boy dies nonetheless. The story ends with the mothers of the boy and of the executed revolutionary meeting at the graveyard where the two youths are buried. A wreath of flowers, which has miraculously appeared on the revolutionary's grave, gives a ray of hope that someday things might be better.

In this story, debilitating illnesses include ignorance, superstition, and fear of revolutionary change, as well as the boy's tuberculosis. The medicine that the father obtained for his son clearly was not effective against the tuberculosis, and Lu Xun leaves unanswered the question of what can cure the ills from which the rest of the characters suffer.

"The True Story of Ah Q"

Lu Xun's most famous story is "The True Story of Ah Q" ("A Q Zhengzhuan"/"A Q Cheng-chuan") (1921), a long and episodic tale of the adventures of a down-and-out villager named Ah Q. Strictly speaking, Ah Q does not have a name; the narrator of the story claims not to know the man's real name, so he just refers to him by the familiar prefix "Ah" and the Roman letter "Q." Chinese readers have generally taken this to mean that Ah Q represents a kind of Chinese Everyman.

Ah Q's adventures are both humorous and tragico-pathetic. He lives in a world where status and face are of utmost importance, and his main concern is to impress and toady to people higher on the status ladder, and to lord it over the people lower down. His great skill is his capacity to gain a "psychological victory" over his rivals and tormentors, and thereby gain face and status, at least in his own eyes. Thus, after he is beaten up by a rival who insists that Ah Q confess that he is a "beast being beaten by a man," Ah Q calls himself not only a beast but an insect; then he congratulates himself on having won the battle because he was the "foremost self-belittler," and if you take off the term "self-belittler," you are left with the fact that he is "foremost," which is something to be proud of.

Ah Q is not always able to win. He feels dejected, for example, when his companion is able to find more numerous and fatter lice in his padded jacket than Ah Q can, and to make louder popping noises when biting the lice between his teeth. Ah Q joins the revolutionaries so that he can loot people's houses the way they do, and in the end he is executed as a criminal. The final paragraph describes the villagers" disappointment that he was shot instead of beheaded, because shooting was not as exciting a spectacle for them to watch.

In this story not only Ah Q but virtually all the characters embody the qualities that Lu Xun despises in his fellow Chinese. There is not a trace of compassion, kindness, generosity, or nobility to be found, but only selfishness, pettiness, laziness, greed, self-deception, and cruelty. As usual, Lu Xun provides no solution to the problem, but he presumably hopes that readers will recognize themselves in the satirical portraits, and perhaps be shamed into changing their own behavior. Most readers can see their neighbors clearly in this story, if not themselves, and the name Ah Q has come to stand in the Chinese language for the pervasive negative qualities in the national character.

Not all Lu Xun's stories are as harsh as the three outlined above. Two autobiographical sketches, "My Old Home" ("Guxiang"/"Ku-hsiang") (1921) and "Village Opera" ("Shexi"/"She-hsi") (1922), deserve mention as poignant reminiscences of childhood. But most of his stories, like "New Years" Sacrifice" ("Zhufu"/"Chu-fu") (1924), a scathing account of how cruelty and superstition drive a servant woman to her death, or "In the Wine Shop" ("Zai jiulou shang"/"Tsai chiu-lou shang") (1924), a portrait of two intellectuals who have lost all their youthful idealism and now live only to get by, portray a corrupt and corrupting society that holds out very little light or hope.

Wild Grass

Though Lu Xun's volume of prose poems, Wild Grass (Yecao/Yeh-ts'ao) (1924), totals only 80 or so pages, the works contained in it deserve attention both because of their aesthetic interest and because they often present Lu Xun's major themes in a starker form than the stories do.

From a young age Lu Xun was fascinated by traditional Chinese woodblock prints, and later by the prints of European artists such as Kathe Kollwitz. He liked the directness of the prints and the way they made a strong, unforgettable impact through powerful images, without presenting unnecessary details. Lu Xun tries to use similar principles in his fiction, and he applies them most purely in his prose poems. In one or two pages he is able to paint a vivid, visual scene and conjure up a psychological mood that leaves an indelible impression on the reader's mind. Many of the prose poems also contain an allegorical message that would be out of place in a work of realistic fiction.

"Snow" ("*Xue*"/"*Hsüeh*") (1925), for example, sketches children making a "snow Buddha" from dazzling, moist snow. After a day of sunshine its skin melts; but a cold night gives it a coat of ice that looks like opaque crystal. The piece seems mainly to be a reverie on different kinds of snow, the "ghosts of rain."

"Dead Fire" ("*Sihuo*"/"*Ssu-huo*") (1925), on the other hand, describes a dream in which the narrator finds himself on a mountain of ice that contains a dead fire. The narrator picks up the frozen flame and puts it into his pocket. The warmth from the man's body revives the flame, which burns a hole in the man's clothing. The man and the fire then discuss which would be better: to take the flame out into the warmth, where it would live and eventually burn itself out, or to leave it on the icy mountain, where it would be preserved forever in its frozen state. In this sketch Lu Xun is able to express more vividly and directly than in his stories his personal struggle with (or against) hope.

Essays

Lu Xun's essays cover a wide range of subjects, from random thoughts on the role of youth in society to observations on how best to toady to one's superiors, to the need for reform of the Chinese writing system. Most of the essays were written in response to current events, and most exhibit a strongly satirical tone.

The themes found in his short stories and prose poems are repeated in the essays—almost every essay contains at least one reference to a weakness in the Chinese national character—but the essays differ from Lu Xun's other works in that they often contain calls to action and strategies for accomplishing reformist goals from within the corrupt environment of the time.

One of Lu Xun's most famous essays is "What Happens After Nora Leaves Home?" ("*Nuola zouhou zenyang*"/"*Nola tsou-hou tsen-yang*") (1923), the title alluding to Ibsen's play *A Doll's House*, which was popular in China at the time. The essay points out the need to work towards economic rights for women, and indeed for all people, if they are ever to expect to enjoy the privilege of freedom. Another essay, "Waiting for a Genius" ("*Weiyou tiancai zhiqian*"/"*Wei-yu t'ien-ts'ai chih-ch'ien*") (1924), points out that a receptive public is as important to nourishing genius as good soil is to nourishing a rose. Lu Xun urges his readers to be good soil, supporting those who are working for the public good, rather than waiting critically for a genius to emerge full-blown.

Long after he stopped writing short stories, Lu Xun continued writing timely and pointed essays, struggling to the end with his own fear of the futility of his efforts.

JEANNETTE L. FAUROT

Further Reading

Translations

Yang, Xianyi, and Gladys Yang. *Lu Xun: Selected Works.* 4 vols. Beijing: Foreign Languages Press, 1980. A representative selection of stories, prose poems, and essays.

Lyell, William. *Diary of a Madman and Other Stories.* Honolulu: University of Hawaii Press, 1990. Lively translation of the best of Lu Xun's fictional works.

Related Studies

Lee, Leo Ou-fan, ed. *Lu Xun and His Legacy.* Berkeley, CA: University of California Press, 1985. A collection of essays by leading scholars in the field.

———. *Voices from the Iron House: A Study of Lu Xun.* Bloomington, IN: University of Indiana Press, 1987. A thorough study of Lu Xun's life and role in modern Chinese literature.

Lyell, William. *Lu Hsun's Vision of Reality.* Berkeley, CA: University of California Press, 1976. A biography of Lu Xun and reconstruction of the fictional world portrayed in his stories.

THE SHORT STORIES AND NOVELS OF XIAO HONG (HSIAO HUNG)

Author: Xiao Hong (Hsiao Hung) (Pseudonym of Zhang Nai Ying/Chuang Nai Ying)
Born: 1911, Hulan City, Heilongjiang Province, China
Died: 1942, Hong Kong
Major Short Stories: "The Death of Wang Asao" (1932), "Night Wind" (1933), "Hands" (1936), "Bridge" (1936), "The Family Outsider" (1936), "On the Oxcart" (1937), and "Spring in a Small Town" (1941)
Major Novels: *Field of Life and Death* (1934), *Market Street* (1935), *Tales of Hulan River* (1939–1940), *Ma Bole* (1940–1941, unfinished)

Major Themes

Life at war is hard and sometimes very ugly.
Oppression of females and the poor must be stopped.
Love among fellow human beings and between man and woman is difficult to find.

Born of a wealthy landlord family in the cold Heilongjiang Province, Xiao Hong's tumultuous life can be described as one that is comparable to that of an exile. Xiao's father was a mean and authoritarian landlord who oppressed his subordinates. After her mother died, when Xiao Hong was nine years old, she grew up in her grandfather's warm arms. This kind and generous old man appears in many of Xiao's stories. He not only gave her love and protection but he was also able to send her to school. Yet before Xiao could finish her high school education, her grandfather died, leaving her to fend for herself.

Before this time, Xiao had painted and written poetry. Moreover, as an active high school student, she had participated in the movement against Japanese invasion in the northeastern part of China. Because of her ultra-political ideals and her refusal to marry under her father's order, Xiao was disowned by the family. Hence, her lonely wandering began at the age of 19.

In the beginning, Xiao sent her poems and essays to local newspapers and journals to be published. In 1932, encouraged by her friends, Xiao wrote her first story "The Death of Wang Asao" to enter a story-writing competition sponsored by *International News*. From then on, she continued to write.

But her debut into the national literary arena did not happen until she came into contact with the literary giant, Lu Xun (Lu Hsün). In 1934, while living in abject poverty in Qingdao, Xiao wrote to Lu and asked him to read her manuscript, *Field of Life and Death*. Lu agreed and invited Xiao to come join him in Shanghai, the city of the intellectuals. The appearance of Lu in Xiao's life had a big impact on her career as a writer. Lu introduced her to publishers and other writers who helped her to establish her place in the literary world.

During the short 30 years Xiao lived, she wrote approximately a hundred short stories, essays, and poems, as well as a pantomine. The bulk of her work was written between the ages of 21 and 30, including the last few years when she was ill. Xiao's life as a daughter, a woman, a mother, a writer, and a revolutionist was filled with loneliness, sadness, tears, and sneers from others. The daughter she gave birth to died soon after she was born. The three men she loved during her lifetime failed to give her comfort and happiness. In 1942, when the Japanese Imperial Army occupied Hong Kong, where Xiao was hospitalized, she died a lonely death caused by tuberculosis.

Xiao was one of the pioneer woman writers in China in the pre-war period. The greatness of her works lies in her outspoken criticism of politics, tradition, and a sexist society. Given her education and family background, the amount of work she produced in those 10 years can be described as, on one hand, prolific, and, on the other, amazing. Like Lu Xun, Xiao was a humanistic writer: she cared for her people. Thoughout her life, she lived among chaos and war, but she never gave up the endless search and hope for love, perfection, and happiness.

A Speaker for the Peasants

Born of a landlord's family, Xiao Hong witnessed the toil and suffering of the peasant class. As a child, she saw her father taking over a peasant family's only horse and cart in lieu of rent. The stricken family begged for mercy, because the horse meant survival for them, but Xiao's father lent them no ears. Chinese peasants in the 30's lived on the brink of poverty and famine. After years of civil unrest and political instability since the fall of the Qing dynasty (1644–1912), Chinese peasants barely managed to survive. They had been overtaxed by the corrupted Nationalist government, exploited by the merciless landlords, and robbed by the starving bandits. It was the time when communism began to give them hope and a future to look forward to. Xiao Hong, following her mentor Lu Xun's footsteps, joined the League of Left Wing Writers. Her sympathy for the poor peasants urged her to speak up for them as she did in many of her works: "The Death of Wang Asao," "The Family Outsider," "Bridge," "Flying the Kite," and chapters from the *Tales of the Hulan River*.

Xiao's first story, "The Death of Wang Asao" relates the tragic story of a woman from the labor class. Wang Asao's husband dies when Landlord Zhang (Chang) sets fire to the haystack where he is sleeping. He had hidden himself there because of frustration and despair. A week earlier, while Wang was using the landlord's horse, the horse had fallen and broken its leg, after which the landlord cancelled six months of Wang's pay for his carelessness.

Wang Asao is pregnant when her husband dies. In order to make a living, she works in the fields picking potatoes until, one day close to the end of her pregnancy, she is kicked in the belly by the landlord. After that she cannot get up and for days lies in bed in pain. When her child is born, both mother and child struggle for life, which they both lose at last.

Xiao's first story is successful in her description of the reality of the peasant's life under oppression. In the landlord's eyes, a peasant's life is worthless. A laborer is useful only when he or she is able to work and produce. When the pregnant Wang Asao sits down to take a break from working in the fields, she provokes her master's anger. When her husband is driven to frustration and anger by his loss of pay due to an accident, he is considered insane by his master and thus useless. A peasant is born to work as an ox or a mule in a landlord's home. Not only that, their children and generations after will suffer the same fate if not worse.

Stories of Peasant Life

Obviously, Xiao Hong is sympathetic to the suffering peasants whom she knows so well from her childhood. In "Bridge," a woman who works on one side of the river as a wet nurse for her master's baby, watches her own baby crying for her on the other side. She dreams of a new bridge being built, so that one day her child can come over to join her and she can feel his face once again. Some time later, money is raised to repair the old bridge. When her happy child runs over to meet her, he trips, falls into the river and drowns.

"The Family Outsider" talks of an old time servant's serious beating by his master. Family members just stand by and watch; nobody comes forth to stop the beating because he is just a servant. Thereupon, two ducks clamber up to where the servant lies and with their beaks peck at the blood on the ground.

Chapter seven of *Tales of Hulan River* tells of Feng (a "slanted-mouth" peasant who works in a mill), who does not receive understanding from his master when he decides to have a family. His master and mistress, despite the bitter cold, drive his wife and the newborn baby out of the mill. The three stay in a barn borrowed from a kind old man and cover themselves with hay while the temperature outside is below zero. His wife works hard to take care of the child and the family. A year later, after she has a second baby, she dies of malnutrition. Alone, Feng raises the two children, feeding them with leftover food from his master's table. What is admirable about him is that he remains strong and hopeful about life even after suffering repeatedly from defeat and disappointment.

In the story "Hands," a young girl named Wang, from a family of dyers tries to get an education by attending a nearby school. But her dye-tainted hands become an indelible mark of her background. She is segregated by her fellow students and sneered at by school authorities. She does her best to accede to her father's wishes—to learn and then go home to teach her brothers and sisters so that they can all get out of the dyeing business. Because she receives no help, encouragement, or support from the school, she is forced to leave after a year. Her father cannot come up with enough resources to keep her in school any longer. A pair of hands covered with dye has led to the shattering of the laborer's dream of improvement and change.

Xiao's depiction of the so-called intellectuals is vivid. The female principal bars Wang from attending morning calisthenics because she has a pair of black hands that will catch the attention of the passers-by because the school wall is not high enough to keep passersby from looking into the school yard. The principal also tells Wang to go home before the final exam because she will not be able to pass it anyway.

When Wang is driven to sleep on a bench in the hallway because no other student is willing to share a bed with her, the housemother pretends not to notice. The doorman refuses to open up for Wang, who has been waiting outside in the snow. Even the society outside the school abuses the Wang family. A doctor declines to treat Wang's mother because he is afraid that the poor dyers will not be able to pay him. In this story, Xiao expresses her ideas about the future of the peasants. Their fate is deter-

mined for generations to come. They suffer the ordeal of trying to free themselves from poverty and oppression, but the intellectuals and the rich do nothing to help them. As far as the laborers are concerned, there is no way to improve their social status, no matter how hard they try: education will be denied to them even if they are able to pay for it as others do; society will not accept them but will forever see their "black hands" that cannot be hidden.

Two stories in *Field of Life and Death*—"Flying the Kite" and "Night Wind"—portray the suffering of peasants from the Japanese invasion of their villages. Every day, they carry dead bodies to their graves, watch their wives and daughters being raped, and suffer at having their food and property snatched away by the foreign army.

These peasants may be superstitious, stubborn, and selfish in their daily life, but when their sons are killed and their daughters are sexually molested, they stand up to defend themselves and their country. Many of them vow to give their lives and all they own for their purpose. In "Flying the Kite," young Liu runs away from his aged and helpless father to join the people's army in order to save more people. Zhang, the exploiting landlord from "Night Wind," is finally executed by the united peasants, made up of hired hands and women, both young and old.

Oppression brings about a unifying national consciousness. Villagers (in the story told in chapter 13 of *Field of Life and Death*), after months of being ravaged by the Japanese, gather together to make a covenant with heaven. Since no rooster is available, they use a goat at the altar. All the peasants, including the old and the widows, for the first time, get together and swear with a gun pointing to their hearts. They all promise to die for their country, so that they will be worthy of having a Chinese flag covering their grave mounds.

To Right Wrongs

A number of Xiao Hong's stories, like many of those written by Lu Xun, tell of the oppression of women that stems from tradition and superstition.

Chapter five of *Tales of Hulan River* shows what it means to be a young bride from a poor family. The Hu family buys a young bride who is 12 years old. Instead of being the shy, gentle, and slim adolescent they had expected from their first impressions, the child bride is a happy, sociable youngster who is bigger than her age. The mother-in-law from the Hu family begins to "tame" her, hoping that eventually the child bride will be "normal." The child bride's hearty laughs, her striding about confidently without downcast eyes, and her good appetite at dinner bother the family. Their conclusion is that something is wrong with the newcomer. Neighbors, witch-doctors, and a Taoist priest come up with herbal prescriptions, magic dances, and scalding hot baths to drive the devil out of her. The Hu mother-in-law hangs the child bride upside down on a rope and brands her feet with a flatiron to punish her for her "mistakes." Within a year, the child bride dies, and her mother-in-law mourns for the loss of all the money she has spent on her.

"The Child Bride" reveals the obstinace of the peasant group. Blindly, they uphold traditon and force it onto a healthy and happy girl who does not know anything better. The mother-in-law, in the process of "saving" her daughter-in-law, shows off her power and her wealth. Supersitition is another factor in this young girl's death. Illiterate as these peasants are, they refuse to think, and therefore let archaic traditions be the guide of their lives.

Writing such stories was Xiao Hong's attempt to right wrongs. She wanted to call her reader's attention to the wrong things people were doing. Such people cannot see the truth when they are so caught up with tradition and pride.

"Spring in a Small Town" has a theme similar to that of the "Child Bride." Like all girls born at that time, Jade is betrothed by her parents' order to a man she has never met. Those who have seen him say he is short and ugly. It is not surprising, then, that when the beautiful and talented Jade meets her cousin, who is the narrator's brother, she finds that life is not worth living if she cannot be his wife. Gradually, she becomes ill and loses the will to live. Our heroine, Jade dies before she fulfills her marriage rites with her fiancé. Never in her life

does she tell anybody about her love for her cousin, not her own mother, not the narrator's brother, and not even the cousin himself!

Xiao Hong is making a personal comment in this story. At the age of 19, while still studying in high school, Xiao ran away from home in order to escape a marriage arranged by her father. Paralleled by Jade in the story, Xiao is a warrior who fights against wrongs.

Jade, however, is too weak to fight, she succumbs to her mother's expectations, she adheres to the etiquette practiced by young women of her times— to obey and trust one's parents on the matter of marriage. But she cannot ignore her own heart, which longs for her cousin. Dignity and social decorum prevent her from making such longing known to her lover even when he comes to her deathbed. When the man she longs for comes to visit her, she grabs his hands in hers and cries without telling him about her feelings; she dies with her love unspoken. When spring comes, her grave is covered with green grass.

By writing this story, Xiao Hong speaks for millions of Chinese women who have suffered from marrying according to their parents' wishes or have sacrificed their lives because they did not want to marry a man who was a stranger to them. The author explores the need for freedom and love in a woman's life, a life considered to be insignificant. Xiao herself took what, for her, was the necessary step toward freedom: she ran away so that she would have a chance to find true love. Although Xiao finally attained freedom, she was never able to find a man who truly loved her.

Xiao Hong was not only a fiction writer; she was also a master in writing essays and memoirs. *Market Street* is a collection of memoirs in essay form about her days with her first lover, Xiao Jun (Hsiao Chün). She also wrote memorial essays about Lu Xun, her friend and teacher. Even when she was dying in the hospital, she had plans to write a novel entitled *Evening Bell*, a story about women students in Harbin and their struggles, and another novel called *Muddy River*, a story of pioneers in the northern wastelands. She also had plans for a novel about the long march of the communist army. Her last short story, "The Story of Red Glass" was orally told to a friend.

Xiao Hong's life is itself a touching story. Except for her days with the grandfather, her life of exile was filled with conflicts and insults from others. Her works alone lend her existence meaning and significance.

FATIMA WU

Further Reading

Translations

Goldblatt, Howard. *Selected Stories of Xiao Hong.* Beijing: China Books. 1982. This book contains a short introduction by the translator and nine of Xiao Hong's early short stories. They include: "The Death of Wang Asao," "Bridge," "Hands," "On the Oxcart," "The Family Outsider," "Flight from Danger," "Vague Expectations," "North China," and "Spring in a Small Town."

———— and Ellen Young. *Xiao Hong's Tales of Hulan River* and *Field of Life and Death.* Bloomington, IN: Indiana University Press. 1979. This book contains two of Xiao's important works.

————. *Market Street: A Chinese Woman in Harbin.* Seattle: University of Washington Press. 1986. Xiao's memoirs, with a nine-page introduction and a picture of Xiao Hong and Xiao Jun.

THE FICTIONAL WORKS OF LAO SHE

Author: Lao She (Pseudonym of Shu Xingchun/Shu Hsing-ch'un)
Born: 1899, Beijing, China
Died: 1966, Beijing, China
Major Novels: *The Two Mas* (1931), *Cat Country* (1933), *Divorce* (1933), *Rickshaw Boy* (1936), *Four Generations Under One Roof* (1943), *Cremation* (1944)
Major Plays: *The Face Issue* (1941), *The Dragon Beard Ditch* (1950), *Teahouse* (1957)
Major Operas: *Spring Wind* (1943), *Fifteen Strings of Cash* (1956), *Blue Clouds and White Snow* (1959), *Wang Baochuan* (1964)
Major Short Stories: "The Grand Opening" (1933), "Mr. Jodhpurs" (1933), "Black and White Li" (1934), "The Crescent Moon" (1935), "Tragedy in a New Age" (1935), "A Benevolent Person" (1935), "The Soul-slaying Spear" (1935), "An Old and Established Name" (1935), "This Life of Mine" (1937) and "Going to Work" (1958)

Major Themes

Fiction is a portrait of and a comment on life.
Feudalism and capitalism are responsible for the spiritual erosion and poisoning of the people.
In order to improve the lives of the people, China needs to be rebuilt.
The times and morals are changing, which is confusing and hard on the illiterates and the conservatives.
The people need to overcome their tendency towards individualism and work together for a better society.

When Lao She was a year old, his father, a Manchurian soldier, died in battle. His mother had to support a family of six by washing, cleaning, and sewing for others. Sympathetic relatives sent Lao She to school until he managed to obtain a scholarship at the age of 14. After he graduated from high school, he became an educator. Lao She did not begin to write until the age of 24, when he published his first short story "Little Ling" (1923). His experiences in learning at the Yenching University and in teaching at the University of London opened him to Western literature and sparked his desire to write. His first novel, *Old Zhang's Philosophy (Lao Zhang de zhexue/Lao Chang te che-hsüeh)* appeared in 1925.

During the Sino-Japanese War, Lao She was active in participating in political meetings, serving as chairs for anti-war literary organizations, and at the same time writing plays and anti-war propaganda. During the four years of Civil War (1945–1949), Lao was invited as a lecturer and a visiting professor by American universities. His bourgeois writings as well as his absence during this civil war might be the reason for his persecution by the Red Guards in 1966 at the dawn of the Cultural Revolution (1966–1976), even though in 1951 he had been awarded the title "The People's Artist" by the government in Beijing. In 1966, after an intensive period of persecution by the Red Guard, he either committed suicide or died as a result of beatings by his persecutors.

Lao She distinguished himself by being a master of several literary forms. In his lifetime, he wrote about a dozen novels, 16 plays, about 10 operas and juvenile drama, six volumes of short stories, and many essays and poems. On top of that, he has served as the editor for numerous literary magazines and journals and chaired literary and political organizations. Quite a few of his novels and plays have been made into films.

Lao She's writings provide the readers with the socio-political situations of China during the Sino-Japanese and Civil Wars as well as the corrupted Nationalist period. His favorite characters are the peasants and the women who were victims of society and its changes. With understanding and concern, Lao She made his rickshaw pullers and pros-titutes human beings, brought down only by the corrupted system and the burden of a hopeless fu-ture.

To Reveal the Ugly in Society

Lao She stands out from his contemporaries as a master of satire and humor, which he used to attack the deemed "respectable" and "charitable" intel-lectuals from the upper class society. Three stories—"The Grand Opening" *("Kaishi Daji"/ "K'ai-shih ta-chi")*, "A Benevolent Person" *("Shanren"/"Shan-jen")* and "Mr. Jodhpurs" *("Maku Xiansheng"/"Ma-k'u Hsien-sheng")*—illustrate clearly Lao She's attitude toward the hyp-ocritical upper class.

In "The Grand Opening," the author uses a first-person narrator, one of the founders of the General Hospital, to reveal the deceitful hearts of the doc-tors and administrators. Their aim is to make a profit, not to help the sick. An officer who comes for cure of his veneral disease is given injections of leftover tea. The doctor is assisted by young ivory-skinned nurses hired to attract patients. Patients are charged exhorbitant fees for each service rendered but can do nothing while they are being operated on. When a rich old lady comes in and complains about the hospital regulations and diets, the Gen-eral Hospital, adapting itself to her wishes, be-comes her personal convalescent mansion, with bands of maids and cooks moving in. Each day the hospital founders look for ways to expand their business—by taking in abortion cases, and by hir-ing cars to bring their friends to the hospital in order to create an illusion of popularity. The heav-iest irony comes when they hang up a plaque in the front door that reads "virtuous hearts and benevo-lent actions."

A boorish and overbearing intellectual is por-trayed in the story "Mr. Jodhpurs." The narrator happens to share a compartment on a train with a man wearing a Western jacket and jodhpurs, a pair of plain glass spectacles, and woolen boots. His jodhpurs especially tell of this man's social class, that of a man from a wealthy family educated over-seas. Yet his actions in the cabin are nothing but rude, selfish, and self-centered. While he is loung-ing in his seat he screams for the steward, first for tea, then water, a blanket, napkins, then a hot towel; the reply each time is that only after everyone has settled down can any service be provided.

When no one cares to converse with him in the compartment, he snores aloud, awakens, spits, and bothers the steward again. As soon as he finds out that his cabin mate, the narrator, carries no luggage with him, he expresses regret that he paid for ex-cess luggage when his bags could have been trans-ferred as the narrator's. He worries that the train is heading toward the wrong direction, he kicks his socks around when he wants to sleep, and he com-plains about everything. The story is a graphic and sarcastic portrayal of the so-called upper class liter-ates.

Lao She's purpose in writing his social satires was, in his own words, "to reveal the ugly in soci-ety." He wanted to tear the veil from those who pretended to be something other than what they were, and he was especially critical of those who made others suffer to satisfy their own interests. Although he does so with humor and understand-ing, he expresses a sense of disappointment and sadness in what he writes.

The Plight of the Poor and of Abandoned Women

Lao She, like his contemporary Lu Xun, was very much disturbed by the treatment of the poor and of women in his time. Through the use of his pen, he wrote scathing stories about the effect of a sexist society on abandoned women. "Crescent Moon" is a unique story that describes the tragic lives of a mother and a daughter.

The narrator, a seven-year-old girl, watches her father's corpse being put into a box made with four slender pieces of wood. Then she begins to notice how her mother's hands turn calloused and rough from washing clothes. Her mother finds her a new father who later vanishes without a trace. Soon, more men walk into the apartment shared by the mother and daughter. They come and go, leaving money for the women. When the mother gets old and cannot manage the housework anymore, she finds herself a "home" and tells the daughter to take care of herself. The young woman finds a bed in school where she knits and cleans for others. She begins to look for a job, and the new principal throws her out. Seduced by a handsome young man, she loses her chastity. After being chased away from her lover by his wife, she finds a job at a restaurant where she is asked later to serve the guests with her body. At the age of 19 she quits, trying to find something else since there is nothing available except selling herself. Soon she finds that she has contracted veneral disease. Her mother, who has been abandoned by another man again, rejoins her. Mother and daughter shed tears over their fate. One day, the daughter is picked up by the police on the streets and sent to a rehabilitation center. There, her reckless and careless attitude arouses the anger of an officer who finally puts her in prison, leaving her aged mother to fend for herself.

This disheartening story is told in 43 short monologues connected by the one narrator, the daughter, and one image, the crescent moon. The moon, which shines on things great and small, pays no more attention to this pair of pitiful beings than to anyone else. It is described as shedding "a cold light." Most of the time, the crescent moon gives "a chilling effect" to its viewer, the narrator. Although it is the only thing that bears witness to the two women's destiny, it never betrays its feelings, except that, night after night, it hangs itself up in the sky. The first time the narrator notices the crescent, its light shines on her tears.

The crescent moon, which is beautiful and light-giving, signifies the longing of something good (a full moon later). But never in the story are we given the description of a full moon. The author uses the crescent to symbolize the imperfection of these women's lives in which something is always missing or lacking: something good never arrives.

The life of Chinese women in a sexist society will always be imperfect and lacking. The Confucian ideal of the virtues to be seen in an uneducated woman destroys her chances for independence and

survival. The mother and daughter in the story try hard to survive without a male provider in the house: the mother tries to clean and wash for others; the daughter attempts to knit and clean for her friends in school and later she finds work in a restaurant. These efforts cannot relieve them from their status as servants and sex objects. It is a hopeless life. A woman is considered fortunate if she is able to find a trustworthy man who lives long enough to take care of her.

Rickshaw Boy

Women were not the only ones suffering from social evils in the 20's and 30's; men also had to rely on their strength and labor to survive, and often they failed in the effort.

Camel Xiangzi, the leading character in Lao She's novel *Luotuo Xiangzi (Lo-t'o Hsien-tzu)— Camel Xiangzi* (the protagonist's name) or *Rickshaw Boy*—is an honest, diligent, and self-motivated young rickshaw puller. His only ambition is to own his own rickshaw, but he is devastated when his hard-earned rickshaw is stolen. He starts all over again to sweat and slave in order to save enough money for another rickshaw, only to have the savings looted by corrupt governmental officials.

Tricked into marriage by a young woman, Tiger Girl, who claims she is pregnant, Xiangzi harbors resentment towards his wife even though she later gives him enough money to buy his own rickshaw. But the rickshaw is sold when Tiger Girl dies of childbirth and money is required for burial. When Xiangzi finds out that he is in love with Little Lucky One, who has been forced into prostitution, he decides to work hard so that he can pay ransom for her. But it is too late by the time Xiangzi has saved up enough, because Little Lucky One has hanged herself to deliver herself from suffering. Dejected and frustrated, Xiangzi begins to dissipate. Witnessing what is happening to the old rickshaw pullers in town, Xiangzi doubts the old wise precepts of diligence and thrift. He does not care for work anymore; all day long, he wanders and daydreams.

Rickshaw Boy is the first realistic novel of China, a lot of critics claim. It portrays the labor class struggling to stay alive in the city of Beijing. Little Lucky One echoes the narrator of "Crescent Moon" in her fate. The young, energetic Xiangzi's situation is not a whole lot better than that of the women. Working as hard as a camel under unfavorable conditions, he is defeated time and again by greedy government officers, bad luck, and social snobbishness. Xiangzi and Little Lucky One's lives are controlled not by themselves but others. In the beginning, they both believe that with diligence, honesty, and confidence, they will be able to create a better life together. Yet, their honesty and diligence turn out to be no match for reality. At the end of the novel, Xiangzi pawns his winter coat to buy drinks and amusement, taking care, as he says, of the days one at a time. Lao She's question for the reader is: What is there left in a society or a generation to look and hope for if the hardworking ones are rewarded with dejection and failure?

The Change of Times and Morals

Lao She lived in the midst of a gigantic sociopolitical change in China. The Qing dynasty had just come to an end in 1911 while the new Nationalist Party ruled with corruption and chaos. Western influence and communism enveloped the nation in the hope of ridding the old and advancing to the new. Intellectuals, politicians, and industrialists come up with various solutions for salvaging the country, with the poor and the conservative suffering and paying for the results.

"An Old and Established Name" ("*Laozihao*") shows how the change of times and government affect the Fortune Silk Store which has been around for generations. Through the narration of a senior storekeeper who has been watching the coming and going of managers, the author reveals the effect of Western influence on the conservative group that follows rules generations old. When the story opens, the storekeeper Xin comments on the fact that the store now has deteriorated to such a state that the manager needs to pull customers from the streets. The society has changed and only those

who keep up with the new techniques can survive. The fabric store across the street, the Village Silk Shop, gives discount to buyers; they also provide a gift of candies to those who have purchased with a certain amount. Moreover, Xin can hear music from the phonograph across the street; he can also spot the store in the dark by the gas light that is hanging right in front of it.

But when the new manager Zhou comes in to help, Xin is disgusted by the changes that are initiated. First, Zhou acquires a gas light, then cigarettes and tea, which are served free to customers. Xin thinks Zhou has broken all the rules handed down by the previous managers by lying to the police and the customers. When the police come to confiscate Japanese items, Zhou throws one roll of fabric out on the street, pretending that it is the only one he has. To the customers, cheap Japanese fabrics can be represented as British, German, or Chinese ones. Xin finds Zhou repulsive because he has a glib tongue. When the month-end balance sheet comes out, Zhou brags that, although the store has not made any money, it would actually have made a profit were it not for the extra expenses spent on cigarettes, tea, and the gas light—expenses that would pay off in the long run. When the store across the street comes up with a lucky drawing for a free roll of fabric, Xin knows the old times and ways have come to an end.

Lao She uses this story to talk about the two groups in China having opposite attitudes and values. The first group symbolized by Xin and the Fortune Silk Store holds onto tradition, counting on the fact that they have been around longer than anyone else, so that they need not worry about keeping their customers. The other group, symbolized by the Village Silk Store across the street and by the new manager of the Fortune Silk Store, Zhou, has adopted the new Western style. One must change to fit the times, to find new ways of securing profits, even it means to lie, to cheat, or to coerce. The Village Silk Store also uses sex appeal to attract passers-by when the owner's wife nurses her baby right at the counter. The changes have been effective, but are they right?

Lao She's question is: Is it moral to cheat and to

lie? Does improvement and advancement come only when one cheats? What about the old tradition, how can it be adapted to the new age without losing integrity? Lao can see that change is inevitable, but the question remains: How can one change without losing the values that have sustained the old society?

A positive change is celebrated by Lao She in his "Teahouse" ("Chaguan"/"Ch'a-kuan"), a three-act play that covers three historical periods in China: the end of the Qing dynasty, the Nationalist period, and the Communist regime. Lao She has filled this play with various kinds of characters such as peasants, intellectuals, workers, industrialists, eunuchs, beggar women, and government officials. All these people from different social levels are joined together in this Yutai Teahouse, providing Lao She with the opportunity to pour out his opinions on the oppression of women and the poor, loyalty to the country, compassion for one's fellow men, honor, power, and homosexuality.

Teahouse is a play in which Lao She, through a survey of Chinese history in his time, deals with fundamental questions: What is the best that can happen to a country that is poor and chaotic? How can the people be saved?

Master Qin (Ch'in) believes the answer to be industrialization, which would create jobs and strengthen the country's economy. Qin sells his land to build factories, only to have them snatched away by the greedy government. Fourth Elder Zhang (Chang) sees the importance of helping the poor, to give them food, clothing, and shelter. Yet his kindness is mocked by rich and selfish townspeople who get Zhang into trouble. Pockface Liu is entirely self-serving. He is a flesh merchant, an immoral go-between who sets up marriages between 15-year-old girls and eunuchs. He exploits the poor on the expense of the rich and the powerful. Pockface Liu's philosophy is: make the most of one's actions by hook or by crook.

Qin, Zhang, and the proprietor of the Yutai Teahouse finally agree that the future of the country is over. The three join together to mourn the loss of the old ways; they prepare for the end of the country and their lives. But new hope speaks when, in the *Epilogue*, Lao She introduces Miss Ding Bao (Ting Pao), a woman of the new age. Her appearance symbolizes the coming of communism, which fosters fresh hope for everyone:

Sweet young lady, dry your eyes;
It's a dark night, but the sun will rise.
Sweet young lady, don't you mope;
From the Western Hills flows a bright new hope.
A hope to wash away our grief,
And fill our hearts with new belief.
In a land where neither your nor I
Nor our children shall know slavery.

(HOWARD-GIBBON, TRANS., 1980)

Beneath the Red Banner

Beneath the Red Banner (*Zheng hongchi xia/Cheng hung-ch'ih hsia*), an autobiographical novel that Lao She never finished because of his death, by suicide or murder, also sheds hope for future generations. As in *Teahouse*, Lao is interested in showing the change of time in Chinese history: how the Qing dynasty is rotten to the core; how corrupted and divided the Nationalist bureaucratic systems are; and how after years of turmoil and war, the Chinese people are looking toward a future with hope. To say this novel is autobiographical is to say that Lao She used actual events that involved his family members—for example, his father's death at a grain shop after being injured by the explosion of gunpowder. The characters Cousin Fuhai, Master Ding (Ting), and Duofu, are all based on Lao's relatives.

Besides being prolific and versatile in his writings, Lao She is renowned for his use of language. He believed that the appropriate use of language in literature not only achieves a realistic effect but also enhances characterization. The language of rickshaw pullers in *Rickshaw Boy* contributes to a realistic portrait of that class; the narrative of the young girl in "Crescent Moon" reveals her innocence and confusion; and the short and jerky dialogue in "Mr. Jodhpurs" fully reveals the man's selfishness and awkwardness.

Because of the effective ways he used his narrative gifts to create sensitive portraits of the people of his times, Lao She can be recognized as a master of fiction.

FATIMA WU

Further Reading

Translations

Lao She. *Camel Xiangzi*. Shi Xiaoqing, trans. Bloomington, IN: Indiana University Press, published in association with Beijing: Foreign Languages Press, 1981. This is a lively translation of Lao She's most renowned novel *Luotuo Xiangzi* or *Rickshaw Boy*. This edition contains an Afterword by Lao She, dated September 1954, in which he states that he has "taken out some of the coarser language and some unnecessary descriptions." He goes on to write that "today, 19 years after the writing of the novel the working people have become masters of their own destiny. Even I now understand something about revolution and am very grateful to the Communist Party and Chairman Mao." Also included is a six-page account by Lao She, "How I came to write the novel *Camel Xiangzi*" and a three-page preface (written in 1979) by Hu Jieqing, Lao She's widow.

———. *Rickshaw: the Novel Lo-t'o Hsiang Tsu*. James, Jean M., trans. Honolulu: University of Hawaii Press, 1979. This translation includes an excellent 11-page introduction by Ms. James, in which she argues that "Hsiang Tzu" is "not a victim of a sick society but one of its representatives," suffering from his "Individualism," that is, his selfishness, a malady that pervaded the whole society.

——— [Lau Shaw]. *Rickshaw Boy*. Evan King, trans. New York: Reynal & Hitchcock, 1945. This early translation, although popular in the United States, has come under extensive criticism because of King's juggling of the later chapters and adding a romantic ending in which Happy Boy rescues Lucky Girl, while she is on the verge of death, from the whorehouse that holds her captive, and runs off with her in his arms, exulting in their new-found freedom.

———. *Dragon Beard Ditch*. Liao Hung-ying, trans. Beijing: Foreign Language Press, 1956. With illustrations.

———. *Cat Country*. Lyell, William A. Jr., trans. Columbus: Ohio State University Press, 1970. This is a translation of the novel, *Mao Chengji*, a satirical novel of China in the 1930's. On page 295 of this book, the translator lists all the novels by Lao She available in English translation.

———. *Beneath the Red Banner*. Cohn, Don J., trans. Beijing: Chinese Literature, 1982. This is a translation of Lao She's last, unfinished novel, with an epilogue written by Lao's wife, Hu Jieqing.

———. *Teahouse*. Howard-Gibbon, John, trans. Beijing: Foreign Language Press, 1980. This translation of the three-act play *Chaguan* contains illustrations.

———. *The Two Mas*. Finkelstein, David, and Kenny K. Huang, trans. Hong Kong: Joint Publishing Co. 1984. This is a translation of Lao She's novel *Erma*, with illustrations by Ding Cong.

———. *Crescent Moon and Other Stories*. Beijing: Chinese Literature, 1985. This is a collection of Lao She's short stories by a number of translators. The stories included in this book are: "A Day in the Life," "Filling a Prescription," "By the Temple of Great Compassion," "Mr. Jodhpurs," "A Vision," "Black and White Li," "The Eyeglasses," "Brother You Takes Office," "The Soul-slaying Spear," "The Fire Chariot," "Crescent Moon," and "This Life of Mine."

Related Studies

Kao, George, ed. *Two Writers and the Cultural Revolution: Lao She and Chen Jo-hsi*. Hong Kong: The Chinese University Press, 1980. A collection of articles and translations, many of which appeared originally in the Chinese-English translation magazine (published in Hong Kong), *Renditions*. Opening articles include speculations about Lao She's death, tending to move from the theory of suicide to the conclusion that he died from persecution at the hands of followers of the "Gang of Four." Among the translations are those of the final two chapters of *Rickshaw Boy*, and the stories "Old Liu," "The Drum Singers," and "City of Cats."

Vohra, Ranbir. *Lao She and the Chinese Revolution*. Cambridge, MA: Harvard University Press, 1974. A careful account of the course of Lao She's career as a writer, with attention to the effect of the changing political climate on his work.

INDIA

HYMNS OF THE *RIG VEDA*

Authors: Many anonymous authors over the centuries
Literary Form: Metrical poetry, scriptural hymns
Dates of Composition: 1500 B.C.(?) to c. 800 B.C.

Major Themes

There are numerous gods and deities, but they are features of a pervasive reality that governs the universe.
There are three classes of deities: those of the natural world, those that represent principles of human relationships, and those of the ritual world.
Nature and human behavior are not chaotic; they are governed by a basic law.
Ritual is necessary to worship and understanding.

The Vedas, the sacred scriptures of the Hindus, are the earliest extant religious texts of the Hindus. "Veda" is not the name of a particular book, but of the literature extending almost two thousand years. They are written in Sanskrit; their expressions are highly symbolic and not easily translatable. They are called *Shruti* (from *shru*, "to hear") since they were transmitted orally from teacher to disciple. Although the Aryans who settled in India had no system of writing, they brought with them from Iran a tradition of myths, legends, poems, and hymns which were not systematized as a collection until around 800 B.C. This collection is generally known as the "Four Vedas": the *Rig Veda*, the *Sāma Veda*, the *Yajur Veda*, and the *Atharva Veda*.

The *Rig Veda* is the oldest of the four Vedas. It is the liturgical text of the *hotars*, an ancient order of Aryan priests, who performed sacrifices without help from the experts whose specialty was the performance of sacrifices. Eventually, these specialists were asked to take over certain parts of the performance of sacrifices and in the process developed their own liturgical manuals. As a result, the *Rig Veda* continued to develop for over three or four centuries.

The term "*Rig*" is derived from the root "*ric*," which means "a hymn," "to praise," and "to shine." Each verse of the hymns of the *hotars* was called a *ric* or a "praise stanza." The term "Veda," on the other hand, is a cognate of the English term "wisdom." These terms give the collection its name: the *Rig Veda*, the sacred wisdom consisting of stanzas of praise. These hymns were probably recited by the *hotar* priests, who invoked gods during the rather detailed and complicated ritual sacrifices performed during those times.

The *Rig Veda* contains 1,028 hymns organized in ten books. Interpretation and reconstruction of the *Rig Veda*, as with the other three Vedas, is fraught with peril. In many places, a difficult idea is expressed in simple language; at other places a simple idea is obscured by very difficult language. The *Rig Veda* is replete with half-formed myths, crude allegories, paradoxes, and tropes. These difficulties notwithstanding, it remains the source of the later practices and philosophies of the Hindus.

In the Rig Vedic hymns numerous *devas* ("the shining ones") or deities are addressed and invoked. From a fuctional point of view, these deities can be divided in three classes: (1) the deities of the natural world, (2) the deities that represent the principles of human relations, and (3) the deities of the ritual world.

The Deities of the Natural World

The deities were often personified natural forces: the Sun was *Sūrya*, the dawn was *Ushas*, the wind was *Vāyu*, and so on. The degree of personification, however, varied significantly.

Vedic seers were interested in nature. They were interested in establishing a correlation between human activities and nature. An attempt was made to read natural phenomena in terms of human behavior: a flood meant that the river was angry: spring signified peace and prosperity and the fact that the deities were pleased. They projected their own emotions upon nature.

The Deities of the Principles of Human Relations

The most important deity in the *Rig Veda* is Indra. In the *Rig Veda* there are more hymns addressed to Indra than any other deity. In fact, a quarter of the *Rig Veda* is dedicated to him. His *vajra* (the thunderbolt), horses, and chariots receive much attention in the hymns. He drinks *soma* (the divine drink of immortality) and bestows fertility upon women, at times by sleeping with them. At times, he is referred to as an *asura* (demon), although most of the hymns emphasize his heroic deeds.

Indra is addressed as at once as the war-God and the weather-God. As war-God, he was usually accompanied by warbands *(Maruts)* through the skies in chariots singing martial songs. He was responsible for destroying the Dāsa fortress. However, his most famous deed is the unloosening of the water with his thunderbolt. He slew the demon Vrita, who prevented the monsoon from breaking. Vrita had dammed the water inside a mountain, which resulted in a massive drought that caused much human death and suffering. Indra is also represented as a benevolent power and mediator. In the Vala episode, he helps the worshipers to obtain the cows that had been hidden in a cave.

Varuna is the most important deity from an ethical point of view, because he oversees moral behavior. Varuna is a celestial God *par excellence*, a universal monarch. Guilty human beings confess to Varuna. He is an enemy of falsehood and is also the punisher of sin. He resides in a thousand-column golden mansion and surveys the deeds of human beings. His eye is the Sun, who is also his spy. The Sun sees everything and reports to Varuna. Varuna has a number of other spies in addition to the Sun; their sole duty is to report on the evil doings of human beings. Varuna is a just and inscrutable God, who inspires the sense of guilt and the feeling of

awe. Human beings are destined to sin; only Varuna can release them.

In the later hymns, Varuna's function is replaced by *rita*, an abstract principle that ensures justice and order in the universe. Varuna is the custodian of *rita*.

No term in English can connote what is meant by the concept *rita* in the Vedic context. Etymologically, *rita* signifies "the course of things." It is the Vedic counterpart of the later notion of *dharma*. It is at once the ordered universe and the order that pervades it. It represents the law, unity, and rightness that underlie the orderliness of the universe. *Rita* enables natural events to move rhythmically, day following night; it governs the cycles of birth, growth, decay, succession of the seasons, and so on. It provides balance and guides the emergence, dissolution, and reemergence of cosmic existence. In short, the central idea permeating the *Rig Veda* is that nature in all its diversity and multiplicity is not chaotic but is governed by a basic cosmic law.

Not only natural phenomena but also truth and justice are subject to *rita*. It is the moral law that regulates the conduct of human beings. When *rita* is observed by human beings there is peace and order. In social affairs, *rita* is propriety and makes possible harmonious actions among human beings. *Rita* is truth in human speech. *Satya* "agreement with reality," and *anrita*, "negation of *rita*," later confined to truth and falsity of speech, respectively appear in moral contexts to represent virtue and vice. In human dealings, *rita* is justice. In worship, *rita* assures correct performance of ritual, which in turn results in harmony between human beings and the deities, human beings and nature, and among human beings.

The Deities of the Ritual World

In the *Rig Veda* there are hymns that allude to numerous complicated and detailed rituals in which the Gods are invoked to attend the sacrifice. Accordingly, one finds abundant interest in the two deities essentially associated with ritual, namely, *Agni* and *Soma*.

Agni is the deva second most addressed in the Vedic hymns. He is indispensable in the performance of sacrifices. He symbolizes the renewal and interconnectedness of all things and events. On the one hand, he is greater then heaven and earth; on the other hand, he is a householder—he is the household fire, which even today is the center of domestic rituals. Fire serves as the medium and transforms the material gifts of the sacrifice into the spiritual substance from which the Gods draw their strength and of which they can partake. In Agni, both the divine and human world coalesce. He acts as the mediator between the Gods and human beings. The meeting point is the sacrificial altar where Agni as fire consumes the oblation in the name of the gods, and in so doing transmit their virtues to human beings whom he represents. Soma is the divine plant of immortality. The juice of soma plant is ritually extracted in the famous soma sacrifice, a very important feature of many Vedic rituals. This juice is filtered in a woven sieve which is identified with the sky, and the pouring of the juice, water, and milk is identified with all sorts of cosmic processes. Both Agni and Soma relate to the fundamental needs and values of humankind.

Other deities mentioned in the *Rig Veda* are: Mitrā, who is concerned with compacts and vows and is associated with Vrita; Vishnu, who was known for the three strides by which he measured the universe; and Yama, the god of death. Surprisingly, the deities that become so important in later Hinduism, namely, Vishnu and Shiva, are rather insignificant in the Rig Vedic hymns.

Vedic Religion and Polytheism

A superficial study of these hymns has led scholars to conclude that the Vedic religion is polytheistic. It is indeed true, as we have seen so far, that many divinities are invoked in these hymns. However, most of the conceptual apparatus that gives rise to polytheism in the strict sense of the term is absent in the Vedas. Therefore, the Vedic religion, in the strict sense, cannot be said to be polytheistic. In polytheism, gods are fully personalized entities having a precise function. The Vedic divinities, on the other hand, are not fully personalized entities; nor are they divided in watertight compartments. They are interrelated. For example, Indra is assisted not only by the Storm Gods, but also by Visahnu in the breaking of the monsoon. Indra was the recipient of the soma sacrifice aimed at promoting rain and fertility. It was believed that the soma juice was highly intoxicating and was the source of inspiration for the Gods to do good deeds. Indeed, it is the copious imbibing of soma that gives Indra the power to overcome his enemies. As Indra assumes a position of greater supremacy in the pantheon, Somā becomes so associated with his activities that at times he is praised as a mighty warrior.

The Rig Vedic hymns extol a particular divinity; they even exaggerate its importance at the expense of the other deities. They glorify the deities they invoke by using terms or epithets generally applicable to other deities (power, wisdom, brilliance) and often attribute to a god mythical traits and actions that characterize other deities. In these hymns the interconnections among the deities are glorified, their distinctions implicitly rejected.

This interconnection among various gods is not found in polytheism in its technical sense. For example, in Greek polytheism, many gods are hierarchically arranged in a patriarchal family with Zeus as the head. The gods have a very clearly defined function and symbolism. Their place in the hierarchy is determined by their relationship to Zeus. Therein one finds goddesses of wisdom and sex, of marriage, of beauty, of war, and so on. However, their power is limited in that they too must answer to Zeus who has the power to modify the results of their actions. The gods are fully personalized entities and are regarded as distinct individuals. It is important to note in this context that there is no counterpart of the Greek Zeus in the Vedic pantheon.

In the later Rig Vedic hymns, on the other hand, there is a movement away from a series of more or less separate deities toward the notion of a single principle. The hymn X.90, for example, addresses the unity of organic and inorganic being in the form of Purusha. By the end of the *Rig Veda*, Prajāpati appears as the Lord of being who existed prior to the universe and produced the universe, gods, and human beings through his sacrifice to himself.

The Hymns as Poetry, Scripture, and Philosophy

A study of the hymns of the *Rig Veda* is indispensable for any adequate account of the Hindu thought. It represents the starting point of the Hindu tradition. The text is an anthology of disparate, individually complete hymns, and a selection does not destroy its beauty and originality. One need not read the *Rig Veda* in its entirety to enjoy its wisdom and the beauty of its poetic language. These hymns have exercised a tremendous effect on Hindu orthodoxy and still remain the highest religious authority for all Hindus. The importance of Vedic rituals has remained central. In modern Hinduism, all the obligatory rites of the Hindus at birth, death, and all the main celebrations marking the progression of life stages are performed in accordance with Vedic rituals. It is not an exaggeration to say that a modern Brahmin in his prayers three times a day utters the same Vedic verses a Brahmin did three thousand years ago.

BINA GUPTA

Further Reading

Translation

Macdonell, Arthur Anthony, trans. *Hymns from the Rig Veda.* 2 vols. London: Oxford University Press, 1923. A good and readable metrical translation of selected hymns of the *Rig Veda.*

Related Studies

de Nicolas, Antonio T. *Meditations Through the Rig Veda.* Stony Brook, New York: Nicolas Hays, 1976. This work explores the intentional connotations of the Rig Vedic hymns.

Panikkar, Raimundo. *The Vedic Experience.* Los Angeles: University of California Press, 1977. A clearly written collection of teachings from the Vedas, Brahmanas, and Upanishads.

BRĀHMANAS AND ĀRANYAKAS

Authors: Many anonymous authors
Literary Form: Prose mixed with verse
Dates of Composition: Tenth to fifth centuries B.C.

Major Themes

To understand the significance of ritual is to understand reality and its powers.
All things have a unity and order that lies beyond appearances.
Mantras and other recitations, as well as ritual actions, have a connection with observable reality.
By the power of speech the creator brought earth and fire into existence, and by earth and fire the world was created.

The primary Vedic literature of India consists of four sets of texts: the *Rig Veda*, which has come down to us in a single textual recension (critical revision) or branch; the *Sāma Veda*, which has three recensions; the *Yajur Veda*, with six distinct recensions; and the *Atharva Veda*, with two. Each of these Vedas is in turn divided into four parts: *Samhitā*, *Brāhmana*, *Āranyaka*, and *Upanishad*.

Samhitās are the oldest of the four, containing, in the *Rig Veda*, hymns of praise to various deities, descriptions of the pressing of the soma plant, cosmological speculations, and occasional historical references; in the *Sāma Veda*, adaptations of Rig Vedic hymns to ritual song cycles; in the *Yajur Veda*, mantras to be used in sacrificial rituals and legendary material connected with the sacrifices; and in the *Atharva Veda*, spells and other material reflecting more popular religious sentiments, ideas, and actions. In general, the Brāhmanas and Āranyakas contain ritualistic and to a lesser degree mythic explications of material presented in the Samhitās. The Upanishads are more recognizably philosophical, more or less completing the transition from an emphasis on sacrificial ritual reflected in the earlier texts to an emphasis on interiorized ritual and meditation.

In spite of this broad characterization, very few of the texts are monolithic in content. All the texts and divisions of texts are in fact quite diverse, presenting a wide range of material, from mythic to devotional to ritual to philosophical.

Brāhmanas

We know from references within classical Sanskrit texts that many more Brāhmanas existed in antiquity than are extant today. Although the Vedic textual and religious traditions are remarkable for their survival into the present day through more than 3,000 years of social and religious change, many texts were nevertheless lost over the course of the centuries.

The most important surviving Brāmana texts are the following: the *Aitareya* and *Sānkhāyana (or Kausītaki) Brāhmanas*, belonging to the *Rig Veda*; the *Pancavimsha* and *Sadvimsha Brāhmanas*, belonging to the Kauthuma recension of the *Sāma Veda*; the *Jaiminīya Brāhmana*, belonging to the Jaiminiya recension of the *Sāma Veda*; the *Shatapatha Brāhmana*, belong to the Yajur Veda recension known as the *White (Shukla) Yajur Veda*; the *Taittīriya Brāhmana*, belonging to the Taittiriya recension of the *Black (Krishna) Yajur Veda*; and the *Gopatha Brāhmana*, belonging to the *Atharva Veda*.

Surviving in addition are several minor Brāhmanas of the *Sāma Veda* that deal with technical details of ritual chant, as well as fragments of several others. The latter survive largely through quotations in related texts and commentaries. The distinction between the texts of the *White* and *Black Yajur Veda* is that in the former the ritual mantras are included in the Samhitā sections while the explanatory or Brāhmana sections are separately constituted. In the texts of the *Black Yajur Veda*, mantra and Brāhmana sections are mixed. Thus the important Samhitās of the *Kāthaka* and *Maitrāyaniya* recensions of the *Black Yajur Veda* contain extensive Brāhmana sections, as does the *Taittirīya Samhitā*, in spite of the existence of a separate Brāhmana of that recension or school. Many of these texts, including some of the minor Brāhmanas of the *Sāma Veda*, are still consulted today by learned ritualists in south India as reference works in the performance of sacrificial ritual.

The Style and Language of the Brāhmanas

Stylistically, the Brāhmanas are varied. Some, notably the technical works belonging to the *Sāma Veda*, are little more than lists of chants along with succinct and arcane instructions on how to break up verses used in the chants. These works, while not composed with a sense of secrecy, are comprehensible only to ritual specialists who already know the primary texts on which they are based. However, most of the Brāhmanas are not condensed to the point of incomprehensibility—a goal of certain other genres of Indian literature that are composed in many cases as mnemonic tools with an assumed dependence on oral explication. While diversions into technical details of ritual and recitation are not uncommon, most of the subject matter of the Brāhmanas is accessible.

All of the Brāhmana texts listed above are written in a narrative prose which is occasionally lyrical and is usually readable. Poetic passages do appear, however, in many of the texts, especially the Brāhmanas of the *Rig Veda*. These passages are particularly important because many are artifacts of a more archaic period, and therefore shed a rather different light on the liturgical anecdotes and mythology that occupy major sections of the Brāhmanas. In general, it is clear that whatever the styles, the texts were designed for oral transmission. Most of the texts were doubtless chanted in near-rhythmic fashion, and a few of the older texts (those of the *Yajur Veda*) are accented, a characteristic of the early language that helped determine

meaning and assisted in memorization and recitation. Almost never will a passage be so long that its full meaning cannot be ascertained in a few words. The effect is one of very loose verse, a feature consonant with the textuality of traditional and oral cultures elsewhere.

In sum, the Brāhmanas—and the Vedic literature generally—are on the whole concrete, poetical, and narrative rather than abstract or conceptual, features which contribute to their durability. Where the Vedic literature stands out from other oral discourse, however, is in the surprising degree to which it is abstract and conceptual. Narrative philosophy as found in Plato or later European thought is absent, but very elaborate abstractions and concepts are very much present, often poeticized into concrete imagery. As noted, this imagery is largely ritual, but it has always held an appeal much broader than the comparatively restricted circles of Vedic ritualists. The abstractions and concepts illuminated by the ritual, mythic, and grammatical imagery of the Vedic texts, exemplified by the Brāhmanas, held a fascination that spread into all schools of Indian philosophy, religion, art, political and social science, and traditional history.

The language of the Brāhmanas is not uniform, but reflects linguistic change occurring over the approximately five centuries of their composition. In addition, the language to a great extent betrays the technical idiom of the sacrificial ritual, a vocabulary and style to which the Brahmanas contributed immensely. In spite of much mythic and other material of general interest in the Brāhmanas, the reader can make little headway without extensive knowledge of the Vedic rituals.

Because of their style, esotericism, and emphasis on ritual knowledge, the Brāhmanas were severely denounced by the very scholars who first studied them at the end of the nineteenth century. To cite two out of perhaps dozens of examples: F. Max Müller, perhaps the best known of the nineteenth-century Vedic scholars, regarded them as "the twaddle of idiots" (*A History of Ancient Sanskrit Literature*, London, 1860: p. 389); and Julius Eggeling, who worked for twenty-five years on a masterly translation of the Shatapatha Brāhmana, introduced his work with the following statement: "For wearisome prolixity of exposition, characterized by dogmatic assertion and a flimsy symbolism rather than by serious reasoning, these works are perhaps not equaled anywhere" (1882: ix).

Recently these assessments have been revised. Jan Gonda, the most prolific Vedic scholar of this century, wrote in 1975 that the quest of the authors of the Brāhmanas for a general explanatory theory led them to "place all things in a causal context wider than that provided by common sense, a desire to penetrate the mysteries of the world, to find that unity, order and regularity which underlie apparent diversity, disorder and anomaly" (1975: 342). Now, at last, we can see that the Brāhmanas were at the fountainhead of later Indian speculative and philosophical thought.

The Meaning of the Vedic Sacrifices and Ritual

The Brāhmanas proposed to explain the origin and meaning of the Vedic sacrifices and their ritual elements, and to demonstrate that the mantras and other recitations, as well as the actions themselves, had a connection with observable reality. The principal reasons for this were firstly to influence or gain control over the flow of nature through knowledge of these esoteric connections, and secondly to demonstrate to themselves and others the relevance of what was already a body of ancient religious practice. The very word *brāhmana*, "comment on *brahman*," the absolute principle, the Veda itself, indicates the grand design and significance of the texts. The primary methodology was the *bandhu*, a stated connection in which, for example, the individual Vedas were equated or brought into other types of connection with poetic meters, animals, specific sacrifices, and social classes. Sacrifice was ultimately effective because of knowledge of the connections between aspects of the ritual and various natural forces, a knowledge that was effective because it appeared to the initiate, the ideal ritualist, through the sacred word, the Brāhmana text. A Brāhmana passage from the *Taittirīya Samhitā* says "The sacrificial post (to which an animal is tethered prior to immolation) is of udumbara wood; udumbara is strength; cattle are strength; thus by strength he wins for himself strength and cattle" (2.1.1.6). One of the primary means in the Brāhmanas for expressing these connections or *bandhus* was through arcane etymologies, often pursued relentlessly. Two (or more) ostensibly dissimilar items or notions could be very easily linked through similarity of sound, regardless of whether or not a true etymological connection existed. For example, the Jaiminīya Brāhmana says: "Of him when he has caught fire the smoke *(dhūma)* shakes off the body. Because it shakes off *(dhunoti)* therefore it is *dhūna*. In fact it is *dhuna* by name. They call it mystically dhūma in a mystic way of speaking. For the gods are fond of the mystic" (Bodewitz, 1973: pp. 115–116). In this way, ordinary phenomena are given extraordinary significance. Indeed, we frequently meet with passages which reflect everyday attitudes, such as those towards sex, violence, and death. Two of the primary subtexts of the Brāhmanas are reproduction and contestation, each of which commands a special discourse that is woven thickly through these otherwise ritual commentaries.

The Great Fire Altar and the Legend of Shunahshepa

As further illustration of Brāhmana material, it must suffice to mention two remarkable passages that are as concerned with questions of general ontological and soteriological concern as with ritual. One is the tenth book of the Shatapatha Brāhmana, containing the cosmological speculations of the sage Shāndilya. The text is an explication of the construction of a great fire altar *(agnicayana)* built of a thousand bricks, two hundred in each of five layers, the whole in the shape of an eastward facing bird. Through increasingly complex strategies of identifying ritual accessories, actions, and mantras with cosmological notions, entities, and objects, the sacrificial fire is identified with the bird-shaped altar, the altar with a creator god named Prajāpati, Prajāpati with the year, and the year—time personified—with Death. Thus the construction of the altar holds the secrets of life and death—for one who knows.

The second example is the legend of Shunahshepa from the seventh book of the *Aitareya Brāhmana*. This legend does not purport to comment on any ritual, though ritual lies at its heart, and the story is to be recited at the time of ritual enthronement and consecration of a king. Very briefly, the story is as follows: King Harishcandra, devoid of heirs, prays to Varuna, the god of righteousness and cosmic order, to grant him a son, vowing to sacrifice that very son to Varuna if the wish is granted. A son is born, Rohita, who learns of this arrangement when he reaches maturity. He flees to the forest, a result of which is that his father is afflicted with dropsy. However, not wishing to disappoint his father, Rohita searches for a substitute. He finds a starving Brahmin priest named Ajīgarta (One-Who-Has-Nothing-to-Swallow) and agrees to purchase his middle son, Shunahshepa (Dog's-Penis), to be sacrificed in his place. When no one can be found to undertake the slaughter, Ajīgarta agrees to bind and slay him for an extra one hundred cows for each action. Shunahshepa then takes refuge in various Vedic gods, praising them with verses from the *Rig Veda*. Finally, the gods release Shunashepa from his fetters and King Harishcandra from his disease. Shunashepa "sees" a new ritual and is adopted by the famous sage Vishvamitra as his son, who is so impressed that he appoints Shunashepa his sole heir, over his one hundred natural sons.

The Āranyakas: The Forest Books

The main Āranyakas are the following: the *Aitareya* and *Shānkhāyana Āranyakas* of the *Rig Veda*, the *Taittirīya Āranyaka* of the *Taittirīya* recension of the *Black Yajur Veda*, and fragments of a *Katha Āranyaka* of the *Kāthaka* recension of the *Black Yajur Veda*. Certain Brāhmana texts include short Āranyaka portions, including the *Shātapatha Brāhmana*. Various Āranyaka texts belonging to the *Sāma Veda* are found whose sole contents are very complicated variations of Sāma Vedic chants. That textual identities were occasionally unclear is

seen from the titles of some works, for example the *Brihad-Āranyaka-Upanishad*, appearing at the end of the *Shatapatha Brāhmana*, and the *Jaiminīya-Upanishad-Brāhmana* of the *Sāma Veda*.

The term *āranyaka* is derived from *āranya*, the Sanskrit word for forest. Āranyakas are texts regarded as so secret, dangerous, and esoteric that they must be studied only by advanced students in the seclusion of the forest. Like the Brāhmanas, Āranyakas have as their main subject the explanation of Vedic sacrificial ritual. More than the Brāhmanas, however, the Āranyakas attempt to explain the symbolical and philosophical significance of obscure ritual text passages. Much of the significance of the Āranyakas is that they represent an important transitional stage in the development of Vedic literature. In the Āranyakas, the esoteric explanations of ritual approach independent speculation, paving the way for the more philosophically based Upanishads and their partial suppression of ritualism. This is further emphasized by the fact that the Āranyakas were enjoined to be studied not just by ritualists, but often by ascetics, thus demonstrating their divergence from the Vedic ritual, which is explicitly intended for householders.

As a transitional genre containing titles that are often difficult to place, it is not surprising that the contents of the Āranyakas are not extremely varied. Included in these self-proclaimed esoteric texts are discussions and enumerations of mantras, explanation of ritual, mystical identifications and etymologies, legends, references to effects of rituals, descriptions of rituals that were neglected in the Brāhmanas, a lengthy description of the details of Veda study *(Taittirīya Āranyaka)*, and meditations on causation and life processes. The structure and style of the Āranyakas are as varied as their contents, occasionally presenting lists and straightforward descriptions, and sometimes powerful speculative ruminations.

The *Aitareya Āranyaka* deals at length with an ancient festival called *mahāvrata*, containing considerable music, dance and revelry, preserved ritually within a normal soma sacrifice. Other rituals discussed at length in the Āranyakas are an important variation of the construction of the great fire altar *(agnicayana)* called Arunaketuka *(Taittirīya Āranyaka)*, and a very important rite called *pravargya (Taittirīya Āranyaka)*, that is to be performed at least six times prior to the performance of any soma sacrifice. Among other topics, the *Shānkhāyana Āranyaka* covers topics usually found in the Upanishads, including the internal performance of certain fire sacrifices, the rivalry of the senses, and the premonitions of death.

One citation from these texts must suffice to illustrate the content and style of the speculative sections. In describing the manifestations of the creator, the *purusha*, the *Aitareya Āranyaka* (2.1.7) states: "By his speech earth and fire are created. On (this) earth plants grow; fire renders them palatable. Saying "take this, take this," these two, earth and fire, serve their father, speech. As far as the earth extends, so far extends this world. And as long as the world of earth and fire does not decay so long does the world not decay of him who knows thus the manifestation of the power of speech" (Gonda, 1975: p. 426).

FREDERICK M. SMITH

Further Reading

Translations

Bodewitz, H. W. *Jaiminīya Brāhmana 1, 1–65.* Leiden: E. J. Brill, 1973.

———. *The Jyotiṣṭoma Ritual. Jaiminīya Brāhmana 1, 66–364.* Leiden: E. J. Brill, 1990.

Caland, W. *Pañcavimśa Brāhmana.* Calcutta: Asiatic Society of Bengal, 1931.

Dumont, P. E. [Important sections of the *Taittirīya Brāhmana*] *Proceedings of the American Philosophical Society,* 92.6 (1948): 447–503, 95.6 (1951): 628–675, 98.3 (1954): 204–223, 101.2 (1957): 216–243, 103.4 (1959): 584–608, 104.1 (1–10), 105.1 (1961): 11–36, 106.3 (1962): 246–263, 107.2 (1963): 177–182, 107.5 (1963): 446–460, 108.4 (1964): 337–353, 109.6 (1965): 309–341.

Eggeling, Julius. *The Śatapatha-Brāhmana, Parts I, II, III, IV, V.* Oxford: Clarendon Press, 1882, 1884, 1885, 1897, 1900. [*Sacred Books of the East,* Vols. XII, XXVI, XLI, XLIII XLIV.] (Reprint: Delhi: Motilal Banarsidass, 1972.)

Keith. A. B. *Aitareya Āranyaka.* Oxford, 1909.

———. *Rigveda Brāhmanas [Aitareya* and *Śānkhāyana Brāhmanas].* Harvard Oriental Series, Vol. 25. Cambridge: Harvard University Press, 1920. (Reprint: Delhi: Motilal Banarsidass, 1971.)

Malamoud, Charles. *Le svādhyāya, récitation personelle du Veda. Taittirīya-Āranyaka II.* Texte traduit et commente. Paris: Ed. de Boccard, 1978.

Oertel, Hans. "The Jāiminīya or Talavakāra Upaniṣad Brāhmana: Text, Translation, and Notes." *Journal of the American Oriental Society,* 16 (1896): 79–260.

Witzel, Michael. *Das Kaṭha Āranyaka: textkritische Edition mit Übersetzung und Kommentar.* Kathmandu: Nepal Research Centre Publications, 1974.

Related Studies

Gonda, Jan. *Vedic Literature (Saṃhitās and Brāhmanas).* Wiesbaden: Otto Harrassowitz, 1975. Contains valuable and accessible descriptions of Brāhmanas (pp. 339–422) and Āranyakas (pp. 423–432).

O'Flaherty, Wendy Doniger. *Tales of Sex and Violence: Folklore, Sacrifice, and Danger in the Jaiminīya Brāhmana.* Chicago: University of Chicago Press, 1985. A very readable account of many stories, with detailed interpretation, from one of the most important Brāhmana texts.

Smith, Brian K. *Classifying the Universe.* New York, Oxford: Oxford University Press, 1994. Drawing extensively from the Brāhmanas, this book elucidates both the massive associations of object, idea, form, ritual act, and so on, of Vedic discourse, and their theoretical underpinnings

Thite, Ganesh. *Sacrifice in the Brāhmana-texts.* Poona: Poona University, 1975. Clearly describes the nature of the sacrifices and the doctrines of sacrifice espoused in these texts.

RĀMĀYANA

Author: [Vālmīki] (by tradition)
Born: ? 750–500 B.C.
Died: ? 750–500 B.C.
Literary Form: Epic poem
Date of Composition: Evolved over several centuries; work took its present form somewhere between the fourth and second centuries, B.C.

Major Themes

Truth wins in the long run.
One must keep one's promises.
Fidelity to father implies unconditional obedience.
An ideal wife serves her husband and remains faithful to him.
Tapas (penance) is necessary to attain the highest goal.

The epic *Rāmāyana* has exercised a profound influence over the lives of Hindus. It is the most popular Hindu book; it has been very widely disseminated. The story of the *Rāmāyana* is often told by Indian parents and grandparents to their children and grandchildren. Vālmīki, traditionally believed to be a *rishi* (sage), is generally considered to be the author of original Sanskrit *Rāmāyana*. It retells in Sanskrit verses the story of the career of Rāma, the prince of the northern Indian kingdom of Ayodhyā. Without the benefit of writing, the story of Rāma was sung as a ballad in the court of kings by wandering bards. The *Rāmāyana* itself recounts that the story of Rāma was recited for the first time in a forest before a gathering of sages, in the streets of Ayodhyā for the second time and, for the final time, in the palace of Rāma after a horse sacrifice.

The text of the *Rāmāyana* is divided into seven books, called *kāndas* (books): *Balakānda* (the book on the childhood of the princes), *Ayodhyākānda* (the book on the city of Ayodhyā), *Aranyakānda* (the book on the forest exile), *Kiskindhakānda* (the book on the monkey citadel of Kiskindhā), *Sundarakānda* (the book on the beautiful island of Lankā), *Yuddhakānda* (the book on the battle), and *Uttarakānda* (the last book).

These seven books deal chronologically with the major events in the lifetime of Rāma, beginning with his birth and ending with his death. Of these, the seventh one, is generally regarded by the scholars to be an addition to the original story of Vālmīki. The epic contains 638 cantos and over 24,000 verses. It is very easy to discern interpolations in the present *Rāmāyana*. Accordingly, it is difficult to date the *Rāmāyana*, because it is the product of the combined efforts of poets belonging to several generations. Stories and verses were being composed throughout the first millennium B.C. Probably, the text took its present form somewhere between the fourth and the second centuries B.C.

The *Rāmāyana* has received many regional renderings in numerous languages and dialects spoken during different periods of time. Accordingly, the text of the *Rāmāyana* has come down to us in several versions. However, they can be grouped under two major versions: the Northern and the Southern. Of these, the Hindi (the Northern) re-creation of the text, Tulsidas's *Rāmacaritmānas* has become more popular than the Sanskrit original. The version of the *Rāmāyana* of Kaman in Tamil (the Southern) is equally popular in the south. Each version bears a close affinity to the others, in spite of linguistic and regional variations. Scholars generally believe that the Northern versions are less homogenous than the Southern ones; both abound in innumerable interpolations.

The Story of Rāma

The prosperous and just kingdom of Kosala, with its capital in Ayodhyā, sets the stage for the story of Rāma. The wise and powerful Dashartha was the ruler of this kingdom. Dashartha had three wives, Kaushalyā, Kaikeyī, and Sumitrā, but no son. On the advice of his ministers, Dashartha performed a sacrifice. Vishnu, one of the gods in the Hindu pantheon, appears to Dashartha in the midst of the sacrifice, and gives Dashartha a magic potion with the instruction that it be divided into four portions to be given to his three wives. As a result, four sons were born to his three wives: Rāma to Kaushalyā, Bharata to Kaikeyī, and Lakshmana and Shatrughna to Sumitrā. The first book of the epic describes these four brothers as partial incarnations of Vishnu.

The four sons were reared as princes in Ayodhyā, and came to be known, especially Rāma and Lakshmana, for their military acumen and prowess. Sage Vishvāmitra seeks their help to establish peace in his *ashram*. Rāma and Lakshmana go to sage Vishvāmitra's *ashram* to kill the demons who were disturbing Vishvāmitra in the performance of his sacrifice. They succeed in killing the demons and restoring peace in the *ashram*. On their way to Ayodhyā, they go to Mithila, the capital of the Videha kingdom of Janaka, who had promised his lovely daughter Sītā to the *kshatriya* (warrior) who could bend the great bow of Shiva. No suitor prior to Rāma was able even to lift this great bow. Rāma, however, has no difficulty in bending the bow. He marries Sītā and returns to Ayodhyā. The first book of the epic closes at this point.

The Second Book: The Ayodhyākānda

The second book of the epic, as the name *Ayodhyākānda* suggests, largely revolves around events that take place in the city of Ayodhyā. Dashartha is approaching old age and he decides to crown Rāma as the king so that Dashartha may retire to the forest. On the eve of the consecration ceremony, Manthara, the evil maid of Kaikeyī, and the second queen of King Dashartha, poisons Kaikeyī's mind by suggesting that if Rāma is crowned, her son Bharata's life would be in jeopardy. Kaikeyī becomes worried. Manthara further suggests to Kaikeyī that she should claim two boons that her husband Dashartha had promised her a long time ago. Kaikeyī agrees. She demands, firstly, the exile of Rāma to the forest for fourteen years, and secondly, the appointment of her son Bharata as the king. King Dashartha, though heartbroken, accedes to Kaikeyī's demands. Rāma, accompanied by his wife Sītā and brother Lakshmana, leaves for the forest. The entire family is grief stricken; Dashartha soon dies of a broken heart. Bharata is brought back to Ayodhyā from his maternal uncle's home. However, he refuses to rule Ayodhyā and goes to the forest to request Rāma to return to Ayodhyā. Rāma, however, was determined to carry out the orders of his father. The brothers reach an impasse. It is resolved when Bharata agrees to rule in Rāma's name; he takes Rāma's wooden sandals and places them on the throne in Ayodhyā as a token of Rāma's sovereignty.

The Third Book: Rāma's Exile to the Forest

The third book gives a picturesque description of the events that take place during Rāma's exile to the forest. They are in Dandaka forest, where they live in a hut. This forest is inhabited by hermits and ascetics as well as by demons. Here, Rāma and Lakshmana destroy many demons who were disturbing the peace. At this time Shurpanakha, a demon sister of Rāvana (King of the island of Lankā), comes to visit Rāma and Lakshmana, is infatuated by them, and wishes to marry either one of them. Both Rāma and Lakshmana reject her offer. She sees Sītā as the obstacle and tries to kill her. This enrages Lakshmana, and he mutilates her by cutting off her nose and ears. She goes to Rāvana and convinces him to punish Rāma and Lakshmana. Rāvana secures the aid of other demons and succeeds in kidnapping Sītā. The third book of the epic closes with a grief-stricken Rāma wandering through the forest in search of Sītā.

Sugrīva, the Monkey King

The next two books recount the events that occur in a monkey citadel in the forest. Rāma helps Sugrīva, the king of the monkeys, and makes an alliance with him. In return, Sugrīva promises to help Rāma to find Sītā. Hanuman, son of the wind, who is the general of the monkey forces and is well known for his prowess as a jumper, appears on the scene. He is an adherent of Sugrīva, who instructs him to find Sītā. Hanuman goes in search of Sītā, leaping over a sea of sixty miles in one jump. He locates Sītā, who has been a captive of Rāvana, on the island of Lankā. He offers to carry Sītā back to Rāma, Sītā refuses; she does not want to be touched by any man other than her husband. She then demands that Rāma come to rescue her. Hanuman decides to return to Rāma. However, prior to his leaving Lankā, he decides to have a little mischievous fun; he destroys trees and buildings, kills servants, and leaping from roof to roof, sets fire to the city. Finally, he returns to Rāma and informs him of Sītā's whereabouts.

The sixth book of the epic describes the battle between the forces of Rāma and Rāvana, the abductor of Sītā. With the help of the monkeys, Rāma builds a bridge across the sea to Lankā so that the princes and their army may cross over the sea. After a fierce battle, Rāma's army succeeds in slaying Rāvana and rescuing Sītā. However, because Sītā had stayed in the house of another man, Rāma refuses to take her back. Sītā proves her innocence and fidelity by throwing herself into a fire. The fire, however, does not burn her, and Agni, the fire God, emerges to testify on Sītā's behalf. She is reunited with Rāma and all of them return to Ayodhyā. Rāma's long-awaited coronation ceremony is duly performed and Rāma rules Ayodhyā in a just and a fair manner.

The concluding book of the epic consists of many different legends and myths. It recounts the story of Rāma's previous life, Sītā's banishment to the forest by Rāma at an advanced stage of pregnancy, and the story of Rāma's ancestors, all of which are only marginally related to the primary theme. The epic ends when Sītā gives birth to two sons, Lava and Kusha, who are reared and educated with Sītā in the forest under the guidance of the sage Vālmīki. Rāma eventually hands over the kingdom to his sons and returns to heaven as Vishnu, having fulfilled the purpose of his incarnation on earth.

The Deity Who Descends to Earth

Whereas the Vedic hymns praise gods, the *Rāmāyana* focuses on human beings and their greatness. The mediator between human beings and God is the *avatāra*, the divine incarnation; the deity who descends to earth and assumes earthly forms. The origin of the concept of *avatāra* is shrouded in mystery. It is not found in the Vedas; probably it is non-Aryan. It is quite likely that it came from Persia, where one finds the notion of discontinuous incarnations in the Bahrām Yāsht of the Zoroastrian literature. Irrespective of its origin, this concept of *avatāra* has greatly influenced Hindu religious life even to this day. Rāma has remained one of the most beloved expressions of the Divine. Regarding the historicity of characters in the *Rāmāyana*, most Western scholars believe that it deals with Rāma as a human hero, who, as the *avatāra* doctrine became important, assumed the form of an *avatāra* of Vishnu. Hindu orthodox, however, look upon Rāma as an historical figure and consider him to be a divine being.

The *Rāmāyana* exhorts people to lead a dharmic life, that is, a life in accordance with *dharma*, the law of moral conduct. Good moral conduct consists in honesty, fidelity, sincerity and loyalty. Rāma, Sītā, and Lakshmana have been the archetypes of conduct for generations. The most striking feature of the *Rāmāyana* is its characterization of Rāma as the ideal man, whose aspects are depicted by the different roles he plays in the family. As an ideal son, he observes strict filial piety; he respects the wishes of his father and goes into exile. He shows total deference to parental authority. He receives the news of his banishment with equanimity, and when Lakshmana argues with him that their father, because of old age, is being irrational and his words need not be obeyed, Rāma reiterates that the wishes of teachers and father are binding, regardless of the circumstances. He also highlights the significance of keeping one's promises even if the person to whom one has made the promise has died. Although his father Dashartha dies during Rāma's banishment, Rāma still completes the term of his banishment. In short, filial piety is articulated in terms of total and unconditional obedience. However, Ramāyana does not provide us with a clear criterion for resolution in cases where a conflict arises in the context of filial piety. When Rāma takes the news of his banishment to his mother, Kaushalyā, she is flabbergasted and asks Rāma to violate her husband's commands. She reminds Rāma that her words as his mother are just as binding as are his father's words. However, although the *Rāmāyana* emphasizes filial piety, in practice the words of one's father are shown to be more binding than the words of one's mother.

The Ideal Woman

Sītā is depicted in the *Rāmāyana* as the ideal woman. Her fidelity to husband is reiterated in the *Rāmāyana* again and again; her duty is to serve her husband and she must remain faithful to him. When Sītā returns from the demon Rāvana's house, Rāma refuses to take her back because she has lived in the house of another man. Although Sītā agrees to take the fire test to prove her integrity and character during the tenure of her captivity and passes with flying colors, the *Rāmāyana* again clearly exhibits the dominance of men and the fact that the society was patriarchal. As the *Rāmāyana* demonstrates, polygamy was quite common at the time in India, and women were subordinate to men.

The *Rāmāyana* emphatically declares that "a woman's first recourse is to her husband, the second to her son, and the third to her kinsmen." It is not an exaggeration to say that in the *Rāmāyana* we find, for the first time, a normative view regarding the status of women; the view became characteristic of Hinduism and later found expression in classics such as *The Laws of Manu*: "In childhood, a female must be subject to her father, in youth to her husband, when her lord is dead to her sons. . . ." A

husband must be constantly worshiped as a god by a faithful wife." (G. Buhler, 1969)

Tapas

The *Rāmāyana* repeatedly emphasizes the importance of *tapas*. "*Tapas*" is a generic term for all sorts of ascetic practices. It literally means "heat." It encompasses a wide spectrum of practices ranging from the recitation of sacred syllables and the chanting of melodies to real self-torture. *Tapas* in the Hindu context has been articulated as voluntary suffering in the performance of one's duties. It not only involves virtually no or minimum enjoyment of worldly pleasure, but also control of the mind and the senses. The *Rāmāyana* refers to Vishvāmitra as a character who became a *rshi* on account of his *tapas*. Not only are Vishvāmitra, Rāma, Lakshmana and other princes referred to as performers of *tapas*, but it is believed that Vālmīki, the original author of *Rāmāyana*, was a highway robber who, because he performed *tapas*, became a sage. The term "Vālmīki" means "born of an ant hill." It is said that he was given this name because he performed deep meditation where he became totally oblivious of his own consciousness and external surroundings and remained so even when the ants built their mounds all around him.

On the whole, the beautiful poetic language of the *Rāmāyana* makes it a favorite to many people. It gives a picturesque description of the emotions, sentiments, and mental states of its characters. Rāma's lament upon learning that Sītā has been kidnapped is vividly described in the *Rāmāyana*. (Rāma wanders in the forest searching for Sītā.) Additionally, the *Rāmāyana* contains many verses that describe the beauties of nature, seasonal changes, and the humming of the birds, as well as the mischievous activities of the monkeys and the magical powers of the demons.

The *Rāmāyana* is a national treasure for Hindus and even non-Hindus. It is appreciated in non-Hindu countries such as Thailand and Cambodia. It is read and sung by innumerable Hindus and performed in *Ram Lilās* every year in big cities and small towns alike. Rāma stands for all that is good and noble; Rāvana for the forces of evil; the story told in the *Rāmāyana* highlights the victories of good over evil. It still remains the main source of inspiration for the *bhakti* (devotional) tradition. That both epics the *Mahābhārata* and the *Rāmāyana* are war stories testifies to the unsettling nature of the times. The *Rāmāyana* brings together in one story the basic beliefs of the Vedic and Upanishadic era and explicates the religious and moral codes contained therein in a dramatic manner that can be understood even by lay persons.

BINA GUPTA

Further Reading

Translations

Goldman, R. P., and S. Sutherland, eds. *The Rāmāyana of Vālmīki*. Vols. I and II. Princeton, NJ: Princeton University Press, 1984. These vol-umes contain a translation and insightful analysis of the first two chapters of the *Rāmāyana*.

Buhler, G., trans. *The Laws of Manu*. In *Sacred Books of the East*, Vol. XXV. New York: Dover Publications Inc., 1969.

Related Studies

Gowen, Herbert H. *A History of Indian Literature*. New York: Greenwood Press, 1968. This book contains a chapter on the *Rāmāyana* that summarizes in a lucid manner the main themes of the seven books of the *Rāmāyana*.

Krishnamoorthy, K. *A Critical Inventory of Rāmāyana Studies in the World*. Vol. I. Delhi: Sahitya Akademi, 1991. This work, as its title suggests, contains an inventory of the academic studies done on the *Rāmāyana*. It also contains a very useful introduction.

MAHĀBHĀRATA

Title in Sanksrit: *Mahābhārata (Great Poem of the Descendants of Bharata)*
Author: Rishi Vyasa
Born: Place and date unknown
Died: Place and date unknown
Literary Form: Epic
Dates of Composition: 400 B.C. to 400 A.D.

Major Themes

Through action fulfill your duty (dharma)*; do not worry about the fruits of effort.*
Fate should not to be blamed; it is individuals who are responsible for their actions.
War is necessary for truth to prevail; it is a sacred duty to kill for the triumph of truth over malicious evil.
Where there is virtue, there is Krishna; where there is Krishna there is victory.
Righteousness is eternal and leads to prosperity; all else is merely ephemeral.
Whatever the circumstances, ultimately truth is victorious.

The *Mahabharata*, an epic poem, grew over centuries, spanning times of varying political, economic, religious, and social ethics. It has deeply influenced the psyche of the people of India. In popular culture the subtle inflections of the *Mahabharata* are not difficult to point out. The theme of the *Mahabharata* and reference to its characters are featured prominently in literary and artistic works, ancient to modern. From Kalidasa's masterpiece *Shakuntala* to the contemporary rendering of *Yayati* by Girish Karnad and *Andha Yug* by Dharamvir Bharati—all are evidence of the latent but constant presence of the epic. The *Mahabharata* has been translated into most of the Indian languages. Again, its themes are verbalized in folklore and folk music, expressed in architecture and sculpture. Films in different Indian languages have the *Mahabharata* as their theme, and a number of films have one or many of the characters plucked out of the epic and juxtaposed into a current setting. The *Bhagvad Gita*, a poem in the Sixth Book of the epic, in itself has become a book of superlative dimensions, a focal point of Hinduism and Hindu Philosophy. Though the *Mahabharata* was presented as a Broadway production by Peter Brook, in the West the epic has not received the attention and appreciation it commands in the East.

The *Mahabharata* is a long epic poem of about 100,000 couplets in Sanskrit, spread over 18 books and numerous chapters. It has been translated not only into the Indian languages but also into many of the European languages. It continues to hold the interest and entrance the minds of readers and critics alike with its heroic proportions.

Originally the *Mahabarata* was composed by Rishi Vyasa. Scholars have differing views about its date of composition. It is felt that many of the chapters and books were added to the original work from time to time. It is largely agreed that the epic was written and additions were made from 400 B.C. to 400 A.D. It is eight times the size of the *Iliad* and *Odyssey* combined.

The War of Succession

The *Mahabharata* is the story of a family feud over succession between the *Pandavas* (sons of Pandu) and the *Kauravas* (sons of Dhritarashtra). It is set in the northern Indian kingdom of Kurukshetra. The descendants of King Bharata, Pandu and Dhritrashtra, are two brothers. Since Dhritrashtra, the older son, was born blind, Pandu becomes the king. After ruling for many years Pandu goes to live in the forest and with the help of the gods his two wives bear five sons for him. When Pandu dies in the forest, Dhritrashtra becomes the king.

The five sons of Pandu and the hundred sons of Dhritrashtra are raised and educated together in Hastinapur under the guidance of the priest Acaharya Drona, a maestro of archery. He was chosen by Bhishma, the "Grand Old Man," great grandfather of the princes, who takes a keen interest in their instruction. The five Pandavas excel in every art, skill, and virtue. Arjuna, the third Pandava, becomes an ace archer and a favorite of Drona. The success of the Pandavas generates resentment and hostility in the Kauravas, typified by the eldest, Duryodhana. This bad feeling is manifested through a series of plots to kill the Pandavas, including an attempt to burn them alive in a house of lacquer (they manage to escape with the help of Vidura, their uncle). Rightfully, the eldest son of Pandu, Yudhistira, should become the king. Because of stubborn Duryodhana's greed for power it is decided to divide the kingdom.

The Pandavas convert their portion, the barren and forested Khandavaprastha, into an architectural marvel, Indraprastha. The Pandavas also have the support of their cousin Krishna, incarnation of Vishnu, head of the Hindu Trinity, born to bring order amidst chaos with victory of *dharma* (righteousness) over *adharma* (evil). However, Duryodhana in connivance with his uncle Shakuni, is able to send the Pandavas into exile for thirteen years, after defeating them in a dice game.

On their return, the Pandavas make a claim to their kingdom, but Duryodhana's covetous nature is backed by his father, Dhritrashtra, who refuses to give the Pandavas what they deserve: the result is war between the two families.

The two armies meet in the battlefield of Kurukshetra. The eighteen-day war results in the fall of great heroes, warriors, and priests. Ultimately, the Pandavas emerge triumphant, and Yudhishtra becomes the king of Hastinapur.

The War Between Good and Evil

The *Mahabharata* is replete with awesome descriptions of events, in particular of the war scenes, capturing the finest details and complexities. Neighing horses, trampling elephants, warriors on chariots at rampage, the clashing steel of swords and maces, battle cries, all reverberate throughout the eighteen-day war.

The *Mahabharata*, in its epic grandeur, has many plots and sub-plots, stories and sub-stories. The epic moves swiftly and dramatically with a myriad of events taking place, but it is character and its development which are quintessential. The archetypes of good and evil are perceptible as the story unfolds: the Pandavas are fountainhead of *dharma*, while the Kauravas are guided by *adharma*. Yudhishtra represents *dharma* and Duryodhana, *adharma*. Bhishma, the great grandfather of the princes, is the epitome of *dharma*; he stands by his word and integrity, never lies, and even in situations of conflict always does what is right.

Dharma and *karma* (fate-determining action) dominate the epic. The narrative recounts a number of occasions during which characters suffer from internal conflicts. Bhishma knew that Duryodhana was wrong in forcing the Pandavas out of their kingdom, that the Pandavas stood for *dharma*, yet Duryodhana led the Kauravas in the battle as he had pledged his loyalty to the protection of the king and throne of Hastinapur. Bound by obligation, Drona, Kripacaharaya, and Shalya too fight under the banner of Kauravas, fully knowing that the Pandavas would be victorious.

It is interesting to note that all these characters were aware of "where there is *dharma* there is victory." Draupadi, wife of the Pandava brothers, is lost to the Kauravas by Yudhistara, who stakes her on the last roll of the dice, and she is then dragged by her hair into the Kaurava court and disrobed. Bhishma, Drona, and Vidura, all find the whole episode abhorrent and shameful but do not say a word. When asked by Draupadi whether Yudhishtara had any rights to stake her in the dice game after having lost himself and his brothers earlier, there is only silence.

Karna, the son of Kunti before she married Pandu, is Duryodhana's friend; Karna is the Pandava's eldest brother, having been fathered by the Sun God, Surya. Since Kunti, the mother of the Pandavas, was unmarried when she gave birth to him, she put him in a box and set it afloat in a river. Because of his peculiar situation Karna faces many dilemmas. Before the war, Krishna discloses the secret of Karna's birth to him. For Karna, it is a conflict of interest, fighting in Duryodhana's camp against his brothers, but he has vowed to kill his younger brother Arjuna. Karna comes out of this moral battle victorious and a hero. It is more important for him to honor the solemn promise of allegiance made to Duryodhana than to give priority to his own feelings. Considering he had just found out his real parentage, a major issue here, his integrity and righteousness impress Krishna.

Later on Karna is approached by his mother Kunti who begs him not to kill Arjuna. Again he is put in a position of conflicting concerns, but he informs Kunti that one way or the other she will remain the mother of five sons after the great battle. When Karna was earlier approached by Lord Indra, Arjuna's father, in the guise of a Brahmana (priest), asking for Karna's armor and earrings that will protect him from anything, Karna gives them to Indra despite knowing who the Brahmana really is. Again, virtue takes precedence for Karna.

Karna's mother, Kunti, who is also the mother of Yudhistira, Arjuna, and Bhima, is similarly involved in a moral dilemma. When she hears that Karna has been killed by Arjuna, she struggles with her grief: none of the Pandavas are aware that they had slain their own brother, and they rejoice. Dhritrashtra, the blind king, is morally blinded by the love for his son Duryodhana. Very much aware of Duryodhana's evil intentions, as a father he ends up giving silent approval to his plans. He vacillates and resorts to blaming fate for whatever happens.

Arjuna, the great warrior, is not faced with moral dilemmas. In his case the greatest conflict occurs when he is in the battlefield, facing his cousins and kinsmen, priests and teachers. A despondent Arjuna says,

> *The magic bow slips*
> *from my hand, my skin burns,*
> *I cannot stand still,*
> *my mind reels.*
> *I see omens of chaos,*

> *Krishna; I see no good*
> *in killing my kinsmen*
> *in battle.*

(MILLER, TRANS., 1986)

It is important to take note of the armed outer battle and the inner conflict that accompanies it. In fact, this is the fundamental feature of the *Mahabharata*. As V. S. Sukthankar said, "Kurukshetra is at the same time the battlefield of the different emotions and passions in the heart of man, and the holy battleground of the eternal war between the higher nature and lower nature of man."

Krishna, the eighth incarnation of Vishnu, is Arjuna's charioteer in the war, as well as his counselor. Arjuna's moral dilemma results from weakness in the execution of *dharma*. Action is the key word here. Krishna's advice to Arjuna is analytical and clarifying; the relationships between duty, discipline, knowledge, and action are emphasized.

Krishna's moral philosophy is expressed independently of the main story in the *Bhagvad Gita* section, now the holy book of Hindus. The essence of the *Gita* is that regardless of rewards one must act in accordance with *dharma*. It is only such action that has the power to liberate the inner self. The *Gita* also elucidates the permanence of the human soul. It shows how the control of one's senses and of what is transitory can lead to contentment of mind and bliss. Geared for battle, by the end of the sermon Arjuna is able to "see" the full divine form of Lord Krishna, the protector of *dharma*.

As an epic, the *Mahabharata* involves characters engaged in devious methods to attain their ends. Clearly Karna is tricked by Indra into giving up his armor and protective earrings, which weakens him on the battlefield. Spurred by Krishna's encouragement, Arjuna kills Karna, despite Karna being without arms and trying to push his chariot's wheel out of the mud. Bhishma is also handicapped when Shikhandi (a woman reborn as a man) becomes Arjuna's charioteer in place of Krishna. The Pandavas, with Krishna's guidance, make this change, knowing Bhishma will not attack a woman. When Drona proves difficult to conquer, Yudhishtra, even though he is *dharma* incarnate, lies too. He tells Drona that "Ashwatathama" (using the name of Drona's son) is dead, even though this is false. (The "Ashwatathama" referred to is actually an elephant.) Drona, who knows that Yudhishtra would never lie, is overcome with grief and is beheaded by Dhristadyumna while in a yogic trance. When Bhima is unable to kill Duryodhana after a long fight, Krishna, standing aside, tells Bhima to strike Duryodhana on his thighs (Duryodhana's whole body had become like stone when he was embarrassed to have his mother Gandhari see his naked body, except for his loins, which he had covered with a banana leaf). Krishna was aware of this and by his advice to Bhima was instrumental in bringing about Duryodhana's death. (Here it would be appropriate to compare him with Satan.) Even in defeat Duryodhana's spirit was invincible. As he was dying flowers were showered on him from the heavens.

These different acts of killing either by lying or by laying deceitful traps, are justified in the epic as necessary to bring order and uphold *dharma*. The driving force is so overwhelming that people like Yudhishtra are caught in its vortex and adopt sinning as a means. Here the philosophy of doing a wrong or resorting to deceit in order to eliminate evil and to bring order is put into perspective. Krishna, the incarnation of cosmic power, advises and encourages various characters to do what is "wrong" or what is against their values and beliefs. As an incarnation of Vishnu he has the power to see and foresee consequences and to determine right and wrong. When the moment requires a negative act, the negative act achieves *karma* for the glory of virtue and *dharma*. This is the moral justification for war and acts of violence—that by such means peace and justice are attained. The unwavering focus here is entirely on *karma*, forceful action that determines the future.

The *Mahabharata* concentrates upon male characters. Women are not given the same importance as men and are viewed as subordinates. Gandhari, Dhritrashtra's wife, spends her life with a band tied over her eyes, so as to be like her husband, who is congenitally blind. This act is admired as a sacrifice required by a wife's duty towards her husband. Hardly ever is it seen as unfair. Her helplessness in knowing that her son is following the path of *adharma* (opposed to *dharma*) and not being able to do anything is expressed only as a silent lament. As a woman Gandhari is far stronger, and has a clearer vision of *dharma*, than the weak and vacillating Dhritrashtra, her husband. Kunti, the Pandavas" mother, is also a silent sufferer, as she cannot acknowledge to the world or even to the five Pandavas that Karna (born before her marriage to Pandu) is also her son and their brother. Draupadi (the wife of the five Pandava brothers), who is a major character of the epic, is often accused of being the cause of the great war. To some extent she reflects the woman of her times: she can freely choose her husband; she can sit beside him in the court. She then suffers, however, from being staked in the dice game by her husband, Yudhishtra; her individual rights are violated and nobody utters a word. She suffers the humiliation of being disrobed in front of the court of Hastinapur; her Pandava husbands witness the whole scene with their heads hanging in shame. Once again the nature of *dharma* is the focus here. This whole act is justified as required of Yudhishtra in order that he follow the path of righteousness; as a loser in the game of dice, he has no rights and has to accept whatever his opponents say or do, no matter how immoral and abhorrent it is. (To the modern reader, Yudhishtra's inaction may seem like moral impotency; he allows his wife to be humiliated because he has lost everything, including her, in a game of dice. Only the intervention of the gods saves both him and her.)

The *Mahabharata* is a monumental work—an epic involving colorful characters, acts of deceit and valor, great battles, philosophical lessons, religious injunctions, practical guidance—and it is not surprising that it came to be venerated by the Hindus and resorted to for information, inspiration, moral advice, and—last but not least—as a story of exciting and compelling drama.

PRABHJOT PARMAR

Further Reading

Translations

Lal, P. *The Mahabharata of Vyasa.* New Delhi: Vikas Publishing House Pvt. Ltd., 1980. The author has skillfully condensed the epic centered on the Kauravas and the Pandavas, and has eliminated the extrapolations and trappings that have little connection with the two families. The introduction, with a well made genealogical chart, is an illuminating critique in itself. Another highlight is the bibliography with brief reviews of the books.

Miller, Barbara Stoler. *The Bhagavad Gita: Krishna's Counsel in Time of War.* New York: Columbia University Press, 1986. Capturing the essence of Krishna's philosophical "sermon," it is a work well worth reading. The book provides helpful insights into the *Gita* and the epic itself.

Rajgopalachari, C. *Mahabharata.* Bombay: Bhartiya Vidya Bhavan, 1952. A simple translation of the Tamil version of the stories of the epic. It is a reading for first-timers and those who shun voluminous books. Even in such a short rendering of the epic, the author has managed to convey the underlying philosophy.

Van Buitenen, J. A. B. *Mahabharata.* Books I–V, 3 vols. Chicago and London: The University of Chicago Press, 1973, 1975, 1978. A successful effort. This translation from Sanskrit into English reflects the laborious work and scholarship required to capture the spirit of the *Mahabharata.* It is well written, with an introduction that throws light on the authorship, themes, and other translations of the epic. The notes on the text are of help for those looking for detailed study of the epic. It is based on the critical edition of Bhandarkar Oriental Research Institute, Poona.

Related Studies

Matilal, Bimal Krishna. *Moral Dilemmas in the Mahabharata.* Shimla: Indian Institute of Advanced Study in association with Motilal Banarsidass, Delhi, 1989. The editor has compiled a collection of papers on moral dilemmas explored in the epic. Most of them offer interesting perspectives and some challenge certain of the implications of the epic. This book is very useful for those trying to understanding the complexities of the characters and events.

Sukthankar, V. S. *On The Meaning of Mahabharata.* Bombay: The Asiatic Society of Bombay, 1957. Authored by an accomplished scholar, this book provides substantial insights into the *Mahabharata* and its characters. The "mundane," ethical, and metaphysical aspects of the epic are examined. Contains a critique of other works about the *Mahabharata.*

THE SONG OF THE LORD (BHAGAVAD-GĪTĀ)

Title: *Bhagavad-gītā*
Author: Unknown. Tradition assigns the work to Vyasa, the legendary author of the *Mahābhārata*
Literary Form: Religious, devotional poetry
Date of Composition: The exact date of composition is unknown. The *Gita* has been dated as early as 500 B.C. and as late as A.D. 100. Most scholars situate the work between the fifth and first centuries, B.C.

Major Themes

God is the absolute source, ground, and end of all being.

The Divine forms all reality and by doing so reveals his creative energy.

The Absolute becomes human in order to teach humanity and establish righteousness.

The human being is both spirit and matter, the imperishable and the perishable, eternal and temporal.

The eternal human soul is the essence of the individual and a minute part of God.

The goal of human life is a perfect union with God, which also results in perfect self-knowledge and a union with all being.

Humanity achieves salvation through acts of wisdom, work, and love.

Wisdom is the mystical intuition of the one in the many, rather than attachment to the changing world of senses, mental images, and ideas.

Work must be done in accord with caste requirements.

When liberated persons act, they never seek the fruits of their actions.

Love is complete self-donation to the other and to God; it is the essence of sacrifice and devotion.

Within the 100,000 couplets of the great Hindu epic, the *Mahābhārata*, a work of only some seven hundred verses has attained the status as one of the world's great religious classics. The *Bhagavad-gītā* is revered as literature that throughout the centuries has offered to countless millions spiritual comfort and religious inspiration. Its pages are searched for insights into all of life's complexities, while its verses are often found on the lips of the pious Hindu as death approaches. As religious literature, it calls the believer to focus on God alone, who is presented as revealing the many ways to salvation. As philosophical literature, it challenges the thinker to reflect on the meaning of life and, as such, to know the one in the many. As dramatic poetic literature, it captures the distress and confusion of the seeker and the compassionate smile of the Divine one who is sought. The *Gītā* presents a grand view of the whole of life, serving as one of the most beloved guides for the perplexed in the history of Eastern literature.

The work opens with the warrior Arjuna facing his enemies across a great battlefield. There he stands in his own existential situation (as, of course, does the reader) on the battlefield of life—both having the same question: "What ought to be done with one's life?" Arjuna is stunned by the dilemma that to fight would involve either the death of those he loves, his family and respected teachers, or his own demise. Krishna, the Divine Incarnate who serves as Arjuna's charioteer, proceeds to offer insights into the whole of reality. It is these ideas that form the substance of the *Gītā*.

The ideas at the core of this work of literature are religious and philosophical. These ideas can be delineated issue by issue, but within the work they are all interrelated, forming a coherent whole. The themes range from discussions regarding the nature of Divinity and humanity to the various expressions of the human intellect and will as the person struggles to achieve salvation. The *Gītā* is a work noted for its ability to hold together a rich complexity of ideas in a synthesis of seemingly contradictory conceptions. The catholicity of the *Gītā* appreciates the whole of being with its diversity and unity as it celebrates the many different paths to the same divine end.

The Divine

Arjuna's focus on his own particular duty is set by Krishna within the context of the nature of God and, as such, raises the issue of the meaning of all human duty. To make it clear what humanity ought to do, the author of the *Gītā* sets forth two themes regarding divine nature: first, the absolute character of the Divine who is the source, ground, and end of all reality; second, this Absolute as a compassionate personal God who offers Himself to struggling humanity. Both themes are held together throughout the work: the God of being and the God of grace.

As the absolute source, ground, and end of all being, the Divine throughout the *Gītā* is described in terms such as the "imperishable," the "incomprehensible," and the "all-knowing." In such images there are echoes of the earlier tradition of the *Upanishads*, which saw Brahman as the absolute unity at the core of all the fleeting images of this world, the One who cannot be captured by the grasp of the senses. Also upanishadic is the *Gītā's* attention to the creative power of God to form all aspects of being. This creative energy is called *maya* (from "*ma*" meaning to form). All reality has its source through divine *maya*. To capture this, the text uses a rich assortment of images (light, time, death, goodness, fear, knowledge, courage) to speak of the vitality within all acts that is the Divine. Thus, we read of God as the primeval seed of all contingent beings, the death that snatches all away, and the time that causes the world's destruction. These images, rooted in the claim that all things flow from the Divine, tend to approach pantheism. However, the work often affirms that the Absolute is never trapped in *maya*, for all nature is within the transcendent God.

Pantheism is further rejected in the personal theism throughout this song of the beloved. The impersonal Absolute is the personal self-conscious reality with intellect and will who becomes human in an act of divine descent *(avatāra)*. This incarnation is presented in the *Gītā* as Krishna, the supreme gift of grace of the absolute God. These avataras are said to happen throughout history in order for God to establish righteousness, reward the good, punish the evil, and offer a focus for all pious devotion. This monotheism, while not rejecting the sacred Vedas, does move away from the vedic pantheon. For the *Gītā*, God is the one Absolute, both within and beyond all being. This is a personal incarnate Absolute, the goal of all human longings; that end which alone satisfies human nature.

Humanity

To seek the Divine, the person, according to the *Gītā*, must understand the nature of humanity. Thus, the first topic addressed in the work is the nature of the "embodied self." This discussion is immediately relevant to Arjuna who is risking his very self in the impending battle. Krishna's teaching on the nature of the person (along with an understanding of divinity) becomes the foundation for all subsequent discussions on the various yogic paths to salvation. All comes from the Divine—the spirit *(purusha)* and the body *(prakriti)*; however, there is a fundamental distinction between these two worlds. This dualism expresses itself in the famous line of advice offered to the perplexed warrior: " . . . everlasting is this self. . . . It is not slain when the body is slain" (2:21). The soul, unchanging and immortal, abandons old bodies as if they were only old clothes.

The spiritual self belongs to eternity, while all that is material remains caught in time. This immortality is affirmed in the *Gītā* because at the core of the self is the Absolute, the imperishable. The divine macrocosm is linked with the human microcosm, for the soul of a person is said to be a minute part of God. Here is the upanishadic tradition of the unity of humanity and divinity in the essence of the human soul. Because of the *Gītā's* personal theism, the Divine remains not only within, but also the other, distinct from the soul. This other is the One with Whom the person seeks unity.

What is, is not obvious, for the self is caught in the ever-present material field, the *maya* of all that changes. The world, the senses, the fleeting mental images, all have transitory qualities or strands *(gunas)* of pleasure or pain or indifference. These constituent elements of being are ever changing (light, purity, passion, energy, darkness, dullness). As the soul draws the world of the senses and of the imagination into the self, the self becomes attached to the fleeting shadows. Enjoyment of the world leads to suffering, to a bondage to all that perishes. In such a situation, a person in ignorance thinks that the transitory really concerns the self. Desires, as in Buddhism, lead to the bondage of attachment.

The Yogic Paths

Desire for the creative energy of the Divine but for not the Divine Self is the result of a lack of awareness. The unenlightened are lost, as was Arjuna in the expectation of the battle, in the world of outer appearances and ego driven preoccupations. The liberated, like God, merely behold the flow of time. They, like a tortoise, withdraw all external inclinations either mental or sensual, and remain undisturbed. Or, as another *Gītā* image puts it, they are like the ocean that while unmoved draws all water to itself. Since the core of self is the Divine, the ideal of humanity and divinity is presented as the image of the unattached spectator who beholds all. To achieve this state of perfection, spiritual exercises *(yoga)* must be undertaken.

The term *yoga*, as used throughout the *Gītā*, implies a joining and a corresponding disjunction. The goal of all spiritual exercises is to join the self with what it is in essence (a part of God) by actively disengaging from all the attachments to what it is not. Redemption is an awareness of one's true nature. As Krishna puts it in the sixth chapter: "Who sees me in all, and sees all in me, for him I am not lost, nor is he lost to me."

To achieve the Divine, according to the *Gītā*. there is a twofold yogic path: the way of knowledge *(jnana yoga)* and the way of works *(karma yoga)*. For those who are inclined to be oriented by their intellect, Krishna offers advice on the elements of meditation. For others, oriented by their wills, lessons are offered on life's duties *(dharma)*, and ac-

tion in the world and loving devotion *(bhakti)*. These two great paths and their many expressions are ultimately to be integrated throughout a person's life in the attempt to achieve salvation.

The Enlightened Intellect

The wise who control their mental inclinations *(prajna)* practice a discipline of knowledge *(jnana yoga)*. They do not permit their wisdom to be swept away by manifold desires, but have achieved freedom in the truth. A life of wisdom is celebrated throughout the *Gītā*. It is likened to a sacrifice to God, a boat that crosses over the sea of evil, a fire that burns all false deeds, and a shining lamp that dispels all darkness. As the sun enlightens all, so also even the worst of evildoers can, by the light of wisdom, be lifted to the Absolute. For the *Gītā*, nothing on earth resembles wisdom in its power to purify.

Wisdom, according to the *Gītā*, is achieved through mystical intuition, rather than through rational argumentation or sense experience. It is the intuitive grasp of the permanent unchanging riverbed that sustains and gives direction to the flowing river of being. The ideal is a contemplative gaze of the mind on the infinite in the finite, a union with the beyond that is within.

From this perspective, attachment to the Divine requires detachment from the fleeting shadows of life's experiences. The enlightened are not scattered by multiple distractions caused by sense and reason. This accounts for the often repeated advice from Krishna to Arjuna to center his thoughts on Krishna alone. With such a centering, the eternal self will remain absolutely undisturbed by the experiences of life. This is a state of awareness called by the *Gītā* "sameness" *(samatva)*, where equanimity of mind judges all opposites as the same. This is why Krishna teaches Arjuna that no matter what the outcome of life's battles—success or failure, life or death, victory or defeat—it is really all the same. God-like, the silent sage observes all, but is attached to none.

In all this there are numerous similarities to early Buddhism, with the important difference that in the *Gītā* there remains an eternal soul at the root of knowing. Thus, the teaching of Krishna is that a person whose self is integrated sees the self as abiding in all beings, and sees all beings as in the self.

The Liberated Will

The person without attachments, having joyful thoughts fixed on the Absolute must, nevertheless, still act. Arjuna is told by Krishna to fight, for it is his duty as a warrior. For the *Gītā*, the path of work *(karma yoga)* done according to a person's duty also serves as a vehicle of salvation. The *Gītā*, in its strong support for the traditional social order *(dharma)*, may be seeking to repudiate the growing influence of Buddhism and Jainism with their radical renunciation of the world. This is why the *Gītā* demands that the warrior must fight, for this is the obligation of his caste; duty and honor demand it.

We read that the traditional social divisions were established by God and that the demands of the specific caste are set at birth. Some are called to offer sacrifices *(Brahmins)*, others have the duties of commerce and husbandry *(Vaisyas)*, while others serve as serfs *(Sudras)*. The warrior class *(Kshatriyas)* must do its duties even if it violates the more general moral precept imposed on all castes of non-violence *(ahimsā)*. These rigid divisions maintain and conserve the social order. It is God who decides which person is best suited for a specific caste, based upon the inner tendencies of the person acquired throughout previous lifetimes. Far from escaping from the demands of the world, the *Gītā* claims, a person discovers the Divine only by performing his or her assigned duties.

The call is to act, but to do so in a way whereby a person does not become trapped in the ever changing *maya*. To accomplish action but not attachment requires work that remains detached from the fruit of the work; not a quietistic life but rather selfless action, utterly indifferent to its success or failure. The seed of the deed is the motive. For the *Gītā*, the unselfish, humble, and loving abandon all egocentric desires. They are unlike those who follow the vedic demand to sacrifice in order to receive the benefits of the gods. Indeed, for the *Gītā*, the habit-

ual round of rituals and sacrifices cannot achieve liberation *(moksha)* if these acts have, as their motive, self-centered gain. Mere external formalities rooted in pride lead away from salvation.

The way to salvation is through acts done in wisdom and informed by love *(bhakti)*. An action that serves as a sacrifice to God is an act which offers the self. Detachment from the fruit of an action is completed in acts of attachment to the merciful Krishna. So Krishna tells Arjuna that none who love God are lost, for Krishna will deliver them from all evil. *Bhakti*, a term from the Sanskrit root *bhaj*, meaning "to serve," captures the ideal impulse of both humanity and divinity. In the ninth chapter we read: "They who revere Me with devotion, they are in Me and I am in them." And elsewhere (18.58), we find the source of the widespread Hindu custom of thinking of God at death: "Fixing thy thoughts on Me, thou shalt, by My grace, cross over all difficulties." The personal God of the *Gita* is a God who offers different paths as the gift of His compassion. All is grace, all a gift. None of those who love God is lost to the God of love.

The Influence of the Gītā

The *Bhagavad-gītā*, a text that has transcended its ancient context, can rightly be said to be one of the world's most influential religious works. There are many reasons for its influence. The work is beloved because of its ability to speak to the common person, as a comfort for the distressed, and as a source for piety and devotion. The learned have found in its pages a rich deposit of philosophical ideas all woven together like the threads of a complex tapestry; all together an interplay of opposites, a diversity in unity, a unity in diversity. Written before the rise of rigid and precise systems of thought, the *Gītā* reveals mysteries that defy complete intellectual penetration. Little help is offered the reader who seeks to comprehend the interplay of divine providence and the reality of free choice. For the *Gītā*, the mystery is contained in the action of Arjuna, who picks up his bow declaring that his doubts are dispelled, and he will now fight because of Krishna's words.

Immensely fruitful for the Hindu tradition is the *Gītā*'s image of the Divine. The Absolute is both completely impersonal and completely personal; the ground of all being and the one Incarnate in specific times and places. God is both the serene silent unattached observer and the passionate lover who desires to be the gracious helper of all. God is the absolute source of the good but also of the evils and illusions of life; the root of life and death, eternity and time.

Since its composition, the *Gītā* has served as an encyclopedia of the multiple spiritual paths. Salvation is celebrated as unity and enlightenment, a oneness with all in a perfect act of self-knowledge. The ways of knowledge, of work, and of love are all acts of worship. Each serves a different disposition while all together call the whole person: intellect, will, and emotions.

Much Hindu social thought discusses the *Gītā*'s traditional reaffirmation of the vedic and upanishadic ideals of sacrifice, caste, and liberation. According to a popular idea, the *Gītā* is the milk from the upanishadic cow. The *Gītā* has served as a layman's *Upanishads*, for it is more accessible with its shorter length and its easily memorized and memorable poetic lines.

On the other hand, centuries of Hindu social thought discuss the *Gītā*'s critique of the older tradition. Vedic sacrifices are purified by the call for personal sacrifice through acts of ego-destroying devotion. Vedic polytheism and upanishadic monism are understood from the perspective of the *Gītā*'s theism. Caste and duty are important not only for social cohesion but also as vehicles for human perfection. While offering passing attention to the liberation from the cycles of birth and rebirth, this *Song of the Lord* is directed to elaborate descriptions of union with God.

Interpretations of the Gītā

The elasticity of the text has permitted the *Gītā* to be interpreted within a wide variety of contexts, at different times, for different aims. Shankara (d.c. A.D. 820), one of Hinduism's most famous metaphysicians, offered a commentary *(bhasya)* on the

Gītā that remains an important statement of a non-dualistic *(advaita)* philosophy. With Shankara, the *Gītā* entered the world of brahmanic scholarship with much attention to the complexities and subtleties of the intellectual life. For Shankara, liberation is achieved only through an insight into the Absolute as the only reality; all else is mere appearance conditioned by ignorance. Only the learned few can rise to a comprehension of the real purpose of the *Gītā*: to teach true knowledge.

In reaction to this monistic reading a later Hindu, Ramanuja (d.c. A.D. 1137), argued in his commentary that the *Gītā* is a work that above all reveals the personal dimension of the Divine. Influenced by the piety traditions of Southern India, he saw the *Gītā* as a call to surrender to the Incarnate God through acts of ego-transcending devotional furor. All castes could thus achieve salvation through acts of love.

Ramanuja's inclusive reading reappears in modern times in the writings of India's social reformers. Seeing the *Gītā* as a call to selfless action, writers such as B. G. Tilak (1856–1920) and Mohandas Gandhi (1869–1948) understood their struggles in part through the *Gītā*. They argued that the *Gītā* embodied the essence of a Hindu Eastern spirituality, which alone could strengthen emerging Indian nationalism against the political domination and cultural materialism of the British Empire.

Today, the *Bhagavad-gītā* has transcended national boundaries. The internationalizing of the work, begun with the first Western translations (1785), has come to full flowering with every year witnessing hundreds of translations, commentaries, and studies in all the modern languages. To the world community, the *Gītā* has become an essential expression not only of the spirituality of Hinduism but also of the deepest of human longings: the desire for perfection.

LAWRENCE F. HUNDERSMARCK

Further Reading

Translations

Bolle, Kees W., trans. *The Bhagavadgītā*. Berkeley: University of California Press, 1979. An unrhymed English verse printed without commentary facing the critical Sanskrit text. A helpful feature of this work is its relating the basic Sanskrit terms to their English equivalents and their location in the text.

van Buitenen, J. A. B., trans. *The Bhagavadgītā in the Mahābhārata*. Chicago: The University of Chicago Press, 1981. A narrative prose rendering with the critical edition on the opposite page. This translation has been greatly praised by professional Indologists for its learned control of the Sanskrit text. The focus is away from the philosophical and religious themes of the work, in favor of a precise rendering grounded in text criticism and philology.

Edgerton, Franklin, trans. *The Bhagavad Gītā*. Cambridge: Harvard University Press, 1944. This famous translation was first published as volumes 38 and 39 of the Harvard Oriental Series. It was also reissued in 1964 through Harper and Row Publishers. Edgerton's work imitates the verses *(sloka)* of the Sanskrit in syntax and cadence. At times the English is awkward, but it remains a faithful reproduction of the original. Edgerton's introductory discussions of the key ideas of the *Gītā* have been influential. The Harvard edition also reproduces the *Gītā* as translated by the nineteenth-century English poet Edwin Arnold. It was through this poetic version that Gandhi, when studying in London, first encountered the *Gītā*.

Parrinder, Geoffrey, trans. *The Bhagavad Gītā*. New York: E. P. Dutton, 1975. A rhymed iambic meter version designed to help readers memorize verses of the *Gītā*.

Radhakrishnan, Sarvepalli, trans. *The Bhagavadgītā*. London: George Allen and Unwin, 1948. After each verse is offered a gloss in the tradition of Shankara's views, but generalized in an apologetic way, designed to demonstrate the universal relevance of the *Gītā*. The work is important as a vehicle for Radhakrishnan's neo-Hindu idealism presented as an antidote for Western materialism.

Sargeant, Winthrop, trans. *The Bhagavad Gītā*. Albany: State University of New York Press, 1984. An unrhymed verse translation with an extensive concordance. The value of this effort is that the translation is offered as a word-for-word interlinear Sanskrit to English. This text is very helpful for those who are using the *Gītā* as an introduction to the vocabulary and morphology of Sanskrit. Also of value is a complete list of epithets used throughout the *Gītā*, with their exact English meanings.

Zaehner, R. C., ed. *The Bhagavad-Gītā, with Commentary Based on Original Sources*. London: Oxford University Press, 1969. The best single volume in terms of the harmony of translation and commentary. The *Gītā* is presented in three ways: first, as continuous narrative prose; second, as a verse-by-verse with commentary; finally, as a thematic arrangement of the most important passages illustrating the work's key themes. No other work in English has such an extensive and sophisticated commentary grounded in the broad spectrum of classical Sanskrit sources.

Related Studies

The following three books, if taken together, offer the reader a broad and intelligent introduction to the rich history of *Gītā* exegesis:

van Buitenen, J. A. B. *Ramanuja on the Bhagavadgītā: A Condensed Rendering of His Gītābhasya with Copious Notes and an Introduction*. Delhi: Motilal Banarsidass, 1968.

Minor, Robert, ed. *Modern Indian Interpreters of the Bhagavad Gītā*. Delhi: Sri Satguru Publications, 1991.

Sharma, Arvind. *The Hindu Gītā: Ancient and Classical Interpretations of the Bhagavadgītā*. La Salle: Open Court Publishing Co., 1986.

DHAMMAPADA

English Translation of Title: *The Path of Righteousness* (or *Virtue*)
Author: The *Dhammapada* consists of sayings attributed to the Buddha (Siddhartha Gautama); finally translated into Pali by unknown writers.
Literary Form: Aphorisms, some in poetic form
Date of Composition: Around third century B.C.

Major Themes

Practicing what the Buddha preached is a sure path of freedom from suffering.
Suffering follows from bad conduct as surely as peace follows from good conduct.
Mental states are caused by our perceptions; therefore, we must purify perceptions.
Cultivating awareness eventually leads to Nirvāna.
There are Four Noble Truths: Life is sorrowful; Craving is the cause of sorrow; Removing craving removes sorrow; By following the Eightfold Path one destroys sorrow.
The Eightfold Path consists of: right knowledge, right intention, right speech, right action, right livelihood, right effort, right mindfulness, and right concentration.

After the death of the Buddha, his disciples were concerned about the preservation of his teachings. All of Buddha's teachings had been imparted orally. His followers assembled at the first council of Rajagriha, India in 477 B.C. to rehearse and commit the Buddha's discourses to memory. From this source evolved the Pali canon of Buddhist scriptures, which was divided into three baskets (the *Tipitaka*), the most important of the three being the *Suttapitaka* (the basket containing Buddha's discourses). The *Suttapitaka* itself was divided into five collections. The fifth of the five collections is called *Khuddanikāya* and consists of several books, which are works of poetic art—collections of aphorisms, songs, poems, fairy tales, and fables. The *Dhammapada* is the second book of the *Khuddanikāya*.

The title *Dhammapada* has been translated as "The Path of Virtue," "The Way of Truth," "The Way of Righteousness," or "Words of Truth."

The *Dhammapada*, in its Pali version, is an anthology of 423 sayings of the Buddha in verse. It is divided into 26 chapters, each chapter dealing with one subject. In one recension or another the *Dhammapada* was dispersed throughout the Buddhist world. The next most noteworthy versions are the four Chinese versions from the Sanskrit, the ear-

liest of which, an anthology of 500 stanzas, was brought from India in A.D. 223. One of these, together with the rest of the *Tipitaka*, was printed from blocks in A.D. 972, nearly seven centuries before Gutenberg. Next in importance is the *Udānavarga* in a near-Sanskrit version found in Turkestan, and comprising some 1,050 stanzas. There are two other versions known as the *Gāndhāri Dharmapada* and the *Patna Dharmapada*.

The Pali version of the *Dhammapada* is the most well-known version. Since the stanzas of the *Dhammapada* are pithy sayings of the Buddha, the Buddhists of Sri Lanka found it necessary to compose a commentary on the *Dhammapada*, which explains the meaning of each stanza and tells where, when, and why each stanza was uttered by the Buddha. The *Dhammapāda Commentary* was composed about 450 A.D. and its compiler remains unknown. Its authorship is mistakenly attributed to Buddhaghasa.

The *Dhammapada* is composed in a very lucid, chaste, and elegant Pali. The entire work is in verse. The majority of the verses are in a meter very close to the vedic *anushtubh* (eight syllables in each foot), while some verses are close to the vedic *trishtubh* (eleven syllables in each foot) or the vedic *jagati* (twelve syllables in each foot). The work is rendered in a charming and smooth style. The verses display a wealth of similes drawn from everyday life. There are flashes of humor produced by the clever use of puns, and the verses are easy to memorize.

Since *the Dhammapada's* appearance in a Latin version in 1850, it has been repeatedly translated into the principal European and Asian languages. The depth and universality of its doctrine, and purity and earnestness of its moral teachings, combined with the refined simplicity and pellucid poetical beauty of its language, has earned for it an honored place in world literature.

The *Dhammapada* is also the most important single work belonging to the canonical literature for practicing Buddhists. Through the centuries, the *Dhammapada* has been memorized by novices who were expected to recite the entire text from memory before they received the higher ordination as monks. The *bhikku* (friar) Kassapa in the Foreword to Narada Thera's translation of *the Dhammapada* writes, "If I were to name any book from the whole *Tipitaka* as having been of most service to me, I should without hesitation choose the *Dhammapada*. And it goes without saying that, to me, it is the best single book in all the wide world of literature. For forty years and more it has been my constant companion and never-failing solace in every kind of misfortune and grief. There is no trouble that man is heir to, for which the Lord over Sorrow cannot point out cause and prescribe sure remedy."

The Contents of the Dhammapada

The *Dhammapada* is divided into twenty-six chapters, offering sage advice in a pithy and metaphorical manner, and dealing with such topics as the mind, the self, the world, the awakened one, happiness, the path, hell, the elephant, the mendicant, and the Brahmins.

The book is short, amounting to something like thirty-four printed pages in a modern English edition.

Chapter one, called "The Pairs," presents pairs of possibilities for human conduct, each leading to a different kind of destiny. The negative is presented first, leading to unhappiness, and this is followed by the positive, leading to happiness.

The first verse of chapter one states the fundamental principle of Buddhist psychology. Our mental states depend on our perception, not on how things are in themselves. If we perceive a red-faced, wildly gesticulating person as an angry, hostile attacker, our mental state will be quite different from that which would arise if we saw the same person as rehearsing a play or as releasing his own inner tensions. Therefore, the *Dhammapada* declares that if one acts with polluted perception, suffering follows as a wheel follows the draught-ox's foot, whereas if one acts with tranquil perception, happiness follows him, as a shadow that never leaves.

The Buddha's half-brother Nanda was infatuated by sensual pleasure. It was this state of mind that the Buddha described in verse 13: "Even as rain penetrates an ill-thatched house, so does lust penetrate an undeveloped mind." Nanda was afterwards completely converted to Buddhism when verse 14 was uttered: "Even as rain does not penetrate a well-thatched house, so does lust not penetrate a well-developed mind." Mind is purified by concentration and contemplation.

Chapter two is entitled "*Appamādo-vaggo*." "*Appamādo*" means awareness, heedfulness, vigilance, and watchfulness. The importance of awareness was the Buddha's greatest discovery. In history, it ranks with the taming of fire, agriculture, or the Pythogorean theorem as a milestone in humanity's journey upwards. The Buddha discovered that if awareness is focused with deep concentration and equanimity upon all aspects of human experience, suffering is overcome and replaced by tranquility and quiet joy. Verses of chapter two highlight the supreme importance of awareness. It is said that the first verse of this chapter, verse 21, which states that the path to the deathless (that is, *Nibbāna*, or *Nirvana*, (the ultimate freedom) is awareness, whereas unawareness is the path of death, completely transformed the character of King Asoka the Righteous, who was originally stigmatized as Asoka the Wicked.

Control of the Mind

Control of the mind is the theme of chapter three. The verses remind us that the quivering, wavering mind is hard to guard against and hard to check. Yet, as the last verse, verse 43, states, "What neither mother, nor father, nor other kinsmen can do, a well-directed mind does." The *Dhammapada* commentary states that a well-directed mind is directed towards the ten kinds of meritorious deeds: (1) generosity, (2) morality, (3) meditation, (4) reverence, (5) service, (6) transference of merit, (7) rejoicing in others' merit, (8) hearing the Doctrine, (9) seeing Buddhas, and (10) straightening one's right views. The well-directed mind is contrasted with the ill-directed mind which turns to ten kinds of evil: (1) killing, (2) stealing, (3) unchastity, (4) lying, (5) slandering, (6) harsh speech, (7) vain talk, (8) covetousness, (9) ill-will, and (10) false belief.

Chapter four, "*Puppha-vagga*" ("Chapter on Flowers") uses the imagery of flowers to illumine the spiritual path. For example, the last verse states that a disciple of the Buddha outshines the wretched, ordinary folk just as a sweet-smelling, lovely lotus could bloom upon a heap of rubbish.

Chapters six and seven contrast the behavior of the childish and immature to that of the wise and sagacious. Verse 64 conjures up an attractive poetic image: "Though the fool associates with a wise man all his life, he no more understands the *dhamma* [righteousness] than a spoon the flavor of soup." Verse 97 is a good example of an Indian riddle. Taken one way it means, "The man who is not credulous, who understands Nibbāna, who has cut off the links, who has destroyed opportunities [of good and evil], who has ejected all desires, he, indeed is the supreme man." But, depending on a series of puns, verse 97 might mean, "The man who is faithless, who is ungrateful, and who has cut off alliances; who has destroyed opportunities, and is an eater of vomit, is the supreme man."

Chapters nine and ten deal with evil conduct and punishment. They highlight the Buddhist theory of *karma*, which states that evil deeds will return to haunt a person not only in this life but also in the next, for evil deeds form an evil character and such

a person must inevitably face increased suffering. Similarly, good deeds bring happiness.

Chapter eleven contains the two verses, 153 and 154, the first paean of Joy (*udāna*) uttered by the Buddha, immediately after his Enlightenment. "Through many a birth I wandered in *samsāra*, searching for, but not finding, the house-builder. Misery is birth again and again" (153). "House-builder, you are seen. The house you shall not build again! All your rafters are broken, your roof-beam destroyed. My mind has achieved the end of cravings and attained the unconditioned" (154).

Chapters twelve and thirteen deal with the self and the world. By conquering the self, one conquers the world. Verse 171 points to the false attractiveness of the world, adorned like a royal chariot, where fools flounder.

Chapter fourteen, "The Buddha," describes the qualities cultivated and perfected by the Buddha, the Awakened One. Verses 183, 184 and 185 were originally recited by Buddhist monks every fortnight, as they indicate the ideal life of a monk.

Chapter fifteen, "Happiness," points out that happiness comes from returning good for evil. The Sakyas, members of the Buddha's own clan, quarrelled with their neighbors, the Koliyas, about the use of the water of the river Rohini. The Buddha dissuaded both clans from fighting, finally uttering verses 197 and 198.

Chapter sixteen, "The Pleasant," sets forth the fundamental Buddhist teaching that the pleasant leads to attachment, attachment results in craving, and craving is the root cause of suffering.

Chapter seventeen, "Wrath," dwells on the dangers of anger. Verse 222 asserts that whoever can hold back arisen wrath, like a swerving chariot, is a real charioteer, while other folk merely hold the reins. Verse 223 advises us to conquer anger by love, evil by good, the miserly one by giving, and the liar by truth.

The Four Noble Truths and the Eightfold Path

Chapter twenty, "The Path," provides a summary of the Buddha's philosophy of life. Verses 277, 278, and 279 state the three pillars of Buddhist metaphysics: (1) all compound things are transitory (*anicca*); (2) all compound things are sorrowful (*dukkha*); and (3) everything that is, is without self (*anattā*). Verse 273 states that the four Sayings are the best of truths and the Eightfold path is the best of paths. The four sayings are Buddha's four Noble Truths, namely: (1) life is unsatisfactory and sorrowful, (2) craving is the cause of sorrow, (3) removal of craving will remove sorrow, (4) the Eightfold Path leads to the destruction of sorrow. The Eightfold Path consists of: right knowledge, right intention, right speech, right action, right livelihood, right effort, right mindfulness, and right concentration.

The opening verse of chapter twenty-one captures the entire theme of the *Dhammapada*: "If by giving up a limited pleasure, one may behold a larger happiness, let a wise man give up the limited for the greater." The last six verses of this chapter are some of the most lyrical in the *Dhammapada*. They give a memorable picture of the "greater happiness" of those who follow the Noble Eightfold Path.

Chapter twenty-four focuses on craving. Buddhism has elaborated an extensive psychology of desire—a great understanding of its nature, its arising, and its conquest. After all, the Buddha attributed all sorrow finally to craving and Nibbāna is equivalent to the cessation of all craving.

Chapters twenty-five and twenty-six describe the Buddha's spiritual elite. They are identified by their conduct, not by externals. The last two verses describe the sage as the fearless, the noble, the hero, the conqueror, the desireless and the enlightened.

NARAYAN CHAMPAWAT

Further Reading

Translations

Carter, John Ross, and Mahinda Palihawadana, trans. *The Dhammapada*. Oxford: Oxford University Press, 1987. Best available translation, with Pali text and "Explanation of Verses" from the *Dhammapada Commentary*.

Rashakrishnan, Sarvepalli, and Charles A. Moore, eds. *A Source Book in Indian Philosophy*. Princeton, NJ: Princeton University Press, 1957. The entire *Dhammapada* is translated here in a clear and fluid way. The text also contains explanatory material.

Thera, Narada, trans. *The Dhammapada*. Boston: Charles E. Tuttle Co. 1993. This work was originally published in London by John Murray in 1954. Accurate translation with copious explanatory footnotes.

Related Study

Burlingame, E.W. *Buddhist Legends*. London: Luzac & Company, 1969. First published in 1921 by Harvard University Press. These legends are drawn from the original Pali text of the *Dhammapada Commentary*.

VEDĀNTA SŪTRAS

Title in Sanskrit: *Vedāntasūtras* or *Brahmasūtras* or *Shārīraka-mīmāmsā-sūtras*
Author: Bādārayana
Birth and Death Dates: Unknown. Possibly second century B.C.
Literary Form: Sutras (aphorisms)
Date of Composition: Probably c. 200 B.C.

Major Themes

Brahman (the ultimate principle, absolute reality) is real.
Brahman is both the material and the efficient cause of the world.
Moksha (release) is the highest goal of life.
One must follow an ethical discipline to achieve moksha.

Vedanta is the most important and the most well known school of Indian philosophy. The *Vedanta Sutras* are the texts on which various schools of Vedanta are based. The term *Vedanta* literally means "the end of the Vedas," and is derived from the conjunction of the terms *"Veda"* and *"anta."* The term "Veda," as a derivative of the root *"vid"* meaning knowledge, refers to the achievement of knowledge. The term *"anta"* (end) has two meanings: the final place reached as a result of effort, and the goal (objective) towards which all effort is to be oriented, namely, an understanding of the Upanishads. In other words, the term *Vedanta* refers to the doctrines set forth in the Upanishads, and the Upanishads are generally taken to signify the esoteric teachings imparted orally by the *guru* (spiritual teacher) to his disciples—referred to by the term *Upanishads* (*upa*, "near"; *ni*, "down"; *shad*, "to sit"). In this oral erudition, the guru and the pupils engaged in discussions and debates that added to the body of learning and eventually became an essential part of the textual tradition.

On the other hand, such an oral tradition by its nature is very vulnerable to distortion. One could never be sure of the fidelity of the pupils to the teachings of the guru. A pupil might bend the tradition by emphasizing those parts which suited his subjective framework, while either forgetting or deleting those parts with which he did not agree. Moreover, if no systematic records were kept, the likelihood of the original teachings getting lost be-comes great. On the other hand, this vunerability to change might be viewed as a strength for a living tradition, insofar as it would be much easier to modify the tradition to meet the needs of the people as the culture changed.

The Origin and Character of the Vedanta Sutras

The principal Upanishads, the subject matter of the *Vedanta Sutras*, were primarily composed between 600 and 300 B.C. They were composed by different individuals, living at different times and in different parts of North India. Additionally, the individuals who put the Upanishads into their final written form introduced their own teachings into the Upanishads. Thus, the Upanishads are not systematic philosophical treatises by any means. They are not a coherent system and do not contain a systematic and logical development of ideas. Indeed, the Upanishadic teachings are full of inherent ambiguities, inconsistencies, and contradictions. Therefore, it became imperative that the different texts be systematized and, more particularly, harmonized. Several attempts to systematize the teachings of the Upanishads were made; one such attempt was made by Badarayana in his *Vedanta Sutras*.

The *Vedānta Sūtras* authored by Badarayana are variously known as the *Brahma Sūtras*, the *Shārīraka-mīmāmsā Sūtras*, and the *Uttara-mīmāmsā*. They are called the *Brahma Sūtras* because they deal with Brahman as the ultimate reality; the *Shārīraka Sūtras*, because they discuss the embodiment of that which is unconditioned; and the *Uttara-mīmāmsā*, since it is a *mīmāmsā* or investigation of the later part of the Vedas, as distinguished from the earlier portions of the Vedas that concern themselves with rituals.

It is difficult to date the *Vedanta Sutras*. However, since these sutras contain a refutation of all the orthodox and nonorthodox schools of Indian philosophy, which are dated from 500 B.C. to 200 B.C., these sutras could not have been composed earlier than 200 B.C.

The collection entitled *Vedanta Sutras* contains 555 sutras. They are divided into four chapters and each chapter is divided in four sections. Each section is subdivided on the basis of topics, which may cover one or a group of sutras. The first chapter on "harmony" teaches that the Upanishadic texts deal with Brahman as the central reality. In this chapter, one finds a detailed account of the nature of Brahman, its relation to the world and to the individual soul. In the second, the objections that may be raised against Vedanta metaphysics are discussed. The principal objector is a representative of the Sankhya, one of the six orthodox schools of Indian philosophy. The third chapter discusses the ways and means of attaining the highest knowledge *(brahma-vidyā)*. The fourth chapter deals with the result of attaining the highest knowledge. It discusses in detail the theory of the departure of the soul after death, as well as the character of the released souls.

The elliptical character of these sutras has given rise to various interpretations within the fold of Vedanta. The term *sutra* literally means "thread," and is related to the verb "to sew." It refers to a short aphoristic sentence, and, collectively, to a text consisting of such statements. Sutras generally do not consist of more than two or three words each; they are characterized by brevity and terseness. For example, the first four sutras of the *Vedanta Sutras* state: (1) *athātobrahma-jijñāsā*, "Then, therefore, the desire to know Brahman"; (2) *janmādy asya yatah*, "from which [proceeds] the origin [subsistence and destruction] of this

[universe]"; (3) *shastrayonitvāt*, "because its [knowledge's] source is scripture"; and (4) *tat tu samanvayāt*, "[that Brahman is the cause of the Universe] follows from the total harmony [of the scriptural passages]."

Since these sutras are packed with meaning, and were not comprehensible without a commentary, commentaries, and commentaries on commentaries were written to unpack their meanings. The laconic contents of these sutras gave rise to various divergent interpretations within the Vedanta school, of which three are generally considered to be most important: Shankara's Advaita, Rāmānuja's Vishistadvaita, and Madhva's Dvaita. There are other well-known commentators— Bhaskara, Vallabha, and Nimbārka, to name just three. The interpretations fall under two basic groups: non-dualistic, and theistic. The following discussion of the content of the sutras will reflect these main strands of interpretation.

The Nature of Brahman

No matter how one interprets the *Vedanta Sutras*, there is no doubt that all the interpreters agree that according to these sutras, Brahman is the supreme reality. The most important question discussed has to do with the nature of Brahman. What kind of reality corresponds to Brahman? The nature of Brahman becomes the most important consideration since the answer to this question determines, or at least, conditions the answer they give to other metaphysical and epistemological questions. Although all schools of Vedanta regard Brahman as the highest reality, they answer differently the question regarding the nature of Brahman.

As indicated above, these answers and the solutions might be divided in two basic groups. The first answer articulates Brahman as *nirguna*; the term stands for *undifferentiated* being, being *without* qualities or distinctions: Brahma is *non personal* being. The second answer articulates Brahman as *saguna*; this opposing term stands for *differentiated* being, being *with* qualities and distinctions: Brahma is a *personal* being.

The first answer is essentially non-dualistic *(ad-*

vaita); the second is dualistic *(dvaita)* or "theistic." Although Vedantic philosophers combine these answers in different ways, these still remain the two basic alternatives given.

Other important questions are also discussed: Who created the world? What is the relation between Brahman and the world? What is the nature of the soul? What is the status of the self in relation to Brahman?

Brahman: The One Reality

Regarding the creation of the world, the *Vedanta Sutras* do not give us any clear leads. The very first chapter of the text makes the following terse claims: Brahman is the cause of the origin of the world (1.1.2); Brahman as consciousness is different from the non-conscious Prakriti of Sankhya (1.1.5–11); Brahman is the golden person in the Sun, the cosmic space, and the cosmic light (1.1.20–23). A little later, it is said that Brahman is not only the efficient but also the material cause of the world (1.4.23–37). Finally, it states that Brahman and the world are *ananya*, that is, they are not different as a clay pitcher is not different from the clay (2.1.14, 1.1.4, 1.4.22).

For Shankara, these texts teach non-difference *(advaita)*. Brahman is the only reality; it is the one reality without a second. Brahman does not possess any determinations. No attributes can be ascribed to it; it is *nirguna*. It is a state of being where all subject/object distinctions are obliterated. Brahman is both the material and the efficient cause of the world. However, only the cause is real; the effect is only an appearance of the cause. The world belongs to a level of being that is different from Brahman; the world is only an appearance of Brahman. The world is real only empirically; it is not ultimately real. The world exists only for those who are ignorant in a way very similar to those who mistake a rope coiled in the corner of a dark room for a snake. The world's appearance is due to *avidya* (ignorance). *Avidya* not only conceals the real nature of Brahman; it makes Brahman appear *as* the world.

Ramanuja denies the non-dualism of Shankara.

For Ramanuja, the sutras quoted above teach both difference and non-difference. The world and souls are different as well as non-different from Brahman. Brahman is perfect, whereas the world and the souls are imperfect, and therein lies the difference between them. The world and the souls are also non-different from Brahman, because they are the body and the attributes of Brahman. In his scheme, Brahman is the supreme reality; the world and the souls are organically related to Brahman. Ramanuja in his commentary emphasizes the creative aspect and makes *saguna* Brahman the highest reality. The knowledge of Brahman is to be gained from the characterizations given in the second aphorism, which articulates Brahman as the cause of the origin of the world, omniscient, all-powerful, and so forth. Brahman has wonderful powers; he uses these powers to create the world. He possesses, as in Christian teachings, conscious will, but unlike the deity of Christian teachings, He creates the world out of Himself.

Brahman and Individual Souls

Regarding the nature of the soul, the *Vedanta Sutras* simply state that the soul is *jna*. Shankara interprets *jna* as intelligence. Brahman is intelligence and appears as individuals owing to its contact with the limiting adjuncts, the bodies.

Ramanuja, on the other hand, interprets *jna* as an intelligent knower. Regarding the question of the relation of the individual soul to Brahman, the *Vedanta Sutras* do not provide any clear answer. The questions remain: Is the individual soul a *part* *(amsa)* of Brahman? Or, is it a reflection of Brahman? The *Vedanta Sutras* mention several views without supporting any.

Brahman, for Shankara, is not composed of parts. Therefore, he contends it is ridiculous to suppose Brahman has parts in the literal sense. Accordingly, the text that the individual soul is a part of Brahman is construed by Shankara to mean that the soul can only be an imagined part, "a part as it were" (2.3.43). For Ramanuja, on the other hand, the individual soul is a real part of Brahman, just as the spark is part of fire, and is not merely an appearance as Shankara suggests. In fact, for Ramanuja, both individual souls and matter are real parts of Brahman.

Ethical Discipline and the Release of Souls

The issues of the ethical discipline that leads to release *(moksha)* and the character of the released selves are discussed in the third and fourth chapters of the *Vedanta Sutras*. While these chapters discuss the general rules laid down in the Upanishads for the acquisition of the highest knowledge, they do not recommend a specific discipline to attain release. In 3.4.26, release is said to be the result of knowledge, not actions. Actions are said to be useful only as a means to knowledge. However, in 3.2.38–41, release is said to be the result of actions. A devotee who meditates receives the rewards of his/her meditation, namely, release.

Regarding the character of the released souls, the *Vedanta Sutras* do not give us any definitive statement. 4.4.5 simply states that the released soul possesses the nature of Brahman. Ramanuja takes this to mean that the released soul possesses the qualities mentioned in the Upanishads, namely, all-knowing, all-powerful, and so forth. On Ramanuja's interpretation, the empirical world is not non-real, and he thus emphasizes devotion as a means to *moksha*. God bestows salvation on his creatures. Brahman is supreme; he is Vishnu, and *moksha* is union with him. Shankara, however, does not agree with this interpretation. For him, 4.4.5 states that the released soul is Brahman because *moksha* is the realization of the individual's identity with Brahman, which was forgotten during the embodied existence. Attainment of *moksha* is not anything new; it is the realization of that which always was there. Wisdom is necessary to attain release. Prayer and worship do not take one to the final goal of *moksha*.

The sutras of the *Vedanta Sutras* reflect the ambiguity that characterizes the Upanishads. Thus, it should come as no surprise to anybody that these sutras have given rise to several conflicting interpretations. Any attempt to arrive at a definitive and precise characterization of the teachings of the *Vedanta Sutras* will only distort the real intent of these sutras.

BINA GUPTA

Further Reading

Translations and Studies

Gambhirananda, Swami. *Brahma-Sūtra Bhāṣya of Śaṇkarācārya.* Calcutta: Advaita Ashrama, 1983. This book gives a very useful and reliable translation of the *Vedanta Sutras* from an Advaita point of view.

Radhakrishnan, Sarvepalli. *The Brahma Sutra: The Philosophy of Spiritual Life.* New York: Greenwood Press, 1968. This volume contains a very useful introduction and a readable translation of the sutras from several different Vedantic perspectives.

Thibaut, George, trans. *The Vedanta-sutras with the Commentary of Śaṇkarācarya.* Vols. XXXIV and XXXVIII of *The Sacred Books of the East*, edited by Max Muller. Oxford: Clarendon Press, 1890 and 1896. These volumes contain useful introductions and readable translations of the sutras from Advaita and Vishistadvaita perspectives.

PANCHATANTRA

Title in Sanskrit: *Panchatantra (The Five Books)*
Author: Unknown, sometimes attributed to the narrators: Vishnusharman or Vasughaga, depending on the version
Literary Form: Collection of animal fables
Date of Composition: Unknown, likely c. 200 BC.

Major Themes

Hostility among comrades is caused by deceitful intriguers.
Collaboration among friends provides security.
Cunning reverses losses.
Accomplishments are not achieved by dreaming.
Hasty action leads to regret.

The *Panchatantra* is a Sanskrit collection of animal fables and anecdotal tales, whose original has been lost. Research on later recensions, versions, abridgments, and translations has led to a reconstruction of the original work, but no extant text can be claimed to be the exact replica of the original that engendered the different variants of the work.

The title, *Panchatantra*, is made up of two words: *pancha*—sometimes written as *panca*—which means "five," and *tantra*, which means "book," "chapter," "lesson," or "religious teaching."

The genesis of the *Panchatantra* is conjectural. It was probably collected from oral narratives and fables that were circulating in India before the Christian era and were rendered in a literary form some time between the fourth century B.C. to the fourth century A.D., in central India. The prologue of the famous Arabic translation of the *Panchatantra* dates it to the era of Alexander the Great (356–323 B.C.). From there the *Panchatantra* travelled to north and south India, and later on to Europe and Southeast Asia respectively.

Such migrations of the text caused alterations of slight or extensive dimensions. The north Indian branch is often known as the "Vishnusharman Panchatantra" or simply the *Panchatantra*; the south Indian branch as the "Vasughaga Panchatantra" (after the narrator mentioned in the opening section of each branch and sometimes presumed to be the author). The southern branch traveled through Sanskrit and through translations to Kannada, Tamil, and other languages of South India, and from there to Java, Laos, and Thailand where indigenized forms of the collection are found. The northern version was translated into Pahlavi (middle Persian) in the reign of King Khosru Anoshirvan (A.D. 531–579), by the court physician Burzoe. This translation has not been preserved, but a Syriac (ancient Semitic language) translation by a certain Bud based on it survives, and it has been translated into German by modern scholars.

The more celebrated translation of the *Panchatantra* from Pahlavi is the Arabic rendering by Ibn al-Muqaffa' (A.D. 750), entitled *Kalila wa-Dimna*, after the names of the two minister jackals of the first book. This translation became very popular in the medieval Arab world and its prose style became a model for the literati of the time. It is this version that was disseminated in medieval Europe and the Islamic world and came to be known as the *Fables of Bidpai*, after the transformed rendering of the name of the narrator, presented as a philosopher, in the Arabic version. This Arabic work was then translated into Greek in the eleventh century by Symeon Seth, and from Greek it was translated into different Slavonic languages in the following century. The Arabic was also translated into Hebrew (presumably by Rabbi Joel) and in the reign of

Alfonso the tenth, the Arabic was translated into Castilian (Old Spanish), c. A.D. 1251, and from that translation into Latin by Raymond de Béziers in the early fourteenth century. It is said that the rich picaresque Spanish novel has been influenced by the episodic structure of the *Panchatantra*. From the Hebrew translation, John of Capua made a Latin translation in the thirteenth century. On that Latin translation were based further translations into the different vernaculars of Europe, including an Italian translation by Doni, which was the basis for the first English translation by Sir Thomas North entitled *The Morall Philosophie of Doni* (1570).

The different texts of the *Panchatantra* vary in their inclusion or exclusion of certain stories, by their use of different titles, and by stylistic variations. The *Panchatantra* has been called by the Indian novelist and anthropologist Amitav Ghosh "the Mother of Folklore." It is said to be the most translated work in the world after the Bible. It has engendered parallel fables and translations in countries that extend from Korea to Central Africa, from Iceland to Ethiopia. Its widespread influence can be glimpsed, but not always documented, as in Aesop's fables of ancient Greece, Welsh medieval ballads, and the French fables of Jean de la Fontaine (1621–1695).

The *Panchatantra* has contributed immensely to studies in comparative folklore and comparative literature. Illustrations in manusripts of translations of the popular fables of the *Panchatantra* constitute an important contribution to Islamic visual arts. The Arabic translation has also inspired a symphonic suite by the contemporary Egyptian composer Adel A. Afify.

The Structure of the Panchatantra

The structural features of the *Panchatantra* can be summarized as a loosely episodic narrative with a prologue leading to five frame stories, each of which includes in its turn a number of stories. What triggers this narrative's unfolding is the king's desire to educate his three sons. The teacher is a wise instructor who prefers to convey knowledge of practical wisdom *(artha)* and polity *(niti)* through fables and tales rather than through the regular curriculum. Such knowledge covers one field of the three-fold human quests in Hindu thought; the other two are religion and morality *(dharma)* and love *(kama)*.

The Brahman instructor opts for the allegorical mode and places his practical philosophy in indirect discourse and fictionalized events, narrated mostly, but not entirely, through animal characters. These stories demonstrate modes of action or principles of conduct. Within each story, examples and comparisons are given in the form of yet other stories, using the structure of emboxing or embedding, which is also typical of the *Arabian Nights*.

The complex enclosing of stories-within-stories sometimes distracts the reader from the point of the frame story, and at others, reinforces and elaborates the thrust of the enclosing story. The protagonists tend to be stock characters: the crafty jackel, the powerful lion, the loyal mongoose, and the curious monkey. The tales are often interspersed with poetry to reinforce a point or to include a moral or to introduce a principle of behavior. The language of the stories is fairly simple and uses maxims and aphorisms, thus reflecting its oral origin. The thematic concerns of each book are displayed in its title. The first three books are elaborate and extensive, while the last two are short.

The Loss of Friends

The first book opens with a friendship between the lion and the bull that is spoiled by the jealous intrigue of Karataka, the minister jackal, who insinuates the bad faith of the bull into the lion and vice versa, as a result of which the lion kills his friend the bull. Afterwards, torn by remorse and grief, the king of the beasts is consoled by his other minister jackal, Damanaka, who convinces him of a dictum that lacks morality but implies Machiavellian political realism: the king has to kill whoever threatens him, even if it is a relative or a friend; rulers should shun tenderness, for common morality does not apply to kings.

Within this story other fables are embedded that

demonstrate that one should not concern oneself with what is not one's business ("The Ape and the Wedge"), that appearances are deceptive ("The Jackal and the Drum"), that afflictions at times are self-caused ("The Monk and The Swindler," "Rams and Jackal," and "The Cuckold Weaver and The Bawd"), that guile can do what violence cannot do ("The Crows and the Serpent"), that greed causes death ("The Heron and The Crab") and that wit is power ("The Lion and The Hare").

This fable "The Lion and the Hare" narrates how the hare, who is offered as a meal to the lion, manages through his cunning and wit to escape his doom. He arrives late and explains his delay by contriving a story about another fierce lion he met on the way. Intrigued by a possible rival, the lion follows the hare to a well. Seeing his reflection in the water and taking it for another lion, he jumps into the well to fight with it and is drowned.

The Winning of Friends

In the second book of the *Panchatantra* a number of stories display how communal solidarity and group collaboration can overcome traps and predicaments. The birds caught in a hunter's net co-ordinate to fly in one direction and thus move up and away with the net. The birds' friend, the mouse, chews away at the thongs and liberates them.

Within this frame story, there are others that display related points. The story of the captivity of the deer and his being turned into a pet, and of his longings to join the herd, points to the natural yearning to be with one's own kind and the folly of going against nature. The frustration of this desire leads to the strange illness of the deer's owner, which is cured only upon the release of the deer.

Other embedded stories condemn the hypocrisy of monks and the greed of jackals.

War and Peace

The third book deals with the war between the crows and the owls, which ends with the spectacular victory of the owls. One of the crows asks his fellows to pluck his feathers in order to pretend that he has been deserted by his fellow crows and to gain access to the dwellings of the owls. Thus, he succeeds in spying on his enemies and eventually sets fire to them. The point of the elaborate story is to signify that to welcome a foe among your ranks is like standing on "the blade of a sword" [Edgerton].

There are other tales interspersed within this tale which reflect an implied point of the frame story, namely the necesssity of submission before ultimate victory.

The Loss of Gains

Book four is about two-sided losses: those of an ape as well as those of a crocodile, and the end of their friendship because of the wiles of women. The exiled ape befriends a crocodile, but the crocodile's wife, unhappy with this friendship that keeps her husband away, claims that the doctor has recommended that she eat an ape's heart for her illness. The crocodile is torn but eventually decides a wife is more important than a friend, and invites the ape to his home. On the way, the crocodile divulges the nature of his wife's illness, and the threatened ape tries to save himself by counter-cunning. He informs the crocodile that he had left his heart behind on a tree. So they go back to pick up the heart, but once the ape returns to shore, he escapes, and refuses to be tricked again by the promises of the crocodile.

Hasty Action

The last book of the *Panchatantra* has two stories that have migrated wide and far: One is about the Brahman who dreams of wealth and calculates how he will sell the goodies in his jar and buy goats, then cows, then marry and have a child, and on and on, until he gets in his daydreaming to the point of disciplining his wife; waving his cudgel, he hits the jar and his dream collapses.

The other story is that of a Brahman who left his child alone protected by the mongoose. In the meantime, a cobra approaches and the mongoose tears it apart. When the Brahman returns and sees the bloodstained mongoose, he assumes it has devoured the child, and he instantly kills it, only to discover the truth when it is too late.

FERIAL J. GHAZOUL

Further Reading

Translations

Edgerton, Franklin, trans. *The Panchatantra*. London: George Allen and Unwin, 1965. This is a reprint with minor revisions of Edgerton's translation from Sanskrit of his own reconstructed version of the work. It has an introduction, aimed at the general reader, which situates the *Panchatantra* in world literature. Footnotes in the translation explain the wordplay of the original and relevant Hindu concepts. Words are provided in parentheses in the text by the translator to clarify meaning, but this intrusion into the body of the narrative text diminishes the pleasure of reading.

Ryder, Arthur W., trans. *The Panchatantra*. Chicago: The University of Chicago Press, 1925. A smooth-reading translation from Sanskrit of a twelfth-century text of the *Panchatantra* that was edited by J. Hertel. The translator's introduction comments on the themes of the work.

Related Studies

Huilgol, Varadraj. *The Pañcatantra of Vasughaga: A Critical Study*. Madras: New Era Publications, 1987. This thorough study compares the northern branch and the southern branch of the *Panchatantra*, pointing out elements of overlap and of divergence, with an attempt at a reconstruction of the southern variant. Differences are outlined and expansion of the southern version in Southeast Asia is documented.

Barthakuria, Apurba Chandra. *India in the Age of the Pañcatantra*. Calcutta: Punthi-Pustak, 1992. This study deals with the social, economic, political, religious, academic and anthopological aspects of ancient India that produced the *Panchatantra*, in an attempt to contextualize the tales and see them against their background.

DEEDS OF THE BUDDHA

Title in Sanskrit: *Buddha-carita*
Author: Ashvaghosha
Born: First century A.D.
Died: Second century A.D.
Literary Form: Poetic biography
Date of Composition: Late first to mid-second centuries A.D.

Major Themes

All things are impermanent, and selfhood and the soul are illusory.
Suffering is rooted in desire, and peace is attained by extinguishing desire.
Meditation, self-control, and the suppression of passions and attachments, rather than ascetic mortification of the body, are the true path to enlightenment and nirvana.

Ashvaghosha, the author of the "Deeds of the Buddha," is renowned both as a master poet and as the author of some of the most influential Buddhist texts in Sanskrit. While later Buddhist tradition attributes dozens of texts to him, modern scholars recognize as the authentic surviving works of Ashvaghosha, besides the "Deeds," only his other epic poem "Handsome Nanda" (*Saundarananda*), and the drama "Shāriputra" (*Shāriputra-prakarana*).

As is often the case with the authors of Sanskrit texts, very little reliable information is available about Ashvaghosha, apart from later pious legends of dubious historical authenticity. From the colophons of his own compositions, we know that he was a native of Sāketa in northeastern India, whose mother was Ārya-suvarnkshī. He was almost certainly a Brahman by birth and was at some time in his life converted to Buddhism; this explains the intimate acquaintance with Brahmanical (or "Hindu") lore and tradition demonstrated in his works, his choice of literary genres associated with Brahmanical culture for the purpose of propagating his new faith, and his mastery of the Sanskrit language.

Later Buddhist traditions consistently associate Ashvaghosa with the court of the great emperor Kanishka of the Kushāna dynasty of Northern India, and it is probably true that they were contemporaries. Unfortunately, Kanishka's dates are uncertain, but he probably reigned at some time in the later first century or the first half of the second century A.D.; this estimate provides the only firm ground for Ashvaghosha's dates. The question of Ashvaghosha's exact sectarian affiliation within the contemporary Buddhist tradition has been extensively debated by modern scholars, but without definitive conclusion. Judging from the tone and content of his works, it would appear that he was an adherent of the basic doctrines of Buddhism in general, without any strong interest in promoting a particular sectarian viewpoint.

Importance and Influence

The "Deeds of the Buddha" is widely held to be Ashvaghosha's master work, both in terms of its literary qualities and of its veneration by, and influence on, Buddhist tradition. Of the several biographies of the Buddha in Sanskrit and other Indian languages, Ashvaghosha's rendition held a special place as the most polished and appealing to the general public, and was widely popular in ancient times, as attested by the words of the famous Chinese Buddhist pilgrim Hsuan Tsang who reported that it "is widely read or sung throughout the five divisions of India and the countries of the Southern Sea [i.e. Southeast Asia]. He [Ashvaghosa] clothes manifold meaning and ideas in a few words, which rejoice the heart of the reader, so that he never feels tired from reading the poem. . . . It contains the noble doctrine given in a concise form." This popularity is also reflected by the fact that it was translated into Tibetan and Chinese, which is especially important since these are the only complete versions of the "Deeds" which have survived into modern times. For with the decline of Buddhism in its Indian homeland in the medieval period, the original Sanskrit text was neglected to the point that only a few incomplete manuscripts survived which contain slightly less than the first half of the entire poem. The contents of the second half of the poem are thus known only from the Tibetan and Chinese translations.

The literary genre of the "Deeds" was the Sanskrit ornate epic (*mahā-kāvya*, literally "great poem"), of which it is the oldest surviving specimen. It originally contained 28 cantos (*sarga*) ranging in length from 41 to 121 verses. Of these, only cantos 2 through 13 survive completely in the original Sanskrit; the first 7 verses of canto 1 and the last 77 verses of canto 14 are lost, as are all of cantos 15–28 except for a few fragments of canto 16 preserved in an old manuscript from Central Asia.

The Life of Buddha

The biography of Buddha as recounted in *Deeds of the Buddha* can be summarized as follows: After a miraculous birth accompanied by prophecies of future greatness (canto 1) and an idyllic childhood in the city of Kapilavāstu (2), the young Prince Sarvārthasiddha (elsewhere known as Siddhārtha), the future Buddha, ventures out of the palace for the first time and begins to question the value of things of this world when he sees an old man, a sick man, and a dead man, who were actually set in his path by the gods in order to fulfil his destiny of bringing enlightenment to the world (3). He rejects the beautiful women whom his father Shuddhodana, King of the Shākyas, assigned to seduce him in the hope of keeping him at home (4). In his dissatisfaction, the Prince wanders outside the palace again, where he sees a mendicant ascetic and requests his father's permission to become an ascetic himself. The king again tries to have him seduced by the women of his harem, but the prince resists again and flees the palace by night (5). Taking leave of his faithful groom Chandaka and his horse Kanthaka (6), Sarvārthasiddha visits a Brahman hermitage but finds the ascetic practices there to be superficial and unsatisfactory (7). Meanwhile, in Kapilavāstu the King and the Prince's wife Yashodharā, along with the people of the city, bitterly lament the Prince's departure (8); the King sends his priest and minister to persuade him to return, but they are rejected (9). The future Buddha then goes to the great city of Rājagriha, where Shrenya, the King of Magadha, similarly attempts to persuade him to return home (10); but his entreaties are rejected by the Prince (11). The prince then visits Arāda Kālāma and other sages, but refutes their doctrines of the liberation of the soul and goes off to practice ascetic meditation for six years (12). Remaining steadfast when Māra, the god of love and passion, attempts to distract him with threats and temptations (13), he finally attains true enlightenment (14).

In the latter half of the *Deeds* preserved in the Tibetan and Chinese translations, the Buddha proceeds to the holy city of Kāshī (Benares) to preach his first sermon in the Deer Park (15), and begins winning over many converts including the King of Magadha (16). After continuing to win over converts with his sermons (17) and establishing a monastery at Shrāvastī (18), the Buddha returns to visit his father, who receives him with great joy (19). Returning to Shrāvastī, he converts Prasenajit, King of Kosala (20). While wandering around India gaining ever more adherents, he calms the mad elephant which his jealous cousin Devadatta sent to kill him (21). In Vaishālī he converts the courtesan Amrapālī (22) and preaches to the Licchavis (23). After announcing to them his intention to leave his body (24), he goes on his final journey to Kushinagara (25) where he speaks his last words to his followers and passes on to nirvana (26). As gods and humans mourn him and sing his praises, the Mallas cremate his body (27). His relics are divided and distributed among the Mallas and the neighboring kings, and his followers assemble to collect his sermons and establish the canon (28).

Style and Literary Qualities

Unlike most early Buddhist literature, the *Deeds of the Buddha* is written in an early form of the classical style of Sanskrit poetry, characterized by the use of elaborate similes and metaphors, complex syntactic structures, vivid visual imagery, and learned allusions. The author saw fit to justify his choice of this unusual literary medium for Buddhist propaganda in his concluding verse (28.74):

This poem has been composed for the good and happiness of all people in accordance with the Sage's Scriptures, out of reverence for the Great Sage, and not to display the qualities of learning or skill in poetry.

(ADAPTED FROM JOHNSTONE, 1937)

Here, Ashvaghosha wishes to make it clear that he composed his poem only in order to benefit his readers by presenting to them in an attractive form the salvific message of Buddhism. As he put the point more concretely in the conclusion to his other poem ("Handsome Nanda," 18.63), he used the medium of ornate poetry "as one might mix honey with a bitter pill so that it may have the desired effect." The specific choice of the formal classical style, and indeed of the Sanskrit language itself, no doubt reflects the poet's desire to present Buddhism to members of his own original social stratum, namely the Brahman elite, in terms that would appeal to and be comprehensible by them.

Regardless of his original intention, in the "Deeds" and his other surviving works Ashvaghosha did create major monuments of the classical poetic tradition, and moreover significantly affected its development. In fact, his poems and dramatic compositions are the oldest specimens of classical Sanskrit literature that have come down to us, although they seem to presuppose an earlier body of Brahmanical literature which Ashvaghosha remodeled to his own ends. Although they lost their popularity with the decline in Buddhism in later centuries, his works were known and even imitated by the authors of the high classical

period of Sanskrit literature (fourth to sixth centuries A.D.), including the great Kālidāsa whose compositions frequently echo Ashvaghosha's imagery and phrasing. Ashvaghosha's two poems, and especially the *Deeds*, in effect set the standard for the later, non-Buddhistic development of the ornate Sanskrit epic.

From the point of view of purely poetic appreciation, some of the finest parts of the *Deeds* are those which portray worldly scenes, as in this description of the ladies of the town clamoring for a glance of the young Prince as he comes out of the palace for the first time (3.19–20):

The faces of the ladies as they peered from the windows, their earrings jangling together, looked like lotuses pinned to the balcony. And with those balconies bursting with the women as they gleefully tossed open the shutters, the whole city looked like flying chariots packed with the nymphs of heaven.

Here, Ashvaghosha merely develops one of the conventional scenes of early Sanskrit poetry, but later in the poem he turns such stock descriptions around to his own ends. In the following extract, he illustrates the Buddhist doctrine of the impermanence and superficiality of all worldly pleasures in describing a woman of the harem who was magically put to sleep by the gods when she tried to seduce the Prince (5.61):

She lay there as if in a drunken stupor, mouth gaping open and drooling saliva, body splayed open shamelessly; now her misshapen body had lost all power to charm.

(JOHNSTONE, 1972)

Similarly, in his description of the attack by Māra's army of demons on the meditating Buddha, Ashvaghosha employs the vivid descriptive force of Sanskrit poetic style to contrast the chaos of the passions with the peace of enlightenment (13.41–43):

One monster rose up in the sky like the blazing sun, and cast down on him a mighty rain of blazing coals. . . . But as it burst in a shower of sparks on the seat of enlightenment, it was turned into a shower of pink lotus petals by the power of The Sage's love. And even as all manner of distractions bodily and mental were hurled at him, The Wise One wavered not from his meditation; for he embraced his own determination like a dear friend.

Although it is these vivid word-pictures that tend to capture the attention of the reader, the author's real message is imbedded in the various sermons spoken by the Buddha throughout the poem, summarizing in poetic language the fundamental concepts and metaphysical foundations of Buddhist belief; for example, this passage from the dialogue with the King of Magadha, in which the Buddha-to-be explains the urgency of turning one's attention to spiritual matters (11.62–63):

When the wicked hunter, Death, is ever lurking near to hand, striking down his prey, the mortals, as they wander through the forest of fate, with his bow, old age, and his arrows, disease, how can you cling to the illusion of longevity? Therefore whether you are young and old, or even a child, if you know what is right you must hasten to make up your mind whether to continue to strive in worldly activity, or to turn away from it.

It is this unique combination of poetic skill and rhetorical power that enabled Ashvaghosa's *Deeds of the Buddha* to stand as both a monument of world literature and a work of inspiration revered by Buddhists throughout Asia.

RICHARD SALOMON

Further Reading

Translations

Note: Passages from Deeds of the Buddha *quoted in this article and not otherwise attributed are translations by Richard Salomon.*

Beal, Samuel, trans. *The Fo-sho-hing-tsan-king: A Life of the Buddha by Asvaghosha Bodhisattva.* Oxford: Clarendon Press, 1883. (*Sacred Books of the East*, 19.) English translation of the Chinese version of the *Deeds of the Buddha*, which was translated from the Sanskrit by Dharmaraksha in A.D. 420.

Cowell, Edward B., trans. *The Buddha-Karita or Life of Buddha by Asvaghosa.* Oxford: Clarendon, 1894. Based on an early and inaccurate edition of the text, this translation was superseded by that of Johnstone.

Johnstone, E.H., ed. and trans. *The Buddhacarita: Or, Acts of the Buddha.* 2 vols. Calcutta: Baptist Mission Press, 1935–36. Reprinted in 1 vol., Delhi: Motilal Banarsidass, 1972. The standard scholarly edition and translation. It is a masterpiece of textual scholarship, but it does strive more for scholarly accuracy than literary grace. It is therefore entirely faithful to the original but does not do it full justice as a work of literature.

———, trans. "The Buddha's Mission and last Journey: *Buddhacarita*, xv to xxviii." *Acta Orientalia* 15, 1937, pp.26–62, 85–111, and 231–292. Translation of the portion of the "Deeds of the Buddha" lost in the original Sanskrit, on the basis of the Tibetan and Chinese renditions. An indispensable supplement to the previous item.

Miller, Barbara S., trans. [Forthcoming translation of the *Deeds of the Buddha*]. This recently deceased master translator's version, to be published posthumously, will undoubtedly become the standard version.

PURĀNAS

Author: Vyāsa (legendary author). Revised by many unknown writers.
Birth and Death Dates: Unknown
Literary Form: Poetry, with some prose sections
Date of Composition: First century A.D.

Major Themes

The best path to moksha *(salvation), the highest goal for human beings, is* bhakti *(devotion) to a chosen deity (usually Vishnu or Shiva, but occasionally the Great Goddess, Devi).*

The Universe is created, sustained, and destroyed by Brahman in the form of the Great God (Vishnu or Shiva).

Stories of Avatārs (incarnations of God), sages, kings, and great devotees inspire and instruct us so that we may live good lives and attain moksha.

The *Purānas* form a class of books written in Sanskrit, expounding ancient Indian theogony, cosmogony, genealogies, accounts of kings and *rishis* (sages); religious beliefs, forms of worship, observances, philosophy; personal, social and political ordinances and other miscellaneous things. The whole is enforced by tales, legends, old songs, anecdotes, fables, and myths. The Purānas are written mainly in verse, generally in the common *shloka*, but there are certain prose passages.

There are eighteen major works entitled *Purānas* (or more accurately *Mahapurānas*). The names of these works are: (1) *Vāyu* or *Shiva Purāna*, (2) *Brahmānda Purāna*, (3) *Mārkandeya Purāna*, (4) *Vishnu Purāna*, (5) *Matsya Purāna*, (6) *Bhāgvata Purāna*, (7) *Kūrma Purāna*, (8) *Vāmana Purāna*, (9) *Linga Purāna*, (10) *Varāha Purāna*, (11) *Padma Purāna*, (12) *Nāradīya Purāna*, (13) *Angi Purāna*, (14) *Garuda Purāna*, (15) *Brahma Purāna*, (16) *Skanda Purāna*, (17) *Brahmavaivarta Purāna*, and (18) *Bhavishya* or *Bhavishyat Purāna*.

There exist, also, minor *Purānas*, called *Upapurānas*, sometimes numbered as eighteen; but in fact there are more than a hundred *Upapurānas*.

The *Purānas* claim for themselves a divine origin. According to the Purānas, the god, Brahmā, originally uttered the *Purānas*. In their original form they number a hundred million. In our age,

Vyāsa, the author of the *Mahābhārata* and the editor of the Vedas, organized the *Purānas* into eighteen texts by abridging them. The *Purānas* should be looked upon as works-in-progress, whose original form might be placed as far back as the eighth or ninth century B.C. The earlier *Purānas* were composed, in their present form, during the first centuries of the common era. The *Bhāgvat Purāna*, written in the sixth century A.D., is the best and most popular literary production among the *Purānas* due to its language, style, and meter.

The *Purānas* were the most important instruments in the founding and growth of the Hindu civilization. The Vedic civilization, which was the precursor to the Hindu, was based on the teachings of the Vedas. Vedic religion was ritualistic and mainly confined to the upper classes. The original *Purānas* were encyclopedias, embodying the total knowledge of the Vedic people. They dealt with stories and myths relating to creation and dissolution of the Universe and the genealogies and history of gods, sages, and kings. They included Vedic cosmology and philosophies. They showed a person how to live so as to attain happiness here, and in the hereafter.

About the sixth century B.C., the Vedic civilization faced a severe crisis. The crisis was occasioned by the rise of the Buddhist and Jain ideologies. In order to meet their challenge, Vedic religion transformed itself into Hinduism. The most conspicuous change was the replacement of the Vedic gods by the Hindu trinity of Brahmā, Vishnu, and Shiva. With the rise of the new Gods, especially Vishnu and Shiva, came a new form of religious practice: *bhakti*, that is, devotion and surrender to one's God. The ritualistic upper-class religion was transformed into a popular and emotional religion. It is a reasonable conjecture that the leaders of the new sects took the extant Purānas and transformed them into vehicles for their own faiths. So it turns out that most of the present *Purānas* are sectarian in nature, eulogizing either Vishnu or Shiva.

These transformed *Purānas* proved to be wonderfully powerful instruments of culture transmission. The *Purāna* recital has been a central feature of Hindu religion. In almost every city and village, frequent *Purāna* recitals area organized. The reciter, a learned and entertaining public speaker, educates and entertains his audience every evening for weeks on end by reciting and commenting on the verses of the chosen *Purāna*. His audience consists of men and women, old and young. Each gets from the recital whatever he or she is capable of absorbing, for the *Purānas* contain all the information a person needs to live a good life. To top it all, each *Purāna* itself declares that just by listening to its recital a person attains salvation.

The *Purāna* recital itself mirrors the literary structure of the *Purānas*. Every *Purāna* is a dialogue in which some person relates its contents in reply to the inquiries of another person. The immediate narrator is commonly, but not always, Lomaharshana, the disciple of Vyāsa. But no narrator ever directly narrates. Each narrator only claims to relate what he himself has heard from another, and so on, till the chain reaches backwards to a divine or semi-divine source.

The *Vishnu Purāna* provides an excellent example. The first two verses are a salutation to Vishnu. The third verse reads: "Having adored Vishnu, the lord of all, and paid reverence to Brahmā and the rest. . . . I will narrate Purāna equal in sanctity to the Vedas." (Wilson, 1972, p. 2)

As the narration begins, we are told that Maitreya makes the following request of his teacher, Parāshara:

"I am now desirous . . . to hear from thee, how this world was, and how in the future it will be. What is its substance and whence proceeded animate and inanimate things? Whence proceeded the gods and other beings? What are the situation and the extent of the oceans and the mountains, the earth, the sun and the planets? What are the events that happen as the close of a kalpa [the Great Age], and the terminations of the several ages: the histories of the gods, the sages and kings . . . the duties of the Brahmans and other castes?" (Wilson, 1972, p. 3)

Parāshara now proceeds to answer these questions, but only as a retelling of what he himself has heard from his teacher. The brief reply to the basic questions about the world is that the world is produced by Vishnu and exists in Vishnu: He is the cause of its continuance and cessation; He is the world. The longer reply to Maitreya's questions constitutes the whole of *Vishnu Purāna*.

The Vishnu Purana

The *Vishnu Purāna* is divided into six books. The first book deals with cosmology. Its account of the creation of the world basically follows the Sāmkhya concept of the evolution of every object from a primordial nature to its present form (*prakriti*). But the authorship of the personal deity, Vishnu, is superimposed on the Sāmkhyan impersonal nature.

From Vishnu's body comes Brahmā. Brahmā creates the Universe. The world is peopled by the mind-born sons of Brahmā and their progeny. This created Universe lasts through a day in Brahmā's life. A day of Brahmā (a *kalpa*) covers 1,000 Great Ages (*mahayuga*). A *mahayuga* lasts for 4,320,000 years. Each *mahayuga* is divided into four ages (*yugas*): *Krita, Treta, Dwapara,* and *Kali*. The first is the golden age; humanity deteriorates in each succeeding age until *Kaliyuga* is reached, where everything falls apart. (Our age is a *Kaliyuga*). At the end of *Kaliyuga*, Vishnu appears as Kalki, one of his incarnations, to save mankind. Thus one *mahayuga* follows another till the end of Brahmā's day. At this point the great dissolution occurs. The world is burnt up by fire and a deluge of rain dissolves everything into one vast ocean; life is reabsorbed in the god, Vishnu, who sleeps on that ocean. Everything remains quiescent through Brahmā's night. Then a new day in Brahmā's life dawns and the Universe is re-created. This cycle continues through Brahmā's life, which lasts a 100 years. At the end of Brahmā's life, an even more radical dissolution occurs. The whole process then starts all over again.

Book one of *Vishnu Purāna* also recounts the legends of Dhruva and Prahlada, both of whom attain glory and salvation due to their unwavering devotion to Vishnu in the face of awesome difficulties. In fact, Dhruva is raised to the sky to become the pole-star, the very symbol of steadfastness.

Book two of *Vishnu Purāna* deals with geography and astronomy, describing different regions of the world, and locates India in Jambudvipa. It also recounts the story of King Bhārata, who gave India its Sanskrit name, Bhārata.

Book three gives the history of the Vedas and describes the fundamental institutions of Hindu society, namely the four classes and the four stages of life, and all the duties pertaining to each of these categories.

Book four gives ancient history, focusing on the two major dynasties of India's prehistory, the Solar and the Lunar. This account of dynasties culminates in the historical era of the Mauryas in the fourth and third centuries B.C.

Book five is given to the life of Krishna, the most important incarnation of Vishnu. It aims at inculcating and fostering *bhakti* (devotion).

Book six relates the dissolution of the world. It ends by describing the methods of Yoga as means for a person to attain final release.

Although the *Vishnu Purāna* is regarded as the most perfect of the extant *Purānas*, all of the *Purānas* deal with similar themes. The most conspicuous feature of the *Purānas* is the cultivation of *bhakti*. The *Bhāgvat Purāna* claims that it was composed by Vyāsa on the advice of the sage, Nārada, who asserts that in *Kaliyuga* humans can attain salvation only by *bhakti*. The major deity in six of the *Purānas* is Vishnu, in six others it is Shiva. In the rest of the *Purānas*, it is either the goddess Devi, or Brahmā, or Sūrya (the Sungod).

The Kurma Purana

Whenever a Purāna extols one of the deities as the supreme one, it describes the other major deities as his other forms. For example, one of the *Purānas* dedicated to the Devi (Goddess) claims that Shiva, Vishnu, and Brahmā are all Devi's sons and hence are equally worthy of devotion. It is noteworthy that the *Purānas* are sectarian but also liberal-minded.

In the *Kurma Purāna* the following story is recited: some of the sons of Kārltavirya worshipped Vishnu, while the others worshipped Shiva. When they could not agree as to which god was the more worthy of worship, the seven Rishis (sages) decided the dispute by declaring the deity worshipped by any man is that man's deity.

Having chosen a deity, a Hindu is to worship the deity with total *bhakti*. His *bhakti* is strengthened by hearing the wondrous tales of Gods, sages, and the great devotees of the past. With love in his heart, he visits great temples and undertakes difficult pilgrimages. The Great God assures him that he is guaranteed *moksha* sooner or later. Life will have a happy end.

The *Purānas* are truly unique creations in world literature, providing non-Hindus a mirror in which to view Hindu culture, and providing Hindus a comprehensive guide to life.

NARAYAN CHAMPAWAT

Further Reading

Translations

Venkatesananda, Swami, trans. *The Concise Srimad Bhāgvatam.* Albany, NY: State University of New York Press, 1989. Abridged version of the most popular Purāna.

Wilson, H. H., trans. *The Vishnu Purāna.* Calcutta: Punthi Pustak, 1972. Elegant English translation by a pioneering Indologist.

Related Study

Winternitz, Moritz. *A History of Indian Literature.* Vol. I. New York: Russell and Russell, 1971; first printed 1927. Comprehensive, general treatment of the *Purānas.*

YOGA SŪTRA

Author: Patanjali
Birth and Death Dates: Uncertain, second to fourth centuries A.D.
Literary Form: Sutras (aphorisms)
Date of Composition: Perhaps second to fourth centuries A.D.

Major Themes

Yoga aims at the suppression of the movements of the mind.
Yoga is achieved through dispassion and practice.
Three practices—austerity, the study of sacred literature, and the surrender to God—comprise the Yoga of Action.
The Eight-limbed Yoga consists of moral principles, observances, the development of physical postures, control of breath, restraining the senses and directing the mind inwards, concentration, meditation, and samādhi, a state of contemplative consciousness in which the essence of the object of meditation is fully identified with the mind.

The *Yoga Sūtra*, composed by a sage known as Patanjali sometime in the early first millennium A.D., has had enormous impact on the theory and practice of yoga and meditation in India and beyond since virtually the time of its composition. Very little can be said about the author, as nothing of him is revealed in the *Yoga Sūtra*. The only other work credited to a Patanjali is a well-known work on Sanskrit grammar, entitled *Mahābhāshya*, which was, however, written (in all likelihood) several centuries before the composition of the *Yoga Sūtra*.

The *Yoga Sūtra* was composed in the clipped aphoristic "sutra" style, common to many early works of Indian scientific and systematic thought. This style espoused brevity as a cardinal principle, in which substance prevailed over aesthetics. Linguistically, adjectives and verbs were pared down to a minimum, leaving much to be assumed from context. The purpose of a Sūtra was mnemonic: to facilitate memorization in what was largely a tradition of oral transmission of knowledge. Sutras were then employed as foci for practical instruction as well as critical analysis. A major consequence of such employment was a large commentarial prose literature, and a much larger body of oral explanations, each purporting—often at odds with other,

competing, authorities—to explain the meaning and significance of the sutras.

There is hardly a set of sutras that commands a more diverse set of viewpoints than the *Yoga Sūtra*. Nevertheless, a certain set of indisputable themes emerges from the text, which consists of four chapters containing 194 sutras. It is convenient that the themes of the *Yoga Sūtra* generally follow the order of the text.

Yoga and Meditation

The first chapter of the *Yoga Sūtra* defines yoga, and describes, in turn, the nature of the mind and various states of consciousness, the nature of God and the utilization of God in meditative practice, obstacles to achievement in yoga, aspects of the enlightened personality, and, interspersed throughout the chapter, the nature of the highest state achievable during meditation, called *samādhi*. In fact, the title of the first chapter is "The Chapter on *Samādhi*."

Yoga, etymologically related to the English "yoke," literally means "union." It is defined at the very beginning of the text as the "suppression of the movements of the mind." This goal is to be achieved by employing two fundamental methodologies. The first is dispassion *(vairāgya)*, in which the practitioner recognizes the duality consisting of self and the objective world, and ceases to identify with the latter. The second is practice *(abhyāsa)*, in which one identifies with the self through meditative absorption and *samādhi* or ecstasy. *Samādhi*, literally "putting together," is described as the pinnacle of the practice of yoga. This problematic word is often translated as "deep contemplation," "concentration," or "tranquility," but also has the sense of unifying disparate elements of consciousness during blissful or ecstatic meditative states. Patanjali describes several different levels of *samādhi* which may be experienced as the result of determined practice of yoga, moral development, and intellectual understanding. *Samādhi* is represented in chapter three of the *Yoga Sūtra* as the final step of the "eight-limbed yoga."

It is important for both the internal cohesiveness of the yoga school of philosophy as well as its position in relation to other schools of thought that its goal of expansion of consciousness and personality be achieved by detachment from the very contents of the mind, including the ideas that contribute to this withdrawal. This inherently recognizes the validity of the objective world, consistent with the dualistic Sānkhya system of thought with which it was related, and opposed to the pure idealism of Buddhist philosophy, to which it was opposed. This also highlights Patanjali's view of the soul *vis-à-vis* that of Buddhism, which perhaps ironically was the major influence on the *Yoga Sūtra*. While employing many of the important terms and concepts of Buddhism, Patanjali, whose agenda was in part the refutation of Buddhism, asserts the existence of a god and of a permanent self. This is the opposite of Buddhism, which denies both. In fact, employing identical concepts, Buddhists developed a meditation practice that worked in the opposite direction from that of Patanjali: the Buddhist practice focused on the contents of the mind and body in order to demonstrate their emptiness and the non-existence of a soul.

The Yoga of Action and the Eight-Limbed Yoga

The second chapter, which addresses practice *(sādhana)*, contains two major sections. The first sutra mentions three attitudes—austerity, study of sacred literature, and surrender to God—which comprise the "Yoga of Action" *(kriyā-yoga)*. The text then describes at length the nature of the ignorance *(avidyā)* and psychic afflictions *(klesha)* which this yoga is designed to surmount. The second half of the chapter describes the first five limbs of the "eight-limbed" *(astānga)* yoga. The first limb consists of five moral principles *(yama)*. These are non-injury, truthfulness, abstention from stealing, chastity, and non-covetousness. The second limb consists of five observances *(niyama)*. These are bodily purification, contentment, austerity, study of sacred literature, and surrender to God. Inclusion among the observances of the three defining elements of the Yoga of Action suggests that Patanjali was drawing from at least two distinct schools of yoga, a suggestion which receives confirmation in several other places in the text. It is characteristic of the traditions of practice and commentary that developed from the *Yoga Sūtra* that disparate elements of the text are presented as a seamless whole. This is characteristic not only of the yoga traditions but also of other schools of Indian religion and philosophy. Most notably, the *Bhagavad Gītā*, probably the best known religious text of classical India and the one referred to most frequently in religious and philosophical discourse, contains glaring contradictions which have been woven together in dozens of creative ways by countless commentators over thousands of years in order to present the text as containing a unified, seamless discourse.

The third limb of the eight-limbed path was the development of physical postures *(āsana)* suitable for the practice of yoga. The general rules were that the postures should be comfortable, easy, and stable. Their purpose was to provide a firm foundation for meditation, to allow the mind to attend to the tasks of meditation without being constantly drawn back to the body due to pain or discomfort. Though a long tradition of postural yoga *(hatha-yoga)* existed prior to the *Yoga Sūtra*—as early Buddhist texts attest—virtually all schools of postural yoga claim descent from the brief discussion (three sutras) in the *Yoga Sūtra*. The fourth limb was control of breath *(prānāyāma)*. This was also regarded as preparatory for the final three limbs. Patanjali was clearly acquainted with a wide range of yoga practices, the essences of which he extracted and set down in very general and concise form. The fifth limb was the mental act of restraining the sense organs and directing the mind inwards *(pratyāhāra)*. The image given throughout the commentaries is of a tortoise drawing in its limbs. It is significant that Patanjali ends the second book here, after completing the more active, anticipatory, aspects of yoga practice. It should be mentioned here that the only yogic or spiritual practice *(sādhana)* actually prescribed by Patanjali is repetition of the mystic syllable *"om"* and meditation on its meaning. All other instructions are general rules that can be applied to any form of meditation or yoga. Patanjali's instructions on *"om"* occur in the first chapter. He states that devotion to God *(īshvara)* is one method of bringing about *samādhi*, and that the syllable *"om"* is a designation of God.

The Accomplishments of Yoga Practice

The third chapter discusses the "perfections" or "accomplishments" *(vibhūti)* of yoga practice. It is often overlooked that the final three limbs of the eight-limbed path are regarded as accomplishments. Patanjali distinguishes these internally-generated limbs of yoga from the earlier five limbs, the only ones which he designates as practice *(sādhana)*. The final three limbs are concentration of the mind on a particular point or object *(dhāranā)*, meditation on that point or object *(dhyāna)*, and *samādhi*—a state of mind and consciousness in which the essence of the object of meditation is fully identified with the mind. As a result of the processes of yoga and meditation, a perceived object or thought will lose its objectification and identity. This is accompanied by a state of profound

mental stillness, a perceived unity of internal and external form, and an absence of boundaries to full and absolute knowledge of the possibilities offered by both nature and mind. The remainder of the chapter is occupied with the results possible through mastering a state called *samyama*, in which the final three limbs—concentration, meditation, and *samadhi*—are taken together and applied to various external and internal phenomena. Among the dozens of supernormal possibilities mentioned are knowing the meaning of the sounds produced by all beings, knowledge of one's previous lives, physical disappearance, flying through the air, omniscience, and finally liberation *(kaivalya)*. Most of these "perfections" are brought about by bringing discrimination of subtle entities, ideas, and objects into the field of *samyama*.

The fourth chapter discusses liberation *(kaivalya)* in a notably obscure manner. The main theme is the relationship of mind, individuality, causality, and the self. External objects are held to be real, subject to natural evolutionary forces. Knowledge of an object, however, is colored by an individual's state of mind. It is this coloration, born of past actions, memory, and the strength of impressions, that defines individuality—which is nothing other than the individual's unique identification with objective reality. Liberation ensues when the interdependence of cause and effect, brought on by continued participation in patterns of action, recognition, and identification, is broken by the influence of yoga. An object, entity, or idea may then be known in its true essence. The mind occupies an ambivalent position. On the one hand it is colored by both the object of perception and the self, and on the other it necessarily mediates between them. As the mind becomes still, stable, and clear, less colored by the vicissitudes of action and objects, one gains the ability to distinguish between object and self. The individual then ceases to cultivate a personal reality and gravitates naturally towards liberation. Ultimately, however, a state of highest and continuous virtue is brought about only when one can discriminate between the self and the subtlest levels of mind. Absolute consciousness is established in itself at this point, when the elemental building blocks of nature lose their purpose of engaging the self and are absorbed back into their original harmony.

Other Yoga Texts

The literature in Sanskrit on yoga begins much earlier than the *Yoga Sūtra*. The later Vedic literature, particularly some of the Upanishads, speaks of different forms of breath control and a few yoga postures. India's great epic, the *Mahābhārata*, which also predated the *Yoga Sūtra*, devotes considerable space to yoga. These discussions appear not only in the justly famous *Bhagavad Gītā*, which forms a part of the *Mahābhārata*, but also in many other passages. Long discourses on yoga are delivered on his deathbed by Bhisma, one of the great heroes of the war which constitutes the main action of the epic. In these discourses, the theme of yoga is intimately tied to the theme of proper livelihood. Independent of this was an extensive early literature on Buddhist meditation, which had its own, rather different, eight-fold path. More directly connected with the *Yoga Sūtra* was the Hindu tradition of yoga.

The primary exponents of Patanjali's yoga were the philosophers and religious teachers who wrote voluminous commentaries on the *Yoga Sūtra*. The earliest commentator was Vyāsa, whose date was probably not much later than Patajali's, and who was regarded as equally authoritative by most of his successors. Most translations of the *Yoga Sūtra* also contain a translation of Vyāsa's commentary. Many latter day Upanishads were written espousing specific yogic practices. These have become known collectively as the Yoga Upanishads. In addition, texts prescribing postures, breathing practices, and allied subject of *kundalinī* became increasingly common from the eighth to the seventeenth centuries.

Another major set of texts containing information on yoga is the *Purānas*, poetic sectarian texts dating from about the fifth century to the nineteenth century. These texts, which describe the exploits of deities such as Krishna and Shiva, all contain major sections on yoga theory and

practice. All of these texts are to some extent indebted to Patanjali.

FREDERICK M. SMITH

Further Reading

Translations

The number of English translations of the *Yoga Sūtra* probably number well over 100. Almost any translation will do for a casual reader, but anyone with a serious interest is advised to compare at least three translations. The differences are often astonishing. This is due to both the difficulty of the language and the differences in interpretive viewpoints, both of which tend to draw translators into manufacturing their own, usually highly idiosyncratic, technical language.

Aranya, Swami Hariharananda. *Yoga Philosophy of Patañjali*. Albany: State University of New York Press, 1983. A translation of the *Yoga Sūtra* and its principal Sanskrit commentary, by Vyāsa, along with supplementary discussions by Aranya.

Shearer, Alistair. *Effortless Being: The Yoga Sūtras of Patañjali*. London: Wildwood House, 1982. A relatively simple and comprehensible translation.

Related Studies

Eliade, Mircea. *Yoga: Immortality and Freedom.* Princeton: Princeton University Press, 1969. A study of different philosophies, practices, and sectarian forms of yoga that remains the starting point for all students of yoga.

Feuerstein, Georg. *Yoga: The Technology of Ecstasy.* Los Angeles: Jeremy P. Tarcher, Inc., 1989. An updated and user-friendly guide to the literature and practice of yoga, not just in its Hindu form, but also according to Buddhism and Jainism, with sections on Tantrism and alchemy.

Iyengar, B. K. S. *Light on Yoga*. New York: Schocken Books, 1977. The definitive book on hatha yoga; includes step-by-step instructions and more than a hundred photographs. Also excellent is Theos Bernard's *Hatha Yoga,* New York: Samuel Weiser, 1968. This book is a report of the author's study of yoga in India during the 1930s and contains translations of several important Sanskrit texts on hatha yoga.

Leggett, Trevor. *The Complete Commentary by Śankara on the Yoga Sūtras.* London, New York: Kegan Paul, 1990. This translation of Shankara's commentary is important because Shankara, who lived in the eighth century A.D., is one of the most important figures in Indian philosophy, and his commentary was lost until the 1950s, when a single manuscript of it was found in the southeast corner of India.

Varenne, Jean. *Yoga and the Hindu Tradition.* Delhi: Motilal Banarsidass, 1989. (English translation of *Le yoga et la tradition hindoue,* Paris: Loisirs, 1973.) Describes the philosophical and textual background of classical Indian yoga, along with many of its allied doctrines and forms, including Tantrism and Kundalini.

SHAKUNTALĀ

Title in Sanskrit: Śakuntalā (Shakuntalā). The work is also known by its longer title: *Abhijnānashakuntalā (Shakuntalā and the Ring of Recollection)*.
Author: Kālidāsa
Born: c. 390
Died: c. 470
Literary Form: Drama, heroic romance *(nataka)*
Date of Composition: Middle of the fifth-century A.D.

Major Themes

Mutual love will grow if the lovers realize and develop the relationship between love and duty.
There is a perfect harmony of humanity with the natural world.
The natural and the supernatural are one integrated whole in an ordered universe.

Shakuntalā is considered by many critics to be the finest example of Sanskrit drama. It is a work which celebrates the harmonious interplay and ultimate unity of complementary aspects of reality. Unity emerging from diversity pervades the entire work at many levels. Most obvious to those who read or watch the drama is the struggle of two different individuals to overcome their alienation and achieve the unity of love. At a deeper level, the work dramatically presents the universality of the struggle between duty and the desires of love, while leading the audience to a realization of the interdependence of the two. This play also expresses the interconnection of the world of the human with the world of nature. Further, throughout *Shakuntalā*, the visible realm (the human and the natural) is ever present to the realm of the invisible (the gods). Finally, this is a work acknowledged as a masterpiece of composition, with its parts in harmony with the whole. The interpenetration of prose with poetry and the intense emotional flavor of the drama have delighted audiences for fifteen hundred years.

Very little is known about the life of Kalidasa, the author of *Shakuntala*. He lived at a time when northern India was ruled by the Hindu Guptas (c. 320–c. 570 A.D.), and was enjoying an intense revival of traditional Hindu culture. To distinguish themselves from the preceding five hundred years of foreign domination, these native rulers energet-ically worked to revive the traditional Vedic ideas regarding sacrifice, the role of the Divine, and the established hierarchy within society (the caste system). This time was remembered in Indian history as one of stability and order which encouraged a development of the humanities, especially mathematics, astronomy, logic, and literature. Sanskrit, perfected by the efforts of the grammarians, richly re-expressed itself in the poetry and dramas of the period. This renaissance in learning, combined with a marked Hindu traditionalism, expressed itself throughout the seven poetic works and three dramas of Kalidasa. Of all his compositions, *Shakuntala* has been praised as the supreme example of his art, both in terms of its modes of expression and its mastery of the depth of human emotions.

King Dushyanta and Shakuntalā

The basic plot of the play is as follows: The King of India, Dushyanta, in hot pursuit of a deer, finds himself on the grounds of a forest hermitage. Descending from his chariot out of respect for Kanva, the chief hermit, the King puts a halt to his hunting and proceeds on foot toward the sacred grove. The sage, Kanva, is not at the hermitage but his beautiful foster daughter, Shakuntalā, is present watering the plants. She is the offspring of a warrior-turned-ascetic and a nymph. The nymph was sent by the god Indra to seduce the ascetic, whose austerities were threatening the throne of the god. Hiding behind a tree, the King sees a bee lustily attacking Shakuntalā and recognizes his chance to present himself as her protector, and he steps forward. In their conversation after his gallant rescue, he learns of her semi-divine origins. He is overcome by her exquisite beauty and falls deeply in love. Ordering his retinue to return to the capital, the King remains at the sacred grove under the pretense of defending the hermitage from wild animals and evil demons. In reality, his desire and hers only deepen until Dushyanta and Shakuntalā consummate their love in a secret marriage of mutual consent. Shakuntalā, who is pictured as the essence of vitality, becomes pregnant. The King, not knowing of the pregnancy (and thus of the joyful possibility of an heir), leaves for his capital soon after the marriage. Before leaving he gives his wife a signet ring as a sign of their commitment and promises to send for her in a short time.

Shakuntalā, distracted by her thoughts of her lover and thus neglecting her religious duties in the hermitage, fails to greet the irascible hermit Durvasas, who is greatly insulted by her lack of attention. In anger, Durvasas pronounces a curse on Shakuntalā such that whomever she is thinking of will completely lose all memory of her. She remains ignorant of the curse, but it is overheard by her female attendants who beg the hermit for leniency. The only concession he offers is that the curse will dissolve if the King sees from her some token of affection (hence, "the ring of recollection" in the longer title of the drama). Her attendants, in the hopes of sparing Shakuntalā any anxiety, tell her nothing of the hermit's words.

Kanva now returns and, learning from a supernatural voice that his foster daughter will give birth to a son who will rule the world, gives his permission for her to leave the hermitage to join the King. On her way to the capital with her escorts, Shakuntalā loses the ring at the river shrine of Indra's consort, Saci, and thus brings Durvasas's curse into actuality.

King Dushyanta does indeed fail to recognize her and repudiates her claims of love and marriage. She is rejected by the King and in her shame and

anger calls upon the earth to open and receive her. Before the eyes of the astonished priests a strange winged being, the nymph mother of Shakuntalā, flies down to the palace gardens, picks up her daughter and carries her up into heaven. When this event is reported, the King is greatly disturbed.

Meanwhile, a fisherman has found the King's ring inside the belly of a fish and is arrested as he tries to sell the precious item. Brought before the King for punishment, he receives a reward instead, for when the King sees the ring his memory is immediately restored. Overwhelmed with remorse, Dushyanta refuses to be comforted. Another nymph, who remains invisible, is moved by the King's distress and calls upon the god Indra to send a chariot to transport Dushyanta to heaven for a reunion with his beloved.

In heaven, the King finds a young boy playing fearlessly with a lion and, feeling a strong attraction to him, picks up an amulet that had fallen from the child's neck. Rather than being injured by the amulet, as had all others, in the hands of the boy's parents it proved not to be harmful. The little son is called the All-tamer (*Bharata*). The mother and child readily forgive the King upon hearing of the curse. The gods, happy to see them all reunited, send the family back to earth to enjoy many years of happiness.

The Origin of the Story

This story has its origin in the first book of the famous epic poem of 100,000 verses, *The Great Story of the Bharatas (Mahabharata)*, where Bharata is the great ancestor of all the princes who act throughout the poem. Kalidasa changes the story from the that of the *Mahabharata* by introducing the curse and the ring. This change results in the elevation of the moral character of the King and, thus, an enhancement of audience identification with his noble qualities.

Kalidasa, in his appreciation for the complexities of drama, introduces a number of lesser characters (attendants, hermits, nymph, fisherman, police, and the King's clown). Each enhances the interplay of the main players in the drama. The most important,

Shakuntalā, under the genius of Kalidasa, seems to grow throughout every act. The audience feels ever closer to her as they experience the transformation of an innocent maiden embodying all the beauty and perfection of nature, to a courageous suffering wife falsely accused by her cursed husband, to an all-forgiving nature-mother capable of assuming her duty as the Queen of the kingdom.

Love and Duty

Shakuntalā's growth throughout this drama was possible because of her transformation from a maiden who is the embodiment of the sensual vitality of love (*kama*) into a wife who brings this vitality into the sphere of social duty (*dharma*). As a symbol of loving desire she is presented in the beginning of the play as an intimate with all the natural forces in the forest. The purity of her innocent self-giving and her natural beauty arouse the King's desire who, upon seeing her, likens her to a flower in full bloom. Thus, there is little surprise that a bee would aggressively seek her and so manifest nature's longing for union. Dushyanta, like the bee, also longs for union. However, as the King, fully conscious of his place in society, he first reveals himself to Shakuntalā as her protector. It is an heroic act befitting the *dharmic* demands of his position. In this, he is revealed as the embodiment of duty.

Shakuntalā's strength is also her weakness. Failing to fulfill the duties of protocol and hospitality because of her loving preoccupation with thoughts of her lover, she occasions the curse. Her desires blocked from her consciousness the duties of social relatedness. Similarly, the King's strength becomes his weakness. The King, in his cursed ignorance, rejects her claims in his duty to protect the crown from what he thinks are false claims, this duty leads him to forget the passion of their love. He is pictured as unable to carry on the affairs of state. She, no longer a part of either the forest or the palace, finds her salvation in an escape to the heavenly realm.

Earlier, in act four, the wise sage of the forest hermitage, Kanva, tells his foster daughter about the complementarity of love and duty. He knows that Shakuntalā's place is with her husband. Overcome with great sorrow at her necessary departure, he exclaims that if this is how a disciplined ascetic so suffers, how much more do fathers bear at their daughter's parting? Turning to the trees, Kanva calls on them to recall that in her pure life they had offered her blossoms; now as she leaves, they are to speed her down the road of life. She is to return with her husband to the forest grove after her royal labors cease; they are to come and end their days in peace. Kanva embodies the unity of duty and love, and as such prefigures the resolution of the drama.

The seventh and last act presents the King meeting his son, who brings together his mother's vitality and intimacy with nature and his father's kingly rule. This child is the fruit of their love and the continuance of the throne. In their union, Shakuntalā is both Queen and beloved; Dushyanta is her King and lover. Together they are the interdependence of love and duty. At the end of the drama the audience experiences a joyful reaffirmation of the twin values that underpin much of Hindu civilization.

The Sentiment or "Flavor" of the Drama

Kalidasa's *Shakuntalā* follows the theory for Sanskrit dramas set forth in the *Natyasastra*, an encyclopedic textbook on dramaturgy written sometime between 100 to 300 A.D. According to this text the aim of good drama is to produce an emotion or sentiment in the audience. In the tradition set forth in Aristotle's *Poetics* (c. 334 A.D.), on the other hand, drama is driven by acts of volition whereby conflicts achieve resolution. This Western tradition of external activity consisting of the struggle between good and evil is quite different from that found in the Eastern tradition exemplified in the *Shakuntalā*.

In this Sanskrit drama, action is subordinate to the various emotional states of the major characters. The focus is on their inner life, not their external acts. The goal of the play is to explore human feelings. The soul of this drama is the changing sentiments of the soul. *Rasa*, the Sanskrit word for sentiments, has its root in the idea of flavor. Just as all foods have their particular taste, so should a good Sanskrit drama leave its taste, not in the mouth, but in the very soul of the audience. The *rasa* is the dominant emotion that persists throughout the play, despite the flux of transitory feelings. Just as the competent cook is wary of allowing too many spices to destroy the unity of taste that pervades the whole, so also Kalidasa avoids an excess of contradictory sentiments that would confuse and distort the main impact of the drama.

The *rasa* of this drama is love *(rati)*. The struggles of separation and union expressed through the energies of passion and the constraint of duty's self-control are all aspects of love. The erotic, the heroic, and the paternal all express the taste of this drama. The attractiveness of the major characters arouses a sympathy for them so that the audience experiences compassion, a true "suffering-with." No other woman competes with Shakuntalā for the audience's attention. Her love objects (nature, father, King, and child) mold the increasing intensity of her love.

Kalidasa has created a drama which keeps the audience at an intense level of feeling as they enter into the longings of the human heart. Kalidasa's choice of literary forms furthers the goal of *rasa* enhancement. Use of prose moves the plot along, and is often on the lips of minor characters. This is why the King's clown, the fisherman, and the police, all of whom provide comic relief, speak for the most part in prose. Poetry is reserved for the lofty flights of emotion expressed by the main players in the drama. These poetic utterances seek to excite the emotions of the audience. This is poetry which, like music, arouses deep feeling. These verses, without the prose, read like a grand sonnet. The perfect harmony of prose and poetry is not unlike that found in Shakespeare, with whom Kalidasa is often compared.

Perfect harmony is the final gift to the audience, the fruit of love. The serenity of the peaceful hermitage and the charm of the celestial paradise leave the audience with the deepest sentiments of peace and optimism. Sanskrit drama, in general, repudiates the tragic. The extreme popularity of this expression of Eastern thought is that it serves as a vehicle of self-purification by calling one to internalize the ideals of love.

The Natural and the Supernatural

The perfect harmony of the King and his beloved is the human expression of the cosmic harmony of the human, the natural, and the supernatural. This drama manifests the unity of all being. Kalidasa stands in the Hindu tradition of rejecting self-absorbed individualism. His play seeks to draw the audience into a communion with the beauty of nature and the providence of the supernatural. He wishes his audience to feel what Shakuntalā experiences.

When Shakuntalā sees a spring creeper enveloping a tree (realizing that it symbolizes the care and love of her foster father), she exclaims in joy, "Wonderful, wonderful!" Kalidasa intends every scene to arouse and deepen his audience's loving wonder. To accomplish this his drama celebrates the worlds of the visible and the invisible.

Nature is described with precision and detail. *Shakuntalā* speaks of the rain, trees, moon, sun, air, rivers, and animals. The flowers are pictured with their colors and fragrances, while the forest grove is sketched down to the roots of the trees washed by many streams and the breezes that ruffle the leaves.

There is much space devoted to the symbolic power of nature to reveal the drama of the human world. The bee is the King who desires, while the vine that embraces reveals human intimacy. In the opening scene, the deer the King hunts turns out to be the dear friend of the maiden who is now the new object of his energies. To leave her beloved hermitage she is like a vine twisted in the wind, a tree uprooted. His conflict between love and duty is described as a stream divided by a rock.

Shakuntala's feminine beauty is described by the use of the images of flowers and a pure pearl. Dushyanta's royal power is like that of an elephant. Their son's royal destiny is symbolized by his intimacy with a lion. The resolution of the curse is through the fish who swallows the ring of recollection.

Wonder at the beauty and symbolic power of the world of nature sustains an openness to the source of this richness. The audience of this play finds itself at home in the traditional religious and philosophical values of Hinduism. The visible is sustained in the invisible.

The drama opens and closes with a prayer to the god Shiva, the lord of the water that creates, of the fire that sacrifices, and of the moon and sun that divide time. All the vitality of the earth reveals the Divine, as do the struggles of humanity.

Heavenly voices reveal Shakuntalā's pregnancy and then bid her farewell from the forest. The King is encouraged to stay in the forest to protest, in the absence of Kanva, the sacrificial fire from the evil spirits. At the moment of greatest distress, Shakuntalā's nymph mother rescues her. In the King's depression, upon realizing his error, he fails in his duty. Because of this failure we are told that the gods are impatient for their sacrifice. To bring about a return of cosmic harmony, they will soon cause him to welcome his true wife. No person in the audience could fail to see the profound interrelationship of the sacred and the secular. They, with the King, approach the forest grove. As the King enters he experiences the good omen of a trembling right arm. He questions, in wonder, what success this omen portends, for everywhere there are doors to destiny.

The Expression of Hindu Culture

Shakuntalā reinforces the ordered world of traditional Hindu customs and laws. The values and mores of Kalidasa's culture are encapsulated in his drama. An earlier collection of the obligations for each caste, *The Laws of Manu (Manava Dharmasastra)*, (c. 200 B.C.–100 B.C.), casts light on a number of customs smoothly integrated throughout the play.

The King must ascertain if the forest maiden is the daughter of a priest (Brahmin) or, like himself, a member of the warrior class *(kshatriya)*. To his joy he discovers her to be the offspring of a warrior; thus, he is permitted by Hindu law of caste to continue his romance. Later, in his ignorance, he hesitates to speak to her for fear she may be married to another man; hence, preserving the order of social propriety. Their marriage is in accord with a declaration of mutual consent permitted for the warrior castes (called in Hindu law *Gandharva*). His beloved remains under the authority of her foster father for, according to the Law of Manu, women are not thought fit for independence. Thus, as a daughter, she remains under her father's authority until he offers her to her husband. This is why Kanva teaches her to obey her elders, and not be angry nor prideful; for, a self-willed woman is a curse of life. Her duty is to become a noble husband's noble wife.

The crisis occasioned by the curse becomes intelligible when we remember that Hindu culture demands extreme attention to the welcoming of a guest. If a guest leaves disappointed, the guest's sins are thought to be transferred to the householder. Elsewhere, traditional values are illustrated by the attention given to the use of grass to prepare the sacred fires, and by the rough treatment of the fisherman. The police feel free to have their way with him for, as a destroyer of fish, he was considered to be a member of a low caste.

Through the hierarchy of caste the audiences of Kalidasa are reinforced in their belief in an ordered universe, a belief that enhances the feelings of harmony and peace. Further, this ordered universe is rooted in the Hindu traditions of reincarnation and liberation. We read in act five the speech of the King who affirms that there are recollections of things not seen on earth, as there are loves earlier than birth. The very last words spoken in act seven are those of the prayer the King addresses to Shiva, asking that the gods see his faith and make him free from all rebirths.

The Influence of the Drama

Shakuntalā is now recognized as the highest expression of Sanskrit drama; the play is read and performed throughout the world. Beyond its own time, its great influence is a phenomenon of the past two hundred years. For, by the year 1000 A.D., Hindu drama had ceased to be a living force in the life of India. Successive waves of invasions left northern India in ruins. Court life, the traditional promoter of the arts, collapsed. While few had the leisure or resources for education, only a few Brahmins were able to understand Sanskrit. Nevertheless, after the year 1000 through to modern times, various manuscripts of the drama were produced, often with attached commentaries. The most famous commentary was produced around 1500 by Raghavabhatta, who argued for the interplay of love and duty as a key to Kalidasa's work.

In 1789, Sir William Jones translated *Shakuntalā* into English. His efforts created a great sensation throughout Europe. At a time when very few Hindu works were known to European audiences, this work was the first drama to be presented from the Sanskrit into a living European tongue. Quickly it was translated into German (1791), and French (1830). In less than a hundred years it appeared in a dozen different languages.

These multiple translations reflected the fascination of Europe with *Shakuntalā*. The efforts of numerous scholars with the text expressed the emergence of, and an important catalysis for, the modern Western appreciation of Eastern literature. This appreciation focused on Kalidasa's play, for many saw it as the source for archetypal Eastern values, as a summation of the spirit of India. The exoticism of the drama attracted some, while others saw the text as an important expression of Hindu mythology. The appeal to feeling aroused the impulses of European Romanticism, as did the work's sympathy for nature. Literary critics appreciated the interplay of different literary forms. Learned debates developed over whether the drama was a witness to the pre-modern cosmic harmony of the natural and the supernatural; or evidence of the fatalism of Eastern thought (the curse); or an Eastern celebration of enlightened Western humanism (the sage Kanva, and the growth, struggle, and redemption theme). The present international respect for the work stands in continuity with J. W. von Goethe's assessment in his *Deutsche Monatschrift* (1791), that the enchanted reader of *Shakuntalā* receives not only the

bloom of youth and the fruit of later years, but earth and heaven as well.

LAWRENCE F. HUNDERSMARCK

Further Reading

Translations

There are four recensions of the Sanskrit from different locations in India: Kashmiri, Bengali, Southern Indian, and Devanagari (central India). There is no critical text of all the recensions. Each is considered to offer a good reading of the play, even though each has numerous interpolations at the hands of scribes of different regions. The following four translations are all respected efforts:

Devadhar, C. R., trans. *The Works of Kālidāsa* (Vol. I, Dramas). Delhi: Motilal Banarsidass, 1966. Follows the Devanagari recension of the text with facing Sanskrit and English texts. The extensive notes often deal with philological issues. The translation style captures the tone of formality in the Sanskrit.

Lal, P., trans. *Great Sanskrit Plays in Modern Translation.* New York: New Directions, 1957. *Shakuntalā* is here translated along with the plays of five other Sanskrit dramatists allowing for comparisons of styles and themes. Less formal than the translation of Devadhar, with more attention to unrhymed poetry.

Miller, Barbara Stoler, ed. and trans. *Theater of Memory: the Plays of Kalidasa.* New York: Columbia University Press, 1984. A learned attempt to present the best texts that are the most faithful to Kalidasa's style. The translations are smooth and clear with helpful notes. This book offers the reader the three dramas of Kalidasa with introductory essays that situate him within his literary and historical context.

Monier-Williams, M., trans. *Śakuntalā, or Śakuntalā Recognized by the Ring.* 2nd edition, Oxford: Clarendon Press, 1876. A very influential nineteenth-century translation of the shorter Devanagari recension. The work is famous for its exhaustive notes on Hindu traditions.

Ryder, Arthur W., trans. *Kalidasa: Translations of Shakuntalā and Other Works.* London: J. M. Dent and Sons, 1912. A famous early-twentieth-century translation of the Bengali recension, known for its beautiful rhymed poetic verse. An added benefit of this book is translations of Kalidasa's poetry.

Related Studies

Scholarship on Kalidasa has been extensive throughout the past 150 years. For reference to the great number of manuscripts, translations, and studies, see S. P. Narang, *Kalidasa Bibliography.* Delhi: Heritage Publishers, 1976. See also the following studies:

Figueira, Dorothy Matilda. *Translating the Orient: The Reception of Śakuntalā in Nineteenth-Century Europe.* Albany: State University of New York Press, 1991. A very-well-written, sophisticated study of the various ways European translations reflect a wide set of competing values.

Gerow, Edwin. "Plot Structure and the Development of Rasa in the *Śakuntalā.*" Parts 1 and 2. *Journal of the American Oriental Society,* (1979), 99(4): 559–72; (1980), 100(3): 267–82. A very detailed representation of the themes of love and duty first set forth in the sixteenth-century commentary of Raghavabhatta.

Harris, Mary B. *Kalidasa: Poet of Nature.* Boston: The Meador Press, 1936. A thematic study of the place of nature in all of Kalidasa's work.

Krishnamoorthy, K. *Kalidasa.* New York: Twayne Publishers, 1972. A good first introduction to Kalidasa's plays and poetry with attention to their contents.

Mirashi, Vasudev V. *Kalidasa: Date, Life and Works.* Bombay: G. R. Bhatkal, 1969. A more in-depth study than that of Krishnamoorthy, with careful attention to modern scholarship on issues of historical context for the poems and plays.

Wells, Henry W. *The Classical Drama of India.* New York: Asia Publishing House, 1963. A standard introduction to the range of dramatic expression in India. This work complements an earlier classic of Arthur Berriedale Keith: *The Sanskrit Drama: Its Origin, Development, Theory and Practice.* Oxford: Clarendon Press, 1924. Both, taken together, offer the student a broad overview of the whole field.

TREASURY OF WELL-TURNED VERSES

Title in Sanskrit: *Subhāsita-ratna-kosa*
Compiler: Vidyākara
Born: Mid- to late-eleventh century
Died: Early- to mid-twelfth century.
Literary Form: Anthology of classical Sanskrit poetry
Date of Compilation: c. A.D. 1100 (revised version c. 1130)

Major Themes

A well-turned verse provides an image of a scene that captures its emotive essence.
Poetry offers devotional invocations of the Buddhist and Hindu deities.
Only poetic fancy can yield metaphors that express the anguish and delights of lovers.
The everyday life of the villagers is more worthy of poetic expression than is the effete world of the court.

As is the case with many authors of Sanskrit literary works, nothing is known of the compiler, Vidyākara, other than what can be deduced from the collection itself. From the contents and general tone of his anthology, it can be determined that Vidyākara lived in the time of the Pāla kings who ruled northeastern India (modern Bihar and Bengal) from the eighth to twelfth centuries A.D. and who were staunch patrons of Buddhism of the Mahāyāna school. Vidyākara was evidently a scholar-monk residing in the Buddhist monastery of Jagaddala in Bengal. His selections prove that he was widely read in the classical Indian literary tradition and was especially fond of the more recent poets of the eighth to eleventh centuries, particularly those of his own northeastern region. Vidyākara probably compiled the first version of his anthology, comprising about 1000 verses, sometime around A.D. 1100, but continued to add to it over the following years so that the final version, probably completed around A.D. 1100, had 1,738 verses. Only two complete manuscripts of the anthology have survived to modern times, one each of the earlier and later versions, which were found in Tibet and Nepal respectively. Modern scholars have reconstructed and translated the anthology from these two texts, plus a fragmentary second manuscript of the revised text.

The Revised Version

The revised version of the *Treasury of Well-Turned Verses* is divided into fifty sections (*vrajyā*s; the first version had only forty-four sections) each concerning a particular topic of poetic interest. The first six sections consist of devotional invocations of Buddhist and Hindu deities; the first three are dedicated to Buddhist figures, namely the Buddha and the Bodhisattvas Lokeshvara and Manjughosha, the second three to the Hindu gods Shiva, the companions of Shiva, and Vishnu. The arrangement here reflects the compiler's Buddhist sentiments, but also the eclectic spirit of his era. Sections 8 through 13 contain descriptions of the six seasons of the traditional Indian calendar. Sections 14 through 25 concern standard erotic themes, as in "The Words of the Messenger" (18) and "The Evidence of Consummation" (20). Sections 26 through 31 are made up of verses describing various times of the day and night; most of this material was added in the revised edition of the anthology. Sections 32 through 49 treat miscellaneous themes, mostly worldly concerns, as in "Good Men" and "Villains" (37 and 38), "Discouragement," "Old Age," and "The Cremation Ground" (42–44). This part also contains technical poetic categories such as "Allegorical Epigrams"

(33), "Characterizations" (35), "Substantiations" (40), and "Inscriptional Panegyrics" (46). The anthology concludes, appropriately enough, with a "Praise of Poets" (50).

Within this broad scheme, this massive anthology contains an enormous range of variety in themes, styles, content, and quality. The verses range from the sublimely inspired to, occasionally, the labored and humdrum; but on the whole Vidyākara's selection reveal him to be a man of subtle sensibilities and fine poetic tastes according to the literary standards of his world.

Sources of the Anthology

Though many verses are cited anonymously, the names of 223 different authors are cited by the compiler in the expanded version of the anthology. The number of verses attributed to a particular author ranges from one to 101. The writers cited most frequently by Vidyākara are the polymath Rājashekhara (101 verses) and the playwrights Murāri (56) and Bhavabhūti (47). These, along with other familiar names such as Bhartrhari (25 verses), Bāna (21), Kālidāsa (11), and Ashvaghosha (1), are well-known authors of the classical tradition. But Vidyākara also cites many gifted poets whose works are otherwise entirely unknown, or are known only from citations in other anthologies. Among this category are several local poets of northeastern India, notably Yogeshwara, a writer of exceptional skill and originality who is cited thirty-two times.

It is interesting that among the poets Vidyākara quotes are several women, notably Vidyā, to whom seven verses are credited. Because of its citations of many otherwise unknown or little-known authors, the *Treasury* is an important source for the dating and reconstruction of the later history of Sanskrit poetry, especially in northeastern India.

In view of Vidyākara's preference for verses from the middle classical tradition (eighth to eleventh centuries A.D.) of northern and especially northeastern India and his relatively sparse citations of well-known early classical poets such as Kālidāsa, Vidyākara's intention seems to have been

to present an up-to-date, "modern" anthology of the literature of his time.

Many of the verses quoted in the "Treasury" are taken from the Sanskrit dramas; this is presumably because they contain large numbers of descriptive verses that can be easily appreciated when taken out of context. Quotations from the ornate epic (*mahā-kāvya*), the other main genre of classical Sanskrit verse, are much fewer, presumably because these narrative verses are typically less amenable to being taken out of context. The third major genre from which Vidyākara drew was that of short poems and pre-existing single-author anthologies such as the *Centuries* of Bhartrhari. Altogether, the sources of approximately two-thirds of Vidyākara's verses can be traced in extant texts, or at least in other anthologies; the remaining third are unknown in any other source.

The Concept of the Well-Turned Verse

Although most of the verses collected by Vidyākara are extracted from larger works, the ideal of the "well-turned verse" (*subhāshita*, literally "thing well-said") that can stand by itself is well grounded in the Sanskrit poetic tradition. A true "well-turned verse," whether compiled independently or as part of a longer poetic or dramatic text, presents a vivid verbal "snapshot" of a scene, event, or situation that captures the essence of its emotional power (*rasa*, literally "flavor"). It is this aesthetic standard, rather than any common feature of style, content, or message, that serves as the thread that ties all the verses in this collection together into a coherent literary unit, and which lends significance to the metaphor of its title: each well-turned verse is a gem, and a well-chosen anthology is a literary treasure-chest.

Place in the Sanskrit Anthology Literature

Vidyākara's *Treasury* is the oldest known specimen of the general anthology of literary Sanskrit verses, though earlier, more limited collections on specific topics are known. After Vidyākara's time many more such anthologies were compiled, down to the modern era, and several of them, such as the well-known *Nectar of Well-Spoken Verses* (*Sadukti-karnāmrta*) of Śridharadāsa, were strongly influenced by it. We cannot be sure that the *Treasury* was actually the first anthology of its kind, since there may have been earlier works that did not survive to modern times, and the rarity of the surviving manuscripts indicates that it did not maintain its popularity through the centuries, probably because of the collapse not long after its composition of the Buddhist monastery culture from which it stemmed. Nonetheless, Vidyākara's *Treasury* did have an major, if largely indirect, influence on the subsequent development of the genre of the Sanskrit anthology, by way of setting patterns for the themes, arrangements, and specific verses chosen by later anthologists.

Stylistic Characteristics

Vidyākara's *Treasury* stands out as the most purely "literary" of the major Sanskrit anthologies. Most other anthologies include at least some verses composed in a more casual style, more like versified proverbs than polished literary gems, but Vidyākara excluded such informal verses from his *Treasury* and accepted only verses in the high classical style. Many of the verses in the *Treasury* are accordingly characterized by learned literary and technical allusions, rarified literary conventions, obscure and learned vocabulary, and complex syntactic structures, so that they are difficult to render in simple English and often require extensive commentary to make them comprehensible to the modern reader. Also typically of classical style, twenty-five different meters are represented in the anthology, of which the most common (used in more than one-third of the verses) is the difficult "Tiger's Play" (*shārdūla-vikrīdita*) consisting of four quarters of nineteen syllables each in a strictly prescribed sequence of light and heavy syllables.

As required by classical aesthetic standards, the poets employ a vast variety of ornate poetic figures of sound and sense, often interweaving them in complex combinations. For example, this verse (no. 257) by Yogeshwara from the section (10) on

descriptions of the rainy season illustrates a masterful application of the technique of multiple or extended metaphors much favored by Sanskrit poets:

> *Now the great cloud cat,*
> *darting out his lightning tongue,*
> *licks the creamy moonlight*
> *from the saucepan of the sky.*

(INGALLS, 1965, P. 134)

Another, anonymous verse (no. 242) from the same section, in describing a traveler returning to his beloved at the beginning of the rains, embodies the exquisite combination of imagination and grace of expression that distinguishes classical Sanskrit poetry at its best:

> *The god of love, angry at the transgression of his*
> *   command,*
> *orders the traveler sent back to his mistress*
> *with limbs constricted in a crystal cage*
> *made by the broad bright stream of water*
> *pouring from his umbrella.*

(INGALLS, 1965, P. 404)

This verse utilizes another favorite device of Sanskrit authors, the "poetic fancy" (*utprekshā*) in which the poet proposes an imaginative interpretation of the scene with is the object of his poetic eye. The same figure is ingeniously put to use in an anonymous erotic verse (404) from the section (16) on the charms of young women, where the author plays on the poetic convention that a beautiful woman should have three folds of flesh across her stomach:

> *The folds of her waist are the exudation of allurement*
> *from the three interstices of the creator's fingers,*
> *as he squeezed her in his fist,*
> *to add weight to loins below and breasts above.*

(INGALLS, 1965, P. 168)

Several of the later sections of the anthology concentrate on themes more appropriate to the later stages of life, as in the grisly descriptions of The Cremation Ground (section 44) that serve as *memento mori* to the wise reader; for example, this famous verse (1532) by the great dramatist Bhavabhūti:

The she-ghouls have made bracelets from intestines
and red lotus ornaments of women's hands;
have woven necklaces of human hearts
and rouged themselves with blood in place of
*   saffron.*
So decked they join their lovers with delight
and drink the marrow-wine from skull-cups.

(INGALLS, 1965, P. 399)

The verses cited above are more or less representative of standard themes and styles in classical Sanskrit literature. But the *Treasury* also contains a significant number of verses that reflect a less conventional and idealized style and focus more on the real experiences of Indian village life, often charming but sometimes also harsh. Such verses, which seem to reflect a distinct regional literary tradition of the northeast, maintain the highest standards of Sanskrit literary artifice and diction even as they distance themselves from the effete world of the court and the urban sophisticate. Several excellent specimens of this class are included in the section (35) on Characterizations, such as the following verse (1178) of Yogeshwara describing the village women at work:

How charming are the women's songs as they husk
*   the winter rice;*
a music interspersed with sound of bracelets
that knock together on round arms swinging
with the bright and smoothly rising pounder;
accompanied by the drone of hum, hum
breaking from the sharply heaving breasts.

(INGALLS, 1965, P. 334)

An anonymous verse (1148) from this section caricatures a fish-eating glutton, poking fun at the regional cuisine of Bengal and revealing a lighter side that is occasionally represented in the *Treasury*:

I rolled them up in a cumin swamp
and in a heap of pepper dust
till they were spiced and hot enough
to twist your tongue and burn your mouth.
When they were basted well with oil,
I didn't wait to wash or sit;
I gobbled that mess of koyi fish
as soon as they were fried.

(INGALLS, 1965, P. 328)

But the harder side of village life is also candidly depicted in several poems from the section on poverty (39), as in this poignant verse of Dharanīdhara (1306):

Somehow, my wife, you must keep us and the
*   children*
alive until the summer months are over.
The rains will come then, making gourds and
*   pumpkins grow aplenty*
and we shall fare like kings.

(INGALLS, 1965, P. 359)

RICHARD SALOMON

Further Reading

Translations

Ingalls, Daniel H.H., trans. *An Anthology of Sanskrit Court Poetry: Vidyākara's "Subhāṣitaratnakoṣa."* Harvard Oriental Series 44. Cambridge: Harvard University Press, 1965. The definitive, and only, complete translation of Vidyākara's *Treasury*, this is a masterpiece which combines the highest standards of scholarship with a readable style of translation for the non-specialist. This original, unabridged edition includes extensive technical notes, indices, and other apparatus. Quotations are from Ingalls' *Anthology*, copyright © 1965 by the President and Fellows of Harvard College; and used by permission of Harvard University Press.

————, trans. *Sanskrit Poetry from Vidyākara's "Treasury."* Cambridge: Harvard University, 1970. An abridged version of the above, containing a selection of slightly less than half of the verses and omitting the scholarly apparatus but retaining most of the valuable general introduction. This volume serves as an ideal introduction to classical Sanskrit poetry.

Kosambi, D. D. and V. V. Gokhale, eds. *The Subhāṣitaratnakoṣa Compiled by Vidyākara.* Cambridge: Harvard University, 1957. (Harvard Oriental Series 42). Contains the critically edited Sanskrit text that served as the basis for Ingalls' translation, with an extensive introduction containing some material of interest to the general reader, though skewed by Kosambi's idiosyncratic Marxist interpretation of Sanskrit literature.

GĪTAGOVINDA

Title in Sanskrit: *Gītagovinda (Song of the Lord)*
Author: Jayadeva
Born: Twelfth century
Died: Twelfth century
Literary Form: Dramatic, lyrical poem
Date of Composition: Twelfth century

Major Themes

The gods are remote until they are loved.
To know Krishna one must know him as his beloved does.
Anyone who can imagine intimacy with the divine can begin to appreciate the range of divine response to human needs.
Through the aesthetic experience of the mutual love of Rādhā, a cowherdess, and Lord Krishna, enjoyment of the divine is possible.
Sexual ecstasy is the image of religious ecstasy.
To know Krishna in this way is to become a blissful and wise person, capable of purifying this dark time.

Perhaps no literature that is inherently contradictory is more valuable than the literature that brings the gods into close, even intimate, relationships with human beings. In all religions, despite the individual personalities sometimes attributed to the gods, there remains the distance factor: the supernatural is above and beyond the natural, maintaining an aura of mystery even while appearing to be within reach through prayer, or at hand in times of need (or too much present in times of mortal sinning).

To envisage the gods, or a god, as human is to utilize paradox (the god, who is divine and not human, is human after all) in the service of emotive—that is to say, spiritual—understanding. To go one step further, to imagine and thereby to experience a god as lover—and the lover as romantic and erotic lover—is to confound the paradox for the sake of miraculous revelation: somehow, god as sexual lover brings into focus, in a startling and incisive way, what it is for a god to be divine, nonhuman but not inhuman, intimately concerned with, and immersed in, the spiritual life of human beings.

Gītagovinda (The Love Song of the Lord) is the story of the passionate love affair between Krishna,

a god, an incarnation of Vishnu, and Rādhā, a cowherdess. The lyrical poem, with its songlike refrains, celebrates the growth of love, its erotic consummation, and the pains of departure and separation, made finally bearable only through memory and faith.

The entire romance, with all the beauty and darkening threat of a summer storm, is a metaphor that uses human erotic love as a kind of foretaste of communion with the divine. Every feature of the affair has both its earthly and its heavenly significance, and the justification for the metaphor lies in this: the feelings of the one are appropriate to the other. The attempt to know and to be close to the lord as, presumably, the lord is to the devotee, is frustrated by the divine "otherness": even when a god seems responsive to one's need, he (or she) is "dark," in the sense that the god is cloaked in mystery and is always, at least essentially, aeons apart from the worshiper. But there is the same problem of the mysterious in instances of human passionate love, as one never quite closes the gap between the lover and the beloved; there is a self that is always an infinite step away from being known and taken.

Just as there is an analogy between the divine as

231

"other" and the beloved as "other," while at the same time there is an intimacy than which none greater can be conceived, so there is an analogy between the beloved as one with the lover—as more immediately concerned about, and in touch with, the lover, than the lover is with any other person on earth—and God as one with the human devotee, as eternally at hand when needed and called for, and more privy to the secrets and longings of the finite self than is any person on earth.

It is not surprising, then, that every religion that has its God or gods attempts to close the gap between the human and the Divine, and to achieve an understanding that is spiritually fruitful by imagining God as lover, the human being as beloved, and the passions of sexual love as the passions of revelation.

Jayadeva

The author to whom the *Gītagovinda* is attributed is a poet who used the name "Jayadeva." The name, which means "God of Triumph," is also given to Lord Krishna, with the result that the meeting of the human spirit and the god is accomplished at the outset in the very act of naming.

According to the tradition, Jayadeva was born a Brahman and showed his genius in the poetic use of language at an early age. He became a wandering ascetic, and in the course of his travels became acquainted with the Jagannatha cult of Puri. Although legend has it that Jayadeva married a Brahman's daughter, Padmāvatī, who danced in the temple while he wrote poetry, references to Padmāvatī as Krishna's divine consort suggest that she is more a symbol than a wife.

Jayadeva as Poet

Although Jayadeva was well-versed in Sanskrit, he did not limit the appeal of his poetry to the educated admirers of complex linguistical devices for the expression of ideas and emotions; his poetry was apparently designed to interest, instruct, and inspire a broad audience that, whether analytical or not, could hardly fail to grasp the significance of

love poetry that is at the same time, and on that account, religious poetry.

The poetry composed by Jayadeva is rich with imagery, enlivened by rhythm, made appealing by alliteration, and strikingly effective in its use of metaphors. (For a scholarly but lively account of the technical aspects of Jayadeva's poetry, including information concerning the origins of the poetic conventions and devices that he employed, see Barbara Stoler Miller's *Love Song of the Dark Lord: Jayadeva's Gītagovinda*, which is also an excellent translation. See Further Reading at the end of this article.)

The Structure of the Poem

The *Gītagovinda* is in twelve parts, each part containing from one to four songs for a total of twenty-four. Each song is prefaced by a short verse that provides the setting for the song, and is followed by another recitative or narrative verse passage that rounds off the scene and prepares the way for what follows (or else draws the religious moral).

The poem begins with a brief eight-line verse that creates the mood and refers to the secretly consummated passions of Rādhā, the cowherdess, and Krishna (here initially called Madhava, a name with a host of associations, including springtime, honey, and killer of the demon Madhu).

Jayadeva, the poet, declares that he writes his lyrical poem to tell of Krishna's passion and thereby enrich the hearts of his readers.

The Love Story of Rādhā and Krishna

After celebrating in the First Song the ten incarnate cosmic forms of Krishna (including the Fish, the Tortoise, the Boar, the Man-lion, and the Buddha), Jayadeva addresses Krishna in the Second Song's invocation as "Hari," the "tawny one," and the "destroyer of pain" (thereby relating him to Vishnu, the Supreme God, of whom Krishna, the cowherd and tribal hero, is an incarnation).

Krishna is then pictured in verse and song as revelling with wanton cowherdesses, a sight that distresses Rādhā when her attention is called to it by her (anonymous) friend.

*One cowherdess with heavy breasts embraces Hari
    lovingly
And celebrates him in a melody of love.
    Hari revels here as the crowd of charming girls
    Revels in seducing him to play.*

> (PART I, SONG 4, VERSE 39.
> MILLER, TRANS., 1977)

Because of her envy, Rādhā is depressed and made angry by Krishna's sexual play with the other cowherdesses. Krishna realizes that his behavior has driven her away, and he finds that his love for her drives him to find her and beg her forgiveness. He is so affected by Radha's longing for him that he abandons the other cowherdesses.

Rādhā's friend, aware of Rādhā's suffering and the cause of it, visits Krishna and tells him how Rādhā "Lying dejected by your desertion, fearing Love's arrows,/ . . . clings to you in fantasy, Mād-hava." (IV, song 8, refrain. Miller.) The friend elaborates: "She raises her sublime lotus face, clouded and streaked with tears,/ Like the moon dripping with nectar from cuts of the eclipse's teeth." (IV, song 8, verse 5. Miller.)

The friend tells Krishna that nothing can ease Rādhā's suffering except to know his love again; if he denies her, Rādhā will die. Krishna, who is himself suffering from the separation from Rādhā, asks Rādhā's friend to reassure her and bring her to him. He prepares the bed of branches in the thicket where they first made love.

*When a bird feather falls or a leaf stirs, he imagines
    your coming.
He makes the bed of love; he eyes your pathway
    anxiously.
    In woods on the wind-swept Jumna bank,
    Krishna waits in wildflower garlands.*

> (V, SONG 11, VERSE 10, MILLER.)

The friend's efforts to reassure Rādhā fail; Rādhā seems powerless to return to Krishna, who she feels

has deserted her. Again, the friend tells Krishna that Rādhā will not survive the night without him.

When Rādhā sees her friend return without Krishna, she begins to suspect that he is enjoying himself in the arms of some other young woman. She tells her friend what she imagines:

*She is richly arrayed in ornaments for the battle of
    love;
Tangles of flowers lie wilted in her loosened hair.
    Some young voluptuous beauty
    Revels with the enemy of Madhu.*

> (VII, SONG 14, VERSE 13, MILLER.)

In two more songs in Part VII, Rādhā tortures herself by imagining Krishna's lovemaking, but she admits that "even when he is cruel/ I am forced to take him back."

Krishna, abashed, bows before Rādhā when "[a]fter struggling through the night . . . wasted by the arrows of love," Rādhā angrily confronts him. She chides him for the marks of passion on his body; she cries out, "Your heart must be baser black than your skin," and she castigates him with the refrain, "Damn you, Mādhava! . . . Don't plead your lies with me!" (VIII, song 17, Miller.)

Rādhā's friend attempts to reason with her. She tells her not to "turn wounded pride" on Krishna, for he has pride also. Since Krishna regrets having deserted her for his wanton play with the cowher-desses, she should be responsive to his protestations of love and not condemn herself to a life of loneliness (Part IX).

Krishna returns with "blissful words." He issues an invitation to her: "Let your moon face lure my nightbird eyes/ To taste nectar from your quivering lips!" He is even more extravagant:

*If you feel enraged at me, Rādhā,
Inflict arrow-wounds with your sharp nails!
Bind me in your arms! Bite me with your teeth!
Or do whatever excites your pleasure!*

> (X, SONG 19, VERSE 3, MILLER.)

Krishna realizes that he has calmed Rādhā and reawakened her love. He goes to the thicket and lies down on the love bed. Rādhā arrives at the thicket, pauses modestly, finally enters, and knows immediately that he loves and desires her. Her passion rises with his; she goes to the bed where he awaits her (Part XI).

As Krishna exclaims, "Consent to my love; let elixir pour from your face!" (XII, song 23, verse 4, Miller) she "launched a bold offensive/. . . And triumphed over her lover." (XII, song 23, verse 10, Miller.)

Rādhā, triumphant, orders Krishna to decorate her: "Pin back the teasing lock of hair on my smooth lotus face!/. . . Make a mark with liquid deer musk on my moonlit brow!" (XII, song 24, verse 15, 16, Miller.)

Jayadeva's Summary Comment on His Poetry

In the next-to-last verse on his *Song of the Dark Lord*, Jayadeva relates his erotic love poem to the gods, bringing out its religious spirit:

> *His musical skill, his meditation on Vishnu,*
> *His vision of reality in the erotic mood,*
> *His graceful play in these poems,*
> *All show that master-poet Jayadeva's soul*
> *Is in perfect tune with Krishna—*

Let blissful men of wisdom purify the world
By singing his Gītagovinda.

(XII, SONG 24, VERSE 21, MILLER.)

IAN P. MCGREAL

Further Reading

Translation

Miller, Barbara Stoler, ed. and trans. *Love Song of the Dark Lord: Jayadeva's Gītagovinda.* New York: Columbia University Press, 1977. The source of the quotations in the above article, this book contains not only an excellent translation of high poetic quality designed to suggest the form and rhythms of the text in Sanskrit, but also a thoroughly researched account of the structure of Jayadeva's poem, its religious significance, information about the music and the songs, reviews of various early editions, a glossary of Sanskrit words, a note on Sanskrit pronunciation, and the *Gītagovinda* in Sanskrit text (script, not romanized). A detailed bibliography is given for each section of the introduction. (Quotations reprinted with permission of the publisher. Copyright © 1977 by Columbia University Press.)

RĀMCARITMĀNAS

Author: Tulsīdās
Born: c. 1532
Died: 1623, Banaras, India
Literary Form: Epic poem
Date of Composition: c. 1574

Major Themes

Lord Rām is the ultimate deity, encompassing and transcending all other gods.

Rām's incarnate acts are infinitely charming and revelatory, and ought to be constantly sung, heard, and meditated upon.

In the present age of darkness and confusion (kali yuga) *the knowledge of Rām's acts and the repetition of his name provide the surest means of salvation.*

The *Rāmcaritmānas*, or "Holy Lake of the Acts of Rām," is an epic poem of some thirteen thousand lines, composed in Avadhi, a pre-modern literary dialect of Hindi. It is the earliest and most famous of a dozen works attributed, on good evidence, to the poet-saint Tulsīdās, who lived in northeastern India—mainly in the sacred city of Banaras or Vārānasī—during the late sixteenth and early seventeenth centuries. The epic retells, with significant modifications, the ancient tale of the adventures of Prince Rām (in Sanskrit, Rāma) of Ayodhya and his wife Sītā: Rām's youthful adventures and winning of Sītā as his bride, his unjust exile to the wilderness together with his wife and his younger brother, Laksman, Sītā's abduction by the ten-headed demon-king Rāvan, Rām's quest and eventual battle to recover his wife, assisted by a race of supernatural monkeys under the leadership of Hanumān, and Rām and Sītā's triumphant return to reign over Ayodhya.

This complex saga of love, obedience, and heroism was first set in literary form in the Sanskrit epic *Rāmāyana*, attributed to the sage Vālmīki and variously dated by modern scholars as being somewhere between the second century B.C. and the first century A.D. It was subsequently retold in numerous other Sanskrit and regional-language renderings throughout India and beyond; indeed, it is estimated that the literatures of South and Southeast Asia contain more than three hundred major Rām-related texts. Due to a combination of factors, however, the Hindi epic of Tulsīdās—the long title of which is often abbreviated simply as "*the Mānas*"—has risen to such popularity and esteem throughout northern India that it has overshadowed its classical antecedents and has assumed a dominant role in shaping many Hindus' conception of the oft-told and beloved story. Celebrated by scholars as the foundational masterpiece of Hindi literature—sometimes compared to Dante's *Divine Comedy* or Goethe's *Faust*—the *Mānas* acquired its extraordinary popularity in the absence of print technology. For nearly four centuries it successfully reached a far-flung and largely illiterate audience through lively genres of oral performance, and it has continued to be powerfully transmitted and reinterpreted in the twentieth century through the mass media of print, film, and audio and video cassettes.

Tulsīdās and His Age

Like his English contemporary Shakespeare (to whom, in breadth of cultural influence, he is sometimes compared), the author of north India's most popular epic appears to modern scholarship as a rather shadowy figure, whose long and productive career left little in the way of historical records. Most accounts of his life rely on a few possibly autobiographical verses scattered through his writings, and on a handful of dated manuscripts believed to be in his own hand, supplementing these with the rich and reverent hagiographical tradition that developed in the centuries after his death. Neither the date nor place of his birth is known with certainty; estimates of the former range from 1532 to 1543, and some seven places in present-day Uttar Pradesh and Bihar states vie for the honor of claiming him as native son.

Tradition holds that Rām belonged to the Brahman caste of priests and scholars, but was born under an unlucky astrological conjunction which led his rustic parents to abandon him soon after birth. A few late, "confessional" poems allude to a childhood of loneliness and hunger, and to an apparent adoption by a group of wandering mendicants devoted to the god Vishnu and his avatars or earthly "incarnations," especially Rām. These holy men may have given the poet his name, which means "servant of the *tulsī* plant"—an herb sacred to Vishnu—as well as his first instruction in the holy story he was to devote much of his life to celebrating.

There must have followed a long period of Sanskritic education (traditionally held to have occurred in a Brahman school in Banaras), for the poet was clearly learned in the sacred tongue and its lore; this may have been followed (as legend holds) by a brief period of marriage, before Tulsīdās ultimately decided to renounce worldly life and journey to the sacred town of Ayodhya, legendary capital of Rām. There (the poet himself records) on the hero-god's birthday in the spring of 1574 he began retelling Rām's adventures in "rustic speech," a task that must have continued for several years. During this time he apparently shifted his residence to Banaras, where he eventually settled in a stone house, built for him by a wealthy admirer and still standing today, on the Ganges at Assi Ghat. Several of his later works—including the anthology *Vinay patrikā* ("the letter of humble petition," his best-known work after the *Mānas*) and *Kavitāvalī* ("song-cycle in *kavitta* meter")—refer to his residence in the holy city, and to criticism from its religious elite, who may have resented

the popular appeal of his vernacular writings; tradition asserts that he died there in 1623.

Tulsīdās's lifework continues a devotional tradition dating back to the seventh-century hymns of south Indian poet-saints. Often termed the "*bhakti* movement," this tradition is characterized by a preference for local languages over Sanskrit, a relative social egalitarianism, and a fervently emotional mood of devotion *(bhakti)* toward a personalized and accessible deity. Although much of the output of *bhakti* authors was lyric poetry, longer narrative works include several regional versions of the Rām story, such as Kampan's (circa eleventh century) *Irāmāvatāram* in Tamil. Like its Tamil precursor, the *Mānas* foregrounds the divinity of the epic's hero, whom it recognizes as the supreme personification of godhead, and invites its audience to ponder his salvific deeds. Set in rhyming couplets, the Hindi epic lends itself to memorization and to chanted or sung performance, and there is evidence that it attained considerable popularity and dissemination during its author's lifetime. In later centuries, the patronage of mercantile and landowning classes and of ascetics of the powerful Rām-oriented Rāmnandi order contributed to its increasingly unique prestige throughout much of northern and central India, suggested by the traditional appelation "the Hindi Veda," and by the British administrators" designation, "the Bible of North India."

Metrical and Narrative Structure

Like most retellings of the Rām tale, the *Rāmcaritmānas* loosely follows the structure of the archetypal Sanskrit *Rāmāyana's* seven *kāndas* or books. In the Hindi epic, these are further divided into more than a thousand stanzas of roughly twelve to eighteen lines, set in the predominant narrative meter of *caupāī*, followed by a pithy couplet in *dohā*, the favored Hindi meter for folk aphorisms. Occasional bursts of lyrical four-line *chand* meter, at moments of high emotion, provide additional variety. All the meters feature end-rhymes, and these, combined with the complex patterns of internal rhyme and alliteration for which Tulsīdās is justly famed, give the work an extraordinarily rhythmic and musical quality, which, needless to say, eludes translation; no fewer than seven complete English renderings, alas, vie with one another in their prosaic bludgeoning of the text.

The narrative structure of the epic is particularly noteworthy, comprising a series of four interlocking dialogs between gods, divine sages, and exemplary devotees that both frame, and offer a philosophical and devotional commentary on, the unfolding adventures of Rām and his companions. One of the four narrators is Tulsīdās himself, who addresses his audience directly in a lengthy invocation, a briefer epilogue, and through periodic "signature verses" (bearing the poet's name) such as are characteristic of much *bhakti* poetry. Another narrator is Shiva, the patron deity of Banaras and, like Vishnu, one of the high gods of classical Hinduism; his fervent devotion to Rām's tale reflects Tulsīdās's evident wish to synthesize diverse strands of the Hindu tradition and to transcend narrow sectarian differences. A further narrative frame is offered by a lengthy allegory that likens the epic to the holy Mānas lake, located high in the Himalayas at the foot of Mount Kailasa, and from which the text derives its name. This complex narrative design ingeniously situates the epic within a multiform oral tradition, and prefigures its own retelling and elaboration by later generations of commentators and storytellers.

Performance and Interpretation

As a text that straddles the divide between written and oral traditions, the *Mānas* is perhaps best understood, in its historical utilization, as a script or blueprint that has been adapted to a variety of individual and collective needs. Chanted recitation or singing of the epic (*pāth* or *gānā*) from a written text or from memory, serves both as a spiritual discipline and recreational pastime, and there are regular systems for reciting it annually, or in nine- or thirty-day cycles, bracketed by appropriate rituals. In the twentieth century, large scale public

recitation programs have become popular festive events. Recitation accompanied by exposition and commentary (*kathā* or *pravacan*) developed early on into a specialized art form practiced by paid performers known as *Rāmāyanīs* or *vyāsas*, who were often itinerant holy men hired by individual patrons or communities. Their insights into the deeper meaning of the epic have been preserved in numerous written commentaries, but modern devotees continue to derive special satisfaction from listening to their rhetorical performances, which now sometimes circulate on audio and videocassette. The tradition of publicly enacting the *Mānas* story though an annual cycle of outdoor dramas held at the time of the autumn *Dashahrā* festival—the *Rāmlīlā* or "Rām's play"—may have developed in Banaras during Tulsīdās's lifetime, and later grew into an elaborate spectacle under the patronage of the Ramnagar Maharajas. More modest local productions sprang up throughout the Hindi-speaking regions, and today virtually every village and town has a resident amateur *Ramālīlā* troupe. In 1987, the Government of India sponsored a controversial television serialization of the Rām story—heavily influenced by the Tulsīdās version and by folk performance genres like *Rāmlīlā*—that ran for nearly two years and created a nationwide sensation.

The Hindi epic shares with other versions of the Rām story a preoccupation with the problem of *dharma*—understood both as individual duty and as cosmic and societal order. In the twentieth century, much debate has centered on the teachings of the *Mānas* with regard to caste and gender roles. The epic's culminating vision of the utopian regime of Rām—*Rāmrāj*—was constantly invoked by Mahatma Gandhi during the independence struggle, and has been prominently featured in the discourse of Hindu nationalism. Quotations and images from the epic are regularly used by politicians of all persuasions, and the text is periodically defended or assailed in public discourse as egalitarian or elitist, liberating or reactionary—all the while remaining immensely popular. What is clear is that, in creating a literary masterpiece convincingly imbued with scriptural authority and set in the common speech, Tulsīdās forged a uniquely powerful medium for the ongoing production, interpretation, and transmission of Hindu culture.

PHILIP LUTGENDORF

Further Reading

Translations

Allchin, F. Raymond, trans. *Tulsi Das, The Petition to Ram.* London: George Allen and Unwin, 1966. An adequate if not lyrical translation of the song anthology *Vinay patrikā*, Tulsīdās's second most famous work, including a solid introduction.

Growse, Frederic Salmon, trans. *The Rāmāyaṇa of Tulasīdāsa.* New Delhi: Motilal Banarsidass, 1978. First published in 1891, this earliest complete English translation remains the most readable, despite occasional lapses into Victorian doggerel.

Hill, W. D. P., trans. *The Holy Lake of the Acts of Rāma.* London: Oxford University Press, 1952. Albeit more scholarly than Growse's effort, this accurate prose translation is regrettably turgid.

Related Studies

Babineau, Edmour J. *Love of God and Social Duty in the Rāmcaritmānas.* Delhi: Motilal Banarsidass, 1979. A textual study of the epic, focusing on the interplay of devotional and ethical themes and their relationship to the cultural and religious context of sixteenth century north India.

Hess, Linda, and Richard Schechner. "The Ramlila of Ramnagar." The *Drama Review* 21 (September 1977): 51–82. An illustrated introduction to Banaras's most famous *Rāmlīlā* pageant.

Lutgendorf, Philip. *The Life of a Text: Performing the* Rāmcaritmānas *of Tulsīdās.* Berkeley and Los Angeles: University of California Press, 1991. An in-depth study, based on extensive fieldwork, of the oral performance traditions (*pāth, kathā,* and *Rāmlīlā*) and cultural impact of Tulsīdās's masterpiece.

Richman, Paula, ed. *Many Rāmāyaṇas: The Diversity of a Narrative Tradition in South Asia.* Berkeley and Los Angeles: University of California Press, 1991. Although it contains relatively little on Tulsīdās's Hindi epic, this scholarly anthology offers an excellent introduction to the scope of the encompassing pan-Indian tradition of Rām narrative.

THE WORKS OF RAMMOHUN ROY

Author: Raja Rammohun Roy
Born: May 22, 1772, Bengal, India
Died: September 27, 1833, Bristol, England
Major Works: *A Gift to Deists* (1803), *Translation of an Abridgment of the Vedanta* (1815), *The Precepts of Jesus, A Guide to Peace and Happiness* (1820)
Literary Form: Prose expositions

Major Themes

There is a single source of creation.
God is one, not many.
All human beings are equal; women are equal to men.
There should be no distinction of caste.

The Hindu Renaissance movement gained considerable strength in the early nineteenth century, the time during which several Western powers had established themselves in India. Among the Hindus there were those who were disgusted with the corrupt Muslim rule and welcomed these modern powers. There were others who resisted the change and clung tenaciously to tradition. For the social reformers of the Indian Renaissance, it was not a matter of either wholesale rejection of the tradition or acceptance of the modern; it was not an "either-or" dilemma. The Hindu reformers embraced those elements of the traditional religion that retained their validity, relevance, and legitimacy, while rejecting obsolete elements that hindered the revival and regeneration of Hinduism.

The first of the really remarkable Hindu reformers was Rammohun Roy (Ram Mohun Roy), who was given the title "the Raja" by the British government. The Raja was born in an orthodox Hindu *brāhmana* family; his father was a *Vaishnava* (a devotee of the cult of Vishnu), his mother a *shakta* (a devotee of the cult of Shakti, adherents of the female principle).

At the age of twelve, Roy went to Patna to study at the Muslim University. He learned Arabic and Persian and became interested in Sufism. As a result, he developed an aversion to idol worship, an issue over which he had a falling out with his conservative father. He left home for Tibet, where he acquired knowledge of Buddhism. Once again, his campaign against Buddhist idolatry aroused the anger of Lamas and he was forced to leave Tibet, returning home. His return rearoused the former tensions at home, and so he left home for Banaras to learn Sanskrit and the ancient Hindu scriptures. During these days, he also began to study English, which resulted in his securing a job in the East India Company as a revenue officer in 1803.

During his tenure in the East India Company, he developed close ties with Unitarian missionaries. He regularly attended Unitarian services for a few years (1824–28) and began to consider himself a "Hindu Unitarian." He soon realized however, that Unitarianisn did not suit his beliefs and principles; he left the Company, and devoted himself to religious and social reforms. He set for himself the task of purifying Hinduism by sweeping away the cobwebs of cruel social customs and religious superstitions. He went to England in 1830, became ill, and died in Bristol, England, in 1833.

A Gift to Deists

The Raja's first publication, *Tuhfat al-Muwāhhiddīn (A Gift to Deists)*, was written in Persian, except for a one-page introduction in Arabic. At the outset of the introduction, Raja notes his belief in one, universal God: "I travelled in the remotest part of the world, in plains as well as in hilly lands, and I found the inhabitants thereof agreeing generally in believing in the existence of one Being who is the source of creation and governor of it. . . ." However, the various worshipers assigned this "being" different attributes and practiced varying modes of worship.

The experiences of diversity of belief led Roy to make a distinction between the natural and the conditioned. Whereas belief in one eternal being is common to all individuals and all religions, attributes assigned to God or gods, forms of worship, religious customs, and beliefs in miracles are accidental features of religion that are the results of habit and training.

This distinction became the basis of his universal religion. For the Raja, intuition yields an all-wise sovereign deity as the source of creation. It is a belief, simple, undefiled, and natural. This forms the starting point of all religions. Differences thus are not over the existence of God but over the nature of God. Some believe in a God qualified by personal attributes; there are others who are atheists; and there are still others who believe in a being that extends over nature. He reiterates that those who make such distinctions do not distinguish between the natural and the acquired; belief in a being as the source of creation is an indispensable characteristic of humankind; it is natural, not acquired.

With this in mind, Roy accepted certain elements of Hinduism, Islam, and Christianity and rejected others. His study of institutionalized religions consisted of a three-fold process of rejection, affirmation, and modification. He studied the ancient scriptures of these religions and made them accessible to all.

Translation of an Abridgment of the Vedanta

With regard to Hinduism, he studied the Vedas, translated several of the Upanishads, and published his *Translation of an Abridgement of the Vedānta*. He studied the Upanishads and the Vedānta Sūtras and arrived at the conclusion that they taught monotheism free of polytheism and idolatry. He opposed the polytheistic ritualism of the Vedas;

God is to be worshiped only in its pure form, a realization of the Divine in every human being. He viewed salvation as union with God, the chief goal of the human religious pursuit. He affirmed that God manifests in many ways, and is both transcendent and omnipresent. He rejected Hinduism's numerous Gods and rituals, practice of idol worship, the notion of rebirth, and many social practices he deemed harmful to the human spirit. His goal was to revive Hinduism as a truly national religion fit to meet the demands of the emergent India.

The Raja rejected Islam's intolerance of the views of other religions and proselytization of its own. However, some aspects of Islam appealed to him. He was impressed by Islam's strict monotheism or emphasis on the unity of the Godhead— "There is none other than Allah." He was also impressed by Islam's rejection of caste, its lack of a priestly class, and its emphasis on the priesthood of all believers and its simplicity and directness. It was Islam that appealed to him first and made him a confirmed monotheist.

The Precepts of Jesus

Finally, with regard to Christianity, Roy again opposed the Christian missionaries proselytization. He was unable to accept the Christian belief in the divinity of Jesus and atonement. He was attracted however, by the basic moral principles of the New Testament. He extracted from Christianity its ethical precepts, and rejected the divinity of Christ just as he rejected the Hindu notion of *avatāra* (incarnation). He presents his secular analysis of the New Testament in *The Precepts of Jesus, A Guide to Peace and Happiness*. In this publication, the Raja rejects irrationality, superstition, miracles, and dogmas in very strong terms, while at the same time expanding on a theme that concerned him greatly, the relation between religion and morality. While this publication strips the New Testament of many of its basic doctrines, it highlights Jesus' humanitarian ethics as the essence of the text. By articulating conceptions of religion in moral terms, he was able to make moral principles the bases of social reform.

In the Raja's world view, we find an acceptance of the philosophy of the European Enlightenment and the nineteenth-century English social and political liberalism that characterizes the works of John Stuart Mill. The emphasis on the dignity of each individual, the value of liberty, brotherhood, justice, and equality are some of the characteristic features of such a world view. He was not a narrow nationalist whose sole concern was with the good of Hindus; he was equally concerned about the well being of humankind as a whole.

Western values appealed to Roy because he himself believed in them. They reinforced his universalistic outlook. He believed in the inherent worth of each individual regardless of their social and economic status. The Raja's belief in equality among human beings led him to oppose the caste system. In the eyes of God, all human beings are equal. Since God did not make any distinctions among human beings, we should not make them either. This further led him to launch a vigorous campaign against the low status of women in India.

The Immolation of Widows

During Roy's time, the practice of *sati* (suttee) was prevalent in Bengal. The term *sati* was originally used for a "true and virtuous" widow who willingly allowed herself to be burnt on the funeral pyre of her husband. Eventually, the act of self-immolation itself incorrectly came to be referred as *sati*. This rite was regarded as sparing widows from impure temptations by forcing them to immolate themselves. When a woman did not willingly commit *sati*, she was often pushed into the fire after being bathed and attired elegantly. As a boy, the Raja witnessed the forced *sati* of his sister-in-law, who was very dear to him. This barbarous ritual of women-slaughter stirred him profoundly, and he vowed to devote his life to the abolition of this inhumane ritual. The British officials allowed this atrocity to go on as part of their policy of non-infringement of religious freedom. The Brahmin pandits provided legitimation for this custom by

their novel interpretations of the Rig Vedic concepts of *karma* and *dharma*.

The Raja organized a movement to abolish *sati*. His opposition to this atrocious ritual took various forms: he submitted petitions to the East India Company, organized vigilance committees, and published two tracts on the issue, the first one in 1818 and the second in 1820. The first tract describes *sati* as "the violation of every human and social feeling." To the traditionalists for whom this was atonement for the sins of their husbands and assurance of heavenly life for the wife with her husband, the Raja emphatically declared that each is responsible for his/her own sins and that there are other ways of accomplishing the atonement. He cited the Laws of Manu, pointing out that it gives the widows another option: the option of leading an ascetic life and performing austere duties.

The first tract was followed by a second in which he questioned the prevailing assumptions about the status of women. He argued that the low opinion of women is responsible for widow-burning. Proponents of *sati* argued that women are naturally inferior to men; they are untrustworthy. The wiles of womanhood are all powerful and dangerously seductive; should they survive their husbands they would bring disgrace to their respective families. The Raja argued that the claim that women are inferior to men cannot be validated because women have not been given equal opportunities; they have been denied education. The claim that women are generally untrustworthy, argues the Raja, is similarly invalid because the number of women deceived is ten times more than the number of men deceived. He further pointed out that virtue belongs in the column of women and not men, because women quietly suffer injustices in a male-dominated society. He campaigned for granting equal property rights to women and men, for widow remarriages, and against child marriage. The Raja was able to demonstrate that *sati* has neither moral nor religious sanctions and that abolition of it was not against the Hindu scriptures. His efforts succeeded, and the anti-*sati* law was passed in 1829 under Lord Bentick's administration.

Belief in One Creator as Basis of Universal Religion

Another of the Raja's important achievements was the foundation of *Brahmo Samāj*. It began in 1828 as *Brahma Sabhā*; it consisted of small groups of people of theistic outlook who practiced purified Hinduism. They recited Vedic texts, read the Upanishads, and sang hymns. It opposed idolatry, the caste system, child marriage, untouchability, and widow-burning, and it supported widow remarriages and intercaste marriages. The various activities of Samāj provided further impetus to the national reform and social awakening in India. The two important pillars of *Brahmo Samāj* were belief in a single Godhead and brotherhood among human beings.

In his *Brahmo Samāj*, the Raja was able to combine the precepts of Hinduism, Islam, and Christianity. Brotherhood among fellow human beings went a long way toward removing the social evils and distinctions Hindu orthodoxy tried to impose, and his conception of monotheism expressed his desire to synthesize the three religions. He made the common essence of them—the belief in the one Godhead as the Creator—the basis of his universal religion, which the Raja believed, would be accepted by all regardless of caste, creed, and religion.

Some philosophers are critical of the idea of universal religion; they believe the essence of all religions cannot be *a* religion. They further deny that the one Godhead of such a universal religion can be part of the essence of all religions.

However, in this context, we must keep in mind the Raja was not a systematic academic philosopher, nor was he a theologian. He was a student of religion, specifically, of comparative religion. In the Hindu Reformation movement of the nineteenth century, social and political reforms went hand in hand with religious reforms. His interest in the subject, combined with his interest in social reforms, resulted in his suggesting changes in several religions. It is not possible to view these changes as stemming from pure theological positions lacking any kind of social and political

agenda. Religion was employed as a tool to effect social reform; the Raja used it effectively to accomplish his goals.

The Father of Modern India

Raja Ram Mohun Roy had a clear vision of India's future. He was very well aware that every national renaissance glorifies the achievements of the past. This nostalgia characterized not only the French Renaissance but also the British Reformation; the Indian Renaissance should be no exception. Therefore, his universal religion, which profoundly influenced the writings of later scholars, such as Gandhi and Radhakrishnan, assimilated the best elements of the traditional religions. His *Brahmo Samāj* became one of the most influential movements in nineteenth-century India. Although the Raja lived for only four years after its inception, the *Samāj* grew in membership and by 1866 there were fifty-four branches of *Brahmo Samāj*. The movement made it possible for Indians in the last two centuries to meet the challenges the British rule had imposed on them without compromising their own tradition. It is not an exaggeration to say that the *Brahmo Samāj* movement was a major force in reawakening a national consciousness which eventually resulted in political regeneration, the formation of the Indian National Congress in 1885, and India's independence from the British rule. Thus, it should come as no surprise that Raja Rammohun Roy was called the Father of Modern India, and was honored as "the Raja," a true monarch among human beings.

BINA GUPTA

Further Reading

Crawford, S. Cromwell. *Ram Mohan Roy: Social Political and Religious Reform in the 19th Century India*. New York: Paragon House, 1987. This is one of the most recent clearly written book on the Raja's thoughts.

Ghose, J. C. *The English Works of Raja Rammohun*

Roy. Calcutta: Srikant Publishers, 1901. This is one of the best studies of the works of Raja Ram Mohun Roy.

Kopf, David. *The Brahmo Samāj and the Shaping of the Modern Indian Mind.* Princeton; NJ: Princeton University Press, 1979. This book con-tains a perceptive analysis of the forces that shaped modern India.

Sarma, D. S. *Studies in the Renaissance of Hinduism.* Banaras: Banaras Hindu University, 1944. This work contains an illuminating analysis of the Hindu Renaissance.

THE POETRY OF GHALIB

Author: Asadullah Khan Ghalib (Mirza Ghalib)
Born: 1797, Agra, India
Died: 1869, Delhi, India
Major Poetic Works: In Urdu: *Diwan-i-Ghalib*, in Persian: *Kulliyat-i-Nasir-i-Ghalib*

Major Themes

Sorrow is inherent and inevitable in life; grief itself gives pleasure and becomes a remedy as man endures it.
Enjoy whatever life has to offer.
The finest antidote for pain is wine: nothing can bring more pleasure.
Life is a perpetual struggle in search of happiness and the fulfillment of desires.
God is the supreme being.
Human beings are prisoners in this world: all events are predestined.
All human beings are equal; so are different religions.

A distinctive survivor of the turbulent decades of nineteenth-century India, Asadullah Khan Ghalib has a unique place in Urdu literature. His verse transcends the constraints of time and space. His verbal ingenuity churned out captivating verses on love, loneliness, complexities of life, and the relationship with God. Ghalib lived in an unsettled era of political and social changes. Between a dying order and an emerging system, we find balance in his poetry.

Ghalib best represents the "newness" in Urdu poetry. He excelled in composing ghazals. (A ghazal consists of a series of couplets, each independent of the other. There is no set length as such, although the least number of couplets in a ghazal is usually five.) Ghalib unshackled the genre of ghazal from the conventional rigidities and infused it with an unequivocal cadence. In fact, he is the finest exponent of Urdu ghazals, along with Mir Taqi Mir, his predecessor. Mundane themes like "the beloved" and "wine," with Ghalib's touch become extraordinary and glorified. He had the beautiful gift of presenting the worn-out in an entirely new light and with entirely meaning. He repeatedly came up with something fresh and palatable:

Though hands cannot move, the eyes at least have
life

Let the jug of wine and the goblet stay in front of me.

(AIJAZ AHMAD, TRANS., 1971)

His is a sound sleep, a profound composure, and his
are the nights
On whose arms have rolled your waving locks.

(ALI JAWAD ZAIDI, TRANS., 1993)

Ghalib was born in Agra. His date of birth is generally accepted as 27 December, 1797. Ghalib's ancestry goes back to Turkish aristocracy, the founders of the Seljuk dynasty. His grandfather had come to India to look for better fortune. Ghalib's father, Abdullah Beg Khan Bahadur, was a soldier who died in a battle in Alwar when Ghalib was only five years old. His mother and siblings were looked after by his uncle Nasarullah Beg Khan Bahadur. Unfortunately, he too died in a battle when Ghalib was eight. This was the beginning of a life of hardships for him. At the age of thirteen he was married to Umrao Begum, a woman from the well-educated, rich family of a Mughal nobleman, and moved to Delhi.

Ghalib started to write verse around the age of nine or ten. As a young teenager he adopted the pseudonym "*Asad*" (Lion). Later, he on preferred "*Ghalib*" (Conqueror) as a *takhallus* (adopted name)—this is how he is known and remembered

TOSA DIARY

Title in Japanese: *Tosa nikki*
Author: Ki no Tsurayuki
Born: c. 872
Died: c. 945
Literary Form: Diary and travel record
Date of Composition: c. 935

Major Themes

Women can write like men, and men like women.

All creatures are given to song, whether in sadness or in joy, and the song of our language is our heart and soul.

To return to the capital is to live again; whatever the hardship, celebrate the journey.

Most precious to the parent is the child.

To each singer and to each occasion there is an appropriate style.

One of the most confounding works of Japanese literature wears a mask more concealing yet more transparent than any other. "A woman will try to manage one of those things called diaries that men write." So begins *Tosa nikki*, a cross-dressed performance by the premier male vernacularist of his day, Ki no Tsurayuki. He was the champion of Japanese letters when male bureaucrats kept daily records in Chinese, and by styling himself a woman in the entourage of ex-governor Ki no Tsurayuki, the author claimed to break through the gender barrier for diarists. Yet he took with him a load of Sinified phrases that betrayed his disguise. Over a millennium later, Tsurayuki entices the reader to mull this impish, but surely meaningful, authorial choice.

Long before the *Tosa Diary*, Tsurayuki was at the heart of a movement to revive native poetics. Descendant of a family with remarkable literary achievements, the young poet made his name in competitive poetry meets and the production of verses for folding screens. The compilation of the first imperial anthology of native *waka* poetry, the *Kokinshū*, or *Collection of Poems Ancient and Modern*, centered on him, and it was he who wrote the vernacular Preface that called for the elevation of Japanese verse to serious art. The compendium includes 102 of his compositions; he is judged a conservative in a tradition that favored creativity within strict bounds. His participation in the anthologizing process secured his prominence, but as a member of the Ki family in an age when the Fujiwara kept all others from the heights of power, Tsurayuki's political future was dim.

Tsurayuki's choice of Japanese for prose ventures that more commonly would have been written in the lingua franca of East Asia was deliberate and politically charged. He was biliterate if not bilingual, because, in their professional lives, men used the written Chinese language. His bureaucratic duties at one point ran to drafting memorials and recording ranks in the imperial secretariat. As a lower-level courtier, he was three times appointed to the provinces. His return from the last of his distasteful posts, the governorship of Tosa, provided the material for his journal. If his bold writing habits did not gain him temporal influence in his own time, they did make him a voice to be reckoned with throughout literary history.

The Narrative Patterns of a Sea Voyage

Tosa nikki follows the ex-governor and his party from their embarkation in southern Shikoku to their homecoming 55 days later. Entries are daily—some terse, most interspersed with verses to this day. Some of his contemporaries fondly referred to him as "*Mirza*." He started writing verses in Urdu at an early age. By the time he was thirteen he was already known for writing quality verses. He had no *Ustad* (teacher), contrary to the prevalent tradition. In his letters, he talks remorsefully about his inadequate knowledge and literary weaknesses. (Some critics, however, believe that he did have a Zoarastrian scholar as a teacher.)

Most of his life, Ghalib struggled to get what he financially deserved. He spent much time trying to restore his family pension—in fact, a major part of his life was spent appealing in vain to the British authorities. In 1869, after a prolonged illness, Ghalib died at the age of seventy-two, and was buried in Nizamuddin, in Delhi.

The Poetry of Ghalib

In the Indian subcontinent, Ghalib is still the most widely read and quoted poet. His verses have the unique quality of being understood by both intellectuals and casual readers. If one can get into the depths of his metaphors and imagery, the other finds pleasure in whatever the poet says. Ghalib refers to his Urdu poetry as "things I write to earn bread." (See *Russell and Islam*, 1969.) It was his *Persian* poetry that he held in high esteem. He wrote it with incomparable style, and order, and took great pride in it:

Look at my Persian ; there you see the full range of
*   my artistry*
And leave aside my Urdu verse, for there is nothing
*   there for me.*

(RUSSELL AND ISLAM, TRANS., 1969)

Elsewhere he remarks:

I make no claims to be an Urdu poet:
My object was to please your Majesty.

(RUSSELL AND ISLAM, TRANS., 1969)

However, Ghalib's personal bias in favor of Persian does not mean that his Urdu poetry is not

written with a felicity and style that is unparalleled. In fact, he continues to be the favorite and most widely read poet in the Urdu language. Ghalib was opposed to following the prevalent and the common. He skillfully used his imagination and sharpness of mind to be unique. The diction of many of his ghazals is highly Persianized, liberally using Persian phrases and words in his Urdu ghazals to embellish them. He exhibited the Persian trait of being indirect in his verses. Through his verbal play and techniques, Ghalib primarily appealed the intellect. This set him apart from most of his peers, who, following tradition, dealt fundamentally with emotions:

If our apprehensions have such intensity of heat, we
*   should abandon*
*   the heart that suffers.*
The glass goblet is about to melt because of the heat
*   of the wine.*

(AHMAD, TRANS., 1971)

Ghalib appeals to the emotions only after the intellectual faculties have been prompted to find in-depth meanings. He presents a profound thought as an image first and then explains it in the second line of the couplet. The flow of his stirring words and ebullient imagery sustains the interest of the reader:

Asad! my shadow runs from me like smoke
My soul is on fire; who can stay near me.

(AHMAD, TRANS., 1971)

The imagery used by Ghalib is often obscure, much like that of the English Metaphysical poets. This obscurity of imagery was not appreciated by his contemporaries, who were more used to direct references to objects.

The wing of the north was perhaps the sail
of the boat of wine, for with the warmth
of the festive company the round
of cups has gathered momentum.

(ALI, TRANS., 1973)

Ghalib's poetry is replete with sorrow and despondency. Yet it is in no way pessimistic. Because of his master craftsmanship couplets are chiselled and refined; the expression of his painful experiences is profoundly moving, rather than depressing:

> When man knows pain, then pain itself
> Disappears. So great
> Have been my sufferings that grief
> Is easy to endure.

> (ALI, TRANS., 1973)

His experiences of suffering included the death of all of his seven children, as well as the death of his wife's nephew, Zain Ul Abidin Khan Arif, who was very dear to the poet. Arif died in 1852, and Ghalib wrote a poignant and moving elegy on the occasion of his death:

> On your way out you said that we shall meet next on
>   the doomsday,
> As if there was yet another day of doom.
> Foolish are they who still wonder why Ghalib is
>   still living;
> It is his fate to stay alive, and wish for his death, a
>   little longer.

> (AHMAD, TRANS., 1971)

Another great sorrow in his life was the death of a woman with whom he had a love affair:

> It was not our good fortune to meet our love.
> However long we lived, we would still be waiting
>   for such an encounter.

> (AHMAD, TRANS., 1971)

Elsewhere, about his misfortunes he wrote:

> You are nightingale, held in a cage
> So that the age may hear your melody.

> (RUSSELL AND ISLAM, TRANS., 1969)

The romantic in Ghalib craved what was not, and bemoaned its absence. This constant strain of

yearning for what could not be is heard in his ghazals. Out of desolation comes his anguished cry for escape into a world of loneliness:

> I wish to go away and live
> In a lonely and forsaken place,
> Where not a soul will talk to me,
> Nor I behold a face.

> (ALI, TRANS., 1973)

Ghalib writes of the universality and inevitability of pain and sorrow:

> The nature of creation itself
>   is sorrowful;
> It is not the kind of pain
> Which can be stopped at will.

> (ALI, TRANS. 1973)

In 1828, in the hope of getting his full pension, he went to Calcutta staying en route in Benaras. Both cities are fondly referred to in his letters. At that time, Calcutta was pulsating with social reform movements and was an active seat of Persian learning, and it bewitched Ghalib. During his two-years' stay, his intellect thrived amidst scholars like Abdul Qadar Rampuri, Nemat Ali, Karam Hussain Bilgrami, and Siraj Ahmad. He was similarly exposed to Western thought and learning. To the poet, it all seemed cheerful and lively after the decadence he had seen in Delhi. The pronounced influence of a modern outlook is discernible in Ghalib's poetry from the very beginning, and the newness and modernity of thought he encountered further enhanced his intellectual capabilities. The Western influences of free thinking and unorthodoxy of styles mark many of his verses. Ghalib was much impressed, and after he returned to Delhi he wrote nostalgic verses of yearning:

> Ah me, my friend! the mention of Calcutta's name
> Has loosed off a shaft that pierces to my very soul.

> (RUSSELL AND ISLAM, TRANS., 1969)

Ghalib had a logical approach towards religion. He had tremendous respect for different sects and religions. His close friends included Hindus, Muslims, and Christians. Despite being a Muslim, Ghalib was known for his love of wine and gambling. Because of his lifestyle, he was accused of being sympathetic to the Shia sect (believing that Ali, the Prophet's son-in-law, was his rightful successor), and an atheist. Unconcerned, he lived and wrote with a style that he held dear. To silence his critics, he makes logical references to what he thought of heavenly bliss and came up with some delicious, mocking couplets:

> *I know the truth of Paradise—*
> *A futile thought but comforting.*

> (ALI, TRANS., 1973)

It is an Islamic belief that after death, a true Muslim goes to Paradise. Ghalib talks of Paradise elsewhere, too, exposing the irony of the situation:

> *For what else should I value Paradise*
> *If not the rose-red wine, fragrant with musk?*

> (RUSSELL, TRANS., 1992)

Ghalib believed in the Prophet, Islam, and prayers. But he did not fast during the month of Ramadan nor say his daily prayers. He could be found gambling, and drinking wine in the company of his friends, rather than in a mosque. He freely admits his own beliefs and conduct:

> *I believe in prayer and worship,*
> *But somehow cannot bring*
> *Myself to practice them.*

> (ALI, TRANS., 1973)

A progressive attitude and modern outlook is clear in his approach towards religion. He was not a fanatic. Many of his ghazals reflect his secular viewpoint. He firmly believed in the unity of existence and the brotherhood of man. He may not have protested explicitly against the establishment, but he did make open references to the narrowmindedness of fundamentalists and hardliners:

> *If your heart be heavy with envy, get lost in the*
> *multitudinous scenes.*
> *May be your narrow outlook broadens in the midst*
> *of the crowded views.*

> (ZAIDI, TRANS., 1993)

The sensuous and the intellectual are both bewildered by the haze of mysticism that wraps beauty and beloved, as Ghalib's mystical temperament unravels itself:

> *Who can tell*
> *Whose is this glorious revelation?*
> *He has let down a veil*
> *Such as none can lift.*

> (HUSSAIN, TRANS., 1977)

And again there is the sense of mystery and its preservation:

> *I fear the secret of the beloved*
> *May become known, otherwise there is*
> *No mystery in dying.*

> (ALI, TRANS., 1973)

Ghalib's ghazals are manifestations of a mind and personality that saw a civilization in flux. With their eloquent intensity the ghazals express a thought process in which the emotional and the intellect become one. In his own words:

> *Take the word which appears*
> *In the poems of Ghalib*
> *To be a treasure*
> *Full of the magic of meaning.*

> (ALI, TRANS., 1973)

PRABHJOT PARMAR

Further Reading

Translations

Ahmad, Aijaz, trans. *Ghazals of Ghalib*. New York and London: Columbia University Press, 1971. A collection of thirty-seven selected ghazals by Ghalib from his Urdu collection; provides an interesting insight into his verses. The translations are literal, with some explanatory notes touching on different themes, as well as Ghalib's philosophy. Most of the ghazals have been further interpreted by various American poets, reflecting Ghalib's poetic spirit. Quotations used in this article from *Ghazals of Ghalib*, copyright © 1972 by Columbia University Press, are reprinted with the permission of the publisher.

Ali, Ahmed. *The Golden Tradition: An Anthology of Urdu Poetry*. New York and London: Columbia University Press, 1973. This collection has about eighty of Ghalib's finest ghazals. The translations are eloquent and are expressive of the poet's spirit. The introductory chapter, "The Molten Flame—The Age of Ghalib," is a detailed historical and creative perspective on the poet. There is also a comparison of style, technique, and themes of Ghalib and certain Western poets, such as Donne and Eliot. A satisfying introduction for the Western or non-Urdu-speaking reader. Quotations used in this article from *The Golden Tradition* by Ali Ahmed: copyright © 1973 by Columbia University Press. Reprinted with permission of the publisher.

Hussain, Yusuf. *Urdu Ghazals of Ghalib*. New Delhi: Ghalib Institute, 1977. A translation of Ghalib's Urdu *Diwan* and also selected verses from the Bhopal Edition *(Nuskha-i-Hamidia)* of his ghazals. The translator has captured the beauty and poetic sensibility of Ghalib, overcoming the language barrier. The meter of the verses is mixed (rhyming and blank), to incorporate meaning and message. The book also contains ghazals in Urdu script, for bilingual readers to read, compare, and enjoy. This is a noteworthy translation, revealing the richness of Urdu literature.

Russell, Ralph, and Khurshidul Islam. *Ghalib: Life and Letters*. London: George Allen and Unwin, 1969. An excellent collection of translations, chiefly of Ghalib's Urdu and Persian letters, his diary, and Hali's *Memoir of Ghalib*. Highlighting his struggles and achievements, this book is invaluable for those who want not only to read but also to understand Ghalib.

Related Studies

Russell, Ralph. *The Pursuit of Urdu Literature: A Select History*. London and New Jersey: Zed Books Ltd., 1992. The essay "Ghazals of Ghalib" reveals the outstanding qualities of the poet. It encapsulates the essential Ghalib with smoothness and cohesion.

Zaidi, Ali Jawad. *A History of Urdu Literature*. New Delhi: Sahitya Akademi, 1993. The chapter entitled "The Twilight and Ghalib" presents Ghalib in a historical perspective in the saga of Urdu literature, emphasizing the changing sociopolitical milieu and its effects. The brief essay also explores the elements of grief and mysticism in Ghalib's poetry.

THE WORKS OF BANKIM CHANDRA CHATTERJEE

Born: June 27, 1838, Kanthalpara, West Bengal, India
Died: April 8, 1894, Calcutta, India
Major Works: *Rajmohan's Wife* (1864), *The Daughter of the Feudal Lord (Durgeshnandini)* (1865), *Mrinalini* (1869), *The Poison Tree (Bishabriksha)* (1873), *Indira* (1873), *Chandrasekhar* (1875), *Krishnakanta's Will* (1878), *Anandamath (Abbey of Bliss)* (1882), *Rajsinha* (1882), *Sitaram* (1887)

Major Themes

Self-control through purification of the mind and body is necessary to happiness and progress.
British rule in India has been a mixed blessing.
Lord Krishna teaches that self-restraint, a religious spirit, and a love that is dutiful lead to the perfection of one's character.
Those who obey the social conventions will prosper, while those who defy them—such as those who break the marriage vows—will suffer.

Bankim Chandra Chatterjee was a deputy magistrate and a deputy collector in the British India Civil Service, but simultaneously he led a life as a writer to satisfy his intellectual, creative, and artistic talents. As a prose writer his versatility earned him the reputation as "father of modern Indian literature." His novels, short stories, and essays covered a wide range of topics including history, romance, mystery, science, religion, politics, nationhood, and social issues. He rose to fame because of his radical change from the tradition of writing in verse or lyrics to writing in a narrative prose style, thus giving new life to Bengali literature. He was not a man of action but remained a concerned thinker regarding the British rule in India and the destiny of his people, and he emphasized the importance of patriotism as a kind of spiritual loyalty to "Mother India."

Like his contemporary Bengali intellectuals—for example, Madhusudan Dutta—Chatterjee began his literary career by writing, in English, *Rajmohan's Wife* (1864). He was perhaps prompted to write in English because he had his high school and college education in that medium. (It is noteworthy that Macaulay's recommendation of the English system of education for India was introduced in 1835, just three years before Chatterjee's birth.) Bankim was a product of this new education with its emphasis on the use of English. But he soon switched to writing in Bengali, his mother tongue, so that his works could be read and understood by the masses and not only by the English-educated alone. His subsequent works were translated into several Indian languages and also into English and he came to be venerated all over India as "*rishi*" or "prophet." Sri Aurobindo Ghose, who translated the patriotic verse *Bandemataram (Hail to the Mother)* into English called him, "a seer and a nation builder."

In spite of his preoccupation with a highly responsible job, Bankim unfolded new facets of his literary talent as he became more mature and gathered life-experiences, especially after witnessing the plight of ordinary people. He lived through a transitional stage, the Bengal Renaissance, and the formation of new social classes under the British administration. It was in 1858 that the Crown took over the rule of India from the trading East India Company (which had not been particularly sensitive to the needs of the natives) and it was in the same year that Bankim began his professional career. He evolved his own sociopolitical and religio-ethical idealism, often reflecting the influence of the East and the West. At the beginning, he addressed social, political, and patriotic issues through historical and romantic novels, but slowly moved to develop spiritual thoughts explaining the manifestation of the Divine. As Professor Sengupta has remarked, "There is one common point in all his writings and that is an emphasis on the necessity for self-control as the key to happiness and greatness."

In his early novels he paints a beautiful picture of social and domestic life in a historical setting mostly of medieval and eighteenth-century Bengal. The descriptive plots and characters are colored by a lively literary imagination and style. His heroes and heroines belong largely to the upper class or nobility, and give new signals to the changing Bengali society, as with the pre-marital love affairs in *Chandrasekhar.* His upper-class upbringing is reflected in these early writings. His father also belonged to the Civil Service (a deputy collector) and had a large estate in Kanthalpara, near Calcutta. It was here that Bankim had his education in Sanskrit and Bengali languages and literature.

The historical novels have a romantic theme as well. Chatterjee did not strictly adhere to established historical facts, but the location, characters, and plots were basically historical. His literary expressions excel in style. *Durgeshnandini* portrays the Muslim Pathan and Muslim Moghul conflicts in sixteenth-century feudal Bengal. For the historical background, he essentially follows Charles Stewarts' *History of Bengal* (1847). In the romantic part of the story he paints a changed attitude toward traditional life. For example, Ayesha, one of the female characters, defends her pre-marital love in opposition to the prevalent practice in Hindu society of arranged marriages.

Mrinalini is designed to show how the last Hindu king of Bengal, Lakshman Sen, was defeated by Muslim Pathan Bakhtiyar Khilji in the thirteenth century. Although Chatterjee was criticized for expressing an anti-Muslim sentiment, he defended his position by saying that the account was primarily designed to show the weaknesses of the Bengali national character. The message was a defense of patriotism.

In this vividly descriptive story he addressed such much-debated and time-tested social issues such as widow remarriage and polygamy. The heroine, Mrinalini, is sacrificial. The message the author gives is that chastity is the greatest virtue for women. A widow should not think of finding a new love. At the same time, he thought it was important that she decide her own fate, arguing that remarriage is not good for everyone. If a widow does fall in love, she should try to overcome it for the sake of *dharma.*

In *Chandrasekhar*, historical incidents are in the background; what is important are human feelings, passion and emotions. Chatterjee portrays the childhood love between Pratap and Shaibalini but shows that the latter marries Chandrasekhar by arrangement. Through Chandrasekhar's character, Bankim develops his belief in "yoga," self-control, purification of mind and body. There were two kinds of love: pure love and socially acceptable love.

Rajsinha, the only historical novel where the setting is outside Bengal, essentially describes the struggle between the Rajput Hindu king and the Mogal emperor. It focuses on the heroic effort and patriotism of the Hindu king. Many critics have argued that this work displays Chatterjee's anti-Muslim attitude, but the author defends his position by stating that since there are good rulers and bad rulers in history, this is what he concentrates upon, rather than the influence of race or religion.

The influence of ancient Sanskrit literature is evident in *Poison Tree (Bishabriksha)*, *Rajini*, *Krishrakanta's Will*, and *Indira*, all of which are concerned with social and domestic issues and values.

Krishnakanta's Will

Krishnakanta's Will is the story of a married man, Govindlal, the nephew of Krishnakanta, who, despite being married to the faithful Bhramar, falls in love with the flirtatious widow Rohini (who by Hindu code is not to marry again). Rohini is persuaded by Haralal, Krishnakanta's elder son, to steal Krishnakanta's will and to put in its place a forged will that provides Haralal with the bulk of the inheritance and deprives Govindlal of the portion due him because of the death of Krishnakanta's brother Ramkanta. The story, told with charming simplicity and a kind of seductive literary intimacy between the author and the reader, is the story of the fall of Rohini and Govindlal, and its moral is clear and unconditional: If one departs from duty and virtue, the outcome will be calamitous, and peace will be found only if one realizes one's guilt and puts oneself in the hands of God.

After murdering Rohini and being acquitted of the killing, and also suffering from the death of Bhramar, from whom he did not have the humility to ask for forgiveness, Govindlal disappears for twelve years of a penitential retreat and returns briefly at the end of the period of penance to bless his nephew Sachikanta, who has inherited the property. When Sachikanta urges him to stay and enjoy his share of the property, Govindlal replies, "I have found a treasure which is greater than all properties and estates . . . and it is sweeter and more holy than even Brahmar. I have found peace. I have no need of the property. Let it remain yours." (Ghosh, trans., 1962).

When Govindlal is asked whether peace can be found in asceticism, he replies, "No, never. I only put on this monk's garment because it is suitable to a life of obscurity. Only by offering one's mind at the feet of God can peace be found. God alone is now my property, my Brahmar, and my more than Brahmar." (Ghosh, trans., 1962) He then disappears again.

Prophet of Nationalism

Much of what Chatterjee wrote in his novels was in the guise of historical fiction or romances, but the underlying theme was the championing of Bengali and national patriotism, culminating in his widely admired novel, *Anandamath (Abbey of Bliss)*.

Sri Aurobindo has commented that Chatterjee converted the Indian masses to a "religion of patriotism." Having become aware of pervasive lawlessness, the misery of the people, and the persistence of social injustice in Bengal, Chatteerjee devoted his time to writing to improving society through fostering an allegiance to a nation under the influence of the Hindu ideals.

As Chatteerjee was a government employee, he did not take a direct part in politics or political agitation. In his writings, he made a national appeal to the people to search their own rich nonsectarian cultural heritage and to take pride in their mother tongue. Inspired by him, the revolutionary "*Swadeshi*" ("Rule your own country") movement gained momentum. His novel *Anandamath* incorporated varied themes—romance, history, religion, natural calamity, human sufferings, atonement, and so forth. But the dominant theme remained a new patriotism inspired by Hindu values.

The novel suggests that British rule in India had both its good and bad features. It has been argued that to some degree Chatterjee's attitude was contradictory because, in the opinion of the political critics, patriotism and British rule could not go hand in hand. Sisir Kumar Das, for example, writes: "He makes an attempt to harmonize the contradictory ideas—one that of militant patriotism directed against the British rule and the other that of necessity as well as the beneficial aspect of British rule."

Anandamath contains the poem *Bandemataram* ("Hail to the Mother"), equating love of Bengal, the "Mother," with love of the female aspect of the Hindu deity. The poem as a song became the Indian national anthem.

Anandamath is a novel based on the Sannyasi ascetics' rebellion in Bengal in the late eighteenth century. The story centers around a rich householder, Mahendra, whose wife and daughters are kidnapped by a group of Sannyasis, who have resorted to raids and robbery to further their cause. When Mahendra finally locates his family at Anandamath (the Abbey of Bliss), he is intrigued and even charmed by Bhavananda, both a mild anchorite and a warring hero. The song *Bandemataram* is sung by Bhavananda to Mahendra, and it becomes clear that the Sannyasis regard Bengal as the mother goddess, to whom all must give allegiance. Bhavananda argues that the Sannyasis are not really robbers because what they take from the Mussulman (Muslim) king does not rightfully belong to him, but rather to the people. Mahendra is tempted to join the group, but when he is told that he cannot be with his wife and daughter until the mission of deposing the Mussulman king is completed, he refuses to take the vow.

The novel inspired the Bengalis and encouraged a swelling of the forces of Hindu nationalism, but at the same time it handicapped the moderate reformers and added to the antagonism between Hindus and Muslims.

The Prophet of Hinduism

In his writings Bankim Chandra Chatterjee moved slowly toward new interpretations of Hindu philosophy, scriptures, and popular religious beliefs. He was far removed from any positivist philosophy (which to some degree had earlier appealed to him) when he stated that society is essential to the practice of *dharma*. His religious views were developed in such essays as *Dharmatattwa, Krishnacharitra,* and *Letters on Hinduism*, and in his incomplete commentary on the *Bhagavad Gita* (Song of God).

Chatterjee believed in Lord Krishna and worshiped him. In *Krishnacharitra*, he wrote that Krishna preached something vital and universal for all mankind. He emphasized that to build a perfect character one must practice self-restraint. He portrayed Lord Krishna as "God incarnate," the embodiment of the true religious spirit.

His critical commentary on the *Bhagavad Gita* contended that the work provided a perfect doctrine of the spiritual life, and of human culture. He placed the sacred text as supreme among all the religious texts of the world.

Chatterjee started and edited the journal *Bangadarshan* in 1872. It encouraged intellectual contributions from eminent writers. It published articles on history, science, philosophy, and literature, and featured reflections on the temper of the age. Finally, it became an important organ for writing in Bengali about cultural and social issues, especially concerning the transitional society under British rule. It was in this journal that many of his articles were serialized. He also popularized the positivism of Auguste Comte (1798–1857) and the Utilitarian theory of John Stuart Mill (1806–1873) by writing in Bengali about these Western ideas. He encouraged harmony between the East and the West, but he also argued that the native art forms— singing, music and dancing—must also be cultivated.

Although Chatterjee played a significant role in the growth of Hindu nationalism (and thus shares the responsibility for the difficulties that the movement caused), he is perhaps best remembered as a consummate literary artist who made the Bengali language an effective instrument for both the expression of ideals and the portrayal of the conflicts and triumphs of human beings in their interaction with one another.

KRISHNA LAHIRI

Further Reading

Translations

Ghosh, J. C., trans. *Krishnakanta's Will.* New York: New Directions, 1962. A beautiful translation of a novel that many consider Chatterjee's best. Ghose's introduction is both informative and critically appreciative of Chatterjee's accomplishments as a Bengali writer.

Ghose, Aurobindo, trans. *The Abbey of Bliss: A Translation of Bankim Chandra Chatterjee's Anandamath.* Calcutta: P. M. Neogi, 1906.

———. *Collected Poems and Plays.* 2 vols. Pondicherry: Sri Aurobindo Ashram, 1942.

Related Studies

Das, Sisir Kumar. *The Artist in Chains: The Life of Bankimchandra Chatterji.* New Delhi: New Statesman Publishing Co., 1984.

Halder, M. K. *Renaissance and Reaction in Nineteenth Century Bengal: Bankimchandra Chattopadhyay.* Calcutta: Minerva Associates, 1977.

THE POETRY OF RABINDRANATH TAGORE

Author: Rabindranath Tagore
Born: May 7, 1861, Calcutta, India
Died: August 7, 1941, Calcutta, India
Major Works: In English: *Gitanjali* (1912), *The Gardener* (1913), *The Crescent Moon* (1913); in Bengali: *Prabhat Sangeet (Morning Songs)* 1883, *Mānasi (The Lady of the Mind)* 1890, *Sonār Tari (The Golden Boat)* 1894, *Naibedya (Offerings)* 1901, *Gitānjali (Song Offerings)* 1912, *Balākā (Wild Geese)* 1916, *Patra-put (Plate of Leaves)* 1936, *Naba-jatak (The Newly Born)* 1940, *Ses Lekhā (Last Writing)* 1941.

Major Themes

The human being is at home in nature, and beauty of nature evokes human love.
Human love is a prelude to love for the Universe.
The infinite manifests itself in the finite.
The human and nature, the human and the human, the human and society, the human and the Divine—all are bound to each other by love.
Human beings attain their highest good by transcending their egos.

Rabindranath Tagore has been acclaimed as perhaps the greatest literary figure in Indian history. In sheer quantity of work, few writers can equal him. His writings include more than one thousand poems and over two thousand songs, in addition to thirty-eight plays, twelve novels, two hundred short stories and innumerable essays and letters covering every important social, political and cultural issue of his time. He was awarded the Nobel Prize for Literature in 1913.

Tagore shines forth as one of the brightest stars in the firmament of world poetry. He wrote poems covering virtually every theme important to man. Above all, he was the poet of love—love of humanity, nature, children, nation, the Universe, God, and death. His love poured forth in magical verses for almost sixty years—from his first book of poems when he was twenty to his last book published after his death. He dictated his last poem on his deathbed.

Rabindranath Tagore was born into a very distinguished Bengali family. His grandfather, Dwarkanath (1794–1846), became one of Calcutta's leading business magnates and cultural leaders. "Prince" Dwarkanath was a friend of Raja Rammohun Roy, the architect of Indian Renaissance. Rabindranath's father, Debendranath (1817–

1905), although competent in business affairs, was spiritually inclined and spent much of his time in religious pursuits. He was called *Maharishi* (the Great Sage). The Tagores lived in an exciting ambience of culture, music, and amateur theatricals, and it was natural that young Rabindranath was drawn to the arts. His most important childhood experience was a tour of the Himalayas with his father. The beauty of nature, the religious personality of his father, and the daily recital of verses from the *Upanishads* made an indelible impression on him.

Tagore started writing poetry in his early teens. In 1882, his first major volume of poetry, *Sandhya Sangeet* (Evening Songs) was published. This was the beginning of a steady stream of poems that flowed from the poet throughout his long life. His command of Bengali verse in his very first book was greeted by the public. Bankim Chandra Chatterjee, Bengal's preeminent literary figure, was among his admirers. *Sandhya Sangeet* was a work of subjective lyrical poetry, expressing the yearnings of an isolated and brooding self, in despair and longing for love and freedom. The emergence of the self into light and life in the next work, *Prabhat Sangeet* (Morning Songs), was the direct result of Rabindranath's formative spiritual experience. The poet writes, "When I was eighteen, a sudden breeze of religious experience came to my life for the first time and passed away leaving in my memory a direct message of spiritual reality" *(My Reminiscences)*. He continues, "One morning I happened to be standing on the verandah. . . . The Sun was just rising through the leafy top of those trees. As I continued to gaze, all of a sudden a covering seemed to fall away from my eyes, and I found the world bathed in a wonderful radiance, with waves of beauty and joy swelling on every side. This radiance pierced in a moment through the folds of sadness and despondency which had accumulated over my heart and flooded it with this universal light.

"That very day the poem, 'The Awakening of the Waterfall,' gushed forth and coursed on like a veritable cascade. The poem came to an end but the curtain did not fall upon the joy aspect on the universe."

From then on, Tagore's best poems were suffused with the idea that a deeper reality underlies all phenomena and that the universe is the music of the Infinite playing through finite forms. Tagore wrote, "I had long viewed the world with external vision only . . . when of a sudden, from some innermost depth of my being, a ray of light found its way out, it spread over and illuminated for me the whole universe. . . . This experience seemed to tell me of the stream of melody issuing from the very heart of the universe and spreading over space and time, re-echoing thence as waves of joy which flow right back to the source . . .

"And as we become aware our love goes forth; and ourselves are moved from their moorings and would fain float down the stream of joy to its infinite goal. This is the meaning of the longing which stirs within us at the sight of beauty . . .

"The stream that comes from the Infinite and flows towards the finite—that is the True, the Good . . . Its echo which returns towards the Infinite is Beauty and Joy" *(My Reminiscences)*.

Tagore is renowned as a poet of human love and of nature:

*Hands cling to hands and eyes linger on eyes: thus
begins the record of our hearts.*

*It is the moonlit night of March; the sweet smell of
henna is in the air;
my flute lies on the earth neglected and your
garland of flowers is unfinished.
This love between us is simple as a song.*

(THE GARDENER)

However, *Endless Love* from *Mānāsi* transforms simple human love into a play between the Divine and the human:

*I seem to have loved you in numberless forms,
numberless times,
In life after life, in age after age, forever.
. . .
Today it is heaped at your feet, it has found its end
in you,
The love of all man's days both past and forever:
Universal joy, universal sorrow, universal life,
The memories of all loves merging with this one
love of ours—
And the songs of every poet past and forever.*

(THE GARDENER)

Tagore experienced and expressed an uncanny sense of the unity of the universe. He sang:

*The same stream of life that runs through my veins
night and day runs through the world and dances
in rhythmic measures.
It is the same life that shoots in joy through the dust
of the earth in numberless blades of grass and
breaks into tumultuous waves of leaves and
flowers.*

(GITĀNJALI)

Tagore felt that he was one with Nature in the beginning of creation. The joy and wonder of that unity permeated his consciousness:

*Mother Earth, thou art mine since time
immemorial.
Through ages countless, day and night, thou hadst
taken me with your dust to scour the trackless
universe with untiring steps.*

The green-blades have danced upon me;
The flowers in reckless abandon have blossomed
  over me.
The ancient trees have showered their leaves,
    flowers and fragrance over me.

("MOTHER EARTH")

So, sitting alone midst immense solitude, the poet does not merely remember, but feels "the mighty bond of the earth through time immemorial" in every fiber of his being:

Of a day, sitting idly on the Padma bank all alone,
    my entranced eyes spread far sway,
I sense, I feel in every limb and vein,
    in all my body and soul,
how deep in your bosom, O Mother,
    quivers and sprouts the tiny grass-blade;
how the fountain of life streams incessantly night
    and day;
how, with what mad ecstasy, the blossoms sway
    on the stems that sway in the air;
with what mute, ravishing joy plants and creepers,
    blades and brushwood, dance in the morn-
    ing sun,
like the child dreaming and smiling in happy sleep,
    after feeding full at mother's breast.

("MOTHER EARTH")

The anguish of inevitable loss was the poet's lot. Tagore suffered many bereavements: the first was the suicide of his sister-in-law, Kadambari Devi, to whom the poet was greatly attached and whose memory haunted him all his life. The decades that followed were marked by the deaths of his wife, a daughter, a son, and his father.

Tagore's poems exhibit a great variety of forms and subject-matter. "One could fill a whole book talking about his technical skills—his double and triple rhymes, and those composed of two words which pounce on the reader like an animal waiting in ambush, and those which run in tercets, or in quatrains where the third line is left hanging on an echoing half-rhyme. . . . One could show that although Bengali poetry had existed for nearly a

thousand years before him, he was the first to exploit the full resources of the language" (Buddhadeva Bose, *Tagore, Portrait of a Poet*, p. 44).

Buddhadeva Bose goes on to give us a glimpse of Tagore's personality and his impact on Bengal:

"He was a marvel of a man, a peer of da Vinci and Goethe, handsome, powerful in physique, abundant, versatile, superbly poised in himself: a veritable god among men. . . . He refined our manners and our language of everyday speech, he taught us to love and honor our mother-tongue, he even metamorphosed our handwriting. Would it surprise you if I say modern Bengali culture is based on Tagore?"

When Tagore celebrated his fiftieth birthday, he had published eighteen books of poetry and established himself as the greatest poet of Bengal. The intelligentsia of Bengal celebrated his jubilee on January 28, 1912, in the Town Hall of Calcutta. The *Modern Review* described the reception and address as "an unparalled ovation—the first time that such an honor has been done to a literary man in India."

But he was unknown outside Bengal, even in India. His advent on the world stage is a strange tale. Tagore was due to sail on March 19, 1912, for his third voyage to Europe. On the night before his departure he fell ill and had to retire to Shelidah on the banks of his beloved river Padma. It was here that he began to translate, for the first time, some of his *Gitānjali* songs into English. Recollecting that time, Tagore wrote, in a letter, "Yet I had not the energy to write anything new, so I took up the poems of *Gitānjali* and set myself to translate them one by one. . . . The pages of a small exercise book came to be filled gradually, and with it in my pocket I boarded the ship. . . . When my mind became restless on the high seas, I would recline on a deck-chair and set myself to translate one or two poems at a time." These were the poems that excited tremendous appreciation from Yeats, Eliot, Gide, and other Western thinkers, and resulted in Tagore's receiving the Nobel Prize in Literature in 1913.

The poems of Tagore's English *Gitānjali* are a perfect poetic expression of the perennial philosophy. The Infinite, the Divine, God or Ultimate Reality forms the canvas on which the Universe is painted. The Universe is the Infinite expressing itself in the finite. God and man are tied to each other by mutual love:

Thus it is that thy joy in me is so full. Thus it is that thou hast come down to me. O thou lord of all heavens, where would be thy love, if I were not?

. . .

And for this, thou who art the King of kings has decked thyself in beauty to captivate my heart. And for this thy love loses itself in the love of thy lover, and there art thou seen in the perfect union of two.

(GITĀNJALI)

Nature is created both as man's home and also as a thing of beauty whose contemplation awakens man's heart and directs it towards the Beloved:

"When I bring to you coloured toys, my child, I understand why there is a play of colour on clouds, on water and why flowers are painted in tints—when I give coloured toys to you my child."

(GITĀNJALI)

Tagore's meteoric rise to fame proved to be both a blessing and a liability. Without the English *Gitānjali* and the Nobel Prize, he might have remained but a Bengali poet. Now, his claim to be a world poet gained substance. However, his fame in the West was short-lived.

The main problem lay with the translations. In the best of circumstances, translating poems is a difficult and thorny enterprise. Tagore's own recreations of his poems in his first three English books—*Gitānjali, The Crescent Moon,* and *The Gardener*—were excellent. But his later efforts were hastily done and lacked vitality.

Furthermore, Tagore's reputation suffered from hasty stereotyping by his English critics. He was labeled a romantic and a mystic. These were half-truths. He *was* a romantic, but his romantic imag-

ination was founded on the robust belief in the Infinite manifesting itself in the finite. Therefore, his romanticism led to a joyous affirmation of all aspects of life—the Apollonian as well as the Dionysian. His mysticism, too, was life-affirming: "Deliverance is not for me in renunciation. . . . No, I will never shut the doors of my senses. The delights of sight and hearing and touch will bear thy delight" (*Gitānjali*).

Besides being a romantic and a mystic, Tagore was also a realist and a humanist. His poems record all moods of nature, benign as well as malevolent. For example, *Sea Waves,* in the book *Manasi,* gives us a picturesque description of the cruel and terrible aspect of nature. It was composed on the occasion of the sinking of a pilgrim-ship carrying eight hundred passengers to Puri, in 1887. The poet describes the raging fury of the sea and the utter helplessness of 800 men and women. The poem nevertheless ends with affirmation of human love even in the face of imminent death and destruction. For Tagore, even realism is tinged with redemptive love.

Rabindranath's humanism embraced all mankind—men, women, and children, of all castes, nationalities, and races. He wrote poems about Bengal and Africa, about villages and cities, about young people and old men. His poems affirmed the basic human values—truth, justice, and love. He chided his countrymen for clinging to superstitions instead of listening to reason. Tagore had sung his people into a nation, said Ezra Pound. Tagore had the unique distinction of having his songs chosen as the national anthems of two nations: India and Bangladesh.

In 1931, Tagore published a book *Bana-bani* (*The Message of the Forest*) which brought together a number of poems and songs about trees. The poet writes:

O Tree, life-founder, you heard the sun
Summon you from the dark womb of earth
At you life's first wakening; your height
Raised from rhythmless rock the first
Hymn to the light; you brought feeling to harsh
Impassive desert.

. . .

Man, whose life is in you, who is soothed
By your cool shade, strengthened by your power,
Adorned by your garland—O tree, friend
Of man, dazed by your leafy flutesong
I speak today for him as I make
        This verse-homage,
As I dedicate this offering
        To you.

(IN PRAISE OF TREES)

Rabindranath's versatility as a poet is astounding. Besides his lyric poems, he wrote myths, heroic stories, and children's nursery tales in verse. He wrote humorous poems and nonsense poems for children. One critic has remarked that an entire course in poetry-appreciation can be built around Tagore's work.

At seventy, Tagore was still writing fresh poems. Many critics believe that his greatest poetry was written in the last decade of his life. He had already come to terms with death as a necessary part of life. "And because I love this life, I know I shall love death as well." His last poems reveal the poet's encounter with pain and the possibility of annihilation. But his sturdy faith in love as an amalgam of joy and sorrow brought him consolation. He had already recorded his farewell to this world in *Gitānjali* 96.

When I go hence let this be my parting word, that
what I have seen is unsurpassable.
I have tasted the hidden honey of this lotus that
expands in the ocean of light, and thus I am
blessed—let this be my parting word.
In the playhouse of infinite forms I have had my
play and here have I caught sight of him that is
formless.

My whole body and my limbs have thrilled with his
touch, who is beyond touch, and if the end come
here, let it come—let this be my parting word.

It is revealing of Tagore's universal appeal that the great British poet Wilfred Owen, in his last letter to his mother, quoted this poem.

NARAYAN CHAMPAWAT

Further Reading

Translations and Works in English

Tagore, Rabindranath. *Collected Poems and Plays.* New York: Macmillan (1936).
———. *My Reminiscences.* London: Macmillan (1917). Tagore's autobiography.
Kabir, Humayun, ed. *One Hundred and One: Poems by Rabindranath Tagore.* Bombay: Asia Publishing House (1966). Very good translations of a wide selection of Tagore's poems by some of the most well-known Bengali scholars.
Radice, William, trans. *Rabindranath Tagore: Selected Poems.* Harmondsworth: Penguin Books Ltd. (1985). Very good translations of some of Tagore's best poems.

Related Studies

Kripalani, Krishna. *Rabindranath Tagore: A Biography.* New York: Grove Press (1962). Best English biography, by a scholar well acquainted with the Tagore family.
Mukherjee, S. B. *The Poetry of Tagore.* New Delhi: Vikas Publishing House (1977). A comprehensive treatment by a scholar well versed in Bengali as well as European literature.

THE POETRY OF MUHAMMAD IQBAL

Author: Shaikh Muhammad Iqbal (Allama Iqbal)
Born: November 9, 1877, Sialkot, Pakistan
Died: 1938, Lahore, Pakistan
Major Works: (In **Persian**) *Asrar-i-Khudi (Secrets of the Self)* (1915); *Rumuz-i-Bekhudi (Mysteries of Selflessness)* (1918); *Payam-i-Mashriq (Message of the East)* (1923); *Zabur-i-Ajam* (Persian Psalms) (1927), *Javidnama (The Book of Eternity)* (1932), *Pas Chi Bayad Kard Ay Aqwam i Sharq? (What then is to be done, O Peoples of the East?)* (1936). (In **Urdu**) *Bang-i-Dara (The Caravan Bell)* (1924); *Bal-i-Jibril (Gabriel's Wing)* (1935); *Zarb-i-Kalim (The Blow of Moses' Staff)* (1936); *Armaghan-i-Hijaz (The Gift From Hijaz)* 1938.

Major Themes

In freedom life burgeons and flourishes.
The revival of old values can uplift the world from its decadent state.
Resurgence of Islam to the heights of its glorious past could inspire Muslim spirituality with a new vigor.
God's will controls the course of our lives; life can be improved by exalting one's "Self" to the highest level.
The discovery of the potentialities of the Self can lead to control over events.
Wealth and power are worthwhile if attained by effort, instead of being inherited.
Those in constant search are really alive; others are merely living.

At the turn of the twentieth century, literary circles in India witnessed the emergence of a poet-philosopher who seized the imagination of younger generation of Indians and jolted others out of their slumber. Muhammad Iqbal (later Sir Iqbal) inspired Indians at a time when the struggle for independence was gaining momentum. His vigorous verses appealed to all. His call for confidence, thought, and action motivated the Indian masses.

Iqbal wrote verses in Urdu, his mother tongue, as well as in Persian. In Urdu literature, Iqbal remains a close second in popularity to Mirza Ghalib, the renowned nineteenth-century poet.

A Punjabi-Muslim, Iqbal was born in 1877 in Sialkot (in undivided India). His ancestors were Kashmiri Brahmins who had converted to Islam. His mother, Imam Bibi, and father, Shaikh Noor Mohammed, were devout Sunni Muslims. Iqbal was raised in an orthodox and deeply religious environment and started reciting the Holy Quran at an early age. The influence of religion during his formative years later found expression in Iqbals' poetry, philosophy, and political outlook.

Maulana Mir Hasan, a friend of Iqbals' father,

instilled in Iqbal a lifelong enthusiasm for Persian and Arabic. At the age of fifteen, Iqbal married Karim Bibi (later he also married Sardar Begum and Mukhtar Begum). In 1895, he moved to Lahore to further his studies. At that time, Government College Lahore was the hub of cultural and intellectual pursuits in India. It was here that Iqbal came into contact with Sir Thomas Arnold, his teacher, whose philosophy left a lasting impression on him. Iqbal studied English and Arabic and completed his Masters in Philosophy in 1899, following which he taught in the University Oriental College and Government College Lahore for some years. By this time, he was already a popular Urdu poet.

In 1905, Iqbal went to Trinity College in Cambridge, England, where he studied Philosophy under the Hegelian J. M. E. McTaggart and James Ward. Subsequently, in Munich, he submitted his Ph.D. thesis on "The Development of Metaphysics in Persia." The philosophies of Goethe, Nietzche, and Hegel were all influences on the development and refinement of his own philosophy. After this, he qualified as a Barrister in London and was called to the English Bar in 1908. That same year he returned to India and started teaching in Lahore.

As a lawyer Iqbal was undistinguished, but his skill as a poet gave him better satisfaction. As the years passed he became a renowned poet in India and in the West, in acknowledgement of which a British knighthood was conferred on him in 1924. He became quite active in Indian politics, in particular with the Muslim League. In fact, it was Iqbal who first introduced the idea of a separate nation for Indian Muslims, a proposal which later resulted in the birth of Pakistan. Iqbal's health deteriorated in his last years. After a long period of illness, he died on 20 April, 1938. He was buried in the Badshahi Mosque in Lahore, a place of pilgrimage for the lovers of the Urdu language.

The Love of Nature

The development of Iqbal as a poet is evident from a reading of his poetry. In his early poems, the love of nature and traces of pantheism are apparent. Also, the influence of English Romantics like Shelley, Byron, and Wordsworth is obvious in poems such as "The Moon," "A Wish," "Solitude," "The Glow Worm," and "The Mountain Cloud." The famous poem "Himala," the very first in *Bang-i-Dara (The Caravan Bell)* is an ardent tribute to the glory and grandeur of the Himalayas. (The Kauser and Tasneem rivers mentioned in the poem are the fabled rivers of Paradise.)

From your heights
cascade rippling waters,
surpassing the rivers Kauser and Tasneem,
holding a mirror up to nature,
frolicking around the scattered pebbles.
O wanderer!
Touch this poet's lyre with your music,
for he hears your melody
with inspired genius.

(BURNEY, TRANS., 1987)

Nationalism, and the Call for Unity

The socio-political milieu in which Iqbal grew up was charged with the spirit of freedom. It is this

spirit and fervor that pulsates through many of his verses. Many of the poems in *The Caravan Bell* celebrate his country:

Think of your country, oh, thoughtless ones!
Trouble is brewing.
In heaven there are signs of your ruin
See that which is happening
and that which is to happen!
What is there in stories of olden times?
If you fail to understand this,
You will be exterminated
Oh, people of Hindustan!
Even your story will not be preserved in the annals
of the world!

(ANAND, TRANS., IN NICHOLSON, 1978)

He wrote with intensity and abounding energy and motivated the desolate, downtrodden, and disheartened:

In bondage life shrinks to a mere rivulet;
while in freedom it is a boundless ocean.

(BURNEY, TRANS., 1987)

The real signs of life in races in this age are
That morn and eve their fortunes change.

(SINGH, TRANS., 1981)

In *Naya Shivala (A New Shrine)*, a remarkable poem, Iqbal talked about unity and brotherhood, reaching beyond the boundaries of temples or mosques:

Come let us lift this curtain of alien thoughts again,
And reunite the severed, and wipe division's
stain.

(KIERNAN, TRANS., 1947)

The poem ends with a simple and pure thought:

Strength and peace too shall blend in the hymns the
votary sings—
For in love lies salvation to all earth's living things.

(KIERNAN, TRANS., 1947)

Iqbal wrote primarily for Muslims, not only of India but of other countries. For this reason perhaps, he chose to write in Persian:

I am of India; Persian is not my native tongue,
. . .
Although the language of Hind [India] is sweet as
*   sugar,*
Yet sweeter is the fashion of Persian speech.

(NICHOLSON, TRANS., 1978)

This is similar to what Mirza Ghalib had expressed some decades earlier, preferring Persian over Urdu for the writing of poetry. The Persian that Iqbal used was the classical form taught in Indian schools; it was archaic and quite different from the Persian spoken in Persia (Iran) itself. Like Ghalib, Iqbal's Urdu poetry is also marked with a noticeable use of Persian phrases and expressions. In some of his poems, this increases the degree of difficulty in understanding, especially when there is ample use of perplexing Persian metaphors. In sharp contrast to such poems are the pure, simple, and flowing verses and songs composed by Iqbal, comprising some of his most quoted poems. Interestingly, these also include poems where Iqbal has made liberal use of Hindi words and phrases.

Most of his poetry written after 1905 has Islamic religious philosophy as its base. Iqbal had a firm faith in Allah. Devotion, loyalty, and the glory of Allah was the purpose of a Muslim's life. In "*Jawab-i-Shikwa*" ("Answer to Complaint"), the Prophet tells how the destiny of the world could be in the hands of Muslims:

If you break not faith with Muhammad, we shall
*   always be with you;*
What is this miserable world? To write the world's
*   history, pen and tablet we offer you.*

(SINGH, TRANS., 1981)

Iqbal makes passionate reference to Muslim conquerors, who spread the name of Allah in distant lands. He confesses, "The goal of poetry is, to me, not to get fame and honour but merely to show

religious convictions." (Schimmel, 1989). He condemns Muslims "infected by Western values and ways of Brahmins" and gives the clarion call, "Convert to Islam India's millions who still in temples dwell." (Singh, 1981).

The Life of Action

A great admirer of inspired action, Iqbal held a life of struggle and strife in great esteem, and denounced inactivity. For him, action is imperative if there is to be spiritual progress:

"Tis how we act that makes our lives;
We can make it heaven, we can make it hell.
In the clay of which we are made
Neither light nor darkness [of evil] dwells.

(SINGH, TRANS., 1981)

In "A Portrait of Sorrow" he declares:

This is the law of nature!
This is the inexorable logic of the universe!
He who swings into action
is God.

(BURNEY, TRANS., 1987)

He gives precedence to action over thought:

May God bring a storm in your life;
The sea of your life is placid, its waves devoid of
*   tumult.*

(SINGH, TRANS., 1981)

Action is explored and emphasized in the Persian poem *Asrar-i-Khudi* (*Secrets of Self*), the first of Iqbal's poems on religious philosophy:

Be ashamed if you want to inherit a Ruby from your
*   forebears*
This cannot give the pleasure that lies in looking for
*   the Ruby.*

(ANAND, TRANS., IN *NICHOLSON*, 1978)

A similar strain is heard again, where asking is begging and a symbol of inaction:

A whole ocean, if gained by begging, is but a sea of fire;
Sweet is a little dew gathered by one's own hand.
Be a man of honour, and like the bubble
Keep thy cup inverted even in the midst of the sea.

(NICHOLSON, 1978)

Asrar-i-Khudi, published in 1915, "took the young generation of Muslims by storm. Iqbal has come amongst us as a Messiah and has stirred the dead with life" (Nicholson, 1978). In the poem, Iqbal renders ghazals of exquisite beauty. Replete with artistic brilliance, *Asrar* emphasizes the manifesta tion of the latent Self. To realize and recognize the potentialities of the Self is akin to conquering the world:

Man wins territory by prowess in battle,
But his brightest jewel is the mastery of himself.

(NICHOLSON, TRANS. 1978)

Iqbal sets forth three stages in the education of Self: obedience, self-control, and divine-vice-gerency. He used religious and traditional metaphors to arouse the spirits of Muslims and affirm the importance of the Self. His verses are marked by strength of feeling and a compelling charisma:

Endow thy will with such power
That at every turn of fate it be so
That God himself asks of his slave
"Tell me, what is it that pleaseth thee?"

(SINGH, TRANS. 1981)

PRABHJOT PARMAR

Further Reading

Translations

Burney, S. M. H. *Iqbal: Poet Patriot of India.* Dr. Saeda Saiyidain Hameed, trans. New Delhi: Vikas Publishing House Pvt. Ltd., 1987. A collection of verses from Iqbal's various volumes, this book presents the dominant elements of nationalism in his poetry. Iqbal's patriotism and the influence of Indian philosophy on his thought are highlighted. Persian and Urdu poems are written in English script, followed by English translation. Besides the English reader, a great reading for those who understand spoken Urdu or Persian but cannot read them.

Kiernan, V. G., trans. *Poems From Iqbal.* Bombay: Kutub Publishers Ltd., 1947. The volume has translations of some of the finest poems from Iqbal's three Urdu volumes; *Call of the Caravan, Gabriel's Wing,* and *The Sword of Moses.* It is an admirable representation of Iqbal's thinking and style. Maintaining the style of the ghazal, the translator has excellently preserved the rhyme scheme, a formidable task indeed. Added bonus are two essays on Iqbal as a poet and as a philosopher.

Nicholson, R. A., trans. *The Secrets of the Self: A Philosophical Poem.* New Delhi: Arnold Heinemann, 1978. A long poem first translated by Nicholson in 1920, introduced Iqbal to the Western reader. It concisely states the essentials of Iqbal's philosophical ideas. The introduction by Nicholson discusses the different sections and is a prelude of merit. This edition also has an afterword by Mulk Raj Anand, concerning the humanism in Iqbal's poetry.

Singh, Khushwant, trans. *Muhammad Iqbal: Shikwa and Jawab-i-Shikwa; Complaint and Answer: Iqbal's Dialogue with Allah.* New Delhi: Oxford University Press, 1981. This eminent writer and critic has captured the fire and spirit of two of Iqbal's most evocative Urdu poems about the glorious past and the decadence of Islam. The translation is set between the original work in Urdu and Hindi.

Sud, K. N. *Iqbal and His Poems (A Reappraisal).* Jullundur and Delhi: Sterling Publishers, Ltd., 1969. A sincere and fine attempt to render the eloquence of Iqbal's poetry into English for those knowing neither Urdu nor Persian. Iqbal as a poet is discussed briefly in the introduction.

Related Studies

Haq, Q. M., and M. I. Waley. *Allama Sir Muhammad Iqbal: Poet Philosopher of the East.* London: British Museum Publications Ltd., 1977. A distinct and succinct account of Iqbal. A brief biographical portrayal is followed by a sequential summary of his works, including poetry, lectures, and speeches. An excellent introduction to the poet-philosopher.

Jafri, Ali Sardar, and K. S. Duggal. *Iqbal: Commemorative Volume.* New Delhi: All India Iqbal Centenary Celebrations Committee, 1980. This book contains a series of papers written by eminent writers and critics, analyzing Iqbal's philosophy, technique, and style. One section is devoted to a comparison of Iqbal other poets and philosophers (Goethe, Tagore, Milton, and others), revealing to his brilliance and greatness.

Schimmel, Dr. Annemarie. *Gabriel's Wing.* Lahore: Iqbal Academy Pakistan, 1963. (Reprinted 1989). A comprehensive study of Iqbal's views of Islam. The influence of West and East on his thought and mysticism are explored with constant references to his poetry.

Zakaria, Rafiq. *Iqbal, The Poet and the Politician.* New Delhi: Viking, 1993. An outstanding and well-balanced approach to Iqbal. There are excellent and perceptive translations of a variety of verses, punctuated with description about Iqbal's beliefs and philosophy. The book has an introduction by Khushwant Singh.

KAMAYANI

Author: Jaishankar Prasad
Born: 1889
Died: 1937
Literary form: Epic poem

Major Themes

Moksha *(bliss) is the highest goal of life.*
Moksha *is attainable, not through pure reason but through faith.*
Masculine and feminine are not two opposite powers; they are two aspects of one reality.

In the concluding stanza of *Kamayani*, Jaishankar Prasad presents his vision in the following words:

> *Spirit and matter were harmonious,*
> *Beauty took form,*
> *One consciousness was all-pervading,*
> *There was indivisible profound bliss.*

(BANDHOPADHYAY, TRANS., 1978)

The attainment of "indivisible profound bliss," celebrated in the above stanza, is the principal theme of *Kamayani*. In this epic poem, Jaishankar Prasad makes a passionate plea for the salvation of human beings through a nonrational faith.

The term "*Kamayani*" etymologically means "the daughter of Kama [desire]." In Hinduism, however, *kama* is much more than what is generally connoted by "libido." It encompasses libido as well as the Eros of the Greek mythology; it signifies in human beings the basic urge to live, to preserve, to protect, and to expand. The three principal characters in *Kamayani* are Manu, Shraddha, and Ida. Manu represents the mind; the thoughts of Manu equal the different conditions of the human psyche. Shraddha epitomizes faith, love, and determination to live with *satya* (truth) as the basic principle of life. Ida represents rationality.

Kamayani is divided into fifteen cantos, each named after a character that appears in the canto: Chinta (Anxiety), Asha (Hope), Shraddha (Faith), Kama (Desire), Vasana (Passion), Lajja (Bashfulness), Karma (Action), Irshya (Jealously), Ida (In-

tellect), Swapana (Dream), Sangarsha (Struggle), Nirved (Renunciation), Darshan (Vision), Rahasya (Mysticism), and Ananda (Bliss).

The Hindu myth of the Deluge forms the basis of *Kamayani*. In the mythology, the "Deluge" does not mean simply a physical and universal inundation; it signifies the end of the urge to live. It stands for inertia and annihilation. At the outset of this epic poem, the reader finds Manu, the protector of humankind, at the peak of a Himalayan mountain surrounded by death and destruction.

The very first canto entitled "Chinta" (Anxiety) describes the lonely Manu watching, from a mountain peak, the devastating aftermath of the Deluge around him:

> *Quietude! Death! Devastation! Darkness!*
> *Void turned to naught*
> *This is the truth, Oh immortality*
> *Do you have any place here at all?*

(BANDHOPADHYAY, TRANS., 1978)

Manu is desperate and desolate. He is trying to come to grips with the dreadful reality of the loss of a civilization. With the recession of the water, the green bushes begin to reemerge, which gives him Hope ("Asha," second canto). Manu is in awe of nature. Soon, Shraddha (Faith, third canto) appears, and steers Manu in the direction of action and fulfillment. She is the daughter of the King of Gandharvas, who is stranded in the Himalayas. She exhorts Manu to a life of action and offers her company to him. This companionship breeds temptations in Manu's mind and Kama (Desire, fourth canto) illustrates this feeling. Kama, the mythic God of love, exhorts Manu to become worthy of Shraddha.

Manu falls in love with Shraddha. He wants Shraddha all to himself and expresses his feelings to her (Vasana, or Passion, fifth Canto). Shraddha surrenders herself to Manu. However, this act of surrendering raises all sorts of doubts in Shraddha's mind, which are picturesquely described in Lajja (Bashfulness, sixth Canto). She is reassured by Rati, her mother. Shraddha's submission restores Manu's confidence and his old self soon returns. He wants to perform a sacrifice (Karma or Action, seventh canto). Manu performs this sacrifice with the help of two demon-priests who talk Manu into killing Shraddha's favorite deer for the sacrificial rite. Shraddha finds Manu's behavior reprehensible; she feels dejected, her faith in Manu is shaken and her dream of a new order begins to shatter. Shraddha is pregnant by now, and Manu is becoming tired of his old routine and craving for new adventures. Shraddha is excited about her unborn child; she takes Manu to show him the cave in which she is planning to nourish their child. Shraddha shares with him her plans, her dreams of the future, of the kind of life the three of them could lead. Shraddha's attention to their unborn child makes Manu jealous (Irshya, eighth canto); he leaves Shraddha and goes away to pursue his own dreams. He finds himself in the land of Ida (Intellect, ninth canto), the queen of the Saraswat kingdom. He helps Ida restore peace and prosperity in her kingdom.

In the meantime, Shraddha is by herself and dreams about Manu and Ida, Manu's attempt to seduce Ida, and the resulting rebellion against Manu (Swapana or Dream, tenth canto). She becomes worried about Manu. The eleventh canto ("Sangarsha or Struggle) corroborates Shraddha's dream by actual events. Manu faces the consequences of his own misdeeds. He disobeys the very laws he himself had made at the expense of others. His transgressions result in a rebellion. There is a fight and Manu is knocked unconscious. When Manu regains consciousness, he finds Ida sitting nearby and Shraddha standing near him along with their son. Shraddha and Ida meet each other for the first time. Manu is filled with remorse and is unable to face Shraddha; he leaves his wife and son again (Nirved or Renunciation, twelfth canto). Shraddha in the thirteenth canto (Darshan or Vision) points out to Ida the shortcomings of reason and offers to help her build a kingdom in which reason and emotion coexist harmoniously. She leaves her son, Kumar, with Ida and goes to look for Manu. She succeeds in finding Manu, who is feeling very dejected. He asks for Shraddha's forgiveness. Shraddha forgives him. In the final two cantos (Rahasya Mysticism; and Ananda Bliss) Shraddha takes Manu on a mythological voyage where they have the vision of the blissful dance of Lord Shiva; they reach the abode where there is harmony among desire, action, and knowledge.

The Influence of Kashmir Shaivism

In reading *Kamayani,* readers immediately notice the influence of the philosophies of Kashmir Shaivism on Prasad. Kashmir Shaivism postulates a belief in Param Shiva as the ultimate reality with its two aspects: Shiva, the unchanging aspect, and Shakti, the changing power. It affirms a belief in two kinds of orders: impure and pure. In the impure order, human beings because of ignorance (*māyā*) perpetuate divisions and distinctions. *Māyā* not only conceals the real nature of truth but makes it appear as something else. It reinforces the distinction between experiences and what is experienced. In the pure order, on the other hand, the distinction exists only as an idea. In *Kamayani*, this ontological vision of Kashmir Shaivism is brought into play via the trinity of desire, knowledge, and action. In the impure order, there is a lack of harmony among the three; in the pure order one attains harmony which gives rise to integral insight.

The entire story of *Kamayani* can be divided into those two orders. The first twelve belong to the first order, the next three to the second order. Manu, in the first twelve cantos, repeatedly asserts his supremacy over all living creatures. At the outset, we find Manu on the Himalayan peak, desolate and dejected. Shraddha attempts to steer him in the right direction, but to no avail. Being governed by *māyā*, he fails to realize the purpose of Shraddha. He desires lust, passion, and enjoyment. He tries to possess Shraddha and succeeds. However, this does not satisfy him. He leave Shraddha and meets Ida who takes Manu to the world of pleasures and longings. Desires breed further desires; he tries to possess Ida and fails. This is the predicament in which most embodied souls find themselves.

The Attainment of Bliss

The last three cantos belong to the pure order where Shraddha helps Manu attain bliss. She takes him to a place where one finds eternal peace. He has the vision of Lord Shiva—a vision of the delightful dance of Shiva. He sees three luminous dots and asks Shraddha:

What are these spheres? asks Manu
Tell me, what are these, explain, explain!
To what Universe have I travelled into
Oh! Free me from this illusion, this chain.

(BANDHOPADHYAY, TRANS., 1978)

Shraddha explains to Manu that these three dots represent the three spheres of will, knowledge, and action. Each sphere is a universe in itself. The red represents the universe of desire, the realm of *māyā;* the dark-hued is the sphere of action, the realm of conflict and turmoil; and the bright, silvery one represents the sphere of knowledge, the sphere that is indifferent both to pain and pleasure. Each of these three spheres, though luminous, is imprisoned within itself. A harmony among these three is essential in order to obtain *moksha*. With the saying of these words, Shraddha smiles, and her smile spreads into these realms rendering them "one," resulting in bliss:

Dream and slumber and awakening vanished
As wish and wisdom and action dissolved

The heavenly music filled the earth and sky
And Manu in Shraddha's spell was lost.

(BANDHOPADHYAY, TRANS., 1978)

They attain bliss that is free from any kind of dichotomy, a single pure consciousness remains.

It is significant that Prasad closes his epic poem with the idea that Faith (Shraddha), not Intellect (Ida), helps one achieve harmony among desire, knowledge, and action. Ida, in the poem, represents the rational and the intellectual. However, intellect cannot take one all the way. Prasad was aware of the powers of intellect. That explains why Shraddha leaves her son Kumar (Compassion) with Ida (Intellect) when she goes to look for Manu. A harmony between the two is essential. Faith epitomizes *sattva* (pure goodness). Manu benefited from Ida's company; however, Faith brought him bliss.

Brain is the inspiration of reason
Faith is the Queen of hearts
Perfect Harmony of the two
Is the immortal story of life.

(BANDHOPADHYAY, TRANS., 1978)

In this poem, Prasad shows that both masculine and feminine principles are two significant and complementary parts of reality. In the first canto, Manu is desperate; he has lost the desire to live. Shraddha motivates him and inspires him to act; she gives him will to live and towards the end of the poem helps him attain bliss. Throughout *Kamayani*, the idea of *moksha* (bliss) is articulated vis-à-vis the masculine-feminine symbolism; bliss represents the harmonious union of the two as well as their transcendence.

Kamayani may be viewed from two perspectives: the first one portrays *Kamayani* as an historical account of the propagation of the human species; the second depicts *Kamayani* as an allegory in which a human being abandons faith in favor of reason and logic which results in destruction. In the Vedas (the sacred scriptures of Hindus), there are references to Ida. Manu is taken to be the progenitor of human kind, in the literature from the Vedas to the Puranas. "Doomsday Deluge" represents an event which inspired Manu to promulgate a new era different from that of the gods. Manu is generally taken to represent the first-born in Indian history. In the *Rig-Veda*, Shraddha and Manu are depicted as seers. In one of the aphorisms, Shraddha is said to be the daughter of Kama, the god of love. For Prasad, the Hindu scriptures and the Puranas, on which he bases the story of *Kamayani*, are historical documents. Accordingly, although he believed that in *Kamayani* he was giving an historical account, he was willing to concede it is also an allegorical commentary on human civilization.

In the preface, Prasad notes that the episodes presented in *Kamayani* have ancient roots. However, he concedes that "allegory has also crept in. . . . These three (Manu, Shraddha, and Ida) form the basis of *Kamayani* coupled with my imagination."

Prasad belongs to the Chhayavada movement in the history of Hindi literature—a romantic movement against the didactics, the superficial, and the straitjacket of conventionality. Love of nature, sensuousness, mysticism, musicality, and so on are the chief characteristics of the Chhayavada movement. These characteristics are particular to all of Prasad's writings; *Kamayani* is no exception.

Kamayani deals with the struggles in which human beings find themselves, their conflicts, their shortcomings, and how these conflicts might be resolved. In *Kamayani* Prasad achieves an equilibrium that encompasses within itself conflicting and opposing claims. In this universe, everything is organically related. Masculine and feminine are not two opposite powers; they are two aspects of one reality. Both must be taken in account and given due recognition. The hallmark of *Kamayani*, as in Prasad's other works, is assimilation—that and syntheses of the opposing claims of tradition-modernity, reason-faith, intellect-emotion, action-inaction, within-without, and masculine-feminine.

BINA GUPTA

Further Reading

Translations

Bandhopadhyay, Manohar, trans. and ed. *Kamayani*. New Delhi: Ankur Publishing, 1978. A good and readable English translation of Prasad's *Kamayani*.

Sadani, Jaikishandas, trans. *Kamayani*. Calcutta: Rupa and Co., 1975. Another useful translation of Prasad's *Kamayani*.

Related Studies

Gupta, Bina. "The Masculine-Feminine Symbolism in Kashmir Saivism," in *Sexual Archetypes: East and West*, edited by Bina Gupta. New York, Paragon House, 1987, pp. 71–105.

Prasad, Jaishankar. *Kamayani*. Allahabad: Bharati Bhandar, 1964–65. For those who are interested in reading the original *Kamayani* in Hindi.

Singh, Rajendra. *Jaishankar Prasad*. Boston: Twayne Publishers, 1982. A very good and useful discussion of Prasad's life and works.

JAPAN

THE COLLECTION OF TEN THOUSAND LEAVES

Title in Japanese: *Man'yōshū*
Compiler and Major Authors: Ōtomo no Yakamochi (718?–785) and other (unidentified) compilers; Princess Nukada, or Nukata (b. 630), Kakinomoto no Hitomaro (d. 708–715), Yamanoue no Ōkura (660?–733?), Ōtomo no Tabito (665–731), Lady Kasa (dates unknown).
Literary Form: Poetry, including *chōka, tanka, sedōka, tanrenga, bussokusekika*
Date of Compilation: Late eighth century

Major Themes

Poetry consists of lyric and narrative expressions of human response to the world of nature and to human events of all sorts.

Poetry may be composed by persons of many classes and backgrounds, who couch their personal emotions in powerful language, drawing on metaphor, natural imagery, rhythmic repetition, fixed epithets, and incantatory language.

The world is one harmonious realm in which human and nature, past and present, public and private feelings are all unified.

Man'yōshū (*The Collection of Ten Thousand Leaves*), the oldest collection of Japanese poetry, compiled in the late eighth century from a variety of sources, including oral tradition and collections otherwise lost, is one of the most revered works of Japanese literature. The period best represented in the collection is from about A.D. 600 to 759 (the last datable poem is from 759), but many of the poems may predate the seventh century. The primary compiler seems to have been Ōtomo no Yakamochi, who is also one of the principal poets of the collection. It is divided into 20 books, though the method of organization seems haphazard—varying from topic to chronology to poetic form. Many of the poems are accompanied by headnotes or endnotes detailing the circumstances of composition, or offering editorial comment upon a particular poem.

The *Man'yōshū* contains several forms of poetry, many of which became extinct as the composition of *tanka* came to dominate poetic production in Japan in succeeding centuries. There are 265 *chōka*, 4,207 *tanka*, 62 *sedōka*, 1 *tanrenga*, 1 *bussokusekika*, and 4 Chinese poems. The collection is written entirely in Chinese characters, used chiefly for their phonetic value (*man'yōgana*) rather than their semantic value.

The range of topics and tones is also much greater in the *Man'yōshū* than in anthologies compiled in later centuries when Japanese poetry had become largely a vehicle for elegant expression of private lyrical moments: the *Man'yōshū* includes poems on public topics, such as war, affairs of state, the discovery of gold, the history and descent of the imperial family, and historical events of various sorts, as well as elegies, philosophical musings, and expressions of intimate emotion in lyric and nature poetry. This diversity of topics and approaches is matched by a rich vocabulary, including many words and expressions that were eliminated as insufficiently elegant from the later poetic vocabulary. Some of the poems reveal Chinese influence, in Taoist celebrations of wine, Buddhist religious attitudes, or Confucian concern with society. Chinese influence is also seen in the increasing regularity of form, in the formal parallelism used in some verses, and in the sudden appearance of sophistication of expression.

The Early Poems

The earliest poems of the *Man'yōshū* have the qualities of folk song or ritual poetry and are often irregular in meter and form, and unclear as to their topic. Some are attributed to early rulers and members of the aristocracy, such as the Emperor Yūryaku (r. 457–479), whose poem "Your basket, with your pretty basket" is given the place of honor at the head of the collection:

> *Your basket, with your pretty basket,*
> *Your trowel, with your little trowel,*
> *Maiden, picking herbs on this hill-side,*
> *I would ask you: Where is your home?*
> *Will you not tell me your name?*
> *Over the spacious land of Yamato*
> *It is I who reign so wide and far,*
> *It is I who rule so wide and far.*
> *I myself, as your lord, will tell you*
> *Of my home, and my name.*

> (NIPPON, 1965)

This poem, seemingly a simple pastoral, presents, on closer inspection, numerous difficulties of interpretation: Why should the emperor use honorifics to address a country maiden? Why the exchange of names? Is there a significance to the herbs the girl is gathering? Why is this gentle, romantic song coming from a ruler otherwise remembered for his cruelty? Is the poem in fact a single song, or perhaps a melding of two early songs? Still, the rhythms and elegant simplicity of expression have attracted readers for centuries.

Many early poems, including elegies and *kunimi* (land-praising) poems, are believed to have been composed by court women whose duties consisted of composing poetry on formal occasions in their own voices or as substitutes for others. Chief among these women is Princess Nukada (or Nukata; b. 630), who often incorporated Chinese themes or approaches into her Japanese poetry.

Kakinomoto no Hitomaro

Little is known of the life of Japan's first major poet, Kakinomoto no Hitomaro, a court poet who was master of the *chōka* (long poem), which consists of alternating phrases of five and seven sylla-

bles concluding with a couplet of seven syllables. Sometimes an envoy in *tanka* form (5,7 5,7,7) was appended to the *chōka*. Nineteen of Hitomaro's *chōka* are included in the *Man'yōshū*, along with about 75 *tanka*. There are also about 380 poems selected from the no longer extant *Hitomaro Poetry Collection*, but it is unclear which of these, if any, were written by Hitomaro.

Many of Hitomaro's poems were written on public topics, such as an imperial journey or the death of a ruler; others appear to be more private expressions—of sorrow at parting, or grief at the death of his wife—although couched in the language of public presentation that emphasizes the universality of the emotions expressed.

Hitomaro is particularly noted for the complex paratactic syntax of his beautiful *chōka*, many of which consist of a single architecturally organized syntactic construction, impossible to capture in English. This poem, composed by Hitomaro for Princess Hatsusebe as an elegy for Prince Osakabe, demonstrates both the expert construction of Hitomaro's poetry and his mastery of imagistic patterns:

> *Sleek seaweed streams*
> *from where it grows*
> *on the upper shallows of the Asuka,*
> *   where the birds fly,*
> *to touch and touch again*
> *the lower shoals.*
>
> *   Asleep*
> *without the folds of his wife's*
> *soft skin,*
> *   that once he kept beside him*
> *   like his swords,*
> *when she, like sleek seaweed,*
> *bent toward him, swaying to and fro—*
> *now desolate lies the bed*
> *of his pitch-black nights.*
>
> *So, inconsolate, yet hoping*
> *she might meet him,*
> *she sojourns,*
> *   grass for pillow,*

on the broad, jewel-trailed fields of Ochi,
her pearly hems muddied in the morning dew,
her robe drenched in evening mist,
for the Prince she cannot meet again.

Envoy

> *The Prince who crossed the sleeves*
> *of his evening robe with hers*
> *has passed beyond the jewel-trailed*
> *fields of Ochi. How could she hope*
> *to meet him again?*

(LEVY, 1981)

Post-Hitomaro poets

Among the poets of the early eighth century, Yamanoue no Ōkura stands out for the philosophical content and continental influence in his work. Appointed a member of an embassy to China in 701, Ōkura remained on the continent for several years. He composed, prose and poetry not only in Japanese but also in Chinese, some of the latter also included in the *Man'yōshū*. Upon his return to Japan, he produced a series of *chōka* treating the impermanence of human life, the sufferings that accompany old age, poverty, or separation from children and family, and other topics that seem to have their roots in Confucian or Buddhist thought. In his celebrated "Dialogue on Poverty" (*Man'-yōshū* 892–893), for example, Ōkura presents statements first by a poor man who wonders how those worse off can possibly survive, and then by a destitute man, who indirectly replies by describing the misery he and his family suffer:

> *No fire sends up its smoke,*
>   *And in the pot*
> *Only a spider drapes its web—*
>   *We have forgotten*
> *Even the manner of cooking food,*
>   *And like the night finch*
> *We raise weak-throated cries.*

(BROWER AND MINER, 1961)

Ōkura's contemporary, Ōtomo no Tabito, shows another aspect of Chinese influence, a Taoist pleasure in plum blossoms, strong drink, and friendship, in a series of poems he and members of his salon composed. One *tanka* presents the blossoms addressing the company of revelers:

> *The plum blossoms*
> *spoke to me in a dream—*
> *"Most elegant*
> *flowers are we. Please*
> *let us float in your sake."*

(BROWER AND MINER, 1961)

Tabito's son, Ōtomo no Yakamochi, is the last major poet of the *Man'yōshū* and, evidently, its principal compiler. Yakamochi's work stands as a transition to the elegant court poetry found in later Japanese court anthologies. Of his many *Man'yōshū* poems, including 46 *chōka* and 433 *tanka*, the most memorable celebrate the beauties of the natural world and the pleasures and disappointments of human relationships, the inexorable passage of time and the melancholy, bittersweet feeling that awareness of time's passage brings.

> *Though I know*
> *the world of the living*
> *is not eternal,*
> *yet how the cold autumn wind*
> *makes me remember her!*

(LEVY, 1981)

Yakamochi exchanged numerous love poems with Lady Kasa (Kasa no Iratsume), but evidently his ardor cooled, while she continued to yearn for him. Many of her poems lamenting her unrequited love are included in the *Man'yōshū*:

> *Longing for you*
> *leaves me helpless with despair;*

I lean against a little pine
on Nara Mountain,
        grieving.

If longing were a thing
one could die from,
death would have come to me
        and come again
a thousand times!

                    (LEVY, 1981)

The compilation of the *Man'yōshū* was followed by a lengthy period during which Chinese poetry took the place of public poetry composed in Japanese. When Japanese poetry again emerged from the shadows of the bedchambers of the court aristocracy with the compilation of the *Kokinshū* in the early tenth century, it had been largely reduced to a single form, the *tanka*. Its topics, themes, and materials also were restricted to suit to elegant tastes of the authors and patrons of the court. Not until the twentieth century did Japanese poetry again achieve the variety represented in this early collection.

                    LAUREL RASPLICA RODD

Further Reading

Translations

Levy, Ian Hideo. *The Ten Thousand Leaves*. vol. 1. Princeton, NJ: Princeton University Press, 1981. Translation into colloquial English of the first five books of the *Man'yōshū*.

Nippon Gakujutsu Shinkokai. *Man'yōshū*. New York: Columbia University Press, 1965. Translation of one thousand poems representing all twenty books of the *Man'yoshu*.

Related Studies

Brower, Robert H., and Earl Miner. *Japanese Court Poetry*. Stanford, CA: Stanford University Press, 1961. The standard critical study of Japanese court poetry, this remarkable book places the *Man'yōshū* in the context of the Japanese literary tradition.

Doe, Paula. *A Warbler's Song in the Dark*. Berkeley: University of California Press, 1982. A biographical and critical study of Ōtomo no Yakamochi, the chief *Man'yōshū* compiler.

Levy, Ian Hideo. *Hitomaro and the Birth of Japanese Lyricism*. Princeton, NJ: Princeton University Press, 1984.

TALES OF ISE

Title in Japanese: *Ise monogatari*
Authors: Unknown. Possibly, among others, Ariwara no Narihira (825–880)
Literary Form: An *uta monogatari* or "poem tale." This genre contains numerous poems or groups of poems with short prose settings.
Date of Composition: First part of tenth century.

Major Themes

Long ago the ideal courtier displayed remarkable elegance, especially in the composition of poetry appropriate in diction and treatment to the occasion.

Time passes, everything fades away, love and beauty offer only a brief respite from the uncertainty of human existence.

Tales of Ise belongs to a unique genre commonly referred to as the "poem tale." These were collections of short prose pieces that provide a setting for a *waka* poem or an exchange of poems. The term *waka* means Japanese poetry as opposed to Chinese verse. Each *waka* poem contains approximately 31 syllables arranged in five lines of 5-7-5-7-7 syllables respectively. The typical *waka* of the Heian period (794–1186) was an occasional poem in which the circumstances of composition might be described in headnote in an anthology or with a short prose passage in a poem tale such as *Tales of Ise*. In the poem tale, the authors of the poems are usually left unidentified, but it is sometimes possible to determine authorship if the poems appears in anthologies with a named author.

The poem tale as a genre may have grown out of the poetic anthology. The headnotes in an anthology were short statements that detailed the subject or the circumstances of the composition of the poem. In the poem tale the compiler or compilers created prose setting for individual poems, exchanges of poems, or small groups of poems. These prose settings were often completely unrelated to the original poems. In the anthology, the arrangement of poems can create a certain narrative aspect. For example, the first six books of an imperial anthology are always devoted to the four seasons. Reading these books is like unrolling an especially long landscape scroll where elegant, courtly gentlemen and ladies go about their daily lives amidst scenes representative of the special beauty of each season. In the poem tale, groups of episodes may be centered around the same character or similar situations, but in *Tales of Ise* there is no overall unity to the narrative.

Even with the context provided by the prose setting in the poem tale, *waka* poetry may seem trivial to those unfamiliar with the tradition. However, a careful reading of *Tales of Ise* can provide one of the clearest statements of the ideal of "courtly elegance" that was so important to Heian culture. For this reason this collection of subtle little vignettes was one of the most influential works in traditional Japanese literature.

The exact origin or authorship of *Tales of Ise* is unknown. Considering the lack of organizing principle, it seems likely that *Tales of Ise* is the product of several authors over a period of time. Because certain groups of episodes form short biographical sketches focusing on several events in the life of Ariwara no Narihira (825–880), there is speculation that these episodes may have been the original core of the work. Alternative titles for *Tales of Ise*, such as *Tale of Narihira* and *Narihira Journal*, suggest a stronger biographical tendency in the work than what is generally recognized today.

Love in **Tales of Ise**

The fragmentary structure of *Tales of Ise* makes it nearly impossible to pinpoint any single theme in the work. Most of the episodes deal with romantic adventures. The predominant tone is a certain sense of sadness and resignation over the passing of time that permeates much of Heian literature. Perhaps the best-known example of this is the forth episode, in which a young man, presumably Narihira, has visited a certain woman who was in service to the Empress. The lady has suddenly moved away, and although he knows where she is, there is no way to visit her. In the early spring of the next year, when the plum trees are in bloom, the young man once again visits the place where he had met the young lady. Unable to recapture the past, he is overcome with grief and composes this poem:

> *Is this not the moon?*
> *This spring, is it not the*
> *spring of old?*
> *Myself alone, only I*
> *am the same as before.*

The poem invites metaphysical interpretation in a way that is unusual for Japanese poetry of this period. The nuances are difficult to capture in translation, but the poem first asks the rhetorical question: Are not the moon and the spring different this year? Of course they are not, but since they appear so different, perhaps it is the author who has changed. The overall impressions from the poem are of time passing, uncertainty, and subjectivity. Obviously from the context, the subject is grief over the end of a brief, but intense, love affair. Perhaps more than any other single poem in the work, this forms the clearest statement of what might be called a theme in *Tales of Ise*.

Love is the thread that unites most of the episodes in *Tales of Ise*. Part of the charm of the work is the variety of kinds of love and the variety of situations. Another famous episode, number 23, concerns what might be called innocent love. Two young people meet again after having grown up together. They fall in love and the boy sends this poem to the girl:

> *Rail around the well—*
> *against this railing we measured*

> *our heights—*
> *we have grown, it seems*
> *since last we met.*

She replies to him:

> *That once we compared—*
> *this hair that now I part,*
> *grows past my shoulder.*
> *For whom should I put it up*
> *if not for you?*

Both boys and girls had shoulder-length hair until they reached a certain age. The hair of the boys was cut upon maturity while girls' hair was allowed to grow. In his poem the boy observes that they have both grown in height. In reply the girl observes that her hair has also grown. It is time for her to marry. An exchange of poems in this manner was an important part of the ritual of courtship in Heian Japan. There are numerous examples of such exchanges in *Tales of Ise*. In this case, the two eventually marry, but all does not go well. The man takes a mistress in a far-off province, which worries his wife. He overhears her composing this poem:

> *When the wind blows,*
> *white waves upon the sea*
> *rise as Rising mountain,*
> *which this night you must*
> *cross all alone.*

This poem contains a play on words (*kakekotoba*). The white waves out at sea are said to "rise" (*tatsu*) as does "Rising (*tatsuta*) mountain." The husband is so moved by the poem that he gives up the mistress he has been visiting. The man and mistress end up exchanging poems, but he still does not go back to her. This episode serves as the kernel for a well-known noh play, *Izutsu* (*The Well Rail*).

The art of poetry is central to *Tales of Ise*. In some cases the composition of poetry is the actual subject of an episode. The opening story is a good example. It begins with a young courtier on a hunting excursion who catches a glimpse of two beautiful young sisters. He is so impressed by their beauty that he tears off a strip from his hunting robe and sends it to them with a poem comparing his feelings to the confused pattern of the dyed cloth:

> *On Kasuga plain*
> *grow the young purples—*
> *those used to dye cloth as*
> *confused in pattern*
> *as this heart of mine.*

The narrator of the episode then points out how the young man has taken this occasion to compose a poem that is a variation of an earlier poem:

> *In far off Michinoku*
> *the random patterns of dyed cloth*
> *for whose sake,*
> *is it so confused*
> *this heart of mine.*

Since *waka* is a conventional verse form, poems are often only slight variations on common themes or images. In the late classical period, this borrowing became formalized with the use of the technique called *honkadori* (variation on a poem). The poet would take two or three lines from a well-known poem, and give them a new twist by adding several lines of his own composition. In the poem quoted above, the poet has used the same imagery of the confused pattern on dyed cloth to represent the confused state of the heart of someone in love. The latter poem exists in several different versions and is attributed to Minamoto no Toru in anthologies.

Love, Politics, and Exile

Some of the episodes in *Tales of Ise* can be taken together to form a sort of narrative. For example, the poem about the moon by Narihira in episode four is part of a number of episodes that form a tale of romantic intrigue and exile very similar to the story told in the first third of the eleventh-century Japanese novel, *The Tale of Genji*. In *Tales of Ise* the narrative begins in episode three with a young man sending a poem to the lady who would eventually become the Empress. After she moves and he is no longer able to visit her, he composes the poem about the moon (translated above). Then, in episode five, he visits her again, when she is living in a different place. In the seventh episode he carries her off to continue the affair somewhere safe from interference. She is eventually rescued by her brothers. It seems doubtful that this is a factual account. Most likely it is a mixture of fact and legend.

If the story were completely factual it would certainly have been a serious political scandal. At this time, although the Emperor was the titular head of the government: the real power was being wielded by the Fujiwara family. They controlled the throne by marrying their daughters to Emperors, thus becoming the grandfather of the next Emperor. The old Emperor was often forced into retirement before he could really exercise power, leaving the new Emperor under the influence of a Fujiwara regent who would be the child's grandfather. For someone such as Narihira to carry off a young girl who might someday bear the Emperor an heir would be a grave crime against the Fujiwara. It is this subversive aspect of the story that makes it such a powerful myth.

The eight episodes that follow this story detail Narihira's exile to the eastern provinces with poems about various sights to be seen on the journey and love affairs with country maidens. This again parallels the story of the hero of *The Tale of Genji* where the hero also goes into self-imposed exile after being caught having an affair with a young lady destined for the imperial entourage.

Perhaps the best known single episode in *Tales of Ise* is number 69. It involves a young man on a hunting excursion in the provinces who visits the chief priestess at the Ise Shrine. One theory has it that the title, *Tales of Ise*, comes from this episode. The priestess would have been the unmarried daughter of a noble family who was chosen by the emperor to serve in this capacity. The young man and the priestess have a brief affair and eventually she sends him the poem:

> *Did you come here?*
> *Or did I go to you?*

I cannot recall,
was it dream or was it real?
Was I awake or was I asleep?

The young man replies:

In utter darkness
my heart is clouded
and I am lost.
Was it dream or was it real?
You will have to decide.

This clever exchange is characteristic of early-tenth-century Heian poetry. Love is seen as such a powerful emotion that it creates an intense state of confusion. There are hints at the Buddhist concept of worlds of reality and illusion behind this exchange, but the charm lies in a blend of cleverness and controlled emotion. For later generations expressions such as these would become nothing more than trite convention, but in *Tales of Ise* they are still fresh. This sense of freshness is a large portion of the charm of this pivotal work in traditional Japanese literature.

Both the poem tale and the imperial anthology deal with the topic of love. The five books devoted to love in the imperial anthology describe a typical affair from the first meeting to the inevitably un-happy conclusion. Thus the passing of time and the complexities of human emotion are used to craft a portrait of an aesthetic ideal in the courtly life of the Heian period. In *Tales of Ise* the only links between many of the episodes is the unidentified hero, a "certain person," or the "man of old," who is gallant, elegant, charming, and, above all, witty. Love as a subject matter is essentially the same in both genres, but *Tales of Ise* goes much further in anchoring the portraits of love in a real world populated by real people. In this sense the poem tale can be seen as bridging the gap between poetry and the great flourishing of the novel that would soon take place.

JON W. LACURE

Further Reading

Translations

Translations in this article are by Jon W. LaCure.

McCullough, Helen Craig. *Tales of Ise: Lyrical Episodes from Tenth-Century Japan.* Stanford, CA: Stanford University Press, 1968.

Harris, H. Jay. *The Tales of Ise*. Rutland, VT: Charles E. Tuttle Co., 1972.

COLLECTION OF POEMS OLD AND NEW

Title in Japanese: *Kokinshū*
Anthologizers: Ki no Tsurayuki (d. 945?), Ki no Tomonori (d. 906?), Ōshikōchi no Mitsune (fl. c. 900–920), Mibu no Tadamine (fl. c. 900–920)
Literary Form: Poetry: *tankas* (short poems)
Date of Compilation: Early tenth century

Major Themes

Poetry is a lyrical expression of human response to nature and the passage of time.
Poetry is a vehicle for the expression of such emotions as love and regret, sorrow and grief, joy, and loneliness.

The *Kokinshū* was the first of 21 anthologies of Japanese poetry compiled at the behest of the Japanese sovereigns between the tenth and fifteenth centuries. It consists of 1,111 poems, with all but 9 in the 31-syllable, 5-line form known as the *tanka* (short poem), which so dominates the Japanese poetic tradition that it is also known simply as *waka*, or "Japanese poem."

The anthology was compiled in the early years of the tenth century and marked a return of Japanese poetry to the public arena after a century and a half of the vogue for Chinese writing. There are two prefaces to the *Kokinshū*, one in Japanese written by Ki ho Tsurayuki, and one in Chinese that is attributed to Ki no Yoshimochi. These, along with the inventive organization of the anthology, make it clear with what seriousness the compilers, four courtiers and poets appointed by Emperor Daigo, took their charge to demonstrate the qualities and elevate the status of Japanese poetry.

The compilers selected poems composed in earlier centuries, as well as poems that they and their contemporaries had written, but their work did not stop with the task of selection. Rather than arrange their materials by date of composition or by author, they chose a novel, thematic arrangement. Through this thematic organization, the 20 books of the *Kokinshū* are made to form a unified whole illustrating the topics most commonly treated in Japanese court poetry: nature and the natural progression of the seasons, love and the progress of the love affair, celebration, mourning, travel and parting, and combinations of these themes. Within the larger topics, care was taken in the ordering of individual poems: each one is linked to those before and after by a chronological or geographical progression, by imagery, or by subtle shifts in theme or event. Thus the anthology may be read as a unit from beginning to end, as one poem woven from bits composed by multiple authors—a pattern followed in later Japanese court anthologies and one which influenced the development of other genres of Japanese literature.

Poetry in the Early Heian Period

In the early ninth century, as the vogue for Chinese poetry ran its course, Japanese *waka* served primarily as a means of private communication among the sophisticated members of the courtly aristocracy who whiled away their hours in the practice of music, dance, calligraphy, painting, the blending of incense, and other arts. The style of *waka* most heavily represented in the *Kokinshū* thus developed at a court dominated by adaptations of Chinese culture. Among the characteristics of the style are an intellectual, conceptual approach in which human life and the world of nature are presented through a process of reasoning; a blurring of the boundary lines between the natural world and human experience; treatment of both nature and man in terms of the passage of time; and a subdued, elegant, graceful tone.

An "obliqueness" of presentation came to dominate the poetry of the ninth century: perceptions were expressed not in the simple language of the moment but in more highly contrived terms. Clever reasoning and use of decorative figurative language, especially metaphorical interplay between the worlds of nature and of human life, were much admired. This poem by Ise is typical of the *Kokinshū* style:

harugasumi	as patches of warm
tatsu o misutete	spring mist float upward fickle
yuku kari wa	wild geese forsake us—
hana naki sato ni	are they accustomed only
sumi ya naraeru	to a village without blossoms

(*KOKINSHŪ* 31)

By the last decades of the ninth century, *waka* was no longer confined to private communication, but was taking on a new public role: it had been elevated to art, and new occasions for its practice and public display came into being. Courtiers commemorated imperial excursions with Japanese poems, and court ceremonies in which the courtiers had previously composed Chinese poetry now included *waka*. Poetry competitions, termed *utaawase*, and the composition of *byōbu-uta*, or screen poems, provided other public opportunities for the recognition of Japanese poems. These also led to the practice of composing poems on set topics—topics chosen for the competition or based on the scenes depicted on the screens—rather than on topics inspired directly by the poet's own experience.

Compilation of the Kokinshū

Around 905 Emperor Daigo ordered four of the well-known poets of the court, Ki no Tsurayuki, Ki no Tomonori, Ōshikōchi no Mitsune, and Mibu no Tadamine, to gather old poems not previously anthologized, as well as their own, into a new anthology, a collection representing the best Japanese poetry. Despite the obvious prestige of these four men in early-tenth-century Japan, very little is known about them. Tsurayuki is revered as the leader of the group of compilers, and as author of its Japanese preface, the preface to the "Waka from the Imperial Excursion to the Ōi River" and the *Tosa Diary*; but little is known of his personal life. He is credited with defining the aesthetic of the *Kokinshū*. Of the other three compilers, even less is known. Tomonori died during or soon after the compilation. Tadamine virtually dropped from sight after the *Kokinshū*, while Mitsune was supported by Retired Emperor Uda and Tsurayuki's patron, Fujiwara no Kanesuke, until his death around 925.

The Aesthetics of Kokinshū Poetry

Tsurayuki's Japanese preface to the *Kokinshū* reveals the beginnings of a critical consciousness in Japanese literature: the preface defines the nature of Japanese poetry, its origins and history, and the circumstances that gave rise to poetry in Japan; describes the work of six poets (the "six poetic geniuses") of the generation preceding that of the *Kokinshū* compilers; and tells of the circumstances of compilation of the anthology. The intent of the author is to describe the realm and achievements of Japanese poetry and to establish it as an art equal to Chinese poetry. In the preface, Tsurayuki introduces three important critical terms: *kotoba, kokoro,* and *sama.* By *sama* he seems to mean specifically those new techniques adapted from Chinese poetry: obliqueness, witty reasoning, and a focusing on the poet's mental processes rather than on the natural scene described. *Kotoba* and *kokoro* refer, respectively, to diction (including choice of material, subjects, and decorum) and spirit (attitude, approach, and theme). Tsurayuki emphasized the need for balance between the two. He criticized such poems as this one by Archbishop Henjō for overemphasis on *kotoba* ("the style is good but he lacks sincerity"):

asamidori
ito yorikakete
　shiratsuyu o
tama ni mo nukeru
haru no yanagi ka

along slender threads
of delicate twisted green
translucent dewdrops
strung as small fragile
　jewels—
new willow webs in spring

(*KOKINSHŪ* 27)

Similarly, Tsurayuki found in such poems as the following by Ariwara no Narihira "too much feeling" burdening the brief expression:

tsuki ya aranu
haru ya mukashi no
haru naranu
waga mi hitotsu wa
moto no mi ni shite

is this not that moon—
is this spring not that spring
we
shared so long ago—
it seems that I alone am
unaltered from what I was
then

(*KOKINSHŪ* 747)

The "Rules" of Court Poetry

The *Kokinshū* came to serve as a model for composition of court poetry, establishing implicit rules for both topical and lexical decorum. The serious poet could no longer write of the pleasures of drink, the harsh realities of war or sickness, or the pain of poverty. None of these topics fit the newly established decorum of court poetry. The poet had to limit the vocabulary of the poem to native Japanese words, and, of these, only those sanctioned by tradition as being poetic. He or she had to give priority to metaphorical and decorative language, particularly for the expressions of deep emotion, and of feelings of wonderment, puzzlement, confusion, and longing.

In addition to the indirect, roundabout expression of admiration, wonderment, or questioning through metaphor, other rhetorical devices were commonly used in *Kokinshū* poetry to elevate the language or to allow the poet to express multiple meanings in a limited number of words. The *makurakotoba*, or pillow word, which had its ori-

gins in earlier poetry, is a fixed epithet that serves to amplify or enhance the effect of a particular word, its use often creating a ritualistic or hieratic tone. The *kakekotoba*, or pivot word, is a type of pun in which a series of sounds is employed in two different senses, functioning as a pivot between the preceding and the following phrases. *Engo*, or word association, enables a poet to bring out secondary meanings by developing an imagistic pattern in addition to that of the surface statement of the poem.

Poems of the *Kokinshū* fuse the worlds of nature and human affairs, keeping the subjective responses of the poet at the center of the experience, but giving those responses voice through metaphor drawn from the natural world. Central to the perception of the world expressed in *Kokinshū* poems is a concern with time: everything is treated in terms of the shifting moments of time. The emotion such poetry calls forth in the reader is a keen appreciation for the passing beauties of life and a poignant awareness of their brevity.

Arrangement of the Anthology

The arrangement of the poems in the *Kokinshū* also points up the poets' and compilers' acute awareness of the passing of time. The organization of poetry to illustrate the changing of the seasons or the course of human affairs marks the first occurrence of an intricate structure in which poems are arranged by formal categories, within which is a natural sequence of chronological or geographic progression and imagistic association. The *Kokinshū* became the model for editors of Japanese anthologies, as well as for other types of poetic texts. The 20 books of the anthology are organized by topic: spring, summer, autumn, and winter; felicitations, parting, travel, and wordplay; love and grief; and miscellaneous, and court ceremonial. Within each book, the poems are linked by subtopics: in the books of seasonal poems, there is an orderly progression beginning with the first signs of spring and moving through the year. Shorter sequences of poems move through the hours of the day. In the books of love poems, the classic pattern of Japanese courtly love is drawn: the books open with poems on the first glimpses of the beloved, and move on to love after meeting, fear of the loss of love, sadness, and ultimately, resignation that come with the end of the love affair.

The concept of integrating poetry into prose texts or into poetic sequences is an ancient one in Japan. Both the brevity of *waka* and its lyric tone lend themselves to the development of such compound literary forms as the *nikki* (diary), *utamonogatari* (poem tale), lyric novel, and integrated sequence of poems or linked verse. Thus, the unique structure of the *Kokinshū*, with its integration of the individual poems into a whole and its emphasis on the whole collection rather than the individual poem or author, established a pattern that had enormous influence on subsequent Japanese literature. The concept of integrating a series of poems or a body of short prose passages by means of topical and imagistic association, and by the progression of seasonal change and narrative event is a fundamental one in Japanese literature. It was basic to the structure of nearly every succeeding premodern collection of poems, and led to the development of such types of poetry as the linked-verse forms *renga* and *haikai*.

Even twentieth-century prose fiction bears the mark of this method of linking images and events.

Laurel Rasplica Rodd

Further Reading

Translations

Translations in this article are by Laurel Rasplica Rodd.

McCullough, Helen Craig, trans. *Kokin Wakashū.* Stanford, CA: Stanford University Press, 1985.

Rodd, Laurel Rasplica, with Mary Catherine Henkenius, trans. *Kokinshū: A Collection of Poems Ancient and Modern.* Princeton, NJ: Princeton University Press, 1984.

Related Studies

McCullough, Helen Craig. *Brocade by Night: "Kokin Wakashū" and the Court Style in Japanese Classical Poetry.* Stanford, CA: Stanford University Press, 1985. This study treats the Chinese heritage as well as the tradition of Japanese poetry and song and shows their impact on *Kokinshū* style.

of assorted modes, both the child-like and the laughable, as well as the poignant and the finely crafted. Although scholars believe all 56 of the *waka* compositions for the text were written by Tsurayuki himself, he invents a series of presenters including "the ex-governor," a seasick old woman, a young child, "a certain person," the ship's captain, and the woman narrator herself, each of whom is portrayed as producing likely verses when the occasion arises.

One of the key organizing principles of the diary is the journey itself—the spatial and temporal progress of travelers on a boat. Linear motion is punctuated by occurrences and recurrences such as would mark sea travel, at once fraught with danger and utterly mundane. Refrains of "we are in the same port as yesterday" or "still the wind blew" liken the quality of the voyage to an ebb and flow, every day much like the next, while incidents both amusing and frightening spike the narrative at convincing intervals. The inconveniences of travel are enumerated, and there is even a point when the women get out and take a dip, with what they reveal in their undress duly noted.

Numerous patterns pull the text along, and other themes sparkle across its surface. As the sorrow of parting mounts, anticipation for homecoming swells. Celebratory poems relate the joy and blessings of life. The account begins with much reveling—five days and nights of it before departure—both because of hopes for an auspicious trip and because of anticipation of the new year. Seasonal delicacies—or the lack thereof—receive comment, because the focus on the calendar is necessarily a focus on the beans and greens that must be served as part of ritual observance. Inasmuch as they are returning to the hub of the world, the passengers are anxious to behave as capital residents, to counter their hardships with increasing layers of affirmation that they will safely reenter the community from which they have endured such long separation.

A deeper level of the trope of return is explored due to the fact that one member of the party that originally set out for Tosa in 930 never came back. It is this absent person, the daughter of the ex-

governor, who pulls most at the heartstrings of retinue and reader alike. The brave face they try to put on their loss show in the relatively small number of poems that deal with sorrow over the dead child—9 of the 56—even though it is this theme that reverberates in the emotional space of the diary. When one passenger proposes to alight and collect "forgetting shells" to ease the pain, another counters that it is memorialization that must take the fore.

> *Sending waves,*
> *Send yet more, please.*
> *Then I will come collect*
> *shells to help forget*
> *the one I long for.*

At this, someone who could bear no more recited the following to relieve the pain on the boat:

> *I will not collect*
> *forget-me-shells.*
> *But my longing for her,*
> *a white pearl,*
> *will I take as my memento.*

These verses are sometimes interpreted as being by Tsurayuki and his wife, or vice-versa. The narrative ends with two verses by a man whose grief demands expression, followed by the observation that the sadness can never be set down on paper. In the final comment, the narrator suggests that the only solution is to tear up the pages. Thus is the incommensurability of words and feeling allowed; but in the end, of course, the text survives as memorial, and as testament to Tsurayuki's faith in the power of *waka*.

Poetry Courts the Heart and Soul

Japanese poetry, confined in the standard form, the *waka*, to 31 syllables, exploits a number of rhetorical devices to intensify the resonance of the short lines. In Ki no Tsurayuki's day, poets fashioned elaborate conceits, equating such images as snowflakes and foam. The majority of the poems rely on a studied confusion between things—gulls and waves, sea spray and snow. Such wordplay was the essence of courtliness. Unlikely juxtapositions and other witticisms are common as well, and we can only suppose that readers were amused at the suggestion that the pressed salt trout that touched the travelers' lips might have found it romantic to be treated so.

Much of this word play centers on noteworthy locations, especially those famous for pines. The lasting green of the pine is a sign of long life, and so here it is a distressing irony. Pine, or *matsu*, is also homophonous with the verb, *matsu* (to wait), and by the 44th day the travelers are heartily sick of rowing past trees that postpone their arrival.

> *Though we go on and on,*
> *we cannot pass beyond them—*
> *the pine stands on the*
> *beach at Ozu, that long*
> *strand wound by a paramour.*

Any of the vicissitudes of travel (with the exception of pirates) could become a subject for treatment within the poetic code, even wind, waves, and displeased divinities. Rituals of pacification, culminating in the ex-governor's casting a mirror into the sea to calm the deity of Sumiyoshi, dot the narrative.

Not the least significant aspect of the diary's subtexts is Tsurayuki's own portrait. In places, the narrator seems to be a convenient device for lionizing the author. People—even those who stand to gain nothing—treat the ex-governor with extraordinary good will. When it comes to poetry, however, the Tsurayuki character (the master on board, whom a few commentators distinguish from the ex-governor) is usually reluctant to compose, and then, as on the first day of the second lunar month, suffers the whispers of his fellows over his lack of skill. Strangely, he presents himself as not up to the refined activity of versifying. Modesty, perhaps?

Tsurayuki's Promotions—Poetry, Self, or Women?

Many theories have arisen regarding Tsurayuki's effort. It is plainly a salvo in his campaign to pro-

mote *waka*. The *Tosa Diary* demonstrates the proper creation of poetry for specific motives and by various kinds of authors, all invented for the purpose. Children frequently come up with lines so that a reader can see what constitutes an immature style. Even the rough and heartless captain, who has embarrassing difficulty with predicting the weather, breaks out in song that fits the metric requirements of true poetry, in accord with Tsurayuki's statements in the Preface that all beings are given to verse. Lines by the Japanese poet par excellence, Ariwara no Narihira, surface, as does the Chinese of Abe no Nakamaro (modified for a woman's style), who found Japanese poetry worthy without knowing the language. Some of the poems gain the narrator's approval. As with much Japanese critical literature, however, evaluative commentary is pithy, brief, and frequently ambivalent. It contains precisely the kind of remarks that would inspire a lively discussion among a group of cultivated readers.

The diary is also without doubt Tsurayuki's literary attempt to ease his reentry into capital society. The provincial governor class to which he belonged was frustrated in its pursuit of rank and high office even when, as in Tsurayuki's case, the talent was obvious. Fresh from his tour of duty in what was, by court standards, the non-world, the ex-governor sought patronage; it mattered not if he had to perform a masquerade to do so. In this way he could be self-deprecating—a social necessity vis-à-vis a potential patron—with a broader wink at the truth than usual. One can only imagine how fine the holograph might have been, for Tsurayuki was a well-known calligrapher. Pieces attributed to him are brushed on fine papers covered with delicate tracery in mica. *Tosa nikki* would also have made a fine hand scroll with illustrations, although it is pure speculation to suggest that such might have been part of his ploy for a heightened reputation.

Official career records tell us that Tsurayuki was not successful in impressing the right people with his journal. We do know, however, that the tradition took up The *Tosa Diary* as a classic. An unusual work by the chief compiler of what became the central literature at the court for centuries, it was destined to retain a high profile. Indeed in modern literary histories it appears as "the first" of several genres—diary literature, travel records, and feminine vernacular prose.

The author's gender becomes an issue in any such treatment. In the traditional view, Tsurayuki is a liberator of feelings and a pathfinder for the women writers who would follow. Tsurayuki repeats his own success from the Preface, in which he had used vernacular prose to justify native poetry as fully worthy of imperial patronage. The narrative centers on the longing for home and the grief of a parent who has lost a child. To write as a woman, the theory goes, was to rationalize the unleashing of the tenderest responses, otherwise unavailable or unseemly to a professional man. Japanese men were not socialized to the avoidance of tears, however; they were lachrymose in the extreme. Tsurayuki's experiment with point of view may have been less in the interest of emotional license than a writer's freedom and play.

The traditional interpretation depends on a belief that women were not well established as writers, at least not of diaries. But is it possible that this too was a fiction, and that his emancipatory gesture was in fact a usurpation, an infringement on the writing that women had done? Perhaps this was Tsurayuki's motive—to intervene as a male, albeit a masked one, in the production of the feminine vernacular. Tsurayuki's influence was a relativizing one, however. He certainly helped make it acceptable for women to write in a male genre. Likewise, when his identity became known, he made it appropriate for men to use the vernacular that was almost exclusively identified with women. Whatever his intentions, the effect for later readers and writers was great. The first anthology, *Man'yōshū*, of the eighth century, names women as singers of some third of the poems, with no special notice attached to that fact. Tsurayuki activated gender as a concern. In that sense, his diary covers vastly more ground than the journey from Tosa to his home.

LINDA H. CHANCE

Further Reading

Translations

Translations in this article are by Linda H. Chance.

Carter, Steven D., trans. *Traditional Japanese Poetry: An Anthology.* Stanford, CA: Stanford University Press, 1991. 100–116. A selection of Tsurayuki's best poems, and a short sequence from the *Kokinshū*, make a manageable introduction to his poetics in action.

Keene, Donald, comp. *Anthology of Japanese Literature.* New York: Grove Press, 1955. An abbreviated translation by G. W. Sargent appears here.

McCullough, Helen Craig. "A Tosa Journal." In *Kokin Wakashū: The First Imperial Anthology of Japanese Poetry*, 263–91. Stanford, CA: Stanford University Press, 1985. Provides romanized versions of the poems as well as a map of the journey.

———, comp. and ed. *Classical Japanese Prose: An Anthology.* Stanford, CA: Stanford University Press, 1990. A very slightly modified version of the translation above appears in this anthology.

Miner, Earl. *Japanese Poetic Diaries.* Berkeley: University of California Press, 1969. Contains a complete translation with map, as well as an essay placing the work in the context of others in its genre.

Related Studies

Keene, Donald. *Travelers of a Hundred Ages.* New York: Henry Holt and Co., 1989. An extended treatment of the travel record genre, offering essays on each of the major works.

McCullough, Helen Craig. *Brocade by Night: 'Kokin Wakashū' and the Court Style in Japanese Classical Poetry.* Stanford, CA: Stanford University Press, 1985. An extended history of *waka* up to and including Ki no Tsurayuki's time, it elaborates on the compositional methods and themes of the imperial anthology for which Tsurayuki was chief compiler. A chapter on

"Tsurayuki and the Kokinshū Legacy" includes a section on *Tosa nikki*. Provides detailed consideration of the role of *waka* in the journal.

Marra, Michele. *The Aesthetics of Discontent: Politics and Reclusion in Medieval Japanese Literature.* Honolulu: University of Hawaii Press, 1991. See chapter 2: "A Lesson to the Leaders: Ise monogatari and the Code of Miyabi" for the disenfranchisement of the Ki and Ariwara families and the effect this had on their literary activities.

Miller, Marilyn Jeanne. *The Poetics of Nikki Bungaku: A Comparison of the Traditions, Conventions, and Structure of Heian Japan's Literary Diaries with Western Autobiographical Writings.* New York: Garland Publishing, 1985. An extensive study of the diary form in Japanese literature with comparisons to many Western exemplars.

Miyake, Lynne. "Woman's Voice in Japanese Literature: Expanding the Feminine," in *Women's Studies* 17:12 (1989): 87–100. This article concentrates on *Tosa nikki* in the course of offering Japanese women's writing as essential evidence in feminist arguments over the possibility of a specifically feminine voice in literature. It includes analysis of the elements that betray Tsurayuki's male voice.

Viswanathan, Meera. "Poetry, Play, and the Court in the *Tosa Nikki*," in *Comparative Literature Studies* 28:4 (1991): 416–32. Discusses Tsurayuki's text in terms of the courtly tradition in literature worldwide. Establishes the importance of games, play, indirection, display, power, and hierarchy in the *Tosa Diary*, thus accounting for the puns and levity that may puzzle a reader of the translation.

KAGERO DIARY

Title in Japanese: *Kagero nikki*
Author: Michitsuna's Mother (*Michitsuna no Haha*)
Born: 936?, Kyoto, Japan
Died: 995?, Kyoto, Japan
Literary Form: Poetic Diary, an autobiographical text interspersed with poetry
Date of Composition: c. 971

Major Themes

Life is insubstantial and ephemeral.
Marriage, even to a prince, may not be a happy ending.
Communication also takes place in what is not said.
Prose can be as beautiful as poetry.

The *Kagero Diary* (also known to the English-speaking world as *The Gossamer Years*, after the first translation into English by Edward Seidensticker in the late 1950s) is the first of a number of major prose works by women in the latter half of the Heian period, (794–1185) that laid the foundation for the classical literary canon in Japan. This situation, in which it is the works of women writers that established the canon, is unusual in world literary history. The *Kagero Diary* commands our attention as the work that opened the way for this remarkable production of women's literature as well as being an evocative record of human consciousness in its own right. Through this text, we have direct access to what it felt like to be a woman 1,000 years ago, and although the difference in culture somewhat distances the text from the twentieth-century western world, a reader of this text will be surprised at the familiarity of the psychological states expressed in the diary.

This diary, divided into three books and covering about 20 years of the author's life, is a lyrical rather than a metaphysical exploration of the meaning of a person's life. As the author attends carefully to the currents of emotion that constitute life for her, she is struck by the insubstantiality and emphemerality of human existence. As she says at the end of Book One in a famous passage from which the title for the work is taken, "... all the more, I sense how ephemeral everything is, wondering am I or the world really here or not, this could be called the diary of a *kagero*." *Kagero* is a pun meaning both mayfly, an insect that lives only a day and is therefore an emblem of emphemerality and, the shimmering haze on a warm day, which is an example of something that is both there and not there at the same time.

Michitsuna's Mother

Michitsuna's Mother was born around 936 into the middle level of the Heian aristocracy. She married "up" by becoming the wife of Fujiwara Kaneie (928–977), third son in the most powerful line of the Fujiwara family that monopolized political power at the Heian court. At this time, polygamy was the custom of Heian aristocrats, so the author actually became Kaneie's second wife. Marriage in the Heian period was normally a "visiting" arrangement; the husband did not actually live with any of his wives but visited them in the homes of their mothers. This meant that, unlike the situation in China, the wives did not have to live together in the homes of their mother-in-law. Also unlike China, as there were no regulations determining and guaranteeing the hierarchical relationship between principal wives, secondary wives, and concubines; marriage was fluid and the wives of one man could never be sure of where they stood. One of the certain ways for a wife to rise in status and secure her position was to have a lot of children. Michitsuna's Mother was not fortunate in this regard, as she gave birth to only one son, Michitsuna, from whom she gets her name. Nonetheless, her marriage lasted for 16 years.

Around 971, there was an emotional crisis in her marriage followed by a gradual estrangement. Internal evidence in the text suggests that she started to write her diary around the time of the crisis. When the diary ends in 974, she is living in the suburbs of the capital more or less as a "divorced" woman; the expression in Japanese is *toko banare*, or "separated from the bed." From the evidence in her poetry collection, which was compiled posthumously and appended to most manuscripts of the *Kagero Diary*, it is known that she lived at least until 995 and continued to be an active poet throughout her life. Her life, then, is an example of a married woman secluded at home in contrast to the backgrounds of all the other major women writers of the period, who all at one time or another served at court. Nevertheless, there is a surprising amount mentioned of her in contemporary documents. She is noted as one of the great beauties of the age and as a skilled poet. Indeed, many of her poems were included in successive anthologies of poetry commissioned by the throne. The diary itself bears witness to the exceptional nature of her artistic talent.

Declaration of the Author's Intention

The opening statement of the *Kagero Diary* expresses the author's intention with remarkable self-awareness:

> [I]t is just that in the course of living, lying down, getting up, dawn to dusk, when she looks at the odds and ends of the old tales, of which there are so many, they are just so much fantasy, that she thinks perhaps if she were to make a record of a life like her own, being really nobody, it might actually be novel, and could even serve to answer, should anyone ask, what is it like, the life of a woman married to a highly placed man, yet the events of the months and

years gone by are vague, places where I have just left it at that are indeed many.

The "old tales" of which she speaks are the elegant tales of courtly romance such as the *Tales of Ise* or a classic Cinderella story like the later *Tale of Lady Ochikubo*, in which the couple lives happily ever after. The Heian period was a great age for the "romance." Underlying the *Kagero Diary*'s author's dismissal of the old tales as "just so much fantasy" is the awareness that while the outline of her own life might fit the romance story, (although of relatively low status she married a very highly placed man), the marriage did not ultimately fulfill the romantic myth. A paraphrase of her story of the marriage might be, "I married a prince but we didn't live happily ever after." Thus an explicit part of her project is to write an "anti-romance," that is, an account of a "real life." The originality of this idea at that time, in the context of world literature, merits underlining.

Moreover, this passage also demonstrates that the author is aware of the fact that in giving an account of a real life, it will still be a kind of story. Note that while she says it could serve as an example, she does not claim it for the absolute truth but rather commends her narrative to the reader as something "novel" and even admits the distorting power of memory. Moreover, she starts her account in the third person, which also creates the effect of telling a tale.

Outline of the Content of the Kaegero Diary

The three books of the diary have distinctively different characters. Book One is more like a poetry anthology as it tells the story of 15 years of the author's married life focusing on the occasions of poetry exchanges between her and her husband. Even though a comment here and there indicates that she is recollecting the past from the vantage point of seeing how her marriage turned out in the end, she narrates the past as though it were reoccurring before her eyes. The poems assist her in doing so because they stand as crystal moments in a timeless present. The latter part of Book One records a three-day pilgrimage she took to Hase Temple. Her description of nature in this section has been widely admired for its originality and evocative power.

Book Two covers only three years, detailing with particular intensity the author's growing dissatisfaction with her marriage. In a stream-of-consciousness style, she captures her hypersensitive reactions to each sign of her husband's neglect. She seeks relief from her anguish by going on two pilgrimages that again give rise to some superbly lyrical descriptions of nature. However, whenever she returns to her home in the city, the mental agony grips her again; so she withdraws to a mountain temple to consider becoming a nun. She does not take the drastic step and is finally forced to leave the temple through the combined efforts of her husband and son. Even though she does not come down from the mountain of her own choice, she returns as a different person. She is able to accept the situation of her marriage and achieves some peace of mind.

Book Three begins with the author declaring that her "gloom and pain have quite cleared away." It also covers only three years and, of the three books, is most like a conventional diary with frequent entries recording recent events. The emotional intensity of the first two books has abated and an objective point of view prevails. The author begins to bring into the narrative stories of other people, notably the story of the mother of a daughter the author adopts, accounts of the courting adventures of her son, and the pursuit of her adopted daughter by a rather determined older man. As the author relates the stories of herself and others in an objective way, her subjects, including herself, begin to appear like characters in fiction. In the choice of details for description and even the choice of events themselves, there is evidence of the desire to make a good story. It is as though the diarist were turning into a novelist.

Realistic Portrayal of Human Interaction

While being an intensively personal and lyrical narration of a life, the *Kagero Diary* nonetheless gives a realistic portrayal of human interaction. It should be realized that the exchange of poetry was a perfectly normal part of social life in the Heian period, so the presence of poetry in the narration is natural. The impression of realism arises from the acuity of psychological observation apparent in the author's descriptions of personal interchange. One striking aspect of her narrating powers is the ability to convey the communication taking place in what is not being said. Take for example the following excerpt that comes from a time about two years into the marriage, when, just after the birth of their first and only child, her husband starts an affair with another woman to which Michitsuna's Mother reacts with intense jealously. At this point, they have reached a strained accord and he has resumed seeing her and is just now about to take his leave after a short visit.

[I]t was painful between us as always.

As the late rising moon was just about to emerge from behind the mountain ridge, he makes as though to depart. Then, perhaps seeing the expression on my face as I think, *Surely, tonight at least he doesn't have to go*, he said, "Well, if you really think I ought to stay . . . ?" But I didn't want him to think me desperate, so I say,

ikaga semu	What is there to do?
yama no ha ni dani	Since your heart is like the moon
todomarade	that does not linger
kokoro mo sora ni	at the edge of the mountain
idemu tsuki woba.	but emerges into the open sky.

He replies,

hisakata no	You say this heart-moon
sora ni kokoro no	emerges into the o'er-spread sky,
idzu to iheba	yet will it leave
kage wa soko ni mo	its reflection
tomarubeki kana	behind in this pond.

and so he stayed.

She wants him to stay but she will not say so for fear of the humiliation should he turn down her request. Moreover she wants him to stay of his own volition, not as a favor. She indicates this to the reader by narrating her silent thoughts. By his response, we know he has heard the request in her silence. The exchange between them in this passage is something between a tug of war and a dance. The multi-meanings of poetry allow them to express themselves ambiguously, never commiting themselves to a direct statement. In the end she wins; the power of her poem has him stay without her having to ask. This complex interchange in which all the communication takes place in the gaps between what they actually say has been rendered with amazing acuity and economy. There is nothing like this in Japanese prose before this text.

jectivity vibrates in the prose even when the description is of the external world.

Readers of *The Tale of Genji* will know that the realistic portrayal of human relationship and a prose as lyrical as poetry are also the hallmarks of the *Genji* style. There is no doubt that the example of *Kagero Diary* contributed to the creation of *The Tale of Genji*. Moreover, the *Kagero Diary* is a rich piece of literature in its own right, inviting exploration from such critical perspectives as the construction of the self—particulary the feminine self—in literature, the paradox of truth and fiction in the autobiographical form, the cross-cultural aspect of stream-of-consciousness as a writing mode and so on, but beyond that, and perhaps most important of all, it may be commended to the reader as an exquisitely beautiful text.

SONJA ARNTZEN

Poetic Prose

Another original aspect of Michtsuna's Mother's prose is the blurring of the distinction between poetry and prose. No less than her poetry, her prose is often a rich tapestry of natural image, sensual perception, and expression of emotion. Here is an excerpt from Book Two when the author is returning by boat from a pilgrimage to Ishiyama Temple:

> I look up at the sky; the moon is very slender, its reflection mirrored on the surface of the lake. A breeze springs up and busies the surface of the lake; with a whispering sound the ripples stir. Just hearing one of our young men sing out the song with the line, "Your voice is weak, and your face so pale," the tears fall drop by drop.

There is a montage effect to her natural descriptions as they move from visual image to auditory perception. It is also characteristic of her prose descriptions, as here, to embed bits of song and poetry, which further erases the distinction between prose and poetry. Moreover, an intense sub-

Further Reading

Translations

Translations in this article are by Sonja Arntzen.

McCullough, Helen Craig. "The Gossamer Journal" in *Classical Japanese Prose: an Anthology.* Stanford, CA: Stanford University Press, 1990. This translation of only Book One of *Kagero Diary* puts effort into rendering the poetry but otherwise follows the same conservative translation strategy as the Seidensticker version, which entails chopping up the long sentences of the original into short units, putting the narrative solidly into the past tense and removing all ambiguity.

Seidensticker, Edward. *The Gossamer Years: a Diary by a Noblewoman of Heian Japan.* Rutland, VT: Charles E. Tuttle Co., 1964. Seidensticker originally prepared this translation for publication in 1955 by the Asiatic Society of Japan. Deft and readable, this translation conveys the content of the diary with accuracy. However, it makes no attempt to recreate the style of the original and paraphrases the poems.

Related Studies

Mostow, Joshua. "The Amorous Statesman and the Poetess: The Politics of Autobiography and *Kagero Nikki*" in *Japan Forum*, vol. 4, no. 2, October, 1992. 305–315. This article examines the literary and political conditions that enabled the production of the *Kagero nikki*.

———. "Self and Landscape in the *Kagero Nikki*" in *Review of Japanese Culture and Society*, December, 1993, pp. 8–19. In this article, Mostow reveals the "painterly" aspect of the *Kagero Nikki* style, challenging Watanabe Minoru's thesis that the *Kagero Nikki* author fell short of being able to describe something in purely objective terms.

Watanabe Minorou. "Style and Point of View in the *Kagero nikki*" in the *Journal of Japanese Studies,* 10:2, 1984, 365–384. A translation of a chapter from Watanabe's *Heiancho bunshoshi* (Tokyo: Daigaku Shuppankai, 1981). The article analyses the intense subjectivity of the *Kagero nikki* style showing how the author narrates all events and refers to all persons exclusively from her personal perspective.

THE PILLOW BOOK

Title in Japanese: *Makura no soshi*
Author: Sei Shonagon
Born: c. 966
Died: c. 1021–1028
Literary Form: Essays, miscellany
Date of Composition: c. 993–1010

Major Themes

Under the tutelage of a superior being, such as Empress Sadako, women can attain the highest levels of taste and accomplishment.
Aesthetic sensibilities are the sole acceptable indices of character and quality.
Aesthetic merits are displayed only by the members of court society living in the capital.
Do not suffer fools lightly, especially if they are male.

About the year 1000 in the capital city of Heiankyō, groups of women mounted an ongoing aesthetic competition. Because of their encounters with the opposition, utilizing poems, silk robes, and the struggle to preserve a snow mountain, these women were serious, meticulously trained for their literary showdowns, and as much a part of elite power politics as any government leader. That their investment in things literary was no trivial matter is attested by the achievements of two of them, one the author of *The Tale of Genji*, Murasaki Shikibu, and the other, Sei Shōnagon. The latter's miscellany records her times at length in gem-like prose, and is valuable, among other reasons, because it relates episodes involving historical figures, whereas one can only speculate on real models for Murasaki's fiction.

Because Sei Shōnagon evaluates those around her, commenting often, and sometimes scathingly, on who and what is elegant, amusing, praiseworthy, disgusting, or just in poor taste, the reader gains a sense of a lively, intriguing female mind. *The Pillow Book*'s aesthetic judgments are not solely the product of a single imagination, however. Through them, Shōnagon represents her salon, the talented women surrounding the empress Sadako (b. 977). Sadako (or Teishi, as her name may also be pronounced) entered the imperial palace at the age of 14, become the consort of the emperor Ich-

ijō, and progressed to empress. Sadako's position as the favored wife was something she could not afford to take for granted. Her father, Fujiwara no Michitaka, would not have tolerated her complacency either, as it was his desire to manipulate the future heir to the throne that led him to present her to the emperor. Such marriage politics were common among the elite, and they made high-ranking women vulnerable not only to jealousy, but also to the cultural coups of their rivals. Sadako invited a formidable array of court poets to be among the 30 or 40 women who served her.

Few facts survive on the writer who came to epitomize Sadako's group, the woman we know only as Sei Shōnagon. *Sei* is the Sinified pronunciation of the first character in the surname Kiyohara. Kiyohara no Motosuke (908–90), her father, although perhaps only by adoption, was a compiler of the second imperial poetry collection *Gosenshū*. Possibly Shōnagon was exposed to Chinese literature in more than the usual measure for a female due to her father's interests; certainly, she was conscious of her literary heritage. She was also aware of her origins in the provincial class, an awareness that she shows by an extreme distaste for anything rural or the slightest bit out of fashion. Motosuke was posted to the western province of Suō when she was nine, and thus was inflicted by a grave inconvenience on her youth and adolescence. In 981, she married Tachibana Norimitsu, whose mother had been wet nurse to the crown prince. Kazan's ascension to the throne in 984 enhanced Shōnagon's connections and her literary activities. She bore a son, Norinaga, in 982, but the marriage dissolved by about 990. Sometime in 993 she entered service at court, where she was called Shōnagon, a title meaning "minor counselor."

Court life agreed with Shōnagon; but it was fraught with political dangers. After her father, Michitaka's, death in 995, Sadako's fortunes turned. Her brothers were exiled the next year, and Sadako herself left the palace and received the tonsure. All three were redeemed in 998, but in the following year, Fujiwara no Michinaga, the new power, installed his daughter Shōshi, or Akiko, as consort to Ichijo. This occurred in the same month that Sadako bore him a son, normally the crowning moment for an empress. In 1000, Sadako died in childbirth, which probably signaled the end of Shōnagon's career as well. A possible second marriage to Fujiwara Muneyo after her retirement is a matter of speculation, although we know she had a daughter.

Parts of *The Pillow Book* circulated while the author was at court, but scholars think she composed some of it as a tribute to Sadako after her death. Shōnagon's court service is the subject of much of her writing, but we have little beyond legend of her life after the year 1000. These legends are quite widely distributed, and tend not to be complimentary. Medieval moralists were no doubt being spoilsports when they wrote of her miserable old age as fitting recompense for a life of display and self-promotion. The dark tone of some poems from Shōnagon's later years surely also contributed to this image.

A Fascinating Style of Composition

As a cultural achievement, *Makura no sōshi* is of the highest caliber. The prose style has long been recognized as the most beautiful and accessible in the Japanese language, which, with its agglutinative capacity, can tend toward unwieldy sentences.

At its most accomplished, Shōnagon's prose calls on all the senses, juxtaposing the unexpected and inverting the familiar in a process that leaves the reader marveling. The collection expresses a delightful wit, as when the narrator skewers the sort of clumsy lover who cannot find his way out of a woman's room without banging his head or scrounging for his belongings in the dark. In fact, it has been dubbed the literature of *okashi*, meaning "charming," "splendid," or "interesting," in contrast to *The Tale of Genji*, called the literature of *aware*, or "a sense of deep feeling or pathos." The contrast is an artificial one, but telling nonetheless.

Even the compositional mode, which those fond of narrative order or categorization might deride as unorganized or desultory, affords a reading experience of surprise and fascination. A description of how a lover returning home at dawn is tempted to dally with another woman whose lattice happens to be open when he passes by—a narrative that itself grows out of remarks on the heat of the seventh month—leads into a discussion of flowering trees, and then to a list of ponds with comment on their names. Thanks to this meandering style, *The Pillow Book* is often seen as the precursor of a literary type that may be Japan's quintessential prose idiom, the *zuihitsu*, literally meaning "to follow the brush." This is a useful comparison, but it is an anachronism. It is not until late in the eighteenth century that this work becomes associated with the *zuihitsu* genre, which before that point refers more to scholarly compendia than to personal jottings. In Shōnagon's day, the genre category was apparently *makura no sōshi*, since her work was called *Sei Shōnagon makura no sōshi*, and other authors' collections were similarly named after them. At the time, the translation "pillow book" came into English, many believed it referred to notebooks kept in drawers inside wooden pillows. The current theory is that *makura* is related to the poetic terms *makura kotoba* (fixed epithet) or *utamakura* (place names famous in verse). The numerous lists in Shonagon's work, it is felt, were most likely there for use in poetry.

Scholars normally divide the contents of *Makura*

no sōshi into three categories—the lists, diary-like recitals of incidents, and essayistic or *zuihitsu*-like passages that may touch on any subject. A key listing feature is the many observations as to which things have which qualities. Not only does Shōnagon record "elegant things" and "wonderful things," she inventories "embarrassing things" and "hateful things," including crows, mosquitos, and gossips, whom she describes in all modes of operation. When she lists "things that have no value," she comments that she has license to bring them up because no one will look at her notes, thus implying that the book was meant for private consumption; this seems to be a pose, however, as it is typical for the time to include self-disparaging comments. The origins of her lists are unclear, for no one recorded such before her, but they surely come out of an oral context, and may reflect a salon pastime. Evidence exists of a parlor game involving lists, a variety of which may also have been used to teach children. Hidden riddles have been discovered in some of the catalogs. Punning lists surface in Chinese literature; the nearest possible model is the late Tang poet Li Shang-yin's miscellany, the *Ishan zazuan* (*I-shan tsa-tsuan*). Contemporaneous Japanese works on poetic topics may additionally have inspired her.

Judgments of Social Propriety

Sei Shōnagon could be cutting in her sketches. Those whose mastery of etiquette left something to be desired were the target of laughter, while commoners could be ridiculed simply for breathing. The faults of men are enumerated in excrutiating detail. Shōnagon's disdain for those of low rank is as unrelenting as her belief that the only life worth living is that of the court woman. She repeatedly complains about the unsuitable behavior of servants, and promotes the striations in society. The court is the universe, and all women of rank should participate without fear. It is a life of many shared activities, not the least significant of which is sexual concourse between men and women. Etiquette demanded that women be shielded behind screens

much of the time, but the spaces people inhabited were still quite permeable, especially with sound. The author exposes the pressures of living at close quarters by means of overheard conversations and peeping through cracks.

Shōnagon was notorious in her own day, if the remarks of Murasaki Shikibu in her journal are any guide. Murasaki's Shōnagon is a self-important, conceited woman who oversteps her abilities in the use of Chinese characters. It is true that Shōnagon records numerous episodes in which she saves a situation by pulling out a rare reference from Chinese poetry or otherwise showing up whoever can be bested. We moderns may find it endearing, since it combats our image of the reticent Japanese woman. Sei Shōnagon appears in *Mumyōzōshi*, a critical discussion of vernacular literature most likely written by the daughter of Shunzei in about 1200, as do many women authors. The judgment of women a few centuries later was evidently much kinder, as they roundly praise *Makura no sōshi* for capturing the atmosphere of the palace.

The Influence of The Pillow Book

The textual history of *Makura no sōshi* is so complex as to have fostered, some say, a lack of scholarly attention. Of the four main textual groups, two contain manuscripts in which the segments unfold at random, while two marshal the sections into classifications. The oldest known manuscript is the classified sort, but this may only mean that readers from early on have tried to impose order on Shōnagon's dilations. The earliest literati to produce full-scale commentaries, however, preferred the miscellaneous texts. The Japanese seem to appreciate a reading experience that allows participation by the reader, who must find connections and tie the disparate pieces together. Most believe that this disorder was intended by the author to encourage the reader to match wits. Indeed, the flexibility of the text reflects an aesthetic quality that mattered to Shōnagon and her contemporaries—the ability to improvise in a potentially poetic situation.

Opinions differ as to how widely *The Pillow Book* was read during the medieval era. Two early commentaries are known only by title. Yoshida Kenkō, the author of *Essays in Idleness*, not only read but imitated Shōnagon's style in parts of his work. The most famous commentary, the *Sunshoshō* by Kitamura Kigin (1614–1705), made the text accessible beyond the elite by providing detailed notes on vocabulary and ancient court practices. Thus the text could be used, as it is today, in educational settings. Because of the gender of its author, who was blamed for "immoral" and "weak" tendencies in the work, *The Pillow Book* was always slightly less likely to be in a curriculum than *Tsurezuregusa* (*Essays in Idleness*). Now, however, it is generally understood that the difference between the two is as much social as gender-related.

Random Patterns

While *The Pillow Book* may not be what Westerners would call logical, it is rich with pattern and layering that is not unreminiscent of the formal women's "twelve-layer" costume, or *jūnithitoe*. Naturally the adjective *okashi* appears repeatedly, as do other evaluative terms. Seasonal activities in the captial come to the forefront in intervals, perhaps in the way that certain occasions drifted into the author's memory. A small cast of characters makes appearances here and there, providing a kind of tension to the flow. By the end we may feel as though we have glimpsed the swirl of many ladies' layered sleeves, subtly joining colors and textures that were thought out with extreme care by each wearer (however she may seem to deny it). The context of the palace frames them all, the more strongly when they venture beyond the pale to the countryside. And always, at the center, the image of the compassionate, elegant Sadako, whose merest word can shame or delight the company, makes its presence felt. Shōnagon's literary form, then, far from being a hodgepodge, reveals itself as a near-perfect match for the experience the text tries to convey, that is the aesthetic and temporal superiority of Sadako's salon.

LINDA H. CHANCE

Further Reading

Translations

Bowring, Richard. *Murasaki Shikibu: Her Diary and Poetic Memoirs.* Princeton, NJ: Princeton University Press, 1982. Murasaki's record of the rival salon led by Empress Shōshi is an excellent companion piece. At its core is a depiction of the birth of Shōshi's first son (Atsuhira) in 1008, an extended look at high court ritual and glory, but other passages also bear comparison.

Morris, Ivan, trans. and ed. *The Pillow Book of Sei Shōnagon.* 2 vols. New York: Columbia University Press, 1967. The complete translation. Abridged versions are also available in Penguin and Columbia University Press editions.

Related Studies

McCullough, William H. "Japanese Marriage Institutions in the Heian Period." In *Harvard Journal of Asiatic Studies* 27 (1967): 103–67. Valuable treatment of marriage customs in the Heian period.

Marra, Michele. "*Mumyōzōshi*: Introduction and Translation." In *Monumenta Nipponica* 39:2–4 (1984): 115–45, 281–305, 409–34. This work of informal literary criticism, written by a woman in the form of a talk among women, not only speaks of Sei Shōnagon, but gives further context for the activity of women in salons, despite coming from a different historical period.

Morris, Ivan. *The World of the Shining Prince: Court Life in Ancient Japan.* Oxford: Oxford University Press, 1964; reprint, Baltimore, MA: Penguin Books, 1969. For many years the only introduction to the cultural world around the major literary monuments of the mid-Heian period, this is still worth reading. Readers should, however, take Morris's perspectives on "superstition" and the gender balance of the time with a grain of salt.

Morris, Mark. "Sei Shōnagon's Poetic Catalogues." In *Harvard Journal of Asiatic Studies* 40:1 (June 1980): 5–54. An excellent and most informative article that explores all known explanations for the derivation of the list style that comprises nearly a third of The Pillow Book.

Wakita, Haruko. "Marriage and Property in Premodern Japan from the Perspective of Women's History." In *Journal of Japanese Studies* 10:1 (1984): 73–99. Translated and introduced by Suzanne Gay. Offers a more up-to-date perspective on marriage in Heian, and critiques McCullough's version.

THE TALE OF GENJI

Title in Japanese: *Genji monogatari*
Author: Murasaki Shikibu
Born: c. 973
Died: c. 1014
Literary Form: Novel
Date of Composition: The bulk of *The Tale of Genji* was probably written and circulated chapter by chapter between the year 1003 and the author's death, as early as 1014. There is no known original holograph. Extant textual variants fall into three major categories: the Kawachi recension, the Aobyōshi recension, and a group of other dissimilar variants called *Beppon*.

Major Themes

We are compelled to seek substitutes for those we have lost, retracing the present and future through patterns established in the past.

Maternity, nurturing, loss, and death are points on a continuous line, one leading inevitably to the next. Transgression invokes retribution, be it political, personal, social, or psychic in nature.

Nature, the seasons, and human existence are inextricably linked, each reflecting and commenting upon the other.

Beauty is intrinsically and necessarily fragile and fleeting.

The Tale of Genji is widely acknowledged to be not only a masterpiece of Japanese literature, but one of the greatest works of prose fiction ever created. For centuries, the *Genji* has held countless Japanese readers in thrall, prompted endless interpretive debate, and spawned numerous guidebooks, secret teachings, and commentaries. The tale has served as a repository of classical allusions and a sourcebook for generations of poets, essayists, and fiction writers. Characters, themes, episodes, and allusions to the *Genji* haunt almost every genre of Japanese literature, from essay to short story or haiku. Medieval Japanese Nō drama is permeated with references to the *Genji*, whether to characters, themes, and episodes from the tale, or merely in the incorporation of text and allusion to increase lyrical impact. In the exuberant Edo period (1600–1868), the tale took on a new vitality in printed format, which allowed for the further dissemination of the text and numerous digests and commentaries. While few of the newly emerging bourgeoisie actually read the entire text, everyone was familiar with the plot, key characters, and major episodes. Thus, the tale became integrated into the common cultural mainstream to such an extent that there even emerged a rash of satires and spoofs. In the twentieth century, several celebrated writers, among them Tanizaki Jun'ichirō and Enchi Fumiko, have produced translations into modern Japanese. The *Genji* frequently finds its way into the pages of modern novels and short stories; it has been dramatized in television serials and even recycled into the popular comic book format.

The impact of the *Genji* in Japanese culture has extended well beyond the world of *belles lettres*. In pictorial art, it has inspired countless illustrated scrolls and screen paintings. It has served as a sourcebook for etiquette manuals, a wide swath of textile patterns, color designations, and graphic motifs. Woodblock print artists were quick to exploit the graphic possibilities of the world of courtly love and aesthetics inherent in the tale, and even Edo period houses of pleasure were populated by a fair number of courtesans named after female characters of the *Genji*, their interaction with customers acquiring depth and spice through reference to it. In modern times, scholars frequently refer to the text for clues to such diverse areas of historical inquiry as social customs, religious ceremonies, diet, and clothing. Indeed, it is difficult to imagine Japanese culture expunged of the tale. With the appearance in 1935 of the hauntingly beautiful English-language translation by Arthur Waley, and, more recently, the excellent translation by Edward Seidensticker, and rendition into several other major languages, *The Tale of Genji* has assumed a canonical position in the ranks of world literature as well. Often called the world's first pyschological novel, it has invoked comparison with Proust's *Remembrance of Things Past*, and its insight on the complexities of human life continues to impress an ever-widening contemporary audience.

Murasaki Shikibu

It is a matter of considerable literary irony that this work of almost universal appeal was initially produced by a relatively obscure writer for an extremely narrow audience of elite court ladies. We know precious little about the putative author, Murasaki Shikibu. Even her name is a construct, composed of a court title (*shikibu*) once held by her father, and the sobriquet (*Murasaki*) of a major female character in the tale itself, this latter nickname probably bestowed in jest by a fellow courtier. Most scholars agree that the author was born around 973 to a minor branch of the illustrious Fujiwara clan. Well educated in both Chinese and Japanese, unusual for a woman at the time, she married a man considerably her senior and was widowed two years later. In 1007 or 1008, she entered the service of the empress Shōshi, consort of the emperor Ichijō, where she acted as attendant and tutor. It is unclear when she first commenced work on the *Genji*: it may have been that portions of it were already known to the court, prompting her appointment. In any event, certainly by 1008, portions of the tale were known and circulated among members of the court. In addition to her masterpiece, Murasaki Shikibu left a diary, *Murasaki Shikibu nikki*, and a poetry collection, *Murasaki Shikibu shū*. Although no longer extant in its complete form, the diary is an important work in its own right, and is counted among the four major

diaries of the rich and productive Heian period (794–1185); the poetry collection is autobiographical in nature and was probably consciously compiled by the author late in life as a kind of literary self-portrait. Both diary and poems reveal a devout, thoughtful, and intelligent woman of a retiring nature, and somewhat inclined to be overly critical of herself and others. The year of her death is uncertain: the last reference to her is dated 1013, when she would have been around 35 years old. She might have died shortly thereafter, or survived as late as 1025. Her name is missing from a roster of Shōshi's ladies compiled in 1031.

Textual Generations

Within 50 years of its initial appearance, versions of the *Genji* were in circulation among the literate elite. Because each copy was transcribed by hand in a painstaking, labor-intensive process, few had access to the entire work, and most had to make do with such chapters as they could acquire in whatever order they could acquire them. As a result, we have no way of knowing to what degree the texts now available represent the text that Murasaki Shikibu originally committed to paper. Even while she was in the process of writing, her own copies tended to disappear into the hands of overly eager readers, and she was obliged to reconstruct the manuscript from memory. Thus, each copy assumed a life and authority of its own. Over the years, later copyists added interpolations and embellishments, and scrambled the chapter sequence, either by accident or intention. Moreover, admirers could not resist adding their own contributions, such that entire chapters are of questionable authenticity. In the subsequent medieval period, there were several attempts to sort out this tangle. The Aobyoshi recension collated by Fujiwara Teika from a number of different versions now forms the basis of the standard text, but even this is not without its problems, the most pernicious of which is its chapter sequence.

The Story of Genji

One of the longest novels ever written, *The Tale of Genji* comprises 54 chapters, spans 3 generations and 4 imperial reigns, and is populated by over 400 characters, some 30 of whom are of major importance. Most Japanese scholars divide the tale into three sections: first: the hero's youth, rise to power, and halcyon years; second: conflict, tragedy, and decline, culminating in Genji's death; and finally, the "sequel," devoted to Genji's descendents, which is increasingly preoccupied with Buddhist themes. But, as we will see, to describe and divide is not necessarily to conquer the complexities of the *Genji.*

The shining prince, Genji, is the sole issue of the union between an emperor and his favorite lady Kiritsubo, who, lacking strong paternal backing at court, is persecuted by the emperor's primary consort Kokiden, daughter of the powerful minister of the right, and her allies. When the lady sickens and dies, the distraught emperor finds a substitute in her kinswoman Fujitsubo, who closely resembles her. The emperor bows to political realities by naming Kokiden's son (the future Suzaku emperor) as heir apparent, and demotes Genji to commoner status, thereby negating his eligibility for the throne. At the age of twelve, Genji is married to the haughty Aoi, daughter of the minister of the left. Genji's childhood devotion to his stepmother, Fujitsubo, turns amorous, and he contrives a secret meeting with her. This indiscretion results in the birth of Reizei, assumed to be Genji's half-brother, who eventually assumes the throne.

Seemingly propelled by a discussion of women among fellow courtiers, Genji has a series of dalliances, to varying degrees of success, with a variety of women. Textual critics group together the chapters focussing on these affairs, which appear to function as counterpoint to the main narrative. Aside from his own lost mother and her substitute, Fujitsubo, Genji's greatest love is Murasaki, a distant cousin of Fujitsubo, whom he discovers when she is a child. Unable to secure from her guardians permission to adopt her, he kidnaps and rears her until she is of an age for the relationship to become one of husband and wife.

Aoi is afflicted by the jealous spirit of Genji's spurned lover Rokujō and dies after giving birth to a son, Yūgiri. An ill-advised affair with Kokiden's sister sparks a decline in Genji's political fortunes; and he goes into exile. There he meets and impregnates the Akashi Lady, daughter of an ambitious monk. When a series of ill omens in the capital prompts Genji's recall from exile, he builds a new mansion at Nijō and assembles there his numerous women, including the infant Akashi Princess, whom the childless Murasaki rears as her own. With his putative stepbrother Reizei on the throne, Genji assumes a prominent position at court, dabbling in marriage politics by successfully installing Akikonomu, daughter of the now-deceased and spurned Rokujō, as empress to the new emperor Reizei and, later, his own daughter the Akashi princess, to the crown prince, son of the retired Suzaku emperor. A series of chapters is devoted to the story of Tamakazura, daughter of Yūgao, whom Genji once loved, and Genji's close friend and rival, Tō no Chūjō. Tamakazura is courted by a number of suitors (including Genji himself), but unexpectedly marries the uncouth but powerful General Higekuro.

Genji takes the youthful third princess, daughter of the Suzaku emperor, as primary consort, causing great anguish to the faithful Murasaki. The third princess is seduced by Kashiwagi, son of Tō no Chūjō, and bears a son, Kaoru, whom Genji raises as his own; Kashiwagi languishes and dies, while the third princess, wracked by guilt and shame that Genji has discovered her infidelity, takes the tonsure. Murasaki's death presages that of Genji himself, and the story turns to the sober Kaoru and dashing Niou, Genji's grandson, and their courtship of the daughters of a retired prince living outside the capital. Kaoru pursues Ōigimi, the elder sister, who eventually dies rather than succumb to his advances; Niou marries Nakanokimi, the younger sister. Their half-sister, Ukifune, who resembles Ōigimi, seeks refuge with Nakanokimi, where she is pursued by Niou. Ukifune takes flight, to be discovered by Kaoru, who also attempts to woo her. Unable to choose between the two, Ukifune attempts to drown herself, and is presumed dead, but she survives in hiding at a nunnery. Upon discovering her whereabouts, Kaoru attempts to contact her, but she refuses to reply. The novel ends on this inconclusive note.

It will be obvious that the tale does not reach any semblance of what Westerners would call a conclusion. Opinion is divided on whether or not available texts represent the full extent of the tale. Certainly the tale breaks off at a point very close to conclusion, such that barring any new major plot developments, any missing material would probably comprise no more than a chapter or two. Dissatisfied readers yearning for a sense of closure have written their own sequels, while others have found the very note of suspension with which it ends to be entirely consistent with the dreamlike, inconclusive nature of the work as a whole.

Nature of the Work

The Tale of Genji is best described as a novel that vacillates between romance and realism. In Japanese, it is considered the primary exemplar of the *monogatari* (literally, telling things, or the person who tells) narrative tradition. The first few chapters of the tale, relating the doomed love between the emperor and his favorite, and the amorous adventures of a handsome young prince evoke themes and overtones of the Japanese classical romance. Earlier works of this genre, most of which are now lost, related fantastic adventures and improbable romances, often featuring the "stepdaughter" theme, in which a young woman is tormented by a stepmother, but eventually marries a nobleman well above her station. The *Genji* resonates with other familiar narrative patterns derived from myth and folklore. The hero's lonely exile described in the "Suma" and "Akashi" chapters, for example, is enriched by reference to the "exile of the noble" theme, wherein a young man endures hardship and proves his mettle before assuming power in the society that cast him off. The "stepdaughter" theme also plays a role in these chapters, as well as in several other chapters relating the tribulations of young women whose families are blind to their merits. But the *Genji* has a way of subverting its own generic referents, becoming an ironic commentary on the ideals of courtly love and the monogatari tradition itself. Even early chapters such as "Utsusemi" ("The Shell of the Locust") and "Suetsumuhana" ("The Safflower") parody the amorous quest, casting the hero in an unflattering light and revealing the realities that can lurk behind the ideal. In fact, Genji is notably unsuccessful in three of his first four amorous encounters. Women who become entangled with the hero—particularly those of the lesser ranking zuryō class of provincial governors—often live to regret their lots. Initially, the story of the lady of Akashi resembles a fairytale romance, but as the tale progresses, we see the lady herself become increasingly aware of the price she must pay for her liaison with Genji.

Gender Relations

The bulk of *The Tale of Genji* concerns love and its ensuing complications. Among the aristocracy of the Heian period, primary marriages were arranged in accordance with political considerations, often at an early age. But secondary and tertiary connubial arrangements were also possible, so long as discretion was maintained and social proprieties observed. But men had few opportunities for direct social intercourse with their female counterparts: the more high-born a woman, the less accessible she was to male company, remaining indoors behind her screens, accompanied by a bevy of attendents, often speaking through an intermediary. Male ardor was aroused not by the sight of a woman's face or body, but by stolen glimpses—of her long hair, handwriting, trailing sleeves, or other signs of allure. Passivity, delicacy, and sensitivity were key to the contemporary feminine ideal. If a woman had no powerful relative who might block an amorous idyll, so much the better. Thus, the romance of the *Genji* often reveals itself in the male search for, and discovery of, beautiful hidden women, aided and abetted—and sometimes even witnessed—by attendents of both parties. As a paragon of male beauty and accomplishment, Genji has considerable attractions. While he is a perennial favorite of many ladies, his affairs are often marked by tragedy and pain; some women, aware that romantic entanglement with Genji would harm their public reputation or cause them pain, elude him altogether. Others, like the complacent Lady of the Orange Blossoms (Hanachirusato), are content to remain minor constellations in Genji's universe. Still others, having once been bathed in Genji's light, retain fond memories of the past and maintain contact with him over the years.

Readers disturbed by the seeming promiscuity, occasional brutality, and sheer frequency of love affairs in the *Genji* should keep in mind that it is dangerous to try to extrapolate from a literary text a sense of the social realities of the Heian period. *Genji* is a fictional construct, larger—and sometimes smaller—than life.

Narrative Style

The Tale of Genji was the first work of extended prose fiction to be composed in the vernacular, as opposed to either Chinese or Sinicized Japanese, which was encumbered by Chinese phrases, rhetorical devices, and references. The use of Chinese marks previous monogatari as of probable male authorship, for knowledge of Chinese was considered unseemly for women. By a fascinating twist of linguistic fate, women, limited to the simplified *kana* script (whereby the sounds of native Japanese could be written through simplified characters), had the opportunity to develop the expressive nuances of their own language unfettered by the demands imposed by a foreign language. The vernacular not only allowed for a greater subjectivity and emotive power, but its very structure, based upon a complicated system of verbal endings and honorifics, made possible a subtlety of expression impossible to duplicate in translation. Even modern Japanese readers find that this maddening, glorious imprecision makes the text difficult going indeed. Moreover, characters are referred to not by a fixed name but by their rank, office, or function, which change as the tale progresses, or equally often, by a sobriquet based upon an association established through the text. Thus, the Rokujō lady is so designated

after her place of residence, Rokujō—sixth avenue; her daughter Akikonomu (literally, autumn-loving) derives her sobriquet from her preference for autumn over spring.

In the Japanese text, the presence of the narrator is marked by this same system of verbal endings and honorifics, which situates her rank below that of the main characters, but sufficiently high to serve at court—an attendant, perhaps, who has witnessed or heard of the events. This narratorial presence, both covert and overt, creates a number of textual effects, not the least of which is an increased sense of versimilitude. Occasional narratorial digressions provide interpolative commentary upon the action and the character's motivations. Sometimes the hero is lavishly praised: "I could have enjoyed a millennium of his company, . . . so serene and sure did he seem." (Seidensticker, trans., *The Tale of Genji*, 329). Other times, he is undercut: "She was a shallow woman, but to his less than pure heart she was not a prize to be flung away." (51). "He seemed a little self-satisfied at times." (140). And sometimes doubt is cast upon the reliability of the narrator herself: "Sometimes . . . one is deluded by rank or an elegant hand . . . and afterwards, in attempting to describe it, made to feel that it was not so at all. It may be that I have written confidently and not very accurately." (351)

The Place of Aesthetics

The Tale of Genji reflects what Ivan Morris has called a "cult of beauty": a small society of aristocrats who valued beauty so highly that they turned almost every pastime into art. Often the art was of a public, collective nature, such as shell-matching contests, incense competitions, musical and dance performances, and, of course, poetry. Central to this pursuit was the demonstration of a refined sensibility, upon which rested one's reputation. Careful note was taken of clothing: an unseemly color combination in the layering of her many robes might dash a lady's hopes for a good marriage. A courtier's performance in a court poetry contest might affect profoundly his prospects in the annual round of promotions. In private matters as well, the rules of taste were equally important. Upon receiving a note from a woman, Genji would scan it carefully, noting such details as the choice of paper and calligraphic style as indicators of the lady's worth. The sniffling Safflower lady is made an object of ridicule as much for her worn, out-of-date robes as for her bulbous red nose. Once codified in the *Genji*, the intricacies of style—from court ceremonies to informal amusements, from courtship etiquette to the mixing of incense—guided practice for centuries. Passages from the *Genji* have provided the basis for a considerable amount of literary and art criticism. The debate between Tamakazura and Genji on the relative merits of fiction in the "Fireflies" chapter is considered the first Japanese defense of fiction. "A Picture Contest" offers an extended—and often cited—disquisition on the relationship between literature and painting.

In its abundance of poems, poetic repartee, and poetic references, the text of the *Genji* reflects the social importance of poetry in the Heian period and enriches the narrative with a deep lyricism. References to Po Chu-i's "Song of Everlasting Sorrow," about the love of a Chinese emperor for his most favored concubine, dominate the opening chapter; and echo later in "The Wizard," in which Genji mourns his dead Murasaki. Other poetic allusions, such as Fujiwara Kanesuke's "The heart of a parent is not darkness; and yet / He wanders lost in thoughts upon his child." (Seidensticker, 9) act as a leitmotif in the developing narrative. In addition to the many poetic allusions, the *Genji* contains over 800 poems, most of only middling poetic merit, through which characters communicate both everyday matters as well as their deeper emotions.

Nature

Anyone scanning the chapter titles of *The Tale of Genji* will be struck by the overwhelming preponderance of seasonal references, flora and fauna, and natural phenomena; indeed, nature serves as the dominant metaphor for artistic expression and human sentiment throughout the novel. Traditional Japanese aesthetics are in large part derived from

human empathy with nature, in particular, with seasonal progression. In particular, the evanescence of all things implied in the term *aware*, a keenly felt appreciation of beauty and the transience inherent to that beauty, struck a responsive chord. The *Genji* is suffused with this sense of *aware*, both as perceived by the characters and as transmitted thematically.

Most major characters are identified with seasons, flowers, or natural phenomena. While each season has its charms, spring and autumn are the most valorized. In Genji's residence at Nijo, ladies occupy quarters in keeping with their particular seasonal affiliations and social rank. The ever-faithful Lady of the Orange Blossoms lives in the northeastern summer wing and cultivates the flowers of summer; Murasaki (and her adopted daughter, the Akashi princess) occupy the southeast corner, planted with spring flowers and foliage; the autumn-loving Akikonomu, the southwest, planted with maples and autumn grasses, and the Akashi lady, the northwest winter garden. Nature informs human life in other ways as well: the moon often appears in conjunction with death, and, quite predictably, storms presage upheaval in human affairs.

Repetitive Patterns

It has often been remarked that *The Tale of Genji* is motivated by a dynamic of desire and replacement, set in motion by the original loss of Kiritsubo, Genji's birth mother. When Genji's father, consumed by desire for his dead love, replaces her with Fujitsubo, he sets off a pattern that spirals repeatedly throughout the novel. The drive to replace is sparked by resemblance, a physical or spiritual identification of a person—usually a woman—with another now lost. Each woman has her shadowy predecessor, whom she can never completely eclipse because she can never fully *be* that woman, who is unknowable and unattainable. Genji, of course, seeks Kiritsubo through Fujitsubo; later, he is drawn to Murasaki by her resemblance to Fujitsubo, and begins to move into the role of father. He attempts to create the ideal mate in his relationship with Murasaki, psychically combining the roles of son, husband, and father. Such is the brilliance of the novel that Genji and Murasaki never produce children: the perfect union is a sterile union.

Relationships in the *Genji* are seldom stable. Rather, they are under almost constant threat of encroachment by a third agent, expressing the impossibility of equilibrium. These relationships, too, are marked by another dynamic of resemblance. Sometimes, the triads are of an oedipal nature, linking a child figure to a male paternal and female maternal figure. For example, the Genji-Old Emperor-Fujitsubo triad is repeated in the Kashiwagi-Genji-Third Princess grouping. Other triads are patterned after the love triangle, although this too may be informed by the oedipal triangle, and often extend through generations as well. Genji's rivalry with Tō no Chūjō over Yūgao, an early love of each, is later echoed in Yūgiri's attempts to win Tō no Chūjō's daughter, and in Tō no Chūjō's son's attempts to secure the affections of Tamakazura, Yūgao's daughter, for whom Genji nurses a secret desire.

Transgression and Retribution

In the heavily Buddhist and deeply superstitious world of *The Tale of Genji*, every transgression leads to retribution. Transgression in the *Genji* generally is of a political, social, or spiritual nature, and retribution may come in physical or psychic form. The best known example is that of the lady Rokujō, the haughty, high-born widow of a retired crown prince. The young Genji has a fleeting affair with her but, weary of her persistent attentions, he neglects her. Outwardly, she maintains her pride and elegant composure, but her inner rage is transformed into an evil spirt, which possesses Genji's wife, Aoi, who has additionally slighted Rokujō in the famous carriage dispute recounted in the "Aoi" chapter. Even after Rokujō's death, the spirit afflicts Murasaki and Genji's young new wife, the Third Princess. Thus, the feckless Genji pays dearly for his unwitting arousal of Rokujō's pride and jealousy, while Rokujō's emotional excess and burden of guilt also doom her own spiritual aspirations.

Within the political sphere, Genji's sin of dallying with Kokiden's sister, Oborozukiyo, who had been promised to the Emperor, results in exile; underlying this, however, is the greater sin of having violated the imperial line by secretly siring the crown prince. But the knife of retribution cuts both ways: for their willful machinations, the Kokiden faction is visited by a series of misfortunes that forces them to reinstate Genji to his former position. For his own sin, Genji suffers further when his wife is violated by another man and gives birth to a son. Only the guilty parties and Genji himself are aware of Kaoru's true paternity, retrospectively raising the possibility that Genji's father had been aware of Genji's own transgression. Kaoru grows up with a heavy burden of yearning that he tries to assuage first through religion, and later, through his doomed love for the devout, motherless Ōigimi.

In this way, the *Genji* grows in a spiral fashion, each development reflecting upon and modifying earlier developments, with new characters informed by their predecessors, each different from, but reminiscent of, another. As Haruo Shirane puts it, "In a manner reminiscent of a locust, which transforms itself as it grows, the *Genji* is repeatedly 'reborn' from within and leaves intact its former self or selves, which continue to make their presence felt even after they are 'outgrown.' "

The Tale of Genji is amenable to almost as many interpretations as it has readers. In recent years, a number of theoretical approaches—Marxist, myth criticism, semiological—have been applied to the text, with interesting and provocative results. Yet the tale is too immense and complex to be pinned down by a single approach or even a single reading. It might be said to resemble the character of Ukifune (literally, the boat upon the waters). To Kaoru, Ukifune is a memento of his lost love; to Niou, an erotic object to be added to his harem; to her mother, a steppingstone to social recognition; to a nun who rescues her, a surrogate daughter. Intriguing, mysterious, enigmatic, and beautiful, Ukifune is a vessel filled by the meaning others assign to her, but whose own identity remains unfathomable. Similarly, the *Genji* invites the reader to explore its intimations and partake of the desire that motivates it, to feel the ebb and flow of its gentle rhythms, and to trace its patterns as they expand and spiral back upon themselves without ever reaching the closure of definitive interpretation.

In casting about for a statement that epitomizes the work as a whole, a line from Fitzgerald's *The Great Gatsby* seems particularly fitting: "So we beat on, boats against the current, borne back ceaselessly into the past. . . ." While such borrowing might strike the specialist as heresy of the highest order, that a line culled from a twentieth-century American writer might be so applied is, I think, testimony to the universal truths embedded in *The Tale of Genji*.

VIRGINIA SKORD WATERS

Further Reading

Translations

Seidensticker, Edward, trans. *The Tale of Genji.* New York: Alfred A. Knopf, 1976. Considered by most to be the authoritative and preferred English-language translation. While certainly more prosaic than that of Waley, the style is spare and cooly elegant, and the accuracy is unquestionable. Given that neither this nor the Waley translation contains much by way of explanatory notes or guidance, the inquisitive reader will find it necessary to refer to secondary sources for background information or interpretive guidance. Those listed below will be particularly helpful.

Waley, Arthur, trans. *The Tale of Genji.* London: George Allen and Unwin, 1935. A classic in its own right, this densely lyrical translation is highly regarded for its evocation of the spirit of the original, but is marred by inaccuracies and the translator's free-wheeling interpretation, which omitted certain parts altogether and overly embellished others.

Related Studies

Bowring, Richard. *Murasaki Shikibu: The Tale of Genji.* Cambridge, MA: Cambridge University Press, 1988. A brief guidebook outlining the plot, major themes, and historical context of the tale.

————. *Murasaki Shikibu. Her Diary and Poetic Memoirs.* Princeton, NJ: Princeton University Press, 1982. Translations of and commentary on Murasaki Shikibu's other works.

Field, Norma. *The Spendor of Longing in the Tale of Genji.* Princeton, NJ: Princeton University Press, 1987. An interesting reading of the tale as disrupted myth, with the Genji character coming in for a pummeling. Dense and eloquent, but prone to retelling.

Morris, Ivan. *The World of the Shining Prince: Court Life in Ancient Japan.* New York: Knopf, 1964. The standard reader's companion, relating information on such topics as Heian-period Japanese religion, marriage customs, politics, and court ceremonies.

Okada Richard. *Figures of Resistance: Language, Poetry, and Narrating in The Tale of Genji and other Mid-Heian Texts.* Durham, NC: Duke University Press, 1991. Basing his study upon close reading of the original text, Okada demonstrates how traditional approaches skew our understanding. Difficult going for the non-specialist.

Pekarik, Andrew, ed. *Ukifune: Love in the Tale of Genji.* New York: Columbia University Press, 1982. An excellent collection of essays centered upon the last 10 chapters of the book. Illustrates the range of readings that may be fruitfully applied to the *Genji*.

Shirane, Haruo. *The Bridge of Dreams: A Poetics of the Tale of Genji.* Stanford, CA: Stanford University Press, 1987. A graceful and accessible study of the interrelated themes and meanings of the *Genji* that takes pains to situate the novel within its contemporary historical, political, and social contexts.

Stinchecum, Amanda. *Narrative Voice in the Tale of Genji.* Illinois Papers in Asian Studies. vol. 5. Urbana, IL: Center for East Asian and Pacific Studies, University of Illinois, 1985. A sophisticated and refreshingly jargon-free study of the operation of the narrative voice in the tale.

AN ACCOUNT OF A TEN-FOOT SQUARE HUT

Title in Japanese: *Hōjōki*
Author: Kamo no Chōmei
Born: 1155, Kyoto
Died: 1216, Kyoto
Literary Form: Essay
Date of Composition: 1212

Major Themes

Human beings and their dwellings are impermanent.

Tranquility and peace of mind are attainable if one lives in a thatched hut, separated from the mundane world and its attachments.

The cultivation of religious sensibility can be accomplished through artistic endeavor in a life close to nature.

The essay *An Account of a Ten-foot Square Hut* by Kamo no Chōmei is one of the undisputed classics of Japanese literature. It belongs to the medieval tradition of literature of the thatched hut—writings with strong Buddhist coloration that speak of the life and aspirations of the recluse and the wandering monk. It contributed much to the definition of the basic themes and concerns of this literature. The *Ten-foot Square Hut* is not, however, a religious tract or purely confessional work. In its focus on daily life within a framework of religious concerns, and its fusing of aesthetic activities and sensibilities with otherworldly aspirations, it expresses a fundamental current of thought that manifests itself in such traditional Japanese arts as the tea ceremony, nō drama, and linked verse.

Kamo no Chōmei (1155–1216) was born into a family of Shinto priests at one of the most distinguished shrines in Kyoto. His father was Kamo no Nagatsugu, the head priest of the Shimogamo Shrine, and for much of his youth, it appears that Chōmei was to succeed his ancestors in the priesthood, which would have afforded him court ranking and a comfortable position. When he was about the age of 20, however, his father died, leaving him without strong sponsorship for obtaining an appointment. Although he would have several opportunities thereafter for posts in Shinto shrines of lesser status, they all in the end failed to bear fruit

in the competitive environment of the Kyoto court. This pattern of frustrated expectations was to characterize Chōmei's efforts to gain standing in the world.

After his father's death, Chōmei directed his energies into literary and musical pursuits, in which he displayed considerable skill. He studied poetry (*waka*, the classical 31-syllable poem) under Minamoto Shun'e, one of the leading poets of the day and a Buddhist priest of Tōdaiji temple. Chōmei became involved in court literary circles, and even came to serve as a judge at poetry gatherings at the imperial court, eventually gaining appointment to the court poetry office. In this field, however, he found his activities limited by his low social standing, and was barred from participation in the most exalted meetings for poetic composition. Throughout his life he maintained strong interest in poetry, and even wrote an influential work of criticism, chiefly in anecdotal form of advice he had received from Shun'e, but he seems to have found the path of complete devotion to the art closed to him.

Chōmei was also an accomplished musician of the *biwa* (lute) and koto. Here again, however, influential backing was necessary for genuine advance, and Chōmei found himself at a disadvantage. Further, it appears that he imprudently performed in public a piece traditionally transmitted only secretly, and was censured by others engaged in the art. In any case, we see in Chōmei a man of diverse and notable talents, but lacking the social ranking that could provide the opportunities to nurture them fully and also, perhaps, the patience to fare well within the hierarchical social structures of the day. It may be noted that during this period he seems also to have married, but after a time to have separated from his wife and children.

When about the age of 40 (in his writings, he tends to exaggerate his age), Chōmei, as he explains in his essay, "abandoned homelife and turned from the world," becoming a Buddhist monk. He went first to Ōhara, an area northeast of Kyoto that was favored by wandering monks and recluses—some descending from the Tendai temple on Mount Hiei—who carried on their religious practice away from the institutional setting of monastic centers. Chōmei's lifetime was during a period of upheaval—when warrior clans battled for power, seizing authority from the imperial court and establishing a military government at Kamakura. The armed clashes and the new warrior rule are not directly touched on in Chōmei's *Ten-foot Square Hut*, but they form part of the backdrop against which he depicts the uncertainties of life in society. During this period, there were many monks who left the temples in disgust with either the worldliness of the ecclesiastical establishment or their own inability to fulfill the prescribed practices. They often did not return to the society they had abandoned, however, but took up lives of seclusion and wandering, seeking to discard once more all attachments and mundane concerns. Further, there were also many who adopted such a life without a settled dwelling, even without formal ordination as Buddhist monks. They might live in retreat, or travel from village to village, preaching and performing services of sutra chanting and living a mendicant life. It was among such men that Chōmei first passed several years at Ōhara.

The Buddhism of these wandering monks was often of the Pure Land tradition, based on the vow of Amida Buddha, the personification of wisdom-compassion, who brings to the Pure Land of enlightenment all who simply say his Name, *Namuamida-butsu*, entrusting themselves to his vow. The practice of saying Amida's Name is termed *nembutsu*, and spread widely in Chōmei's time as a path to religious attainment available to common people, not simply the aristocracy who could afford to have religious rites performed, or the spiritually endowed who could fulfill rigorous discipline and meditative cultivation. The *nembutsu* was a practice accessible to all, whether monk or lay, and was spread among the people by wandering monks who had turned away from the elitism of monastic life. It was this form of Buddhism that Chōmei adopted.

Chōmei did not, however, adopt a life either of wandering preacher or religious ascetic. Rather, he left Ōhara for the hills southeast of the capital, in an area known as Hino, where he built his small hermitage and lived the last decade of life in relative isolation. It is of his life there that he writes in *Ten-foot Square Hut*.

An Account of a Ten-foot Square Hut

Chōmei's essay, written when he was nearly the age of 60, falls into two parts. The first, a reflection on life in the world of society, takes as its focus the nature and vulnerability of human dwellings. The second is a description of Chōmei's own hermitage and his way of life secluded in the hills of Hino. By framing his account with the theme of dwellings, Chōmei is able both to impart unity to the range of his concerns in the essay—the reasons for his decision to withdraw from society and the joys of his day-to-day existence at his hermitage—and to give free rein to his skills of observation and of literary expression. *Ten-foot Square Hut* achieves a stately rhetorical tone through its passages of intricate parallelism influenced by Chinese literature, and also through the Buddhist theme of impermanence; but it may be said that, throughout, it is not Chōmei's rejection of the world that most deeply imbues the work, but rather his lively interest in it—his inquisitiveness, his insistence on seeing with his own eyes the events of his period, and his attention to incisive details. Thus, it is the tension between his abandonment of mundane life and his keen perception of the things of the world that animates his essay and contributes to its status as an influential classic of Japanese literature.

The Fragility of Dwelling in the World

Chōmei sets forth the theme of the first section of his essay in the celebrated opening passage:

> The river flows ceaselessly, but the water is not the same. Bubbles floating in still pools vanish and form, never remaining long. So it is with human beings and their dwellings in the world.

Chōmei seeks to elucidate the Buddhist teaching of impermanence by challenging the illusion of permanence with which people commonly view the fixtures of their lives. He does this by pointing out that, although residences, cities, and populations may give the impression of unchanging existence, in fact they are like constantly changing rivers, always in flux, with no single person or structure remaining untouched. Thus, human beings are more appropriately viewed as but foam on the stream:

> If some die in the morning, others are born in the evening; it is precisely like bubbles on the stream. Of those born and dying, we know not whence they come or whither they go. Nor do we know, of this temporary shelter, for whose sake we so trouble ourselves over it, or why it should please the eye. Persons and their dwellings vie in impermanence; in this, they differ not at all from the morning glory and its dew. The dew may fall away and the blossom remain; but though it remains, it withers utterly in the morning sun. The flower may wilt and the dew not yet disappear; but though it stay, it does not await the evening.

In Chōmei's image of the ephemeral blossom sheltering the dew of life effectively conveys both his perception of impermanence and his sense of the interconnectedness of shelter and human existence.

His underlying theme, then, is the quest for genuine refuge.

In the first half of the essay, Chōmei pursues his depiction of residences as far more precarious than ordinarily perceived, and of the folly of investing them with much care and concern, by describing a number of "extraordinary events" he himself has witnessed, disasters that seem to be occurring with increasing frequency. Again exercising his skill in shaping his material, he suggests that most of the disasters involved one of the four elements of the universe—fire, air or wind, water, and earth. At the same time, each disaster is presented not in abstraction, as a type, but with telling detail that reveals Chomei an informed and compelling reporter.

Proceeding in chronological order, he begins with a fire that burned a large "fan-shaped" swath across Kyoto one windy night in 1177, and vividly describes the smoke and glare as the flames leaped through the night. In 1180, a whirlwind swept through part of the city, ripping up structures and drowning out voices in its fury. Later that year, the military ruler, Taira no Kiyomori, decided to move the 400-year-old capital for strategic reasons. Although Chōmei does not discuss the reasons behind the move, he describes how the mansions of the prominent were dismantled and floated down-river toward the new location, the former sites quickly reverting to fields. In the end, the capital was returned to Kyoto before the year was out. Then, in 1181–1182, drought, typhoons, and floods led to widespread famine, with corpses thick along the Kamo river, and about the same time, a tremendous earthquake occurred. Chōmei comments that although the elements of water, fire, and wind often wreak havoc, it is rare for the earth to cause such damage.

Having completed his account of disasters revealing the dangers that press upon human dwellings, particularly in the crowded urban conditions of the capital, Chōmei concludes the first half of his essay with a question: "In what place, engaging in what sort of activity, can one shelter one's existence even briefly and give repose to one's heart and mind?"

Reclusive Life

In the second half of his essay, Chōmei applies the same method of close observation and description to depict his own life in his ten-foot square hut. We find here an aesthetic preference for the consideration of concrete particulars over the abstractions of doctrine and religious principle. This preference not only accounts for the literary qualities of the essay, but also gives expression to the nature of Chōmei's life as a fusion of aesthetic and religious pursuits: the life of the Buddhist recluse as infused with aesthetic pleasures, or the life of the cultivation of aesthetic sensibilities as fundamentally religious in aspiration.

At the beginning of the second part of the essay, Chōmei describes the process by which he gradually came to live in smaller and smaller dwellings, largely as his fortunes in the world of society declined. Though inheriting a large residence through his father's relatives, he failed to gain a position by which to maintain it, and was forced to move into a house one-tenth in size. Even with that, he met with further disappointments, and finally withdrew to the hills of Ōhara. We see, then, that it was not a sudden religious awakening or resolve that led him to take up the life of a Buddhist hermit, but the growing realization that no suitable path was open to him in society, and a disillusionment with secular life. In Chōmei's account, his reclusion appears almost the result of an inevitable process, one possessing a logic in consonance with the law of impermanence that he has sketched concretely in part one.

After five years at Ōhara, Chōmei moved to Hino, where he built his ten-foot square hut as a temporary dwelling no more than one-hundredth the size of his second house. He explains that it is built with hinges so that it may be dismantled and moved easily to another site. Thus, it escapes all the vulnerabilities of attachment to place or vain embellishment. Chōmei had two models in particular for constructing his hut. The first, which he speaks of directly, is the "ten-foot square hut" of the Buddhist layman Vimalakirti, depicted in the sutra that bears his name as a Mahayana sage who, while maintaining his life in society, surpasses even bodhisattva-monks in wisdom. Chōmei comments at the end of his essay that, though his dwelling may be modeled on Vimalakirti's, he himself is less able than even the most foolish of the Buddha's disciples; thus he contrasts the reclusive form of his life and his inability to dedicate himself fully to religious aspirations.

Chōmei's second model is Yoshishige Yasutane (931–1002), a court scholar who built a small chapel on a pond at his residence in the capital, which he used as a retreat after returning from his daily duties. In this way, he simulated a hermit's life of religious devotions, based on nembutsu chanting and study of the Lotus Sutra, even while carrying on life in society. He left an account of his hermitage, "Record of the Hut on the Pond" (Chiteiki), and Chōmei deliberately echoes passages from it in his own essay.

While in the cases of Vimalakirti and Yasutane, the hut represents a fusion of mundane life with the transcendent, Chōmei's actual seclusion presents a different configuration of these elements, one of which influenced later thinking about the arts in Japan. In the tiny space of his hut, Chōmei placed his bedding along the eastern half of the room. The other half of the room was divided by a low partition, on one side of which he hung scrolls depicting Amida Buddha and Fugen Bodhisattva, with a copy of the Lotus Sutra placed in front. Here he performed his religious devotions. On the other side of the partition, he placed his biwa and koto. On shelving above these instruments, he placed leather-covered cases in which he kept writings on poetry, music, and religious practice. We see, then, that the hut as a site for religious life within the secular has become, for Chōmei, a locus in which both aesthetic activity and religious cultivation can be carried on. Regarding religious practice: "When I do not feel like saying the nembutsu or being diligent in reciting the sutras, I rest and am lazy. There is no one to prevent me from this, and no one who makes me ashamed." At such times, he engages in arts: "My artistic skill is poor, but I do not seek to please the ears of others. I play alone, compose poetry alone, and thus bring peace to my own spirit." He speaks of playing songs that express a sensitivity to impermanence and the pathos of things, and of observing, in each season, things of nature conducive to contemplation:

> When the night is still, seeing the moonlight at the window, I recall friends who have departed this world, and hearing the cries of monkeys, I shed tears in my sleeves.... Listening to the calls of mountain pheasants, I wonder if it might be my mother or father.

At the conclusion of his essay, after recounting the advantages and pleasures of his way of life, Chōmei reflects on the lingering attachments he feels: "Now, love of my thatched hut is a fault; attachment to tranquility is an obstruction." He has not attained religious liberation, yet he has never sought personal perfection, but rather the apprehension of reality in an aesthetic mode. Just as his entrance into reclusive life seems to have come about through various conditions rather than personal deliberation and resolve, so now, when doubts assail him, Chōmei can only allow his life to run its course, aware of the human weaknesses of his own character and of a sense of compassion nurtured by his artistic endeavors: "I simply employ the tongue alone in saying two or three times, without ardor, the Name of Amida Buddha; then I fall silent."

DENNIS HIROTA

Further Reading

Translations

Translations in this article are by Dennis Hirota.

Kamo no Chōmei. "An Account of My Hut." Trans. Donald Keene. In *Anthology of Japanese Literature: from the earliest era to the mid-nineteenth century.* Compiled and edited by Keene. Rutland, VT: Charles E. Tuttle Co., 1955, 197–212.
———. "An Account of My Hermitage." Trans. Helen Craig McCullough. In *Classical Japanese Prose: An Anthology.* Stanford, CA: Stanford University Press, 1990, 379–392.

Related Studies

Hirota, Dennis. *Plain Words on the Pure Land Way: Sayings of the Wandering Monks of Medieval Japan.* Kyoto: Ryukoku University, 1989. Buddhist background of the thatched hut tradition.
Keene, Donald. *Seeds in the Heart.* New York: Henry Holt, 1993. 759–768. Treatment of Chōmei in a history of Japanese literature.
LaFleur, William. *Chōmei as Hermit: Vimalakirti in the "Hojo-ki."* In *The Karma of Words: Buddhism and the Literary Arts in Medieval Japan.* Berkeley, CA: University of California Press, 1983. 107–115.
Yamaori Tetsuo. "Kamo no Chōmei, The Recluse." *Chanoyu Quarterly* 64 (1991): 30–45 and 65: 29–42.

NEW COLLECTION OF POEMS ANCIENT AND MODERN

Title in Japanese: *Shinkokinshū*
Anthologizers: Fujiwara no Teika (Sadaie) (1162–1241), Minamoto no Michitomo (1171–1227), Fujiwara no Ariie (1155–1216), Fujiwara no Ietaka (1158–1237), Fujiwara no Masatsune (1170–1221), Jakuren (d.1202).
Imperial Sponsor: Retired Emperor Gotoba (1180–1239).
Literary Form: Anthology of poems (*waka*)
Date of Compilation: First decade of thirteenth century

Major Themes

Poetry is a michi, *or "artistic vocation," both a worthy secular pursuit and a path that can lead to religious enlightenment.*

Waka *can convey depth of emotion through complex poetic technique, allusion to the literary traditions of Japan and China, and seriousness of purpose.*

Descriptive poetry can make symbolic reference to an underlying perception of the world or to human experience.

Aesthetic ideals in waka *include* yōen *(ethereal beauty),* sabi *(desolation, a sere beauty), and* yūgen *(profundity, mystery and depth).*

The *Shinkokinshū* is the eighth, and, by general agreement, the finest, of the 21 *chokusenshū*, or imperial anthologies of Japanese poetry compiled at the behest of various emperors between the early tenth and mid-fifteenth centuries. This anthology was produced during the first decade of the thirteenth century. At that time, the rise of the military clans had deprived the court aristocracy of most of its political power. Yet the court retained a social cache that enabled it to establish cultural standards and values. The anthology is characterized by a neoclassical search for models in the past, particularly in the *Kokinshū* and *The Tale of Genji* of the tenth and eleventh centuries; a feeling of profundity; mystery and beauty of expression; and the emergence of individual poetic voices.

The Character of the Collection

The collection comprises 1,979 poems, all in the 31 syllable, five-line form known as *waka*. Although some poems date from earlier periods of Japanese literature, including the eras of the *Man'yōshū* and *Kokinshū*, the majority are by contemporaries of the compilers. The poems are divided into the traditional 20 books: six books are devoted to the seasons (with spring and fall poems each filling two books); one book each to poems of congratulations, condolences, separation, and travel; five to love; three to miscellaneous, or compound, topics; and one each to Shintō and Buddhist poems. Two prefaces give a brief history of the *waka* in Japan, describe the criteria for inclusion of poems in the anthology, and tell how Gotoba ordered the compilers to conduct their task. One preface, in Japanese, is by Fujiwara no Yoshitsune (1169–1206); the other, in Chinese, is by Fujiwara no Chikatsune (1151–1210).

Within the books of the *Shinkokinshū*, the poems are organized by principles of chronological and geographical progression, imagistic association, and similarities of language. Many of the individual poems have titles that come from topics assigned for poetry competitions at court or for private contests, such as "lingering snow," "young herbs," "mountain thrush at the barrier," or "moon on spring mountains." The books of seasonal poetry are a temporal progression of the seasons, with natural images appearing in order throughout the year. In the books of love poetry, the poems record the moments of a love affair from the first kindling of interest to the sorrowful realization that the affair is over.

A banquet to celebrate the completion of the *Shinkokinshū* was held in 1205, although editorial work continued until 1210 and a later revision was completed by Retired Emperor Gotoba during his exile on the island of Oki.

Poets of the **Shinkokinshū**

Gotoba, emperor from 1183 to 1198, was a devotee of popular folk songs, court football, hunting, and other pastimes during his boyhood on the throne. After abdicating at the age of 20 in favor of his eldest son Tsuchimikado, he turned his attention to *waka*. Free of his official duties, he quickly developed a passion for *waka*, becoming a superior poet himself and sponsoring numerous competitions (*uta-awase*) among the major poets of the day. Many of the poems included in the *Shinkokinshū* were originally composed for such competitions, which became an increasingly important forum for composition and establishment of aesthetic values in the twelfth and thirteenth centuries.

The *Shinkokinshū* is striking because of the group of exceptional poets represented in its pages: compiler Fujiwara no Teika and his father Shunzei, sponsor Retired Emperor Gotoba, the courtiers Fujiwara no Ietaka and Fujiwara no Yoshitsune, the priests Jien and Saigyō, the Daughter of Shunzei, and Princess Shikishi are the foremost among many outstanding poets of the *Shinkokinshū*. These poets' poems represent a new style of the Japanese *waka*, one with less focus on intellectualization and arch confusion of natural images that typify the first imperial collection, the *Kokinshū*. The *Shinkokinshū* style instead relies more heavily on the intense and moving expression of emotion and a prevailing tone that is darker than earlier collections and more in keeping with an era of warfare and dramatic social, political, and religious change.

While a gentle melancholy pervades earlier collections, the *Shinkokinshū* poets often express a more profound grief, even despair, and their imagery runs to the bleak and monochromatic.

Allusive variation

The new style of the *Shinkokinshū* was founded not on rejecting the past, but on taking inspiration from, and playing variations on poetry of earlier eras, particularly poems from the first three imperial anthologies, the *Kokinshū*, *Gosenshū*, and *Shūishū*. Many of the poems in the *Shinkokinshū* are allusive variations on source poems (*honka*) in these earlier collections. Poets were expected to draw inspiration not only from their perceptions of the world around them and their own experiences and emotions, but also from their reading of literature of the past. Readers were expected to recognize such allusions and to appreciate the changes recent poets were ringing on literary works of the past by the technique called *honka-dori*. This practice of incorporating poetic experience of the past into new expression is one of the aspects of the new poetry that produces the extraordinary richness of language and the complex layers of meaning in the best of *Shinkokinshū* poems.

One of the most famous poems of Fujiwara no Teika, *Shinkokinshū* 38, is a good example of the use of allusive variation and of the atmosphere of delicate, dream-like beauty called *yōen*, "ethereal charm" found in many *Shinkokinshū* poems:

haru no yo no	the floating bridge of
yume no ukihashi	the dream of a brief spring night
todae shite	breaks off and in
mine ni wakaruru	the sky ribbons of trailing
yokogumo no sora	cloud drift away from the peak

Teika's poem is included among seasonal poems on spring, but the image of the "dream of a brief spring night" implies a love affair, either real or imaginary. Awakening at dawn, the speaker must part from the beloved, in dream or reality, while outside the clouds pull away from the mountain peak. "Floating Bridge of Dreams" is also the title of the last chapter of the eleventh-century *The Tale of Genji*, which tells the pitiful tale of Ukifune ("floating boat") and her decision to break off her affair with her suitor Kaoru and to become a nun. Teika's readers would immediately have made the association.

In addition, Teika alludes to two earlier poems. One is *Kokinshū* 601 by Mibu no Tadamine:

kaze fukeba	when the breezes blow
mine ni wakaruru	the white clouds drift from
shirokumo no	the peaks
taete tsurenaki	without regret cut
kimi ga kokoro ka	off from me can they be as
	cold hearted as my lover

The other *honka*, by Teika's friend Fujiwara no Ietaka, is also included in *Shinkokinshū*, where it immediately precedes Teika's variation:

kasumi tatsu	curtains of mist rise
suenomatsu yama	veiling Suenomatsu
honobono to	Mountain dimly seen
nami ni hanaruru	breaking away from the
yokogumo no sora	waves
	trailing clouds drift through
	the sky

The linking of the worlds of dream and reality, the layers of potential meanings, and the beauty of the sound and rhythm of his language mark Teika's poem as an exemplar of the *Shinkokinshū* style.

Poetry as Religious Expression

By the time of the *Shinkokinshū*, the concept of poetry as an "aesthetic vocation," or *michi* was widely accepted. The poet who meditated on his topic in order to penetrate its depths rather than merely describe its surface appearance was believed most able to convey the essence, or "*hon'i*," of the topic. Such a poet would achieve an almost mystical identification with the topic and discover the truth beneath the surface in the same way the enlightened mind discerns the truth behind the illu-

sions of the phenomenal world. Teika's father Shunzei argued that this process of intense concentration and meditation was the equivalent of the practice of *shikan*, "concentration and insight," taught by the Tendai sect of Buddhism.

The Buddhist rejection of worldly phenomena and experience as illusory and deceptive surely influenced aesthetic ideals of the *Shinkokinshū*: *sabi* ("lonely, sere beauty") and *yūgen* ("profundity, mystery and depth") are generally conveyed by natural images that are somber, colorless, even bleak. A poem (*Shinkokinshū* 625) by the Buddhist priest Saigyō conveys these ideals:

tsu no kuni no	spring in Naniwa
naniwa no haru wa	in the province of Tsu was
yume nare ya	it but a dream now
ashi no kareha ni	cold gusts of wind rustle
	through
kaze wataru nari	the withered leaves of dry
	reeds

The lonely winter landscape has lost all trace of the spring charm Saigyō had once admired, and the green reeds for which Naniwa was famous now exist only as dry stalks. Such melancholy beauty is the essence of *sabi*.

The profundity of *yūgen*, derived from an attempt to grasp the essence of an object rather than its superficial aspects, is conveyed by a mysterious ambiguity and muted imagery and tone, as in *Shinkokinshū* 40 by Teika:

ōzora wa	the broad heavens are
ume no nioi ni	misted over with the scent
kasumitsutsu	of the plum blossoms
kumori mo hatenu	the bright moon of the spring
	night
haru no yo no tsuki	is not quite hidden from
	view

The aesthetic ideals and modes of expression represented in the *Shinkokinshū* mark the beginning of a new era of Japanese literature that succeeded the first flowering of classical literature in the Heian period. The *waka*, the linked verse form called *renga*, *nō* drama, and the military tales and other prose genres of the thirteenth to fifteenth centuries all are marked by the neoclassical search for models in the past; the aesthetic ideals of *yōen*, *sabi*, and *yūgen*; subtlety; and fragmented expression united by the methods of chronological and geographical progression and of imagistic association that characterize early-thirteenth-century *Shinkokinshū*.

LAUREL RASPLICA RODD

Further Reading

Translation

Translations in this article by Laurel Rasplica Rodd.

Brower, Robert H. *Fujiwara Teika's Hundred-Poem Sequence of the Shōji Era, 1200*. Tokyo: Sophia University, 1978. Translation and introduction to a sequence of poems composed by Teika, the head compiler of *Shinkokinshū*.
————, and Earl Miner. *Fujiwara Teika's Superior Poems of Our Time*. Stanford, CA: Stanford University Press, 1967. Translation and study of a collection of poems admired by Teika.
Carter, Steven D. *Waiting for the Wind*. New York: Columbia University Press, 1989. Translations of poems mainly by late medieval poets, but including sections *Shinkokinshū* poets Fujiwara no Teika and Fujiwara no Ietaka.
LaFleur, William R. *Mirror for the Moon*. New York: New Directions, 1978. Translations of poetry by Saigyō.
Watson, Burton. *Saigyō: Poems of a Mountain Home*. New York: Columbia University Press, 1990.

Related Studies

Brower, Robert H. *Japanese Court Poetry*. Stanford, CA: Stanford University Press, 1961. Seminal study in English of Japanese court poetry.
Keene, Donald. *Seeds in the Heart: Japanese Literature from Earliest Times to the Late Sixteenth Century*. New York: Henry Holt and Company, 1993. This highly readable, clearly organized, and thoroughly researched history of Japanese literature includes chapters or sections on *Shinkokinshū*, the imperial poetry collections that preceded and followed it, poetry competitions, literary politics, and poetic form and language.
Konishi, Jin'ichi. Earl Miner, ed. Aileen Gatten and Mark Harbison, trans. *A History of Japanese Literature. Volume Three: The High Middle Ages*. Translation of an influential history of Japanese literature by the first scholar to explicate the principles of association and progression by which Japanese poetic anthologies and other genres of literature are unified.

THE TALE OF THE HEIKE

Title in Japanese: *Heike monogatari*
Author: Unknown
Literary Form: Composite of fictional and nonfictional tales
Date of Composition: Thirteenth century

Major Themes

The prosperous and powerful will inevitably fall from their position of glory.
Nothing is permanent; the Buddhist law (mappō) will prevail.
Rebirth and karmic retribution account for the downfall of the Heike clan.

The Tale of the Heike is considered to be the most influential work of Japanese literature after *The Tale of Genji*. It is as much a part of the Japanese consciousness as Shakespeare's plays are in the West. The stories told in the *Heike* have been retold in the *nō*, *kabuki*, and puppet theaters of the medieval and early modern periods. They have been the subject of numerous tales and historical novels throughout Japanese history. And they have also been produced on television, recited on the radio, made into movies, turned into comics, and recorded on compact discs in the modern era. As Donald Keene has said, the *Heike* is "in the blood of the Japanese."

As Japan's greatest war tale, the *Heike* is a work of epic proportions. There are villains and heroes, goblins and horses. There are sweeping battle scenes and tender moments of human interaction. There are detailed descriptions of battles and armor and long contemplative passages that recall the past. There is poetry and prose; there are documents and letters. Though the *Heike* is classified as a "war tale" (a translation of the term *gunki monogatari*, or "tales of martial accounts"), it is much more than just a recounting of skirmishes and battles. It is an evocative and resonant work that weaves anecdotes, myths, legends, and Buddhist sermons with the methodical, and partially fictional narration of events that brought about the fall of a great military family. These events—known as the Gempei War (1180–1185)—also set the stage for the more cataclysmic political changes that brought an end to four centuries of aristocratic and

imperial rule during the Heian period (784–1185) and led Japan into what is often called its feudal era (1185–1600).

The story told in the *Heike* is about the fall of the Heike (the Sinicized reading of "Taira clan"), a once militarily powerful family that gained political control of the imperial capital of Heian-kyō (present-day Kyōto) for about two decades in the latter half of the twelfth century. The events that led up to the expulsion of the Heike from the capital and that culminated in the clan's demise involved the participation of a broader cross section of Japanese society than ever before. The participants included the military families (led by the Genji, the Sinicized reading of "Minamoto clan") and their supporters in the eastern provinces, the powerful ex-Emperor Go-Shirakawa and his attendants in the capital, and the common people in the western provinces, as well as the Buddhist monks and priests in the influential ecclesiastic centers in and around Nara and Heian-kyo. Because of the involvement of so many people in such tragic events, the stories surrounding the fall of the Heike traveled quickly through the country and touched the hearts of the populace in a way that nothing ever had before.

The opening lines of the *Heike*, some of the most famous in all of Japanese literature, express the pathos and sense of ephemerality to which the medieval audiences were particularly responsive: "The sound of the Gion Shōja bells echoes the impermanence of all things; the color of the *sāla* flowers reveals the truth that the prosperous must decline. The proud do not endure, they are like a dream on a spring night; the mighty fall at last, they are as dust before the wind." It is in these lines that we see not only an encapsulation of the story to come ("The proud do not endure . . . the mighty fall at last") but also an expression of the Buddhist ethos which provides the fundamental religious framework for its telling ("The sound of the Gion Shōja bells echoes the impermanence of all things . . ."). While courtly refinement is that quality to which every good aristocrat aspired during the Heian period, it was a pervasive feeling of impermanence *(mujō)*, overlain with a fear that the effectiveness of the Buddhist teaching was coming to an end, that came to govern Japanese sensibilities in the centuries to follow.

Any final pronouncements about the authorship of the *Heike* seem unlikely given its unusual textual development, but recent scholarship seems inclined to accept Yoshida Kenkō's account in the *Tsurezuregusa (Essays in Idleness*; 1330–1331). In this work we find the following sentence in a passage about the *Heike*, "Yukinaga wrote the *Heike Monogatari* and taught a blind man named Shōbutsu to recite it." The two important elements of this statement are, one that the text was originally a written one and, two that a recited text developed from this original written text. Most scholars now seem to agree that the original version of *Heike*, which is no longer extant, was composed in Chinese in the early part of the thirteenth century—probably by the ex-courtier and lay priest Nakayama Yukinaga—and later developed into a Japanese text interspersed with many Chinese grammatical and lexical elements. This transformation occurred primarily due to its recitation by itinerant blind lute players *(biwa hōshi)* such as Shōbutsu. While the Yukinaga/Shōbutsu texts probably existed in some form or other in the first quarter of the thirteenth century, the "final" text, which is most commonly read today and from which most translations are made, dates from 1371 and is credited to a blind priest by the name of Kakuichi.

In part it is the tonal qualities of the language in the *Heike* that has helped it to endure. It is a rich mixture of Chinese and Japanese sprinkled with a variety of words of Sanskrit origin. Its sentences are often grammatically structured into parallel couplets like Chinese poems or syllabically structured into phrases of five and seven syllables in the manner of Japanese poems. This kind of patterning makes them very melodic to the ear. Though it is a beautiful text to read, it is an even more beautiful one to hear. One only has to listen to the recent recordings of the Heike by Mari Uehara and Junko Ueda to be able to imagine what the original storytellers sounded like.

The Fall of the Heike

The *Heike* is divided into 12 untitled chapters (and an epilogue—possibly a later addition entitled "The Initiates' Chapter") with each chapter subdivided into short titled sections. The brevity of each section is a testament to the origins of the *Heike* in an oral tradition. The narrative techniques that sustain the telling of the story also arose in response to the storyteller-audience relationship. In some cases, these techniques serve to highlight the action, as in the description of a warrior's armor. In other cases, the techniques have a more didactic purpose, as, for example, when Chinese legends are interjected into the story. Whatever the case, however, these techniques are all essential to the nature of the *Heike* text and should not be dismissed as superfluous digressions from the basic story.

There are hundreds of characters in the *Heike*—warriors, wives, courtiers, emperors, princes, dancers, and consorts. There are some who are so crucial to the plot that they are unforgettable. There are others who play a tangential role to the plot, yet whose stories are known to all Japanese because they have been memorialized in plays, poems, and novels throughout the centuries. As an example of the first type of character, none is more important than Taira no Kiyomori, the head of the Heike clan, the political ruler of the country, and the character around whom the first half of the *Heike* revolves.

Kiyomori's downfall is foreshadowed by the actions of his grandfather, Tadamori, who once entered the inner sanctum of the imperial palace with a dagger hidden beneath his robes for protection. This affront to the Emperor and the imperial family is minor, however, compared to the disrespect Kiyomori exhibits towards ex-Emperor Go-Shirakawa (the actual head of the government and as much a sacred figure as the Emperor himself), various courtiers at the palace, and the monks and priests at the major monastic centers. His arrogance and intractability win him few friends among the refined aristocrats in the capital and eventually precipitate a mutinous conspiracy that is the focus of the first two chapters. Kiyomori's crimes do not go unpunished. His death scene is one the most dramatic in the entire work. While his sons and his warriors are marching east to punish the encroaching Genji, Kiyomori himself is dying of a fever so hot that water poured on him turns to flame. Eventually, unable to eat or drink, he dies in a fit of convulsions.

The members of the Heike family are not all depicted as treacherous and demonic, however. Kiyomori's son, Shigemori, and his grandson, Koremori, represent the aristocratic society Kiyomori shuns. While Kiyomori is threatening to execute both ex-Emperor Go-Shirakawa and the court noble, Narichika, for their role in the conspiracy to oust him, it is the sensitive and rational Shigemori who comes to their aid in the name of Buddhist compassion and Confucian decorum. And later, when the Heike are fleeing the capital and the Genji, Koremori reveals himself to be more of a devoted husband and father than a loyal warrior. He is torn between the practicality of leaving his family behind and the fears he has for their safety if they are discovered by the enemy when they reach the capital.

Among examples of the second kind of character found in the *Heike*—that is, minor characters whose stories have captured the imagination of the Japanese people—Shunkan and Atsumori are the most well known. This is partly due to the fact that their stories have both been made into *nō* plays.

Shunkan is one of the conspirators who wants to drive Kiyomori from the capital. He is exiled along with two others to a faraway island in the Japan Sea for his part in the plot. While Kiyomori eventually pardons Shunkan's two compatriots, he decides against pardoning Shunkan, as it was in his villa where the plans for the conspiracy were hatched. As the boat that has come to fetch the two pardoned exiles is about to leave, Shunkan holds onto the bow and ropes in a desperate attempt to be taken even part of the way home to the capital. In the end, however, Shunkan fails in his attempt and ends up spending "the night on the beach, his feet washed by the waves and his garments wilted by the dew." When we encounter Shunkan several scenes later and just before he dies, he has become a ghost of his former self, a person to whom bits of seaweed and debris cling, whose joints protrude, and whose skin dangles from his bones.

The story of Atsumori comes much later in the work, after the Heike have fled to the island of Shikoku. Here at the battle of Ichinotani, a certain warrior by the name of Kumagae no Naozane is viewing the aftermath of the battle when he notices and enemy warrior and worthy opponent riding his horse near the sea. He pursues the warrior, captures him, and is about to cut off his head when he notices that he "was sixteen or seventeen years old, with a lightly powdered face and blackened teeth—a boy just the age of Naozane's own son Kojiro Naoie, and so handsome that Naozane could not find a place to strike." The poignancy of the particular scene is heightened when Naozane realizes that Atsumori is carrying a flute along with his weapons, an act of such singular refinement and elegance that Naozane is moved to tears. Even though Naozane would clearly prefer to spare the young boy's life, he kills him rather than surrender him to those who would not offer prayers for Atsumori's spirit. The ironic point of this story—and the one that would have affected its listeners the most—is that it is a musical instrument used for "profane entertainment" that impels Naozane to renounce his life as a warrior for one on the Buddhist path.

The characters of the *Heike* may be a memorable

in the book, but it is the flights from the enemy, the suicides, the executions, and the battles themselves—at Yokotagawara, Hiuchi, Shinohara, Hōjūji, and Mikusa among others—that tell the real story about the demise of the Heike. None of these battles is more important or more well known than the final one at Dannoura. Here the Heike and the Genji set out to sea with bows and arrows in hand fighting more desperately and more recklessly than they ever had before. As the Genji warriors board the Heike vessels, sealing the fate of the occupants, the eight-year-old Heike Emperor, Antoku, jumps into the sea, along with scores of Heike warriors, intoning the sacred name of Amida Buddha and hoping to be reborn into the paradise of the Pure Land. In the few concluding sections of the book, most of the remaining Heike warriors either commit suicide or are executed, leaving no room for misunderstanding about the outcome of this once great family: "This did the sons of the Heike vanish forever from the face of the earth."

Buddhist concepts in the Heike

Though an awareness of impermanence (*mujō*) may be identified as the underlying sentiment informing the *Heike* (and much of medieval Japanese literature), there was an equally pervasive belief at this time that the Buddhist teachings had entered a period of irreversible decline *(mappō)* starting in the year 1052. It was widely believed that during the period of *mappō*, people would neither understand the teachings of the Buddha nor have any way to put those teachings into practice. This belief may not have provided the kind of solace that we often associate with hope, but at least it did provide an explanation fro the serious upheavals and turbulence people were experiencing.

The term *mappō* appears frequently in the *Heike*, but its usage in the final section of the first chapter is typical. In this section we are told of a conflagration at the imperial palace, an event that occurred during Kiyomori's rule in the Angen era (1175–1176). The final sentence of the last section reads: "Because the power of the state has waned in these latter days of the Law [*mappō*], the hall has not

been rebuilt since the Angen fire." By using the word *mappō* in this way, both excesses and deficiencies of the government—in fact, any act that was detrimental to the status quo—could be attributed to the natural order of things.

Along with this tendency to rationalize disorder and chaos came a belief in the inefficacy of one's own power *(jiriki)* to effect personal salvation. This belief was supported by one of the new Buddhist sects known as Pure Land Buddhism. Pure Land Buddhism, unlike the other Mahayana sects common to China, Korea, and Japan, advocated surrendering one's fate to the salvational powers of Amida Buddha, the Buddha of the heavenly Pure Land or the Western Paradise as it was also known. In other words, salvation required the intervention of some otherworldly power *(tariki)* or one was doomed to constant rebirth in this world of suffering. The only religious act that was required of a Pure Land believer was the intonation of Amida's name in the phrase "*Namu Amida Butsu.*" In the battle at Dannoura discussed previously, just before the child-Emperor Antoku drowned himself, his mother instructed him to "turn to the west and repeat the sacred name of Amida Buddha, so that he and his host may come to escort you the Pure Land."

The fate of the Heike clan is attributed to the evil deeds of Kiyomori. This final section of "The Initiates' Chapter" states this in no uncertain terms: "It was all the fault of the Chancellor-Novice Kiyomori, the man who held the whole country in the palm of his hand and executed and banished as he pleased, unawed by the Emperor above and heedless of the myriad fold below, with no concern either for society or for individuals. There seemed to be no room for doubt that the evil deeds of a father must be visited on his offspring." Fate, then, is karmic retribution, a belief that our actions—in particular our wrongful deeds—will result in some kind of punishment in the present or in a future life. The nature of these deeds, of course, is never clear, but the severity of the punishment is considered to be an indication of the degree of their iniquity.

Stephen D. Miller

Further Reading

Translations

Kitagawa, Hiroshi, and Bruce T. Tsuchida, trans. *The Tale of the Heike.* Tokyo: The University of Tokyo Press, 1975.

McCullough, Helen Craig, trans. *The Tale of the Heike.* Stanford, CA: Stanford University Press, 1988. This is the translation used in the preceding article.

Related Studies

Butler, Kenneth. "The Textual Evolution of the *Heike Monogatari.*" In the *Harvard Journal of Asiatic Studies*, vol. 26, 1966. The only English-language article to deal in depth with the textual origins and developement of the *Heike* as a narrative work of literature. It theorizes that the reclamation of an original source text along with the discovery of the interaction of the written and oral traditions will provide the basis for a "formulaic, structural, and thematic study of the narrative of the manuscripts."

———. "The *Heike Monogatari* and the Japanese Warrior Ethic." In the *Harvard Journal of Asiatic Studies*, vol. 29, 1969. A study of the process by which the warrior code came to be incorporated into the narrative structure of the *Heike*. Some attempt is also made to contextualize and historicize the depictions of this code.

Varley, Paul. *Warriors of Japan: As Portrayed in the War Tales.* Honolulu: The University of Hawaii Press, 1994. A very well-respected historian presents a cultural history of the warrior tradition as it has been depicted in literary tales from the tenth to the fourteenth centuries. The third and fourth chapters deal exclusively with the characters and battles in the *Heike* as well as with some of the historical foundations of the Gempei War.

ESSAYS IN IDLENESS

Title in Japanese: *Tsurezuregusa*
Author: Urabe Kenkō
Born: c. 1283
Died: c. 1352
Literary Form: Essays on various subjects
Date of Composition: Composed c. 1319 to c. 1350

Major Themes

Beauty is best found in that which is least obvious.
Life is fleeting, and for that very reason, precious.
Restraint is the mark of a good man.
The one important thing is the Buddhist path (although enjoying oneself at the races is acceptable).
In all things prefer the customs of the past, except where the present is more useful.

Japanese scholars and lay people alike have long regarded *Tsurezuregusa* as one of their most important and typical literary works. Assembled from a variety of segments that represents most of the genres popular in its day, from narratives of courtly heroes parting the dewy grasses in the moonlight to exhortations on the practice of the Buddhist Way, this collection of prose gems is unusual only in its marked lack of poetic interpolations and its virtuoso range. The sentiments within, while in an aggregate uniquely expressive of the author, are those common to many classical pieces—the majesty of the imperial house, the sadness of fate, the pleasure of meeting a friend with taste, astonishment at the habits of the common people, and the advantages of the Buddhist path. There is, however, a resonance between themes and their execution that finds few parallels elsewhere. Here are the characteristic elements of the medieval aesthetic, many of which survive as Japan's elite standards for beauty, not only explained but demonstrated. Thus, the quality of suggestion, which permits the viewer to exercise the imagination, is praised in a discussion that moves quickly from a preference for torn scroll wrappers and incomplete sets of books, to imperial palace buildings, to the missing chapters of the classics. The classic version of *Tsurezuregusa* itself is not uniform, but leaves open the possibility of many readings across its gaps. Furthermore, the author's contention that the world is a place of unease in which one's pursuit of equanimity may be interrupted at any time is embodied in the flow of the text, which is far from predictable.

Kenkō hōshi, the lay priest Kenkō, as Japanese literary history most often styles him, was born in about 1283 to a family of lower level courtiers, the Urabe, whose members occupied shrine posts. His popular designation, Yoshida Kenkō, derives from the Yoshida Shrine in Kyoto, with which he was probably not associated in his lifetime. Kenko advanced to the post of chamberlain of the sixth rank, serving as tutor to Emperor Go-Nijō. Factional politics were severe, and sometime before 1313, during a temporary eclipse of his patrons, the Horikawa, he took Buddhist orders and retired from the world for reasons that remain unclear. He spent a time studying religious texts and practice, but the death of a leading poet in the Nijō school and its resulting need for reinforcements in the poetic world brought him back to the capital. Although he was a lay monk, or perhaps because of that fact, which ameliorated his low rank, Kenkō spent the rest of his life active in poetry circles, while offering his expertise in court custom and ceremonial to anyone who would pay. Kenkō is known to have advised some unsavory creatures among the parvenu warriors, whose power he recognized without approving.

Kenkō lived in "interesting times," when the imperial court split into two branches, each maintaining its own emperor. While the monk has nothing to say about this political development, nor about the battles that raged around him (court literature traditionally ignored such affairs), he was not ignorant of the wider world. Kenkō traveled east to Kanezawa, where his grandfather had resided, on at least two occasions, and included the differing customs and ethos of the warrior in his text. Records show he was alive until at least 1352, and while some believe *Tsurezuregusa* was written between the years 1330 and 1331, others date the beginning sections to 1319. It is also easy to imagine that parts date from a wise and reflective old age. In modern editions its preface plus 263 sections cover many moods and stages of life.

Tsurezuregusa *and its Readers—Making Sense of Contradictions*

After the seventeenth century, *Tsurezuregusa* was widely read. It became a preferred source for lessons in literacy among townsmen and warrior classes, in addition to the Buddhist monks and nobles who had read it previously, and an active tradition of commentary, parody, and legend arose. Kenkō was seen as a paragon of virtue and knowledge, but one who had such human foibles as love affairs. Partisans of many a world view laid exclusive claim to *Tsurezuregusa*, from believers in its Confucian import to sectarian Buddhists, to merchants who found the secrets of successful business in its pages. Even the most modern interpreters see it as having a core meaning, although it may be as generalized a theme as "a resource book for human life." Nowadays, no one is likely to argue that the text has only one ideology or that it "belongs" to the followers of a single school of thought. The openness of the bricolage, its entropy, or as some put it, its contradictions, are thorough enough to invite controversy.

A look at any of its topics confirms this. Kenkō condemns liquor, for example, in terms that a temperance activist could love, only to close his discussion with an admission of the benefits of drink for social occasions. He makes statements both for and against having children, and veers from homage to scorn toward women. Some may be tempted to attribute this flexibility to an inferior capacity for logical thought, which is not the problem: *Tsurezuregusa*'s readers' focus through recent centuries on resolving its contradictions is testament to that. Japanese are as likely as anyone to prefer the easily unified, the pedantically complete, and the hopelessly obvious. Kenkō was determinedly opposed to these tendencies, as exhibited in his aesthetic call for the "sidelong glance." To fill the eyes with sights of spring or the hands with refulgent blossoms, he argues, is both to exceed the limits of good taste and to lose touch with the truth that all things must perish.

Idleness and Impermanence—the Classical and the Medieval Meet

The mutability of phenomena, a chief Buddhist tenet, informs much of *Tsurezuregusa* on both aesthetic and philosophical levels. With awareness of insubstantiality comes the motive for embarking on the path to enlightenment, a goal that medieval Japanese valued even when they could not submit to its strictures. Kenkō's enticements to the pursuit of Buddhist wisdom are numerous and rhetorically effective. He exploits every means to convince the reader to reach the same conclusion as he does, sometimes cajoling, sometimes shocking, and always seeming to anticipate objections to the quiet life of unattached discipline. The work is deeply colored by a belief that this is the true good.

And yet *Tsurezuregusa* is no religious tract. Forsaking any stiff Chinese compound, Kenkō often uses the term *tsurezure* to indicate the state of calm solitude. Popular in the writings of women around the year 1000, *tsurezure* signifies the boredom and idleness of days when long rains fell or there was nothing to amuse the females of the house. Joined with a suffix meaning "writings," *tsurezure* takes its place in the title of this work that is intimately bound to the classical literary tradition in all its feeling and sensibility. The following passage is typical:

To seclude oneself in a mountain temple and attend the Buddha relieves idleness and seems to clear the spirit of its tarnish.

(SECTION 17)

Narrative vignettes in the style of women's writings spin the beauty of a woman not long for this world glimpsed from the shadows, or of a young man espied on a spring day. For a poet of note (he was called one of the "Four Deities of Verse" in his day), he neglects poetry per se to a surprisingly extent, but the prose is sufficiently lyrical to compensate.

We can intuit Kenkō's dedication to poetry through his pronouncements on the attitude befitting artists and experts. A rare comment on versifying is this:

There is nothing so depressing as when someone begins speaking of poetry and the poems are bad. Anyone with the slightest knowledge of that path would not say he thought them good. In all cases, it makes one uncomfortable to sit by and listen to someone speaking about a path he knows nothing of.

(SECTION 57)

The topic here is not only poetry but appropriate behavior for the cultured. In Japan's medieval period, to take up a path, whether religious or artistic, was the best way to cultivate the self, and *de rigueur* for a gentleman. Elsewhere Kenkō advises total commitment, respect for anyone who has achieved much in the arts, and modesty in displaying accomplishments.

Tsurezuregusa is shot through with the feeling of longing for a soul mate. Wickedly dismissive of the insensate, the stupid, the undignified, and the uneducated, Kenkō imagines in section 12 what it would be like to have the perfect companion: of course he would respond to his friend's temperament and not flood him with extraneous conversation; such a person would also not try to make a fool of his friend in front of others, and would rise above the coarseness and degeneracy of the present age. When it comes time to name in a few words who

would be the best friend to have, however, Kenkō finishes his short list with "a friend who gives you things." Such is his practical streak.

Kenkō and His Times

In the early fourteenth century many social anomalies required adjustments from members of the aristocracy such as Kenkō. Some of the more humorous and puzzling sections are stories of his contemporaries. One anecdote tells of monks who created an elaborate ruse to attract the affections of a young boy by burying a hamper of treats, which they intended to "discover" while on an outing with him. They are humiliated and enraged when they cannot find it again. Other narratives concern a monk who gets his head caught in a pot (losing ears and nose in the effort to remove it), a young woman who eats nothing but chestnuts, and a monk who squanders his fortune on potatoes just because he likes them. There are vast collections of such episodes extant, but few are as compelling as *Tsurezuregusa*'s deft versions.

One of the best known stories involves a master tree climber who instructs a beginner not to think about what he is doing until he reaches the bottom branches on the way down. It is at that point, he explains, that people forget themselves and fall. When speaking of the Buddhist Way, or advising practitioners of an art, Kenkō is clearly hortatory. In other places where we might expect Kenkō to take a didactic tone, such as these tales, he fails to do so. Most striking among the types of segment in which he evades the expected is his commentary on court customs, which manages to condemn present practice while not always giving the correct procedure. We know from him that people had forgotten how to fashion a rack for torture or tie offenders to it, but we do not find out how they should do it or even what they were doing in his day. Many passages of *Tsurezuregusa* begin and end without telling the reader what he might have expected to hear, and then move on to something that seems utterly unrelated. Ultimately, it is the slippage among all these categories of subject that most intrigues the reader, and brings home the messages of impermanence, the right way, and aesthetics.

Tsurezuregusa is often compared with Montaigne's *Essais* as a broad sampler of the thought of a cultivated man aware of his own time and on the brink of a new era. While the parallel is informative, Montaigne probes topics in order to portray his own psychology. *Tsurezuregusa*, on the other hand, is not especially revealing of its author, for all that it seems a record of his thoughts. He remains detached, and leaves us to wonder what could be in the mind of a person who arrives at the races, remarks on the pointlessness of wasting the few days of our precious lives at such amusements, and takes the offer of better seats for the contest from the spectators on the front row that he impressed with his comment. Perhaps there is some argument for interpreting the opening lines of *Tsurezuregusa*, as some do, to mean fairly literally that the long days at his inkstone have driven him insane. If sanity means gorging in fulsome dullness on life as it is, then Kenkō is truly bereft of that quality.

LINDA H. CHANCE

Further Reading

Translations

Translations in this article are by Linda H. Chance.

Keene, Donald. *Essays in Idleness: The Tsurezuregusa of Kenkō*. New York: Columbia Univer-

sity Press, 1967; reprint: Rutland, VT: Charles E. Tuttle Co., 1981.

Related Studies

Chance, Linda H. *Formless in Form: Tsurezuregusa and the Rhetoric of Fragmentary Japanese Prose*. Stanford, CA: Stanford University Press (forthcoming). A study of the literary form of *Tsurezuregusa* with special reference to generic comparisons and the Buddhist sources of its aesthetic.

Keene, Donald. "Japanese aesthetics," in *Philosophy East and West* 19:3 (July 1969): 293–306. This article shows the relation of Kenkō's aesthetics to the characteristic Japanese preference for suggestion, irregularity, simplicity, and perishability.

Marra, Michele. "Semi-Recluses *(tonseisha)* and Impermanence *(mujo)*: Kamo no Chomei and Urabe Kenkō," in *Japanese Journal of Religious Studies* 11:4 (Dec. 1984): 313–50.

———. *The Aesthetics of Discontent: Politics and Reclusion in Medieval Japanese Literature*. Honolulu: University of Hawaii Press, 1991. See chapter 6: "The Ideal Court: Kenkō's Search for Meaning," which includes some of Kenkō's poetry and elaborates on the political in his life and text.

THE NOH PLAYS

Authors: Kan'ami Kiyotsugu (1333–1384), Zeami Motokiyo (1363–1443), Kanze Motomasa (1400–1432), Komparu Zenchiku (1405–1468), and others.
Literary Form: Drama in linked verse, with song, dance, and masks
Dates of Composition: Fourteenth through sixteenth centuries

Major Themes

An atmosphere of subtle beauty and suggestion, rather than plot development or character, is what attracts and pleases the audience.

The geographical site of a profound attachment provides an intersection of the sacred and mundane.

Obsessions can lead to spiritual salvation.

The pity of the human condition lies in the nature of attachment to things of this world.

Japanese drama, like theater in most other parts of the world, began as a ritual performance in celebration of the gods. For Japan this meant the gods *(kami)* of Shinto and, the land which the kami inhabit. The islands of Japan are important to popular Shinto belief because the kami were responsible for their creation. To become manifest the kami descend onto particular sacred sites in Japan, usually mountain peaks, tall pines, or auspicious rocks. Early theater appears to have been performed as an offering for the kami who were thought to be integrally involved in every aspect of man's life, from the bestowal of bountiful harvests to the easing of the pains of childbirth or illness.

Shinto influence can still be seen in the noh (nō) stage, which was originally attached to a Shinto shrine. Today the stage is an independent structure, complete with a tiled roof and small garden, and housed within a theater building. It is composed of a cedar floor, hollow stage, open to the audience on two or three sides, with a bridgeway (*hashigakari*) off to the left, leading off-stage. Because of its asymmetry, the stage allows for a free flow of space and enables the actor to suggest great distances simply by gazing out from the bridgeway. The absence of barriers between the audience and stage such as we find in a traditional proscenium-arch stage contributes as well to a sense of timelessness. On the back of the stage is painted the Yōgō pine of Kasuga shrine in Nara. According to legend, the god of the shrine was observed dancing beneath the pine. This dance has been preserved in the New Year's ritual play *Okina Sanbasō*, as a dance commemorating longevity. The principal noh actor wears the laughing mask of an old man, the god of the shrine. In this sense the actor is a vehicle for the gods and the Yōgō pine represents the point of the god's descent. While especially significant in the Okina play, the presence of the Yōgō pine reminds the audience of the early origins of theater in Shinto ritual.

Zeami and the Transformation of Noh

By the mid-fourteenth century noh emerged as a secular form of entertainment (*sarugaku noh*) distinct from its antecedents in Shinto shrine dance (*kagura*) and from other early dramatic forms such as *sarugaku* (originally a variety performance probably from China) and *dengaku*, which began as a folk agricultural dance celebrating the harvest. *Sarugaku* and *dengaku* had already become difficult to distinguish in the fourteenth century, both having incorporated dance as well as mimetic plays. What would later be the Kanze school of noh began as one of the Yamato sarugaku troupes. Three other schools of noh emerged at this time: Komparu, Hōshō, and Kongō. The fifth school, Kita, did not appear until the seventeenth century.

Noh was transformed from a simple folk dance or play into the sophisticated form known today in the fourteenth century by two exceptional actors,

Kan'ami Kiyotsugu (1333–1384) and his son Zeami Motokiyo (1363–1444). They were members of one of the four Yamato sarugaku troupes affiliated with Kōfuku-ji, a Buddhist temple in Nara. Yamato refers to the area around Nara. Kan'ami is responsible for the introduction of a dance form known as the *kusemai*, a rapid dance with a strong beat, sometimes found in the *kuse* scene of a noh play. We know very little of Kan'ami's life, and we cannot attribute to him with certainty any of the plays in the current repertory. Zeami, on the other hand, was a prolific playwright as well as the author of the first treatises on the art of noh. To him, we owe the transformation of noh into a truly significant art form.

Like most performers in the fourteenth century, Zeami was a member of the commoner class. The social status of performers was so marginal that in later centuries they were sometimes referred to as riverbed dwellers *(kawara mono)*, due to the fact that the actors occasionally performed in the dry riverbeds around Kyoto. As a child, he was observed in performance by the shogun, Ashikaga Yoshimitsu, a great patron of the arts. Yoshimitsu seems to have been awestruck by his beauty and invited him to stay at the palace where he associated with the practitioners of high culture, poets of *waka* (the classical poetic form in 5 lines of 32 syllables) and *renga* (linked verse), as well as zen masters who frequented the palace. The language of noh is the language of linked verse, the popular verse form of the day. The poetic devices, imagery, and specific lines of verse have their origins in the poetic manuals popular among the linked verse poets. The atmosphere of the noh, the subtle and refined beauty of gesture and speech, reflects the nostalgia in many of the arts in this period for the refinement of earlier times when the imperial court was at its zenith.

Unfortunately, Zeami's life was not entirely one of ease and gracious living. Ashikaga Yoshinori, who succeeded Yoshimitsu as shogun, banned both Zeami and his son, Motomasa (1400–1432), from the stage. Finally, in 1434, Zeami was exiled to the remote island of Sado. Although there is no clear record of the reasons for the exile of Zeami,

Yoshinori does seem to have preferred Zeami's nephew, On'ami (1398–1467), who was to continue the line of succession much against Zeami's wishes. Zeami chose, instead, to pass on his treatises to his son-in-law, Komparu Zenchiku (1405–1468).

In his treatises, Zeami speaks of the importance of mastering the two arts of song and dance, as well as the three role types: the old man, the woman, and the warrior. In other words, he emphasizes both the central importance of role playing *(monomane)*, and dance and song. Much of his writing is of a practical nature addressed to his followers. However, he also writes in more abstract terms of the esthetic of his art. One of the central terms he uses is the "flower" *(hana)* of the actor. The flower appears to mean the inner art of the actor, his imagination, which he expresses outwardly through his body. The flower of the actor is what attracts the audience; it is both fascinating and novel. He also speaks at length of *yūgen*, the gracious, refined outward form of the actor regardless of his role. The model for *yūgen* of this type was the courtier. *Yūgen* is used more expansively to refer to the atmosphere created on stage when a performance reaches the highest level of achievement. In this case, he describes a subtle beauty, with a suggestion of mystery. This is the beauty towards which an actor must strive.

In a section called *Sandō*, Zeami discusses the writing of a noh play. Of single importance is the selection of a source *(honzetsu)* based on an easily recognized line of poetry or scene from a well-known work of literature. Here, we can see Zeami's concern for his audience, which continues throughout his writing. The audience to which he refers includes both commoners and the elite. For Zeami, a performance is successful only in so far as the entire audience is moved by it. Allusions in the text, therefore, must be those to which the audience can easily respond. For sources, Zeami chose those works that provided source material for linked verse as well. His aim was to present images that would reverberate with associations for the audience and promote an atmosphere on stage beyond the effect of a single word or line itself. He structures the plays according to a progressive rhythm known as *jo-ha-kyū* (opening, break, rapid finish). The rhythm is not new with Zeami; it is found in court *bugaku* as well. Zeami, however, adds a psychological dimension to the rhythm in his plays that is missing from the earlier uses of it. The build up of the rhythm coincides with the heightening of tension as the play proceeds to its finale, providing a rapid emotional release at the end of the play. There is no sequential plot enacted and no attempt at resolution of the action. Instead, we are offered an emotionally intense atmosphere based on a well-known incident often from literature and, then, a moment of release. The *jo-ha-kyū* rhythm is also used to order the plays within a formal program so that the day's performance begins with the more stately, god plays, and concludes with a rapid demon play.

Performance

A noh performance usually consists of only two or three actors (although there may be more), a chorus of eight members, and three, sometimes four, musicians seated at the rear of the stage. Movement on stage is highly stylized. Some gestures are symbolic, such as the raising of the hand to the face to indicate weeping, but others are entirely abstract. The main actor is known as the *shite*, and he appears masked and dressed in elaborately embroidered robes. In a typical, two act play, he will appear twice: once in the first half as the *maejite* and again in the second half as the *nochijite*. During the course of the play, the thread of his emotion will be taken up by all of the elements of performance to create an atmosphere of emotional intensity on the stage. The secondary role, the *waki*, is there primarily to witness the display of the shite. Without his presence, the shite cannot reveal his identity. The waki wears neither mask nor elaborate robes.

In most cases, the actors are born into acting families that specialize either in waki or shite roles, and begin performing from a very young age. The chorus is made up entirely of shite actors so there are more opportunities for shite actors to perform.

Unlike the chorus in Greek tragedy, with which it is frequently compared, the chorus in noh has no character of its own. Rather, the noh chorus performs the role of narrator as well as taking up the shite's lines and reciting them for him. This helps to decentralize the character of the shite and to abstract the emotion, removing the focus from the shite performer. In addition to the shite and waki, there may be companions known as *shite tsure* and *waki tsure*. In most cases their roles are minimal, although in the play *Pining Wind (Matsukaze)*, by Zeami Motokiyo, the character of Autumn Rain is essential to the play and almost as central as that of the shite, Pining Wind. In the majority of plays, two hand drums and the transverse flute are used. The hand drums, the *ōkawa* (a large hip drum) and the *kotsutsumi* (a small shoulder drum), are struck with the flat of the palm in an eight beat interlocking rhythm. The drummers accompany their playing with wild, vocal cries *(kakegoe)* which form part of the eight beat rhythm. The flute *(nōkan)* is reedless and has a high sound like the whistling of the wind. The dancer follows the lead of the flute during the dance sections or, in some cases, may direct the melody. In some plays, a large stick drum *(taiko)* is used to create a stronger beat. As is true for the other elements of performance, the musical segments are created as modules which interlock to form musical patterns. However improvisational the music may sound to the novice, the arrangements of the musical segments are set for each play.

Comic Interludes: Kyōgen

In addition to the main roles of shite and waki in the noh, there is also a comic character who appears within a noh play usually as a man of the neighborhood or perhaps, a god of one of the tutelary shrines. The comic actor known as the *kyōgen* actor also performs independently in short, one-act skits that appear between noh plays in a program of noh and kyōgen. The role within the noh play is known as the *aikyōgen* and usually consists of a simple retelling of the play in the vernacular of the medieval period, the style of aikyōgen preferred by Zeami. Some aikyōgen, those that seem to have been created later in the fifteenth century, have a more integral part to play.

There are approximately 210 independent plays of the kyōgen theater. Two or three character types appear in each. They represent the life of the common man in medieval Japan and are realistically presented in terms of clothing, speech, and mime. However, kyōgen, like noh, is a stylized theater and is entirely choreographed down to the least gesture, so we would be mistaken if we expected to see anything remotely akin to western realism. The characters include: the tender, yet shrewish, wife and her henpecked spouse, the master and his mischievous servant, priests, mountain ascetics, blind men, great and small lords, and even the popular folk gods of hearth and home. In each case, the main character is known as the *shite* and his partner as the *ado*.

The plots are simple and the devices familiar from western farce: plot reversals, deception, mistaken identity, and so forth. Whoever the shite character of kyōgen may be, the kyōgen actor aims at revealing his universal human failings and inviting the audience to laugh, not at the character, but at the same failings within all of us. Although the plays may once have displayed a more satiric wit, this has largely been displaced in favor of a gentle ironic commentary on the nature of humankind. The master or lord may be outwitted by his wily servant, but no one is threatened or hurt by the situation, and the relationship continues whatever occurs during the course of the play.

The Importance of Place: Shintoism and Noh

While a number of the 230 plays in the current repertory of noh celebrate the *kami*, the influence of Shinto is most apparent in the emphasis on place that is integral to noh. Just as the kami are associated with particular natural sites in Japan, the main character of a noh play, whether kami or human, is usually drawn to one particular spot that becomes for him an intersection, both geographically and temporally, of the sacred and mundane. For example, the play *Pining Wind* (*Matsukaze*) takes place

on the shores of Suma where the spirits of two maidens appear to a travelling priest. The maidens appear to the priest in the hope of attaining a spiritual release from their attachment to a lover. At the opening of the play, the priest notices on the shores of Suma a single pine with a tablet. The tablet has been affixed to honor two faithful salt makers, the maidens Pining Wind and Autumn Rain. The presence of the pine at Suma beckons the maidens back into this mundane world. One of the girls, Pining Wind, relates the story of their love for the courtier, Yukihira, who promised to return to the shores of Suma but never came again. He left behind only a court robe and hat as mementos of his love. As she retells the story in the kuse section of the play, Pining Wind ceases to distinguish between her memory and the event itself; in other words she goes mad. The pine before her becomes Yukihira.

The image of Suma, as it is picked up in the poetry of the play, calls up other associations as well: a poem of Suma by Yukihira in the tenth-century collection of court poetry, the *Kokinshū*; a chapter on Suma in the tenth-century novel, *The Tale of Genji*; and a story in the ninth-century work, *The Tales of Ise*, said to be by the brother of Ariwara Yukihira, Ariwara no Narihira. In each case, we have a story of exile from the capital to Suma, a love affair with a fishergirl *(ama)* or a provincial maiden, and the subsequent abandonment of the girl. In other words, a place name such as Suma is charged with meaning and highly significant to the play. This is true for other noh plays as well.

Obsessions Leading to Release: Buddhism in Noh

The most intense plays in the noh repertory are about people tormented by an obsession, or in Buddhist terms, an attachment such as we see in *Pining Wind*. Buddhist and Shinto concepts coexist and intermingle in the noh as they did in Japanese society as a whole by the fourteenth century. The themes of these plays and the dilemmas of the characters originate in the chaotic realm of emotion that does not lend itself to easy articulation. The emotional state of the main character (the *shite*) is generated by music, poetry, and dance rather than by any reliance upon plot.

The stories are usually well-known from their literary sources or from legends that are a mixture of Buddhist and Shinto folk belief; no plot such as we would expect in Greek tragedy is spun out before our eyes. The attraction of noh lies instead in the creation of an authentic emotional state on stage and in the possibility of release from that emotion. This state of mind is premised on the Buddhist belief that attachment to objects of the senses leads to pain. An inability to release oneself from one's obsession can cause the spirit of the living or dead to be drawn to and, in the case of the dead, return endlessly to the geographical spot where the attachment occurred.

For Lady Rokujo, the vengeful spirit of *Aoi no ue* (revised by Komparu Zenchiku), it is the bedside of Lady Aoi, the wife of her lover Prince Genji of *The Tale of Genji*. For Atsumori in the Zeami play by the same name, it is the battlefield of *Ichi no tani* where he was slain by the Minamoto warrior Kumagai no Jiro Naozane, as recorded in *The Tale of the Heike*. No release is possible without the added element of interpersonal interaction that allows the tormented being to relive the story of the obsession and thereby to exorcize it from the self. The second character on stage (the *waki*) is often a travelling priest whose vocation is to save lost souls through prayer. He is the receiver of the tale. In *Atsumori*, the priest is the former warrior and slayer of Atsumori, Kumagai, who has himself returned to the spot of the battle in order to pray for Atsumori's soul. There are many variations on this theme and indeed, in some plays, no salvation seems to occur. Lady Rokujo, a living being, reveals the demon of her jealousy, but there is no indication that this revelation has led to release.

Despite the symbolic nature of a noh performance, the subject matter is sympathetic and reassuringly human. The audience of noh is not asked to believe in extreme acts such as we might expect from classical Greek theater: Oedipus putting out his eyes, for example, or Antigone following her brother into his tomb. Jealousy over a lover (as in *Aoi no ue*), bitterness over a failure in battle *(Atsumori)*, or grief over the loss of a child *(Sumidagawa* by Motomasa) are the events which torment the characters of the noh.

Stories of obsessions exist in the Western tradition as well, but the character is left with no hope of salvation, as is the case for Oedipus in his quest to find his father. In the *Poetics*, Aristotle speaks of the fatal flaw in character that causes the downfall of the hero. There is no fatal flaw in the characters of noh. Their condition is the normal condition of man, only more intense. No one is concerned with the nature of the attachment, or whether it constitutes good or evil. The attachment of the mother to her child, one of the most difficult to break, according to Buddhism, would hardly constitute a flaw in a Western sense. Rather, the intensity of the attachment and the attendant pain are what serve to lift the individual up out of the norm, and to open up the path which may lead to enlightenment. Obsessions that are given a spiritual dimension in the noh offer the sufferer dignity and eventually repose. Moreover, in spite of the anxious wandering of the spirit, he/she is anchored to a definite place and moment in time. The obsession adds to the aura of the place, attracting visitors. The place itself, occasioning the return of the spirit, lends further meaning to the obsession.

The character in the *Well-Curb (Izutsu)* by Zeami Motokiyo is able to tell her story only because of the well that draws her back to the love of her childhood, a love already made famous in *The Tales of Ise*. The tormented being in the noh plays exists within a meaningful cultural and geographical context. He is not abandoned to his fall but rather given a path to release from the karma of his existence. He does not fall into hell because his obsession is already his hell. The only path, then, is deliverance. For the audience this feeling of release is accomplished through the subtle interplay of the arts of music, poetry, and dance on stage, which build in tempo and complexity until they reach the finale. Instead of feeling pity or fear for the condition of the character, the audience experiences the chaos of untamed emotion brought on by attachment and the feeling of release at the conclusion of the play.

CAROLYN MORLEY

Further Reading

Translations

Brazell, Karen, ed. *Twelve Plays of the Noh and Kyōgen Theaters.* Ithaca, N.Y.: Cornell University East Asia Papers, 1988. Contains translations of plays not readily available and some of which are no longer performed. Contains a provocative afterword by Brazell in which she argues that noh and kyōgen are one, rather than two, distinct dramatic form.

Keene, Donald, ed. *Twenty Plays of the No Theater.* New York: Columbia University Press, 1970. The classic collection of translations of twenty plays of the noh theater. Includes a sensitive introduction to the noh by Donald Keene.

Tyler, Royall, ed. *Japanese Nō Dramas.* New York: Penguin, 1992. A collection of translations of 24 noh plays with insightful introductions to each of the plays. Translations are of exceptional quality.

Waley, Arthur. *The Nō Plays of Japan.* London: Allen and Unwin, 1921. Reprint. New York: Grove Press, 1957. The first collection of translations of noh plays.

Related Studies

Bethe, Monica, and Karen Brazell. *Nō as Performance: an Analysis of the Kuse Scene from Yamamba.* Ithaca, N.Y.: Cornell University East Asia Papers, 1978. A detailed analysis of the performance of noh with a video tape that accompanies the text.

Goff, Janet. *Noh Drama and The Tale of Genji: the Art of Allusion in Fifteen Classical Plays.* Princeton, NJ: Princeton University Press, 1991. A sophisticated textual analysis of the noh plays based on the tenth-century novel *The Tale of Genji.* Contains translations of the 15 plays studied.

Keene, Donald. *Nō and Bunraku: Two Forms of Japanese Theater.* New York: Columbia University, 1966, 1990. Provides a clear introduction to the history of noh and the appreciation of noh as literature and as drama. Includes photographs illustrating performance, stages, and masks.

Rimer, Thomas J., and Yamazaki Masakazu, trans. *On the Art of the Nō Drama: The Major Treatises of Zeami.* Princeton, NJ: Princeton University Press, 1984. The first complete translation of the nine treatises by Zeami Motokiyo. Includes an introductory chapter on the historical backround to the treatises by Thomas Rimer and a chapter analyzing the artistic theories of Zeami by Yamazaki Masakazu. Photographs of noh performance as well as illustrations of the treatises are provided.

THE FICTIONAL WORKS OF IHARA SAIKAKU

Author: Nagai Saikaku
Born: 1642, Osaka, Japan
Died: 1693, Osaka, Japan
Major Works: *The Life of an Amorous Man (Kōshoku ichidai otoko)* (1682); *Five Women Who Loved Love (Kōshoku gonin onna)* (1686); *The Life of an Amorous Woman (Kōshoku ichidai onna)* (1686); *The Great Mirror of Male Love (Nanshoku ōkagami)* (1687); *The Japanese Family Warehouse (Nippon eitaigura)* (1688); *Tales of Samurai Honor (Buke giri monogatari)* (1688); *Some Final Words of Advice (Saikaku oridome)* (1694)

Major Themes

Excess breeds disaster; security is found in moderation.
Versatility and ingenuity foster worldly success.
No set theory can entirely predict the outcome of human actions.

Ihara Saikaku created from elite prose and poetic traditions a plebian form of fiction that became a wellspring of Edo (1603–1867) literature. A major figure in the popularization of the arts, he championed the oppressed townspeople by reflecting their immediate concerns in amusing, exemplary stories. Often based on actual events, these stories center on an unfixed ideal of savoir-faire and show that strategies born of human desire are in practice not consistent. These works do not embody theme so much as attitude, balancing a healthy skepticism of rules with an intuitive faith in human versatility and ingenuity, existential virtues equated with the dynamism of the townsfolk. Saikaku's genius is literary, not philosophical; his vigorous, elastic style quotes classical literature as easily as it reports gossip fresh from the street. His sophisticated narration may seem flippant and cynical in making entertainment out of the cruel ends of the unscrupulous or unlucky, but when his enormous talent embroiders cold fact into a tapestry of brilliant poetry, winning humor, and effective pathos, it belies a stoic humanism that applauds life's defiance of tyrannical rules.

Saikaku was born in 1642 to a wealthy merchant family in Osaka, at the time a second-rate trading port. He first gained renown as a talented member of a major poetry school. His wife died in 1675, and no children survived past infancy. Two years later he shaved his head (like a monk taking orders), put a trusted clerk in charge of the family business, and devoted himself to travel and writing.

In 1682, Saikaku published a startling new work of prose that changed the course of Japanese literature, and won him a large following. Saikaku (whose name is a pen-name, with a homonym meaning "ready wits" or "business acumen") capitalized on this success to become Japan's first author of best-sellers. Never giving up poetry, he produced numerous prose works of remarkable diversity until his eyesight began to fail around 1689. By the time of his death in 1693, he had produced some 25 books that gave shape to his society.

Saikaku's greatness rests on a sharp eye for details that bespeak the concerns of his townspeople (*chonin*) readers, who occupied the lowest caste of a social system borrowed from China by a late-sixteenth-century shogun. Propped up by a simplified Confucian ethic, this rigid system placed the imperial court first, samurai (warrior) second, farmers and artisans (producers) third, and "non-producing" townspeople fourth, just above outcasts. Upward social mobility was not an option; caste and even profession were nearly frozen into hereditary patterns. Chōnin managed to succeed as speculators, money-lenders, merchants, artists, actors, and geisha, though the shogun, who held absolute power, could harass them at will with sumptuary rules and taxes. Protest or petition of any form usually cost one one's life; indeed, capital punishment was meted out with shocking frequency at gruesome execution grounds located just outside each city. Stoic indifference was the best assurance of a chōnin's survival. Caught between life's unforeseeable hardships and harsh autocratic rules, the chōnin inhabited a fleeting, floating world, the *ukiyo*.

Ukiyo, an Orthodox Buddhist term for the "ephemeral world" that deprived non-*bonzes* (non-monks) of *satori* (interior illumination), lost this meaning as later sects taught simple salvation attainable even by worldly chōnin. By Saikaku's day, ukiyo had taken on a sharp, sarcastic ring—a buzzword for an island of style, extravagance, and abandon, floating in a sea of spartan samurai with a stiff code of honor and duty. The ukiyo revolved around the pleasure quarters and kabuki theaters, chōnin-run demimondes, in which money and savvy alone determined status. Though off-limits to them, samurai and bonzes were discreet patrons. Chōnin ambition, politically denied and economically curtailed, found an outlet in the ukiyo, a market for chonin tastes and (to a lesser extent) their vaguely defiant antipathy. A cultural revolution ensued. Mass producing and marketing freed artists from patrons. Kabuki and *bunraku* (puppet) theaters thrived on the crowds they drew. Literature was no longer confined to hand-written scrolls circulated among nobles, thanks to improved bookmaking methods and the high rate of literacy accompanying the rise of commerce.

The Life of an Amorous Man

Saikaku filled the need for a popular fiction by redefining the *kōshoku* ("loving love") form of semi-didactic, mechanical romance with the crisp form of *haikai* poetry. His first prose work, *The Life of an Amorous Man*, appeared in 1682, the year he became head of the Danrin School of haikai. Haikai was a "comic" version of the nobility's *renga* ("linked verse"), itself derived from the poetry-writing contests integral to Heian court life. Renga sequences usually were composed in one

sitting by poets who rotated turns. Poets had to be fluent in the intricate rules of composition that encouraged linking poems by imagery or allusion. Displaying the author's ability to link verses of diverse topic and sentiment being the measure of poetic prowess, a good renga sequence is a verse collage of the gamut of human sentiments. Haikai popularized renga with looser rules of composition, common language, and "vulgar" subject matter. The Danrin School produced sequences on a single theme, such as love, mocking the elegant aesthetics of court poetry with rapid, mass composition. Saikaku excelled at haikai, writing at the speed of stream-of-consciousness, and blurring the distinction between poetry and prose. His record still stands: 23, 500 verses recited in a single day and night in 1684.

Saikaku's early fiction grew out of mass-produced verse and cannot be appreciated without a sense of the haikai-like links at work. *The Life of an Amorous Man*, for instance, is hardly a novel. Its 54 chapters (mimicking *The Tale of Genji*), each detailing the erotic exploits of a year of the roué Yonosuke's life, offer little emotional or psychological insight and advance no theme or plot. The one-dimensional Yonosuke is reduced to an insatiable sexual appetite for women and even boys, and actions devoid of consequences. Lust incarnate, this caricature is at the mercy of the prose (unpunctuated in the original), which flows forth in a torrent of wit and invention. Since the prevailing force of impromptu haikai linking, the feeble storyline all but disappears in sudden shifts in narrative voice, tone, and subject. Billed as a koshoku, *The Life of an Amorous Man* was recognized, within a generation, to be the first of a new genre, the *ukiyo-zōshi* ("ukiyo book").

Ukiyo books are defined by skepticism and vulgarity, a reflection of their audience's tastes and of government censorship. Subject matter included illicit (and explicit) romances, get-rich-quick schemes, and the latest vogues in food, drink, dress, and sex. The detached loftiness of classical literature (*koten*), the condescending preachiness of Buddhist parables, and the dour nay-saying of Confucian tracts were all targeted for earthy lampoons.

When Saikaku sardonically chastises "uncouth" chōnin for preferring to gaze at gold and silver instead of the autumn moon and cherry blossoms (sacrosanct to court poetry), the back-handed jab at aristocratic preciosity is intentional. His books revel in aloof frivolity: puns offset the pathos of his account of an unjust execution. Ukiyo books may fail to fulfill the didactic purpose of "serious" literature, but for oppressed chōnin, the slapstick must have been cathartic, and the finely wrought actuality, magical.

Saikaku's checkered career as a writer of ukiyo is not documented in contemporary sources, and publication dates (especially of posthumous works) may not reflect order of composition. Among his 11 miscellaneous books are a play, a biography of an Osakan merchant playboy, a collection of tales of judicial trials, and an illustrated guidebook to Japan. These works are not among his best, and not easily discussed as fiction. The remaining 14, when examined chronologically as koshoku, sumarai, and chōnin books, give clues to his stylistic development. Narrowly defined, he produced eight kōshoku books (seven published 1682 to 1688, one posthumously in 1693), three samurai books (1687 and 1688), and three chōnin books (1688, 1692, and 1694).

Kōshoku Books

Kōshoku books owe the most to older literary conventions, that limited them thematically. By definition, erotic works meant to amuse, these paeans to fleshly pleasure are not without a hint of social criticsm, warning that imprudence can lead to ruin. Of course, Saikaku's libertines do not represent the norm; his extensive treatment of male bisexuality and homosexuality is also remarkable. His kōshoku are noteworthy for their sophisticated style and systematic treatment of sex. *The Life of an Amorous Man* (which has a lesser 1864 sequel) focuses on socially condoned sex from a male perspective. Three more masterpieces follow: *Five Women Who Loved Love*, a third-person narrative of five famous illicit affairs; *The Life of an Amorous Woman*, a first-person, female companion piece to *The Life of*

an Amorous Man; and *The Great Mirror of Male Love*, a third-person narrative of 40 homosexual stories. These four major kōshoku thoroughly survey contemporary sexuality (excepting lesbianism, portrayed only once, in *The Life of an Amorous Woman*). They also represent large advances in Saikaku's perfection of his fiction. Lastly are three later "repentant" kōshoku that describe rich brothel patrons who have fallen on hard times. Of the eight kōshoku, Japanese critics laud *The Life of an Amorous Man*, undeniably Saikaku's greatest contribution to literary history, while Western critics tend to prefer *Five Women Who Loved Love*.

Samurai Books

Having exhausted the topic of sex, Saikaku found new material in ancient and contemporary samurai tales. He may also have hoped to win favor and a larger audience. Yet these are not the work of a sycophant, as is evident by comparing the vendettas of the sober *Tales of Samurai Honor* (his best samurai book) to *Chushingura (The Treasury of Royal Retainers*; c. 1748) by Takeda Izumo, Miyoshi Shōraku, and Namiki Senryu. Saikaku's tone is one of cautious curiosity and bemused respect for the sword-bearing men who were, in both senses, keepers of the ukiyo. As a chōnin, he could not write about samurai without pinpointing their ideal of bravery and loyalty, and his best efforts show it to be the dynamic of their conduct. Admittedly, the samurai work is Saikaku's weakest, as he was at pains to write credibly about a world he did not know first-hand. Yet the chōnin attitude finds expression in an objective investigation into the arbitrariness of the worldly rewards for the samurai virtue, *giri*, echoing the kōshoku theme, that excesses lead to ruin. Saikaku's viewpoint developed through the samurai books, which more fully capture the values and ideas behind human actions.

Chōnin Books

The samurai books challenged Saikaku to give his unrepresented caste its own literature, chōnin books on three themes: *The Japanese Family Storehouse*,

30 stories of fortunes made or lost; *Worldly Mental Calculations*, 20 stories about debts collected or avoided; and *Some Final Words of Advice*, 23 stories about changing fortunes.

Writing for merchants, Saikaku simplified his ornate style and employed an authoritative voice that is at times downright earnest. Set against the samurai books, the chōnin books carry the obvious message that chōnin are fundamentally different from samurai and must make the most of their lot. Each story is a test case of strategies, both successful (*The Japanese Family Storehouse)* and dubious (*Worldly Mental Calculations* and *Some Final Words of Advice*). A principle, such as filial piety or frugality, incurs reward in one story but disaster in another, because success depends on circumstances. The moral is that since the floating world offers no sure-fire solutions or guarantees, chōnin must know how to manipulate opportunity and avoid disaster. From this philosophical gristmill emerge forces propeling chōnin society: integrity, diversity, and adaptability. The extremely popular chōnin books announced the arrival of a new class with its own ethos and culture. Their revolutionary concern for getting the most out of life may seem obvious now; but much can be learned from Saikaku's clinical, unsparing exposition of the tyranny of rigid rules. By demonstrating that the common sense of common people prevails over all theories, he was the first to tap into a deep undercurrent of Japanese civilization, the desire for self-reliance and determination.

Five Women Who Loved Love

Saikaku's most accessible kōshoku breaks from the mechanical conventions of the form, allowing action to tell five contemporary incidents of illicit relations. The collection is framed by a pleasing fugue-like symmetry, showing a strong haikai influence also evident in the alternating of humor and pathos, and authorial aside and storyline. The surprising, delightful ending to the last story casts the work in a positive light. Even without character development, psychological truth is found in the depiction of the mentality that leads to committing crime in the name of love. The long-awaited, frantic moments of love-making provide each story with a dramatic hiatus in which time seems suspended. That four of the stories end in tragedy only makes these fleeting moments of passion larger than life. Saikaku views his five women with a knowing, loving eye, arousing our envy and portraying their sexual awakening as a liberation from social confines. As the 15-year-old Oshichi naively asserts after a too-short night of love-making, "The world is wide enough—there should be one land where night lasts throughout the day." In discovering how narrow the world actually is, the five heroines delimit the boundaries of ukiyo society.

The Life of an Amorous Woman

The third major kōshoku, *The Life of an Amorous Woman,* presents Saikaku's most formidable fictional creation, a tragicomic old debauchée who recounts, in vivid detail, her numerous affairs. In scope and form, the work complements *The Life of an Amorous Man*, though the progress is reversed as she slides from daimyo's mistress to the lower ranks of courtesan, and finally becomes the meanest of streetwalkers. Her many exploits, pleasurable and otherwise, even include an incident of lesbianism. The rich variety echoes haikai composition. Finally, unable to ensnare even desperate men, she becomes a nun, and attains a truly climactic enlightenment.

The work is a sharp attack on the orthodox Buddhist doctrine of denial, which condemned both sex and money-making, and was anathema to chōnin. Though her personality is sometimes lost in efforts to amuse the reader, she is depicted as an intelligent woman of complex emotions and conflicting desires. There is an arresting immediacy to her frank, ribald reflections as she pursues her desires with gusto and optimism. If her character is reminiscent of Fanny Hill, she inhabits a world almost as brutally absurd as that of Sade's Justine. In her, Saikaku created a new kind of heroine who speaks knowingly of the best and worst of the floating world.

The Great Mirror of Male Love

Homosexual relations among samurai and boy-actors, past and present, are the subject of this last major kōshoku. Saikaku's haikai-like prose style is shown to best advantage and the stories have been reduced to a minimum of the most telling and precise details, especially in the stories of boy-actors. Clever plot twists make some stories among the most engaging in his canon.

The work is pivotal because its subject matter, though erotic, looks beyond sex to the ideals behind human conduct. Certainly the samurai stories could not have been written without an awareness of the samurai code of conduct, and *The Great Mirror of Male Love* is also a samurai work, most notably in the stories that focus on vendettas. With its two-part structure, the book hints at a comparison between samurai and boy-actors, a dichotomy that will find fuller expression in the ensuing samurai and chōnin trilogies.

Some Final Words of Advice

Saikaku's last important work is his most complex and original, and contains his most articulate and mature ideas. It consists of two parts, aptly titled, "Some Reflections on Japanese Townsmen" and "People's Hearts in This World of Ours" (which may have been two incomplete manuscripts put together as one book by a disciple). Both sections contain the usual hodgepodge of characters and outcomes, but the theme uniting these stories is not as simple as love, revenge, or money-making.

The predominant subject matter of these stories—happiness in this world—demonstrates a real sensitivity to the human condition. There is an earnestness to many passages, especially in the second part, out of character with the rest of the Saikaku canon, and for the first time, he concludes that people are capable of evil.

The realization that conduct praised in one tale leads to disaster in another is jarring at first. Saikaku seemed to have grown tired of the truisms of his age, and he set them up against one another to show their practical inconsistencies. He repeatedly demonstrates that nothing and no one in this world is completely reliable. His skepticism finds mature expression, and he employs all his gifts, including a sharp analytical eye, to expose the dangers inherent in oversimplification and the uncritical application of rules. A humanism latently present in earlier works comes to the fore, and Saikaku leaves us with a raw and poignant work that shows human life to be as frail as it is unruly.

DAVID C. EARHART

Further Reading

Translations

Ihara Saikaku. *Tales of Samurai Honor.* Caryl Ann Callahan, trans. Tokyo: Sophia University Press, 1981. A fine translation of the best samurai book, well documented, with helpful introduction. Of interest for its chōnin perspective on samurai.

———. *Five Women Who Loved Love.* Wm. Theodore de Bary, trans. Rutland, VT: Charles E. Tuttle, Publishers, 1956. Very readable masterpiece on tragic love delineates the boundaries of the ukiyo.

———. *Some Final Words of Advice.* Peter Nosco, trans. Rutland, VT: Charles E. Tuttle, 1980. Superb posthumous chōnin book. Saikaku's fullest expression of his ideas about his age and his own caste. Solid, standard introduction.

———. *The Japanese Family Storehouse.* G. W. Sargent, trans. Cambridge: Cambridge University Press, 1959. Classic chōnin book about money-making and the arbitrary nature of success formulas, expertly translated. Supplemented by an invaluable analysis of the poetics of Saikaku's prose.

———. *The Great Mirror of Male Love.* Paul Gordon Schalow, trans. Stanford, CA: Stanford University Press, 1990. Top-notch, transitional collection of 30 stories about boy-actors and samurai. Excellent introduction to the work, the age, and homosexuality.

Related Studies

Hibbett, Howard S. *The Floating World in Japanese Fiction.* New York: Grove Press, 1960. Pioneering, standard study of ukiyo fiction. Gives an excellent introduction to the genre and the age, and includes a fine chapter on Saikaku. Includes a translation of parts of *The Woman Who Spent Her Life in Love* (also known as *The Life of an Amorous Woman*).

Keene, Donald. *World Within Walls.* See "Ihara Saikaku," 167–215. New York: Grove Press, 1976. This chronological survey is informative about even obscure works in the Saikaku canon. The literary analysis should be considered in the context of the age and weighed against the scant biographical data.

THE HAIKU POETRY OF MATSUO BASHŌ

Author: Matsuo Bashō
Born: 1644, Ueno, Iga Province, Japan
Died: 1694, Osaka, Japan
Major Works: Some thousand extant haiku; *The Journal of a Weatherbeaten Skeleton (Nozarashi kikō)* (1684); *Collected Verses (Atsume ku)* (1687); *The Narrow Road to the Deep North (Oku no hosomichi)* (c. 1689); *Saga Diary (Saga nikki)* (1691)

Major Themes

There is a meaning to what one sees and hears, but it has to be found inwardly.

There are striking aspects of natural things that have to be grasped all at once, at the right time, and in the right way.

To sense the depth of mystery in the world, one must begin with what is simple and striking.

When Bashō was born in 1644 to a samurai family, his name was Matsuo Kinsaku. His family at that time was in the service of the lord of Ueno in the town of Iga, near Kyoto. By this time Japan was enjoying a pacified, stable, and secure society under the shogunate, a military government established by Tokugawa Ieyasu. The early part of the Tokugawa period (1603–1868) was marked by the official closing of Japan to the rest of the world. This seclusion policy in turn brought about a remarkable cultural enlightenment in the second half of the seventeenth century—Bashō's times.

When Bashō was eight years old or so, he was taken into the service of Ueno Castle in Iga. There he became the page and close friend-companion of the lord's son, Sengin, a few years older than Bashō. Encouraging each other, the two were both interested in the art of poetry. The friendship came to an end, however, when the young lord died suddenly in 1666. His death caused an important change in Bashō's life in his early 20s. Stricken with sorrow and retiring from service at the castle soon after, Bashō withdrew to the monastery at Kōyasan. At the age of about 28, he moved to Edo (the present Tokyo), where he devoted himself to becoming a master of *haiku* (the unrhymed verse form, having phrases of five, seven, and five syllables, in that order, and usually including a seasonal reference). Living in a cottage called *Bashō An*

(Banana Tree Hermitage), given to him by a rich merchant, he came to be known by the name Bashō.

Bashō established himself as a mature poet during his 30s, dealing with more profound themes than before. He also developed the "new style," taken as a model by many poets later, a style associated with his name. During his 40s, Bashō's poetry came to bear the true Zen spirit, although few of his poems were obviously religious. In the last 10 years of his life, Bashō wandered around on pilgrimages, often with one or two companions, sometimes by himself. He visited famous places and met with fellow poets as well as with his disciples. He died on one of his wanderings, surrounded by many of his friends and pupils, in 1694, at the age of 50.

Bashō is influential and admired not only as the master of the haiku but also as the most creative interpreter of haiku theories. Furthermore, his travel journals are regarded as sensitive and perceptive works of prose literature. He is regarded by many, if not most, critics as Japan's greatest poet. In a very proper sense, he is still a living poet of Japan.

"The Old Pond and the Frog"

Written in 1686, when Bashō was 42 years old, a poem generally known as "The Old Pond" may well be one of the best haiku Bashō wrote; certainly it is one of the most famous. While there are many English translations of the poem, it is interesting to look first at the original, then at a word-by-word translation, and finally at my [Ko Won's] rendering of the poem; this pattern of attending to Bashō's poetry is one followed throughout this article.

> *Furu ike ya*
> *kawazu tobikomu*
> *mizu no oto*

> old pond!
> frog jumps in
> water's sound

> *The old pond!*
> *A frog jumping in,*
> *the sound of water.*

It is said that, sitting one day in the garden of his little house in Edo with some friends and pupils, Bashō, when a sound suddenly broke the silence, came up with the phrase, *kawazu tobikomu mizu no oto*. In the poet's realm of imagination, the sudden sound of water brought about by a frog's jumping into the pond immediately prompted, it seems, an "internal comparison" or internal association between the old pond and the sound. As the reference to the frog suggests, the time is probably twilight in late spring. A mossy "old" pond may have been to the poet a timeless and endless body of something perfectly serene, the presence of potent being.

Deep and esoteric, perhaps mysterious, in meaning, the poem demonstrates the characteristics of Bashō's finest poetry—work written in the last 10 years of his life, a period marked by mature thoughts and emotions that find expression in economical and striking imagery.

The Crow, the Locust, and the Cuckoo

In another poem written in the "new style" developed by Bashō, we also see the technique of the "internal comparison":

> *Kare eda ni*
> *karasu no tomari keri*
> *aki no kure*

> withered branch on
> a crow perched
> autumn's dusk

> *On a withered branch*
> *a crow has settled:*
> *autumnal nightfall.*

Simplicity and brevity prevail in this picture. At the same time, a withered branch and the autumnal nightfall present a mental landscape with the small body of the crow contrasting with the vast darkness of the dusk. One may say that all these are symbolically suggestive of something more than what is actually seen. A little man, "nobody," is perched temporarily on a dead branch in the autumn of life.

Stillness, of course, is one of the fundamental qualities that characterize haiku in general and Bashō's art in particular. In a poem included in *The Narrow Road to the Deep North* we hear the shrill of a locust piercing the rocks:

> *Shizukasa ya*
> *iwa ni shimi-iru*
> *semi no koe*

> stillness
> rocks into pierce
> the locust's voice

> *Absolute stillness!*
> *Piercing into rocks,*
> *the voice of the locust.*

A favorite bird in Basho's haiku is the *hototogisu* (a bird resembling a cuckoo). The following two haiku deal with this somewhat mythical bird:

I.

> *Hototogisu*
> *kie yuku kata ya*
> *shima hitotsu*

> cuckoo
> vanish-going direction
> island one

*Out there is the direction
the cuckoo goes and disappears,
a lone island.*

II.

*Hototogisu
otake yabu no
moru tsukiyo*

cuckoo
big bamboo thickets
seeping in moon night

*The cuckoo
through a large bamboo grove
moonlight seeping.*

The cuckoo in these poems can be associated with life, human beings, or the poet. Whatever else the reader may find in the metaphor, Bashō's poetic skill of figurative association in such an appropriately intense, yet simple, fashion seems to coincide with the matureness of his view of life.

Autumn and Nightfall

Bashō's favorite season is, as with many other haiku poets, the fall, and his favorite time of day is the evening or night. The following poem, written in 1694, is a characteristic expression:

*Kono michi ya
yuku hito nashi ni
aki no kure*

this road
going person none
autumn's nightfall

*This road
with no one going
autumn coming to an end.*

The Japanese word *kure* in the above poem appears to be ambiguous: it could mean either late autumn or nightfall (or both). It was written in the year Bashō died: *kure* could be the fall season, the nightfall of his own life.

In the same year, he wrote the following:

*Aki fukaki
tonari wa nani o
suru hito zo*

autumn deep
the neighbor what
does a person

*Autumn deepened.
What kind of things
does my neighbor do now?*

Leaves of Trees

Back in 1692, Bashō wrote poems about leaves of trees, the leaf being symbolic of life:

*Matsutake ya
shiranu konoha no
hebarizuki*

mushroom
unknown tree's leaf
sticking on

*The mushroom.
A leaf from an unknown tree
sticking to it.*

And another:

*Sabishisa o
toute kurenu ka
kiri hito ha*

loneliness
visit will you not
paulownia's one leaf

*Won't you come
and see loneliness?
One leaf from paulownia tree.*

While the leaf in the first of the two leaf poems appears to be objective and positive, even powerful and yet mysterious, the leaf of the second poem seems very personal and frail, even negative.

Bell Tones

Bell tones also play a significant role in Bashō's poetry, as do birds' songs. The following poem, written in 1673, is another perfect example of Bashō's art of association, a sort of auditory-visual perspective:

> *Kane kiete*
> *hana no ka wa tsuku*
> *yube kana*
>
> bell fading
> flowers' scent strikes
> evening
>
> *Bell tones fading out,*
> *blossom scents come up with ringing*
> *this evening.*

Zen Poems

What one might call the "Zen" spirit or "flavor" is probably the most significant prevailing quality of Bashō's poetry. Although all the poems can be understood as having the Zen spirit, which affects the quality of the imagery and the resultant atmosphere, the following two seem particularly effective:

I.

> *Oki yo oki yo*
> *waga tomo ni semu*
> *neru kocho*
>
> wake up wake up
> my companion will make
> sleeping butterfly
>
> *Wake up! Wake up!*
> *I want to make you my companion,*
> *sleeping butterfly.*

II.

> *Meigetsu ya*
> *ike o megurite*
> *yomosugara*

> bright moon
> pond going around
> night is over
>
> *Bright moon!*
> *As I wander around the pond,*
> *the night is already gone.*

In order for the reader to recognize and understand the delicacy of the Zen "waves" in Bashō's poetry, it seems only reasonable to say that he or she should try to see and hear what is neither visible nor audible. Although Bashō was at one point in his life a serious student of Zen, the influence of Zen in his work is subtle and indirect. If one appreciates the beauty and contemplative significance of the world as Bashō presents it—portraying things that are not necessarily beautiful or meaningful—then one has the kind of unique aesthetic experience that the genius of Bashō has made possible through his mastery of the haiku.

KO WON

Further Reading

Translations

The translations in this article are by Ko Won.

Stryk, Lucien. *On Love and Barley: Haiku of Bashō.* New York: Penguin Books, 1985. 253 haiku by Bashō, with an emphasis on the Zen aspects.

Ueda, Makoto. *Bashō and His Interpreters: Selected Hokku with Commentary.* Stanford, CA: Stanford University Press, 1991. The indispensable guide to Bashō's *hokku* (the term Professor Ueda uses to refer to all 17-syllable verses written before the end of the Edo period [1600–1868]; the term *haiku* is used for "independent 5 7 5 syllable" poems of the modern period). This remarkable book contains 255 hokku written by Basho, given in romanized Japanese, with literal and final translations into English by the author; abbreviated commentaries on individual hokku by some 90 critics from the seventeenth century–on; with notes on the commentators, a glossary, bibliography, and extremely useful indexes of the hokku in both English and Japanese.

Yuasa, Nobuyuki. *Bashō: The Narrow Road to the Deep North and Other Travel Sketches.* Baltimore, MD: Penguin Books, 1966. Bashō's masterpiece, together with other important travel journals.

Related Studies

Aitken, Robert. *A Zen Wave: Bashō's Haiku and Zen.* New York: Weatherhill, 1978. An informed study of Bashō's work from the Zen perspective.

Cohen, William Howard. *To Walk in Seasons: An Introduction to Haiku.* Rutland, VT: Charles E. Tuttle, 1972. An appreciative study of haiku, with critical attention to Bashō.

Henderson, Harold G. *An Introduction to Haiku: An Anthology of Poems and Poets from Bashō to Shiki.* Garden City, NY: Doubleday, 1958.

Keene, Donald, comp. and ed. *Anthology of Japanese Literature from the Earliest Era to the Mid-nineteenth Century.* New York: Grove Weidenfeld, Grove Press, 1955. A very useful, well-translated, and intelligently selected collection of major Japanese poetry and prose from the ancient period (to A.D. 794) through the Tokugawa period (1600–1868). Useful introduction by Keene.

Ueda, Makoto. *Matsuo Bashō.* Tokyo: Kodansha International Ltd., 1982. (Previously published by Twayne Publishers, 1970.) An excellent introduction to Bashō containing a chronology of his life, a map of his journeys, a chapter on his life, discussion of Bashō's haiku, renku, and prose, a review of the critical commentaries, and a consideration of Bashō's permanence. Contains many of his poems in both Japanese and English translation.

THE PLAYS OF CHIKAMATSU MONZAEMON

Author: Chikamatsu Monzaemon (original name Sugimori Nobumori)
Born: 1653, Echizen (now in Fukui prefecture)
Died: 1725, Osaka
Major plays: *The Soga Heirs* (1683), *Victorious Kagekiyo* (1686), *Double Suicide at Sonezaki* (1703), *The Battles of Coxinga* (1715), *The Woman Killer and the Hell of Oil* (1721)

Major Themes

Life is an illusion, the pains of birth and death prescribed before our coming.
Love and duty often conflict, sometimes fatally.
Art is something that lies in the slender margin between the real and the unreal.

Chikamatsu, often called the Japanese Shakespeare, wrote between 100 and 150 *joruri* (puppet plays) and 30 *kabuki* plays, the two major dramatic genres of his time. His works consist mainly of historical romances and domestic tragedies. Many of the plots reflect themes derived from Japanese classical literature, legend, and religion. The element of fantasy is observable in his historical works for the puppet theater. His domestic tragedies, with their sentimental stories of love and death and emphasis on tragedy found in ordinary life, tend to be much more realistic. Modern readers may wonder whether *kabuki* or live theater would have been a better vehicle for Chikamatsu's highly sophisticated drama, but even his most acclaimed *kabuki* plays are inferior to his best puppet plays.

Little is known about the life of the man who is generally considered Japan's first professional and greatest playwright. He belonged to a samurai family from a province near Kyoto, the imperial capital. His father apparently gave up his feudal duties and moved the family to Kyoto sometime between 1664 and 1670. There Chikamatsu worked serving various members of the court aristocracy and acquired a considerable knowledge of Buddhism, Confucianism, and Japanese and Chinese literature. Although he may have already written as many as 15 plays earlier, Chikamatsu established his reputation with the production in 1683 of *The Soga Heir (Yotsugi Soga)*, an old style puppet play and the first play definitely attributable to him. His first *kabuki* play was performed the following year.

In 1685, Chikamatsu began to write new style puppet plays that treated the life of townspeople for the chanter Takemoto Gidayu. By 1693, however, he was writing almost exclusively for the *kabuki* theater, particularly for Sakata Tojuro, the greatest actor of the day. Upon the retirement of Sakata in 1703, he resumed writing for Gidayu; and two years later moved to Osaka to write until his death for Gidayu's puppet theater, the Takemotoza.

Ancient Style Puppet Plays

The puppet theater of Chikamatsu's day was fairly small in scale. The puppets were manipulated by one man who inserted his hands from below. Both outdoor and indoor staging was very simple. A chanter delivered the words while being accompanied by a samisen player. The material that Chikamatsu wrote consisted not only of the text for the chanter but also a complete description of the scene settings and comments related to the production.

From 1673 to 1685, Chikamatsu principally composed play scripts in the "ancient style" (*kojoruri*) for the chanter Kaga-no-jo. The dialogue in these drama is quite cursory at the beginning and takes an increasingly important role as the amount of commentary gradually diminishes. Although many elements found in these awkward early plays are similar to those of Chikamatsu's contemporaries, the plays show signs of the later genius of the playwright—more fluid style, greater imagination, involving romanticism, sharpened drama, and a sense of humor recalling classics of the past. Occasionally, he caters to tastes of the day for fantasy by having his puppet characters perform super-human feats; however, some of his scenes of ordinary life treat the subjects of love and war more realistically than had ever been done before. Although some sections in *The Soga Heir*, for example, border on the burlesque, it contains beautiful passages and the union of two incongruous worlds, the battlefield and the brothel, that foreshadowed Chikamatsu's later work.

"New Style" Puppet Theater and Domestic Tragedies

From 1686 to 1703, Chikamatsu wrote for two major chanters, Takemoto Gidayu (1651–1714; up to 40 plays) and Sakata Tojuro (1647–1709; 10 or more). The dialogue in these plays is lively and incisive with increasingly well-delineated characterization. The linear plot of early plays cedes in this period to complex dramatic situations with concomitant lengthening of plays (sometimes from dawn to dusk). While many of the plots reflect religious themes or those derived from the classics of Japanese and Chinese literature, Chikamatsu deliberately avoids well-worn paths, using comedy to alleviate the dramatic atmosphere and humanize the characters.

In 1703 Chikamatsu for the first time broke with established tradition by staging his domestic tragedy, *Double Suicide at Sonezaki* (*Sonaezaki shinju*), written within a few weeks of an actual double suicide. Such themes had already been addressed in *kabuki*; however, Chikamatsu's approach differs from that of *kabuki* dramatists whose work occasionally incorporated the sordid aspects of town life. To his audience of townspeople used to the stories and adventures of nobles and heroes of the past, Chikamatsu instead presented an unperceived dimension of their own life. The amorous intrigues and voluntary death of a lowly shopkeeper and prostitute are described and analyzed with captivating candor. In contrast to Chikamatsu's earlier, noble, even superhuman heroes, Tokubei is pitiable in his ineffectuality. It is the strength of his love for Ohatsu

that makes him a hero. The depth of their love is highlighted in the final scene where Chikamatsu relies on a "poetic journey" (*michiyuki*; a trip conducted under extreme duress described with a great deal of allusion to places traversed) to impart tragic stature to his characters. Their suicides have meaning. They are assured that they will someday attain Buddahood.

The success of Chikamatsu's play, which rested on Chikamatsu's ability to detect the stuff of tragedy in the fate of an ordinary clerk and prostitute, not only saved Gidayu's theater from bankruptcy, but also inspired Chikamatsu to produce at least 15 more domestic dramas often inspired by contemporary events and exploring many situations of town life with increasing realism. All of these dramas are marked by vivid dialogue, a characterization that tends to avoid stereotypes, and occasional poignant passages such as that of the journey to suicide in the grove at Sonezaki.

Historical Plays

With the exception of his 30 or so domestic dramas, most of Chikamatsu's theater is based on historical themes or legends, mainly drawn from the chronicles of feudal wars. In contrast to the merchant class characters of the domestic plays, those of the historical plays include traditional heroes of Japanese and Chinese history—nobles, generals, and the like. Many of these plays contain new dramatic elements such as the poetic journey and the high-principled mistress. The character Akoya, Kagekiyo's mistress in *Victorious Kagekiyo* (*Shusse Kagekiyo*; 1686), is a prime example. She is a character of genuine tragic intensity, and Chikamatsua presents her as a believable woman with a full range of contradictions and complexities.

Nine of Chikamatsu's historical puppet plays deal with the adventures of Yoshitsune and his faithful sidekick, Benkei, a colossal monk-warrior. It is not Yoshitsune's victories that interest Chikamatsu and his audience so much as his youthful feats and even more the end of his life, when he flees before the henchmen of his brother, Yoritomo, the shogun, who is instigated by the calumnies of the traitor, Kajiwara. Chikamatsu retains the virility and the sufferings of the epic hero, but he also adds a sense of romantic allure and is not averse to humanizing his character by placing him in awkward, even ridiculous situations.

Even more popular as a subject than Yoshitsune is the story of the Sogas, found in 11 dramas. Chikamatsu keeps most of the epic dimensions of the prowess of the two brothers, who introduce themselves one night in the camp of the formidable Yoritomo in order to kill, by themselves, their own uncle, the murderer of their father. However, as with Yoshitsune, the playwright makes ordinary men of the Sogas as he recounts their amorous adventures with two courtesans.

The death of Gidayu and the succession of the chanter Masadayu at the Takemoto theater, Takemoto in 1714, influenced Chikamatsu to change direction again. The result was the production of his most popular puppet play, *The Battles of Coxinga* (1715), a historical melodrama whose plot is complicated and full of strange conventions. The work is a romance in the life of a Sino-Japanese soldier of fortune, who after having served the last two emperors of the Ming dynasty, made himself master of the island of Formosa. The work, long been considered Chikamatsu's masterpiece, had a 17-month run, having been seen by more than 200,000 spectators (Osaka had a population around 300,000 at the time). Chikamatsu's most important historical works were produced mainly in the last decade of his life.

Social Critique Mixes with Drama

To suppress political criticism, it was forbidden in Chikamatsu's time to stage any event that occurred after the establishment of the Tokugawa shogunate in 1603. Nevertheless, Chikamatsu often bypassed this interdiction by introducing allusions to the present in a story from the past. These allusions sometimes take the form of satire, when, for instance, a character praises the power of the spade over the sword or another points out suffering brought on by tyranny or harsh feudal taxation. Chikamatsu also managed to transport contemporary events transparently back into the past. One example is the story of

the 47 faithful vassals who killed their master's assassin in defiance of the law. Chikamatsu manages to transplant the entire affair to the fourteenth century, barely changing the names of the principal personages. Likewise, he places the last Japanese Christians, who perished in the Shimabara Rebellion, back in the twelfth century. Because any allusion to the Christians was also forbidden, he created a strange sect, inspired by Taoist magic, whose actions closely paralleled recent events.

Although less popular than his historical plays, Chikamatsu's domestic dramas were nonetheless quite successful and carried a new type of message. The characters that people these plays are merchants, housewives, prostitutes, thieves, and others who lived in the towns of his day, not the superheroes of yesterday. The most prominent theme, as already mentioned, is that of the double suicide, usually precipitated by economic and social constraints on amorous liaisons—especially exacerbated by bullying spouses or abusive parents. Several of these works deal with adultery, a capital crime at the time. What is new here is the author's explication through the dramatic action of the psychology behind the character's actions without excusing the act itself. In two cases, for example, the drama centers on the wives exposed to temptations during the long absences of their warrior husbands. In another, because of a fatal error, a very young woman married to her father's creditor falls in love with her husband's assistant.

Chikamatsu's domestic dramas are concerned with other types of crimes, such as *The Woman Killer and the Hell of Oil* (*Onna-goroshi abura-jigoku*; 1721), one of the last and most profound of his plays. The principal character of this play, Yohei, leads a debauched life in the pleasure quarters, eventually committing murder after attempting to steal money to pay a debt. At first, he is disinherited by his mother, a woman of samurai origin. However, a sense of duty leads her also to steal money to give to her wayward son. In this sordid drama, Chikamatsu lays bare the souls of humble personages and succeeds in revealing their fates with great sympathy. Through his domestic tragedies, one finds an implacable criticism of the society and morality of his time—rigid for the common person, but tolerant for the rich and powerful.

Views on Literature and Art

Some of Chikamatsu's views on drama have been preserved in a work written by a friend in 1738. There Chikamatsu describes his own art as "something that lies in the slender margin between the real and the unreal." He felt that he had to compromise some of his advanced views on dramaturgy in order to accommodate contemporary tastes—for example, at the insistence of the theater manager in the interests of winning popular favor, introducing scenes that spoil the dramatic integrity of his play. Accordingly, in his works he apparently tried to steer between the fantastic elements found in earlier puppet theater and the tide of realism increasingly evident in other genres of contemporary literature, particularly the novels of Saikaku Ihara (1642–1693). Chikamatsu was probably the first Japanese dramatist to sign his name (his pen name) on his scripts (starting in 1687), evidence of the growing importance of his art and of the literary scene in the Tokugawa period.

KENNETH G. KOZIOL

Further Reading

Translations

Keene, Donald. *The Battles of Coxinga, Chikamatsu's Puppet Play*. London: Taylor's Foreign Press, 1951.

———. *Four Major Plays of Chikamatsu*. New York: Columbia University Press, 1961.

Miyamori, Asataro. *Masterpieces of Chikamatsu: The Japanese Shakespeare*. New York: E. P. Dutton, 1926.

Shively, Donald H. *The Love Suicide at Amijima*. Cambridge, MA: Harvard University Press, 1953.

Related Studies

Gerstle, C. Andres. *Circles of Fantasy: Convention in the Plays of Chikamatsu*. Cambridge, MA: Harvard University Press, 1986. Examines theater conventions in the dramas of Chikamatsu.

Pringle, Patricia, ed. *An Interpretive Guide to Bunraku*. Honolulu: University of Hawaii at Manoa, 1992. Surveys the world of puppet theater, particularly that of Chikamatsu.

THE HAIKU POETRY OF KOBAYASHI ISSA

Author: Kobayashi Issa
Born: 1763, Kashiwabara village, Shinano province
Died: 1827, Kashiwabara village
Major Works: *Journal of My Father's Last Days (Chichi no Shuen Nikki)* (1801); *The Year of My Life (Ora ga Haru)* (1819)

Major Themes

Life in Edo is unpleasant, but one can find solace and beauty in the countryside.
One may have difficulty with members of one's family, but there is comfort and hope in Pure Land Buddhism.
Even if one is disappointed and lonely, there is a sense of a larger encompassing and embracing presence. In Japan, even the grasses flower.

Kobayashi Issa is regarded as among the greatest haiku poets, ranked with Bashō and Buson, and perhaps, in modern times, Masaoka Shiki. Further, while Bashō and Buson are often read for the loftiness or elegance of their haiku, Issa's verse is seen to be free of all pretensions to special refinement or sensibility. This is not to say that he was not a trained and disciplined poet. A standard edition of this verse includes more than 18,000 poems, showing him a prolific writer for whom the composition of poetry pervaded his daily life for 40 years. Nevertheless, his use of animated, colloquial expressions, his focus on subjects from common life, including animals and insects, and, in particular, his empathic stance with the weak and downtrodden in the world have endeared him to readers of all ages and walks of life, making him one of the most beloved literary figures of Japan.

Issa's Hardships

Issa's biography is an integral element in the reading of his work, for it is thought that the hardships he endured in his life—especially the early loss of his mother, his bitter relationship with his stepmother, and his often difficult economic circumstances—tested his basically sympathetic outlook on the world and left a lasting mark on the direction and tone of his work.

Issa was born into an average farming family in a rural area of present Nagano prefecture. He was the first son of his father Yagohei, but his mother died when he was three years old, and he was nurtured largely by his grandmother. Reflecting back on his childhood, Issa was later to write:

Ware to kite	Come play
asobe ya oya no	with me, sparrow
nai suzume.	without a parent!

When he was eight, his father remarried a woman named Satsu, who soon bore a son, Senroku. From a later account by Issa, it appears that he was forced to care for his infant half-brother, and that he keenly felt the enmity of both his mother and father when any troubles arose. After his grandmother died, Issa was sent away as an apprentice to work in Edo, present Tokyo. He was 15 years old. It was not uncommon for seasonal workers to migrate to the cities, and nothing is known of Issa's day-to-day life for the following ten years.

About 1785, when he was 23 years old, Issa began to study haikai under teachers of the Katsushika school, particularly Niroku-an Chikua and Konnichi-an Genmu, and his name begins to appear in records associated with the school from about two years later. This school advocated the use of colloquial expressions in haiku, a characteristic of Issa's style throughout his life. By 1789, he was composing verse under the name Issa, which means "one [cup of] tea," and emerged as a notable talent in the world of haiku.

After Chikua died in 1790, Issa became a prominent figure in the school. He returned home in 1791 to see his father, having now spent half his life away in Edo, but the following spring set out once more, this time on a poet's journey that would take him to the western part of Japan, to visit locales associated with poets of old and to engage in verse composition with practitioners in Kyoto and Osaka, and as far away as the islands of Shikoku and Kyushu. Issa traveled thus for six years, then returned to Edo. There, he assumed the leadership of the Katsushika school, taking the names Chikua and Niroku-an, but he was unable to establish himself financially as a teacher, and was forced to live an unsettled life, depending on friends for board and shelter. During this period, a "rustic style" was popular in Edo among poets seeking novel effects not available in the witty and allusive "urbane style." Issa shared some of the themes and methods of this rustic style, but employed it not to affect a tone but to express his discontent with life in Edo and his genuine love of life in the country:

Iza inan	Now, let's return!
Edo wa suzumi mo	Edo is so hot
mutsukashiki.	it's hard to stay.

Ta no kari ya	Wild geese in the fields!
sato no nin zu wa	Again today, people of village
kyo mo heru	grow fewer.

The second poem describes the birds occupying the autumn fields as people depart for winter work in the cities.

In 1801, at the age of 39, Issa again returned home to Kashiwabara after another long absence. At that time, his father fell ill with a high fever, and despite Issa's efforts to nurse him, died after a month. Issa recorded the course of his sickness in a moving diary, "Journal of My Father's Last Days." Two elements that significantly influenced Issa's later life emerge in this diary. One is a sense of reconciliation with his father, who expresses regret for having sent Issa away as a youth, and who in his

will divides his property between Issa and his half-brother. This reconciliation, however, is combined with Issa's portrayal of his step-mother and half-brother as callous and completely lacking in understanding for his father. Although Issa's account cannot be taken as completely objective, after his father's death his brother contested the will, and it was 13 years, with Issa making repeated trips from Edo seeking his share of the inheritance, before he was able to obtain it and return to his village. During this period, he found that other villagers often sided with his stepmother and half-brother:

Furusato ya	My home village:
yoru mo sawaru mo	all approach, all encounters—
bara no hana.	the rosebush.

The second prominent element present in Issa's journal of his father's illness is his father's dedicated and deep engagement with Pure Land Buddhism of the Shin tradition. Issa records, for example, his efforts to dissuade his father from attempting to perform his usual service before the family altar on the memorial day of Shinran, the founder of the Shin tradition. This aspect of religious devotion extends to Issa's perceptions also, as he strives to deal with the animosities of his stepmother and brother, and at times his father's querulousness, with Buddhist reflection on the attachments and egocentric feelings that warp one's perceptions of the world. This strain of self-reflection forms the foundation of Issa's resilience, his sensitivity to others, and his buoyancy despite the frustrations and disputes that dog his life.

A settlement with his stepmother and half-brother was finally reached in 1813 through the mediation of the local priest, and Issa returned to his village. He was then 50 years old. He was able to settle down and marry for the first time, and he expresses a certain contentment:

Ora ga yo ya	This world of mine—
sokora no kusa mo	even that grass there
mochi ni naru.	gets mixed into rice cakes.

His disappointments were not to end, however. His wife bore him three sons and a daughter, but they all died, one after the other, and after 10 years, when not yet 40 years old, his wife also died. After his daughter's death, Issa edited a journal into a work that remains one of the foremost classics of mixed haiku and prose, *The Year of My Life*. In this work, he speaks of his daughter:

Tsuyu no yo wa	This world of dew
tsuyu no yo nagara	is but a world of dew,
sarinagara.	and yet, and yet.

Issa married again, but this marriage failed after several months. A third marriage took place in 1826, but shortly after, a fire swept through the village and destroyed his house. Looking over the site of his property, Issa wrote:

Yake tsuchi no	In the warmth
hokari hokari ya	of the baked earth
nomi sawagu.	the fleas, agitated.

Issa moved into a storehouse that was spared by the flames, but died the next year.

For a haiku poet of Issa's stature and remarkable, lifelong output, he had surprisingly few students and left behind no band of disciples to carry on his highly distinctive and personal style. His influence on the haiku that came after him was therefore limited.

Issa's Themes

Issa's body of haiku writings includes a variety of styles and topics, but there are several themes that are closely associated with him. One is his ambivalent attitude toward his home village, and, more broadly, toward the circumstances of his life. As noted before, the loss of his mother while he was a young child is thought to have influenced his outlook, and to have instilled in him a longing for the love he never received as a child. When about 50 years old, he wrote:

Naki haha ya	My departed mother—
umi miru tabi ni	each time
miru tabi ni.	I see the sea.

Here, Issa expresses his yearning. His sense of loss, however, left him not embittered, but with a profound sense of compassion for the pain of other living things. Further, in the image of the sea, we find that his own sense of loneliness is, in each actual moment of his immediate experience, imbued with a larger sense of encompassing and embracing presence. There is, then, a disappointment that constantly undermines his expectations, together with an unflagging trust that draws him, in his life and his work, to his home village, and to an acceptance of the straightened conditions of his life:

Furusato wa	My home village—
hae made hito o	even the flies
sashinikeri.	bite.

Yuki chiru ya	Flurries of snow.
odoke mo ienu	No room for words of humor:
Shinano-zora.	the sky of Shinano.

This concern with his village extends to an unusual expression of love of the land of Japan in his haiku:

Waga kuni wa	In my land,
kusa sae sakinu	even the grasses flower:
sakura-bana.	the cherry blossoms.

Perhaps the most distinctive aspect of Issa's work in his grasp of the daily realities of the world is his transcendence of an anthropocentric view. This is apparent above all in his treatment of other living things. On watching the mating battles among male frogs:

Yasegaeru	Meager frog!
makeru na Issa	Don't give in.
kore ni ari.	Here stands Issa.

Ari no michi	The path of ants
kumo no michi yori	continuing down
tsuzukiken.	from the clouds' peak.

Toyama ga	Dragonfly!
medama ni utsuru	The distant mountain
tombo kana.	shines in its eye.

Underlying Issa's poetic achievement is his ability to transform the stuff of ordinary life, including its conflicts and contradictions, by infusing it in his haiku with a warmth of human life fully and wholeheartedly engaged, whatever failings there might be by other measures. This is, ultimately, the religious dimension of the ordinary in Issa's poetry, rooted in Japanese Buddhist tradition:

*Tomokakumo
anata makase no
toshi no kure.*

This and that
I leave all to you,
at year's end.

*Mida butsu no
miyage ni toshi o
hirou kana.*

As souvenirs
for Amida Buddha—
these years I gather.

DENNIS HIROTA

Further Reading

Translation

Translations in this article are by Dennis Hirota.

Huey, Robert N. "Journal of My Father's Last Days: Issa's *Chichi no Shuen Nikki.*" *Monumenta Nipponica*, XXXIX:1 (Spring 1984), 25–54.

Mackenzie, Lewis. *The Autumn Wind: A Selection from the Poems of Issa.* Tokyo: Kodansha International Ltd., 1984.

Yuasa, Nobuyuki. *The Year of My Life: A Translation of Issa's Oraga Haru.* Berkeley: University of California Press, 1960.

THE WORKS OF MORI ŌGAI

Author: Mori Ōgai
Born: 1862, Tsuwano, Japan
Died: 1922, Tokyo, Japan
Major Works: *The Dancing Girl (Mahime)* (1890), *Vita Sexualis* (1909), *Youth (Seinen)* (1910), *Delusions (Mōsō)* (1911), *The Wild Goose (Gan)* (1911–13), *The Abe Clan (Abe ichizoku)* (1913), *Incident at Sakai (Sakai jiken)* (1914), *Suibue Chūsai* (1916)

Major Themes

Literature is an intellectual undertaking, a vehicle for exploring ideas, values, and the complex role of an individual in society.

Serious literature must come to grips with the effects of modernization upon culture and the arts.

Commercialization and popularization have debased artistic production and cultural values.

Traditional culture is a wellspring of value; historical and biographical writings are effective literary vehicles for its appreciation.

There are negative consequences of romantic individualism.

The career of Mori Ōgai, which spans one of the most crucial periods in Japanese history, is virtually synonymous with the project of cultural and literary modernizaion carried out during the Meiji period (1868–1912). Together with his great contemporary Natsume Soseki (1867–1916), Ōgai may be said to have established the ideological and artistic framework for a modern literature in Japan.

Born into a samurai household in the declining years of the Tokugawa Shogunate (1603–1868), Mori Ōgai received the rigorous classical education befitting his family's elite status. His was the final generation of Japanese to receive such an education, and the first to be exposed to the full breadth of Western learning. This extraordinary mix of literary and intellectual forces imbue the author's work with a level of complexity—and at times daunting erudition—that stands in stark opposition to the products of a burgeoning popular culture. Ōgai's penetrating critique of what he came to regard as a commercialized and debased literary currency would mark much of his later work and in effect distance him from many of his contemporaries. At once a mainstay of the *bundan*, the Tokyo literary establishment, and among its staunchest critics, Ōgai earned a reputation as Japan's consummate belletrist, a stylist of unparalled authority and intellectual force. His dedication to the moral and ideological dimensions of literature, to the seriousness and elevation of literary endeavor, set a standard that few would succeed in attaining. Mori Ōgai is all but enshrined as a patriarch of modern Japanese letters.

Early Career

Following in his father's footsteps, the young Mori Rintaro ("Ōgai" is a pen name) pursued a medical education and went on to serve in the army medical corps, where he would eventually rise to its highest administrative post. His celebrated dual career as a physician and writer has become part of Japanese literary legend. Having graduated from the medical college of the Imperial University, where he was educated by a German faculty, Ōgai spent four years in Germany, reading widely in European literature and thought. He returned to Japan in 1888 and immediately began to make his mark upon the *bundan*, introducing major writers and new schools of thought to a Japanese public eager for enlightenment from the West. Indeed, the occasion of Mori Ōgai's return from Germany has been proclaimed as a turning point in Japanese literary and intellectual history.

The young writer's attainments as a fledgling figure on the mid-Meiji literary scene are nothing short of breathtaking. Most noteworthy is his publication of a trilogy of stories based on his experiences in Germany. The first of these, *The Dancing Girl,* is among the best-known works of modern Japanese literature. The story tells of Ōta, a young student sent to Berlin in an official capacity, who meets an impoverished dancing girl named Elis. They fall in love; Ōta abandons his schooling, moves in with Elis, and the couple live in Bohemian bliss until the young Japanese, admonished by his friend Aizawa, awakens from his romantic reverie. He leaves Elis, who is now pregnant and descending into madness, and returns to Japan, recording his pained confession on shipboard as he makes his way back home to duty and respectability—and the burden of modern self-consciousness.

Ōgai's so-called German trilogy *(Doitsu san-busaku)* stands as a landmark of modern Japanese literature. A brilliant "translation" of German romantic fiction, the stories introduced a radically new conception of the individual and literary self-referentiality. Their popularity was in part due to the widespread assumption that the author himself figured as hero of the exotic adventure. *Maihime* in particular was a stunning achievement, whose compelling romanticism and personalism opened up new avenues for young writers weary of outmoded conventions and hackneyed moralism.

It is ironic, therefore, that creative fiction *(shōsetsu)* appeared to hold so little fascination for the author, who, having succeeded so brilliantly with his German trilogy, abandoned the writing of fiction for nearly 20 years (1890–1909), during which time he pursued other literary interests. One such activity, which remained a lifelong passion, was literary translation.

The Modernization of Japanese Culture

We need to understand the extent to which the modernization of Japanese culture was in effect a vast translation project. Ōgai's mastery of German and his dedication to the art and craft of literary translation resulted in a body of work fully as significant—and influential—as his original writing. In the realm of poetic translation, for instance, Ōgai organized a group that produced *Omokage (Vestiges)* (1889), a landmark volume of verse, largely romantic, by such figures as Byron, Goethe, and Heine. His translations of fiction and drama cover a wide range of national literatures. Of particular significance is a translation of Hans Christian Andersen's romantic novel *Improvisatoren;* the translation is regarded by many as superior to the original work. There would develop a particular affinity for Goethe, who became something of a patron saint. Indeed, Ōgai's translation of *Faust* remains a standard. Ōgai's renderings of Ibsen and Hauptmann, among others, inspired a generation of Japanese modernists seeking to comprehend Western individualism and selfhood. In short, Mori Ōgai's crucial role as disseminator of new ideas and modes of expression—the naturalism of Zola, the idealism of Hartmann, and the revolutionary works of Nietzsche, Strindberg, Clausewitz, and Freud—places him at the very center of Japan's project of cultural modernization.

Literary careers in the Meiji period inevitably involved the *bundan*, with its network of coteries and competing literary journals. Writers were obliged to abide by the conventions and practices of literary journalism, and many became editors and critics. Ōgai was among the most prominent. As founder and editor of many journals of literature and the arts (and several medical journals as well), he established himself early on as a major voice on the literary scene, creating outlets for his own writing in addition to the work of his circle. Benefiting from his prolonged exposure to the entire range of Western criticism, Ōgai introduced a new sophistication to Japanese critical discourse. Indeed, he ranks among the pioneers of modern literary criticism in Japan, writing with a precision and intellectual rigor that set him far above his contemporaries.

Ōgai's Fiction

As an army medical officer, Ōgai saw service in Manchuria in both the Sino-Japanese (1894–95) and Russo-Japanese (1904–05) wars. In the interim, he spent three years posted in northern Kyūshū, at some distance from Tokyo.

A major turning point occurred in 1909. In response to an outpouring of writing in the new literary vernacular *(genbun itchi)*—much of it a genre of fictionalized confession produced by the naturalist school—Ōgai returned to creative fiction. In *Vita Sexualis*, he employs a style of confessional narrative whose ironic detachment and clinical objectivity, while clearly "autobiographical," serves rather to parody the tawdry, self-pitying work of his contemporaries. Ōgai was particularly disdainful of the vogue for accounts of sexual repression and domestic tedium. A literature of private disclosure and emotional frankness held little interest for him. Yet fiction exerted a certain appeal, and he recognized the genius of Natsume Soseki, whose probing psychological novels had gained widespread popularity.

This essential ambivalence toward *shōsetsu* resulted in several works of longer fiction "in the Soseki style"—most notably *Seinen (Youth)* (1910–11) and *Gan (The Wild Goose)* (1911–13). Each plays upon the popular theme of Tokyo's modern youth and its troubled path to maturity. *Youth* details the intellectual and emotional quest of a young university student, serves primarily as a vehicle for philosophical rumination. *The Wild Goose*, perhaps Ōgai's best-known work, tells of a young woman, Otama, forced by her poverty to become the mistress of an uncouth moneylender, Suezō. She becomes infatuated with Okada, a young medical student whom she observes from her lonely balcony. And Okada finds himself drawn to the woman he sees gazing down at him. The two eventually meet, but circumstances intervene to thwart the incipient romance. Okada will depart for Germany, leaving Otama resigned to her sad fate, unable to free herself from the gilded cage.

Ōgai's suspicion that fiction did not merit serious literary endeavor, a notion that was shared, incidentally, by other major writers of his generation—for instance, Futabatei Shimei (1864–1909) and Kōda Rohan (1867–1947)—has deep roots in the Buddhist and Confucian traditions of East Asia. As *shōsetsu* came to dominate the Japanese literary marketplace—a case, perhaps, of bad currency driving out good—the author sought more congenial avenues for expressing his commitment to writing as a serious intellectual vocation.

Essays, Events, Lives

While seeking to establish himself as a writer of longer fiction (and serving, at the same time, as Japan's Surgeon-General), Mori Ōgai also wrote plays, composed poetry, and produced a number of shorter pieces, some fanciful, some serious. Some are in the form of "essay-stories" in which he crafts a distinctive style of personal narrative, told in the voice of a slightly world-weary intellectual trying to fathom his own past and the vicissitudes of modern society. Thus freed from the constraints of complex plot and character development, the author was able to foreground his intellectual concerns. What resulted was a unique mix of observation, lamentation, Kulturkritik, and learned ephemera reflecting simultaneously the need to craft a personal voice and an aversion to overt self-disclosure. The narrator of *Mōsō*, an oft-cited autobiographical essay, expresses the spiritual malaise that marks a number of these works.

Although I study medicine . . . and make rigorous scholarship my life's work, somehow I've come to feel spiritually starved. I find myself thinking about life. I wonder if what I do can in any way be said to constitute the substance of life. From the time of my birth until this day, what is it that I have been doing? Throughout, as though whipped and goaded by who knows what, I have slaved away at my studies, thinking that this will make me useful, that this will perfect me. And who is to say that some sort of goal might not be thus attainable? Yet it seems to me that what I do is no more than what an actor does who comes onstage and performs his role.

(MARCUS, 1993, 105–6)

Ōgai was by no means alone among Japanese writers in exploring the alienation of the modern intellectual, but his work rises above the narrow confessionalism that prevailed in the *bundan.* Like Soseki, he sought meaning in a world increasingly devoid of enduring values. Much of his literature became imbued with an attitude of detachment and resignation *(teinen),* whose Buddhist undertones are evident.

The ever-quickening pace of Japan's modernization in the second decade of the twentieth century constitutes the backdrop for some of the great literary works of the period. A pivotal event was the death of the Meiji Emperor (July, 1912) and the subsequent ritual suicide of Nogi Maresuke, one of Japan's greatest military leaders. The Nogi suicide, which conjured up the specter of Japan's feudal past, prompted Ōgai to develop a new vehicle for his examination of Japanese values, namely, historical fiction *(rekishi shōsetu).*

Long fascinated by the legend and lore of the Tokugawa period and its ruling samurai class, the author produced a series of stories, based on meticulous historical research, that explore the obsessive loyalty and dedication of the samurai. In beautifully crafted works such as *Abe ichizoku (The Abe Clan)* and *Sakai jiken (Incident at Sakai),* which blend stark factual documentary and bone-chilling drama, Ōgai calls upon his readers to ponder the meaning of ritual sucide *(seppuku)* and the authoritarian structures that promoted it as an ultimate value. Overall, this brilliant body of work elevated the stature of historical fiction in Japan while enhancing the author's reputation as culure critic.

Mori Ōgai had a particular affinity for historical research—the result, perhaps, of his rigorous scientific training. In the course of this research, which he pursued with analytical precision, he happened upon accounts of many individuals, both obscure and renowned. Several of the unknowns— a circle of Confucianist physicians *(jui)* and literati of the late Tokugawwa—aroused his curiosity. They appeared to be kindred spirits, but the historical record is woefully thin. Much concerned about the deteriorating cultural climate, Ōgai set himself to the task of researching the lives of virtuous

forebearers, whom he knew, paradoxically, by only the faintest of documentary traces. What ensued was an extraordinary undertaking that would consume the final years of the author's life.

Between 1916 and 1921, Ōgai engaged in an ongoing project of biographical research that resulted in the serialized publication of three massive works, whose titles bear the names of their central subjects: *Shibue Chūsai, Izawa Ranken,* and *Hōjō Katei.* Collectively referred to by their genre designation *shiden* (historical biography), these works constitute a vast documentary history of nineteenth-century Japan. But they also detail the course of the biographical quest itself and incorporate a host of revealing anecdotes recalled by surviving kin whom the author had managed to locate.

The centerpiece of the trilogy, *Shibue Chūsai,* has been cited as a crowning achievement of modern Japanese literature. Having established a spiritual kinship with his subject, Ōgai positions himself as inheritor of the literati spirit of civility and quiet virtue that the man came to represent for him.

> Chūsai walked the same path that I have walked. But his legs were that much sturdier, and his vigorous pace far outstripped my own. He has come to earn my respect and admiration. . . . If the two of us had been contemporaries, no doubt our paths would have crossed in some mud-splattered alleyway. Such are the bonds of intimacy that join us. Such is the depth of affection I feel for this man.
>
> (MARCUS, 1993, 149)

Mori Ōgai would pursue his biographical project with unflagging devotion until his death. The latter works of the trilogy, however, would largely present undigested documentary fragments with a minimum of interpretation. It was enough, in the final analysis, to preserve a faithful record of exemplary lives. The indifference to popular trends and tastes understandably alienated the mass readership, but a core of devotees—including many of

Japan's finest writers—continued to sing his praise.

Some critics conclude that Mori Ōgai had in old age become a curmudgeon, an unrepentent antiquarian in flight from a world he found distasteful. Others regard him as Japan's greatest modern writer, unmatched in the sheer weight of his intellectual and literary sophistication. Quite telling is the fact that Ōgai has been spoken of both as the last of the traditional literati *(bunjin)* amd the first of a new breed of modernists—testament to the extraordinary age that produced him.

MARVIN MARCUS

Further Reading

Translations

Dilworth, David, and J. Thomas Rimer, eds. *The Historical Literature of Mori Ōgai.* 2 vols. Honolulu: University of Hawaii Press, 1977. A collection of Ōgai's historical and biographical writings in English translation. The prefatory essays in each volume are of particular interest.

Rimer, J. Thomas, ed. *Mori Ōgai: Youth and Other Stories.* Honolulu: University of Hawaii Press, 1994. A wide-ranging collection of translated works, featuring the full-length novel *Seinen.* Includes as well the German trilogy, a number of the essay-stories, and one original play, *Kamen (Masks)* (1909).

Related Studies

Bowring, Richard. *Mori Ōgai and the Modernization of Japanese Culture.* Cambridge, MA: Cambridge University Press, 1979. An excellent intellectual and literary biography, and the most exhaustive English-language treatment of the author.

McClellan, Edwin. *Woman in the Crested Kimona.* New Haven, CT: Yale University Press, 1985. An elegant and moving retelling of the Chūsai biography, centering on the crucial role on Chūsai's wife, Io.

Marcus, Marvin. *Paragons of the Ordinary: The Biographical Literature of Mori Ōgai.* Honolulu: University of Hawaii Press, 1993. A literary study of Ōgai's biographical trilogy, focusing on *Shibue Chūsai.* Contains considerable material in English translation.

Rimer, J. Thomas. *Mori Ōgai.* Boston: Twayne Publishers, 1975. A brief but eminently readable and insightful literary biography.

THE NOVELS OF NATSUME SOSEKI

Author: Natsume Soseki (original name Natsume Kinnosuke)
Born: 1867, Edo (now Tokyo)
Died: 1916, Tokyo
Major Novels: *I Am a Cat* (1905–6), *Botchan* (1906), *Red Poppy* (1907), *Sanshiro* (1908), *And Then* (1909), *The Gate* (1910), *To the Spring Equinox and Beyond* (1912), *The Wayfarer* (1913), *Kokoro* (1914), *Grass on the Wayside* (1915), *Darkness and Light* (1916)

Major Themes

If you are determined enough to devote your life to literature, you cannot be satisfied with a simple aesthetic product.

The phenomenon that looks like love is merely the struggle of creatures eager to harm and conquer others. Become one with Heaven, liberated from the self.

Because of his deep understanding of his own culture and his penetrating insight into human psychology, Natsume Soseki can be said to be one of the most important novelists of the Meiji period, a period of tremendous change brought on by Japan's encounters with the West. His style and imagery were greatly influenced by classical Chinese and Japanese literature, while the influence of English models, particularly the novels of the late nineteenth century, can be seen the structure of his works and in certain themes. It was through him that realistic novels took root in Japan. His work is sometimes difficult, and always exigent; but he has remained one of most-read authors of the twentieth century. Besides his novels, Soseki also contributed a significant body of fine poetry in Chinese, haiku, essays, and other types of literary work as well as important additions to literary criticism.

The eighth, and last, child of a once well-to-do family, Soseki led a very insecure childhood, spending the early part of his life off and on with either a foster family or his own depending on the financial situation. His early education included an intensive study of classical Chinese; later, however, he began the study of English and entered the University of Tokyo with the intention of becoming a scholar of English literature. After teaching in the provinces, he was sent on a government scholarship to London where he came to know not only English literature but also that of the continent. This period

in Soseki's life was marked with serious bouts of depression. Upon returning to Japan in 1903, he replaced Lafcadio Hearn at Tokyo University and lectured on literary theory and literary criticism. His creative career began with the publication of two comic novels: *I Am a Cat* (*Wagahai wa neko de aru*) (1905–6) and *Botchan* (1906). After 1907, Soseki abandoned teaching to become literary editor of the daily paper, *Asahi Shimbun*, making a commitment to write a novel a year, which he managed to meet, but for a few gaps, until his death in 1916. During this time he produced works that deal with man's struggle to fight frustration and loneliness.

The Comic Works

Soseki's early period of creative writing is characterized by works of humor and satire. His first book, *I Am a Cat*, defied the traditional literary categorization of his times. Strictly speaking, it is not a novel but a series of episodes. When he started this work, Soseki had no definite idea about making it a full-length novel. However, the favorable reception of the first episode encouraged him to write more. For this reason each chapter is written as an independent story or essay. Though each individual story is whole in itself and often very insightful and entertaining, there are some weaknesses in the development of the plot of the work as a whole.

I Am a Cat reveals the life of scholars and teachers of Soseki's day, depicted with humorous, satirical touches. The narrative is told from the viewpoint of a professor's cat who takes in the conversations between its master and his friends. Readers find themselves reflecting on their own lives and those of their friends. Skillfully combining the attitude of criticizing society through satire that was characteristic of eighteenth- and nineteenth-century English literature with the spirit of laughter found in the Japanese vernacular comic story (*rakugo*) popular in his day, Soseki succeeded in producing an art of his own that greatly influenced satirical literature in Japan.

Whereas in *I Am a Cat* Soseki is critical of the intellectual class, in *Botchan*, which quickly followed in 1906, Soseki depicts the average Japanese as virtuous and very lovable. *Botchan*, a medium-length novel, is based on the author's experience teaching at a middle school on the island of Shikoku. The hero who goes there as an instructor of mathematics after graduating from the Physics School is a man of righteousness—straightforward, with no worldly sense of compromise. While most of the main characters in modern Japanese literature are meditative individuals, hard to please yet irresolute, the hero of *Botchan* is hasty in judgment and has a habit of risking his job in the cause of justice—a perpetual source of friction between him and those around him.

Maturation of the Novelist

Soseki's major literary interests shifted away from satire as he began to develop fiction for the *Asahi Shimbun*. His first installment novel, *Red Poppy* (*Gubijinso*) (1907), criticizes modern civilization through its portrayal of various types of youths and their relationships to their families, teachers, and peers. This interest in youth and relationships is continued in a series of novels, comprising *Sanshiro* (1908), *And Then* (*Sorekara*) (1909), and *The Gate* (*Mon*) (1910), that established Soseki as a mature and masterful novelist. Though not bound

together specifically as a trilogy, these works deal with related themes in a progressively serious manner, and portray a recognizable, if not identical, hero through the advancing stages of life.

In the first novel, the bitterness of lost love that the modern youth Sanshiro tastes is contrasted with the absurdity of the youthful experiences recalled by his mentor, Hirota. Using a stream-of-consciousness technique, Soseki examines with gentle irony the shifting psychological state of Sanshiro and unfolds the bewildering set of social relationships that an individual creates within the modern city. Nagai Daisuke, the main character of *And Then*, is a further development of Sanshiro, this time in the role of the lover. Daisuke, as opposed to Sanshiro, possesses Hirota's clear moral view of civilization. Nevertheless, Daisuke has an affair, and the experience threatens his intellectual integrity. Finally, the melancholy outcome of this moral dilemma at the end of the second novel is alleviated by the quiet love between the hero, Sosuke, and his wife in *The Gate*. In these works Soseki displays the full range of his literary art and his philosophical and psychological insight through his treatment of the ingenuous hero of *Sanshiro*, the free play of the intellect at the beginning of *And Then*, and the moral dilemma's resolution in the final novel.

Waxing Philosophical

In the summer of 1910, Soseki fell seriously ill with a gastric ulcer while staying at Shuzenji spa. This illness marked the beginning of the author's late period, where his earlier criticism of modern society softened somewhat, but his philosophical and psychological analyses further deepened. In such works as *To the Spring Equinox and Beyond* (*Higan-sugi made*) (1912), *The Wayfarer* (*Kojin*) (1913), and *Kokoro* (1914), Soseki sharpens his examination of the solitary, intense, and occasionally demented mind. In *To the Spring Equinox and Beyond*, he writes about the conflict between love and self. Through his character, Sunaga Ichizo, Soseki discloses his profound understanding of real human solitude in which the individual is fully

conscious of the self as cut off from others—
something the author had achieved while bedrid-
den from illness.

In *Kokoro*, one of Soseki's most famous novels,
Soseki returns to the theme of mentorship. Set
within the historical framework of the death of the
Meiji emperor in July 1912 and the subsequent
ritual suicide of General Maresuke Nogi and his
wife on the morning of the imperial funeral, the
novel is the story of Sensei, a middle-aged man,
and an admiring young boy. The plot consists of the
confession of Sensei's past and his subsequent
death. The motive of his suicide is given in great
detail, and constitutes the main part of this work.
Sensei vied with his best friend for a girl, won, and
married her. His friend committed suicide as a result. Throughout his otherwise happy marriage,
Sensei is constantly tortured by his past. At last he
takes his own life.

Kokoro clarifies Soseki's almost Spencerian, social evolutionist view of life in his later years that
wherever a person comes in contact with another,
he will, without exception, fight against and hurt
the other party. According to this view, once severed from traditional values, man becomes the
center of the world and can no longer love anyone
but himself. In an effort to resolve the ambivalence of living among others and yet feeling apart,
Soseki was forced to conclude that man's very
existence in this world is sinful, and that there are
just two alternatives: for man to assert himself
boldly to the extent of eventually falling into a
state of madness (the theme of his novel, *The
Wayfarer*) or for man to annihilate his existence
through suicide, as seen in *Kokoro*. If incapable of
enduring either of these solutions, man has no
choice but to endure his ugliness and isolation
until his natural end, condemned never to forget
his own wickedness.

Soseki's last novels, *Grass on the Wayside*
(*Michikusa*) (1915) and *Darkness and Light*
(*Meian*) (1916), represent a return to the world of
an outwardly uneventful, but inwardly dramatic,
domestic existence. One finds little intrigue in
these works, only ordinary people who act out life
in ordinary ways. *Grass on the Wayside* is an
autobiographical novel, his only "I" novel. It covers his birth, his youth in the house of his adoptive
parents and his own household, his studies, and
the constant antagonism between himself and his
wife. In *Darkness and Light*, the novel left unfinished at his death, the characters are depicted as
fighting with every mean at their disposal—force,
wisdom, charm, reason, money, and even flesh—
to live up to what they believe and to make life
conform to their wishes. The phenomenon that
looks like love is merely the struggle, as already
seen in *Kokoro*, of creatures eager to harm and
conquer others.

Views on Literature and the Individual

Soseki's first major contribution to literary criticism came in his *Theory of Literature* (*Bun-
gakuron*) (1907), which dealt mainly with the
search for a common denominator between Oriental and Occidental literature. Soseki worried about
the relationship between Europe and Japan. What
is to be laughed at, Soseki asserts, are Japanese who
prostrate themselves too easily before Western authority. Soseki was generally opposed to naturalism, which came into being around 1905 or 1906
when he started writing, and the "I" novel with its
basis in the author's personal experiences. While
naturalists sought the truth by writing honestly
about their experiences, Soseki, regarding the
novel as a kind of art, insisted on the importance of
the form and style of writing. His concept of literary form was primarily moral: A novel has a moral
message to convey through its form.

Soseki believed that the conscious mind, when it
is ethically disciplined, will finally impose its will
on the chaos of life. Accordingly, he believed that
the chief function of literature is its ability to disperse fear of the chaotic and unknown. The essential problem for Soseki is the difficulty of the
individual to adapt to changes in society. His works
are pervaded with leitmotifs that reflect Confucian
values (especially in *Kokoro*). There is an underlying fear in many of Soseki's later works that people,
freed from these traditional values, will become
egocentric, untrustworthy, cold, and even cruel.

Soseki's identification of his own severe physical and spiritual problems reflects the perplexity that many in Japan faced in the early period of Westernization: Who am I? and What is my place in the world?

The function of literature, particularly of fiction, then, is to awaken the reader to questions of existence and identity, to enlighten, and perhaps to cure the self or to find some sense of accommodation with the realities of the modern world.

KENNETH G. KOZIOL

Further Reading

Translations

McClellan, Edwin, trans. *Kokoro, A Novel*. Chicago: H. Regnery, 1957.

———. *Grass on the Wayside, A Novel*. Chicago: University of Chicago Press, 1969.

Mathy, Francis, trans. *Mon: The Gate*. London: Peter Owen, 1972.

Moorefield, Norma, trans. *And Then*. Baton Rouge, LA: Louisiana State University Press, 1978.

Ochiai, Kingo, and Stanford Goldstein, trans. *To the Spring Equinox and Beyond*. Rutland, VT: Charles E. Tuttle, 1985.

Rubin, Jay, trans. *Sanshiro: A Novel*. Seattle: University of Washington Press, 1977.

Sasaki, Umeji, trans. *Botchan*. Rutland, VT: Charles E. Tuttle, 1967.

Turney, Alan, trans. *The Three-Cornered World*. London: Peter Owen, 1965.

Viglielmo, V. H., trans. *Light and Darkness: An Unfinished Novel*. London: Peter Owen, 1971.

Yu Beongcheon, trans. *The Wayfarer*. Detroit: Wayne State University, 1967.

Related Studies

Doi, Takeo. *The Psychological World of Natsume Soseki*. Cambridge, MA: Harvard University Press, 1976. A study of the philosophy and psychology of Soseki's fictional works.

Iijima, Takehisa, and James M. Valdaman, Jr., eds. *The World of Natsume Soseki*. Tokyo: Kinsedo, 1987. Examines the literature and philosophy of Natsume Soseki.

McClellan, Edwin. *Two Japanese Novelists: Soseki and Toson*. Chicago: University of Chicago Press, 1969. Compares the novels of Natsume Soseki with those of Shimazaki Toson.

Turney, Alan. *Soseki's Development as a Novelist until 1907*. Tokyo: Toyo Bunko, 1985. Explores Soseki's early period as a writer of fiction.

Yu, Beongcheon. *Natsume Soseki*. New York: Twayne Publishers, 1969. Surveys the literary works of Natsume Soseki.

THE PROSE AND POETRY OF YOSANO AKIKO

Author: Yosano Akiko
Born: 1878, Sakai, Japan
Died: 1942, Tokyo, Japan
Major Works: **Poetry**: *Midaregami (Tangled Hair)* (1901); "My Brother, You Must Not Die" (1904); "*Sozorogoto*" ("Verses in Idle Moments") (1908)

Major Themes

Literature is the overflow of "true feelings" that well up within any individual who is open to the events of the world.

A work of art is a product of individual creativity.

A poem is both verbal music and verbal sculpture and must contain nothing but pure emotion.

Human beings should cultivate their personal strengths and apply themselves in any areas in which they are interested, without regard for social stigma or convention.

Women are not inferior to men, and they should enjoy equal access to education, to work, and to activity in the public arena.

A married couple should each be self-sufficient and should each contribute to the family's income, child-care, and other needs without artificial gender distinctions; marriage should be based on cooperation and respect.

Yosano Akiko achieved immediate fame with the publication of her first volume of poetry in the traditional Japanese *waka*, or *tanka* (short poem), form in 1901. In this stunning volume, entitled *Midaregami (Tangled Hair)* Akiko expresses sensuous pleasure in her own youthful body and in the beauties of love and the world, choosing to convey her feelings not in the newly introduced, Western-influenced free verse form, but in the centuries-old and stultifying *tanka*. In doing so, she demonstrates the possibilities for revitalizing this traditional poetic form in the twentieth century.

The cover of *Midaregami* depicts a woman's face in profile, gazing upward from a heart filled with swirling locks of red hair. The heart, from which the title falls in drops of blood, is pierced by an arrow whose tip has been transformed into three violets. This romantic fantasy foretells the bold expressions of passion and engagement with the world contained in the 399 poems within the covers. Akiko's early romantic poems are tightly wrought, sometimes so grammatically tangled or elliptical that their meaning can only be intuited; but they are always stimulating:

shion saku / the asters have
waga kokoro yori / bloomed in hues pale as
noboritaru / the color of
kemuri no gotoki / the smoke that rises
usuiro o shite / from my burning heart
mune no shimizu / the crystal waters
afurete tsui ni / overflowing my breast
nigorikeri / have become sullied
kimi mo tsumi no ko / now you are a child
ware mo tsumi no ko / of sin
I too am a child of sin

waga idaku / in the depths
kokoro o kimi wa / of the heart I hide
soko ni min / you will see
haru no yuube no / fragments of the golden
kigumo no chigire / clouds
of an evening in spring

tokigami ni / heavy hair unbound
muro mutsumaji no / the fragrance of the lily
yuri no kaori / in the room of love
kie o ayabumu / in danger of disappearing
yo no toki iro yo / the pale pink color of night

356

The woman's point of view was sorely lacking in the turn-of-the-century literary world in Japan, although classical Japanese literature of the Heian period (eighth to eleventh centuries) had been dominated by women and what has been termed "feminine sensibility." Critics, both literary and political, focused on Akiko's unconventional behavior: she had run away that same year from a sheltered upbringing as the daughter of a middle-class shopkeeper to join her lover, Yosano Tekkan, a well-known poet and editor of the romantic arts journal *Myōjo (Morning Star)*. Although the couple married a few months later and settled into a fairly quiet, stable family life—producing 13 children, of whom 11 lived—Akiko retained her reputation as a rebel and independent thinker, publishing frank expressions of her emotional life in her volumes of poetry, and of her opinions on social, political, educational, and literary issues in her essays.

In 1904, during the peak of the chauvinistic fervor occasioned by the Russo-Japanese War, she published a free verse poem, "My Brother, You Must Not Die." This cry from the heart included such lines as these:

> *Whether the fortress at Port Arthur falls*
> * or not—what does it matter?*
> *Should it concern you? War is not*
> * the tradition of a merchant family.*
>
> *My brother, you must not die.*
> *Let the Emperor himself go*
> * off to war*
> *"Die like beasts,*
> * leaving pools of human blood.*
> *In death is your glory."*
> *If that majestic heart is truly wise,*
> *He cannot have such thoughts.*

Publication led to the denouncement of Akiko as a traitor, and her pacifist outpouring probably later cost her the prize offered by the prestigious Society of Literary Artists, which was founded by the Ministry of Education in 1912.

During the subsequent years, through the 20s and 30s, as various small groups of Japanese women united to work for suffrage or other goals

coalesced and dissolved under pressure from the increasingly repressive and militaristic government, Akiko's solid literary reputation and thoughtful literary and social criticism gave her the role of elder stateswoman. As changes in twentieth-century Japan eroded the feudal bonds in Japanese society, Akiko's poetry came to seem prophetic of a new era, and she became the "queen" of the literary world. The editors of a new women's journal *Seitō* (Bluestocking) sought a contribution from Akiko for their first issue in 1908, and Akiko provided a long series of poems, "Verses in Idle Moments" (*Sozorogoto*), including "The Day the Mountains Move":

> *The day the mountains move is coming.*
> *Though I tell them, people do not believe that*
> *The mountains have but slumbered a while.*
> *Long ago, they moved. They burned with raging*
> * flames.*
> *It is all right not to believe this,*
> *If only—oh, you people—you believe:*
> *The sleeping women are about to waken and move.*

The poem, with its metaphor of the rumbling volcano, long dormant in the earth, for the awakening power of women, has become a hallmark of international feminism.

In addition to the astonishing body of superior poetry she produced, Akiko was a superb essayist. Her contributions to the debate over "woman's role" continue to be influential. In 1913, two of Japan's most important journals, *Taiyō* and *Chūō kōron* sponsored a series of debates and published special issues on "women's problems." Other women argued for the importance of women in "improving and preserving" the race. They felt that the price women paid for this vital role was relinquishing the outside world in favor of "woman's mission," motherhood, and they sought special protection and economic support from the state for mothers and children.

Akiko, herself the mother (and very nearly sole support) of a large family, not only thought this demand degrading, but saw state support for women and children as signifying less, not more, dependence for both women and their children. She argued that what women needed was education and equality of opportunity, training for self-sufficiency and the opportunity to achieve it. In 1921, Akiko joined educator Nishimura Isaku in founding a school, the Bunka Gakuin (Cultural Academy) to provide a model education for women, and she served as a superintendant and instructor there until the year before her death. In her literature classes, Akiko introduced children to great literature of the past and the best literature by contemporary writers, inviting such authors as Kawabata Yasunari, who later received the Nobel Prize, to lecture on their work. She condemned the standard textbooks and argued for a "great books" approach, insisting that great art be presented in the classroom and that children be challenged and stimulated to recognize the finest products of human endeavor.

In her poetry, Akiko sought most of all to capture "actual feelings" *(jikkan)*, whether emotions inspired by the real world or "visions" (her term for dreams or fantasies). In her essays on writing poetry, she describes the process by which these feelings gradually increased in intensity until they reached "combustion" and resulted in a poem. She wrote that, just as it takes time for water to come to a boil, so does it take time for "actual feelings" to reach "combustion." The process was comparable to pregnancy and childbirth for her: a poem that is the product of imperfect combustion is like a premature baby delivered by Ceasarean section.

Akiko's insistence on individuality ("A work of art is an image of the self. It needs: first, the self; second, the self; third, the self; . . . absolutely, the self.") is what makes her the harbinger of a new, modern way of thinking in Japan; and it is a quality that inspired a generation of poets who looked to her for guidance. Her voice is the voice of an individual expressing her candid emotions in language of considerable beauty, as in this moving free verse poem about her family:

AN INSTANT

As I stroke my small daughter's hair,
memories of home float through my mind.
My mother, my dead sister, my aunt,

this and that, incoherent ramblings—
and for an instant golden raindrops fall on me.

LAUREL RASPLICA RODD

Further Reading

Translations

Translations in this article are by Laurel Rasplica Rodd.

Cranston, Edwin A. "Carmine-Purple: A Translation of 'Enji-Murasaki,' the First Ninety-Eight Poems of Yosano Akiko's *Midaregami*," in *Yosano Akiko*, special issue of the *Journal of the Association of Teachers of Japanese* 25:1 (April, 1991).

Goldstein, Sanford and Seishi Shinoda. *Tangled Hair*. Lafayette, IN: Purdue University Studies, 1971; Rutland, VT: Charles E. Tuttle, 1987. Excellent translation of many of the poems from *Midaregami*, with a short introduction to Yosano Akiko's life and poetry.

O'Brien, James. "A Few Strands of Tangled Hair," in *Yosano Akiko*, special issue of the *Journal of the Association of Teachers of Japanese* 25:1 (April, 1991).

Related Studies

Beichman, Janine. "Akiko Goes to Paris: The European Poems," in *Yosano Akiko*, special issue of the *Journal of the Association of Teachers of Japanese* 25:1 (April, 1991).

———. "Yosano Akiko: The Early Years," in *Japan Quarterly* 37:1 (1990), 37–54.

———. "Yosano Akiko: Return to the Female." *Japan Quarterly* 37:2 (1990), 104–28.

———. "Yosano Akiko, Poet of Modern Japan." *The Japan Times*, April 5, 1990 through March 21, 1991.

Cranston, Edwin. "Young Akiko: The Literary Debut of Yosano Akiko (1878–1942)," in *Literature East and West* 28:1 (1974), 19–43.

Larson, Phyllis Hyland. "Yosano Akiko and the Re-creation of the Female Self: An Autogynography," in *Yosano Akiko*, special issue of the *Journal of the Association of Teachers of Japanese* 25:1 (April, 1991).

Rabson, Steve. "Yosano Akiko on War: To Give One's Life or Not—A Question of Which War" in *Yosano Akiko*. Special issue of the *Journal of the Association of Teachers of Japanese* 25:1 (April, 1991).

Rodd, Laurel Rasplica. " 'On Poetry' by Yosano Akiko, with a Selection of Her Poems" in *New Leaves*. Aileen Gatten and Anthony Hood Chambers, eds. Ann Arbor, MI: Center for Japanese Studies, 1993.

———. "Yosano Akiko and the Taishō Debate over the 'New Woman' " in *Recreating Japanese Women*. Gail Lee Bernstein, ed. Berke-ley, CA: University of California Press, 1991.

———. "Yosano Akiko and the Bunkagakuin: 'Educating Free Individuals' " in *Yosano Akiko*. Special issue of the *Journal of the Association of Teachers of Japanese* 25:1 (April, 1991).

———, ed. *Yosano Akiko*. Special issue of the *Journal of the Association of Teachers of Japanese* 25:1 (April, 1991).

Rowley, G. G. "Making a Living from *Genji*: Yosano Akiko and Her Work on *The Tale of Genji* in *Yosano Akiko*. Special issue of the *Journal of the Association of Teachers of Japanese* 25:1 (April, 1991).

Ueda Makoto. "Yosano Akiko." *Modern Japanese Poets and the Nature of Literature*. Berkeley, CA: Stanford University Press, 1983, 53–94.

THE NOVELS OF NAGAI KAFŪ

Author: Nagai Kafū
Born: 1879, Tokyo, Japan
Died: 1959, Chiba, Japan
Major Works: *The River Sumida (Sumidagawa)* (1909), *Geisha in Rivalry (Udekurabe)* (1916–17), *A Strange Tale from East of the River (Bokutō kidan)* (1937), *A Daily Account of the Calamity (Risai nichiroku)* (1946–48)

Major Themes

Intellect and creativity require freedom of thought and expression
Genii loci are an expression of the enduring force of culture.
Personal convictions are an individual's greatest responsibility.
Nationalism is a distortion of culture that denies human diversity.

The novelist Nagai Kafū was also a poet in Chinese and Japanese, translator and professor of French literature, shamisen player, and amateur painter. Though he despised the literary cliques of the day, he called Mori Ōgai (1862–1922) his mentor, and Tanizaki Jun'ichirō (1886–1965) was nominally Kafū's disciple. Literary history places Kafū in the "decadent" anti-naturalist school; but his scandalous eccentricity and unyielding individualism were part of an earnest attack on authoritarianism and superficiality. His oeuvre demonstrates a steadfast devotion to personal ideals of civil liberty and authentic beauty, no small feat considering that his career—which began in the semi-bourgeois, authoritarian Meiji period (1868–1911)—witnessed the rise of militaristic nationalism, the catastrophic defeat of Japanese fascism, and the dawn of the "economic miracle." Initially, his fiction criticized this course of events; but because of stricter censorship he could do little more than record its devastating impact on traditional culture. The largest achievement of his novels is that, collectively, they form an antihistory of modernization that spans the wide gulf separating post–World War II Japan from the slower world of the Edo period (1603–1867).

Kafū's earliest fiction, which was inspired by the novels of Émile Zola (1840–1902), found its strongest critic in Kafū's father, a middle-ranking bureaucrat, who sent him abroad in 1903 to learn a new vocation. Four years spent mostly working for Japanese firms at several locations in the United States, followed by one year in France, gave him a real appreciation for the ideals of Western civilization and a mature critical perspective on his own society. Two volumes of anecdotes about his experiences abroad, in which he loosely compares the liberty of Western society with "despotic" Japan, propelled him to literary stardom. In the productive decade following his 1908 return, he was among Japan's most popular and respected writers.

Having returned to Meiji Japan, Kafū found nothing praiseworthy. He thus submerged himself in studying artists and writers who had been Edo's arbiters of culture and attitude, hoping to emulate them. This is obvious in the early masterpieces *The River Sumida* and *Geisha in Rivalry*, sly updates of the popular fiction of late Edo. The ornate, lyric Edo-like language is piquantly punctuated with sarcasm about garish, faddish things, and the sheer force of the fluid prose, which nimbly jumps from extolling the best to ridiculing the worst in either East or West, carries the message that Japan's modernization is a catastrophic marriage of the worst of both worlds. His novels therefore have a skeptical, subversive dimension and should be read for their implicit social criticism as well as for their intrinsic literary value.

With greater popularity came closer government scrutiny. Three of Kafū's books were censored between 1909 and 1917, first for caustic comments about contemporary society, but later for frank depictions of amorous relations. Censorship began to play a vary large role in what Kafū did or did not write. He clearly saw that Japanese culture was being undermined in the name of progress and that this devolution meant stricter controls of civil liberties, education, and the press. Kafū faced an artistic dilemma because restrictions prevented him from freely publishing social criticism, and he could not bring himself to write uncritical works.

Kafū was dismayed that he succeeded as a popular writer while failing as a social critic. Sarcastically upholding "backwards" Edo over "enlightened" Meiji was a ruse much too sophisticated for most of his readers. Between 1916 and 1920 a number of events attest to a creative and personal crisis. In 1916 he took the unusual measure of resigning from a prestigious professorship, and two years later he all but severed relations with his family after two short-lived, failed marriages that led him to vow to live alone. He had no children. Finally, in a 1919 essay, he announced that he was retiring from the literary world because he could not write works with a social conscience while confronted with both an indifferent public and an unpermissive government.

In an isolated section of Tokyo, in 1920 Kafū built his austere-looking *Henkikan,* (literally, "Eccentricity Manor"), a legendary hermitage in which he passed 25 years of self-imposed internal exile. Casting himself as an aloof eccentric, he concentrated on his diary and rarely broke his vow of silence. One exception is the brilliant *A Strange Tale from East of the River*, a return to the concerns of *The River Sumida* and *Geisha in Rivalry*—the need for creative freedom, and the cultural invalidity of Japan's modernization—that mellows the earlier, harsh appraisal of Meiji Japan with nostalgia. Evidently, the "bad old days" were preferable to the brave new world of 1930's fascism. *A Strange Tale* pits an enduring, instinctive humanism against the alarming militaristic nationalism responsible for the failed coup d'état of 1936. In an age in which secret police detained, tortured, and even killed dissenters, *A Strange Tale* was a coura-

geous appeal on behalf of an older world capable of tolerance and diversity.

Unable to publish during the war, Kafū produced a profusion of works after the defeat, including *A Daily Account of the Calamity*, the wartime section of the diary he had kept since 1917. It relates his experience of the war, including being burnt out in three air raids, and it includes his meticulous observations of the cultural ramifications of fascism as it distorted tradition and denied human diversity. His personal convictions are unequivocally stated, as are ideas that could only be implied or suggested in the necessarily vague prewar fiction. *A Daily Account of the Calamity* gains credibility and poignancy by being an artistic (if not private) mea culpa, Kafū's acceptance of responsibility for writing novels that failed to offer significant resistance to the tide of history.

As one of the few surviving writers who had had both the foresight and the means to avoid cooperating with the war effort, Kafū became a celebrity in the postwar period; and both old and new works sold well. Though his postwar fiction is mostly unmemorable, he received the Imperial Cultural Decoration in 1952, in part for his "elevated form of social criticism." Yet with nearly every trace of Edo wiped out during the war, he was a writer and a man who had outlived the world his literature and lifestyle hoped to revive. In 1959, he died alone at his home in Ichikawa, Chiba, not far from the plebian section of Tokyo immortalized in his books.

Kafū's singular place in Japanese letters remains controversial. As the last writer to emulate Edo's arbiters of culture and attitude, his defiance of the status quo in order to adhere to personal beliefs anticipates postwar writers such as Ōe Kenzaburō. Japanese society still shuns dissent; and his critical, noncomformist stance is often derided and belittled. Kafū, however, continues to attract readers who, dissatisfied with society's contradictions, seek a deeper sense of self. This alone is sufficient proof that his skepticism is genuine and that his literary art is exceptional and enduring.

The River Sumida

The River Sumida is a bittersweet portrait of the fading stage of Edo, set against a backdrop of "modern" Meiji. Kafū skillfully evokes the ambience of the plebian Shitamachi ("low town") district of Tokyo and its Sumida River, the cultural heart of Edo, leaving the characters and plot as mere sketches. Meant to be savored, this elegy to a beautiful world in decay gains power by leaving the obvious unstated: The decay is as unstoppable as a factory's despoiling, by its release of chemical wastes, a cool summer stream that is otherwise the very picture of an Edo woodblock print. Such sensuous evocation invests genii loci with a haunting gravity that carries the weight of an admittedly thin story. This implied social criticism appeals more to instinct than to intellect.

The River Sumida sets the parameters for most of Kafū's subsequent novels, which also employ ornate, Edo-like language, use the setting of Shitamachi and its demimonde of pleasure quarters and kabuki theatres, and are informed by the wry observations of an aloof Kafū alter-ego. Tempo is created by the interplay of lyrical and descriptive passages, melancholy evocations of the past that express with maudlin sincerity and deadpan sarcasm a near-stoic resignation to change. Such constitute Kafū's distinct voice.

The novel is more tightly constructed than Kafū's later novels, its story neatly framed within two visits of a Kafū alter-ego, the poet Ragetsu, and his widowed sister, O-Tomi, a shamisen teacher. The protagonist, O-Tomi's teenage son, Chōkichi, is caught between his mother's "modern" bourgeois expectations and his attraction to the now-dated profession of kabuki actor. Ten short chapters, many of which could be scenes of a kabuki play or prose versions of woodblock prints, serve to reveal Chōkichi frozen in time, incapable of embracing the future or escaping into the past. Kafū uses evocation to equate Chōkichi's dilemma to a crisis in Japanese culture as the Meiji period reaches its pinnacle: In a nation rushing to industrialize and bureaucratize, traditional culture loses its ability to render life meaningful.

Geisha in Rivalry

Geisha in Rivalry, Kafū's most popular and intricate novel, throws a cynical light on the struggle between tradition and change, the theme of *The River Sumida*, by showing Edo virtues losing ground to vulgar, superficial mores. Edo literature lends *Geisha in Rivalry* its main characters—the protagonist, the geisha Komayo, and her paramour, the kabuki actor Segawa Isshi—and a crew of stock characters, including the uncompromising old brothel keeper Kitani Chōjirō and his faithful wife, Jukichi; the ruthless, geisha-keeping businessman, Yoshioka; and the cunning hack writer, Yamai Kaname. Yet despite this strong Edo presence, the outcome is thoroughly, repugnantly "modern."

Though Kafū's diatribe against change is quieter than in *The River Sumida*, the very subject matter mocked the government's efforts to distance itself from the pleasure quarters it licensed after they had become an international embarrassment. The malicious gossip about Diet members visiting the quarters was a provocation, and sales of the magazine serializing *Geisha in Rivalry* were suspended, ostensibly because of their sexual explicitness. A 1918 abridged version sold well until 1944, when the fascist government seized and destroyed the entire stock. The unabridged *Geisha in Rivalry* was not published until 1946.

Geisha in Rivalry borrows its plot from the "duty-versus-feeling" romances of Edo literature: Komayo must choose either duty to her patron, Yoshioka, or love for the dashing Isshi. Though phrased in the dramatic terms of classical literature, her predicament is reduced to a mere economic problem by a supporting cast that cannot transcend the faults that typify the nouveau riche of Japan's World War I boom years: insincerity, cunning, and ruthlessness. The charming, passionate Komayo is no match for these up-to-date characters, and *Geisha in Rivalry* is ultimately a cynical work. This pessimism is echoed by the Kafū alter-ego Kurayama Nanso, a successful novelist who grew disgusted with society and retired his pen. Where Ragetsu (of *The River Sumida*) expressed cautious optimism, Nanso reflects Kafū's deepening despair, cynically accusing the audience of reading *Geisha in Rivalry* for its ribaldry and insight into a geisha's thoughts, but not for its sarcasm and social commentary.

A Strange Tale from East of the River

Kafū's self-referential tour-de-force anticipates by a quarter century the postmodern movement in literature, employing subterfuge to circumvent the suffocating restrictions of militaristic Japan. *A Strange Tale from East of the River* is a symbolic, minimalist reworking of Kafū's earlier fiction, being set almost entirely in a cheap red-light district that the middle-aged Ōe Tadasu, a thinly disguised Kafū, frequents in order to gather material for a novel. Ōe is the main character, and the prostitute Yukiki the only other significant character. There is almost no plot to *A Strange Tale from East of the River*; it is a novel about Ōe's attempt to write a novel, tellingly entitled *Whereabouts Unknown*.

A Strange Tale from East of the River includes sections of Ōe's novel, which is quite Kafu-like: a middle-aged English teacher, Taneda, decides to leave her job and family for a new life in a shabby rented room with a young woman, Sumiko. Ōe hopes to model Sumiko after Yukiko, whose simple sincerity and genuine compassion remind him of the Meiji period. As Ōe becomes involved with Yukiko and her lodgings become his sanctuary, his fiction begins to mirror his life: Ōe's life becomes fiction, and writing becomes impossible. When *Whereabouts Unknown* evaporates into fictional air, *A Strange Tale from East of the River* comes to a paralyzing, heavy silence that conveys the agony of a story, too strange to tell, of the demise of an older, better world. Just as Taneda becomes Ōe, and Ōe becomes Kafū, *A Strange Tale from East of the River* and *Whereabouts Unknown* converge into one elusive book that triumphs in describing the overwhelming frustration incurred by the compromises of fiction and the impossibility of telling the truth.

The long Afterword to *A Strange Tale from East of the River* recounts the conversation of Kafū and an old friend. Though not directly related to Ōe's story, the Afterword contains subtle but incisive comments about Japanese militarism that voice a truth that Ōe's straightforward narrative failed to tell. Kafū likens the 1931 Manchurian Incident, a Japanese act of aggression and deception, to the territorial squabble of sparrows. Long an admirer of Chinese civilization, he hints that this conflict had grave implications for Japan. In another passage he even implies that the people had done nothing to remove evil forces close to the throne and that, once the military began to rule Japan (which it did in 1940), Japanese culture would be ruined. This prophecy was fulfilled within a decade, transforming *A Strange Tale from East of the River* into a relic of a world forever lost.

DAVID C. EARHART

Further Reading

Translations

Dunlop, Lane, trans. *During the Rains and Flowers in the Shade*. Stanford, CA: Stanford University Press, 1994. Fine translations of two later works that anticipate *A Strange Tale from East of the River*.

———. "The Fox" by Nagai Kafū. In *Autumn Winds and Other Stories*. Tokyo: Charles E. Tuttle, 1994. Superbly translated 1909 story that employs evocation to comment on society.

Meissner, Kyrt, and Ralph Friedrich, trans. *Geisha in Rivalry*. Tokyo: Charles E. Tuttle, 1963. Adequate translation of Kafū's most popular work.

Seidensticker, Edward, trans. *A Strange Tale from East of the River and Other Stories*. Tokyo: Charles E. Tuttle, 1972. Entire translations of two masterpieces, *The River Sumida* and *Quiet Rain*, a discursive work that discloses Kafū's ideas about the arts. *A Strange Tale from East of the River* is expertly translated, but lacks the Afterword. Also includes shorter pieces that give some idea of Kafū's versatility.

Related Studies

Earhart, David C. "Nagai Kafu's Wartime Diary: The Enormity of Nothing." In *Japan Quarterly*,

XLI, 4, October–December, 1994. Article devoted to the widely neglected *A Daily Account of the Calamity*. Many translated excerpts.

Keene, Donald. "Nagai Kafū." In *Dawn to the West*. New York: Henry Holt, 1987. Very informative chapter on Kafū's role in literary movements, though the analysis of the works suffers from a lack of socio-historical perspective. Discussion of early works is especially of interest.

Seidensticker, Edward. *Kafū the Scribbler.* Stanford, CA: Stanford University Press, 1965. Good biographical critique, weakest in its failure to account for the impact of censorship on Kafū's career.

THE FICTIONAL WORKS OF SHIGA NAOYA

Author: Shiga Naoya
Born: 1883, Ishinomaki, Miyagi Prefecture, Japan
Died: 1971, Tokyo, Japan
Major Works of Fiction: "The Razor" (1910), "My Mother's Death and My New Mother," *Otsu Junkichi* (1912) "Seibei and His Gourds" (1912), "An Incident," "Han's Crime" (1913), "At Kinosaki," *Reconciliation* (1917), *A Dark Night's Passing* (1937), "Gray Moon" (1945)

Major Themes

To become a self-sufficient individual, one must put parental authority in perspective.
Insincerity leads only to further misunderstanding.
To be close to death makes one more profoundly aware of life.
Nature is inherently good.
One's natural impulses should be trusted; emotion is superior to logic.
Tranquility is found in complete submission to nature.

Shiga Naoya's place in Japanese literature is an anomaly. He outlived most of his contemporaries; yet his literary production—a handful of short stories, several novellas, and only one novel—is meager by comparison. Moreover, with the exception of a few short stories and essays, his literary career all but ended in 1929. And yet Shiga Naoya has been acknowledged by critics and writers alike as the most influential writer of the early twentieth century. Indeed, he has been called "the God of the Japanese novel." Yet there are no literary prizes named in honor of this "God." And though he is considered the "heartland" of Japanese literature, a writer steeped in the Eastern tradition, few read his works today. Western readers are warned by critics Japanese and otherwise that Shiga is an acquired taste.

What is it then that makes Shiga so important? Most would suggest that it is his style and his keen, almost sage-like regard of the human drama. The Shiga style is deceptively simple and has been compared to an ink wash or a Japanese poem. Much is left unsaid. Yet what is provided allows the reader to intuit an often universal significance. Shiga's style has been described as unornamented, economical and concise, yet lyrically beautiful. Shiga was quite capable of crafting believable fictional characters, as is evidenced by several of his more imaginative short stories. But he was known for his relentless, almost obsessive portrayal of moments from his own life. Shiga had a distrust of conscious artifice in storytelling and felt his work was more "sincere" when it delineated his own thoughts, impressions, and experiences "just as they had occurred to him." Shiga's focus was so exclusively on himself that William Sibley has labeled the protagonists who appear in Shiga's stories, as disparate as they may be, as one single "Shiga hero." Shiga wrote deliberately of himself—not because he wished to be purged of some deep sin (as the more confessional writers of his generation did) but because he believed his life was worthy of sharing. "Mine what is in me" he proposed, and so life became writing, and writing, life.

Shiga Naoya was born in a small coastal town in Northern Japan. His parents were descended from high-ranking samurai. Shiga's father was an astute businessman who, over the course of his career, amassed a tidy fortune. Three years after Shiga's birth, the family, paternal grandparents included, moved to Tokyo. Shiga saw very little of his stern, autocratic father who was frequently away on business trips. He saw little as well, of his mother, as he was kept almost exclusively in his grandparents' quarters. An older child had died before Shiga's birth, and it seems the grandparents blamed the mother for the death. To punish her and to ensure the safety of their heir, they insisted on keeping Shiga with them. Shiga adored his grandfather, was spoiled by his grandmother, and seems to have harbored a nostalgia for his mother even while she was alive. She died in 1895 of pregnancy complications. Shiga was 13. Until then a single child, he had been excited by the possibility of a younger sibling, and was devastated by the loss of both his mother and the promised child. But Shiga's attachment to his mother had not been strong enough to prevent him from welcoming the woman whom his father would marry within the year.

These events are depicted in "My Mother's Death and My New Mother" (1912), which Shiga considered his finest work. Shiga tried to recapture the emotions of a 13-year-old boy by recording his memories, as he has said, just as he remembered them. The story is distinctly Shiga. With little background information on the characters concerned, or analysis of the events or the emotions elicited, Shiga provides a sensitive portrait of a young boy's sorrow. As would become Shiga's hallmark, the narrative is terse and unsentimental, and the diction simple. But with a deft sprinkling of detail, Shiga gives the reader insight into the heart of a boy who feels helpless and angry at his mother's untimely death, yet shyly excited by the arrival of her replacement.

Shiga's early story also reveals a distrust of the father, a theme that would continue through most of his works. Shiga's relationship with his father, although never warm, deteriorated precipitously in 1901 over Shiga's involvement in socialist issues. Before the dust had settled on their quarrel, Shiga again enraged his father in 1907 by proposing to marry one of the housemaids, an incident he would record five years later in his novella *Otsu Junkichi* (1912).

Shiga found solace briefly in Christianity, but soon found its insistence on sexual fidelity too confining. He turned next to writing, a choice of profession that did not please his pragmatic father. This discord between the two, and the father's disapproval of his son's occupation, is brilliantly depicted in "Seibei and His Gourds" (1912), one of Shiga's finest fictional pieces. In this simple story, narrated with delightful tongue-in-cheek humor, young Seibei is blissfully obsessed with collecting gourds. His total disregard of every thing proper so enrages his father that he smashes the boy's gourds to bits. No matter, Seibei soon turns to painting. But the wonderful irony comes when readers learn that gourds such as his fetch a handsome price among antique collectors. Seibei, unconcerned with profit, could see value in something his father completely misunderstood.

In 1906 Shiga entered Tokyo Imperial University, only to perform miserably. By 1908 he had begun his association with the *Shirakaba-ha*, or White Birch Society, whose members were sons of the elite, graduates of the Peers School, and uninterested in the morbid, self-loathing of the then-popular Naturalist School. These young men, with little about themselves to loath, advocated cultivation of the individual. Being "sincere" in one's expression and "true to self" were foremost. In 1908 Shiga wrote his first recognized piece, "One Morning." By 1910 he had left the university without graduating to focus on his writing. Between 1910 and 1912 he wrote what for Shiga would be prolifically. But his attention to fiction so displeased his father that Shiga was forced to leave his family home. He was 29. He moved to Onomichi on the Inland Sea and began work on a novel.

While visiting Tokyo in the summer of 1913, Shiga was struck by a streetcar. Ironically, on the very day of the accident he had just completed "The Incident," in which he depicts a little boy similarly injured. Shiga was hospitalized, and upon release went to Kinosaki Hot Springs to convalesce. His brush with death and his sojourn at Kinosaki marked a turning point in Shiga's life and writing. He became even more introverted and less willing to engage society around him. In December 1914, he married without his father's consent, and found it impossible to write for the next several years. In 1917, after the birth of a second daughter (a first, born in 1916 died) Shiga reconciled with his father and resumed writing with "At Kinosaki" and the novella *Reconciliation*, considered by many to be his best works.

After 1929, the year Shiga's father died, he hardly wrote at all. He managed to finish his novel, *A Dark Night's Passing*, in 1937 and continued to publish a sporadic essay or two until his death on October 21, 1971. But for the most part Shiga lived quietly and contentedly. Edward Folwer suggests that writing, having been a cathartic exercise for Shiga, became unnecessary once his pains and problems were resolved.

"At Kinosaki"

Closer to a "prose poem" or a lyrical essay than a story, "At Kinosaki" is considered by many to be Shiga's finest work. Having narrowly escaped death, the narrator journeys to Kinosaki to convalesce. There he witnesses three deaths among the animal realm: the natural death of a bee; the willful and malicious killing of a rat; and his own unintentional killing of a salamander. These observations bring the narrator closer to an understanding of death: its quietness, its potential relation to violence, and its arbitrariness. His own brush with death makes the narrator realize all the more his place alongside other creatures in the cycles of nature. He no longer fears death, but feels an almost warm familiarity with it, which in turn makes him all the more profoundly aware of life.

"At Kinosaki" offers no plot, no dramatic tension. Rather, it provides a dialogue with nature itself. No other human element figures in the work. There is only the narrator's voice and, as the account ends, even that fades quietly into the natural surroundings.

Reconciliation

"At Kinosaki" marked a new phase in Shiga's art. No longer was he concerned with confronting the discordant or the discomforting, as he had been in "Seibei and His Gourds" and other of his earlier works both fictional and personal. His works from 1917 onward reveal more of a conscious effort to strive for harmony in human relationships and a near dissolution of self in nature. This search for harmony is the basis for the novella *Reconciliation,* which charts a coming-to-terms between a father and son.

The narrative direction of *Reconciliation* is retrogressive, as the narrator goes back over his relationship with his father. Although the narrator illustrates the volatile nature of this relationship, nowhere does he explain or attempt to trace the cause of their discord. He is not interested in causes. He is interested in the effects the unhappy past has had on him.

In the course of recounting his struggles with his father, the narrator recalls the joys and sorrows of his adult life: the death of a child and the birth of another. Both events are presented as inevitable stages of the natural process, and, though they evoke diverse emotions, they are equally moving, even beautiful. *Reconciliation*, then, though ostensibly about the relationship between a father and son, is more a discourse on an understanding of and a submission to the forces of nature, much as "At Kinosaki" had been. The narrator, though he knows he needs to apologize to his father if he is to make amends, cannot force himself to utter words that he does not actually feel. To do so would be a betrayal of his true self and would disrupt the natural processes at work in the relationship. The narrator's attitude portrays an insistence on the "sanctity of feeling," a key element in Shiga's approach to life wherein insincerity only leads to further misunderstanding. Once the narrator of *Reconciliation* feels the moment is right, he and his father exchange words and tears, and their discord is dissolved.

The narrator's insistence on "living sincerely" greatly impressed readers of Shiga's generation. The familiar theme of generational quarrels and the "happy" conclusion Shiga provides has made this novella-length work a favorite of many. Moreover, the distinctive "Shiga style," beautifully lyrical yet unornamental, is represented here at its finest.

A Dark Night's Passing

Shiga's most ambitious writing project, the novel *A Dark Night's Passing*, continues the author's quest for a release from discord and a dissolution in the engulfing embrace of nature. Shiga began the novel is 1912. Initially entitled *Tokito Kensaku*, after its hero, the novel originated in Shiga's need to describe his volatile relationship with his father and his struggle to establish himself as a self-sufficient individual. But Shiga's feelings at the time were too rancorous to allow transference to paper; and Shiga abandoned the project. He considered the novel again after his reconciliation with his father in 1917 and began serializing sections sporadically between 1921 and 1928. But Shiga was not able to add a proper conclusion to the work until 1937, when he wrote the final five chapters.

A Dark Night's Passing, consisting of a Prologue and four parts, is a long work, and as the method of creation will attest, a rambling one with little to hold it together save the meditations of the hero. Tokito Kensaku is the disaffected son of a wealthy businessman. Much to the consternation of his father and elder brother, he spends his time in half-hearted dalliances. But Kensaku's malaise is rudely shattered when he learns that he is actually the child of his grandfather, a contemptible man who imposed himself on Kensaku's mother during his father's absence.

Kensaku moves to Kyoto to seek solace in the temples there, only to meet and marry Naoko. Life is not blissful. Moody, with nerves ever on edge, Naoko cannot submit to love. When Kensaku discovers that Naoko has been seduced (more likely raped) by an acquaintance, he feels that he is caught in a morass of illicit passion—the unfortunate incident that caused his own birth now replicated by his wife. Kensaku leaves home to spend time on Mt. Daisen. He finds solace in the wonders of nature, and just when his emotional wounds seem to have healed, he takes ill. As the book concludes, Naoko is with Kensaku. In the bosom of her love, in the bosom of nature, he drifts off to sleep, leaving readers uncertain whether he will ever awaken or not.

The two acts of "seduction" form the pivots upon which *A Dark Night's Passing* turns. But the novel is not about these moments. As in the earlier *Reconciliation*, the narrator makes no attempt to explore the causes or analyze the acts that haunt him so. What matters is not what happened to the women but how the acts affect the hero. The novel presents, therefore, the successive development in the hero's psyche and his search for harmony within himself. The characters who assist Kensaku in his quest matter hardly at all but are more or less markers on his road to discovery. And Kensaku himself, a composite of all of Shiga's heroes, is less a dramatic creation than a succession of mental states. It is fitting, then, that at the end of this novel, which also marked the end of Shiga's career as a writer, his alter ego, his heroic persona, dissolves into nature—left in the interstices of life and death.

REBECCA L. COPELAND

Further Reading

Translations

Dunlop, Lane, trans. *The Paper Door and Other Stories*. San Francisco: North Point Press, 1987. A collection of 17 stories, among them those considered Shiga's most representative.

McClellan, Edward, trans. *A Dark Night's Passing*. Tokyo: Kodansha International Ltd., 1976.

Related Studies

Fowler, Edward. *The Rhetoric of Confession: Shishosetsu in Early Twentieth-Century Japanese Fiction*. Berkeley, CA: University of California Press, 1988. "Shiga Naoya: The Hero as Sage" is a penetrating and stimulating chapter on Shiga as a writer of personal fiction (*shishosetsu*). Fowler's presentation of this genre in this and earlier chapters, helps to explain Shiga's place in Japanese literature.

Keene, Donald. *Dawn to the West: Japanese Literature in the Modern Era*. Vol 1: *Fiction*. New York: Holt, Rinehart and Winston, 1984. His discussion of Shiga Naoya in the chapter "The Shirakaba School" (458–470) is brief and pithy, giving a clear picture of the author's accomplishments and his place among White Birch Society writers.

Mathy, Francis. *Shiga Naoya*. New York: Twayne Publishers, 1974. Mathy provides a thorough and sympathetic biography of Shiga Naoya, though his detailed plot discussions have now been surpassed by translations.

Sibley, William F. *The Shiga Hero*. Chicago: The University of Chicago Press, 1979. This highly provocative study offers a psychoanalytic look at Shiga Naoya's work. Sibley provides readers a cohesive rendering of both Shiga's life and oeuvre. Translations of several short stories are included.

THE NOVELS OF TANIZAKI JUN'ICHIRO

Author: Tanizaki Jun'ichiro
Born: 1886, Nihonbashi District, Tokyo, Japan
Died: 1965, Osaka, Japan
Major Novels: *Naomi* (1925), *Some Prefer Nettles* (1929), *The Secret History of Lord Musashi* (1932), *The Makioka sisters* (1948), *The Key* (1956), *Diary of a Mad Old Man* (1962)

Major Themes

Pleasure, especially sexual pleasure, provides the basis for a successful, fulfilled life.
The basis for the experience of beauty is the pleasurable experience of the physical beauty of the human body.
Beauty is experienced most poignantly in the sadness associated with transience, loss, and attrition.
The artistic and literary accomplishments of the West, however significant, cannot provide deep and lasting fulfillment for one whose traditional culture is Japanese.
Traditional cultural values may provide a means by which people accommodate themselves to change.

The fiction of Tanizaki Jun'ichiro falls into two distinct periods. As a young man, Tanizaki was strongly influenced by the West, in particular by the decadence and aestheticism of Wilde and his contemporaries; and his early work explores the darker side of human nature, especially sexuality and its influence on human behavior. Tanizaki's writing during this period is often sensationalistic, lurid, and extravagant. He rejects the confessional naturalism of his contemporaries for the portrayal of a fantasy world of sado-masochism, transvestitism, and other tabooed subjects. Among the many influences of Western literature on Tanizaki and those who followed his literary example, the most important in his view was "the emancipation of love or, to take it one step further, the emancipation of sexual desire." (Gessel, 1993, pp. 97–99). That in his early work Tanizaki often took it several steps further accounts for his frequent bouts with the censors.

In his later work, dating from the mid-1920's to the 1960's, Tanizaki turned away from the West to focus on traditional Japan and to explore the effects of modernization and change on Japanese society and culture. All of his major work was produced in this period. While he continued to deal with controversial subject matter, he did so with indirection and control: the overt extravagance of his earlier work has been replaced by innuendo, suggestion, and ambiguity. Three key novels from his later years, *Naomi, Some Prefer Nettles*, and *The Makioka Sisters*, chronicle Tanizaki's rejection of the West and his critical exclamation of the effects of modernization on the Japanese life. At the end of his career, Tanizaki returned to erotic subjects in *The Key*, in which he employs parallel diaries to dramatize the attempt of a middle-aged professor to enhance his sex life with his wife by encouraging her to take up with one of his younger colleagues; and in *The Diary of a Mad Old Man*, in which he examines an elderly man's erotic obsession with his daughter-in-law.

Tanizaki Jun'ichiro was born into a merchant-class family descended from the old Edo bourgeoisie, the class that had dominated Japanese life during the late Tokugawa period. His father, a dismal failure in business, repeatedly depended on an older brother to rescue him and his family from financial disaster. His mother was a renowned beauty, to whom Tanizaki remained devoted until her death at 53. From childhood, Tanizaki idealized and worshipped women, being strongly influenced by his devotion to his mother and by western notions of femininity, especially maternal femininity as embodied in the Virgin Mary (see *Childhood Years*, 10). As he grew older and became aware of his sexual nature, Tanizaki's woman-worship would span the full range of the polarity expressed by the "Angel in the House" at one extreme, and the cruelly sadistic prostitute at the other. In his later period, after he had shed the influence of the West, the goddess Kannon replaced the Virgin Mary in Tanizaki's ideal of femininity (see *In Praise of Shadows*, 29–30).

Although he was accused of intellectual shallowness in later life, as a child Tanizaki was recognized as an outstanding student by his elementary school teachers. One of his teachers, Mr. Inaba, believed Tanizaki to be a genius and provided him with attention, encouragement, and opportunities to develop his intellectual talents. At the urging of Mr. Inaba, Tanizaki's family sacrificed to send the future writer to special classes before and after school to learn English and Chinese classics. After following Tanizaki's brilliant career in elementary school, Mr. Inaba convinced Tanizaki's father to allow his son to attend middle school. Of the influence of Mr. Inaba on his writing and his life, Tanizaki later wrote: " . . . there has probably been no teacher or mentor in my whole life who influenced me more than he" (*Childhood Years*, 38).

Another important influence on Tanizaki's development was the Kabuki theater, which he attended as a child, sometimes with his mother, at other times with his nursemaid. Frequent trips to the theater continued until he was 10, when his family could no longer afford the outings. Kabuki performances are often extravagantly colorful and poignantly melodramatic, making the grotesque and lurid seem movingly beautiful. The pleasure Tanizaki derived from attending the theater in the company of these women contributed to his notion that pleasure or joy is fundamental to successful living, a notion set forward in an essay he wrote in 1902 when he was 16, thus establishing the basis for his aesthetic of pleasure. The experience of pleasure took on new meaning for Tanizaki after he enrolled in middle school. For a period of five years, while he continued as a top student, he worked part-time as a *shosei*—a combination tutor and houseboy—in the family of a wealthy restaurateur. During this time, he become romantically

involved with one of the household maids, and in 1907, when someone intercepted a love letter he had written to her, both he and she were discharged.

In 1905, Tanizaki entered the "first higher school," a level of education more advanced than American high schools, enrolling in legal studies, while actively pursuing his interest in literature. During high school, he published stories in the student literary magazine. After graduation in 1908, he enrolled at the Tokyo Imperial University in the Department of Japanese Literature. At university he was a slacker, seldom showing up for classes, preferring instead to frequent the pleasure districts of Tokyo. He became so involved in pleasure-seeking that he ignored not only his responsibilities as a student, but his duties to his family as well.

Around 1909, he began to write for professional literary publication, and he published his first mature fiction in 1910, a story entitled the "Tattooer." "The Tattooer" introduces several characteristic thematic elements that would become increasingly familiar to his readers over the next 15 years. These elements include setting the story in the remote past, foot-fetishism, and sado-masochism under the domination of a cruel, yet beautiful, woman. Tanizaki's use of these motifs persisted throughout his career, figuring importantly in later novels such as *The Secret History of Lord Musashi* and *Diary of a Mad Old Man*.

Tanizaki left the university to pursue a writing career in 1911, and over the next four years, his work attracted considerable attention, more, perhaps, for its lurid sensationalism than for its literary interest. One of his stories caused the issue of the magazine in which it was published to be banned by the police. An important boost to his career occurred in 1914 when the distinguished critic Nagai Kajū praised Tanizaki's writing for its style, its urban settings and subjects, and for the depths of its sadomasochistic effects. Like his fin de siècle European counterparts in decadence, Tanizaki consciously subordinated life to art, pursuing a life of sensual pleasure in secret in order to make the most advantageous use of his experience in the service of art. His pursuit of pleasure led to his exploration in his fiction of the idea that beauty cannot exist apart from its physical manifestations, and that its basis is the beauty of the living human body. The emergence of this theme in his work contributed to his reputation as a hedonist and anti-intellectual.

In 1915, when he was 29, Tanizaki married Ishikawa Chiyo, a 19-year-old, the first of three women that Tanizaki would marry during his lifetime. Ten months later they had a daughter, for whom he felt more fear than love. He was afraid the child would somehow drain his vitality. Over the next few years, Tanizaki developed an interest in film; he made a pleasure trip to China; and he became increasingly infatuated with Western culture. In 1920, he moved to Yokohama Bluff, a Western enclave, where he began wearing European clothes and took up dancing in the European style. He never went to Europe, but was content to imitate Western ways as an exotic lifestyle superficially enjoyed in familiar (and safe) Japanese surroundings. One is reminded here of Shimamura in Kawabata's *Snow Country*, who had become an expert in Western-style dance without ever having seen—or wanting to see—a Western ballet performed.

The earthquake of September 1923 marked an important turning point in Tanizaki's life and career. His first reaction to the temblor was exhilaration. Now, he believed, the old Tokyo would be utterly destroyed and a new, gleaming, Western-style metropolis would rise phoenix-like from the physical and cultural rubble of old Japan. This prediction was not to be realized, however, as the damage was not as great as he had anticipated, and the people were not so easily turned from their traditional Japanese ways. While Tokyo did become more modern, ironically the effect on Tanizaki was to make him grow to dislike the West; and so he turned to his childhood past for artistic inspiration and spiritual fulfillment.

Naomi

In the mid 1920's, he began to visit the Kansai region (Kobe, Osaka, Kyoto, and Nara) for increasingly longer periods. In 1926, after the publication of *Chijin No Ai*, or *Naomi*, he moved permanently

from Yokohama to Kansai, and as he did so, he symbolically left the allurements of the West for the culture of old Japan. *Naomi* marks a literary turning point away from the West. *Naomi* is a portrait of a woman nurtured by her husband in the ways of the modern West. Kawai Toji, the protagonist, is a quiet, frugal, 28-year-old office worker from a well-to-do, middle-class family, who has been trained as an engineer in a technical college. After meeting the 15-year-old Naomi in a restaurant, where she works as a waitress, Toji convinces her to abandon her job and allow him to take charge of her education. Naomi assents with little reflection on the matter, and Toji, Pygmalion-like, undertakes to transform her from a rather insipid adolescent product of old Japanese culture and values into the modern girl of the 1920's.

As *Naomi* progressed through serial publication—first in a newspaper and then in a literary quarterly—Tanizaki's younger readers became fascinated by Naomi and what she came to embody; thus, rejection by women of traditional Japanese values and culture to embrace the ways of the West came to be known as "Naomi-ism." But when the novel reached completion, however, Tanizaki's disparagement of Toji as a fool becomes clear, as, by implication, does the writer's criticism of his own, now fading, fascination with the West.

Some Prefer Nettles

Tade Kuu Mushi, or *Some Prefer Nettles* (1926), is Tanizaki's most penetrating exploration of the psychological and spiritual conflicts arising out of the encroachment of Western values and ideas on Japanese society and culture in the post-Meiji period. By sheer force of national will, Japan had been wrenched over a 40-year period from a semi-feudal, agrarian, and commercial society into a modern, industrial state. The effects of modernization, coming as it did primarily from the West, had produced and continued to produce considerable dislocation in Japanese culture and society, causing many, like Kaname, the protagonist of *Some Prefer Nettles*, to abandon much of their own heritage for the glitter and apparent freedom of the West in the 1920's.

The principal conflict in the novel, a synecdoche for the larger conflict within the Japanese psyche, asserts itself from the first sentence, in which Kaname asks his wife Misako if she will accept her father's invitation to the puppet theatre rather than visit her lover that day. Kaname and Misako have grown apart, and in order to hasten the dissolution of their marriage—while facilitating his own infidelity—Kaname has encouraged his wife to take up with Aso, a Kobe businessman. As Misako becomes increasingly comfortable in her new relationship, Kaname has begun to feel somewhat uneasy, attempting to maintain some semblance of control of the situation by suggesting when his wife should or should not communicate with her lover, and by advising her in the management of her personal schedule. At the opening of the novel, Misako has gained sufficient independence to ignore whatever suggestions Kaname may make regarding her conduct and to resist any unduly public display of marital harmony that might offend Aso, should he hear of it. Hence, she refuses to sit with Kaname on the train on their trip to Osaka to attend the puppet theatre with her father. Her fear of offending Aso suggests that, even as an extramarital lover, the Japanese male is completely dominant in male-female relationships.

While both Kaname and Misako have acquiesced in the disintegration of their marriage, neither seems willing to make a clean, final break. So they procrastinate, making temporary compromises and adjustments, preferring to put off what must be finally an unpleasant event. This same desire to avoid unpleasantness keeps them from informing their son, Hiroshi, a fourth grader, of their impending divorce. Despite his apparent lack of resolve, Kaname does not believe that divorce is wrong: "What [is] wrong," he would say, "[is] outdated convention."

Kaname, the point-of-view character and principal protagonist of the novel, is pictured as a modern Japanese leisure-class male, nominally employed as director of a family business, who chooses to live quietly, "casting no dishonour on his ancestors."

He prefers a Hollywood movie to a Kabuki play, likes jazz, reads classic pornography in English, speculates in U.S. currency, and regularly patronizes a Eurasian prostitute with a gift for languages. He puts women into two categories, the goddess or the plaything, preferring the "loose woman" to the proper wife. He has rejected the traditional, soft, submissive Japanese wife for a Western-style ideal of femininity. Like Tanizaki himself in his younger years, Kaname is a woman-worshipper.

For all of his apparent preference for the West, however, Kaname continues to feel nostalgia for the merchant's section of Tokyo where he grew up, notices the change of the season in the blossoming of the early cherries, and feels more comfortable in a kimono than in Western business clothes. His rejection of Japanese culture for the West is far from complete, and when he accepts his father-in-law's invitation to attend a performance of the *joruri*, the traditional puppet theatre, he feels himself begin to be drawn toward the culture of old Japan. One reason for his renewed interest in things Japanese is the doll-like O-hisa, his father-in-law's mistress-protégée.

In her late 20s, O-hisa is 30 years younger than Misako's father, who schools her in everything from playing the samisen to cooking. As is proper for traditional Japanese concubines, O-hisa shows her devotion by constant attention to her benefactor's needs, although she does complain to Kaname of the old man's nagging. Misako, the modern Japanese beauty, despises O-hisa as "a tranquil, unexcitable Kyoto type, whose conversation . . . seldom [goes] beyond one amiable sentence." At the puppet theatre, where Misako insists on staying for only one act, Kaname thinks, "There [is] much to be said for seeing a puppet play with a bottle of sake at one's side and a mistress to wait on one. . . ."

As the novel progresses, Kaname's restlessness increases, and he feels pressured by his forceful cousin, Takanatsu Hideo, to move forward with the divorce. Without Kaname's permission, Takanatsu has told Hiroshi of his parents' impending breakup. Kaname, however, continuing to vacillate, again turns his attention to his father-in-law, a "son of

Tokyo" who at 59 has "surrendered to Osaka" to spend his retirement indulging in the pleasures of a lifestyle that is passing away even as he enjoys it. Central to Japanese aesthetics is *sabi*, the beauty in sadness resulting from deprivation, attrition, and transience; hence, the old man's love of the old puppet heads, of the older, more authentic puppet theatre at Awajim and of his old fashioned house in Kyoto. Following an extended visit with his father-in-law, during which he reveals the state of his marriage to the old man and O-hisa, Kaname returns to Tokyo, and, after changing into a business suit, pays a visit to his Eurasian mistress, Louise, who is able to satisfy "something of his longing for Europe." Each time he leaves Louise, Kaname resolves not to return, a resolution he repeatedly breaks.

Upon his return home, Kaname receives a letter from his father-in-law, lamenting his daughter's faithlessness, and inviting them to visit him before they finalize their divorce. During the visit, which Misako undertakes with great reluctance, the old man takes his daughter out to dinner, leaving Kaname to dine with O-hisa and to retire with one of his father-in-law's old wood-block books. In the final scene of the novel, O-hisa appears, kneeling in his doorway with a half-dozen more books in her arms.

Some Prefer Nettles ends leaving the reader uncertain as to whether Kaname and Misako will divorce or continue in their marriage while making allowances for one another's sexual needs. What is clear, however, is that Kaname has been drawn to the point of "surrender" to the Japanese way of life symbolized by Osaka, Kyoto, and by the woman O-hisa. Hence whatever decisions he may make regarding his future are likely to be made in the context of his renewed sense of his identity as a Japanese.

The Makioka Sisters

Considered in its totality (some 530 pages in the English translation), *Sasameyuki*, or *The Makioka Sisters*, presents a complex thematic program in which Tanizaki explores the struggle to survive of an upper-middle-class family even as the conventions that define and sustain bourgeois family life are eroded by modernization. As the fortunes and influence of the once-powerful Makioka family diminish in the post-Meiji period, ironically it is the underlying strength and resiliency of Japanese culture and values that provide the means by which the family may adapt to change.

The Japanese are a practical people, whose resourcefulness, adaptability, and willingness to make necessary compromises may be traced to the success of the bourgeoisie during the Edo period. From their position at the bottom Confucian social scale, survival for the merchant class depended on maintaining the appearance of stability, dependability, and respectability, as well as upon the maintenance and protection of family fortunes through arranged marriages. If the Japanese middle classes seem overly conventional and class-conscious, it should be remembered that lacking the support of the Confucian value system, their survival depended up their own system of social vigilance.

Even though, on the surface, the Makioka sisters seem often to exhibit the essence of conventionality with its shallow emphasis on appearances, Yukiko and Taeko, the younger sisters, display enough contrariety and contradiction to resist facile characterization. If the older sisters seem less complex—and thereby less interesting—it should be remembered they *are* older and less susceptible to conflicting social values, and Tsuruko, the oldest, plays a far less significant part in the story than those of her younger sisters.

Tsuruko, the mistress of the main house in O-saka, is a flat character who remains weak, ineffectual, and submissive throughout the novel, despite her presumed authority as mistress of the senior branch of the family. Her wishes and decisions are repeatedly ignored or circumvented by her sisters, especially after she and her branch of the family are forced to relocate in Tokyo. Tsuruko's husband Tatsuo, a management-level bank employee, has taken his wife's family name, thereby becoming the nominal head of the family. After years of sacrificing advancement in order to avoid transfer out of Osaka, Tatsuo is finally transferred to Tokyo, where he moves with his family. In Tokyo the availability and cost of housing forces them to rent a house much smaller than the family home in Osaka, making it impossible to maintain the levels of comfort and privacy they had formerly enjoyed. Moreover, the move to Tokyo causes the "main house" to figure less prominently in the activities of the junior branch of the family who continue to live at Ashiya, a city near Osaka.

Sachiko, the mistress of the Ashiya house, is a youthful and vibrant woman in her 30s, whose attractiveness is set off equally by a formal kimono or a western-style dress. After Tsuruko and Tatsuo move to Tokyo, responsibility for Yukiko and Taeko devolves by default onto Sachiko and her husband, Teinosuke, who are willing to allow the younger sisters to live with them in spite of custom, which demands that they reside at the main house until they are married. By tacit agreement the main house allows the sisters to spend much, and, in Taeko's case all, of their time at the Ashiya house. Sachiko is deeply concerned for the welfare of her younger sisters, spending much of her energy attempting to secure good marriages for them. The level of her self-sacrifice for Yukiko approaches the heroic when, because of exertions she endures in carrying out the rigorous demands of an engagement party, she miscarries her unborn child, a loss for which she continues to suffer years afterward. She has one child, a daughter named Etsuko, a favorite companion of Yukiko. Sachiko's principal source of emotional support and strength is her remarkable husband, Teinosuke.

Like Tatsuo, Teinosuke has taken the Makioka name, but unlike his brother-in-law, Teinosuke is able to maintain his household at a level of security and comfort in keeping with his wife's social position. He is a successful accountant with literary talent and refined aesthetic sensibilities. As head of the junior branch of the family, he is patient, understanding, considerate, and compassionate to all members of his household, including the servants. Yet he can also be decisive, firm, persistent, and courageous when a situation calls for resolve. Examples of such situations range from Teinosuke's

writing a long, carefully-worded, face-saving letter of explanation to a distinguished suitor who has been rudely rebuffed by Yukiko, to his setting out alone on foot across the dangerously flooded landscape in search of Taeko, who has failed to return home from sewing class before the onset of a major flood.

Taeko, called Koi-San because she is the youngest sister, feels completely at home in the modern world. With a tendency to plumpness, she looks better in western clothes than in a kimono, and her talent for sewing and doll-making give her the potential for financial independence and emancipation from control by the family. She is witty, intelligent, and somewhat vulgar, caring less about what people think of her than her sisters do. For all her modernity, however, Taeko displays a remarkable talent for classical Japanese dance, which she studies, practices, and performs with grace and charm. When she was 19, she attempted to elope with Okubata, nicknamed Kei-boy, causing a scandal that reached the newspapers. Unfortunately, the newspapers mistakenly gave Yukiko's name instead of Taeko's, casting a shadow over Yukiko's future marriage prospects, even though the newspaper later corrected the error.

Okubata, an insipid, vain non-entity, is considered, because of his family connections, to be a good match for Taeko, and has remained her tacitly approved, eventual intended over several years while the family has attempted to find an acceptable match for Yukiko, who is older and therefore designated to marry first. Taeko's attitude toward Okubata seems to range between indifference and friendly concern, for it is with his working-class employee Itakura that she falls in love. A talented, self-taught art photographer who has traveled throughout the United States, Itakura is self-assured, good-natured, and, like Taeko, somewhat vulgar. During the flood, Itakura rescues Taeko, her sewing teacher, and her teacher's son from drowning, but because of his social class, Itakura can never be accepted by the family as a husband for Taeko. Fortunately for the family, Itakura dies before such an eventuality can materialize. Less fortunately, perhaps, Taeko later becomes pregnant by a bartender, whom she eventually marries.

If *The Makioka Sisters* can be said to contain a plot, then that plot unfolds as the process of finding an appropriate match for Yukiko, a process that has evolved several years before action of the novel begins. When she was younger, Yukiko was considered such a good match that she repeatedly refused good offers from gentlemen who did not measure up to her particularly high standards. Now, at 30, she continues to pursue her highly selective approach to husband-hunting even though she has been receiving fewer offers lately, and the family believes that, at her, age she should probably be willing to compromise somewhat.

On the surface, Yukiko is quiet, retiring, and self-effacing. In company, she is shy and inarticulate, seldom speaking more than a few words, even when she is on display at the *miai*, the formal pre-engagement party at which the couple begins to get to know one another. Of the sisters, she is the most traditionally Japanese, seldom wearing Western clothes, which accentuate her slimness and make her appear almost consumptive. In a kimono, however, she is attractive and demure, appearing much younger than her 30 years. Beneath her lady-like demeanor, however, Yukiko is self-willed, determined, and manipulative. She seems more willing to remain unmarried, continuing in the Ashiya house as a companion to Etsuko, than to compromise her standards. In the end, thanks in great part to Teinosuki's skill in negotiation, she finds a husband from the nobility, and, as the novel ends, she is suffering from diarrhea on her way to her wedding in Tokyo.

By modern Japanese standards, *The Makioka Sisters* is a mammoth novel, covering with remarkable detail three years (1938–41) in the lives of its protagonists. Through the novel, the focalization is modulated among the family group as a whole, the sisters, and the individuals within the family, thus presenting life in Japan immediately prior to World War II from varying perspectives of age and gender. The family itself is presented as a vibrant, vital, and varied group of people, both capable of deep friendships with two European families, one German and one White Russian, and also unwilling to relinquish the social and cultural activities that bring them closer together and make their lives bearable in difficult times.

Tanizaki began the serial publication of *The Makioka Sisters* in 1943, but the work was suppressed by the military rulers for ideological reasons. After the novel was finally published in 1948, Tanzizaki was awarded the Mainichi and Asahi prizes. In 1949 he dined with the emperor and received the prestigious Medal of Culture. Among his later undertakings was a revision of his earlier translation of *The Tale of Genji* (1954) into modern Japanese, *The Key* (1956), and *Diary of a Mad Old Man* (1962). In 1964 he was made an honorary fellow of the American Academy and Institute of Arts and Letters. Tanizaki died in January 1965.

ROBERT ALAN BURNS

Further Reading

Translations

Seidensticker, Edward G., trans. *The Makioka Sisters*. New York: Alfred A. Knopf, 1957.
———, trans. *Some Prefer Nettles*. New York: Alfred A. Knopf, 1955.

Related Studies

Gessel, Van C. *Three Modern Novelists: Soseki, Tanizaki, Kawabata*. Tokyo: Kondasha International, Ltd., 1993. Detailed critical examinations of the lives and works of three major modern Japanese novelists, these biographies are organized around each novelist's response to the challenge of modernity. This work is intended for a general audience and provides an excellent introduction to the subject.

Keene, Donald. *Dawn to the West: Japanese Literature in the Modern Era: Fiction*. New York: Holt, Rinehart and Winston, 1984. A broad and compendious critical survey of modern Japanese fiction from the Meiji restoration to Mishima, *Dawn to the West* is a thorough and illuminating study, including topics such as the Meiji political novel, naturalism, the "I" novel, war literature, and the revival of writing by woman. Sixteen chapters are devoted to the works of specific authors. This work is an excellent general introduction and reference for the general reader.

Tanizaki Jun'ichiro. *Childhood Years (Yosho Jidai)*. Tokyo: Kondasha International, Ltd., 1989. This is Tanizaki's wonderfully detailed recollection of his childhood, from his earliest memories to his enrollment in the First Higher School. Chronicling his family life, especially his memories of his mother, his experiences at the Kabuki theater, at school, and among his friends and teachers; the novelist reveals the earliest influences on his development as a man and as a writer. While the structure of Tanizaki's memoir is characteristically associative and episodic, *Childhood Years* presents an excellent introduction to the writer by the writer.

————. *In Praise of Shadows (In'ei Raisan)*. Trans. Thomas J. Harper and Edward G. Seidensticker. Foreword by Charles Moore. Branford, CT: Leete's Island Books, 1977. In this work, Tanizaki examines, explains, and presents his version of traditional Japanese aesthetics. Describing beauty in terms of transience, decay, shadow, and darkness, *In Praise of Shadows* is essential for understanding the aesthetic concerns of Tanizaki in his later period.

THE SHORT STORIES OF AKUTAGAWA RYŪNOSUKE

Author: Akutagawa Ryūnosuke
Born: 1892, Tokyo
Died: 1927, Tokyo
Major Works: "The Rashō Gate" (1915), "The Nose" (1916), "Yam Gruel" (1916), "The Bandits" (1917), "A Life Spent at Frivolous Writing" (1917), "Withered Fields" (1918), "The Spider's Thread" (1918), "Death of a Martyr" (1918), "The Hell Screen" (1918), "The Ball" (1919), "Christ in Nanking" (1920), "The Chastity of O-Tomi" (1922), "In the Grove" (1922), "Cogwheels" (1927), "A Fool's Life" (1927)

Major Themes

An artist has to experience what he describes even at the cost of the most terrible sacrifices.
The realization of a dream brings not satisfaction but disillusionment.
Poetic truth is more important than historical accuracy.
In the struggle between the creative passion of art and the humane self, art may triumph at the expense of humanity.
Truth resists discovery because of individual perspectives that conflict with one another.

Akutagawa Ryūnosuke's stature as a writer in modern Japanese literature is attested to by an award named after him: the Akutagawa Prize. Established in 1936, a decade after the death of the author, the award has become the most prestigious literary award for up-and-coming writers in Japan; and the reception of the award assures a bright and promising future for these writers. Akutagawa was also one of the first modern Japanese writers to be known outside Japan. English translations of some of his short stories were available as early as 1930 and one of the best-known Kurosawa films, *Rashomon* (Kurosawa Akira; 1950), was based on two of Akutagawa's short stories: "The Rashō Gate" ("*Rashōmon*") and "In the Grove" ("*Yabu no naka*").

Born in 1892 on a dairy farm in Tokyo, Akutagawa was raised by his maternal grandparents as an infant because of his mother's mental illness, and was later adopted by his maternal uncle. Later in life, Akutagawa was troubled by his mother's madness and its implications for his own mental well-being. This may have contributed to his suicide in 1927, at the age of 35.

Known to English-language readers mostly for his grotesque and exotic tales of the old Japan,

Akutagawa, in fact, possessed a taste for a wide range of literature. A graduate of the English department of the elite Tokyo University, Akutagawa was regarded in his day as a scholarly, intellectual writer. As a young man, he devoured literature of the East and the West, reading not only Chinese and Japanese classical and modern works but also devoting much of his time to European authors from Nietzsche, Tolstoy, and Dostoyevsky to Baudelaire, Strindberg, and Bergson.

Akutagawa's writing was heavily influenced by his reading habits. Drawing inspiration for his narratives both from ancient Japanese tales and from Western sources, he created a unique genre of historical tales that were set in the old Japan, yet employed complicated plots and psychological details that were distinctively non-Japanese. In fact, one of the criticisms he received from his contemporaries, particularly in the barbs from the dominant literary schools of the day, the Naturalists, and later the Proletarians, was that however cleverly fabricated his stories might be, the sources for his writing relied too heavily on knowledge from books rather than drawing on his imagination or personal experience, the perferred modes of literary production at that time.

Born at the very end of the nineteenth century, Akutagawa's writing inevitably reflects the characteristics of the fin de siècle: luxuriant sensuality, cosmopolitan sophistication, and decadent beauty. Sometimes dubbed the Edgar Allan Poe of Japan, he is known particularily as a master storyteller who elaborates abstract ideas by casting them in rich, colorful, somewhat diabolic, plot-driven narratives.

Stories of Times Now Past

The great majority of Akutagawa's popular stories were set in the past and can be seen as historical tales, even though the author's goal was to present poetic truth rather than historical accuracy. Three periods of the historical past fascinated Akutagawa the most. The first was the late-Heian period (twelfth century), when glorious high-court culture fell into chaotic disarray, and the capital was plagued by natural disasters and manmade warfare. This group of stories, many of them either based on or drawing their inspiration from the classical collection, *Tales of Times Now Past* (*Konjaku Monogatari*), typically question men's dignity and value at a time of societal degeneration. The famous "The Rashō Gate" ("*Rashōmon*") tells of an unemployed menial laborer in the war-torn capital city Heiankyō (today's Kyōto) who sought shelter from the rain in the once-splendid but now-dilapidated Rashō Gate. There he chances upon an old woman who is collecting hair to be sold for wigs from the many corpses abandoned there. The man, repelled by this putrid act, seeks revenge by stripping off her kimono and disappearing into the night. The grotesque imagery of a decaying time and place is evoked through vivid, economical language at the same time that serious moral questions are raised.

Another historical period evoked in many of Akutagawa's works is the sixteenth century, when Japan first came into contact with the Portuguese and Spanish missionaries who brought Christianity to Japan. Certainly in this respect, he was influenced by the popular interest in Christianity (specifically, Catholicism) and the fascination with the exotic, so-called Southern Barbarians (*Nanbanshumi*) at the end of the Meiji era. Though never a Christian himself, throughout his brief life Akutagawa was fascinated by the Bible, both as a narrative for religious teaching and as a literary source. Akutagawa was particularly intrigued by the zealotry of the martyrs and maintained a sense of awe and reverence for miraculous mysticism, but never lost the suspicion of a detached observer. "Death of a Martyr" ("*Hōkyōnin no shi*") (1918) and "Christ in Nanking" ("*Nankin no kirisuto*") (1920) are two representative works of this genre, called "Christian tales" ("*Kirishitan-mono*").

Finally, Akutagawa was intrigued by the relatively recent past of the Meiji era (1868–1912), a romantic period in modern Japanese history in which the West was being swallowed whole while Japanese culture and society were being redefined by the newly introduced modernity. The short stories "The Ball" ("*Butōkai*") (1919) and "The Chastity of Otomi" ("*O-Tomi no teisō*") (1922) belong to this category.

The Artist and his Artistry: "The Hell Screen"

Although the author's preferred mode of literary production was to borrow from many different historical, religious, and continental Chinese sources to formulate his own dramatic narrative style, Akutagawa's writing was endearing to its readers because, despite the various genres he worked in, his work grappled with the essential questions that all artists must confront: What is art? How does an artist achieve his art? To what extent should an artist sacrifice for art?

Akutagawa's most important period piece, "The Hell Screen" ("*Jigokuhen*") was an attempt to answer such questions. It was also a prime example of the author's accomplishments in reinventing a tale with a classical frame by injecting into it contemporary psychology, thus transforming the story into something temporally distant, yet psychologically immediate for contemporary readers.

Told in the highly ornate and stylized language of an old court lady, the story centers on an eccentric, ruthless court painter, Yoshihide, whose obsession with creating a screen depicting the horrors of hell costs him the only thing he treasured in the world—his beautiful, gentle daughter. The story was based on a short passage in the *Ujishūi monogatari* about a painter who is so engrossed in studying the right way to draw flames that he could not be bothered to rescue his wife, children, and property from a fire that is about to engulf his house. In "The Hell Screen," the plot is more complicated. Yoshihide's obsession is intertwined with a plot for revenge by a lord whose advances to Yoshihide's daughter had been spurned. When Yoshihide requests a living model for the climatic scene of the screen—a beautiful court lady in a chariot suffering in hell's flames—the lord orders Yoshihide's daughter to perform the task, much to the shock of Yoshihide. Akutagawa elaborated a simple passage into a richly textured, suspenseful tale, juxtaposing good and evil, ends and means. Further, it problematized the inherent conflict an artist often faces in precariously balancing the creative subjectivity and the human self. While Yoshihide watches his most beloved daughter writhing and struggling in the fire, art triumphs over humanity and he is finally able to complete the screen. Nevertheless, the artistic victory ends on a bitter note when Yoshihide committs suicide the day after the completion of "The Hell Screen." Thus, the paradox of life versus art remains unresolved.

In Search of the Truth: "In the Grove"

Another historical fiction that took inspiration from medieval-tale literature was "In the Grove" ("*Yabu no naka*"). The short story stands out from all other historical narratives in that it tells its story by combining seven different testimonies of various characters involved in a murder. A samurai and his wife are traveling through the woods when a bandit named Tajomaru robs the couple, resulting in the death of the husband. Unlike the single narrative viewpoint used in "The Hell Screen," this simple fact of murder is complicated by the different and mutually conflicting accounts of witnesses' testimony.

A work written during what critics consider Akutagawa's maturing period, the short story grapples with the awareness of the impossibility for one to know the truth amidst various, subjective interpretations of an event. The first four segments set up the framework for the story, providing information on its external circumstances and three principal characters. The three confessions, including one as spoken by the ghost of the deceased husband through the mouth of a medium, plunge the story into a suspenseful tale and invite its readers to do the detective work. The irony, of course, is that unlike the usual murder mystery, in which each suspect must prove that he or she is innocent, each of the three characters involved claims responsibility for the death to protect their honor or ego.

Madness and Modernity

The last stage of Akutagawa's literary career marked a distinct shift from his earlier compositions both in tone and in subject matter. These works, quite unlike his earlier historical tales, incorporated autobiographical elements, revealing the agony of a tortured, delirious mind in a state of extreme tension and depression. The boundary between his inner and outer worlds was collapsing. He had not only lost control over his densely crafted literary productions, but also experienced doubts about the aestheticism of those works. In fact, he seems to have distanced himself from the well-structured, event-oriented narratives through which he had made his name in the earlier part of his writing career. In his famous essay "Literary, all too literary" ("*Bungeiteki na, amarini bungeiteki na*") (*Kaizō* 1927, 4–8) he advocated a new kind of "plotless" fiction that quickly prompted a debate between with Tanizaki Junichirō, another writer famous for imaginative fabrication of fiction.

In 1927, the year Akutagawa committed suicide, he wrote several important works that have come to represent this late period. "Kappa" is a biting satire roughly modeled on Swift's *Gulliver's Travels*. It is a cautionary tale of distopia about a madman who claimed to have visited a strange land of water imps, the mythical half-human, half-aquatic creatures who populate Japanese folktales. The Kappa nation is a feminist utopia where gender roles are reversed: female kappas dominate politics and courtship, and cause warfare. According to the Kappa myth, God created the female kappa first, and out of pity molded the male kappa from the female brain. Seen from the eyes of a narrator suffering from dementia praecox, this allegorical fable of social satire is on the one hand a superb fantasy filled with black humor, but on the other hand, a reflection of the disillusionment and distrust the author felt toward a rapidly industrializing capitalist society.

The madness theme grew increasingly darker and more personal as Akutagawa's writing career was buffeted by his ailing health, frayed nerves, and family troubles. His later works demonstrate the all-encompassing disintegration and personal pain of his life; the author was no longer capable of engaging the world around him. Indeed, as he himself wrote in his memo "[Life] is more hell-like than hell. . . . Hell is monotonous, so it is comparatively easy for one to adapt oneself to hell."

Two excellent final works, written in the last year of his life, were published posthumously: "Cogwheels" ("*Haguruma*") and "A Fool's Life" ("*Aru ahō no isshō*"). These stories best illustrate the physical and mental state he was in at the end of his life.

"Cogwheels" portrays a mental state bordering on schizophrenia and paranoia. The resemblance between "Cogwheels" and Strindberg's *Inferno* has been closely studied by Japanese scholars. The protagonist, Akutagawa, constantly hallucinates a transparent revolving cogwheel. He seems unable to shake the ominous death that is rapidly approaching him.

If "Cogwheels" captures Akutagawa's incoherent mental state and an urgent, albeit fragile, awareness of an ominous ending, "A Fool's Life" reflects on the author's short and tragic life. An epigrammatic autobiography, in 51 short, fragmented passages, "A Fool's Life" painstakingly captures key moments that shaped the author's life: events of daily life, references to authors and

books, reflections, parables and metaphors, all constitute a kaleidescopic vision of Akutagawa's inner reality and exterior experiences.

Despite his relatively short life and career, Akutagawa nevertheless left an impressive literary legacy. His masterful literary talents enabled him to synthethize East and West and past and present into literary gems that still glimmer on their own merit. Ultimately, it was his idealist search for artistic truth and his unyielding artistic honesty and principle that won him a very special place in Japanese literary history and in the hearts of his readers.

FAYE Y. KLEEMAN

Further Reading

Translations

Akutagawa, Ryūnosuke. *Hell Screen and Other Stories.* Trans. W. H. H. Norman. Tokyo: Hokuseidō, 1952.

———. *Rashōmon and Other Stories.* Trans. Takashi Kojima. New York: Liveright, 1952.

———. *Japanese Short Stories.* Trans. Takashi Kojima. New York: Liveright, 1961.

———. *Kappa.* Trans. Geoffrey Bownas. Rutland, VT: Charles E. Tuttle, 1971.

Related Studies

Keene, Donald. "Akutagawa Ryūnosuke," in *Dawn to the West: Japanese Literature in the Modern Era,* New York: Henry Holt & Co, 1984, 556–593. This article provides by far the most detailed biographical information on the author. It traces his life and major works, situating Akutagawa in the larger context of modern Japanese literary history. It is useful in that it provides much criticism by Akutagawa's contemporaries.

Tōruta Kinya. "The Hell Screen," "In a Grove," "Kappa," in *Approaches to the Modern Japanese Short Story,* Tokyo: Waseda University Press, 1982, 11–44. Three separate articles that provide thoughtful and illuminating interpretations of Akutagawa's three most important stories.

THE FICTIONAL WORKS OF IBUSE MASUJI

Author: Ibuse Masuji
Born: 1898, Hiroshima
Died: 1992, Tokyo
Major Works: "Salamander" (1922), "Carp" (1926), "Savan on the Roof" (1929) *Waves: A War Diary* (1938), *John Manjirō: A Castaway's Chronicle* (1938), "Tajinko Village" (1939), "Isle-on-the-Billows" (1946), "A Geisha Remembers" (1950), "Station Inn" (1957), *Lieutenant Lookeast* (1961), *Black Rain* (1964)

Major Themes

Human beings are part of the ultimate rightness of the natural order, no more and no less than any other living creatures.
The unadorned voices of the common folk are true reflections of existential reality and history.
The resilience of the human spirit can survive any manmade or natural catastrophe.

Ibuse Masuji represents the last vestige of the literati writer (*bunjin*) in the tradition of Natsume Sōseki, Nagai Kafū, and Kawabata Yasunari. The term *bunjin* (man of letters) refers to the gentleman scholar who engages in literary production and also dabbles in other cultural endeavors such as poetic paintings (*haiga*), and who possesses a refined sensibility to nature and quietly asserts a cultivated philosophy of life. Born at the turn of the century, Ibuse's writing career spanned a remarkable six decades. He is one of Japan's most revered modern authors.

Even though Ibuse is best known in non-Japanese languages and primarily as a novelist and short story writer, he also wrote poetry and was a prolific, polished essayist. Ibuse was also a seasoned traveler and connoisseur of beautiful objects; he wrote about them often. Born in 1898 in a small village in eastern Hiroshima, Ibuse grew up comfortably in an old landowner family (the Ibuse lineage can be traced back to the fifteenth century). Young Ibuse, after graduating from high school, aspired to become a painter. He moved to Tokyo to pursue studies in literature at Waseda University in 1919, but soon quit school to devote himself full-time to writing.

"Salamander"

In 1922, Ibuse published his first short story, a simple, allegorical parable entitled "Salamander"

("Sanshōuo"), which is still standard reading in many Japanese high schools. In this very first short story, Ibuse exhibited several traits that he refined and developed in his later works. His training as a painter gave Ibuse a keen and perceptive eye in observing nature, particularly flowers, birds, insects, and fish. "Salamander" is about a salamander who, through its own carelessness, is trapped in a rock cave under the river. In despair, the salamander curses its fate, laments its loneliness, feels jealousy toward other creatures' freedom, and finally progresses to a sadistic desire to trap others in its prison. One day, quite by accident, a frog, the natural enemy of the salamander, falls into the cave. Thus begins two years of contentious fighting until, one day, realizing they might die of starvation, they finally see the meaningless stupidity of their action and quietly come to peace with each other.

The predicament of these two creatures reflects the confined, predetermined human condition, and the narrative pricks the shallowness of human desires and follies. As Ibuse himself explained, he wrote this story to explore "the process from despair to enlightenment." Even more important than its content was Ibuse's development of a new style purposely modeled on that of direct translation. To the readers of his time, Ibuse's work was different, refreshing and somewhat exotic. It was precisely his unique narrative voice—gentle, understatedly serene, whimsical, and sometimes tinged with comedy—that became the trademark of Ibuse's writing. The subject matter might be serious, or even depressing, but the good humor and light-heartedness of Ibuse's language leavens the weighty tone.

The following two decades are considered Ibuse's most productive years. Some of his more reknowned works, such as his Naoki Award–winning *John Manjirō: A Castaway's Chronicle* (1938) and *A War Diary* (1938), were published during the period of 1930–1940. In 1941, Ibuse was drafted into the army and sent to Thailand and Singapore for about a year. This wartime experience formed the core of his postwar writing. The postwar era marked another fertile period for Ibuse, particularly for his writings on postwar popular culture and society and his subtle criticism of the war Japan waged against its neighbors. Throughout these years, Ibuse maintained his venerable place in Japanese literary circles by steadily turning out quality works that won prestigious literary prizes. He was elected to the Japanese Academy of Art (*Nihon Geijutsuin*) in 1960, and in 1966 he received the Order of Cultural Merit (*Bunka kunshō*), the highest honor that Japan can award to a civilian.

Ibuse's Depiction of Common Folk

Ibuse's writings often drew their inspiration from the life and daily struggles of the masses (*shomin*). However, his interest in the common folk is to be distinguished from that of the Marxist or Prole-tarian writers, in whose philosophy literary works are purely an instrument to serve the masses. Rather than treating the masses as an abstract, collective political entity, Ibuse sought to capture the many distinct voices verbalized by specific, individualistic characters against the backdrop of a changing social fabric.

"Kuchisuke's Valley" ("*Kuchisuke no iru tanima*") (1929), an early example of this genre, presents one of Ibuse's most memorable characters: Kuchisuke. Told from the point of view of a disinterested young narrator, it is a bittersweet tale of

how Kuchisuke, a willful, old-fashioned old man, is forced by the tide of progress and modernization to give up his home and his way of life because of the construction of a dam. A later example is the novel *Proprietor of the Treasure House* (*Chinpindō shujin*) (1959). It relates the disastrous ordeal of a retired schoolteacher's and antique dealer's operation of a resturant. He is defrauded out of his enterprise by a shrewd lesbian and even loses his own girlfriend to her. Some consider this to be the best of Ibuse's writings on the common folk.

Other works, such as the lighthearted "No Consultation Today" ("*Honjitsu kyūshin*") (1950) and the humorous "Station Inn" ("*Ekimae ryokan*") (1956), became well known after being adapted into popular movies.

Humor, Satire, and the Hidden Protest Against the War

Despite Ibuse's deceptively simple depiction of the hopes and woes of everyday folk, he did not lose sight of deeper issues. His refusal to be bound by any ideology, and his clear distaste for authority and warfare emerged early in his writing and are evident through all his works. In the historical fiction *Waves: A War Diary* (*Sazanami gunki*) (1938), the bloody battles between the Genji and the Taira clans are seen through the naive eyes of a defeated Taira teenager. Told in the format of a diary recorded by the young boy, the monotonous day-to-day maneuvering is peppered with occasional outbursts of brutal combat, physical hardships, and a budding sexual awakening. Through the poised and even lyrical narrative voice, we see the unintended acceleration of the narrator's maturation into manhood in a mere eight months' time. The quiet transformation of the boy from an observer to an active participant in warfare reveals the gradually intensifying, militaristic education that encroached on the adolescence of Japanese youth of the author's time. The narrative ends abruptly when the boy is wounded in a battle and can no longer write his own diary. The dramatic irony is even more effective because the reader is fully aware of the calamitous outcome awaiting the boy as he lies silently in a rare moment of peaceful sleep.

The wry humor and subtle irony of *Waves: A War Diary* turned into outrageous, biting satire in Ibuse's postwar writing. *Lieutenant Lookeast (Yōhai taichō)* (1950) illuminates the aftermath of the war through the depiction of a deranged ex–army lieutenant, Okazaki Yūichi. After suffering a head injury in Malaysia, Okazaki is under the delusion that the war is still continuing and that he still commands imperial authority. Whenever he suffers a relapse, he bullies the villagers as if the war is still going on. The title comes from Yūichi's habit of having the army he commanded turn toward the east and bow in the direction of the emperor. The text alternates between village life in the present, and the faraway battlefield as Yūichi oscillates between sanity and derangement. Perhaps one of Ibuse's more-politicized stories, the narrative deals with the price of the war for both those who directed it and those who were led into it. To Ibuse's credit, the narrative's satirical absurdity is neither doctrinaire nor polemical, but rather balanced by the nostalgic kindness of some of the villagers.

Black Rain *and Other Atomic Bomb Writings*

In 1965, nearly two decades after atomic bombs were dropped on Nagasaki and Hiroshima, Ibuse published his most reknowned work, *Black Rain (Kuroi ame)*. A seminal work on the aftermath of the atomic catastrophe, it is more than a literary masterpiece: it also serves as the definitive historical record for the singular most devastating event in modern Japanese history.

In Japan, a genuinely harmonious and relatively homogenous society, there are three groups of people who are discriminated against by mainstream society: the outcasts (*burakumin*), other ethnic minorities, such as the Ainu and Okinawans, and finally the atomic-bomb victims (*hibakusha*). In setting as the theme of *Black Rain* the catastrophic atomic ordeal of Hiroshima, Ibuse took up the greatest challenge of his writing career. He rendered the social and ethical repercussions of the

bombing not through the politics of angry, dramatic events, but through the articulation of an unsentimental, subdued, and almost restrained poetics.

"Iris" (1951) is a good example. This short story deals with the aftermath of the atomic bomb in a visually stunning and emotionally effective way by mixing fact and fiction about Ibuse's own experiences in Fukuyama, a suburban town in the vicinity of Hiroshima, right after the bombing. The disturbing climactic scene subverts the calmer sketches in the preceeding narrative and leaves an indelible imprint on the readers' mind. The narrator recounts his discovery of the body of a young woman floating atop a pond where the irises have suddenly and unseasonably "bloomed crazily." The metaphor of the iris is twofold: its offseason flowering is an indictment of the manmade mass destruction, but it also illustrates the survival of nature despite human stupidity.

Documenting several very personal experiences of the repercussions of the bombing, *Black Rain* was published 20 years after the war. Ibuse felt a near-obsessive need to complete this work two decades after the actual historical incident because he saw the cataclysmic ordeal being turned into a ritual commemorating an abstract, frozen historical moment, while the individual memories of the victims dimmed into the background of this political theater. To Ibuse, the painful but often ennobling memories of the common men are the central core of history, and must be preserved lest they be erased from our collective memory.

The author approached this work as he would historical fiction, conducting excruciatingly thorough research on surviving records and documents before he embellished these materials with his imagination. To personalize the calamity of the Hiroshima holocaust, the author employed the most intimate device of writing—the diary. The novel incorporates records such as diaries, eyewitness accounts, and official reports to fill out the core of the narrative, the diary of the main character, Shigematsu. Shigematsu's diary covers the period of August 6, the fateful day of the bombing, to August 15, the day Japan surrendered. In the frame narrative, set five years after the bombing, Shigematsu's young niece, Yasuko, is having great difficulty getting married because of a malicious rumor that she was in Hiroshima the day the bomb dropped. Shigematsu decides to prove to the world that Yasuko's health is beyond doubt by transcribing Yasuko's and his own diaries of exactly what happened during the few fateful days. However, during the course of his effort, Yasuko starts to show symptoms of radiation sickness. The novel ends with Shigematsu's last entry, in which he shows very little concern over the emperor's surrender broadcast because of his preoccupation with the new lives thriving in the eel pond and his prayers for Yasuko's recovery.

The inhumanity and the horror of atomic warfare is depicted through a detached narrative voice aided by the weight of factual information, but never by hasty political indictments. While the author leads the reader to look directly at a tragedy of historic proportions through the destiny of individuals whose lives were altered dramatically by the event, he never loses his narrative composure. The simple, melodramatic fact of Yasuko's uncertain reproductive capability raises a larger question about the survival and continuity of the whole human race. Ibuse's masterly ability to frame larger, historical issues such as the war, the atomic bomb, and its impact on the communal consciousness through vivid personification is amply demonstrated in *Black Rain*.

The 1994 Nobel Literary laureate, Oe Kenzaburō, in accepting this honor, singled out two writers, Ibuse and Abe Kōbō, as his most respected literary predecessors, and men who had nurtured the modern Japanese literary tradition. It is interesting that Oe chose these two figures. In Abe's surreal, fantastic writing, Oe sees the potential to break down the cultural and literary boundaries between different nations. In Ibuse's narratives, he sees a firm grounding in the Japanese prose tradition, in which subdued language restrains pretentious drama, and compassion and detachment strike a delicate balance. It is this moral commitment, manifest in Shigematsu's feelings of obligation to his niece, embodied in a language totally devoid of

moralistic preaching, that makes Ibuse a unique scribe of the human condition.

FAYE Y. KLEEMAN

Further Readings

Translations

Ibuse Masuji. *Black Rain*. Trans. John Bester. Tokyo: Kōdansha International, Ltd., 1969.

———. *Lieutenant Lookeast and Other Stories*. Trans. John Bester. Tokyo: Kōdansha International, 1971.

———. "Kuchisuke's Valley." Trans. John W. Treat. In Van C. Gessel and Tomone Matsumoto, eds., *The Shōwa Anthology: Modern Japanese Short Stories, 1929–1984*, Tokyo: Kōdansha International, Ltd., 1985, 1–20.

———. *Waves: Two Short Novels*. Trans. Anthony Liman and David Aylward. Tokyo: Kōdansha International, 1986.

———. *Castways: Two Short Novels*. Trans. Anthony Liman and David Aylward. Tokyo: Kōdansha International, Ltd., 1987.

———. *Salamander and Other Stories*. Trans. John Bester. Tokyo: Kōdansha International, Ltd., 1989.

Related Studies

Lifton, Robert J. *Black Rain: Death in Life: Survivors of Hiroshima*. New York: Simon and Schuster, 1967.

Liman, Anthony V. *A Critical Study of the Literary Style of Ibuse Masuji: As Sensitive as Waters*. Lewiston, NY: Edwin Mellen Press, 1992.

———. "Ibuse's Black Rain." In K. Tsuruta and T. Swann, eds., *Approaches to the Modern Japanese Novel*, Tokyo: Sophia University Press, 1976, 45–72.

———. "Carp," "Pilgrim's Inn." In K. Tsuruta and T. Swann, eds., *Approaches to the Modern Japanese Short Story,* Tokyo: Waseda University Press, 1982, 83–101.

———. "The River: Ibuse's Poetic Cosmology."

In Takeda Katsuhiko, ed. *Essays on Japanese Literature*, Tokyo: Waseda University Press, 1977.

Rimer, J. Thomas. "Tradition and Contemporary Consciousness: Ibuse, Endo, Kaikō, Abe." In *Modern Japanese Fiction and Its Traditions.* Princeton NJ: Princeton University Press, 1978.

Treat, John W. *Pools of Water, Pillars of Fire.* Seattle and London: University of Washington Press, 1988.

THE FICTIONAL WORKS OF KAWABATA YASUNARI

Author: Kawabata Yasunari
Born: 1899, Osaka
Died: 1972, Kamakura
Major Works of Fiction: *The Izu Dancer (Izu no odoriko)* (1926), *Palm of the Hand Stories (Tenohira no shōsetsu)* (1926), *Evening Sun (Yūhi)* (1943), *Snow Country (Yukiguni)* (1948), *Thousand Cranes (Senbazuru)* (1949), *Palm of the Hand Stories (Tanagokoro no shōsetsu)* (1950), *Dancing Girl (Maihime)* (1951), *The Sound of the Mountain (Yama no oto)* (1954), *The Lake (Mizuumi)* (1955), *House of the Sleeping Beauties (Nemureru bijo)* (1961), *Beauty and Sadness (Utsukushisa to kanashimi to)* (1965), *One Arm (Kataude)* (1965)

Major Themes

The world is best accessed through the perceptual senses.
Humanity is inextricably bound to nature.
Erotic and sensual pleasures are made ecstatic when consummation is impossible.
Contrasts and transience heighten aesthetic and experiential appreciation.
Art should celebrate the reflected or refracted object, which is far more beautiful than the object itself

Kawabata Yasunari took his place among the great writers of the world as the only Japanese (to date) to win the Nobel Prize for Literature in 1968. Considerable surprise greeted the award, as Kawabata was broadly regarded as so quintessentially "Japanese" an author that he could not be appreciated by non-Japanese. Apparently, his aesthetics resonated with a much larger readership. As a recognized novelist, Kawabata mentored young writers, including Mishima Yukio and Ibuse Masuji, who matured into acclaimed authors.

Early in life Kawabata suffered devastating losses: his parents when he was an infant, his grandmother and sister shortly thereafter, and then his grandfather. Such tragedy undoubtedly contributed to the undercurrent of loss that permeates his work. An early interest in visual arts was superseded by his love of literature. He began to publish poetry and short stories while still in school, and experimented with a literary form of brief vignettes, "palm of the hand stories," which he continued to write throughout his lifetime (hence the two *Palm of the Hand Stories* volumes). He graduated from Tokyo Imperial University in 1924, having studied both English and Japanese literature.

During its formative stages in the 1920s, Ka-

wabata was affiliated with the Neo-Sensualist literary coterie *(shin kankaku ha)*. The coterie rejected the then-dominant naturalist literature that followed the principles of scientific observation and reportage. Kawabata's work emerged as influenced by, yet distinct from, the group. His contribution to their 1925 manifesto, "On the New Directions of Up and Coming Writers," elucidated his belief that giving prominence to sensory perception in the writing of literature would originate a new mode of Japanese literary expression resembling Freudian free association. Kawabata, however, distinguished his associative narrative from the Western avant-garde stream-of-consciousness style (as practiced by James Joyce). Such modernists, he felt, reveled in psychological depravity, and neglected the real world. The associative prose to which Kawabata aspired was inspired by the psychologically balanced, Japanese polysemic tradition. The Japanese classics, moreover, were rooted in mediated impressions of the material world. Kawabata sought to revive in modern prose the associative interweaving of humanity and nature that had characterized the Japanese, premodern canon. Borrowing variously from modern and premodern rhetorical devices, tropes, and genres, Kawabata wrote innovative works independent of the Western novel, modernism, naturalism, and even the Japanese canon.

The first work of Kawabata's to win substantial acclaim, *The Izu Dancer (Izu no odoriko)*, established many themes and stylistic signatures of his later, most celebrated works such as *Snow Country*, *Thousand Cranes*, and *The Sound of the Mountain*. The melancholy young protagonist of *The Izu Dancer* finds solace in a beautiful child-dancer. She is an icon of female purity; and the hero's vaguely erotic desire is reshaped by the impossibility of requital. Humans are bound to the natural world; the prose is lyrical, the sequences episodic, and the mood established through perceptual contrasts—directing the reader firmly along the surface of the text, away from psychological interiority.

Kawabata's works became more erotic as he aged. While his aesthetic of purity had always been brushed with erotic perversion, a bolder fetishization haunts *House of the Sleeping Beauties*, an account of protagonist Eguchi's visits to a unique brothel where elderly, impotent men fondle drugged, unconscious, virgin girls. Kawabata also returned to the surrealism of his youth in *One Arm*, in which a woman detaches and lends her arm (which itself speaks and caresses) to her lover.

While Kawabata's death in 1972 appears to have been a suicide, no note was found. Debates over whether it was suicide, and why he would have killed himself have yielded no satisfactory answers. His works had become increasingly troubled, and the suicide of his protégé Mishima in 1970 may have affected him deeply; yet there were no immediate circumstances to suggest that he was despondent.

Literary Aesthetics

Kawabata's tales frame human events in the cycle of seasonal changes. Heroes observe and record their mental reactions to an ever-changing environment. When heroes become active, their occasional deeds yield only questionable power over the greater forces of time, space, and nature. Trees shed their leaves in fall, human beauty fades over time,

and people age and die—regardless of human effort. Kawabata's primary objective, it appears, is to highlight momentary flashes of perceived beauty, made more lovely against a bleak background. As objects of furtive, unrequited erotic/sensory arousal, appreciated from a physical and psychic distance, women emerge as features of the natural landscape:

> The white in the depths of the mirror was the snow, and floating in the middle of it were the woman's bright red cheeks. There was an indescribably fresh beauty in the contrast. Was the sun already up? The brightness of the snow was more intense, it seemed to be burning icily. Against it, the woman's hair became a clearer black, touched with a purple sheen.
>
> (*SNOW COUNTRY*, EDWARD SEIDENSTICKER, TRANS., 1956)

Characterizations are vibrantly tactile, auditory, and visual: A woman is described by the contrasts of black hair and white skin, the sound of her voice, or the touch of her finger, not by her thoughts, personality, or psychological composition. Contrasts are everywhere: stillness is offset by sudden movement, sadness by a moment of joy, the brightness of red against black, purity against the soiled. Kawabata's episodic brevity and reliance on contrasting images are born of classical Japanese poetics such as the 17-syllable *haiku* and *renga* (long sequences of multi-authored linked verse). As in linked poetry, the separate episodes and images that together comprise the work are not necessarily cumulative; each is intricately related to the words and imagery immediately surrounding it, but not bound to the overall shape of the novel. Kawabata's writing is highly selective of events, and as in the classic *monogatari* (fictional tale) tradition, attention is lavished on decorative details—the scent of perfectly brewed tea, or the crane pattern adorning a kimono. "When a red oleander floods into bloom, the red against the thick green leaves is like the blaze of the summer sky; but when the blossoms are white, the effect is richly cool. The white clusters swayed gently, and enveloped Fumiko" (Seidensticker, trans., 1958).

Beauty is rendered more poignant when it is momentary, when the flow of time is halted to behold wondrous moments that cannot last: the first buds of spring, childhood naivete, and female virginity. At the moment of its fullest blossom, purity already is tinged with decay. Subtle blemishes not only enhance beauty through contrast, but also hint at the deeper stain of perversion underpinning Kawabata's awe of the ingenuous. Desire stripped of the possibility of sexual union is the pinnacle of erotic and emotional arousal for Kawabata's protagonists. Sexual consummation would render the pure impure: beauty can be preserved only by distance.

Just as it is, then, a mental, not physical, processing of femaleness that yields the utmost pleasure, nature in Kawabata's texts is not wild and rampant; it is the garden, tamed by the human hand, or the mountains, made docile in poetry. The ultimate mediations possess the qualities of translucence and reflection. Objects (and women) seen in mirrors or through glass, for example, are transformed into what they "should" or "could" be, which surpasses that which they are. Art repeatedly surpasses reality.

Snow Country

In 1990, when The Limited Editions Club published their edition of Edward Seidensticker's translation of *Snow Country*, the artist Kuwamoto Tadaaki illustrated the text with stark, bold, abstract shapes in red, white, and black. Even for someone expecting a representational rendering of beautiful young women in kimonos, a moment's reflection reveals the artistic brilliance of the artist's decision. *Snow Country* is as much about shape and color as it is about anything else, particularly the colors red, white, and black, which are repeatedly and contrastively copresent; for example, the geisha Komako is a mélange of white powder and black hair, cheeks fire-red, alternating with the cold of the season and the heat of her blood.

The pleasure of *Snow Country* thus lies not in its simple plot, but in the sensualized descriptions of the natural and feminine landscapes. *Snow Country* recounts the repeated sojourns of a middle-aged Tokyo dilettante, Shimamura, at an inn on the snowy Western coast of Japan, and his intermittent erotic dalliance with a young geisha-in-training, Komako. While Komako appears to love Shimamura, he is fascinated by the younger, purer Yoko, with whom he feels a deep, inexplicable connection from the moment he first sees her. Quantitatively, the narrative focuses on Shimamura's encounters with Komako. The qualitatively more powerful passion of Shimamura for Yoko frames, and is embedded within, the dominant story of Komako and Shimamura.

Aboard a train traversing a snowy countryside, Shimamura sees Yoko reflected over the passing scenery in the train window. A light from the mountains shining in the reflection of Yoko's face is to Shimamura "inexpressible beauty." As the modern train travels the old country, the shape and contours of the landscape and Yoko's face, the play of changing light, the sensations of coldness and steam, the high pitch of Yoko's voice in the dark night are each given equal narrative attention. Causal, or plotted elements are subordinated to descriptive aspects.

Distance and the unattainable are established as the enabling conditions for the purest sensual appreciation. Shimamura, a specialist in Western ballet, has refused to see an actual performance. By accessing ballet entirely through distanced representations, such as essays and photographs, he is free to construct his own version of the art, upon which reality should not (and he will not let it) intrude. When Shimamura sets off in search of Chijimi linen, purportedly still woven in the old-fashioned manner, and sun-bleached in the snow, it is no surprise that he never finds it. It can be assumed that, should he have found the Chijimi weavers, he would have discovered impurity there. The erosion of Shimamura's desire for Komako begins with the moment of his physical possession of her. Conversely, the untouched Yoko endures as an object of beauty and desire, her decay halted by untimely death.

The shocking moment of Yoko's death provides a feast for the eyes and the senses, but little emotional catharsis. Yoko's white body, falling from the second floor balcony of a dark, vertical house that is on fire, descends in a perfectly horizontal, physically impossible position, as white water flies up from hoses to meet the red flames. The cold white snow offsets the hot red flames in the framing darkness of the night. Shimamura feels a "flicker of uneasiness" at the thought that her head might drop, or knee bend, and so "disturb that perfectly horizontal line." As Komako carries Yoko's body away, the last line of the novel reads, "the Milky Way flowed down inside him [Shimamura] with a roar."

In Japan, there is a legend about the Milky Way. Two of the stars that flank the constellation were human lovers so impassioned that they were turned into stars. The tragedy is that, inhabiting opposite sides of the Milky Way, they meet only once a year. It is as though the moment of Yoko's death, with its perfect contrasts, is Kawabata's version of the ecstatic condition of separation in the skies above.

The Sound of the Mountain

The Sound of the Mountain is the story of an aging man approaching death, Shingo Ogata, and his erotic attachment to his daughter-in-law, Kikuko. Unhappy marriages and adultery surround the Ogata family: Shingo's own marriage is loveless; his son Shuichi philanders; his natural daughter Fusako divorces. Shuichi's mistress becomes pregnant with his child, while Kikuko aborts her baby. *The Sound of the Mountain* has a deepening darkness. Funerals of Shingo's friends are reported one after another. Death is mentioned page after page. Kikuko and the flora of changing seasons distract Shingo from the disturbed disquiet of the household and mute the roar of the mountain—a premonition of his own death. Shingo idealizes his suffering daughter-in-law, calling her a "window looking out of a gloomy house," and she is devoted to him. A private meeting between Kikuko and Shingo, which has all the intrigue and delight of a tryst is held in a garden where young lovers gather,

and where the "vast green expanse set Shingo free": nature and Kikuko allay his fear of death. Lying beneath his desire for Kikuko is the memory of another unrequited passion—for his long-deceased sister-in-law.

The eroticized women of *The Sound of the Mountain* grace the text as vessels for Shingo's desire, as minimally differentiated symbols of impossible yearning. Characterizations of the women halt at broad strokes sketching the contours of their physical presence—hair, breasts, shoulders, in alternating motion and repose. Shingo's desire is incited by features that suggest purity and by gestures that indicate modesty. Female appearance is female fate. Shingo's natural daughter Fusako's ugliness makes her an ugly person; in turn, her unattractive daughter has a decidedly unpleasant personality.

Shingo's fragmentary, fearsome dreams of death and softer carnal dreams are interwoven with the narrative present. Encroaching senility weakens Shingo's mental acumen; even when awake, he slides easily into reverie. Poignant reminders of his mental confusion are everywhere. One night, awakened by hearing his son returning home drunk, Shingo interprets the voice thick with drink as a repentant, loving one. Yet later he wonders if it were not an "old man's sentimentality" that had led him to fill the voice with love and sadness. Even his fingers have forgotten familiar tasks as he is suddenly, incomprehensibly unable to knot his own necktie. Paralleling Shingo's forgetfulness, events of the narrative present are retold in later episodes in condensed form, as though to fix them in memory, or as if the narrator has forgotten that the reader has already been informed.

More and more, Shingo quotes poetry, or mentions art, progressively retreating from a confusing real world into the mediated realm of artistic representations. Two *nō* masks depicting children's countenances, acquired from a recently deceased friend's collection, fascinate Shingo. The one that Shingo prefers is symbolic of eternal youth. Admiring the mask, Shingo is overwhelmed with desire and almost kisses its lips. Attributing his emotions to having viewed the mask from a perversely intimate distance, he tells himself that it was his "ancient eyes" that had "made the skin more alluring than that of a real woman." Later, when Kikuko tries it on, he is unable to look at her.

In the closing scene, Shingo calls out to Kikuko, but she does not hear him. Nothing is resolved. The events put into motion seem to spill beyond the text into the obvious, unhappy Ogata future—an illegitimate grandson, and Shingo's imminent demise—circumstances symbolized in the oncoming winter and the drooping plants in the garden. One can almost hear the mountain roar.

NINA CORNYETZ

Further Readings

Translations

Kawabata is one of the most translated Japanese novelists, and the following list is by no means comprehensive. Edward Seidensticker, one of the finest translators of Japanese literature, has masterfully translated most of Kawabata's best works. (The quotations used in this article are from works translated by Seidensticker.) For additional titles of works translated into English, some by Seidensticker, and some by other translators, see Petersen's *Moon in the Water*, noted in the "Related Studies" section below.

Kawabata Yasunari. *The Sound of The Mountain.* Trans. Edward Seidensticker. New York: Alfred A. Knopf, 1970. Reprint. New York: Perigee Books, 1981.
———. *Snow Country.* Trans. Edward Seidensticker, New York: Alfred A. Knopf, 1956.
———. *Thousand Cranes.* Trans. Edward Seidensticker. New York: Alfred A. Knopf, 1958. Reprint. Berkley Medallion Edition. New York: Berkley Publishing Corp., 1965.
———. *Japan: The Beautiful and Myself.* Trans. Edward Seidensticker. Tokyo: Kodansha International Ltd., 1968. The translation of Kawabata's Nobel Prize acceptance speech.

Related Studies

Keene, Donald. "Kawabata Yasunari." In *Dawn to the West: Japanese Literature of the Modern Era,* 786–845. New York: Holt, Rinehart, and Winston, 1984. Keene's chapter on Kawabata is rich with biographical anecdotes, and offers a broad, general discussion of his corpus.
Miyoshi, Masao. "The Margins of Life." In *Accomplices of Silence: The Modern Japanese Novel,* 94–121. Berkeley, CA: University of California Press, 1974. An excellent and provocative close analysis of several of Kawabata's best-known works, including *Snow Country* and *Sound of the Mountain.*
Petersen, Gwenn Boardman. "Kawabata Yasunari." In *The Moon in the Water: Understanding Tanizaki, Kawabata, and Mishima,* 121–200. Honolulu: University Press of Hawaii, 1979. Petersen's chapter offers the most extensive biographical information of the four studies noted here, and differs, sometimes emphatically, from Miyoshi's and Ueda's interpretations. There is a complete list of works translated into English through 1979, and a chronology in outline form of his literary activities.
Ueda Makoto. *Modern Japanese Writers and the Nature of Literature.* Stanford, CA: Stanford University Press, 1976. See 173–218, "Kawabata Yasunari," for a fascinating and informative discussion of Kawabata's fictional and theoretical works.
Vernon, Victoria. *Daughters of the Moon: Wish, Will, and Social Constraint in Fiction by Modern Japanese Women.* Berkeley, CA: University of California, Institute of East Asian Studies, 1988. See "Creating Koharu: The Image of Women in the Works of Kawabata Yasunari and Tanizaki Jun'ichiro," 171–204. Vernon offers valuable insights into the construction of women in Kawabata's work, comparing his depictions with typical characterizations of the canon, as well as with renditions by his contemporaries.

THE FICTIONAL WORKS OF ENCHI FUMIKO

Author: Enchi Fumiko
Born: 1905, Tokyo
Died: 1986
Major Works
  Translated: *The Waiting Years (Onnazaka)* (1957); *Masks (Onnamen)* (1958); *Love in Two Lives: The Remnant (Nisei no en-shūi)* (1958)
  Untranslated: *Banshun Sōya* (1928); *Himojii Tsukihi* (1954); *Ake o ubau mono* (1969); *Yūkon* (1972); *Namamiko monogatari* (1965); *Shokutoku no nai ie* (1979)

Major Themes

While social dictates prevented women from active insubordination, literature has long functioned as an outlet for Japanese women to speak honestly on the female experience.

The ethical and moral codes of behavior of the dominant Japanese male have deeply wounded Japanese women over the centuries.

The repressed rage of repeated betrayals suffered by women is formidable if unleashed.

The ongoing suppression of their deepest thoughts and passions have bound women in a female community through the ages.

Enchi Fumiko first entered the literary scene as a playwright, but she is most celebrated for the prose fiction that she wrote after World War II. Born into a family well-educated in the Japanese classical literary tradition, the daughter of the scholar, Ueda Kazutoshi, Enchi's childhood was enriched by access to his extensive library. However, Enchi apparently found her deepest inspiration in the figure of her grandmother, whose actual life and wealthy repertoire of folklore and old tales captured young Enchi's imagination. By the age of 17, frustrated with unstimulating studies at Japan Women's College High School she quit school, determined to be a writer. Privately, with the support of her father, she pursued the study of English, Christianity, and classical Chinese literature.

It is believed that Enchi turned her hand to playwriting in the 1920s, when she first began to write because the dominant literary genre was ill adapted to the exploration of fiction inspired by the classics. Enchi was not interested in writing what was then in vogue: confessional exposés of the author's own life. Conversely, the experimental, socialist-leaning "new theater" *(shingeki)* offered a venue permitting reference to the classics and separation

of theme from realism and naturalism. Enchi enjoyed substantial recognition through the 1920s and '30s, thanks to the patronage of an important male figure in the new theater movement with whom she studied drama, Osanai Kaoru (1881–1928). Her *"Banshun Sōya"* ("A Turbulent Night in Late Spring") (1928) was the first play by a woman performed at the new theater playhouse. During this time she also forged personal and professional friendships with women in the forefront of the literary scene.

Enchi Fumiko's unfulfilling marriage to journalist Enchi Yoshimatsu in 1930 and the birth of her daughter in 1932 were contemporaneous with declining public interest in the new theater, factors that may have been catalysts in shifting Enchi's attention to fiction writing. She published several prose works in 1939, followed by a lengthy creative silence through the second world war and personal hardship. In 1946, Enchi underwent a hysterectomy for uterine cancer, as well as a mastectomy, passing months near death in the hospital. Her recovery seems to have rejuvenated her creative impulses. She began to write again, but for a while her work was repeatedly rejected for publication.

Female writers were still often dependent upon the patronage of powerful men of letters for critical acclaim, and with the death of the leader of the new theater, Enchi had lost hers. Enchi, however, persevered with limited success. Recognition came with her more accomplished *Days of Hunger* (*Himojii Tsukihi*) (1954), which won the praise of a famous male writer, Masamune Hakuchō, and for which she was awarded the Women's Literature Prize. Her most celebrated works followed: *The Waiting Years* (*Onnazaka*) (1957), which won the Noma Literary Prize; *Masks* (*Onnamen*) (1958), and a translation into modern Japanese of the most revered text of the canon, the eleventh-century *The Tale of Genji* (*Genji monogatari*), a project that spanned 1967–1972. Ill health returned to plague Enchi in her later years, and she had lost her sight by the time she had completed the translation of *The Tale of Genji*. Many critics came to consider Enchi the finest modern Japanese woman writer: she was awarded the Tanizaki Jun'ichirō Prize for Literature in 1969, the Distinguished Cultural Achievement Award in 1970, the Grand Literary Prize of Japan in 1972, and was honored with the highest possible award—the Order of Cultural Merit, presented by the emperor in 1985.

It seems that her old-fashioned diction and style, intertextual incorporation of the classics, and the feminist tone of her fiction contributed to her delayed success. Enchi interwove motifs, archetypes, and stories from the canon—most frequently from Heian period (794–1185), women-authored literature—within her own work, resulting in narratives that did not neatly fit existing genre categories. For *The Tale of the False Shamaness* (*Namamiko monogatari*) (1965) she invented a Heian antecedent, and she structured *Love in Two Lives: The Remnant* (*Nisei no en-shūi*) (1958) from a mixture of Ueda Akinari's *The Bond Spanning Two Lives* (*Nisei no en*) (c. 1802) and her own life and imagination. Her works resembled yet deviated from historical fiction—inventing and reinterpreting history, exploring characters' psychological motivations in a thoroughly modern fashion, and depicting women enraged at injustice suffered at the hands of their empowered husbands. The spe-

cific motifs of the canon incorporated by Enchi set the foreground for female spiritual possession, Buddhist doctrines on female sin and female pollution, hidden and unfulfilled female sexuality, and female jealousy. Her renditions expressed the inner lives of female narrative subjects, giving voice to a repressed and angry womanhood disruptive to the harmony and beauty of the old texts. She conversely reconfigured the classical model of feuding women with a harmonious female community forged through the shared experience of oppression. Throughout her work is a stinging indictment of premodern and modern female sociopolitical disempowerment, and depictions of a legacy of female insubordination born of repressed rage and enacted through supernatural empowerment.

Enchi wrote finely crafted fiction, culled from her extensive knowledge of the classics, in a masterful, evocative prose style. Enchi was also important because of her brave and tenacious narrative confrontation of female rage, sexuality, agency, and despondency in a literary period dominated by male writers and critics. Her innovative use of the classics, which employs citations and references to unsettle, rather than echo, many of the dominant paradigms of those classics, has become a mainstay of female narrative expression in the contemporary period. Powerful and honest passions imbue Enchi's work with a strong universalist appeal.

The Waiting Years

Enchi's celebrated novel, *The Waiting Years*, is deeply indebted to the Heian period classic, *The Tale of Genji*. The narrative structure of *The Waiting Years* replicates that of the classical *monogatari* (fictional tale), by tracing the history of a family over many years, yet *The Waiting Years* also overturns much of its "mother" texts. Focused on the inner torment suffered by women at the hands of male polygamy, the book is a heartfelt lament over both premodern and modern female subordination.

Translated as *The Waiting Years*, the Japanese title, *Onnazaka*, literally means "Woman Slope," a metaphor for the relentless, uphill battle of protagonist Tomo's difficult life. Married at the tender age of 14 to a civil servant of moderate position, Yukitomo Shirakawa, Tomo is mother to a dysfunctional son at 15 and a daughter soon thereafter. The book begins as Tomo travels to Tokyo in her early 20s, having been entrusted with the cruel task of finding a mistress for her husband. Beneath meticulous descriptions of kimonos, flower arrangements, and household details, which imbue the work with the flavor of classical romances, is layered an exposé of Tomo's deep, repressed passions, of jealousy and desire, rage and despondency at her husband's insatiably wandering eye. Beholding the innocent girl, Suga, whom she has just selected and purchased for her husband's sexual pleasure, "[p]ity welled up at the sorry fate of the girl fluttering before her like a great butterfly, and with it a jealousy that flowed about her body in a rapid, scorching stream" (Bester, trans., 1971).

Suga is just 15 when she is installed in the Shirakawa household, but within a few years, Yukitomo procures another, younger concubine. Yukitomo's sexual excesses eventually lead him into a liaison with his daughter-in-law, which has the potential to destabilize the family that Tomo has singlehandedly maintained. Overseer of the household finances and business transactions, as well as of the concubines, maids, children, and eventual grandchildren, Tomo tirelessly subordinates her needs and passions to the longevity, reputation, and health of the family, indoctrinated with a "feminine ethic that had taught her to yield to her husband's wishes in every respect, however unreasonable they might seem. . . . barely able to read and write, she ha[s] no shield to defend herself other than the existing moral code" (Bester, trans., 1971). Betrayal follows betrayal at the hands of her despotic husband, and finding nothing for herself in her dependent and sorrowful female plight, Tomo progressively turns to Buddhism and the promise of salvation in the afterlife.

Her final humiliation finds her dying before Yukitomo, in spite of his substantial maturity and her determination to outlive him. It is only in her dying moments that Tomo finally expresses her rage to her husband, demanding that her body be dumped at sea in place of a proper burial. Hearing her words, her husband finally glimpses the depths of her lifelong despair.

Although *The Waiting Years* is structurally organized around the relationship of Tomo and Yukitomo, the book is more accurately described as about the relationships among the women who are bound together by varying degrees of powerlessness against the male-centric social fabric that enfolds them. Tomo has no recourse but to serve her husband lest he abandon her; Suga has no survival skills for a different sort of life. A fierce camaraderie develops between the women in spite of copresent jealousies over the inevitable inequities of their rigidly hierarchical social positions of wife, concubine, or maid. The women who thus might have been bitter rivals are unified through their economic and social dependence on, and suppressed anger at, Yukitomo. Tomo, as household matriarch, is progressively possessed of an awesome inner strength born of her capacity to endure repeated emotional trauma. When Yukitomo seduces his daughter-in-law Miya, Tomo experiences "a fierce wrath that stood up to Yukitomo, the ungovernable male, and took beneath its protective wing Suga, Yumi, and even the offending Miya herself" (Bester, trans., 1971).

Female community as envisioned in Enchi's fiction is a powerful inversion of the conceit of the classical monogatari, in which the jealous spirits of spurned women wreak havoc upon their female rivals. In *The Waiting Years* the women (even rivals) are bound together by subordination, and anger is appropriately directed at the social systems that, and the actual men who, oppress them.

Masks

While *The Waiting Years* is a realistic presentation of Tomo's female endurance, *Masks* is a magical-realist exploration of the explosion of female rage. *Masks* is the story of widow Mieko Togano's relentless pursuit of revenge on her now deceased, previously philandering husband, Masatsugu, which consists of complex manipulations to produce a baby with the Togano name but no Togano blood. Combining the suspense of a mystery with references to old tales of the supernatural, *Masks* reincarnates sorceresses of the Japanese canon in the bodies and psyches of mid-twentieth-century women. Mieko's plan, her supernatural powers, and her motivations are only gradually clarified as the novel unfolds.

By the end, it is clear that as a young bride Mieko suffered a miscarriage caused by Masatsugu's mistress, who had herself been forced to undergo two abortions. Determined to defraud the Togano patrilineage, Mieko gives birth to twins fathered by another man but passed off as Togano offspring. Her son dies before producing an heir, and thus Mieko's retarded daughter Harume (brain-damaged by the pressure of her twin brother's feet on her head in the womb) becomes the only possible vehicle for the continued fraudulent Togano lineage. Mieko's deceased son's wife, Yasuko, becomes her co-conspirator. Together the two women bewitch and trick a man, Ibuki, into impregnating Harume. Harume dies shortly after giving birth to the second Togano heir impostor. Mieko and Yasuko thereby successfully reclaim matrilineage from its subordination to patrilineage through the bitter sacrifice of Mieko's damaged daughter for a healthy, male, false heir.

The present-day tale posits the Rokujō Lady, one of Prince Genji's abandoned conquests from the classic *The Tale of Genji*, as Mieko's prototype. A scholarly essay by Mieko embedded within the primary text, "An Account of the Shrine in the Fields," reinterprets the typically villainized Rokujō Lady as a victim of the paramour Genji and the restrictive social codes of the period. In her essay, Mieko writes that the female author of *The Tale of Genji*, Murasaki Shikibu, "was able to combine women's extreme ego suppression and ancient female shamanism, showing both in opposition to men. . . . Just as there is an archetype of woman as the object of man's eternal love, so there must be an archetype of her as the object of his eternal fear, representing, perhaps, the shadow of his own evil actions. The Rokujō Lady is an embodiment of this archetype" (Carpenter, trans., 1983).

Both Mieko and the Rokujō Lady are likened to the *ryō no onna* female archetype of the noh thea-

ter, as women who will not sublimate their strong wills to male dictates, and whose only outlet for jealousy and passion is revenge through spiritual possession. Mad and obsessed women are often depicted in noh, and function collectively in *Masks* as a motif symbolic of Mieko's sustained, specifically female, supernatural realm, and in conflict with the male, mundane world. In chapter one, "*Ryō no Onna*," Mieko receives the *ryō no onna* noh mask depicting the vengeful spirit of an older woman. The title of the second chapter, "*Masugami*," is the term for the mask used to portray a mad young woman in a sexual and spiritual frenzy. Chapter three is called "*Fukai*" in reference to the mask symbolic of post-traumatic resolution, middle-age, and motherhood. Traditionally, the noh plays portraying mad women end with harmony after the deadly female spirit has somehow been exorcised. Enchi's version offers an ironic, and inverted closure in which frenzy abates through the successful fulfillment of female revenge, and the defrauding of male order with a female one, as the community of spiritually empowered women nurture the false male heir.

Nina Cornyetz

Further Reading

Translations

Enchi Fumiko. "Love in Two Lives: The Remnant." Trans. and Eds. Noriko Mizuta Lippit and Kyoko Iriye Selden. In *Japanese Women Writers*, 97–111. Armonk, NY: M. E. Sharpe, East-Gate Book, 1991. There is an excellent introductory essay on Japanese women writers.

———. "A Bond for Two Lifetimes: Gleanings." [The same story as above.] Phyllis Birnbaum, trans. and ed. In *Rabbits, Crabs, Etc.: Stories by Japanese Women*, 25–47. Honolulu: University of Hawaii Press, 1982.

———. *Masks*. Trans. Juliet Winters Carpenter. New York: Aventura-Vintage, 1983.

———. *The Waiting Years*. Trans. John Bester. Tokyo: Kodansha International, 1971.

———. "Enchantress." Trans. John Bester. In

Modern Japanese Short Stories, 90–117. Seidensticker, Bester and Morris, eds. Tokyo: Japan Publications Trading Co., Ltd. 1961.

Related Studies

Bargen, Doris G. "Twin Blossoms on a Single Branch: The Cycle of Retribution in *Onnamen.*" In *Monumenta Nipponica* 46:2 (1991): 147–172. A meticulously researched and detailed analysis of *Masks'* allusions to, and positioning among antecedent texts, with an informative discussion of the narrative significance of the aborted and miscarried fetuses.

Ruch, Barbara. "Beyond Absolution: Enchi Fumiko's *The Waiting Years* and *Masks.*" In *Masterworks of Asian Literature in Comparative Perspective.* Barbara Stoler Miller, ed. Armonk, NY: M. E. Sharpe, East-Gate Book, 1994. Ruch's chapter on Enchi is rich in both biographical detail and analytic discussion, and includes interesting comparisons with some Western literary figures and works.

Vernon, Victoria. *Daughters of the Moon: Wish, Will, and Social Constraint in Fiction by Modern Japanese Women.* See "Between Osan and Koharu: The Representation of Woman in The Works of Hayashi Fumiko and Enchi Fumiko." Berkeley: University of California, Institute of East Asian Studies, 1988. Vernon's reading compares Enchi's portrayals of women with the archetypes of the canon, and with depictions by several of her contemporaries, including Kawabata Yasunari, Hayashi Fumiko, and Tanizaki Jun'ichiro.

Winters, Juliet Carpenter. "Enchi Fumiko: 'A Writer of Tales.'" *Japan Quarterly* 38:3 (July–September, 1990): 343–55. A good source for biographical information on Enchi.

THE NOVELS OF MISHIMA YUKIO

Author: Mishima Yukio (original name Hiraoka Kimitake)
Born: 1925, Tokyo
Died: 1970, Tokyo
Major Works of Fiction: *Confessions of the Mask (Kamen no kokuhaku)* (1949); *Thirst for Love (Ai no kawaki)* (1950); *The Sound of the Waves (Shiosai)* (1954); *The Temple of the Golden Pavilion (Kin Kajuji)* (1956); *After the Banquet (Utage no ato)* (1960); *Patriotism (Yukoku)* (1960); *The Sea of Fertility (Hojo no umi)* (1970)

Major Themes

Literature aims at an interpretation of the universe and a deep perception of humanity by means of language.

In the ideal world, boxing and art would shake hands without being forced, physical strength and intellectual vigor would run hand in hand, and life and art would smile at one another.

Considered by some as the most important Japanese novelist of the twentieth century, Mishima Yukio was a thinker who expressed himself not only through his fiction, drama, and essays but also through his entire way of life. Mishima's early fictional work was somewhat autobiographical; however, his efforts soon encompassed a large range of fictional form and content. His novels are generally well crafted and often experimental—revealing a sensuous, imaginative appreciation of natural detail, accompanied by probing psychological analysis and a certain sense of irony or understated humor. The central theme of many of his works is the dichotomy between traditional Japanese values and the spiritual barrenness of contemporary life. More than many of his contemporaries, Mishima was steeped in both the literature of Japan and that of the West, especially the classics of both cultures. His works exhibit the harmony and the contradictions that came with this exposure.

Son of a government official, Mishima's early education was spent at the elite Peers' School where he developed a keen interest in the Japanese classics. His literary inclinations and the discovery of his own homosexual tendencies made him feel like an outsider in the military-style school. Having failed to qualify physically for military service, he worked in a Tokyo aircraft factory during World War II. After the war he studied law at the University of Tokyo and for a short time was employed in the banking division of the Ministry of Finance. With the success of his first novel, *Confessions of the Mask*, Mishima began to devote himself full-time to writing. Mishima made his first trip abroad in 1952, traveling to New York, Rio de Janeiro, Paris, and Greece. He was especially attracted to Greece, where he resolved to improve his own appearance through weightlifting, as well as the Japanese martial arts of karate and kendo. Mishima's works were much sought after and although he strove to produce works that were greatly experimental he also produced a great deal of popular fiction in order to be able to live comfortably. Nevertheless, Mishima grew increasingly torn between his Western lifestyle and his rage against Japan's imitation of the West, and became attracted to an austere patriotism and what he perceived as the martial spirit of Japan's past. On November 25, 1970, the day he submitted the final installment of his last novel, *The Sea of Fertility*, he and members of his "private" army broke into a Japanese military headquarters in Tokyo, where he committed ritual suicide.

Desire and Obstruction

At age 16, Mishima wrote his first short story "The Forest in Full Bloom" ("*Hanazakari no mori*") for a literary revue in 1941. The narrator describes his ancestors, who in some sense still live with him, sharing his love for the sea and the sun of the south. The story abounds in metaphors and aphorisms and shows Mishima's pacifist tendencies and a sense of the cult of beauty and death that he was to cultivate throughout most of his later works.

It was not until 1949, when he published his pseudo-autobiography, *Confessions of the Mask*, that he truly revealed his precocious genius. The novel describes in thinly disguised form the traumatic images of the author's childhood, his student life at the Peers' School and the University of Tokyo, his wartime experiences, and his decision to leave his job with the government. Mishima's main intent in the work is to present significant moments of his self-awareness. The title suggests the influence of his mentors at school, who brought him into contact with Japanese romantics, a group of intellectuals who insisted on the uniqueness of the Japanese people and their history. Eroticism and death, youth and beauty fuse as the novel's narrator joyfully anticipates an early death and a final holocaust that will annihilate Japan at the end of the war. He feels cheated when that holocaust never really occurs and he find himself still alive. The work was not fully understood by many readers, who were baffled, for example, by the homosexual proclivities of the hero that prevent him from feeling desire for the girl he loves. Unlike young men found in other works of literature, the young man fails to win the hand of the girl he loves not because she is betrothed to another, but because he can no longer live up to the image society created for him. Instead he recounts the path that leads him to his self-identity.

Mishima followed the success of his autobiographical novel with a series of works of fiction and drama whose main characters exhibit various degrees of physical or psychological torment—often set in places with which the author was not personally familiar. An example is his next major novel, *Thirst for Love*, which is a short work, influenced by the writing of François Mauriac that blends passion and violence with poetic language. Etsuko, the central figure, is a widow who has become her father-in-law's mistress. The neurotic woman lives half in a world of harsh reality and half in a world of fantasy that revolves around Saburo, a young farmer whom she desires. In the end she cannot reciprocate Saburo's love when Saburo discovers her love for him, and she kills him. Etsuko can never obtain what she wants, for she is a intense woman of the inner world and cannot relate to Saburo, a muscular man of the outer world. The chief interest of this work is how Mishima deliberately sets out to create a his own world of fiction, one divorced from that found in the "I" novels of contemporary fiction.

Stretching His Horizons

Renouncing his predilection for darkness and death, Mishima discovered his brighter, more classical side following his trip abroad in 1952. Greece signified sunlit strength as opposed to the weakness of the haunted, martyred Japanese intellectual of his time. The first product of this insight was *The Sound of Waves* (*Shiosai*), written in 1954. Inspired by the ancient Greek romance *Daphne and Chloe*, Mishima brilliantly manipulates the old amorous tale, adding carefully chosen details of the lives of a fisherboy and fishergirl who live on a small isle off the coast of Ise. Mishima seems to have thought of this work as an exercise in style that would demonstrate that he could depict the brighter side of life as well as take a hackneyed story and make it come alive.

Most critics believe that Mishima's finest work is *The Temple of the Golden Pavilion*, a story drawn from an actual event familiar to his readers. The novel, which was widely acclaimed in both Japan and abroad, recounts the events leading up to the burning of a famous Buddhist temple by a troubled young acolyte who cannot attain an inner sense of religion and beauty to match that of the temple. The importance of the novel lies in the author's tracing the circumstances that make the final act unavoidable—similar in effect to the inevitable course of a Greek tragedy. The sumptuous virtuosity of Mishima's psychoanalysis of love turned to hate and his aptitude in translating the language of contemplation give the novel, heavily influenced by Thomas Mann, a philosophical dimension unsurpassed by any of his other works.

Many of Mishima's later works were experimental and uneven in their popular reception. *Kyoko's House* is a long, ambitious, and unsuccessful novel in which the four main characters portray different aspects of himself. It is less a novel then "a study in nihilism." This was followed by the more successful *After the Banquet*, an entertaining book that followed too closely the private life of a gubernatorial candidate. As a result, he was sued for libel and lost the case.

Theater of Death

Starting sometime in the early 1960s, Mishima came to ally himself with the ideology of the extreme right, even while pursuing his own personal phantasms. *Patriotism*, probably his best novella, dramatizes the suicide of a young officer (and his wife) who participated in the abortive nationalist coup d'état of February 26, 1936, the first of several references to this incident in his works. The participants had attempted to wrest power from "corrupt" politicians and restore it to the emperor. *The Voices of Dead Heroes* (1966) reproaches the emperor, through the mouths of kamikaze pilots killed during the war, for having renounced his divine origin—the cement that, according to the nationalists, binds the Japanese people.

From 1965 to the morning of his death in 1970, Mishima worked on his last novel, the tetralogy *The Sea of Fertility*, which he considered to be the summation of his work as a novelist. It is a great work that concerns the transformation of Japan into a modern but sterile society. The length of the work and the abundance of dogmatic material it contains relating to Buddhism are overwhelming. However, it is precisely in the work's totality that its power and the beauty of its architecture are disclosed. Even if the major theme of incarnation does not lead one to conversion, it still conveys to the work a intrinsic sense of dramatic and poetic unity.

The first volume, *Spring Snow* (*Haru no yuki*), invokes the feminine ideals of Japan. It is a romance, told in a florid style and great detail, that evokes the world of the aristocracy at the beginning of the twentieth century. The second, *The Runaway Horse* (*Homba*), in contrast, characterizes the masculine martial ideal. Set in the 1930s, it follows the reincarnation of the hero as a boy so caught up in his devotion to the emperor that he plots political assassination with others. The third volume, *The Temple of Dawn* (*Akatsuki no tera*), which takes place in southeast Asia as well as in Japan, depicts a very corrupt world. The final installment of the tetralogy, *The Decay of the Angel* (*Tenin gosui*), presents the last reincarnation, an ordinary youth destroyed by his tragic destiny and unattainable ideals. Mishima's fascination with the ideals of the February 26, 1936, coup-plotters eventually led him to emulate them in fiction, as well as in his own life.

Views on Life and Literature

One cannot understand Mishima's concept of literature apart from his attitude toward life and reality. Early on, Mishima sought to conquer the world with words. He thought of himself as a "classical writer." By this he meant that his works could be understood only if they and their characters were recognized as classical prototypes—symbols of form, content, and character. The chief function of literature is to disperse fear of the chaotic and unknown. The writer works on raw nature and creates an order out of the disorder.

His concept of literature and its relation to reality changed radically over time. He felt more and more strongly that literature, because it was so personal, was actually powerless to reshape life. Instead, it was action or physical strength, not the mind, that had the potential to reshape nature into an ideal order. The role of literature changed from life-shaper to life recorder. A literary artist was to observe and describe the external world, the world not as what it was but as it changed into an ideal order through the efforts of men of action.

Toward the end of his life, he sought to make concrete these concepts by aligning himself with ultra-nationalist sentiments against the decadence he perceived in present-day Japan.

KENNETH G. KOZIOL

Further Reading

Translations

Bester, John, trans. *Acts of Worship: Seven Stories.* Tokyo: Kodansha International Ltd., 1989.
———. *Death in Midsummer and Other Stories.* New York: New Directions, 1966.
Keene, Donald, trans. *After the Banquet.* New York: Alfred A. Knopf, 1963.
Marks, Alfred H., trans. *Forbidden Colors.* New York: Alfred A. Knopf, 1968.
———. *Thirst for Love.* New York: Alfred A. Knopf, 1969.
Morris, Ivan, trans. *The Temple of the Golden Pavilion.* New York: Alfred A. Knopf, 1959.
Nathan, J., trans. *The Sailor Who Fell from Grace with the Sea.* New York: Alfred A. Knopf, 1963.
———. *Sea of Fertility: A Cycle of Four Novels.* New York: Alfred A. Knopf, 1972–1974.
Weatherby, Meredith, trans. *Confessions of the Mask.* New York: Alfred A. Knopf, 1958.
———. *The Sound of Waves.* New York: Alfred A. Knopf, 1963.

Related Studies

Miller, Henry. *Reflections on the Death of Mishima.* Santa Barbara, CA: Capra Press, 1972. Contemplates the meaning of Mishima's life and death.
Napier, Susan J. *Escape from Wasteland: Romanticism in the Fiction of Mishima Yukio and Oe Kenzaburo.* Cambridge, MA: Harvard University Press, 1991. Compares the two novelists and the influence of Japanese romanticism in their works.
Nathan, John. *Mishima: A Biography.* Boston: Little, Brown, 1974. A detailed biography of Mishima Yukio.
Petersen, Gwenn Boardman. *The Moon in the Water: Understanding Tanizaki, Kawabata, and Mishima.* Honolulu: University Press of Hawaii, 1979. Compares the work of three major Japanese novelists.
Scott-Stokes, Henry. *The Life and Death of Yukio Mishima.* New York: Farrar, Straus, and Giroux, 1974. A definitive biography of the writer.
Wolfe, Peter. *Yukio Mishima.* New York: Continuum, 1989. Examines Mishima's literature and life.
Yourcenar, Marguerite. *Mishima: A Vision of the Void.* New York: Farrar, Straus, and Giroux, 1986. Explores the literature and philosophy of Mishima Yukio.

THE NOVELS OF ARIYOSHI SAWAKO

Author: Ariyoshi Sawako
Born: 1931, Wakayama City, Japan
Died: 1984, Japan
Major Novels: *The River Ki* (1959), *The Doctor's Wife* (1967), *The Twilight Years* (1972), *Kabuki Dancer* (1972)

Major Themes

By investing authority in the oldest male child, the male-dominant Japanese family system encourages unnatural rivalry between mothers and daughters-in-law and diminishes the lives of all the females in the family.

In emergencies and times of crisis, primal matrilineal forces draw children to the family of the mother for assistance and protection.

In Japanese society a woman may draw strength from the cultural traditions that suppress her.

By balancing the modern with the traditional, modern Japanese women may take advantage of the strengths of their traditional culture while achieving greater independence and personal fulfillment.

Modern medical science has lengthened the lives of elder Japanese family members, creating stress and frustration for the younger family members who must, according to Confucian doctrine, care for and honor their elders.

Ariyoshi Sawako was born in Wakayama City, Ki province, the region in which several of her novels are set. Like Tanizaki, Ariyoshi had a keen interest in theater, especially Kabuki, an interest that is expressed not only in her many plays, but also in the skill she displays in the use of dialogue to provide narrative focus and to delineate character in her short stories and novels. As a novelist she pursues a wide range of subjects and issues including environmental problems, racism, the suppression of women in Japanese society, the position of women in the traditional Jaapanese family, and problems associated with aging in modern Japan. Her interest in history, especially women in Japanese history, gives rise to her use of the historical novel form to explore the position of women in Japanese society and the contributions of women to the development of Japanese culture. She is also quite capable of a graphic examination of social issues as they arise in contemporary contexts. Three of her novels, *The Doctor's Wife, The River Ki,* and *The Twilight Years* provide a critique of Japanese society and culture spanning more than 200 years.

The Doctor's Wife

Hanaoka seishu no tsuma, or *The Doctor's Wife*, is a historical novel set in late-eighteenth- and early-nineteenth-century Japan, the middle of the Tokugawa period, a period of peace and stability that lasted 268 years under the shoguns and their samurai feudal vassals. It was during this period that the samurai warrior class abandoned the sword to become wealthy land-owning farmers and bureaucrats who strictly regulated all phases of Japanese life. In *The Doctor's Wife*, Ariyoshi examines the relationship of Hanakoa Kae, the wife of Hanaoka Seishu, a famous historical Japanese physician, and her mother-in-law, Otsugi. In the traditional Japanese family, the father shares authority with his eldest son, not his wife, and so an adult son has authority over his mother. When the father dies, the mother finds herself on a level with the son's wife, her daughter-in-law, with whom she must compete for her son's attention and approval. Throughout the novel, there are references to this perennial problem, a problem exacerbated in *The Doctor's Wife* by the youthful beauty of the mother-in-law, whose rivalry with, and jealousy of, her daughter-in-law has unmistakable sexual overtones.

Hanaoka Otsugi is elegant, graceful, dignified, and beautiful. Always conscious of her appearance, she dresses with impeccable care and taste. The daughter of a wealthy landowner and businessman, she is given in marriage to Hanaoka Naomichi, a poor surgeon who has cured her of a virulent skin condition in exchange for marrying her. Despite the lowering of her social station brought about by her marriage, Otsugi accepts her position dutifully and strives to assist her husband in any way she can. Unfortunately, her husband does not succeed financially, and so he and she put all their hopes in their son Umpei, later to be known as Seishu.

Otsugi's beauty becomes legendary in Kishu province, so much so that eight-year-old Imose Kae, the daughter of a high-ranking samurai family, begs her nurse to take her to see the surgeon's wife. Seeing the famous beauty in the garden of her ramshackle home causes Kae to become deeply infatuated with Otsugi. Because Otsugi's husband is physician to Kae's grandfather, Kae's early memory of Otsugi's beauty and grace is kept alive and strengthened by contrast with Naomichi's ugliness and slovenly manner of dress. During his visits to the Inmose household, Naomichi has apparently taken note of Kae and learned of her character and skill in cooking and sewing, for when Kae is 21, Otsugi calls upon Kae's father to offer her son, Umpei, in marriage to Kae. Because of Otsugi's inferior social position, Kae's father does not seriously entertain the proposal, but Otsugi's persistence, Kae's mother's support, and Kae's delight at the prospect of becoming Otsugi's daughter-in-law finally convince her father to allow her to marry Umpei. Because he is away studying medicine in Kyoto, Umpei does not attend his own wedding. Instead the groom's place at the ceremony is taken by the *Honzo Komoku*, a famous book of herbal remedies.

From the wedding until the arrival of Umpei 18 months later, Otsugi treats Kae with warmth and affection. While awaiting the return of her husband, Kae volunteers to participate with her sisters-

in-law, Okatsu and Koriku, in the family weaving enterprise, all the proceeds of which are sent to Kyoto to support Umpei. Kae quickly learns to weave; and because of her creative designs, her work soon becomes popular with the merchants. Meanwhile, because all of the family's income must go to Umpei, the family remains poor. As time passes, Kae's affection for Otsugi grows, and they develop a close mother-daughter relationship. With the return home of Umpei, however, Otsugi's attitude undergoes a radical change.

No sooner does Umpei arrive home than his mother begins to lavish attention on him, praising his sisters for their hard work and sacrifice in support of his studies, but ignoring completely the part played by his wife. On the night of his arrival, Otsugi suggests that Umpei sleep alone, giving his need for rest as the reason for her suggestion. Later that evening Kae hears Umpei and Otsugi talking and laughing in his room, and to Kae, Otsugi's laugh sounds "lascivious." Later, Kae is irritated by the familiarity of Otsugi's application of the affix "*san*" to Umpei's name, and Kae feels a nagging intuition that "Otsugi's relationship with her son [is] more romantic than motherly." In the days and weeks following Umpei's return home, Otsugi becomes cold and distant from her daughter-in-law, and Kae recognizes that Otsugi has only pretended to be friendly and loving to her. Throughout the remainder of the novel, Kae finds herself in constant competition with her mother-in-law for the attention and affection of Umpei, who becomes known as Dr. Seishu. Although Seishu and Kae have a daughter within two years of their marriage, Kae's vulnerability is complicated by her failure to produce a male heir, a fact Otsugi comments on.

The competition between Otsugi and Kae reaches a climax when they both volunteer to be subjects Seishu's experiments in developing a general anesthesia for use in surgical procedures. His dream has been to develop a surgical procedure to cure breast cancer in women as well as other heretofore untreatable, and therefore terminal, conditions. Before he has developed his anesthesia to the point that it can be tested on humans, his sister

Okatsu dies of breast cancer. Up to this point, Seishu has experimented on hundreds of dogs and cats who have been brought to his clinic by patients and students. Perhaps realizing that the rivalry between his mother and wife are at the root of their willingness to serve as subjects, Seishu accepts both of their offers, allowing his mother to be the first to test the anesthesia. Seishu gives Otsugi a moderate dose of the principal ingredient of his formula, watching her closely as she exhibits symptoms of pain and disorientation before finally becoming unconscious for a few hours. Otsugi revives, believing she has been the instrument of her son's success, whereas Seishu confides in Kae that the dose he mixed for his mother was very mild and contained an antidote. He used sake as a medium for the concoction, and so he attributes his mother's symptoms to the effects of alcohol. Seishu uses Kae for the first real test of his formula. The dose Seishu mixes for Kae is many times more powerful and contains more powerful ingredients than the mixture taken previously by Otsugi. Kae undergoes considerable pain, high fever, and delirium before finally falling into a deep sleep for three days. Seishu remains at her side throughout the ordeal, and he feeds her black bean soup from his own mouth in order to speed her recovery. Witnessing the tender solicitude of her son for his wife infuriates Otsugi, and she insists that her son once more give her the anesthesia. Again, he gives her a mild dose, more to placate her than to learn anything new.

The following summer, Kae's daughter, Koben, dies of pneumonia, and Kae has begun to realize that as a result of her husband's experiment on her, she is slowly going blind. Nevertheless, she once more undergoes a test of her husband's most refined formula, from which she recovers to find herself totally blind. Apparently, however, the blindness was caused by the original experiment, and Seishu becomes totally devoted to her, nearly failing to notice his own mother's death. A few months after Otsugi's death, Kae gives birth to a son, and several years later, at the age of 44, she has another daughter. In the meantime several important events occur in the lives of Seishu and Kae. When Seishu feels

confident enough to try his anesthesia on a patient suffering from breast cancer, he performs the operation successfully and becomes the first surgeon in history to remove a breast cancer surgically under general anesthesia. Ironically, his other sister, Koriku, who, like her older sister Okatsu, had sacrificed the chance for marriage and family for the sake of her brother, contracts an inoperable cancer of the carotid artery.

Kae believes that because of her, Koriku was never able to marry, and so as Koriku lies close to death, Kae asks her forgiveness. Koriku replies that she has nothing to forgive, that she has been aware from the outset of the contention between Kae and Otsugi and of the misery that rivalry caused Kae, including the loss of her sight. Koriku asserts that she is happy she never married, thereby avoiding the suffering of being a daughter-in-law subject to petty and painful rivalry with her mother-in-law and to the manipulation of her husband. Finally, she condemns men and characterizes the relationship between men and women as "disgusting." This scene is the climax of the novel, and Koriku's remarkable speech focuses powerfully the principal theme of *The Doctor's Wife*, that by investing authority in the oldest male child, the male dominant Japanese family system encourages unnatural rivalry between mothers and daughters-in-law and oppresses the lives of all the females in the family. In her final triumph over Otsugi, purchased at the cost of her sight, Kae achieves little more than to replace Otsugi as the model Japanese wife of her era. The final irony of the novel is dramatized by Seishi's enormous headstone hiding the much smaller ones of his mother and wife, suggesting that the figure of the historical physician is all that remains in view of a son, a husband, and a family that sacrificed all for his success.

The River Ki

Kinokawa or *The River Ki* is a sweeping narrative, spanning 61 years, from 1897 in the late Meiji era through the Taisho and post–World War II periods to 1958, the year Hana, the novel's principal protagonist, dies. Set in the Ki River valley in Wakayama Prefecture when Japan was completing its transformation from an agricultural and commercial economy to a modern industrial state, Ariyoshi's novel describes the decline of the wealthy landowning class in the face of modernization, industrialization, and the aftermath of World War II. A novel of character, *The River Ki* focuses on four women: Kimoto Toyono, her granddaughter, Hana, Hana's daughter, Fumio, and Fumio's daughter, Hanako. The narrative begins when Hana is 20 and about to be married. Hana and her grandmother, Toyono, are visiting the shrine at Jison-in to commemorate Hana's leaving the Kimoto family to be married to the eldest son of the Matani family of Musota.

At 76, Toyono, "the matriarch of the Kimoto family," is strong-willed, dignified, and aristocratic in her bearing. Following the death of Hana's mother, Toyono took upon herself the upbringing and education of her granddaughter, whose beauty and achievements represent the "full flowering" of the Kimoto family. Toyono is determined that her granddaughter will achieve the best possible marriage and will experience the lavish wedding that she, Toyono, was denied when her husband was adopted into the Kimoto family. It is Toyono who chooses the less socially distinguished Matanis over several more prominent but less dynamic families into which to marry her granddaughter. Even when she is strongly opposed by her son, Nobutaka, the head of the Kimoto family, her influence with Hana allows Toyono to prevail.

Instructed by her grandmother in all the requisite skills of an elegant aristocratic woman, Hana completed her education at the Girl's School in Wakayama City, where she learned the principle that the role of a Japanese wife is to bear children to preserve the family line. Like her grandmother, Hana is strong-willed and proud, drawing her strength from her willingness to remain a powerful but invisible influence in the shadow of her husband. Hana marries Matani Keisaku, an energetic, up-and-coming landowner and village headman, whose civic commitment and progressive programs of modernization bring him the respect of his peers and propel his political career to the national level.

Ariyoshi's text presents Hana as the ideal traditional Japanese woman—beautiful, intelligent, refined and submissive to her husband. Only once—in a short-lived, undeclared attraction to Kosaku, Keisaku's younger brother—does she waver inwardly from her unquestioning acceptance of her position. While Keisaku is a public man of action, Kosaku is an intellectual and a recluse, the latter circumstance brought on by poor health as well as by choice. Because of her long-standing interest in literature, Hana attempts on several occasions to discuss books with Kosaku but is rebuffed by her brother-in-law's blunt sarcasm. Ironically, Kosaku's behavior toward Hana masks his own infatuation with her. It is Kosaku who identifies Hana with the River Ki in a conversation with Fumio, Hana's rebellious daughter and his favorite niece. Pointing out that Hana is "a good example of a strong woman," Kosaku compares her with the Ki, whose beautiful celadon waters flow quietly, appearing peaceful and gentle on the surface but swallowing up all the weak rivers as it flows toward the sea.

Key Symbols

The river is the central symbol of a complex of four key symbols, all associated with Hana at various stages in her life following her marriage. The remaining three symbols are the branch of a persimmon tree that Toyono sent to be grafted on a tree near the gate of the Matani family estate, a six-foot white snake that lives in the ridge of the storehouse, and the white-walled three-storied central tower of Wakayama Castle. After the birth of Fumio, Hana's second child, Kosaku notices that the grafting of the persimmon branch has been successful, suggesting that having succeeded in fulfilling her function as a wife, Hana is now a full-fledged member of the Matani family.

The snake is presented in Ariyoshi's text as "the true master of the Matani household," bringing to mind a similar symbolic snake in Kawabata's *The*

Sound of the Mountain. It is following her daughter Fumio's wedding in Tokyo that Hana returns to Musota and first glimpses the white snake, a common life-symbol in world cultures. Near the end of the novel, Hana's death is signaled by the death of the white snake at the hands of Fumio's children.

By means of textual opposition, Ariyoshi uses the character of Hana's daughter, Fumio, to dramatize gender issues in *The River Ki*. As she grows through adolescence, Fumio challenges Hana's values as a traditional Japanese wife and mother. Tall and ungainly, Fumio is a rebellious and idealistic tomboy who resists stubbornly her mother's attempts to teach her flower arrangement, the tea ceremony, and koto playing; refuses to submit to the authority of her teachers at the Takayama Girl's School; and takes up the cudgels for a favorite progressive teacher who has been fired for his beliefs in freedom and democracy. After enrolling in the English Department at Tokyo Women's College, Fumio and a coterie of student-radicals establish a magazine which openly espouses women's rights and equality of the sexes. Even though she despises her mother's traditionalism and her father's position as a landowner, Fumio continues to write home for money. Finally, after graduating from college, Fumio is married to an ambitious young bank worker. After her marriage, Fumio becomes a devoted wife and mother, but she maintains her antagonism toward her parents, especially her mother, until shortly before Hana's death.

In Part III of the novel, Hana and her granddaughter, Hanako, have developed a relationship parallel to that of Toyono and Hana. As the final section of the narrative opens, Hana and Hanako are visiting Wakayama Castle, whose tower cannot be seen from within the grounds of the castle. It is blocked from view by tall stone walls, suggesting the walls of convention, poise, and self-discipline behind which Hana has hidden from the world. From a distance, however, the tower can be seen in all its beauty, and when Hana sees it destroyed by an American bombing raid, she staggers and falls to her knees. Even though the castle is later rebuilt, the aftermath of the war brings land-reform and an end to the way of life of the wealthy land-holding class.

In *The River Ki*, Ariyoshi once again presents an idealized portrait of the traditional Japanese woman—this time almost completely without the hidden flaws of Otsugi and Kae—in conflict with a daughter who is a rebellious radical feminist, striving to throw off the burden of male oppression that has made of submissiveness a seeming strength and virtue. Hana's perfection is also contrasted with her husband's weakness: Keisaku's philandering began shortly after his marriage and did not end until his death. Finally, in Hanako, Ariyoshi presents a synthesis of the best features of her mother and grandmother. She is independent, having worked her way through college and having made a career for herself in publishing, but respectful of her grandmother and the traditions that are reflected in the old woman's wisdom, strength, and grace. At 27, having learned that her grandmother is dying, Hanako returns to Musota. The novel ends as she revisits the newly rebuilt Wakayama castle tower to view the River Ki winding through the valley in the distance.

The Twilight Years

In *Kokostu no hito*, or *The Twilight Years*, Ariyoshi calls into question the Confucian notions of filial piety, especially as they relate to one's obligation to care for one's aged parents. The principal protagonist and focal character in *The Twilight Years* is Tachibana Akiko, a middle-aged working wife and mother of a teenaged son about to take his university entrance exams. The narrative is set in a middle-class Tokyo suburb in the late 1960's or early 1970s. Unlike *The Doctor's Wife* and *The River Ki*, both of whose narratives span periods of many years, *The Twilight Years* covers the six months between the sudden death by cerebral hemorrhage of Akiko's mother-in-law and the death of her father-in-law, whose care falls almost exclusively to Akiko as he slowly deteriorates mentally and physically to complete helplessness. By focussing the narrative principally in the consciousness of Akiko, and by using her considerable dramatic skill to evoke Akiko's relationships with her family, her neighbors, and her fellow office workers; Ariyoshi creates a powerful and compelling examination of the complex issues arising from the effects of improved nutrition and medical advances on longevity. It is painfully clear to Ariyoshi's reader that the society she depicts—and it could be any modern industrial society—has simply not made provisions for the population explosion that has taken place among older persons, particularly the frail elderly, who lose not only their physical, but also their mental, independence.

The story begins in late November on a Saturday evening as Akiko is returning home after work. As usual on a Saturday, she has stopped to do some shopping, and she is looking forward to the pleasure that her husband will experience at their evening meal. It has begun to snow, and Akiko is stirred by the beauty of the changing season. Suddenly she meets her father-in-law, striding toward her in a determined manner. Shigezo is over six feet tall, making him look imposing and intimidating to his daughter-in-law, who is diminuitive by comparison. As the old man draws nearer, she notices his distracted manner and his lack of his winter overcoat. She convinces him to accompany her home, where she discovers the body of her mother-in-law, dead for several hours. Following the arrivals of her husband, Nobutoshi, and their son, Satoshi, the family becomes caught up in wake and funeral preparations. Gradually, however, they become aware that Shigezo, or Grandpa as they call him, recognizes no one except for Akiko and Satoshi, not even his own son and daughter. For several years, Shigezo and his wife have been living in a small cottage built nearby by the Tachibanas to allow Akiko relief from her cruel, verbally abusive father-in-law. Because the family rarely saw the old man—a self-involved hypochondriac—they were not aware that he had become senile. Apparently, he had been cared for by his good-natured wife in the spirit of self-sacrifice that would be expected of a Japanese wife of her generation. Even though she is presented as a "modern woman," Akiko's posi-

tion in the family remains inferior to that of her husband, and both she and Nobutoshi agree that their son Satoshi must be given all the time he needs to prepare for his university entrance exam. Therefore, caring for the cantankerous old man must be undertaken almost exclusively by Akiko, whom Shigezo has repeatedly reviled. Fortunately, the old man seems to have forgotten his former attitude toward daughter-in-law. Now he recognizes only her and Satoshi, often referring to Nobutoshi as a burglar and failing to recognize his late wife's funeral picture. As the novel progresses, Shigezo becomes increasingly disoriented, making ever greater demands on Akiko's patience, time, and ingenuity. Because she does not wish to give up her job completely, she seeks out help from various community agencies, including two different senior citizens centers where, for a time, she is able to send Shigezo during the day. In her conversations with officials associated with welfare agencies and senior centers, Akiko learns of the pitiful conditions under which the frail and dependent elderly must live and of the enormity of the problem as thousands must be put on waiting lists for a year or more to enter nursing homes.

Meanwhile, after Shigezo's return home each weekday from the center, Akiko must spend all her spare time attending to the old man's needs. He wakes every night and insists on attempting to go to the cottage to urinate, only to stop in the garden to relieve himself as he is supported from behind by Akiko. Often he wakes up screaming at night, making it necessary for Akiko to get up, go downstairs, and calm him down. Sometimes she even has to sleep with him, as though he were a frightened child. He is insatiably hungry; once Akiko discovers him sitting on the floor, gnawing on bone fragments he has taken from his wife's funeral urn. Each week Akiko must bathe him, forcing herself to scrub his genitals and anus. A continuing problem is his running away, causing the family to conduct far-ranging searches, and, on two occasions involving the police. Repeated awakening during the night causes Akiko to become exhausted, and, consequently, she often misses work.

Fortunately, her employers are understanding, but Akiko dreads losing her job to one of the younger women at the office. The problem of nighttime awakening is alleviated somewhat when Nobutoshi obtains tranquilizers for Shigezo, and Akiko begins using diapers and diaper covers to deal with the old man's incontinence.

Exhausted, frustrated, and sometimes angry, especially with Nobutoshi who remains aloof from all but the most extreme emergencies, Akiko finds herself wishing for her father-in-law's death. A key turning point in the narrative occurs when Shigezo nearly drowns in the bathtub and then comes down with pneumonia. After the doctor indicates that the old man will probably die in three days, Akiko undertakes a heroic effort to nurse him. Surprisingly, Shigezo recovers, but a remarkable change takes place in his demeanor. His illness seems to have brought him a kind of spiritual calm, acceptance, and happiness; he is always smiling contentedly, and never speaking except to say "hello." In his simplicity and contentment, Shigezo seems like a god to Akiko, who takes a leave from her job to spend full time caring for him. With more free time on her hands, Akiko finds herself happily involved in gardening, taking Shigezo along with her whenever she goes to the store for gardening supplies or groceries. Ironically, Akiko has now completely replaced her mother-in-law who had spent her life caring uncomplainingly for Shigezo. After an idyllic interlude of caring for the childlike old man, Akiko gets an opportunity to return to work part-time. When a young couple of married university students agree to care for Shigezo as part of their rent payment for the cottage, Shigezo becomes attached to Emi, the young wife, who willingly takes on even some of the less pleasant aspects of Shigezo's care, such as changing his diaper. The final crisis of the novel occurs when Emi leaves her husband, and Shigezo reacts by running away once again. Because his physical condition has weakened, Shigezo is completely exhausted from his adventure, and dies the following day.

The Twilight Years is a novel of development in which the protagonist assumes the unpleasant, frustrating, and exhausting responsibility of caring for a senile elderly man whom she has never liked and, in the process, achieves a sense of communion, love, and spiritual fulfillment in their relationship. Despite the effects of modernization on her life, Akiko's position as a woman in the Japanese family forces her into an unwanted responsibility. Ironically, the same family system and values that keep her subjected provide her with the strength and determination to fulfill her responsibility and gain a new sense of spiritual fulfillment. Had Shigezo been placed in a nursing home, Akiko's personal development would never have occurred.

When it appeared in 1972, *The Twilight Years* was an immediate success, selling over 1,000,000 copies in the following year. Obviously, the Japanese public related strongly to the issues raised by the novel, issues that transcend cultural and national boundaries as ethical and social development strive to keep pace with technological advances. Ariyoshi continued to write until her death in 1984, winning the Mainichi Prize in 1979. Translations of her work in various languages continue to appear worldwide.

ROBERT ALAN BURNS

Further Reading

Translations

Brandon, James R., trans. *Kabuki Dancer (Izumo no Okuni)*. Tokyo: Kodansha International Ltd., 1993. This is Ariyoshi's fictional account of the career of Okuni, the woman who nearly single-handedly established the Kabuki theater in the late sixteenth and early seventeenth centuries. In this novel the author combines legend and accounts from historical documents in a manner approaching romance in its best literary sense.

Hironaka, Wakako, and Ann Siller Konstant, trans. *The Doctor's Wife*. Tokyo: Kodansha International Ltd., 1981. In the translators' brief but excellent critical introduction, they focus on Ariyoshi's use of 15 dramatic scenes to structure the novel and delineate the characters.

Related Studies

Keene, Donald. *Dawn to the West: Japanese Literature in the Modern Era: Fiction*. New York: Holt, Rinehart and Winston, 1984. A broad and compendious critical survey of modern Japanese fiction from the Meiji restoration to topics such as The Meiji political novel, naturalism, the "I" novel, war literature, and the revival of writing by women. This work is an excellent general introduction and reference for the general reader.

Loughman, Celeste. "*The Twilight Years*: A Japanese View of Aging, Time, and Identity." In *World Literature Today* 65.1 (1991): 49–53. Loughman argues that individual perceptions of time determine personal identity and, in the cases of Akiko and Nobutoshi, affect attitudes toward aging. Having lost his personal identity, Shigezo is freed from time to dwell in an omnipresent trance-like state.

KOREA

KORYŎ SONGS

Authors: Various anonymous authors; a few poets identified by name
Literary Form: Mostly chain verse with refrain
Major Poems (among others): "Ode on the Seasons," "Song of Green Mountain," "Song of P'yongyang," "Song of the Gong and Chimes," "Will You Go?," "Spring Overflows the Pavilion"
Dates of Composition: Twelfth to fourteenth centuries

Major Themes

Songs used to celebrate the beloved are adaptable for celebrating the king.
Wine is the best anodyne for lovers who have lost their beloved.
Love for the beloved (or the king) will cease only when the impossible becomes true.
Were an absent lover to return, he could transform a bamboo hut into a love grotto.

Most Koryŏ songs were orally transmitted for at least two hundred years until they were written down for the first time in the Korean alphabet. An additional incontrovertible proof of orality and performance of these songs is musical notations preserved from the sixteenth century. The reasons for the vicissitudes of textual transmission include the lack of a uniformly used system of writing the language and a general neglect of vernacular poetry by the ruling class during Koryŏ (918–1392), as well as the revision suffered at the hands of censors of the early Chosŏn dynasty (1392–1910).

Sources of Koryŏ songs include the monograph on music in the *Koryŏ sa (History of Koryŏ,* chapters 70–71), *Akhak kwebŏm (Canon of Music)* (1493), *Akchang kasa (Words for Songs and Music)*, and *Siyong hyangak po (Notations for Korean Music in Contemporary Use)* (early sixteenth century). These sources record seventy-two titles of Koryŏ works, thirty-three with texts (twenty-one in Korean; one in *hyangch'al* transcription; two in *hyangch'al* and Chinese; five in Chinese; and four in Chinese with Korean connectives). The remaining thirty-nine titles are not accompanied by texts.

Songs preserved in the *Canon of Music* and *Words for Songs and Music* and performed at court gatherings deal with love, and they were popular during late Koryŏ, when Korean kings married Mongol princesses, who brought with them Mongol entertainments. Musicians and women singers who performed both for royal audiences and townspeople might have introduced popular songs to the court, where most were revised to suit the place and occasion of performance.

The survival of Koryŏ songs is owed to the adoption of their accompanying music for use at court from the beginning of the Chosŏn dynasty. Historical sources may dub the texts as vulgar and unworthy of preservation, but the music books preserve their melodies, an indication that musical notations were in use for several hundred years as part of the repertory of court and official music.

Clear marking of the lyric persona and the abundance of honorific verbal endings in Koryŏ songs indicate the gender not only of the lyric speaker but also of the performer as female—female slaves, entertainers, shamans—as well as the place of performance as court, often in the presence of the king. The occasion of performance sometimes transformed the longing for the beloved in the original into that for the lord/king. Another device was to add the elements of praise to camouflage the realistic contents to suit the occasion (for example, *Tongdong [Ode on the Seasons]*).

To ijang ka (Dirge for Two Generals) (1120) and *Chŏng Kwajŏng (Regret)* (c. 1156) represent a transitional period between the *hyangga* of Silla and Koryŏ songs: the former is an eight-line royal poem written in *hyangch'al*, and the latter, a ten- or eleven-line poem without stanzaic division. The characteristic forms of Koryŏ songs are the *sogyo* (popular songs) and the *kyŏnggich'e ka (kyŏnggi-*

411

style songs). The former's feature includes the refrain recurring at intervals, generally at the end of each stanza, which is used to help achieve a certain mood in each song. They were sung to musical accompaniment and found their place whenever men and women gathered and entertained each other with songs. The refrain serves as a meaningless onomatopoeia of the sounds of musical instruments (drum, flute, or zither) or nonsense jingles to carry the tune and spirit of the songs, as in the "Ode on the Seasons," *Sŏgyŏng pyŏlgok* (Song of P'yŏngyang), *Ch'ŏngsan pyŏlgok* (Song of Green Mountain), and *Isang kok* (Treading Frost). In the *Kasiri* (Will You Go?), however, the refrain has clearly definable parts within itself—an interjection, an imitation of the sounds of a zither, and a poetic phrase, which might have been a later addition.

The refrain in the Koryŏ songs is an indispensable element in chain verse. By means of the refrain a song consisting of several independent parts with different contents is linked together. Each stanza in most Koryŏ songs can be read or detached as an independent unit apart from the entire song. It is the refrain that links the individual units, so that each stanza in each song can play its role in fully achieving the final effect. It should be noted that among the Koryŏ songs, there are also some that do not have stanzaic divisions, several different units linked together, as, for example, in the *Ch'ŏyong ka* (Song of Ch'ŏyong), which consists of six parts including the song written in 879.

Among popular love songs of Koryŏ, only the *Ssanghwajŏm* (The Turkish Bakery) is not a folk song but an original composition made in 1279 by a sycophant of King Ch'unmgnyŏl (r. 1274–1308). In 1274, at the age of thirty-eight, the king married a Mongol princess who was only sixteen. She died in Korea in 1297. The king loved entertainments, lewd songs, and dances, and his sycophants did everything to satisfy his thirst for sensual pleasure. The king had a permanent stage built on the palace grounds, recruited female entertainers from the shamans and official slaves, and had them dress in male attire, a horsehair hat included. The text is enticing, but the refrains, intended for synaesthetic effect, also paint in sounds the arousing of sexual pleasure: *taroro kŏdirŏ* (line 4); *tŏrŏ tungsyŏng tarirŏdirŏ tarirŏdirŏ tarorŏgodirŏ tarorŏ* (line 5); and *wi wi tarorŏ kŏdirŏ tarorŏ* (line 7). The poem consists of four eight-line stanzas, with part of the fourth, fifth, and seventh lines being refrains. The poem is in the first person throughout, and the speaker narrates her adventures in four different circumstances. She speaks directly and her determination finds expression in the last two lines of each stanza: "I will go, yes, go to his bower:/ A narrow place, sultry and dark."

The "Ode on the Seasons" is an anonymous song of sixty-five lines, consisting of a eulogy and a love complaint, and is divided into thirteen four-line stanzas with a one-line refrain, *Aŭ tongdong tari,* at the end of each stanza. The first stanza, a panegyric prologue, was perhaps added later to make the song more suitable for court performance. The twelve stanzas are devoted to each of the twelve months of the lunar year, making reference to monthly observances of folk origin that survive even today.

> *With virtue in one hand,*
> *And happiness in the other,*
> *Come, come you gods,*
> *With virtue and happiness.*

> (STANZA 1)

> *On the feast of irises*
> *I brew healing herbs*
> *And offer you this drink—*
> *May you live a thousand years.*

> (STANZA 6)

The speaker likens herself to "a comb cast from a cliff," "a sliced berry," and "chopsticks." Born into this world to "live alone," she seems to be fated to her plight forever. Following the calendrical song form, she compares the stages of her love to the four seasons, but the sorrow of abandonment and loneliness dominates her. It is the discord between changeless inner turmoil and the changing seasons that is the subject of the song.

In the "Song of Green Mountains," an anonymous song whose text is preserved in the *Words for Songs and Music*, a lost lover takes a pessimistic view of life and tries every means to unburden himself of sorrow. The song is written in eight four-line stanzas, with the same refrain at the end of each stanza, *Yalli yalli yallasyŏng yallari yalla.* The speaker comes to the conclusion that wine is the best anodyne, and the song ends with an invocation and lines in praise of wine.

The "Song of P'yŏngyang" is a dramatic lyric, spoken by a woman, consisting of fourteen three-line stanzas. The third line in each stanza serves to keep the text to the musical tune: *Wi tuŏrŏngsyŏng tuŏrŏngsyŏng taringdiri.* The fifth through eighth stanzas have been popular in and of themselves, apart from the entire song, and recur as the final stanza of the *Chŏngsŏk ka* (Song of the Gong and Chimes).

Were the pearls to fall on the rock,
Would the thread be broken?
If I parted from you for a thousand years,
Would my heart be changed? [Refrain omitted.]

The ninth through fourteenth stanzas are the most intense, with the speaker's plea to a boatman on the Taedong river to not allow her loved to cross over. But she adds that the boatman is in the same predicament as is the speaker—the boatman's own wife is inconstant.

The "Song of the Gong and Chimes" is an anonymous song which sings of an unbroken dynastic line and prays that the life of kings be coeval with Heaven and Earth. The song begins with a three-line introduction and continues in five six-line stanzas. The song offers a series of impossibilities and then declares that only if these ever occur shall "we part from the virtuous lord," as the refrain in the third, fourth, and fifth stanzas states. The use of the *adynaton* as a rhetorical device in the poetry of praise is a commonplace in Korea, as elsewhere. The virtuous lord addressed could be a beloved, or one's parents, according to the occasion, as well as the king. Thus, this song of compliment accom-

panied by the gong and chimes became a popular ceremonial song:

Ring the gong, strike the chimes!
In this age calm and plenty,
Let's live and enjoy.

On a brittle sandy cliff.
Let's plant roasted chestnuts, five pints.
When the chestnuts shoot and sprout,
Then we'll part from the virtuous lord.

(STANZAS 1–2)

The "Treading Frost," sung by a woman, is an anonymous love song of thirteen lines with no stanzaic division, of which the third line is a refrain. The invocation of thunderbolts and hellfire (lines 6–9 in the original) seems to suggest that her relation with her beloved is illicit, or that her passion for him is such that it might bring down punishment upon her.

"Will You Go?" is another love song spoken by a woman. The song consists of four two-line stanzas with a refrain at the end of each. This song has much literary merit: its language is simple but intense, and it is filled with tender sentiments for the parting lover. The court adopted its music for its attractiveness. *Nanŭn* (the personal pronoun "I") appears six times for emphasis at the end of lines 1, 2, 5, 6, 10, and 11, to underscore the plight of the lyric persona.

Will you go away?
Will you forsake me and go?
[refrain]

How can I live if you
Forsake me and go away?
[refrain]

(STANZAS 1–2)

In *Manjŏnch'un* (Spring Overflows the Pavilion), an anonymous love song of twenty lines, the speaker says that a spring in her heart is dead, killed by the loved one. But can there be another spring outside?

After an imaginary coaxing dialogue in the fourth stanza, the fifth transforms the tone of the song by having the treacherous man express his wish for fulfillment: he will be able to transform the icy bamboo hut into a love grotto:

A bed on Mount South, a jade pillow, brocade quilt,
A bed on Mount South, a jade pillow, brocade quilt,
And beside me a girl sweeter than musk,
And beside me a girl sweeter than musk,
Let us press our hearts together, our magic hearts.

(STANZA 5)

The speaker's desire for preservation of love in absence is so strong that he (actually she in disguise) says he can transform a bamboo hut into an ideal place.

The *Samo kok* (Maternal Love) is an anonymous short song of five or six lines in all. The song is simple in structure and compares the difference between paternal and maternal love to the difference in sharpness between a hoe and a sickle.

The Kyonggi Style Song

The *kyonggi* style song is so called because of the refrain that begins *kŭi ŏttŏhaniikko?* and recurs in the fourth and sixth lines of each stanza. The basic form is as follows (syllable counts):

3 3 4
3 3 4
4 4 4
wi 3 3 4
4 4 4 4
wi 3 3 4

(The meaningless sound "wi" precedes the fourth and sixth lines.)

Three Koryŏ compositions include the *Hallim pyŏlgok* (Song of Confucian Scholars) (c. 1216) by a group of literati, the *Kwandong pyŏlgok* (Song of Diamond Mountains) (c. 1328), and *Chukkye pyŏlgok* (Song of the Bamboo Stream) (1348) by An Ch'uk (1282–1348). Texts are either in *idu* and Chinese, or in Chinese with connectives and refrains written in Korean and characterized by enumeration, such as the listing of esteemed Korean scholars in the first stanza of "Song of Confucian Scholars."

This kind of elitist poetry was only for literati who had studied the Chinese classics and literature and became the accomplished writers of their times. The principal trope of enumeration suggests plenitude, with each of the second through seventh stanzas of "Song of Confucian Scholars" devoted to one category in the following order: titles of Chinese classics and works of literature, styles of calligraphy, wine, flowers, musical instruments, and scenic spots. It concludes with a swing scene in the eighth stanza. The recent discovery of five examples by Buddhist monks—Kihwa (1376–1433), for example—written to praise the Buddha and spread his teaching, indicates that the literati did not monopolize the form.

Among eight songs recorded in *Notations for Korean Music in Contemporary Use*, two are folk songs ("Song of the Pigeon" and "Song of the Pestle"), and six are said to be associated with shamanist rituals. The latter are considered to be shamanist in content and function but have not been adequately studied to date. *Narye ka* (Song of Exorcism) is associated with the exorcism ritual held at court and private himes on New Year's Eve in the lunar calendar. At court the ceremony consisted of music, song, and dance, performed by seventy-eight members of the troupe, including twenty-four boys, ages twelve to sixteen, wearing the mask and red gowns. Other songs addressed to shaman gods of mountains and villages, the great kings of the walled cities, and the like are riddled with textual cruzes and require more philological study.

PETER H. LEE

Further Reading

Translations

Translations in this article are by Peter H. Lee.

Lee, Peter H., comp. and trans. *Poems From Korea: From the Earliest Era to the Present.* London:

George Allen & Unwin, Ltd. (and the University Press of Hawaii), 1974. An anthology of Korean poetry from the Silla dynasty (57 B.C.–A.D. 935), the Koryŏ dynasty (918–1392), the Yi dynasty (1392–1910), and the twentieth century. The first comprehensive anthology of Korean poetry in English translation.

———, comp. and ed. *Anthology of Korean Literature: From Early Times to the Nineteenth Century.* Honolulu: The University Press of Hawaii, 1981. Includes a section of Koryŏ poetry; poetry of other periods, including Korean poetry written in Chinese; some prose and some fiction.

SONGS OF FLYING DRAGONS

Title in Korean: *Yongbi ŏch'ŏn ka (Songs of Flying Dragons)*
Authors: Scholars in the Hall of Worthies
Literary Form: Eulogy
Date of Composition: 1445–47

Major Themes

The songs are written to praise the "six dragons"—the four ancestors and the first and third kings of the Chosŏn dynasty.

As a Confucian statesman, Yi Sŏnggye, the first king of the Chosŏn dynasty, brought order and peace to a nation harassed by foreign invaders.

As a Confucian soldier, Yi responded bravely to the demands of destiny willed by Heaven.

A just ruler is moved by love (benevolence), which aims at social order and harmony with Heaven; he is informed by learning, by which moral standards are acquired.

The security of the throne depends upon the ruler's worship of Heaven and his dedication to the people.

Sejong (1397–1450), greatest of all Chosŏn kings and the inventor of the Korean alphabet (1443–1444), was a ruler whose majesty, wisdom, and erudition held his court spellbound. He established the civil service examination system, the examination in literature that began in 1438, and the Academy of Worthies, whose members considered it a virtual haven for the literati. He granted members of his academy leave for further study, showed them genuine affection and encouragement, and became an icon of inspiration in early Chosŏn culture and literature.

The most monumental work among early Chosŏn eulogies is the *Yongbi ŏch'ŏn ka (Songs of Flying Dragons)* (1445–1447), a cycle of 125 cantos comprising 248 poems. It was compiled on King Sejong's order to praise the founding of the Chosŏn dynasty by General Yi Sŏnggye (1335–1408), the king's grandfather, and to test the use of the new alphabet he had invented. Written by the foremost philologists and literary men in the Academy of Worthies, the *Songs* combine poetry and historiography to express the orthodox view of recent history. The *Songs* use mostly themes of praise found in the classics and histories, highlighted with stylistic devices of comparison and amplification, and the fullest exploration of the device of parallelism and formulas.

Preparation began in 1437 with the gathering of both accounts of deeds preserved in the veritable records, and popular traditions circulating among the people. From October 1446 to March 1447, seven members of the Academy completed the Korean verses, and by February–March 1447, a ten-chapter commentary on the *Songs* was completed. Finally, on November 23, 1447, the king distributed 550 copies of the Songs to his subjects.

The first canto, which together with the second, forms the prologue, sets the theme, mood, and purpose of the book: praise of the four ancestors and the first and third kings of the dynasty. These six dragons flying above the land of the Eastern Sea are Mokcho (d. 1274), Ikcho, Tojo (1367–1422), Hwanjo (1315–61), Yi Sŏnggye (1335–1408), and Yi Pangwŏn (1367–1422). The central part of the book includes cantos 3–124, subdivided into two sections: the first, cantos 3–109, praises the cultural and military accomplishments of the six dragons; the second, cantos 110–124, consists of admonitions to future monarchs. Canto 125 is the conclusion. Each canto, except for cantos 1 and 125, consists of two poems, the first relating generally the great deeds of Chinese sovereigns and the second those of the Chosŏn kings. Cantos 86–89 are also exceptions to the general scheme, since each poem celebrates the deeds of the founder.

Also, cantos 108 and 109, the only cantos assigned to women, praise the exemplary deeds of the wife of King Wen; Queen Sinhye (wife of the founder of Koryŏ, Wang Kŏn), and Queen Wŏngyŏng (1365–1420) (wife of Yi Pangwŏn). The compilers assigned five cantos to Mokcho, nine to Ikcho, four to Tojo, six to Hwanjo, eighty-one to Yi Sŏnggye, and twenty-three to Yi Pangwŏn.

The stanzaic scheme characteristic of the Korean verse may be seen in the first verse of canto 2:

> The tree that strikes deep root
> Is firm amidst the winds.
> Its flowers are good,
> Its fruits abundant.

Each quatrain in cantos 2–124 follows the same scheme, the total number of syllables varying from eighteen to thirty, but most commonly twenty-four to twenty-eight. Canto 1 is a single tercet; canto 125, a single ten-line stanza.

A number of cantos celebrate Yi Sŏnggye's marksmanship (cantos 32, 43, 86, 88, and 89), the bow signifying his great military power. Yi wielded a huge bow, cutting his own arrows made of the *hu* tree, instead of the usual bamboo; Yi's arrows made a whirring noise as they flew through the air. Like many heroes, Yi's companion in times of peace and war was the horse. He had eight stalwart steeds, all of which performed miracles of one sort or another. In peacetime, hunting trips, contests, or games provided him with occasions to perfect his horsemanship (cantos 44, 63). Such contests were actually provided by Heaven, or Heaven induced someone to provide them, exemplifying Yi's "august power" (canto 46), as well as inspiring awe in the people and in the king himself (cantos 31–32, 46). With his supreme physical and spiritual qualities, Yi responded to calls to bring order and peace to a nation harassed by successive waves of foreign invaders, the Red Turbans in 1351, the Mongols in 1362 and 1370, and the Japanese pirates in 1377, 1380, and 1382 (cantos 47–52, 58–62).

Yi Sŏnggye fulfilled the duty of a Confucian soldier by withstanding the trials thrust upon him, by bravely responding to the demands of destiny willed by Heaven, and by identifying his own destiny with that of the nation. The ultimate justification, however, is his maintenance and preservation of order, best manifested in good government. The cantos that celebrate the statesmanship of Yi Sŏnggye, therefore, explore the nature and function of kingship, the relations of power and justice, the role of mercy and remonstrance, and the importance of learning and orthodoxy, culminating in the admonitory cantos which conclude the cycle (cantos 110–125).

The Virtues of the Confucian King

The sovereign qualities of the Confucian king enumerated in the *Songs* recall the cardinal virtues of the Christian prince found in the Mirror for Princes literature. Yi Sŏnggye possessed benevolence, justice tempered with mercy, learning, wisdom, temperance, compassion, modesty, and brotherly love. As a defender of the moral order in the universe and a representative of his culture, the ruler's conduct becomes the cause of public order or disorder. The compilers are, therefore, eager to illustrate public doctrine: the special qualifications required of a ruler and the particular functions he is expected to discharge for the good of the human community.

The dominant topic here is *ren (jen)*—benevolence, goodness, or love. Yi Sŏnggye's love, in its various forms, finds expression in his dealings with his subordinates, stepbrother, and rivals and enemies. He was "polite with his men, kind in words," and therefore able to pacify the hearts of his subordinates (canto 76), for regulation of the family is necessary to public order, as is reiterated in canto 119. Yi Sŏnggye furthermore forgave his former rivals and enemies (canto 77) and restored them to their former ranks. He also showed a consistent concern for the welfare of meritorious subjects, thus winning their lasting loyalty.

The Emphasis on Learning

That learning is indispensable to a prince or a gentleman is a commonplace in the tradition. Classics arm man with precepts against every contingency, while history, which embodies the past and teaches by example, provides suitable analogies for each occasion. Both are storehouses of examples, a political and moral mirror in which man finds truth and can know himself. Emphasis on learning is also an affirmation of loyalty to culture, a status symbol of the ruling class which, through the civil service examination in China and Korea, manned the government. Therefore, Yi Sŏnggye, fully accoutered in armor, read books between battles in order to learn the art of government. Regretting that his family had not yet produced a scholar, Yi Sŏnggye urged his sons to pursue classical learning. Yi Sŏnggye's respect for scholarship is also evidenced in his courteous reception of Yi Saek when the latter returned from banishment in 1391.

In the final section of the *Songs*, the compilers directly address King Sejong, their patron and the great fount of their inspiration. The principal concern in the earlier part, we recall, was the celebration of paradigmatic acts of the dynastic founder, or of the virtues he exemplifies, the juxtaposition— and often integration—of native and classical materials becoming the source of resonance. With the final section, we notice a shift to a more poignantly personal utterance, which effects the withdrawal of focus from the comparatively distant and normative to the immediate and real. This effective variation of the compilers' strategy evinces how central, by the nature and tradition of their art, was the impulse to persuade.

The themes in this section include the prevention and treatment of evils that arise from ease and luxury, the role of peace in breeding heroic courage and resolve, the value of modesty and the harm of pride, the evils of flattery and slander, and the transforming power of virtue as the guardian of order. The final canto ends not only with a prophecy of national greatness but with an allusive rhetorical question. The compilers assert again that the security of the throne depends entirely upon the ruler's worship of Heaven and his dedication to the people. They then evoke the figure of T'ai K'ang of Hsia, who was historically

remote enough to protect compilers from the displeasure of the authorities.

A millennium ago,
Heaven chose the north of the Han.
There they accumulated goodness and founded the
*   state.*
Oracles foretold: a myriad years;
May your sons and grandsons reign unbroken.
But you can secure the dynasty only
When you worship Heaven and benefit the people.
Ah, you who will wear the crown, beware,
Can you depend upon your ancestors
When you go hunting by the waters of Lo?

On his way back from a hunting trip to the south of the Lo River, T'ai K'ang is said to have been ambushed by I, Prince of Ch'iung and a famous archer, who subsequently seized the throne. T'ai K'ang's loss of the crown by indulging in pleasures shows how his personal conduct was the immediate source of public disorder. The more important element in constructing the total symbolic structure lies in the meaning of the word "hunt," a "political metaphor for tyranny." The traditional associations of the hunt with war and games are familiar enough, but here emphasis is on the rapacity of the hunt and of the sportive tyrant whose prey included men.

History reveals the fate of the tyrannous hunter after men: he is in turn hunted, deposed, and banished, suffering the consequences of his failure to live up to the rules of his office. The hunt functions as a metaphor for the unbound energy of the tyrant in disregard of the ideal political and moral order; its admonitory appearance in the final canto warns against royal participation in such self-indulgent sport and outlines the cause-and-effect relationship between the moral energy of the ruler and the welfare of his state. Such was the figure of the ideal Confucian prince, whose lasting virtues were vital to the future of the dynasty. Thus, a handbook of education was created, a *summa* of the concerns of Confucian humanism.

PETER H. LEE

Further Reading

Translation and Critical Study

The translations in the above article are by Peter H. Lee.

Lee, Peter H. *Songs of Flying Dragons: A Critical Reading*. Cambridge, MA: Harvard University Press, 1975. The book consists of six critical chapters followed by an annotated translation of the *Songs*. An introductory chapter provides a short account of the Korean events to which the poems refer, followed by an analysis of the form and structure of the work. Two chapters on "The Confucian Soldier" and "The Confucian Statesman" set the themes of the *Songs* into the framework of Confucian politico-moral thought and attempt to explore the Confucian view of man and his conduct in the world. The subject of the fifth is traditional *topoi* and symbolism as well as folklore and myth based on the macro-microcosmic correspondence employed in the creation of hero and the atmosphere of the work. The last chapter, through an analysis of the symbolism of the "sacred" tree, attempts to explore the East Asian view of man and history.

THE POETRY OF HŎ NANSŎRHŎN

Author: Ho Nansŏrhŏn (Nansŏrhŏn is her pen name; her given name was Ch'o-hi)
Born: 1563, Kangnung
Died: 1589, probably in Seoul
Major Poems: "A Woman's Sorrow," "For My Brother Hagok," "Mourning My Children," "A Poor Woman"

Major Themes

Women in Korea during the Chosŏn dynasty suffered from the restraints imposed by a male-centered Confucian society.
Women were expected to be virtuous but uneducated.
Marriages were usually empty and futile, with the wife subservient to the husband.

During the Chosŏn dynasty (l392–1910) a woman's sphere was thought to be only domestic; her life was to be lived entirely within the family home. Except for the *kisaeng*, the professional entertainers who by law belonged to the lowest social class, women, and especially wellborn women, were to have no public life at all, which was the sole preserve of the wellborn man. Since the Confucian creed of the so-called *namjon yobi*, which literally means elevation of men and subjection of women, applied to all areas of public life during this period, all avenues of participation in public life were closed to women, subjecting them to such male-centered Confucian codes of conduct as "The Three Tenets of Obedience" and "The Seven Evils for Expelling a Wife."

Nowhere was this separation between the man's and woman's spheres so clearly drawn as in learning and writing. Since women were discouraged from both, it was a rare woman who was learned, and even rarer was the woman who publicized her learning through writing. According to Yi Ik, a much respected Confucian scholar of the eighteenth century, "Reading and learning are the domains of men. For a woman it is enough if she knows the Confucian virtues of diligence, frugality, and chastity. If a woman disobeys these virtues, she will bring disgrace to the family." Furthermore, one of the seven rules of appropriate behavior for the married woman stipulated that "she should not indulge in study or literature because they were

considered improper for a woman." Lack of learning rather than possession of it was thought to be more conducive to virtuousness in a woman; women of marked intelligence and artistic talent were thought to be "ill-fated."

Despite all these difficulties and opposition to women's studying, writing, and publishing, there were a number of women who became learned, wrote and even published, not only in *han'gul* but even in *hanmun*; that is, in Chinese characters. These were extraordinary, even odd or eccentric women, who had clearly gone against the grain of Chosŏn dynasty Korea, defying the anti-female mores and ideology of their society. They were remarkable women by virtue of their birth, inclination and talent, or circumstances: women who grew up in the households of scholars where they could learn along with their brothers; women with learned grandmothers or mothers who were willing to teach them; women who through their own innate gifts were driven to learning and literature, often becoming "problem women"; and finally talented *kisaeng* who had to be accomplished in learning and literature because it was their job to entertain wellborn and learned men.

Hŏ Nansŏrhŏn (1563–89), elder sister of the better known political and literary rebel Hŏ Kyun, author of *Hong Kiltong chŏn* (The Tale of Hong Kiltong), was one such woman about whose life not much is known. We know her mostly through a small legacy of her poetry—probably no more than a small part of her output. She was born into a distinguished family of scholar-statesmen: her father and her three brothers were all well known such men of the time. She was married to Kim Songnip, an undistinguished son of a distinguished family; she bore him a son and daughter, both of whom preceded her in death; and she seems to have found little joy in her marriage.

No other Chosŏn dynasty woman's life more clearly underscores the tragic plight of a gifted woman than does Hŏ Nansŏrhŏn's. Throughout her short life she had to struggle under numerous restrictions and handicaps, not only because she was born a woman but a woman in Chosŏn dynasty Korea, where to be a woman was to be an inferior being subjected to the so-called "Three Tenets of Obedience": obedience to her father before marriage, to her husband after marriage, and to her son after the death of her husband.

A spirited, beautiful daughter of a high-ranking scholar-official, whose poetic gifts had been recognized from early childhood, and who had been personally tutored by one of the most gifted poets of the time, how could Hŏ Nansŏrhŏn become an utterly silent, acquiescent, obedient daughter-in-law and wife? Although many gifted Chosŏn dynasty women had been able to submerge themselves completely in the role of a compliant, reticent, and obedient daughter-in-law and wife as prescribed by their society, extinguishing whatever individuality or creativity they possessed, Hŏ Nansŏrhŏn was not one of them. Self-expression through poetry could not be denied her even after marriage, when, as a popular saying had it, a married woman was expected be deaf for the first three years of her marriage, dumb for the next three, and blind for another three years. To make matters worse, her husband appears to have been an intellectually inferior man who utterly failed to appreciate her as a woman, wife, or gifted poet.

"A Woman's Sorrow"

Into her poetry she seems to have poured out all her sorrows as well as her dreams. In "*Kyuwŏn ka*"
("A Woman's Sorrow"), her sole surviving *han'gul* poem, a *kasa* of fifty lines, she gives us a vivid portrait of her unhappiness. Because of the evil karma of her three lives—past, present, and future—and a chance connection made in this world, the poet says, she is married to "a shallow, lightweight playboy of the capital," and her daily life is as care-worn as if she were treading on thin ice. What intensifies her pain and bitterness is her dawning awareness of the rapid and irretrievable passage of her youth. The poem begins with the following lines:

> The day before yesterday I was young,
>   but today I am already aging.
> It is no use recalling
>   the joyful days of my youth.

It is this juxtaposition of the relentless passage of time with the futility and emptiness of her marriage that gives power and poignance to the poem. It is as if the passage of time mocks and accentuates her deepening sorrow for the loss of her youth and for a beauty which can never be retrieved. In vain she tries to hush her clamoring heart. Alone in an empty room, as she awaits the return of her uncaring husband, the procession of seasons goes on relentlessly: the plum blossoms outside the window bloom, fade, and fall, spring after spring. She keeps her vigil on a bitterly cold winter night, but when summer returns the drizzling rain of a long summer day makes her heart ache just as much. In the absence of her beloved she unwraps and hugs a lute to play a tune. When she tries to sleep, hoping to see him in her dream, the rustling of leaves in the wind and chirping of insects keep her awake. Lamenting her unhappiness, she remembers the story of the Weaver and Herdboy in the sky. Even though separated by the Milky Way, they are said to never miss their yearly rendezvous. What unpassable river then keeps her husband from her without a word for all these years? As the poem ends, she wonders if anyone in the world could be as wretched as herself, and if she could go on living with so much grief.

"For My Brother Hagok"

But Hŏ Nansŏrhŏn's miseries did not end with her unhappy marriage. The death of her children and the ruin of her father and older brothers, victimized by the vicious political factionalism of the times, added to her unhappiness. In one of her *hanmun* poems, she writes of her grief over one of her older brothers living in exile far from the capital:

FOR MY BROTHER HAGOK

The candle light shines low
*   on the dark window,*
Fireflies flit across the house tops.
As the night grows colder,
I hear autumn leaves rustle to the ground.
There's been no news for some time
*   from your place of exile.*
Because of you,
My mind is never free of worry.

Thinking of a distant temple,
I see a deserted hillside
Filled with the radiance of the moon.

"Mourning My Children"

In one of her most heartbreaking *hanmun* poems she writes of the death of her two children:

MOURNING MY CHILDREN

Last year I lost my beloved daughter,
This year I lost my son.
Alas, this woeful ground of Kangnung!
A pair of mounds stand face to face.
The wind blows through the white birch
And the ghostly lights flicker in the woods.
I call to your spirits by burning paper money
And by pouring wine on your mounds.
Do you, the spirits of brother and sister,
Play together fondly each night?
This child I'm carrying within me
Dare I hope it grow safely to full term?
In vain I chant a magic verse of propitiation,
Tears of blood and sorrow swallow up my voice.

"A Poor Woman"

Rarely did Hŏ Nansŏrhŏn write of a woman's happiness or good fortune. In all her work she seems to have identified most deeply with the pain and sorrow of suffering women, regardless of their social status. For example, she writes of a displaced court favorite or a poor solitary woman who weaves and sews through the frigid winter night making other women's bridal clothes:

A POOR WOMAN

She weaves through the night without rest.
The rattling of the loom sounds lonesome.
This roll of silk in the loom being woven,
Whose dress will it make when it is finished?
Her hand clasps the metal scissors,
The chill of the night stiffens all her fingers.
For others she has made bridal clothes,
Year after year alone in her room.

According to Professor Kim Yongsuk, the scholar who has written most eloquently of the literature of Chosŏn dynasty women, Hŏ Nansŏrhŏn's poetry falls into two categories: the first, the more moving as well as better known, deals with the sorrows and sufferings of women, while the rest deals with the otherworldly affairs of women who are essentially not creatures of this world, because they are creatures of a fairy world. This is an aspect of her poetry which awaits to be further studied, especially in connection with a similar dichotomy found in the work of Hŏ Kyun, her younger brother, also gifted poetically but as ill-fated as his sister.

Hŏ Nansŏrhŏn died at age twenty-seven, preceded in death by all her children. According to one report, just before her death she burned a roomful of her poetry manuscripts. After her death, Hŏ Kyun compiled a volume of her *hanmun* poetry from what had been preserved by him and his brothers, and it is these poems that have come down to us.

KICHUNG KIM

Further Reading

Translations

Translations of Hŏ Nansŏrhŏn's poems in this article are by Kichung Kim.

Lee, Peter H., comp. and ed. *Anthology of Korean Literature: From Early Times to the Nineteenth Century.* Honolulu: The University Press Of Hawaii, 1981, rev. ed., 1990. An excellent selection of Korean literature. Includes Hŏ Nansŏrhŏn's "A Woman's Sorrow" and "Poor Woman." Also contains Marshall R. Pihl's translation of Hŏ Kyun's *The Tale of Hong Kiltong.*

————, comp. and tr. *Poems From Korea: From the Earliest Era to the Present.* London: George Allen & Unwin Ltd. (and the University Press of Hawaii), 1974. (Originally published by John Day Co., 1964.) Although this book contains only "Woman's Sorrow" from the poems of Hŏ Nansŏrhŏn, its concentration on Korean poetry puts her work in a context that gives it an added dimension.

THE POETRY OF YUN SŎNDO

Author: Yun Sŏndo
Born: 1587, Seoul, Korea
Died: 1671, Lotus Grotto, South Cholla Province, Korea
Major Poems: "Dispelling Gloom" (1618), "New Songs in the Mountains" (and their sequel) (1614–1645), *The Angler's Calendar* (1651), "The Disappointing Journey" (1652)

Major Themes

The poet's five friends are water, stone, pine, bamboo, and the moon.
One should be moderate in the pursuit of pleasure.
The wronged courtier longs for the king.
There is harmony between human beings and nature.
The fisherman is a sage.

Poet, musician, and politician, Yun Sŏndo is generally regarded as the most accomplished poet writing in the *sijo* form. (Developed in the fifteenth century, the *sijo* is a poem of three lines, each line consisting of four rhythmic groups, with pauses at the end of the second and fourth groups.)

Yun Sŏndo's lyrics are diverse in mood and technique, and his diction is peerless. Graceful, delicately varied rhythms are natural to him, and his every poem exhibits new techniques and a fresh tone. Yet his invention is so subtle that it becomes noticeable only after repeated close readings of his poems.

The first group of six poems, entitled "Dispelling Gloom" (1618), are the earliest known poems by Yun. They tend to abstractions and a perhaps excessive use of the pathetic fallacy. Nevertheless, these poems sing with an intensity of their own, and the native reader can anticipate in them Yun's later poetic genius. In poem 4, for example, suspense is created by an emphatic repetition of five adjectival verbs.

> *Moehŭn kilgo kilgo*
> *murŭn mŏlgo mŏlgo*
> *Ŏbŏi kŭrinttŭdŭn*
> *mank'o mank'o hago hago*
> *Ŏdŭisyo woegirŏginŭn*
> *ulgo ulgo kanŭni.*

A chain of mountains is long, long;
Waters flow far, far.
Love for parents is endless,
And my heart is heavy.
Far off, crying sadly,
A lone goose flies by.

The long vowels in *kilgo, mŏlgo,* and *mank'o* and the *l*'s in *kil, mŏl,* and *ul* provide a resonant, stately tone.

"New Songs in the Mountains"

Yun's masterpiece in the group of poems entitled "New Songs in the Mountains" is the "Song of Five Friends" (*Ou ka*), written in praise of water, stone, pine, bamboo, and the moon. By naming the five natural objects as his friends, rather than his fickle, mortal fellow men, the poet has won a new domain for himself and his poetry. Indeed, he has established a relationship with nature that is the reserve of those possessing poetic sensibility. In poem 20 (of Yun Sŏndo's corpus of seventy-five poems) tension is achieved by developing the theme with successive contrasts through the fifth line. The tension is resolved only in the sixth line, at the very end of the poem:

> *Kurŭm pitch'i chot'ahana*
> *kŏmkirŭl charo handa.*

Paramsorae malktahana
    kŭch'il chŏgi hanomaera.
Chok'odo kŭch'il nwi ŏpkinŭn
    mul ppunin'ga hanora.

They say the color of clouds is fine
But they often darken.
They say the sound of winds is clear,
But they often cease to blow.
It is only the *water*, then,
That is perpetual and good.

The effect here is achieved by a skillful use of the simple adversative particle *hana* (translated as "but") in the first and third lines, with the reply given immediately following, in the second and fourth lines respectively. The adjectives modifying the subjects "cloud" and "wind" are extremely simple, yet they are at once concise and clear, natural and precise. Even more importantly, they were chosen specifically because their sounds would enhance the rhythmic flow of the poem as a whole. In poem 23 Yun introduces yet another device:

> *Namodo anin kŏsi*
>   *p'uldo anin kŏsi . . .*

You are not a tree,
Nor are you a plant.

First, the omission of a conjunction *ko* between the first and second lines produces a unique intonation and rhythm that quickens the movements of the lines. Second, the ending *i* in this context normally anticipates the interrogative adverb *ŏtchi* or *ŏi* (You are not a tree; but why . . . ?). *Ŏi* appears only in the fourth line, keeping the reader in suspense, and heightening the poem's dramatic effect. The poem moves rapidly through this construction by repetition of *anin* in the first and second lines and the appearance of *nwi* (who) in the third. Furthermore, the poem never specifically mentions the bamboo to which it is addressed, but only its characteristics. Thus, the six lines comprising the poem rush on like a waterfall, keeping the reader's mind ever on the alert.

"At the Beginning of the Feast" and "At the End of the Feast" (Nos. 29–32) are admonitions to the king, and it is uncertain whether they are impromptu poems actually composed at a feast. In the first poem "house" refers to the ideal state, while "straight wood" denotes the benevolent government and moral power of the king. "Straight" in the third line alludes to the ways of the ancient sage-kings. In the second poem, "wine" and "broth" allude to the virtues of the king, while "yeast," "salt," and "prunes" denote the wise ministers who assist in state affairs. The third poem urges moderation in the pursuit of pleasure. Perhaps the poet had in mind the 114th poem in the *Book of Songs (Shijing/Shih Ching)*, in the first stanza of which the monitor says, "So be not so riotous/ As to forget your home./ Amuse yourselves, but no wildness!/ Good men are always on their guard."

"The Angler's Calendar"

Yun's forty poems depicting the four seasons are products of the poet's leisurely life at a favorite retreat, the Lotus Grotto. They are written in intricate stanzas differing from the conventional *sijo* form. The general patern is as follows, the numerals indicating the number of syllables in each metric segment:

First line:	3 4 3 4
envoi:	4 4
Second line:	3 4 3 4
envoi:	3 3 3
Third line:	3 4 3 4

Thus, a pair of four-syllable words is added after the first line, and three-syllable onomatopoeic words after the second line, thus bringing the total number of syllables to fifty-nine. The fortieth poem in this series has an unusual form, the total number of syllables being seventy-two.

The verbs in the first envois of each seasonal set of poems are not only well arranged in narrative sequence, but are identical from season to season: (1) cast off, (2) hoist anchor, (3) raise sail, (4) row away, (5) row away, (6) lower the sail, (7) stop the boat, (8) moor the boat, (9) drop anchor, and (10) bring the boat ashore. Together with the intricate organization, the poems are marked by flawless use of the language and a musical quality that depicts images as well as simulates sounds. Indeed, Yun succeeded in casting an authentic depiction of the life of a fisherman into lyrical rhythms.

The fourth poem in the spring cycle offers an admirable example of the poet's technique (the cuckoo's cry is part of the poem):

> *Is it a cuckoo that cries?*
> *Is it the willow that is blue?*
> *Row away, row away!*
> *Several roofs in a far fishing village*
> *Swim in the mist.*
> Chigŭkch'ong chigŭkch'ong ŏsawa.
> *Boy, fetch an old net!*
> *Fishes are climbing against the stream.*

The poem opens with two questions suggesting uncertainty regarding the senses of sound and sight. In the next two lines we actually do see village roofs, however insubstantial they may appear, as they seem to swim in the twilight. The expression *naraktŭrak* (line 3 in the original) suggests that the vision is a splendid one, even if tinged with unreality. The last two lines are brisk and forceful, and express a practical and immediate concern with nature. In consequence we proceed from a state of near-illusion to one of magnificence dimly perceived, and then finally to one of immediate appreciation and delight, with the suggestion that all these follow in sequence. The poem therefore presents nature's mystery, beauty, and bounty in terms of illusory loveliness, real visual loveliness, and finally the physical sustenance reaped by those who fish. Thus, the poem not only imparts the felt transcendence of the vision, but reveals as well an awareness of the transience of earthy joy and beauty.

The ten poems in the spring cycle depict a day's activities of a fisherman as he sets sail, scanning the river hamlets and distant views. Gulls accompany him and the boy, and he makes sure that a wine flagon has been loaded. Passing hill upon hill, he hears a cuckoo and sees the willow in the distance. He then asks the boy to have an old net ready. But being reminded of "The Fisherman," attributed to Ch'ü Yüan, where the wise fisherman advises the wronged idealistic courtier on the art of swimming in the sea of life, he asks himself if he should catch fish at all, especially when Ch'ü Yüan's soul might reside in a fish.

> *The sun's fair rays are shining,*
> *The water is calm as oil.*
> *Row away, row away!*
> *Should we cast a net,*
> *Or drop a line on such a day?*
> Chigŭkch'ong chigŭkch'ong ŏsawa.
> *The poem of Chü Yüan stirs my fancy;*
> *I have forgotten all about fishing.*

Twilight approaches, the speaker wishes to return to the shore, and he reaffirms that rank and riches are not what he wants. He then realizes that now the moon has occupied the boat, "small as a leaf." The drunken speaker sees the peach blossoms floating down the stream, perhaps from T'ao Ch'ien's literary utopia, Peach Blossom Spring, an indication that he is far away from the world of men. On the boat he wishes to view the moon through a "bamboo awning." Accompanied again by the cuckoo's song, the speaker registers his heart's rapture as he mends his way to his cottage after passing a day as a wise fisherman.

As a seasoned politician who served four kings and spent fourteen years in exile, Yun Sŏndo's allusion to Ch'ü Yüan adds weight to his concern for the relative value of loyal admonition and political action. He is content to bring in harsher realities, as he does in the eighth poem of summer:

> *Let's spread out our net on the sand*
> *And lie under the thatched awning.*
> *Moor the boat, moor the boat!*
> *Fan off mosquitoes,*
> *No, flies are worse.*
> Chigŭkch'ong chigŭkch'ong ŏsawa.
> *Only one worry, even here,*
> *Traitors might eavesdrop.*

The literary source of the "flies" (green flies or bluebottles) is the 219th poem in the *Book of Songs*, where the flies that buzz about and settle on the fence stand for slanderers. A victim of slander as Yun was, he does not banish grim issues from his rural contemplation. "Traitors" in the original is "Minister Sang," Sang Hung-yang (152–80 B.C.) of the Former Han dynasty, probably a metonymy for the poet's political foe. Poetry cannot be divorced from reality; it is involved in history and, as the poet says, we cannot dismiss its political and social engagements.

Judging from textual evidence and rhetorical strategy, some might say that Yun failed to make his self-image as a fisherman. Yun is not writing an account of his life in his poetry, although his biography and other notices in his *Works* testify to his life-style. Educated in the classics and literature, Yun wished to put his ideals into practice, but he learned painfully that he was born for something other than factional politics. In his poetry he accepts the heavenly charge of being a guardian of nature ("Heaven appoints me guardian/ Of peaceful hills and waters") and declares, "Nothing can match my idle pleasures/ Among trees and springs" (*Random Thoughts*, 5). There is no need to separate fact (self) from fiction (role): Who has ever thought that Yun Sŏndo was a simple fisherman-recluse?

Delighting in the manifold richness and beauty of nature, Yun has devoted his life to the truth of feeling. Consider these spontaneous expressions of his freedom and joy as a fisherman:

The Fisherman's Song stirs my fancy;
I have forgotten all about fishing.

("SPRING," 5)

The heart shouts its peak of joy,
I have lost my way in the dark.

("SPRING," 9)

Rod on my shoulder,
I can't still my loud heart.

("SUMMER," 1)

Whelmed by my exalted mood,
I had not known day was ending.

("SUMMER," 6)

I'll angle there, of course, but
My zestful spirit is enough.

("AUTUMN," 4)

In an empty boat, with straw cape and hat,
I sit and my heart beats fast.

("WINTER," 7)

In all these passages, Yun uses the technical term *hŭng*, signifying a surplus of emotion, and its various combinations. Verging on ecstasy, or a sensible ecstasy—for he has not thrown decorum overboard—his subjectivity characterizes his poetry, his sense of himself as individual and center. One is impressed by Yun Sŏndo's sense of craft and vocation, his delight in the exercise of linguistic possibilities to convert experience into art. He sounds most himself. No other *sijo* poet wrote like him, and no other *sijo* poet would prove more exhilerating and rewarding. Yun Sŏndo is a poet for all seasons.

"The Disappointing Journey"

Yun Sŏndo was summoned to the capital by King Hyojong in 1652, but the poet's political enemies defamed and reviled him, and he retired to his retreat after a month's stay at court. There, Yun wrote "The Disappointing Journey" (1652) (literally, "A Dream Visit to Heaven," nos. 73–75), in which the "Jade Emperor" is King Hyojong himself, and the "host of spirits" represents Yun's opponents. In the closing poem, Yun laments the absence of wise ministers who could "raise up" the "White Jade Tower" by delivering the state from the evils of the day.

PETER H. LEE

Further Reading

Translation

Lee, Peter H. *Pine River and Lone Peak: An Anthology of Three Chosŏn Dynasty Poets.* Honolulu: University of Hawaii Press, 1991. Includes a critical introduction to Yun Sŏndo's life and works, together with a complete annotated translation of all of Yun's seventy-five poems. A general introduction relates the poet and his work to the political and cultural context. The book also includes information about and translations of poems by Chŏng Ch'ŏl (1537–1594) and Pak Illo (1561–1643).

THE CLOUD DREAM OF THE NINE

Title in Korean: *Kuun mong*
Author: Kim Man-jung (Kim Man-Choong)
Born: 1637 in Korea
Died: 1692, on the island of Namkae, Korea
Literary Form: Novel
Date of Composition: Most critics believe that Kim in 1687 wrote *Kuun mong* in classical Chinese. Oldest extant version in woodblock print written in classical Chinese dated 1725. Versions in Korean published after 1725.

Major Themes

Life, even at its best, is a dream, an illusion.
Karma is the ruling principle of life.
The Confucian ideal of womanhood should prevail.
One must earn understanding through repeated trials.

Kim Man-jung was born shortly after his father's suicide in 1637. Together with his brother, Kim was brought up by his mother, a learned and noble woman whose family line could be traced to the royal house. Kim and his brother grew up in a strictly Confucian household. At the age of twenty-eight, Kim's name was on the top list of the National Civil Examination. From then on, Kim began a tumultous career at the royal court, which was divided into several factions fighting for power. Rising and falling with the unstable fate of his party, Kim was dismissed from and recalled to service at court many times. He served as the Minister of the Board of Works and as an official in the Board of Rites. Kim was twice exiled, first to Sŏnch'ŏn in 1687 and later, in 1689, to the island of Namhae, where he died three years later.

It was during his exile in Sŏnch'ŏn that Kim wrote *The Cloud Dream of the Nine*, in part to comfort his aged mother during his absence. Besides the *Kuun mong*, Kim also left behind him many essays and poetry, as well as another shorter novel named *Sa-ssi Namiŏng Ki (The Story of Lady Hsieh's Dismissal)*, which was written during his second exile in Namhae. Some critics see this short novel as a satire of King Sukchong and his concubines.

Korean scholars are divided by two theories concerning the origin of the novel. One proclaims that *The Cloud Dream of the Nine* was originally written in Korean and later translated into Chinese. The other insists on the opposite view, arguing that the oldest extant woodblock version that can be found today is written in classical Chinese, the official language of the Korean court where Kim worked. Given his knowledge of classical Chinese and poetry, it would not have been difficult for him to write the *Kuun mong* in Chinese.

The Cloud Dream of the Nine

The Chinese original of the novel is divided into sixteen chapters. Each is preceded by a couplet summarizing the action and theme of the following chapter. This is a very common technique in Chinese classical novels. Of the two translators of the *Kuunmong*, Dr. James S. Gale, follows closely to this structure in his translation, while Richard Rutt puts the whole novel in seven chapters with subsections within each chapter.

The novel is divided into three main parts: (1) the prologue in which the protagonist, Hsing-chen, the young Buddhist monk, because of delaying his return to the monastery on Lotus Peak by flirting with the eight fairies (messengers of a heavenly queen), is sent to Hell and then transmigrated into Yang Shao-yu as a punishment; (2) the story of

Shao-yu's realization of his dream of success at court, and of his happy marriage to eight beautiful and charming women (reincarnations of the eight fairies): Princess Ying-yang (Cheng Ch'iung-pei), Princess Lang-yang, Kuei Ch'an yueh, Ti Ching-hung, Po Ling-po, Chen Niao-yen, Ch'in Ts'ai-feng, and Chia Ch'un-yun; this second part itself has two sections: (a) the story of how Shao-yu comes across the eight women and how he approaches each one of them, and (b) the story of his marriage to all of them, and of how he manages to live in harmony with them all; (3) the account of how, at the end of his mortal existence as Yang Shao-yu, the protagonist becomes once again the monk Hsing-chen, and the eight fairies of Lady Wei become Buddhist nuns.

Life Is Like a Dream

The title, *The Cloud Dream of the Nine* (or *A Nine-Cloud Dream*) signifies a story with the theme of a "dream" that permits the inhabitants of one world to take on new identities and learn from the experiences of living in another world. In this dream the monk, Hsing-chen, undertakes the journey of rebirth in the person of Yang Shao-yu, who excels in both literary and martial skills and so impresses the empress dowager that she chooses him to be her son-in-law. Furthermore, because of Shao-yu's many excellent qualities, eight beautiful women, including a princess, become his wives and amiably work together while sharing one husband. Shao-yu lives the best life that can be lived on earth, with unprecedented success and recognition at court, and with eight outstanding and talented women all serving him with one devoted heart devoid of jealousy and intrigue. This long and happy life continues at court with the royal family until the time comes for his awakening and reincarnation. (Shao-yu and his eight wives are the "nine" of the title.)

In what way is Shao-yu's life a dream? In the prologue, Hsing-chen enters the mundane world or the "dream" by fainting and losing consciousness. When he opens his eyes again, he is reborn as the hermit Yang's child. The last awakening appears in the epilogue when Shao-yu opens his eyes and discovers that he is once again the monk Hsing-chen "dreaming" in his own cell.

Kim's intention in the novel is to present his world view that although life is worth living, it is, even at its best, only a dream. Sooner or later, all of us will have to wake up from it. The idea is not that since life is painful and transient, one must transcend or avoid getting involved with the mundane. It is that even with its utmost bliss, life is just a dream, an illusion. When one wakes up, everything will be gone. These four lines of verse from the Diamond Sutra expounded by the Buddhist master Liu Kuan in the epilogue strengthens the theme of dream:

> *All is dharma, illusion:*
> *A dream, a phantasm, a bubble, a shadow,*
> *Evanescent as dew, transient as lightning;*
> *And must be seen as such.*

(RUTT, TRANS., 1974)

The "cloud" of the title refers to the evanescence and transience of happiness and bliss enjoyed by these nine people; it signifies the mystery of reality, and it suggests the mist that clouds human understanding. The novel begins with an account of China's five sacred mountains and of the clouds that hide their peaks. Near the end of the novel, as Shao-yu is waking from his life-dream, a great cloud surrounds him and then disappears as he discovers that he is once again a poor Buddhist priest. After Shao-yu wakes up as Hsing-chen in his cell, he is joined later by the eight young women in his master's lecture hall. Hsing-chen becomes the master at the Lotus Peak monastery; the eight women become nuns. All nine of them realize that the mundane happiness they had experienced in the past was nothing but a dream, an illusion. In their new life, the eight nuns follow the master's teachings, and all nine together enter Paradise.

A Buddhist Novel

The incarnation of the nine protagonists follows closely a Buddhist theory. The cause of transmigration is karma: since Hsing-chen has carelessly flirted with the eight fairies sent by Lady Wei to his master, all nine of them will be banished from their present existence to expiate their sins. In other words, all nine of them will be reborn with a different identity in the mundane world until their karma is exhausted. As a monk, Hsing-chen had been an outstanding novice to his master Liu Kuan. Although the young man was barely twenty years old, he had mastered all the scriptures. His spiritual accomplishments as a monk earn him merit in his next life as Shao-yu, who possesses most of what a man may desire: beautiful women, literary talents, martial powers, the emperor's favor, a long and blissful life with many prosperous children.

The eight women, by the same token, are reborn as different women who eventually come across Shao-yu and marry him. They are attached to him because of their previous karma with Hsing-chen by the waterfall where they first meet. Since the eight beauties have participated in flirting with the young novice, they are destined to marry him and live out that karma in their next life. In the epilogue, Shao-yu, an old man now, tells his wives that he plans to leave them to pursue a spiritual life. Shao-yu declares to them, "There are three ways on earth: the way of Confucius, the way of the Buddha, and the way of the Taoists. Buddhism is the best of the three." (Rutt, trans., 1974).

There are significant Buddhist overtones invested in the characters" names. For example: "Hsing-chen" means "true to the Buddha nature"; "Ch'un-yun" means "Spring Cloud," something light but fleeting; "Ch'an Yueh" signifies "Moonbeams"; "Niao-yen" is "Wreath of Mist," "Po Ling-po" means "White Waves"—all of these conjure up the image of something illusory and evanescent. Perhaps, the most effective name belongs to Hsing-chen's master Liu Kuan; the name means the "Six Illusions," a term from the Diamond Sutra, meaning a dream, a phantasm, a bubble, a shadow, dew, and lightning. (See *Rutt*, 1974).

Women in Confucian Korea

Korea was still very much under Chinese influence in the seventeenth century. All three Chinese philosophical and religious schools—Confucianism,

Taoism, and Buddhism—existed side by side in Korea at that time. Both Buddhism and Confucianism are significant influences in the novel.

The young scholar Shao-yu braves the pain of leaving his widowed mother behind and decides to come to the capital for the National Civil Examination, an ultimate project for all Confucian scholars. Later, he fulfills his obligation of filial piety by sending for his mother to come to the palace after he becomes successful. The most Confucian aspect of the novel has to do with the eight female protagonists and their relationship with men, especially Shao-yu.

Ch'iung-pei, the first woman offically engaged to Shao-yu, is faced with a great problem when the empress dowager decides that Shao-yu would make the best husband for the princess, Lan-yang. In such a circumstance, Shao-yu cannot and dare not make a decision for himself, since he must stay loyal to the emperor, as the Confucian precept requires. Ch'iung-pei, in this awkward situation, cannot hope to compete with the princess. Luckily, at the end, the empress dowager makes a compromise by adopting Ch'iung-pei as her daughter and marrying both Ch'iung-pei and Lan-yang to Shao-yu as principal wives. The remaining six women, having met and slept with Shao-yu before his marriage to the princess, all become his concubines. None of the women—isolated before marriage and obedient to their husbands afterwards—has any significant control over her destiny.

The novel expresses an unqualified acceptance of polygamy. Once the status of the eight women in Yang's household is set and clarified, there are no further arguments or changes. The principal wife will be the leader and head of the concubines, who must follow and obey her. She will see to it that the family lives in harmony and that all the wives work for the comfort and well-being of the husband, the head of the family. In the society of which they are a part, the eight wives are condemned to lead sequestered and subservient lives; although they manage to enjoy life, there are moments of fundamental dissatisfaction and regret.

The Cloud Dream of the Nine presents an extreme (and implausible) case in which eight women live in peace and happiness serving one husband, thereby enabling Yang Shao-yu to fulfill the Confucian requirement of disciplining his family before giving time and energy to serving his country. The entire situation as pictured in the novel may seem dream-like to the modern reader, but it presents a poignant and sometimes charming portrait of another time and another culture, while underscoring some fundamental convictions about the illusory character of mundane existence.

FATIMA WU

Further Reading

Translations

Gale, James S., trans. *The Cloud Dream of the Nine.* London: Westminster Press, 1922. This is probably one of the first translations of the novel in sixteen chapters. Includes a thirty-nine-page introduction by Elspet Keith Robertson Scott that includes a plot summary and information about the author and translator. There are sixteen black and white illustrations. The seven-page appendix provides footnotes clarifying names, terms, and idioms used in the translation.

Rutt, Richard, trans. Kim Man-jung's *A Nine Cloud Dream,* in *Virtuous Women: Three Classic Korean Novels*, translations by Richard Rutt and Kim Chong-un. Seoul: Royal Asiatic Society, 1974. Mr. Rutt also provides a detailed introduction to the novel on pages 3–15. This is a translation from a two-volume woodblock Chinese edition printed at Naju in 1725. The novel is divided into seven chapters.

THE SONG OF A FAITHFUL WIFE

Title in Korean: *Ch'unhyang ka (Ch'unhyang chŏn)*
Author: Original author unknown
Literary Form: Oldest version in a long poem. Later versions written for singing. Modern rewritings mainly in prose, interpolated with verses.
Date of Composition: Date of origin unknown. Oldest extant version in 1754. The singing version written down by Shin Chae-hyo (1812–1884). Modern rewritings from 1911 on.

Major Themes

A woman must serve only one man in her life, dead or alive, in poverty or in sickness.

Marriage across class boundaries will be blessed by heaven if the couple is devoted and faithful to each other.

Social injustice will be eliminated by faith and persistence.

No one knows the name of the original author of *Ch'unhyang ka*; no one knows when the tale was first written. But every Korean knows the story inside out. *Ch'unhyang ka* has appeared in books, films, paintings, storytelling and singing since its first debut back in the eighteenth century. The earliest version of the story available today is in poetic form written in Chinese by Yu Chin-han in 1754. Between 1866 and 1884, the famous Korean music teacher, Shin Chae-hyo (Sin Chae-hyo, 1812–1884) wrote two Korean versions of the story for singing. After the turn of the century, modern revisions in Korean swamped the literary field with deviations in the plot of the story.

The earliest English translation of *Ch'unhyang ka* by James Gale appeared in September 1917. A sound and scholarly translation of the work, however, did not appear until much later. (The following discussion focuses mainly on Richard Rutt's translation, which is considered by far the most thorough, academic, and professional.)

The *Ch'unhyang ka* is divided into four parts. The first one, which is the longest, depicts Ch'unhyang (Spring Fragrance), her early life and her meeting with the hero, Yi Mong-nyong (Dreaming of the Dragon) in the city of Namwŏn. The two teenagers immediately fall in love with each other and they swear eternal love. Marriage is arranged by Ch'unhyang's mother, Wŏl-mae (Moonlit Plum Blossom), and the young couple are happily united.

In the second part, Mong-nyong is summoned by his father, a government official who is being transferred back to Seoul. Ch'unhyang and Mong-nyong are separated, but the young bride swears devotion and constancy to her husband.

In the third part, a new governor appears, who is attracted by Ch'unhyang's beauty and presses her for love. When she declines his favor, she is tortured and later locked up in prison.

The last part depicts Mong-nyong in Seoul acquiring for himself a government position as a secret inspector of eight different provinces. When he comes to Namwŏn, upon testing his wife and confirming her love and faithfulness to him, he secures her release. The couple is joined once again, and they live happily ever after. They have three sons and two daughters who all rise to the first rank of nobility.

Influence of Confucianism and Buddhism

The story of *Ch'unhyang ka* is almost in all respects indebted to a Confucianism and a Buddhism transmitted earlier from China to Korea. Confucian and Chinese feudal ideology is manifested throughout the work: Yi Mong-nyong aims at the civil examination given by the government as a way of recruiting new talents in the country, a social practice in China since the Han Dynasty (207 B.C.–A.D. 220). Often, the selected candidate will be given a new official title in which he will work as a secret inspector to the provinces to eliminate corruption and injustice. In the story, Mong-nyong is given exactly that post, which eventually enables him to save Ch'unhyang from further imprisonment and possible execution.

Filial piety is also obvious in the relationship between Mong-nyong and his father. Mong-nyong obeys his father's wish that Mong-nyong study hard for the civil examination, and he obediently follows his father back to Seoul, even though he is deeply in love with Ch'unhyang. Since Mong-nyong had arranged his own marriage with Ch'unhyang without his father's knowledge or consent, he has to suffer the separation from Ch'unhyang. In arranging his own marriage, Mong-nyong violated the Confucian ideal of filial piety, but he later redeemed himself by his victory in the civil examination, thereby bringing glory to the family name.

The Confucian orthodox idea of women and chastity forms the main storyline. Ch'unhyang pledges her love to Mong-nyong at their marriage. Her mother Wŏl-mae makes it clear that Ch'unhyang is a headstrong woman when it comes to love and marriage, and both women see the union as one sanctioned by heaven and earth, instead of as a game played by two immature adolescents. After Mong-nyong announces his departure for the capital, Ch'unhyang faints after much weeping and beating herself. She swears constancy and eternal love for her husband, whom she can see only in her dreams.

When the new governor Pyŏn Hak-to comes to Namwŏn, he presents the lonely Ch'unhyang with prospects of a luxurious life. Compared to the young Yi Mong-nyong, Pyŏn is a famous, well-respected writer and official of his time. Ch'unhyang is in fact given a second chance to improve her status as the daughter of a *kisaeng*, a female entertainer for men. Yet she refuses the new governor's offer on the ground that she is already married to another man. Ch'unhyang suffers physical punishment and threats from Pyŏn without flinching. She puts her life and safety at stake because of her constancy toward Mong-nyong. This is a per-

fect manifestation of the Confucian precept concerning women: to starve to death is a small matter, but to lose one's chastity is a fundamental violation of morality.

Ch'unhyang is the epitome of a faithful wife for all to praise and emulate. Her courage during the beatings and her incarceration are particularly admirable. At times, even her mother Wŏl-mae loses faith in Mong-nyong, but not Ch'unhyang, who is prepared to die if worse comes to worst.

Buddhist influence is prominent throughout the story. The birth of the protagonist, Ch'unhyang, amounts to almost a supernatural event. Ch'unhyang's mother, Wŏl-mae, goes to the sacred mountains to make sacrifices to the gods on the fifth day of the fifth month. That same evening, she dreams that a fairy enters her bosom and she becomes pregnant. When her daughter is born months later, the room is filled with fragrant flowers and colorful clouds. The child Ch'unhyang grows up to become a beautiful and virtuous woman.

At Ch'unhyang and Mong-nyong's first meeting, Wŏl-mae discloses that she had a prophetic dream the night before. There was a green dragon swimming in a lake surrounded by peach trees. Dragons and peaches are significant symbols in Asian culture. Yet the predestined meeting between the protagonists in the story illustrates the further influence of fate.

Another strong Buddhist element that can be found in the work appears when Ch'unhyang, suffering from illness and pain in prison, asks her mother Wŏl-mae to find her a fortune-teller. Alone and helpless, Ch'unhyang seeks support from religious sources. The blind fortune-teller's encouraging words put her at ease and give her an incentive to hold on longer for Mong-nyong.

The ending of the story, with good prevailing over evil, is heavily Buddhist. Pyŏn is overcome by Mong-nyong because of his bad karma. Pyŏn has imprisoned an innocent woman just because she refuses to serve him. Also, his lack of care for his people, as well as his extravagance and pride shown during his birthday party, contribute to his final fall. Mong-nyong is able to succeed because of his diligence towards his studies, his filial piety, and his undying love for Ch'unhyang. Our heroine, of course, deserves the happy reunion with her husband because of her devotion, sacrifice, and dedication to love. Through her courageous battle to keep herself chaste, Ch'unhyang achieves the heights of womanly virtue.

The p'ansori

The *p'ansori* is a narrative poem including songs, performed by a single professional singer, a *kwangdae,* who has an excellent voice and memory. A master in this genre, Shin Chae-hyo, wrote down a *p'ansori* version of *The Song of a Faithful Wife* in the late nineteenth century, incorporating the details and songs that had developed during the *p'ansori* performances. The poetry is effective in providing the account of events; the songs sung by Ch'unhyang are lyrical and expressive. Audiences listening to the *p'ansori* performances, involving a single singer and a drummer, were caught up in the events and the passions expressed in the songs; they were able, in effect, to live through the harrowing and inspiring tale.

In the prose narratives of *Ch'unhyang ka*, the reader is drawn into the tale through the author's use of humor and erotic details. Humor is expressed by the servants, valets, and secondary characters, and a romantic eroticism is found in the portrayal of the youngsters' wedding night, when they spend the whole night merry-making with their bodies. Although the author uses euphemisms for the private parts, the love scene continues for ten pages. The importance of the sexual encounter consists in its meaning as the expression of the deep love between the two protagonists, which serves as the motivating force accounting for Ch'unhyang's constancy during imprisonment and torture.

Virtue Overcomes Class Distinctions

Besides the theme of female chastity, *Ch'unhyang ka* also sheds lights on the issues of class boundaries and social injustice. Ch'unhyang is the daughter of a government minister and a *kisaeng*. Her parents are not married, and later Wŏl-mae is responsible for bringing up her daughter on her own. Ch'unhyang is known throughout the city of Namwon as the daughter of a *kisaeng*, not as the child of a minister.

On the other hand, Yi Mong-nyong is the son of a court official, and a successful candiate at court himself. His marriage to Ch'unhyang is not even known to his parents until the very end. In conventional society, such a union could hardly be considered as a legitimate one. Ch'unhyang, at most, could be made into a concubine in Yi's family, according to the social norm of the time. Yet, this story aims at glorifying love, a true love that overcomes class boundaries. Ch'unhyang becomes an exemplary character for all women. Hence, her virtue elevates her above her social class. Her virtue in chastity gives her a moral identity that impresses everyone, even the emperor himself.

Victory over Social Injustice

Another sub-theme in *Ch'unhyang ka* deals with social injustice. The story concerns the abuse of power by civil authorities, illustrated by Pyŏn's attempt to use Ch'unhyang for his own pleasure. In the course of developing the theme that moral virtue is superior to power and can overcome corruption, the damage done by authoritarian abuses and by class distinctions is made clear.

The moral themes of the *Song of a Faithful Wife* are made attractive through a kind of exaggerated portrayal of Ch'unhyang's plight. She is tortured— and breaks into song. With every stroke of the paddle, Ch'unhyang sings another defiant song. The result is that a kind of aesthetic distance is achieved: although the audience understands that she is suffering, they are delighted by her singing response, and they know by the folktale tradition that she will eventually triumph.

Not only does Ch'unhyang have a song for every stroke of the paddle—she manages to fasten on the number of the stroke and to sing about a situation that involves that number. For example, after the first stroke:

One heart undivided,
Faithful to one husband,
One punishment before one year is over,
But for one moment I will not change.

And after the second:

Two spouses are faithful,
Two husbands there cannot be,
Though my body is beaten,
Though I die for ever,
I'll never forget master Yi.

And after the twenty-fifth stroke, as her body is covered with blood and tears, she sings:

Playing the lute of twenty-five strings,
In the moonlight I cannot restrain my sorrow.
Wild goose, where are you flying?
If you go to Seoul,
Take a message to my beloved,
Who lives in the Three Springs Vale:
See what I look like now;
Take care you don't forget.

(RUTT, TRANS., IN LEE, 1981

As a tale of the triumph of virtue, *Song of the Faithful Wife* is thus both instructive and entertaining; it has something of the carefree vitality of folktales or operas in which the villain is starkly evil and offensive, while the hero and heroine are without blemish and have no limits to their courage. But the Confucian and Buddhist context of this tale in poetry and song, together with the features given it by its development in performance in the villages of Korea, make it a unique and much-loved work of literary and musical art.

FATIMA WU

Further Reading

Translations

Gale, James, trans. "Ch'unhyang ka" In *Korea* magazine, September 1917 to July 1918. This appears to be the first English translation of the story, which is completed in eleven installments. Dr. Gale was a missionary from Canada.

Rutt, Richard, trans. *The Song of a Faithful Wife, Ch'unhyang*. In *Virtuous Women: Three Classic Korean Novels*. Pp. 250–333. Seoul: Royal Asiatic Society, 1974. This book contains a complete English translation of *Ch'unhyang ka*. Rutt's translation is based on the Chonju wood-block edition which is usually referred to as the *Wanp'an*, printed in Wangju (no date). It is the longest and fullest of the old versions. The full title of the *Wanp'an* edition is *Yollo Ch'unhyang sujol ka (Song of the Constancy of the Faithful Wife, Ch'unhyang)*.

Related Study and Translation

Lee, Peter H., comp. and ed. *Anthology of Korean Literature: From Early Times to the Nineteenth Century*. Honolulu: The University Press of Hawaii, 1981. In a section entitled "The Art of the Singer: *P'ansori*," pp. 257–284, Lee includes a selection translated by Richard Rutt of *Ch'unhyang ka*, as written for the *p'ansori* by the music master Shin Chae-hyo between 1866 and 1884. It begins with part three of the story, when the new governor of Namwon, Pyon Pak-to, comes to office. The excerpt ends with the happy reunion of Ch'unhyang and Mong-nyong after he delivers her from incarceration. Lee's introduction to the section is a clear explanation of the *p'ansori* and a helpful preface to the selections that follow.

A RECORD OF SORROWFUL DAYS

Title in Korean: *Hanjung nok*
Author: Lady Hong of Hyegyŏng Palace
Born: 1735, Seoul, Korea
Died: 1815, Seoul
Literary Form: Palace literature, autobiographical letter-memoirs
Dates of Composition: 1795–1806

Major Themes

Why does Heaven make humans suffer so unjustly?
Is Heaven totally indifferent to human suffering?

Until the promulgation of *han'gul* (Korean script-writing) in 1447, high-born and learned men had a near-total monopoly of the written word in Korea, because they alone were adequately educated in *hanmun*, that is, the use of Chinese characters. Most women and ordinary people had neither the training nor leisure to become proficient in the use of *hanmun*, a written language alien as well as difficult to learn. Even the women of the *yangban* (gentry) families were discouraged from any systematic training in reading and writing, since book learning was considered both unnecessary and improper for women, their sphere thought to be strictly domestic.

Absence of learning, then, was thought to promote virtue in a woman, and if she was educated, she was expected *not* to exhibit it. If she wrote, therefore, her writing was not to go beyond her family, and for this reason her writings, including letters, were often destroyed by literally having the writing washed off the paper. Even the daughters of the best yangban families were taught only *han'gul* before marriage so they could read in *han'gul* translation of those few works that taught Confucian principles and proper behavior for women.

Thus, one of the real achievements of *han'gul* was that it provided a means of writing for yangban women through a writing system which was not only native and phonetic but also very easy to learn. Besides, because *han'gul* was a phonetic alphabet specifically designed to fit the sound of Korean speech, through it Koreans could represent not only their thoughts and feelings but also the sounds of their own speech, because unlike *hanmun*, *han'gul* could represent the actual sounds of Korean speech with ease and accuracy. While *hanmun* continued to be the written language of the *yangban* men, *han'gul* became the written language mainly of the upper and middle class Korean women who had some education as well as leisure. For this reason, *han'gul* has been called "women's letters" or "female letters."

Palace Literature

"Palace literature" is the name given to those works in *han'gul* written mostly by palace ladies about the lives and events occurring within the palace. The best known works of palace literature are *Hanjung nok* (literally, Records Made in Distress), *Inhyon Wanghu chon* (The Life of Queen Inhyon), and *Kyech'uk ilgi* (Diary of the Year of the Black Ox: 1613). These three works are distinguished not only because they are written in *han'gul* but also because each appears to be written by a court lady who seems to have been an eyewitness to the tragic events recorded in it, thus providing us with invaluable glimpses of the dark underside of life inside the royal palace rarely revealed to the outside world. Of the three, *Hanjung nok* is clearly the most interesting and significant work as literature.

Records Made in Distress

Hanjung nok, most often translated as "Records Made in Distress (or Sorrow)," consists of a series of autobiographical letter-memoirs written by Lady Hong (Princess Hyegyŏng), the widow of Crown Prince Sado (who was put to death in 1762 on the order of his father King Yŏngjo by being buried in a rice chest for seven days).

The letter-memoirs consist of a series of four separate letter-memoirs written by Lady Hong at four different times. The first was written at the time of her sixtieth year, during a brief interval of happiness, in order to leave something of her writing and recollections for the younger members of her natal family. The others were written when she was sixty-seven, sixty-eight, and seventy-one years old, during the extremely trying years after the untimely death of her son, King Chongjo, and they were addressed to her infant grandson—King Sunjo—in an effort to enable him to understand more accurately all the events surrounding the tragic events of 1762 (the year of Imo), and also to clear the names of her own father, uncle, and younger brother who had been variously implicated and punished unjustly by their political foes.

The volume which goes by the name *Hanjung nok* today is thus the modern collations of these four letter-memoirs which have survived in various manuscript versions and forms—one of which is in a manuscript collection at the University of California at Berkeley. (The history and significance of the various surviving manuscripts is too complicated a story to be detailed here.)

The memoirs begin with Lady Hong's happy, though all too brief, childhood in the fold of her family, a distinguished family of scholar-statesmen which had produced a royal son-in-law as well as ministers. At age nine, suddenly and unexpectedly, her childhood came to an end when she was chosen as consort to the crown prince, Sado. To her parents and the older members of the family, her selection must have represented a great honor, but to a nine-year-old girl it was nothing less than a calamity, leaving her both baffled and grief-stricken. Too young to fully appreciate the significance to herself

and her family of her selection, she was devasted by what had befallen her so suddenly and unexpectedly. Her confusion and sorrow seem palpable even half a century later as she reflects on her sorrowful homecoming after the fateful selection:

> When I arrived home, my palanquin was brought in through the guests' entrance, and my father came to help me out, attired in full dress. Both he and mother looked so confused, and were so deferential, that I burst into tears and hugged them both. Mother was also in ceremonial dress, and had covered the table with a red cloth. She behaved very properly, bowing four times on receiving the queen's letter, and twice on receiving Lady Sonhui's [mother of the crown prince].
>
> After that, my parents addressed me differently, using respectful forms of speech. All the family elders, too, treated me with respect, to my great embarrassment. My father, anxious and fearful, kept on instructing me and warning me about so many things, that I felt I had committed some crime, and wished I could hide myself away. I was heartbroken at the prospect of having to leave my parents, and could take no interest in anything.

(CHOE-WALL, TRANS., 1985)

Here we are made to feel not only her dismay over her parents' sudden formality of speech and behavior so upsetting to her, but also her sorrow at the prospect of separation from the family and friends at such an early age. Although her selection was surely an honor to her parents and the rest of the family, such honor mattered little to a nine-year-old child suffering from the grief of separation from her loving parents and family.

The first ten years of her life in the palace were relatively stable and happy. Much loved by King Yŏngjo, her royal father-in-law, and the queen, Lady Sonhui, mother of the crown prince, Lady Hong adjusted to her new life quickly and successfully, and when she gave birth to the royal grandson-to-be, her success as consort to the crown prince seemed assured.

In the meantime, her own family prospered, too. Her father, upon passing the Senior State Civil Service Examination, was appointed to a succession of ever-more-important government posts. But her life was soon caught up in the tragedy which overtook the crown prince, her husband.

Lady Hong locates the origin of the crown prince's growing difficulties with his father in the estrangement which had begun between the father and son not long after the son's birth. She traces it back to the king's decision to house the infant prince in a palace mansion quite a way removed from king's own. According to her, the physical distance had inadvertently led to an emotional distance as well, resulting eventually in a serious estrangement between the father and son.

The crown prince, growing up with little parental guidance or affection and surrounded mostly by female attendants who allowed him to do as he pleased, acquired very little self-discipline, which more and more displeased the king.

Absence of affection between the father and son aggravated the matter. For while the father, lacking in understanding of, and affection for, the son, became increasingly more severe and unhappy with his son; the son on his part became more fearful and resentful of his father's harshness toward him. Whenever the father and son met, "the king's resentment against his son predominated over his affection for him. The son, for his part, was always fearful of seeing the king, and behaved with great caution. . . ." [Choe-Wall].

Coming to what was to her the heart of the matter, Lady Hong writes of the prince's "sickness," which she believed had grown out of his fear of his royal father and his repeated failure to gain the king's favor. Lady Hong writes that it was this "sickness"—a kind of insanity overtaking the crown prince periodically—which drove him to the murders and rapes of court attendants, as well as to brutalities against his own family and herself.

Midpoint through the memoirs there is a poignant illustration of this developing tragedy between the royal father and son. King Yŏngjo, incensed at the crown prince for the numerous murders allegedly committed by him, drops in on him suddenly and unannounced to look into the matter personally. He asks his son if the reports of his misdeeds are true. Making no attempt to conceal them, the prince freely confesses his guilt, and trying to explain his behavior he says:

> "It relieves my pent-up anger, Sire, to kill people or animals when I am feeling depressed or on edge."
>
> The king asked, "Why is that so?"
> "Because I am hurt," answered the prince.
> "Why are you hurt?" the king asked.
> "I am hurt because you do not love me and also, alas, I am terrified of you because you constantly rebuke me, Sire."
> . . . The king seemed to experience a fleeting moment of fatherly compassion for his son. He calmed down somewhat and said, "I will act differently in the future."

(CHOE-WALL, TRANS., 1985)

One of the most dramatic incidents in the memoirs, which also shows Lady Hong's exceptional intelligence, occurs soon after the death of the crown prince through suffocation in the rice chest. Although King Yŏngjo's anger toward his son appeared to have continued unabated even after the son's tortured death, his affection and concern for his royal grandson (and now the designated heir)—the future King Chongjo—seemed actually to have been increased by the tragedy.

Nevertheless, Lady Hong, fully aware of her son's precarious position as heir-designate, tried to do whatever she could to ensure the king's continuing affection for her son. She therefore asked the king to keep his grandson with him and take charge of his education as heir-designate, even though this would mean she would be separated from her son, who was at the time only a ten-year-old little boy.

An especially difficult moment occurred about half a year after the crown prince's death when Lady Hong had an audience with the king and the royal grandson. As she was about to take leave of them, the royal grandson wept inconsolably, unable to contain his grief at being separated from his mother, Lady Hong. Noticing his grandson's sorrow, King Yŏngjo, perhaps a little mortified as well as jealous, suggested to Lady Hong that the royal grandson should perhaps remain with her. Immediately sensing the potential for royal displeasure and the resulting threat to her son's position, Lady Hong managed to do the right thing at this critical juncture, even if it broke her heart. To avoid offending the king she relinquished the company of her son.

What broke her heart was not so much her own loneliness but her ten-year-old son's unhappiness at being separated from her, especially when she saw that her son was weeping because he thought his mother no longer loved him. But suppressing her own emotions, she managed to flatter the aged monarch's ego, thus ensuring her son's position. The old king, understandably pleased with her reply, departed with his little royal grandson, feeling perhaps both vindicated and soothed. By her quick intelligence and self-sacrificing devotion to her son's welfare, she had thus turned a potentially disastrous situation into one of increasing the king's affection and concern for the royal grandson.

Although the main focus of *Hanjung nok* is on the tragedy of Crown Prince Sado and Lady Hong, the letter-memoirs in their entirety present a much larger tragedy. Thus, in her later letter-memoirs, she focuses increasingly on the tragedies that overtook her natal family: not only does her father fall from power, but her uncle and her younger brother are unjustly executed by none other than her own son and grandson, that is, Kings Chongjo and Sunjo. For her brother's death especially, she blames herself, because she believes that her enemies at court, unable to get at her, had directed their venom at him.

Throughout this part of her letter-memoirs, she is also at pains to clear her father of the charges that he had not only conspired to bring about the death of Crown Prince Sado but had also supplied the rice chest in which the crown prince was shut up and left to die. In her own account of the events, she makes it clear that, on the contrary, her father had done everything in his power to protect the crown prince, herself, and the royal grandson.

In the later letter-memoirs, written when she was in her late sixties and early seventies, Lady Hong cries out to Heaven repeatedly, questioning why she and her family have had to suffer so much and so undeservedly. In 1805, at age seventy-one, she returns to her letter-memoirs for one last time in order to give her own account of the events of 1762 so that King Sunjo, her fifteen-year-old grandson, might do justice to her natal family when he becomes king in name, as well as in power. She writes that her life had been "one long series of disasters, and was like a well-frayed cotton thread" and that each word of the letter-memoirs was literally soaked in her heart's blood and tears.

Hanjung nok is thus steeped in what Koreans call *han*, a distillation of long-accumulated bitterness and sorrow which has not been redressed. This probably accounts for the fact that most scholars have construed the title of these letter-memoirs as "Records Made in Distress or Sorrow" rather than as "Records Made in Idleness," for the original title—not of Lady Hong's making—is in *han'gul*, and its first word, *han*, could mean either "distress" or "idleness." Both readings have in fact been used in different editions.

With its powerful though antique prose, steeped in Lady Hong's passionate grief, sorrow, and rage, this record of distress and sorrow is a work of unforgettable vividness, drama, and insight, making it one of the greatest memoirs ever composed in *han'gul*, and a masterpiece of Korean literature.

KICHUNG KIM

Further Reading

Translations

Choe-Wall, Yang Hi, ed. and trans. *Memoirs of a Korean Queen, Lady Hong.* London: KPI Ltd., 1985. The only book-length translation of *Hanjung nok* in English so far that is both accurate and readable. As the translator points out in the introduction, the volume represents the first three chapters of *Hanjung nok* published in Seoul in 1961 under the title *Handyung nok*. (As noted, selections quoted in this article are from Professor Choe-Wall's translation.)

Lee, Peter H., ed. and comp. *Anthology of Korean Literature: From Early Times to the Nineteenth Century.* Honolulu: University Of Hawaii Press, 1990 (Revised). The section entitled "Women Writers" includes a brief introduction to the work of Princess Hyegyŏng and a seven-page translation of an excerpt from her book.

Related Study

Kim, Yongsuk. *Chosonjo yoryumunhak ui yon'gu* (A Study of Chosŏn Dynasty Women Writers). Revised and expanded edition. Seoul: Hyejin Sogwan, 1990. In Korean. This is the best study not only of *Hanjung nok*, but also of the best works of Chosŏn dynasty women writers.

THE WORKS OF PAK CHIWŎN

Author: Pak Chiwŏn. Yonam is his *ho* (pen name)
Born: 1737, Seoul, Korea
Died: 1805, Seoul
Major Works: *Yorha ilgi* (Jehol Diary) (1780); "*Hŏsaeng chŏn*" ("The Story of Master Hŏ"), "*Yangban chŏn*" ("The Story of a Yangban"), "*Hojil*" ("A Tiger's Reprimand"), "*Kwangmuncha chŏn*" ("The Story of Kwangmun"), and "*Yedok Sonsaeng chŏn*" ("The Story of Master Yedok")

Major Themes

One should see things as they actually are, unfettered by past traditions and prejudices.

The real contributors to our society are those who produce the actual goods and services essential to our daily life.

Simple working people are more noble in character than are members of the yongban *class, who inherit privileges they do not earn.*

Pak Chiwŏn, one of the most innovative and creative scholar-writers of his time, was one of the founders of the Northern School of the *Sirhak* movement. To appreciate the intellectual and political climate within which he wrote, a brief review of the *Sirhak* movement is needed.

The Sirhak (Practical Learning) Movement

During its more than 2000 years of recorded history, Korea has suffered few national calamities more devastating than the Japanese invasions of 1592–98 and the Manchu invasions of 1627 and 1636. Not only was the entire country laid waste repeatedly by the successive invasions, the devastations suffered by the people had also exposed just how corrupt and powerless the *yangban* classes (civil and military ruling classes) were, capable neither of protecting the country from foreign invasions nor of restoring the country to any degree of normalcy afterwards by promoting domestic peace, justice, and economic recovery.

A serious self-examination inevitably follows in the aftermath of a national calamity. Many thoughtful observers believed that the root problems of the nation required nothing less than a total and fundamental overhaul of the established institutions. It was in this context the so-called *Sirhak*

(Practical Learning) movement arose. Although there were a few government officials who attempted to bring about the necessary reforms, the main criticism and call for change came from those outside the government, the Sirhak scholars, mostly of the *Namin* (Southerners) faction, who had long been excluded from filling important posts in the government.

The proponents of Sirhak undertook an exhaustive study of Korean society: its political and economic institutions, agricultural technology, commodity exchange system, geography, history, and language. And even though most Sirhak scholars were Confucians, in their investigations into the country's ills they insisted on seeing things as they actually were rather than as they were supposed to be as prescribed by some traditional Confucian theories. They sought truths which could be verified factually or verified through their own study and experiences.

Since the Sirhak scholars were interested first and foremost in remedying the actual ills confronting Korean society, and since the national economy at the time was largely based on agriculture, it was natural that they should focus their attention first on agricultural reforms. Their aim was to improve the living and working conditions of the peasantry by introducing fundamental changes to the system of land ownership, tax collection, corvee labor, and military obligations, as well as many other problems connected with the life of the peasant.

There was also a second school of thought within the Sirhak movement which argued for placing greater importance on manufacturing and commerce. The scholars of this second school, known as the school of Northern Learning, believed that more vigorous and expanded manufacturing and commercial activities were essential to the prosperity of Korean society.

These Sirhak scholars had been greatly influenced by what they learned on their offical trips to Peking, the capital of Ch'ing dynasty China. It was not so much that they admired the Chinese society, for in fact, it was the fashion of the time to despise the Ch'ing China, more in memory of the Ming dynasty than anything else. The scholars of the Northern Learning, on the contrary, thought that Koreans had much to learn from China, such as the Western learning which was then flowing into China. They therefore believed that Koreans should be more rational in their attitude toward China, distinguishing what was inferior in it from what was superior, and thus learn from it what it could teach them and use this knowledge to correct the defects of their own society. What they proposed, as Professor Ki-baik Lee writes, therefore, constituted "a severe indictment of the yangban society of that age."

Pak Chiwŏn: Sirhak Scholar and Writer

Although Pak Chiwŏn wrote everything in *hanmun* (Chinese characters), for he appears to have had little knowledge of *han'gul* (the Korean alphabet), his powerfully provocative stories, sketches, and essays make him not only the outstanding writer of the Sirhak school but also one of the major figures of Korean literature.

Born in 1737 to a distinguished yangban family of little money, he was tutored mostly at home. Instead of sitting for the state civil service examination, the normal path to a career in government, he devoted himself to the study of economics, politics, military science, and literature. Also deeply interested in *Sohak* (Western learning) trickling into Korea through China, he came to believe in the revolution of the earth around its own axis, as did his friend and fellow Sirhak scholar Hong Taeyong.

In 1780, Pak Chiwŏn traveled to Jehol and Peking in an embassy headed by a cousin. While in Peking, he visited both a Catholic church and an astronomical observatory. Appointed to his first government post at age fifty, he occupied a series of minor posts until 1800. Though locally, and on a small scale, he tried to put into practice the reforms he had advocated through much of his life for the improvement of the lives of the peasantry and common people. The year before he retired from government service (1799), Pak Chiwŏn, at the request of King Chongjo (r. 1776–1800), composed and submitted a treatise on the need to limit landownership, and for undertaking agricultural reforms.

Jehol Diary

Pak Chiwŏn's best known work, *Yorha ilgi* (Jehol Diary) (1780), is a record of his journey to Jehol and Peking in northern China (June 25–Oct. 27, 1780). His observations of both people and things in China led him to reflect on the conditions of life in eighteenth-century Korea. For example, he closely observed the many brick-making facilities throughout northern China, which he believed contributed greatly to the improvement of public works, as well as private housing. His account includes lengthy discussions of the superiority of brick over stone for use both in large and small constructions. Bricks, being uniform both in shape and size, unlike stones, are not only easier to transport but also do not require a stonemason to select and to shape them. Even in constructing the *ondol* (a system of heating ducts underneath the floor in traditional Korean houses), bricks would be superior, because not only would they more easily form a smooth flat surface, but heat would be transmitted more quickly and uniformly through them.

More than such observed details, however, what has made the *Jehol Diary* a classic of Korean literature is its inclusion of such wonderful satiric tales as *"Hosaeng chŏn"* (The Story of Master Ho) and *"Hojil"* (A Tiger's Reprimand).

"The Story of Master Hŏ"

"The Story of Master Hŏ" is a utopian tale of sorts, presenting one of Pak Chiwŏn's visionary schemes for Korean society. A utopian vision is, by its very nature, an implicit criticism of the present conditions of society, for by dreaming of a perfect society elsewhere, the dreamer expresses, though indirectly, his profound disaffection with the present order.

Our first impression of Master Hŏ is not very encouraging, for he seems totally oblivious and indifferent to his physical surroundings and to the practical necessities of daily living. While his wife ekes out a living for them both by taking in sewing, he does nothing but read books. He has not even taken the civil service examination, however, and seems to possess no practical skill of any kind which could earn him a living.

Pushed into money-making by the nagging of his wife, however, Master Hŏ proves to be an able man of vision as well as of business enterprise. With 10,000 *yang* (a unit of money) borrowed from the richest man in town, he proceeds to gain an enormous profit by cornering the market, first in fruit, then in horse hair (used in the making of hats). And, most significantly, unlike others of his class who do not wish to soil their hands with money, he not only knows how to make money but also how to use it effectively. For it is in the use of money that he shows himself to be a visionary reformist.

Meeting with a band of thieves who have been disturbing the country, he asks them if they would give up thievery if they were each given a chance to settle down with a wife and ox to become honest farmers. They agree to the condition and give up thievery. Hiring a fleet of ships, Hŏ takes them to an uninhabited island, helps them establish a thriving agricultural community there, and then having culled out all those who can read and write—to pluck "the roots of strife from the soil of this island"—he returns to Korea.

The story concludes with Master Hŏ back in Korea where he finds the yangban rulers of the country unwilling to undertake any reforms which might help save the country. Reality dashes his dreams. And since the real world of eighteenth-century Korea has no use for an able men like him, he soon vanishes without a trace.

Pak Chiwŏn's utopian vision, which forms the heart of "The Story of Master Hŏ," is thus presented like a fleeting dream, preceded and followed by the reality of the Korea of his day.

Money and Commerce

Traditionally, members of the yangban class were not supposed to soil themselves with money or commerce; they were to be concerned mainly with the study of ancient sages, the classics of China, and statecraft. The business of money, trade, and manufacturing was to be left to the lower classes. Pak Chiwŏn challenges this traditional yangban attitude. He sees that money, trade, and manufacturing are the very foundation of a nation's livelihood. Unless these matters are well managed, a nation and its people cannot prosper. Since these were matters of utmost importance to the nation, the yangban, supposedly the ablest members of society, should take an active interest in, and control of these issues.

In expressing this opinion about the yangban attitude towards money and commerce, Pak Chiwŏn emphasizes the main thrust of Sirhak thinking: to see things as they really are, unfettered by past traditions and prejudices, and to try to bring about practical improvements in the life of the people by pragmatic and concrete methods of rectification and improvement.

"The Story of a Yangban"

Himself a member of the yangban literati, Pak Chiwŏn directs his sharpest barbs at his own class, scholars and officials, because he believes they have brought the country to its moral, political, and economic bankruptcy by their own hypocrisy, parasitic life-style, and head-in-the sand attitude.

In his satirical sketch "*Yangban chŏn*" ("The Story of a Yangban")—one of his earlier stories, composed before *Jehol Diary*—Pak Chiwŏn characterizes a yangban as a good-for-nothing who is incapable of earning even his own livelihood. He puts the jeering words into the mouth of the yangban's wife. Her yangban husband is about to be jailed for being unable to repay the loan of government grain on which he had been living. She tells him: "You always love to study, but you're no good at returning the government grain. A yangban you say, but your kind isn't worth a penny." (Lee, trans., 1990).

The yangban is imprisoned and has no way of returning what he owes. However, a rich man volunteers to settle the account if the yangban turns over his title to the rich man. A magistrate draws up a deed and reads from it to the rich man, saying in part, ". . . from now on you must give up mean and base thoughts and imitate the ancients. . . . You must always arise at the fifth watch, light the oil lamp, focus on the tip of your nose and sit with your buttocks on your heels, and recite from the *Critical Writings of Tung-lai* as smoothly as a gourd rolling on ice. . . . You should summon your slave girls with a drawn-out voice, and walk in a leisurely manner, dragging your shoes." (Lee, trans., 1990).

The story suggests that measured against what he ought to be, the yangban of Pak Chiwŏn's time was no more than an empty shell with no real substance; at worst, he's virtually a parasite or thief who lives by preying on other's industry. The magistrate continues:

> "They [the yangbans] do not till the soil or engage in trade. With a smattering of classics and histories, the better ones will pass the final examination [becoming officials], lesser ones will become doctors. The red diploma of the final examination is no more than two feet long, but it provides everything one needs indeed it is like a purse. . . ." (Lee, trans., 1990).

The rich man, upon hearing of the abuse the yangban can heap upon his neighbors, finally interrupts the magistrate and refuses to become a yangban; he then departs, shaking his head.

"A Tiger's Reprimand"

"*Hojil*" (Tiger's Reprimand) provides another amusing but devasting indictment of the yangban. An episode incorporated in the *Yorha ilgi*, it is a fable in which the main character is a famished man-eating tiger, while the object of the satire is one Master Puk Gwak, who is reputed to be at once a profoundly learned and morally exemplary Confucian scholar. But once again the focus of the story is on what is wrong with the yangban. The following is a brief summary of the story: A famished tiger is looking for a man to eat. But he is not too keen on a physician or shaman, because he fears that they might turn out to be unwholesome. They might be poisoned to the marrow of their bones by the unrequited bitterness of their many patients and clients who have been killed off by their lies and mumbo-jumbo. So the tiger decides on Master Puk Gwak, a yangban scholar, since a scholar is supposed to be clean and uncomplicated.

In the meantime, Master Puk Gwak, reputed to be a moral exemplar, is carrying on an illicit affair with a widow in the village who has had five children by five different men. One night at the widow's house, her five children overhear whispers coming from their mother's room. Although it sounds like their mother and Master Puk Gwak are whispering together, how could that be? Since Master Puk Gwak must know full well he ought not to be in a room alone with their mother, a widow, the children decide it cannot be Master Puk Gwak but a wily fox disguised as Master Puk Gwak. So, with sticks and clubs in their hands, they rush into the room. Barely making his escape in the darkness of the night, Master Puk Gwak falls into a pool of excrement, sinking to his neck. When he crawls out of the cesspool, he is confronted by the tiger who has been looking for him. Because of the awful stink, however, the tiger blocks his nostrils and turns his head away.

> "How awful the scholar stinks!" the tiger exclaims, frowning. Master Puk Gwak, terri-

fied of the tiger, prostrates himself before the tiger, and kowtowing three times, begs for mercy:

"Great is the virtue of the tiger, for you set an example for emperors, sons, generals. All look to you. . . ."

"Don't come near me," the tiger tells Master Puk Gwak. "Yes, I've heard that Confucian scholars are wily, and now I know it's true. Whereas you usually have nothing good to say about me, now just because you're in danger and in front of me, you act as if you've never bad-mouthed me. So you flatter me instead. How could anyone believe what you say?"

(KIM, TRANS., FROM YI WUSONG, 1978)

"The Life of Kwangmun"

While Pak Chiwŏn draws his worst characters—idlers, hypocrites, and parasites—from the yang-ban class, he draws his exemplary characters mainly from the lower classes. From them we can get a glimpse of the sorts of people he appears to have respected. They are mostly errand boys or manual laborers, such as night-soil collectors, all of them with little education. In other words, they are people at the bottom of the social order who are despised for their menial station in life, even though it is their labor and service that make possible the yangban's life of privilege and leisure.

In "*Kwangmuncha chŏn*" ("The Life of Kwangmun"), for example, the main character is a man who had been a leader of teenage beggars living in an earthen cave on the bank of a creek flowing through the capital. Kwangmun is a good-hearted and honest fellow who helps others in whatever way he can. When a child-beggar dies, he sees to it that the child is buried decently in a cemetery, and afterwards he prays for the peace of the child's spirit. When Kwangmun's virtuous character becomes known, he is recommended to a wealthy pharmacist who employs him to run errands. In that capacity not only does Kwangmun prove his honesty and trustworthiness but through his comic antics he becomes the town's peace- and mirth-maker. Because he is so homely and funny, he can

break up a fight just by making those fighting laugh at his antics. He is also the favorite manager of the city's most popular *kisaengs* (female entertainers), as well as an arranger of loans, all because he is trusted by everyone. Because he has never married, he is often urged to marry. To this he replies: "Generally everybody admires handsomeness, not only the man but woman as well. Since I'm so homely, how could I expect anybody to be attracted to me?" When his friends urge him to get a house of his own, he replies: "Since I have neither parents, siblings, nor children, what do I need a house for? In the morning I go out into the city, and all day long I wander around singing, and when evening comes I just find a place to sleep in a rich man's house."

(KIM, TRANS., FROM YI WUSONG, 1978)

"The Story of Master Yedok"

Perhaps the most exemplary of Pak Chiwŏn's fictional characters is Om Haengsu of "*Yedok Sonsaeng chon*" ("The Story of Master Yedok"). Om Haengsu is a night-soil man, who carries away excrement, selling it to farmers outside the city who use it as fertilizer. The story is in the form of a dialogue between one Master Son'kyul, a noted scholar, and Cha'mok, his top disciple who has decided to quit his master because of his master's friendship with Om Haengsu. Cha'mok considers it a dishonor that his master should befriend a night-soil man. Master Son'kyul explains to Cha'mok why he respects Om Haengsu:

"Since Om Haengsu makes his living by carrying away excrement, maybe we can say he's extremely filthy, but if you were to look into how he makes his living you would see that his life is actually quite fragrant. Although his body is very much soiled, his adherence to virtue is utterly unbending. For even if all the bells in the world were to rust, his virtuousness would suffer no alteration. Thus there's cleanliness in filth, filth in cleanliness. . . .

How many people could look on Om Haengsu without becoming red in the face? That's why I call Om Haengsu my teacher. How dare

I call him a friend! It's because I could not bring myself to calling him by his name that I have given him the title of Master Yedok.

(KIM, TRANS., FROM YI WUSONG, 1978)

The night-soil man, whose job is to carry off others' filth—one of the lowliest of the lowly in society—turns out to be, when examined more closely, the one who helps feed all those who despise him. For the filth he carries off to the farmers becomes the very fertilizer which is essential to the growth of food which the farmers sell to the city dwellers. Thus, not only does Om Haengsu play a vital role in food production, but the excrement is itself a valuable commodity, as valuable as gold, as Pak Chiwŏn once noted in *Yorha Ilgi*: "Although dung is an extremely filthy thing, they [the Chinese] value it like gold in order to use it in their fields. Thus not only is there no excrement on the road but a man follows closely behind the horses, picking up horse dung."

Pak Chiwŏn's Hanmum Style

One of the ironies of Pak Chiwŏn's life was that though a foremost innovative thinker, a writer, and a visionary of his time, he never recognized the value and significance of the *han'gul*, the Korean alphabet. He had, however, practiced innovation in the writing of *hanmun* (Chinese), for he did not believe in a blind and rigid adherence to the classical style of hanmun. He believed that the style of writing should fit the time and needs of the writer and his subject. But for daring to write in an innovative hanmun style he was severely criticized not only by his fellow scholar-officials but by King Chongjo himself, who ordered Pak Chiwŏn to write in a more standard classical hanmun style; Pak Chiwŏn—a minor official at the time—had no choice but to obey. Yet we can sense his frustration from the words given to one of his fictional characters who protests against having to adhere always to the style of the ancients:

"Even if a single passage or a single word seemed a bit new or idiosyncratic, there's

bound to be the question: 'Is there anything like this in the writing of the ancients?' Should the answer be No, 'How dare you write like this!' is the angry rejoinder. But if such a passage were found in the writings of the ancients, why would I need to write like that?" (Kim, trans., from *Pak Kisok*, 1984).

Despite his neglect of the han'gul, however, Pak Chiwŏn's link to Korea's nineteenth-century reform movement for modernization *(kaehwa)* is significant both personally and intellectually. For Yonam's reformist spirit reappears in his grandson, Pak Kyusu (1807–1876), an important minister under King Kojong (r. 1864–1907), who played a key role in nurturing the first reformers of modernization such as Kim Okkyun and Pak Yonghyo at the dawn of modern Korea.

KICHUNG KIM

Further Reading

Translations

As noted, Kichung Kim has translated, into English, passages in Korean that were translated from the Chinese by the authors indicated.

Lee, Peter H., comp. and ed. *Anthology of Korean Literature: From Early Times to the Nineteenth Century*. Revised Edition. Honolulu: The University Press of Hawaii, 1990. Contains Lee's translations of "The Story of Master Ho," pp. 213–21, and "The Story of a Yangban," pp. 222–25. (Unfortunately *Yorha ilgi* has not yet, except in part, been translated into English.)

Pak Kisok. *Pak Chiwŏn munhak yon'gu* (A Study of Pak Chiwŏn's Literary Works). Seoul: ChmChiwon, 1984. In Korean. Includes some translations of Pak Chiwŏn's works from Chinese into Korean.

Yi Wusong, trans. and ed. *Yijo hanmum tanp'yonchip* (A Collection of Choson Dynasty Hanmun Short Stories). Seoul: Illchogak, 1978. The translations here are from Chinese into Korean.

YOUR SILENCE

Title in Korean: *Nim-ŭi ch'imuk* (*Your Silence* or *The Silence of Love*)
Author: Han Yong-un
Born: August 29, 1879, South Chungch'ong Province, Korea
  Died: June 19, 1944, Korea
  Major Works: *Chosŏn pulgyo yusillon* (The Revitalization of Korean Buddhism) (1913), *Pulgyo taejŏn* (Encyclopedic Dictionary of Buddhism) (1915), *Chosŏn tongnip-ŭi so* (Basis for Korean Independence) (1919–1920), *Hŭkp'ung* (Black Wind—novel) (1926), *Nim-ŭi ch'imuk* (Your Silence—poetry) (1926), *Huhŭi* (Regret—novel] (1938), *Pangmyŏng* (The Ill-starred—novel) (1938)

Major Themes

The loved one is not only the beloved; it is everything yearned for.
The loved one is not only that which is loved but also that which loves.
The beloved is everything, the absolute, the personification of emptiness.
Freedom is necessary to the value of all being.
The freedom to love can be gained only by freedom from love.

It is indicative that the entry for Han Yong-un in the sedate *Handbook of National History* lists him first as poet and second as a leader of the March 1, 1919, Korean Independence Movement against Japan. The achievement for which he is best remembered is the sequence of eighty-eight loosely linked poems, together with the integral preface and afterward, *Your Silence*, love poems addressed to a richly ambiguous "you" or "lover."

Han Yong-un was born on August 29, 1879, in South Chŭngch'ŏng Province to a Korea just beginning to sense the pressures that were ultimately to force the end of seclusion, and the beginning of her intercourse with the West. The disintegrating Yi dynasty, bereft of the Confucian idealism of its founding, was floundering under the weight of a corrupt bureaucracy and pressures from the world outside to end its isolation. Reforms put forth in the eighteenth century had been rejected; repeated uprisings in the countryside had drained the dynasty's resources as the country became a target for the incursion of Western capitalism. Wracked by mutiny within, and barraged by greater guns without, the ship of state was badly buffeted by 1905 when, in the wake of the Russo-Japanese War, Korea lost her sovereignty and surrendered the conduct of her foreign affairs to Japan, followed in 1910 by the abdication of the Korean king in favor of the Japanese Emperor.

So the poet in "Life":

Anchor and rudder lost, the small boat of life adrift on an angry sea, the thread of hope of the yet undiscovered dreamed-of golden land becomes compass, course, and a fair wind, sailing upon a frightful sea where, on one side the waves beat against the sky, on the other, the land.
My love, take this poor life I dedicate to you, hold it tight to your breast.
Even though this poor life crumble against your breast, in that sacred land of happiness the fragments of my fully dedicated life will become the rarest of jewels, each fitted to the next, decorating your breast, a badge of love.
My love! My love is like a tiny bird in the endless desert where there is not even a branch to nest on; hold it to your breast until it crumbles.
And then, one by one, kiss the fragments of my life.

While Han Yong-un was both poet and novelist, he was not a member of any of the many Western-influenced literary coteries which dominated the formative years of modern Korean literature in the first quarter of this century. His profession and dedication were those of a Buddhist monk and reformer, a spiritual leader of his people in the struggle against the yoke of Japanese colonial rule. His poems in *Your Silence*, growing out of that dedication, were meant to be a vehicle along that way. His "Preface" sets both tone and theme:

> *The loved one is not only the loved one; is also everything yearned for. If all human kind be Sakyamuni's loved one, philosophy is Kant's. If the gentle spring rain is loved by the rose, then Italy is loved by Mazzini. You are not only what I love, but are what loves me.*
>
> *If love be freedom, then you are freedom also. But aren't you all helpless, fettered by the high-sounding name of freedom? You say you have a love, even you? If so, it is no love, it is your shadow.*
>
> *I write these poems thinking of lambs wandering the darkening plain searching for their lost way home.*

Despite, or, perhaps, because of this avowed extra-literary purpose, he produced a book which stands very high in the repository of world poetry. His disclaimer in the afterword states his view of the fugitive value of the poems; poor as they may be, they are addressed to the problems of the here and now, and are not a search for immortality:

> *Readers. I am ashamed to set myself up as a poet before you. I know as you read my poems you will be disappointed in me and for yourselves. I have no mind for your children to read my poems. To read my poems then might well be like rubbing a bit of dry chrysanthemum in your fingers and holding them up to your nose in a flowering glade in late spring.*
> *I don't know how far the night has advanced.*
> *As the darkness thins in Mt. Sorak*
> *I wait for the bell of a dawning day as I put my brush aside.*
> *(The night of the 29th day, 8th month, the year of Ŭlch'uk [1925]). The End.*

All this of a book which has been linked with the poetry of the English Metaphysicals because of its similarity in technique with the work of Tagore because of similarity in tone and theme, and which deserves to stand beside the mystic and religious poetry of Blake, Dante, and St. John of the Cross as a profoundly human poetry of the mystic experience.

What could in any sense be called modern Korean poetry was hardly more than a decade old when Han Yong-un published *Your Silence*. "Modern," in this context, means a poetry written in conscious awareness of Western models, both literary and intellectual. But in a very real sense the work of Han Yong-un is an anachronism in the company of modern Korean poetry. *Your Silence* has its roots in tradition and a firm base in Buddhist philosophy and metaphysics. Superficially, what modernisms do creep in—loan words such as "ink," "kiss," "page," or things like button shoes—suggest a dated diction, a sense of the Korean twenties probably much more obvious in the original than in translation. The landscape is traditional, idyllic and rural; the wheel does not appear in the poems, nor does the modern city, the railroad, the electric light, the telephone. Warships there are, off in the distance as they were in the Korea in which he was born, but the sense of his being in real contact with Western ideas of poetry and literature, a sense that gives an imitative tone to much of the poetry of his contemporaries, is not there.

"Traditional" in this context should be taken to indicate a certain cast of mind, rather than being bound to the prosody and trappings of classical poetry or to a blind conservatism that denies the present—a cast of mind that gave Han Yong-un the means to comprehend the present in terms of the past, to accept change without seeing it as a cutting-off.

It was his Buddhist outlook upon change that made this acceptance of "modernization" on Han Yong-un's part possible. As a Buddhist reformer, his thought embodied a view of "making it new" that built upon what existed in order to revitalize Korean life and spirit, accepting, without submitting to, the inrush of the "Modern" and the "Western." While most of his contemporaries floundered in a morass of tradition lost, or washed aside by inflooding disruptions of the "West," he achieved a sureness of touch reinforced by his constant awareness of the base, experiential and metaphysical (one and the same in the world of the poems), that gives both substance and freedom to his poetry. His experiments with verse forms, though they may have found release in the new freedoms imported to Korean poetry from Western models, stem just as powerfully from his sense of the poetry as uniquely his own, free to be the vehicle of the essence of meaning implicit in his experience "My Songs":

There's no set measure, no fixed pitch for my songs,
And so they are not even a bit in tune with the melodies of vulgar song.
But, as for me, I'm not the least bit grieved that my songs don't match common melodies
Because my songs should be different from vulgar songs.
Melody modulates by force the deficiencies of song.
Melody is the chopping up of unnatural song with man's delusion.
To put melody to a genuine song is to disgrace the nature of song.
To paint my love's face is to deface it instead; to put melody to my songs is likewise to deface them.
My songs make the god of love cry.
My songs squeeze the rare crystal-clear water from the youth of a maid.
My songs become the music of the heavens when they enter your ears and become tears when they enter your dreams.
I know you hear my songs far away across mountains and fields.
When I think of my songs reaching out to you my tiny heart throbs with an overflow of glory and sketches out the notes of silence.
When my songs' rhythms tremble about to rise and fail to sound I know they move into your poignant quiet fantasy and vanish.

The poems of *Your Silence* are deliberately shaped by the poet to specific purposes, esthetic, religious, and political. Each poem mediates the space between the public and the private, the secular and the sacred. "The loved one is not only the beloved; it is also everything yearned for. . . . The loved one is not only that which is loved but also that which loves."

The Ambiguous "You"

The "you" of *Your Silence* is richly ambiguous. Just as the one whom the "she" personifies seems to be coming clear, the speaker becomes a woman, and it must then be "he." But this is the least of the problems; the "you" as used in the translations cited here represents a translator's compromise, and, so far as it goes, it works well enough; but the Korean word behind it, "*nim*," means "you" only in an indirect kind of way: it is more an empty marker, a name (noun rather than pronoun) which takes its meanings from its referent, and it is only when the thrust of the poem demands the second person singular in English that "you" can stand. In other contexts "*nim*" is rendered variously as "beloved" (despite Kevin O'Rourke's stricture that once the translator is forced back to "beloved" he has lost the battle), "love," or "lord," for it is open to all these meanings and more.

This "you," this "beloved," has attributes of power, of value, of inducing action, of creating unity. It is not only, to paraphrase the "Preface," that which is loved, it is also that which loves. It has possible referents in the Korean nation and its people, the Buddha, the Absolute, a person, or a personification. But, whatever it might be, it is paradoxically not only object but at the same time subject: "I am at once you."

The use of the beloved to signify the king/nation was nothing new to the Korean tradition. The Yi dynasty scholar-poet banished from court could both protest his wrongs and affirm his loyalties at the same time by this veiled address to the beloved/king in a graceful poem; the wronged national/scholar who has gone or been sent away can, from a distance, present his plea to the nation/king. As utilized by Han Yong-un in *Your Silence*, this convention requires a recognition of the irony of reversal in that it now is the nation/king who has gone, leaving behind the loyal national.

When the poem "Obeying" is read with the full awareness of the Korean King's rescript upon annexation of Korea by Japan, in which he calls upon his subjects to be loyal henceforth to the Emperor of Japan, it becomes clear that from the date of that rescript—29 August 1910—for all loyal Koreans, the Korean king could no longer be considered, except as a hollow convention, to be king/nation; to continue to obey his commands would paradoxically result in disloyalty:

Where others say they love freedom, I like to obey.
Not that I don't value freedom, but, when it comes to
  you, I want only to obey.
Obeying is sweeter than the sweetest freedom where
  obeying is voluntary: that is my happiness.
But, if you tell me to obey someone else, that I could
  not obey,
Because if I obey someone else I cannot obey you.

In the years following the loss of Korean nationhood there took place a general shifting of literary imagery of the nation from the paternalistic extended family headed by the king to Chosŏn (Korea), the nation. The old order had been violated, raped politically, intellectually, morally, and physically. Imagery began to shift from the male to the violated female. In the poetry of the time "more often than not" a beautifully spiritualized and idealized woman stands for the "lost country" as Ko Won points out in the introduction to his *Contemporary Korean Poetry* (1970: xviii). " 'Nim,' " he goes on, "nearly always means the country."

The convention of address to the nation remains, but it is now Chosŏn, the fecund soil that, seeded, gave birth to the people who are Korean. "Chosŏn" no longer represents the reign name of the lost Yi dynasty only; it has become the name in right of the great mother, the lost mistress, the honest though violated keeper of the cheap wineshop by the wayside.

In *Your Silence*, symbols of past greatness are not men such as Admiral Yi Sun-sin or his contemporaries, the Buddhist monks who led in the resistance against the Japanese invaders of the last decade of the sixteenth century, but the two fabled *kisaeng*

(professional entertainers) of the time who gave their lives in the attempt to save their country, Non'gae and Kyewor'yang—violated by the very nature of their profession, but chaste and true to the last to the earth from which they sprang and to which they returned. It is the cold virtue of the enigmatic moon caught in the tree ("I am everybody's love") that startles his nakedness, the "you," the free Korea, free because of her firmness in holding to her vows ("My chastity is free chastity"). The politics of freedom turns into the metaphysics of freedom; defeat at the hands of the Japanese turns into triumph in the mind of silence.

The strength of *Your Silence* lies in Han Yongun's power to reify all abstractions in profoundly human terms, to sing of love in all its aspects, for his poems are first and foremost love songs, as in "Pleasure":

Do you think I am doing just as well as when you
  were here?
If you do, you can't say that you know me.
Since you went away I have not had so much joy as
  the trace of a lone goose flying across a moonless
  sky.
Even the smiles that used to come easy before my
  mirror come no more.
I no longer plant flowers, or water or tend them.
I hate even the whisper of the quiet moon's shadow
  that steps soundlessly up to the thin paper of my
  window.
I find no sweet in the fresh cool in a little grove
  under the ridge of the hill after a shower has
  passed across the searing sky of a dry, hot summer.
I have neither playmates nor playthings.
Since you left I have only one hard-come-by pleasure in this world.
That is to cry now and then until I have cried
  enough.

Faced with the "barbaric" onslaught of Westernization, perhaps only a Buddhist could have remained rooted in tradition and the present, could have maintained the paradoxical position of remaining the same while ever-changing like the

South River that received the body of Non'gae and the pavilion that stands at the spot on the bluffs. ("Night and day the South River flows on, yet it stays./Rain or shine on the bank, Ch'oksongnu stands vacant, yet flees with time like an arrow.")

The power of the beloved of *Your Silence* is, in one of its aspects, absolute; it controls destiny, life, and death. "Ah, who has determined my path for me?/Ah, no one in this world but you can determine my path/ But, if you are the one who has determined my path, why must it be the path of death?" ("My Path"). Even more, the beloved has the power of conscience: "As I was wavering— Should I accept love eternal, should I ink-blot the first pages of human history, should I have a drink?—I saw you" ("I Saw You"). These lines suggest, in the context, the temptations of easy salvation, scholarship, and the secular world, all put away by one glimpse of the Truth and purpose in "you." The attributes of the beloved are many and paradoxical: "Your voice is silence . . . /Your face is darkness . . . /Your shadow is light . . ." ("Inverse Proportion"). And the beloved is all-present, "As you are everywhere my eyes reach. . . ." ("Everywhere").

There is a temptation to see in all this a supreme and all-powerful being of some sort, pantheistically present in all things and exerting its power at all times and places. But no such being is named or evoked in the poems themselves, and it also serves to remember that Buddhism remains in general quite indifferent to the question of an original creator.

The question, then, most clearly is, Where does the power lie that is so absolutely present in the attributes of the beloved? The answer is: In the fruit of meditation, the enlightenment which Han Yong-un posits as the testimony and end of Buddhism. This enlightenment is of the nature of what we commonly call "mystic" and is achieved as the result of disciplined meditation.

In "Waking Dream" the poet draws his love to his breast, after Kom has placed her in his arms, only to embrace himself, leaving the void undisturbed. His love is the void. Suggestive as this is, it is perhaps easier to follow the workings of the

poems of *Your Silence* by shifting the focus from a Buddhist dialectics to the dialectics which Kenneth Burke (*Rhetoric of Motives*, 1969) sees culminating in a "god-term." "Emptiness" cannot be the object of a definite belief, nor can it very well serve the rhetorical necessity for an object of address as does the beloved of the poems. There are two aspects of Han Yong-un's poetry that seem to receive considerable light from Burke's suggestion: first, the nature of the beloved, the "*nim*," as a personification of the absolute, the void; and second, the satisfaction of the need Han Yong-un seems to feel of introducing a specific "god-term" into the poems, though the term occurs only twice, first in "I Talked in my Sleep" and second in the poem "At the Shrine of Non'gae": "Forgive me, Non'gae. If you forgive me, my sins will vanish even if I do not confess before God." In the first case it is the elemental, *Kom*, that warm personification of Korean belief which always seemed somehow to help direct things to their proper working-out. In the second, it is "God," seemingly the god of Roman Catholicism with the implication of the confessional (although it should be noted that the necessity for that God is denied by the statement in the poem).

Insofar, then, as the poetry of *Your Silence* is directed toward the ultimate sources of Han Yong-un's spiritual and religious strength and is a plea for protection on the part of the poet as well as a ritual of protection for his "lambs," his beloved represents the absolute, the depersonalized personification of Emptiness.

Under the aspect of love the beloved represents the Bodhisattva ideal, love in the absolute, compassion for all living things, together with the commitment to work for their salvation: the man who abandons the world yet remains in it. It is this image that informs the poem "Meditation," where the raging seas of "Life" have been calmed to become "moonlit waves that swing and sway endlessly away," where he has "cast adrift" his "tiny boat of vast meditation" and after transversing universe beyond universe has come to a "land of name unknown to man." This is a land of smiles, where all the attachments of the world are unconsidered, all those things which lead to pain in parting or separation are treated as of no value, the ideal land of Buddhism, a paradise beyond the stars, a heavenly kingdom. But the poet chooses not to remain despite the urgings of the land's inhabitants; rather, he would return "in order to build a heavenly land in your heart when you come." Having achieved his own salvation, he renounces it in order to work for the salvation of others.

The way he has had to come has not been an easy one, as the poems so amply demonstrate. He has had to fight inner rebellion ("I Talked in My Sleep"), has longed for emancipation from the bonds of love only to bind them tighter ("The Master's Sermon"), has suffered the temptations of license as opposed to freedom ("Obeying" and "Free Chastity"), has overcome the temptation to retire from the world and not return ("Free Chastity"): "And I have thought deeply about the life with nature away from it all," until the final enlightenment of "Meditation" and the free return to the world.

It is this paradoxical wedding of enlightenment—the realization of the emptiness of all things—to love and compassion for all individuals that creates the dialectical tension of the poetry of *Your Silence*.

The compassionate love of the Bodhisattva informs the poetry as a whole as well as being one of the aspects of the beloved, subject of the poet's "Adoration":

My love, you are gold tempered many times over.
Receive the love of the Heavenly Kingdom until the
    mulberry roots turn to coral.
You! Love! First ray of the morning sun!

Love, you well know the weight of righteousness,
    the lightness of gold.
Sow the seeds of good fortune in the poor land of
    beggars.
My love! Love! Whisper of the old paulownia!

My love, you favor spring and light and peace.
Please become a Bodhisattva who sprinkles tears of
    mercy upon the breast of the weak.
My love! Love! Spring breeze over the sea of ice!

The poem is a paradigm of the three major aspects of the beloved—in the first stanza the protected, Korea, the Korean people; in the second, the ultimate source of power, life, the good, the absolute; in the third, the savior.

It is very much to the point that the metaphors used here suggest images of rebirth, new life and hope in the first and third instance, the protected and the savior, "first rays of the morning sun" and "spring breeze over the frozen sea," while in the second instance the absolute suggests calm and permanence, "the whisper of the old paulownia," the only tree in which the phoenix will nest.

The Beloved as Love

The beloved as love is first suggested in the introduction with "Not only that which is loved but that which loves," and is expanded in "I Love 'Love' ": "When no one else in the world loved me, you alone loved me: I love you, I love your 'love.' "

The task of the Buddhist is to efface the "self," to achieve the greater virtues of compassion and nonattachment rather than the lesser loves with their attendant pains of attachment or grasping. In the dialectic of *Your Silence*, this aim can be achieved only by identification with the beloved in all aspects. Somehow the language has to make significant statements about a reality that is beyond language and its divisions. This goal is achieved in the poems by the radical identification with the beloved in all aspects—a compassionate identification with the beloved as Korea, a passive or spiritual identification with the beloved as the absolute, and an active identification with the beloved as "love." It is through these many identifications that the personification that is the beloved becomes many-faceted and shifting. The poet at one time acts as protector; the beloved is the protector at another; the attributes are not fixed, they shift from one to the other freely, for in the end this world and the other world that the poet crosses over to and returns from, the poet and the beloved, are all one:

If not for you why does this smooth face crease into
*   wrinkles?*
If I had not found you to yearn after I would not age
*   even to the end of time.*
I would stay the same as when first embraced by
*   you.*
But if it's for you, growing old, sick, even dying—
*   I won't mind.*
Do as you will with me, give me life or death.
I am at once you.

The poetry of Han Yong-un, like all major poetry, has universality of theme and appeal. In affirmation of the eternal paradox that freedom to love can be gained only by freedom from love, it gains this, not by generalization and increased levels of abstraction, but rather through the intensity with which it mirrors its time, place, and author: Korea painfully emerging into the "world," tortured and oppressed both by her own slowness in the process and the imposition of Japanese colonial rule; Korea, a place unique and of itself with its own traditions, customs, and feelings; Han Yong-un first a Korean, but also a Buddhist leader in the drive for national independence.

The poet Song Uk's estimate of Han Yong-un's importance for following generations of poets will certainly stand: "It may well be that few Korean poets in the future will turn to *Your Silence* to learn poetics, but they will listen to these magnificent verses every time they come face to face with the problem of how to continue our long tradition while at the same time opening up the future."

But the poet, Han Yong-un, had already said it, though he professed otherwise, in "Ferryboat and Traveler":

I the ferryboat
You the traveler.
You tread on me with muddy feet,
I embrace you and cross over the water.
When I embrace you, deeps or shallows or fast
*   shooting rapids, I can cross over.*

When you don't come I wait dark to dawn, disdain-
*   ing the chill wind, the wet of snow and rain;*
Once over the water you go on without even a
*   glance back at me.*
No matter, I know that sooner or later you will
*   come.*
As I wait for you, day after day I go on growing
*   older.*
I the ferryboat
You the traveler.

S. E. SOLBERG

Further Reading

Translations

Translations in this article of poems by Han Yong-un are © 1972 by S. E. Solberg.

Lee, Peter H. *The Silence of Love: Twentieth-Century Korean Poetry.* Honolulu: The University Press of Hawaii, 1980. This book of well-chosen selections from twentieth-century Korean poetry begins with a substantial section of twenty poems by Han Yong-un, translated by S. E. Solberg.
————. *Modern Korean Literature: An Anthology.* Honolulu: University of Hawaii Press, 1990. An excellent selection of modern Korean literature poetry, fiction, essays, and drama. Includes selections from Han Yong-un translated by Peter H. Lee.

Related Studies

Yu, Beongcheon. *Han Yong-un & Yi Kwang-su.* Detroit, MI: Wayne University Press, 1992. Chapter one reviews Han Yong-un's career; Chapter two discusses his works. There are translations of several of Han Yong-un's poems. The discussion is careful and illuminating.

MIDDLE EAST

THE SEVEN GOLDEN ODES

Authors: Imr'u al-Qays, Tarafa, Labid, 'Antara, Zuhayr, 'Amr ibn Kulthum, Harith
Born: c. A.D. 500–600
Died: c. A.D. 550–650
Literary Form: Seven poems in the *Qasida* form
Date of Composition: Sixth century to early seventh century A.D.

Major Themes

Fate is the agent that separates lover from beloved.
Fate as time wears down all civilizations and brings all aspirations to nothing.
Fate as the allotted moment of death is the final test of human courage.
Meaning is to be found in this mortal life; there are no promises of rewards in an afterlife.

The *Mu'allaqat*, as a collection, comprises the seven most famous poems of pre-Islamic Arabia. According to Arabic legend, the name *"Mu'allaqat"* (the hanging or suspended ones) derives from the fact that these poems were embroidered on black cloth from Egypt and suspended from the walls of the pre-Islamic shrine, the Ka'ba. The poems were selected as the prize-poems in the poetry fair held at Ukaz, near Mecca, when the various tribes would come together for trade, pilgrimage, and cultural events. The *Mu'allaqat* and other great poems in the Qasida (poem form) tradition are, along with the *Qur'an*, one of the two wellsprings of Arabic Literature, and have had a profound influence on other literatures of the Middle East, including Hebrew, troubador poetry (by way of Andalusia), Persian, Turkish, and Urdu.

Some modern scholars have suggested that the legend of the "hanging odes" is an anachronistic attempt to explain the puzzling name, "suspended ones" (*Mu'allaqat*), given to the original collection. But whatever its historical veracity, the legend of the seven odes suspended over the shrine that was to become the central shrine of Islam dramatizes the central importance of these poems, and the tradition of poetry they represented, within the Arabic literature tradition, and, in a more extended way, within the world of Islam.

These poems, vivid in material images and rich in symbolic dimensions, are said by tradition to have been composed in the first two centuries before Islam (A.D. 480–622). Little is known about how and why these particular poems were selected from the vast and magnficent tradition of the Qasida.

What we know of the authors comes from accounts collected decades, even centuries, after the poets lived; how much of the material is historical and how much legendary is impossible to know. Imru'al-Qays is said to have been a prince of the tribe of Kindah and to have lived the life of wandering, warfare, and lovemaking extolled in his poem. Labid is said to have lived for over a hundred years, to have converted to Islam at an old age, and to have given up composing poetry after his conversion. Zuhayr, the author of a *Mu'allaqa* filled with maxims on wisdom and peacemaking, was one of the more respected figures in pre-Islamic Bedouin society. Tarafa was a young man of noble lineage whose poetic and tribal career ended in an early death due to his rash behavior. 'Amr ibn Kulthum, the son-in-law of Muhalhil, one of the greatest early poets, was renowned for killing the oppressive king of al-Hira. The most famous author of a *Mu'allaqa* is 'Antara, whose great poem on warfare both celebrates and intimates the tragedy of the pre-Islamic tribal ethos. 'Antara later became the subject of an oral tradition in the Romance of 'Antar, a romance that continues to be reworked within oral traditions around the Arabic world. The life of the seventh author, Harith, is shrouded in mystery. According to tradition, the original *Mu'allaqat* and all the other poems by these authors were memorized and passed on orally by generations of *rawis* (raconteurs) before being written down from the second to the fourth century of Islam.

Recent scholarship suggests a more dynamic notion of the pre-Islamic Qasida, modeled on the theories of Homeric authorship known as the "Parry-Lord" model of oral composition. According to this model, the poems would have been roughly equivalent to the "standards" in jazz music. Each time the poem was composed, it was created, performed, and transmitted simultaneously as the performer improvised upon a given meter, set of themes, and set of images. Such a theory offers a more robust understanding of poetic culture. The creative moment is not relegated to a distant past to be transmitted thenceforth by rote, but rather continues in each new performance of the poem. It also accounts for the radical variation in manuscripts. Instead of being ascribed to flaws in transmission, the variations show the continual evolution of each poem through different performances.

How far back in history can we trace the tradition of the Qasida? Classical Arabic writers usually cite poets of the mid-fifth century A.D. as the pioneers of Arabic poetry. The poetry is so intricate, however, the similes and imagery so fine-hewn, the meters so complex, the vocabulary so articulated, that it seems likely the poetry may have existed as an oral tradition for generations or centuries before the first named and dated poet given by later scholars.

Genre, Structure, and Symbolism

The seven poems are in the form of the Qasida, a long poem from 40 to 120 verses, in one of several possible intricate meters, and with a single end-verse rhyme or end-verse assonance throughout. The Qasida was divided into three major themes or movements: the remembrance of the lost beloved (the *nasib*), the journey or quest (the *rahil*), and a final movement that could include boast (*fakhr*) or praise of a ruler (*madih*). Although previously dismissed as arbitrary, this tripartite structure has been shown by modern scholars to correspond to basic patterns in human expression and community. In literary analysis of mythopoetic archetypes and in anthropological discussions of the rite-of-passage, a similar three-phase movement has been detected. The loss of an original, idealized community is followed by a central movement of "liminality," during which the hero is outside the bounds and the rules of normal community. The liminal phase is followed by a final reaggregation during which the hero re-engages society in a new, less idealized manner.

The remembrance of the beloved begins with the traces (*atlal*) of the abandoned campsite of the lost beloved. These traces are symbols of both presence and absence. The poet stands within the campsite of the beloved and becomes infused with the poetic voice, sometimes encountering a vision of the phantom of the beloved. The ritual undertones of this motif have been compared to the practice of incubation in the Mediterranean, late antique world. In the practice of incubation, a vigil in a sacred shrine would result in a vision of the god or saint.

The meditation upon the ruins of the beloved's campsite leads to what is commonly called the "description of the beloved." Yet, although the poetic language evokes the beloved powerfully, what is actually described is not the beloved. A simile involving the beloved's mouth, or fragrance, or figure, will lead to a chain of digressive similes that conjure a world of lush vegetation, flowing water, and wild animals in idyllic peace and repose. The remembrance of the beloved turns the barren landscape suddenly into the Lost Garden, which serves as the symbolic analogue of the beloved. Frequently, the poetic voice will attempt to break the spell, pointing out the fact that such an idyllic scene is mere reverie, that the beloved is gone, and that there is no point in lingering over her remembrance. When this voice finally prevails, the second major movement, the journey or quest, begins.

The journey is always solitary, always by camel-mare, and involves a confrontation with the terror of the desert night, the heat of the desert midday, the dangers of starvation, madness, and losing the way, and a confrontation with human mortality. In some poems, such as the *Mu'allaqa* of Tarafa, the journey is dominated by an extraordinary set of similes involving the camel-mare, through which the camel-mare is shown as symbolically multi-valent. It symbolizes the self of the traveler, the world of nature, and the world of human culture. The similes shift back and forth rapidly between the natural and cultural worlds. In other poems, such as the *Mu'allaqat* of Labid and 'Antara, the journey section is made up of vivid and powerful tableaux involving poetic substitutes for the camel-mare: the oryx (a graceful, long-horned antelope), the onager (a wild ass cousin of the zebra, without the stripes), and the ostrich. Recent scholars have challenged the notion that these sections are "objective descriptions" of animal life in the desert. Rather, the key animals have hundreds, even thousands of epithets, and each animal has a key set of associations and symbolic correspondences. Thus the oryx, always at the brink of death in the Qasida presentation, exemplifies beauty, vulnerability, and the fragility of life, and these key themes are woven into the pattern of the poem through what seems like a digression on the oryx.

The journey sometimes ends with a transitional movement, the wine song. The wine song, with praise of the wine and depictions of singing girls, is a form of consolation for the beloved that entails an erotic paradox. The poet drinks to forget the beloved, but the more he drinks the more he remembers; as in Labid's *Mu'allaqa* where the poet, depicted taking a second round before dawn, addresses his absent beloved Nawar to proclaim to her how well he has forgotten her, protesting too much.

The final section of the Qasida shows the poet hero returning to his place in the tribe. The poet can boast of his generosity and leadership in holding the tribe together, of his unflinching firmness in battle, of the virtues of his tribe. Or he can recount a panegyric, that is, the praise of a prince to whom he is offering allegiance. The central ritual moment of the Qasida is the sacrifice of the camel-mare and the division of the meat through the game of *maysir*, a lottery played with notched arrow shafts. This ritual sacrifice is replete with symbolism of the poet-hero's offering of himself to the tribe, while the *maysir* game is associated with the "lot" or "destiny" that each tribesman will find for himself. In the *Mu'allaqa* of Labid, the camel-sacrifice is the moment when the poet/hero as individual becomes Labid, the voice of the tribe. In the *Mu'allaqa* of Tarafa, the camel-sacrifice is improperly done, with a stolen camel, and the result is catastrophe; instead of serving as a unifying ritual for the tribe, the sacrifice goes wrong and serves to drive the tribe into intratribal war. In the *Mu'allaqa* of 'Antara, there is no formal camel sacrifice, but the end of the poem, with its unforgettable depictions of battle frenzy, shows how the battle itself becomes a substitute for the camel sacrifice, and how at the moment of the death in battle, the hero looks into the death grin of his enemy and sees, through tragic intimation, his own reflection.

The three movements are tied together by common symbols and images. Particularly important is the embodiment of fate within material imagery that ties together different aspects of the Qasida. For example, the words "deaf and silent" (attributes of silent fate which never responds to the poet's questions of "why") are applied to several key items. In Labid's *Mu'allaqa*, the ruins of the beloved's campsite, and the abandoned, blackened hearthstones are said to be "deaf and silent" to the poet's question. In Imr'u al-Qays's *Mu'allaqa* the poet remains sleepless, contemplating the loss of the beloved. His sleeplessness is shown by his watching the movement of the stars, stars which suddenly stop moving, as if tied to granite stones that are "still and silent." In the *Mu'allaqa* of 'Antara, the straightened steel sword that takes the life of the enemy is described as "deaf and silent." Finally, in the *Mu'allaqa* of Tarafa, the poet defends his life of drinking and the squandering of all his wealth by stating he might as well quench himself now, in this life, because all humans will end up in graves covered by stone slabs that are "still and silent." In the most subtle ways, the poetry uses what is actually an epithet for fate to weave these four crucial moments of life together around the

central human mystery of destiny. It is this interweaving of symbolic depth and material precision
of imagery (of which the fate/silence corrolation is
only one small example) that gives the Qasida its
power.

The Mu'allaqat *in Arabic Literary Tradition*

The seven poems that make up the *Mu'allaqat* are
the most famous poems of early Arabic, but not all
of them are believed to be the best, and other
poems, not included in the seven, have had an
equally important influence on subsequent poems.
Early on, the critic, grammarian, and collector, al-
Tibrizi, added three other odes to make a collection
of the ten major odes of pre-Islamic Arabic. Several
other influential collections have also been composed. In addition, we have collected poems ("di-
wans") of numerous pre-Islamic poets beyond the
seven authors of the *Mu'allaqat*.

The pre-Islamic poetic heritage is of great lexical and grammatical difficulty, poetic complexity,
and symbolic range. Perhaps for these reasons, it
has been useful to have a small microcosm of this
vast tradition, and the seven *Mu'allaqat* have
served that purpose well. The themes of classical
Qasida that they represent have remained within
Arabic literature to the present day. From the *nasib*
of the Qasida developed two independent forms of
love lyric or *ghazal*: the 'Udhri *ghazal* (associated
with the tradition of the love-mad poet Majnun
and his beloved Layla), and the *ghazal* proper, a
more playfully erotic form in Arabic. The Bedouin
Qasida was later adapted to the urban environments of Aleppo, Baghdad, Damascus, Seville,
and Cordoba by great poets such as Abu Nuwas
(d. 810), al-Buhturi (d. 897), al-Ma'arri (d. 1057),
and Ibn Zaydun (d. 1071), with the ruins of ancient cities often serving as the symbolic counterpart of the traces of the beloved's campsite.
Finally, almost all the elements of the Qasida, but
most particularly the remembrance of the beloved,
became a pervasive and abiding part of the Islamic mystical tradition, with many Sufis, such as
Ibn al-Farid (d. 1235) and Ibn 'Arabi (d. 1240)
writing their own *nasib*s, some of which can be

read both as pure love-poems and as mystical
allegories.

Even non-poetic forms such as the novel and the
short story frequently draw upon the Arabic Qasida
for some of their formal and topical influence. Thus
Tayeb Saleh makes a kind of surrealistic quest
scene the center of his novel *Season of Migration to
the North*, and Naguib Mahfuz in his famous story
"Zaabalawi" uses the themes of the nasib as the
quintessence of classical Arabic sensibility.

Around the year 1000, poets of the two major
world cultures within the Islamic world began to
take of the metrics, structure, and themes of the
Qasida and integrate them into their own traditions:
Jewish poets in Andalusia, and Persian (and later
Turkish and Urdu) poets throughout the eastern
part of the Islamic world. In Andalusia, new forms
such as the *Muwashshahat* (both Arabic and
Hebrew) were developed out of the Qasida. The
nasib, *ghazal*, and *muwashshahat* in turn had a role
in the development of European love-lyrics out of
the Troubadour tradition.

The Qasida, as represented by the *Mu'allaqat*,
offers a symbolic depth that enables the Qasida to
evolve over centuries, always reappropriated, always at the center of Arabic literary sensibility.
Central aspects of the Qasida tradition then became
the common heritage of the rich poetic worlds
within Islam from Andalusia to Indonesia, from
Bosnia to East and West Africa, in languages as far
ranging as Hebrew, Swahili, Serbo-Croatian,
Malay, Urdu, Persian, and Turkish (in its multiple
varieties). The poetry developed by the Bedouin
Arabs in the centuries before Islam and enshrined
in the *Mu'allaqat* includes some of the most artistically compelling and historically influential
poems ever composed.

                                             MICHAEL SELLS

Further Reading

Translations

Arberry, A. J. *The Seven Odes: The First Chapter
in Arabic Literature*. London: George Allen,
1957. The translations are awkward and out-

dated, but the introductions offer valuable accounts of the legend of each author.

Berques, Jacques. *Cultural Expression in Arab Society Today*. Translated by Robert W. Stookey. Poetry translated by Basima Bezirgan and Elizabeth Fernea. Austin, TX: University of Texas Press. This work includes a full translation of the *Mu'allaqa* of Imr'u al-Qays along with discussion of how the values and themes of the *Mu'allaqa* permeate Arabic culture today.

Labid ibn Rabiah (c. 560–c. 661). *The Golden Ode*. Translated with an introduction and commentary by William R. Polk. Photographs by William J. Mares. Chicago: University of Chicago Press, 1974. This volume offers sumptuous photographs with each translated verse of Labid's *Mu'allaqa*, allowing the reader to visualize the Bedouin desert environment of the *Mu'allaqat*.

Sells, Michael A. *Desert Tracings: Six Classic Arabian Odes by 'Alqama, Shanfara, Labid, 'Antara, Al-A'sha, and Dhu al-Rumma*. Middletown CT: Wesleyan University Press, 1989. Includes translations, with introductory essays and notes, of six of the greatest Qasidas, including the *Mu'allaqas* of Labid and 'Antara.

———. "The *Mu'allaqa* of Tarafa." In the *Journal of Arabic Literature* XVII (1986): pp. 21–33. This article presents a new translation of the *Mu'allaqa* of Tarafa, along with an introduction to its major themes.

Further Studies

Stetkevych, Jaroslav. *Zephyrs of Najd: The Poetics of Nostalgia in the Classical Arabic Nasib*. Chicago: University of Chicago Press, 1993. Stetkevych traces the "remembrance of the beloved" motifs from the *Mu'allaqat* through the various strands of medieval Arabic literature, showing how they were adapted and rearticulated in ever new circumstances.

Stetkevych, Suzanne Pinckney. *The Mute Immortals Speak: Pre-Islamic Poetry and the Poetics of Ritual*. Ithaca: Cornell University Press, 1993. This book presents the influential argument that the structure of the *Mu'allaqat* and other pre-Islamic poems is tied to the patterns of the "rite of passage" paradigm found in many cultures.

———. *Reorientations: Arabic and Persian Poetry*. Bloomington, IN: Indiana University Press, 1994. This collection of essays reevaluates the meaning and significance of Arabic and Persian poetry, with five of the essays focusing upon Arabic poems of the period of the *Mu'allaqat*.

Zwettler, Michael. *The Oral Tradition of Classical Arabic Poetry*. Columbus: Ohio State University Press, 1978. Zwettler argues that pre-Islamic poetry was composed, performed, and transmitted in a single process, along the lines of the "Parry-Lord" theory of Homeric poetry. A poem was performed differently each time, always changing and evolving.

QUR'AN

Title in Arabic: *Qur'ān* (*Koran* is a common but less accurate transliteration)
Author: According to Muslim belief, the *Qur'ān* is the Word of God as revealed to Muhammad (Abu al-Qasim Muhammad ibn 'Abd Allah 'Abd al-Muttalib ibn Hashim) over a 23-year period.
Muhammad born: c. A.D. 570, Mecca, Arabia
Muhammad died: A.D. 632, Medina, Arabia
Work Published: C. A.D. 650–655, the "Uthmanic text," named for Uthman, the Third Caliph (A.D. 644–655). This official published text is based upon various collections of the verses. The first such collection goes back as early as the reign of the First Caliph (A.D. 632–634), Abu Bakr.

Major Themes

To enable all persons to remain on the right path, God offers guidance through the words of the Qur'ān. The aim of the Qur'ān is to help the believer achieve union with Allah.
Allah manifests himself as absolute unity, mercy, and power.
The ultimate success or failure of a person's life depends upon the acceptance or rejection of God.
The possibility of eternal rewards or punishments stands before all.
The unbeliever manifests a prideful refusal to submit to God.
Such unbelief expresses itself in a lack of gratitude to the creator for the goods of the creation.
God has been revealing Himself in all of history through the prophets.
Prophetic activity culminates in the perfect revelation spoken by Allah through Muhammad.

The Qur'ān, a collection of 6,252 Arabic verses, is one of the most revered, closely studied, and profoundly influential religious texts in all of human history. The work expresses the essence of Islam. Most of what exists in the 1,300-year Islamic tradition can be traced either directly or indirectly to Qur'ānic sayings. As the source of a living tradition the Qur'ān, to a very great degree, governs and shapes the lives of millions throughout the world. The sayings are believed by Muslims to be the self-expression not of Muhammad, but of God. Thus, the Muslim is one who submits to this Divine word and in this submission finds peace (the Arabic *'slm'* at the root of the term, Islam, means peace and wholeness).

The title of the work implies in Arabic a recitation, a verbal expression connected with acts of worship. Thus, for all of its history, the Qur'ānic verses have been read aloud as instruction, inspiration, and prayer. The oral nature of the text also points to the verbal tradition of Muhammad, who over a period of 22 years expressed orally revelations from God in the form of one or more verses.

The followers of Muhammad retained these revelations as Muhammad conveyed them in different situations at either Mecca or Medina. These followers, shortly after the Prophet's death, organized the verses into 114 chapters (called *suras*) according to length (generally greater to smaller) and identified each *sura* by a key word that appears at or near the beginning of the new division.

This collection, slightly shorter than the New Testament, is not a connected narrative that follows either a chronological or thematic sequence. Rather, verses often stand on their own, moving from one issue to another, while others are grouped around some specific topic. The book offers universal and general demands on a wide range of topics relating to law and religious practice. Islam would develop its comprehensive world view through extensive elaboration upon many topics, all finding their seminal expression in the Qur'ān. Thus, from this book Muslims find answers to questions regarding the nature of the afterlife, prayer, prophets, pilgrimage, marriage, divorce, food, warfare, taxation, government, wealth, slavery, dress, women, inheritance, prohibition of liquor and gambling, and many other matters. The Qur'ān, presented as the very self-manifestation of God, seeks to offer guidance to all humanity in its struggle to achieve salvation. The work is read by Muslims as the fullest and final revelation about divinity, humanity, and their eternal relationship.

Divinity

The divine name, Allah (from the Arabic, "al-Ilah," meaning "the God"), is mentioned hundreds of times in the Qur'ānic text. Fundamental to Islam is the testimonial *Lā illā Allāh*, which means (as Seyyed Hossein Nasr explains in his *Islamic Life and Thought*; see *Further Reading* at the end of this article) that "There is no divinity but the Divine," or "There is no God but God," or "There is no being or reality other than the Absolute Being or the Absolute Reality" or "There is no power, agent, or reality if it is not The Power, The Agent, The Reality."

There are numerous designations for God. Terms such as Sustainer, Provider, Lord (*al-Rabb*) and Merciful, Compassionate (*al-Rahman*) are common. Later Muslim piety would discover ninety-nine different names for Allah in the Qur'ān, all referring to one or another aspect of these activities. Although the source for a wide range of ideas in Islamic thought regarding God, the Qur'ān in its essence is the call to believers to respond with supplication, praise, and gratitude to the merciful, awesome, and omnipotent Allah, and thus to walk on the right path in life. This is why the first *sura*, called the opening (*al-Fatihah*), is thought to contain the aim of the whole Qur'ān, union with God:

In the Name of God, the Merciful, the Compassionate.
Praise belongs to God, the Lord of all Being,
The All-merciful, the All-compassionate,
 the Master of the Day of Doom.
Thee only we serve; to Thee alone we pray for
 succour.
Guide us in the straight path,
the path of those whom Thou hast blessed,

not of those against whom Thou art wrathful,
 nor of those who are astray.

(ARBERRY, TRANS., 1955)

These seven verses, which also serve as the essence of prayer for the pious, articulate the Qur'ānic understanding of the divine as absolute unity, as infinite mercy, and as inexhaustible power.

All praise belongs to Allah, He alone is to be worshiped because, for the Qur'ān, no other reality can claim to be His equal. The Meccans of Muhammad's day knew of a deity named Allah as just one of many other supernatural beings. It is this polytheism that the Prophet absolutely repudiated. In the affirmation of a pure monotheism, the Qur'ān repeatedly affirms the essence of the Muslim creed: "There is no God but Allah." Thus, all attempts to elevate anything to the level of God is severely condemned as the sin of association or partnership (*shirk*). *Shirk* is manifested in all acts of idolatry; be it the elevation of any aspect of the creation as an absolute, or in the claim of Christianity that there are three persons in the Godhead. The absolutely transcendent one God of the Qur'ān does not manifest Himself through an incarnation.

Allah reveals Himself throughout all of history in word and deed. The motive for the self-manifestation of the deity was divine compassion. The most frequent references to Allah in the Qur'ān are under the names of merciful, everforgiving, benefactor, and compassionate. The formula known as the *Basmala*, "In the name of God, Most Merciful, Most Compassionate," begins all but one of the 114 *suras*. God's mercy is manifested in all the acts of creation. A reading of the Qur'ān leaves the unmistakable impression of both God's power and mercy, two interrelated aspects of divine being. He alone is the Lord of all worlds, the Master of the day of judgment. He alone is the object of petition and praise. For the Qur'ān, the themes of creation, guidance, preservation, and judgment all manifest simultaneously Allah's power and mercy.

The sayings of the book do not seek to prove the existence of God but rather point to divine existence by celebrating the order, beauty, stability, magnitude, and utility of the contingent creation. The interrelationship of the parts to the whole of the cosmos is presented as indication that all that is, has purpose. Thus, all the natural world is *"muslim"* (Arabic: "one who surrenders to God") for it has surrendered to God's will and thus gives glory to its creator. The universe in the Qur'ān is a sign (*ayah*) of its maker.

Humanity

The teleology manifested in the creation extends most especially to human beings. Only persons can (to their ruin) choose not to be *"Muslim."* Free will is assumed throughout the Qur'ān, as are the temptations of Satan, whom God permits to attempt a seduction of humanity away from the straight path. Life is an unceasing struggle to conform the human will to that of the divine. Every person is responsible for success or failure in this enterprise. All will be judged at death to be either rewarded in Paradise or punished in Hell.

For the Qur'ān, religion and morality are completely interrelated. All ethical concepts derive from divine commands and prohibitions, while all human acts are judged within an eschatological context. Allah helps those who seek Him, while leading astry those who do not. Later Islamic theology would struggle with this mystery, that is, how both divine providence and human free acts are related to form the essential constitutive elements at the core of human existence. In the Qur'ān both elements of divine providence and human freedom are undeniably affirmed.

When one fails to yield to God, this failure to be a true *muslim* is not rooted in an original sin, a concept foreign to Islamic tradition, but rather a failure of the person's character. It is common throughout the Qur'ān to present this failure in terms of unbelief, knowingly ignoring the gifts of God; in essence, a lack of gratitude. The unbeliever pridefully ignores divine mercy and power while acting toward the creator and the creation with haughtiness, rebellion, and insolence. The unbeliever is an ingrate with a heart hardened to all good that comes from God. The most common

Qur'ānic images used to describe this unbelief are those of blindness and deafness to the signs of Allah. They therefore "go astray" and "wander blindly."

On the other hand, those who have belief (*iman*) have a fear of the Lord, knowing the limits set by divine decree. Their lives manifest piety in prayer, pilgrimage, and almsgiving to the poor. In the believer, according to the Qur'ān, the response to divine guidance takes the form of awe, contrition, gratitude, obedience, and humility. Their energies are directed to an imitation of the justice and mercy of Allah. Their nobility is manifested by lives of generosity, truthfulness, trustworthiness, patience, courage, and peace.

Prophets

The prophets throughout history are understood to have been sent by God to reveal the faith, to embody the faith, and to help others achieve the faith. The prophetic tradition is important in the Qur'ān, where some twenty-five percent of the total book is given to its discussion. Important preachers of the divine message from Adam to Muhammad are considered, for it is claimed that each story serves as a lesson in religious understanding. Important figures from Judaism are set forth with an eye to what they witnessed (Noah, Abraham, Lot, Joseph, Elias, Jonah, Job, David, and Solomon). Excepting for Muhammad, Moses, whose experience is considered most instructive, receives the greatest number of verses throughout the Qur'ān (510 verses). Important figures for Christianity (Zacharias, John the Baptist, Mary, mother of Jesus, and Jesus), as well as the ancient Arab tribes (Salih and Hud) are also presented. These narratives tend to follow the Biblical story, with occasional modifications. All the prophets offer essentially the same message, that is, there is only one God, who alone must be worshiped. This monotheistic revelation was often rejected, and many of the prophets were condemned to death. God, however, often vindicated His message by saving the prophets, such as Noah from the flood, Moses from the Pharoah, and Jesus from crucifixion. (The Qur'ān, while accepting the virgin birth as a sign of the power of the Holy Spirit, and the ascension of Jesus, rejects the claims of Christianity regarding Jesus' salvific acts of suffering, death, and resurrection.) All the prophets were human, and as such serve as examples for humanity. It is said in the Qur'ān that every nation has its own prophet sent by Allah to warn and offer guidance.

Muhammad

Muhammad stands at the end of this long line of divine messengers who by their words and deeds made the invisible visible. As the "seal of the prophets," he is believed to present divine truth so perfectly that none after him can supersede the Qur'ānic revelations. The Qur'ān presents him as the final messenger of God, the perfect manifestation of all antecedent prophets. He is a friend of God who preaches compassion like Jesus; a warrior and lawgiver like Moses; a wise sage like Joseph; and a true preacher of monotheism against all unbelief, as was Abraham. Muhammad's own great success is presented as evidence of divine favor. For the Qur'ān he is "a shining lamp." For the later Islamic tradition he is *"nur al-huda"* (the light of right guidance). In the very mention of his name the pious, out of respect, will often add the words, "God bless him and grant him peace" (the Arabic formula often abbreviated to *"sl'm"* frequently appears in written texts after Muhammad's name).

Social Laws

One important consequence of the Qur'ān was the establishment of an earthly society. The values of this society were quite revolutionary when contrasted with those of the pre-Islamic Arabic world. In the Bedouin tribal society of Muhammad's day, morality was grounded in the requirements of survival, hence, the values of power, pride, and blood relationships. The mighty enjoyed the privileges of the group; the weak, who were outside tribal protection, were often the objects of manipulation. The demands of tribal loyalty often resulted in intertribal warfare that could descend to barbarous levels of violence and exploitation. With little focus on the next life, this world with its pleasures became for many the only good. In this context Muhammad announced an entirely new foundation for society; the will of Allah, where the virtue of submission to this will was the essence of morality. In the Qur'ānic proclamation of the esential equality of all humanity, and of a God whose compassion extends especially to the weak, Arabic society found the values of domination and control to be transcended in favor of kindness and benevolency. Thus, tribal custom is understood as only secular habits to be judged by the awesome Lord of the universe. Indeed, the fear of judgment invests the present with a sense of moral seriousness not common in pre-Islamic times. The ways of justice preoccupy the Qur'ān as its words subject the institutions of Muhammad's day to critique.

One institution modified by the Qur'ān was the customary pre-Islamic pattern of relations among the sexes. In the society of Muhammad's day, women were generally considered of value only as objects of pleasure, and for the creation of sons. Marriage as the established pattern of adult relationships was little practiced. Also, it was an acceptable practice to commit female infanticide. Women in pre-Islamic Arabia held no inheritance rights and were afforded little protection by law.

As a consequence of the Qur'ānic revolution the status of women was dramatically elevated. Both men and women were called to a full participation in the religious obligations of the new faith and were called as equals to divine judgment and eternal life. Marriage was sanctified as the sole locus for sexual intercourse. The veil was required as a sign of female modesty serving as a check on inappropriate male lust. Procedures regarding the dowry, inheritance, and divorce were formalized while in pre-Islamic custom they were not. As for the well-known Qur'ānic permission for men to have up to four wives, the common explanation is that this is designed not to serve the husband's sexual needs but rather as a protection for widows and orphans in an age when war often devastated the male population. A polygynous relationship is acceptable only if all wives are treated equally, an

ideal thought by the Qur'ān to be extremely difficult to achieve. The new husband is also required to
protect the orphan's property rights, scrupulously
avoiding mixing the orphan's property with his
own.

The social laws of the Qur'ān, while not absolutely transcending the age, often led to a humanizing of the traditions of seventh-century Arabia.
Examples of this can be found regarding warfare
and slavery. While many verses call upon the Muslim to take up arms against the unbelievers, and to
strive (*jidah*) with all one's strength, the Qur'ān
does not advocate aggressive violent action for the
secular goods of wealth, territory, or power. The
believer is to defend, with his life if necessary, all
attacks on God's community and by doing so
achieves eternal reward. Warfare is a religious act
under the ethical values grounded in Allah's will.
Thus, in the non-inspired sayings of Muhammad
(the *Hadith*), tradition reports the Prophet admon-
ishing his followers that as they engage in war they
are not to mutilate the dead enemy nor kill women
and children. To serve as a check on rapacioius
grasping for the spoils of war, a revelation in the
Qur'ān after the battle of Badr (624 A.D.) mandated
that one fifth of the goods be assigned to the needy,
orphans, and wayfarers. Those captured in war
could remain as slaves of the victorious. Although
the Qur'ān does accept slavery, its description of
the dynamics of the relationship of slave and master offers another instance of the work's humanizing tendencies. Slaves, often referred to as "those
whom the right hand posesses," are encouraged to
buy their liberty from the believers. The Muslim is
enjoined to offer the slave an opportunity to work
toward emancipation. Elsewhere, the Qur'ān encourages the master to protect the slave-girls from a
life of prostitution. Tradition reports that Muhammad said toward the end of his life (during his last
pilgrimage to Mecca) that slaves were to be fed and
clothed with the food and clothing of the master,
for slaves are servants of the Lord and are not to be
tormented.

In Islamic societies custom and tradition would
work out the specifics of particular laws in voluminous bodies of legal interpretations. The same is
true of the exact types of acceptable governmental
or economic systems which were left unspecified in
the Qur'ān. What is demanded is that all societies
with their different political and economic traditions must conform to God's commands. A number
of these demands are clearly set forth. There are
Qur'ānic sayings that encourage moderation, patience, forgiveness, peace-making, gentleness in
speech, chastity, proper greeting to fellow Muslims, and filial duties toward parents. Religious
obligations regarding prayer, fasting, pilgrimage,
and purity are often enjoined. Private property is
recognized as a value and its uneven distribution is
in accord with God's will. However, those who are
blessed with an abundance of the world's wealth
are obliged to be of assistance to the less fortunate,
hence, the importance of alms (*zakah*). In commercial transactions there is to be a reciprocity of benefits where honesty, justice and the fulfillment of
vows are respected. The Qur'ān prohibits the use of
alcohol on earth, although wine will flow in rivers
for the Blessed to enjoy in Paradise. Prohibited also
are the practices of sorcery, idolatry, fornication,
usury, and the eating of swine.

In the sphere of criminal law the Qur'ān clearly
sets down punishments for some acts. The murderer's life can be taken, but retaliation must be
limited, as in the Mosaic code (Lev. 24:17–21), to
one life for one life. This law of talion holds for
bodily injuries willfully inflicted on another, for
like evil is to be rewarded with like evil. Regarding
theft, the punishment is categorical and well
known, amputation of the hands—a punishment
that later Qur'ānic commentators would seek to
soften through reference to God's forgiveness to
the penitent. Homosexuality is treated as a crime by
reference to the Biblical story of Lot, while adul-
terers and adulteresses shall be given a hundred
lashes. To avoid the possibility of an injustice, the
one accusing another of adultery must produce four
eyewitnesses. This high standard of evidence must
accompany a charge or else the accuser will suffer
eighty lashes and never again be treated as a credible witness.

In all these social laws the Qur'ān demands that
human beings face the fundamental moral choice to

accept or reject God's will. This is the choice that determines the whole worth of a person's life. The specifics of the Qur'ān's social laws set before the Muslim the basic assumptions regarding Allah and his eternal judgment through the requirements of daily life. To the people of Muhammad's time, the Qur'ānic demands regarding the immediate and practical issues of living served as acts of worship and commitment. To recite the text in order to fulfill its demands was to rededicate the self to the divine whose will was believed to be communicated through every verse. For the Muslim, the Qur'ān as the mediation of the infinite in the finite calls for the believer's absolute attention and complete response.

The Influence of the Qur'ān

Aside from its well-known and profound influence on Islamic religious, philosophical, social, and legal thought and practice, the Qur'ān remains to this day the essential reason for the preservation of classical Arabic language and culture. For centuries the Arabic language was learned through study of the Qur'ān. Although Arabic is not the mother tongue of the majority of Muslims in the contemporary world, it remains alive because of the Qur'ān. Arabic serves as the international vehicle of Islamic scholarship. Knowledge of Arabic also acts as a check on the processes of assimilation into non-Arabic cultures while forming the linguistic basis of the cultural and social bonds of a global community. Because knowledge of Arabic is deemed necessary for a proper comprehension of the Qur'ān, Islamic missionaries keep the language vital through the founding and maintaining of schools dedicated to teaching the Qur'ān.

Knowledge of the Qur'ān is achieved not only in formal and structured educational settings, but also through numerous daily and common experiences throughout the Muslim world. Its verses form the inscriptions on the walls of mosques. Often recited in its entirety throughout the month of Ramadan, it remains a mark of piety to learn by heart the entire text. Basic to acts of private and public rituals, it serves as an expression of religious devotion and as

the fountainhead for much proverbial wisdom. The Qur'ān has offered a great number of Arabic phrases suited to the emotion or nature of a particular event that express a full spectrum of human responses to the complexities of life. Daily, millions use Arabic phrases to offer human greetings for every conceivable social situation, as well as all types of blessings and invocations. With this oral tradition the Qur'ānic text passes into the living world of the literate and non-literate, informing and molding the basics of human life.

Finally, motivated by the desire to understand the word of God, Islam has produced many thousands of Qur'ānic Commentaries (*tafsirs*). The work itself (in *sura* 3:7) affirms that some verses are clear while others remain less clear. Further, the lack of punctuation in the original Arabic offered numerous problems for the interpreter. Thus, as with all seminal religious texts, a living tradition labors to understand the meaning of the work through a wealth of classical and modern exegetical literature. Tradition would also focus on one aspect or another of the Qur'ān, giving rise to intense discussions over such issues as the metaphorical and literal meanings of particular passages, or the tension between public law and private mystical piety, or divine predestination and human freedom, or the meaning and extent of anthropomorphic language for the Divine. Throughout Islamic tradition in the heat of theological debates over these issues (and many others), the discussion of the Qur'ānic text occasioned conflict and much polemic literature where all sides would freely cite the Qur'ān as support. Today it is commonplace for authors to produce literature which seeks to make the Qur'ān's teaching relevant to the complexities and demands of modern life. Put simply, the influence of the Qur'ān remains immeasurable.

LAWRENCE F. HUNDERSMARCK

Further Reading

Translations

There are two highly respected Arabic editions of the Qur'ān: *Corani textus arabicus, G. Flugel, ed., Leipzig, 1834, and the "Egyptian Standard Edition" published in Cairo in 1945. These two texts, which differ in their number of the suras,* form the basis for most Western translations. All translations suffer the problems inherent in the task, but even more so when dealing with the complexities and ambiguities of ancient Arabic. Believed by Muslims to be essentially untranslatable, the Qur'ān presents special difficulties because the roots of Arabic terms are often so elastic and comprehensive that they defy the precise analytic equivalence of modern languages. Also, the rhythm, the rhetoric, and the highly emotive character of spoken Arabic presents a great challenge to the translator. However, the great importance of the Qur'ān has led to many attempts to set the text before the non-Arab reader. A complete list of these efforts can be found in the appendix of A. F. L. Beeston, et al, *Arabic Literature to the End of the Umayyad Period*, Cambridge: Cambridge University Press, 1983, and in *The Encyclopedia of Islam* (New Edition), ed. by C. E. Bosworth, et al, s.v. "al-Kur'an (translations of the Kur'an)." 5:429–433. Leiden: E. J. Brill, 1986.

Ali, Abullah Yusuf, trans. *The Holy Qur'an: Text, Translation, and Commentary*. Lahore: Muhammad Ashraf, 1938. This easily readable translation is famous for its very extensive commentary addressed to the modern reader while at the same time demonstrating a great respect for the traditional Islamic commentaries.

Arberry, Arthur J., trans. *The Koran Interpreted*. 2 vols. London: George Allen and Unwin, 1955. Thought to be perhaps the best English translation in terms of critical scholarship and the overall careful reading of the Arabic text. This translation captures in its directness the force of the original while attempting to retain its rhythmical patterns. In 1964, Macmillan publishing house in New York reissued the Arberry translation in one volume.

Bell, Richard, trans. *The Qur'an*. 2 vols. Edinburg: T. and T. Clark, 1937. This translation, while not as smooth as that of Arberry, is often very exact regarding specific terms. Based on the Flugel text, Bell rearranges the traditional order of verses to conform with his theories of text chronology.

Dawood, N. J., trans. *The Koran*. New York: Penquin Books, 1956. This is a rather free, and at times arbitrary, rendition. It has the merit, however, of being very readable.

Palmer, Edward H. *The Qur'an*. 2 vols. Oxford: Claredon Press, 1880. Originally volumes 6 and 9 of the 50 volume series, "The Sacred Books of the East," this translation is respected for its overall accuracy. Palmer's efforts have, however, been criticized by some for his use of colloquial English and thus for diminishing the grandeur of the Arabic.

Pickthall, Marmaduke. *The Meaning of the Glorious Qur'an: Text and Explanatory Translation*. London: A. A. Knopf, 1930. This is a very successful translation reprinted many times in Karachi (Taj Company), London (Allen and Unwin), and New York (New American Library). Some caution ought to be exercised in its use for there is, throughout the translation, the use of inexact modern phrases to capture, as the title puts it, "the meaning of the glorious Qur'an."

Sale, George. *The Koran: Commonly Called the Alcoran of Mohammed*. London: C. Ackers, 1734. This was, for almost 150 years, the only English translation and as such exercised enormous influence throughout Europe. Reprinted a great many times, it was admired for its elegant eighteenth-century style and its use of traditional Sunni exegesis to explain the complexities of the text. Although fair-minded and balanced by the standards of the day, Sale's work has been criticized for its tendency to critique sections of the Qur'ān from a Christian perspective.

Related Studies

Gibb, H. A. R., and J. H. Kramers. *Shorter Encyclopedia of Islam*. Ithaca: Cornell University Press, 1953. Reprinted by E. J. Brill of Leiden in 1974. This valuable work is a one-volume compendium of all the articles dealing with Islamic religion and law from the first edition of the *Encyclopedia* (1913–1938). The articles, alphabetized according to key Arabic terms, can be casily approached through the "register of subjects" which serves as an index to locate all the basic topics. Although a second edition of the Encyclopedia is being prepared and when completed will summarize contemporary Islamic scholarship, the use of this work offers the reader the best nineteenth- and early-twentieth-century Western scholarship on Islamic tradition and its source document, the Qur'ān.

Kassis, Hanna E. *A Concordance of the Qur'an*. Berkeley: University of California Press, 1983. While not a new translation, this work, using the Arberry English text, is of great value. Through an organization of sayings according to key Arabic terms, Kassis offers a very comprehensive thematic arrangement of the Qur'ān. This is the work to consult for the meaning and use of every Arabic term that forms the basis of all the topics presented throughout the Qur'ān.

Izutsu, Toshihiko. *Ethico-Religious Concepts in the Qu'ran*. Montreal: McGill University Press, 1966. This is a very clearly written analysis of the constellation of Qur'ānic terms and their meanings. Izutsu also offers a detailed discussion regarding the Islamization of the old Arab virtues, while considering the key differences between the ethics of tribal solidarity and those of the Qur'ān.

Piamenta, M. *Islam in Everyday Arabic Speech*. Leiden: E. J. Brill, 1979.

———. *The Muslim Conception of God and Human Welfare as Reflected in Everyday Arabic Speech*. Leiden: E. J. Brill, 1983. Written by an expert on Middle Eastern languages and literature, these two works offer to the reader an encyclopedic study of the many ways the Arabic oral tradition keeps alive the essentials of the Qur'ānic text. Because these books set forth common Arabic phrases with English translations arranged thematically, the reader, at a glance, can experience the living vitality of the Islamic world view and its expression in everyday speech.

Rahman, Fazlur. *Major Themes of the Qur'an*. Chicago: Bibliotheca Islamica, 1980. A description of the entire content of the Qur'ān by a well-respected professor of Islamic studies at the University of Chicago. Rahman's work is comprehensive, sophisticated, and reverential.

Sherif, Faruq. *A Guide to the Contents of the Qur'an*. London, Ithaca Press, 1985. (Distributed in North America by Humanities Press of Atlantic Highlands, NJ) Like the work of Rahman, Sherif offers a clear delineation of exactly what the Qur'ān says on a wide variety of topics. In his first chapter he offers an interesting chart that attempts to set forth both the number of verses devoted to a specific topic as well as an indication of the percentage of the whole work that those verses represent. While such a graph cannot be scientifically exact, it does give the reader a quick overview of the entire contents of the Qur'ān.

Watt, W. Montgomery. *Bell's Introduction to the Qur'an*. Edinburgh: Edinburgh University Press, 1970. (Distributed in North America by the Aldine Publishing Co. of Chicago). This is a learned revised edition of Richard Bell's *Introduction* first published in 1953, in which Bell sought to build upon the insights of Western scholars regarding the dating and arrangements of the Qur'ānic *suras*. A reading of Watt's work offers a rich exposition on the state of modern scholarship regarding such issues as the context, history, forms, doctrines, and style of the Qur'ānic text. Much can be learned from chapters on the shaping and chronology of the text as well as on the main lines of Muslim and non-Muslim scholarship on the Qur'ān. Bell and Watt stand in a long tradition of critical Western scholarship beginning with Theodor Noldeke's *Geschichte des Qorans* published in Gottingen in 1860 and its famous second edition, in 3 vols., published at Leipzig in 1938 under the names of two scholars, Gotthelf Bergstrasser and Otto Pretzl. What is common in this tradition are attempts to understand the Qur'ān as a human document with its own literary and historical forms that allow the *suras* to be identified during various points in the Prophet's career.

THE THOUSAND AND ONE NIGHTS
(THE ARABIAN NIGHTS)

Title in Arabic: *Alf Layla wa-Layla*

Authors: Unknown. Product of a long oral tradition.

Literary Form: A collection of tales, realistic or fantastic, of ancient Indian, Greek, Mesopotamian and Persian, and more recent Arabic origins that have been told and retold for thousands of years, especially in the Arabic-speaking Middle East.

Date of Composition: These tales belonged to a primarily oral tradition, the core of which was probably written down in the tenth century. Other tales were added to the corpus over the centuries.

Major Themes

Life, be it tragic or comic, is worth our striving.
With patience, faith, perseverance, and virtue, we can triumph in life.
Civilizations come and go, life is transient, death is omnipotent.
God's world is so immense that all wonders have a place.

In speaking of *The Book of the Thousand and One Nights* (or *The Arabian Nights*), Jorge Luis Borges reminds us that its appeal is in fact suggested by its title: "In the title *The Thousand and One Nights* there is something very important: the suggestion of an infinite book. It practically is." Playing on the implications of the number "one thousand" in Middle Eastern cultures in general, and Arabic culture in particular, Borges expounds on the ways the *Nights* transcends both time and place. Ever since Antoine Galland (1646–1715) discovered and subsequently translated *The Arabian Nights* into French beginning in 1704, the tales contained in it have fascinated the world; they have been translated first into English and later into virtually every major language in the world. *The Arabian Nights'* influence has been so pervasive in the arts throughout history that, according to Robert Irwin, it is easier to name those who have not been influenced than those who have. Its narrative techniques are constantly emulated, its stories adapted and retold, miniatures are created to illustrate the luxurious editions of the book, music is composed in honor of Scheherazade, and films based on scripts adapted from its stories are made. However, being an infinite source of inspiration is only one aspect of the work. It is also a bottomless well of stories; its

narrative structure allows, even compels it to sustain myriad tales of uncountable themes which, though firmly planted in time and place, are universal and timeless because of their insistent celebration of the exhilarating, and excruciating, experience of human life and living. From the stories of love and death, fortune and misfortune, adventure and misadventure, we learn that life, be it tragic or comic, is worth our striving, and that with patience, faith, perseverance, and virtues, life inevitably triumphs. It is no wonder that *The Arabian Nights* remains one of the most popular works in the world today.

The immense popularity of, and esteem for, *The Arabian Nights'* stories at present, paradoxically, has caused certain difficulties in writing the history of this work. In contrast to its status in literature and arts nowadays, *The Arabian Nights* was not an esteemed piece of literature in Arab-Islamic culture in the Middle Ages despite the existence of historical reports attesting to the popularity of its tales. If Antoine Galland had not discovered these tales, and if his translation had not triggered the responses that it did, one may legitimately wonder whether this work would have occupied such prominence in our consciousness. In fact, the history of the text is so intricately woven into the history of its translation that it is impossible to discuss the former without the latter; it is the story of a complex process of cultural exchange, of cross-cultural fertilization that has been taking place for centuries, and of cultural and literary encounter between the East and the West.

Although the tales incorporated into the book now known as *The Book of the Thousand and One Nights* have been in circulation for centuries, and some individual tales were known to Europeans in the Middle Ages and influenced their works, they belonged to a primarily oral tradition of storytelling, most of which were not written down in a final form. The tales were meant to be told, not read: therefore the written texts, when necessary and where extant, consisted of the outlines and essentials of the stories, which the storytellers used to remind themselves of the story line, leaving themselves ample freedom to improvise and embellish, dependent on the audiences they were addressing. These tales were not known as being part of the integral work with which we are familiar today. The writing down of *The Arabian Nights* in its present form took place primarily during the eighteenth and the nineteenth centuries, due to a great extent to the interest the Europeans showed in them.

It all began with Galland, who discovered a manuscript of *The Voyages of Sinbad* and translated and published it in 1701. Inspired by the success of *Sinbad*, Galland obtained a three-volume (some say four) manuscript, dating from the fourteenth or fifteenth centuries, from Levant (now Syria, Lebanon, Jordan, and Palestine) and began translating it. His fruition took the form of the twelve-volume *Les Mille et une nuit*, the first two of which were published in 1704 and the final in 1717. The popularity and influence of Galland's translation were immediate and pervasive in Europe. For almost a century translations of his translation, not of any Arabic version of the *Nights*, were made into other European languages, especially in English.

In the meantime, an earnest search began for the Arabic manuscripts of the *Nights*, and consequently, or subsequently, a series of Arabic texts were put together and published. There are at least twenty-two Arabic manuscripts of the *Nights* of either Egyptian or Syrian origin known to have survived to the present day. Of these manuscripts, one seems to be a copy of a Baghdadi prototype, leading to the speculation that the first Arabic version of the *Nights* might have been put together for the first time in medieval Iraq. However, most of these manuscripts come from a late date and some scholars have conjectured that they, most of which ended in European libraries anyway, may have been produced in the eighteenth and nineteenth centuries in order to meet the demands of European manuscript-hunters in the Near East. Whether this is true or fictitious, we now have four sets of *Nights* texts in print, which were all published in the first half of the nineteenth century: Calcutta I (1814–1828), Breslau (1824–1839), Bulaq (1835), and Calcutta II (1839–1842).

With the publication of these four texts, translation of the *Nights* gained momentum despite some lingering suspicions surrounding their sources and status. During this frenetic translation period, which coincided with the emerging Victorian sensibilities and the European expansion into the Middle East and the Far East—the "Orient"—many translations of the *Nights* surfaced. These translations were welcome commodities promptly devoured by an audience fascinated with the world of the *Nights*. The *Nights* stories, captivating as they are, reflected above all the rediscovered intrigue with the "Orient" and satisfied the hunger for more information about the territories newly acquired by their empires, and their original inhabitants. The translators of the *Nights*—consciously or unwittingly, maliciously or naively—participated in shaping and sustaining the "Orientalist" discourse, which has remained a central issue in the cultural, political, and literary interactions between the "East" and the "West." By the tone they set, the style they chose, the stories they selected to translate, and the format of their presentation, they not only affirmed the vision of their culture, but also provided an interpretation of the "other" culture through which their audiences formed opinions about the "Orient," its peoples and their culture and religion.

Edward William Lane (1801–76), an orientalist preoccupied with the scholarly study of Arabic language and the manners and customs of the Arabs, produced a three-volume translation which appeared first in monthly parts between 1938 and 1940. In contrast to Galland's translation, which embraced the Romantic priorities, Lane's version went after some kind of realism; he was preoccupied with providing historical, cultural, societal, and literary information in copious footnotes, which were later published as a separate work under the title *Arabian Society in the Middle Ages: Studies from the Thousand and One Nights.*

Toward the end of the century, John Payne (1842–1906) translated Calcutta II which, published by the Villon Society, appeared in nine volumes between 1882 and 1884. He also translated additional stories found in Breslau and Calcutta I, which were published as *Tales from the Arabic* in 1884. When a copy of Zotenberg's manuscript of "Zayn al-Asnam" and "Aladdin" became available he translated these as well, publishing them in 1889. About the same time, Richard Francis Burton (1821–90), relying heavily on Payne's rendition, produced yet another English translation of the *Nights*, which appeared first in ten volumes in 1885, and six supplementary volumes between 1886 and 1888. Very similar in taste and style, Payne and Burton gave their translations an archaic version of English and placed much emphasis on the exotic and erotic. Following their example, Powys Mathews produced yet another version the *Nights* in 1923, but his was in reality an English translation of Joseph Charles Mardus's new French translation. Mardus's version, published in sixteen volumes between 1889 and 1904, is at best a loose adaptation of sorts. Claiming to be translating from the Bulaq text first and later from a North African manuscript, allegedly Tunisian that has never surfaced, he produced a version that is often inaccurate and that reflects his own fancies more than anything else.

The misadventures in translation of the nineteenth and early twentieth century are in a sense a reflection of the state of scholarship on the "Orient." Having made progress in both knowledge and methodology, twentieth-century translators, who are often better scholars as well, produced more accurate and readable translations. Enno Littman's (1875–1958) German translation, Francesco Gabrieli's Italian translation, and N. J. Dawood's new English translation of Calcutta II, all provide pleasurable readings. Most importantly, these efforts paved the way for Muhsin Mahdi's scholarly edition of the earliest manuscript of the *Nights*, which appeared in 1984 and was ably translated into English by Husain Haddawy in 1990.

Thanks to two centuries of research and the efforts of Muhsin Mahdi, whose scholarly edition of the earliest manuscript of the *Arabian Nights* appeared in 1984, scholars can now agree on a tentative history of the *Nights*. The *Arabian Nights* is a composite work and the earliest tales in it came from India and Persia. These tales were probably translated into Arabic in the early eighth century under the title *Alf Layla*, or *The Thousand Nights*. An expanded collection that became known as *The Thousand and One Nights* was apparently quite popular in the eleventh and twelfth centuries.

The modern obsession with finding the definitive text of the *Arabian Nights*, and completing the thousand and one nights' worth of storytelling seems in contradiction with the interpretation the moderns have given to the meaning of the title of the work: "infinity." Clearly, this interpretation is supported by the narrative structure of the work; the framing of the tales within another frame which in turn serves as yet another frame for more tales. The primary frame tale—that which links all the tales of *The Arabian Nights*—is that of Scheherazade telling stories to Shahrayar night after night. Within this frame, there are other frames, such as "The Story of the Hunchback," in which a number of people tell tales to a certain king of China. Additionally, the tales themselves may be linked to one another by yet another narrative device: one storyteller tells a tale about yet another storyteller telling a tale. And the chain can go on, literally, forever, making the possibilities of appropriating tales from other sources endless. This is probably what happened, resulting in the incorporation of tales of varying genres, themes, and purposes, not to mention the uneven artistry of the tales in the *Nights*.

Modern preoccupation with locating, or even establishing, a fixed written text, in fact, exposes the contrast between the function of storytelling in the modern West and the medieval Arab-Islamic society. In so much as storytelling is for both entertainment and instruction in the two cultures, stories in Arab-Islamic society were first and foremost meant to be *told*, in the marketplaces, at festivals, in coffee houses, and at homes, and the language of these texts was often in the colloquial, or the spoken language, rarely the literary, except where some members of the educated elite participated in writing them down.

Payne and Burton's renditions of *The Arabian Nights* (see *Translations* under *Further Reading*) into archaic, or pseudo-Shakespearean, English are ironically inappropriate. Yet their efforts, and the overall high regard for this work in the West, paradoxically drew the Arabs' attention to this work, bringing to it the recognition that has eluded it for centuries.

The universal appeal of *The Arabian Nights* stems not only from the universe of the marvels that it portrays, but above all its spell-binding storytelling. The book is ultimately *about* storytelling and *for* storytelling. The storyteller must be like a magician, a sorcerer, who can manipulate words and phrases to put a spell on his or her listeners; for only by doing so, can the storyteller, like Scheherazade and the storytellers whose stories she tells, instruct and save life. As much as they are intrigued by the stories themselves, the modernist Arab writers are even more inspired by Scheherazade's storytelling and her objective. In their writings, novels or short stories, about Scheherazade or emulating her techniques, these writers write to discuss issues central to the survival of the Arabs as a nation in the aftermath of colonialism.

Scheherazade's Storytelling

The Arabian Nights begins with the frame tale; the story of a "nation" on the brink of destruction.

King Shahrayar, as well as his brother king Shahzaman, both witness acts of betrayal by their wives whom they see have sex with their slaves. Outraged, they embark on a journey, hoping to find peace of mind again. They encounter a princess abducted and imprisoned by a demon. The princess forces them to have sex with her and extorts a ring from each despite the presence of the demon, who is asleep at the time. This incident makes both kings lose faith in women, and when Shahrayar returns to his palace he is resolved to wed a virgin every night and kill her the following morning. As the virgins become scarcer by the day, the vizier entrusted with the task of finding the king a bride day after day grows worried. His daughter Scheherazade volunteers to wed the king. She devises a plan to save the womankind, therefore humankind; she takes her sister Dinazad (also known as Dinarzad and Dunyazad) with her and instructs her to ask her to tell a tale at the appropriate time at night. She then proceeds to tell a story throughout the night, always stopping at a critical point in the story at dawn. Yearning to find out the end of each story, Shahrayar postpones her execution day after day. A thousand and one nights later Shahrayar, having fathered three sons by Scheherazade, pardons her.

Scheherazade's tales are numerous, marvelous, and diverse; they defy simple categorization based on genre or theme. Most notably, a sense of the fantastic pervades the stories. The stories—albeit realistic at times—often recount events and circumstances that are incredible, or in Arabic *'ajib* (marvelous) and *gharib* (strange). *The Arabian Nights* is not the only source of stories of the marvelous and the strange, for these aspects of the tales, challenging the imagination as they do, represent a distinctive feature of Muslim thinking in the Middle Ages. Allah's omnipotence exhibits itself in many ways, some understandable and others incomprehensible to the human mind. Scholars have observed this phenomenon *'ajib* and *gharib* in the Qur'ān, the Prophetic Tradition, and the places they have traveled, documenting it in works which often carry these two words in their titles. These works are meant to inspire awe at God's power, and more importantly, to remind us of how limited human comprehension is. Nevertheless, these accounts can additionally serve as entertainment. The *Arabian Nights* stories, much like the stories in *al-Hikayat al-'Ajiba wa al-Akhbar al-Ghariba* (Tales of the Marvelous and Accounts of the Strange), edited and published by Hans Wehr, deal instead with the events occurring to, and circumstances surrounding, humans.

What makes many of these stories fantastic is the role the supernatural elements play in the plot as it unfolds. Demons (*'ifrit, marid,* genie) in *The Arabian Nights*, like humans, have their own social and political organization, with kings, courts and armies; can be evil or good, and are endowed with strong feelings; but unlike humans, they are invisible creatures with bodies of flame and are capable of shape-shifting. They interact with humans, sometimes unwittingly, but at times willingly because they love to meddle in human affairs, especially to matchmake.

The world of *The Arabian Nights* is also inhabited by magicians and sorcerers, reflecting certain social facts and aspects of reality. Just as some believed in the power of demons, they did not doubt the power of magic and talismans. There were, after all, practicing sorcerers, alchemists, and treasure hunters in medieval Baghdad and Cairo. Astrologers were consulted regarding business trips and the outcomes of sporting events. *The Arabian Nights* abounds with stories about demons, about voyages to demon lands, and about luck and charm. In these stories the hero's predestined luck may take a concrete shape in the form of a magic object or charm. Sometimes he obtains a talisman that gives him power over demons, or brings him wealth and fortune.

Alladin and the Magic Lamp

The story of "Alladin and the Magic Lamp" is a superb example of demon stories. In the story, a North African dervish, and sorcerer, determines by astrology that Alladin is the only person who can bring a certain hoard of treasure out from its hiding place. The sorcerer brings the boy to the astrologically determined place and performs a ritual fu-

migation with incense in order to create a hole in the ground. A copper ring attached to a marble slab is revealed by the opening of the earth. The sorcerer bids Alladin raise the slab, for Alladin alone can do this, and descend into the vaults below. He warns him not to touch any of the treasures, for his quest is the magic lamp which confers power over a genie. However, Alladin does touch the treasure and becomes imprisoned in the vault. There he discovers the power of the lamp and with the help of its resident genie he escapes, acquires riches, and marries a princess. Even though he battles the sorcerer again to keep his fortune, the story does end happily.

The story of Alladin crosses literary genres; it is a fantastic journey, a love story, a demon story, and an adventure in treasure hunt. These are not the only genres found in *The Arabian Nights*; there are, to name but a few, fairy tales, romances and novels, legends, didactic stories, humorous stories, anecdotes, etc. If the moral of the story of Alladin is that, destiny aside, good eventualy triumphs over evil, there are many more themes covered by *The Arabian Nights*: there are stories about love, death, fate and faith; about vicissitudes of fortune; about thrills and dangers of travel and adventure; about aspects of life in the cities (crimes); about human virtues (generosity, loyalty, honesty, chastity) and vices (treachery, cheating, greed), and everything else there is in life. In other words, the topics for research on The *Thousand and One Nights*, like its stories, are potentially infinite, therefore, generalizations are impossible. Those scholars who have chosen to work on the book often focus on one story, one theme shared by a number of stories, one phenomenon the stories recount, or one aspect of its storytelling.

The Love Stories

There are, however, themes that are more prominent than others: love, crime, and travel. Love stories in The *Arabian Nights* can be loosely divided into two categories: the hard-earned-happiness stories and the stories of unrequited love. In both, the description of the successive stages of the love affair often draws upon the established convention and its familiar motifs. Love is usually at first sight, and in some cases, at first hearing. In some stories of Persian and Egyptian origin, such as "Ibrahim and Jamila," the hero, usually a prince, falls in love with the faraway heroine, usually a princess, on hearsay, then travels the length of earth to seek and to find her. Love usually involves much pining. The lovers may take no action, but rely on the help of the others, resulting in happy endings in some cases. In "The Story of the Two Viziers, Nur al-Din al-Misri and Badr al-Din Hasan al-Basri," of Egyptian origin, the lovers are first brought together, and separated by demons, and reunited at the end by the uncle of the hero who is also the father of the heroine. However, some heroines may show resourcefulness, like Zumurrud in the Egyptian " 'Ali Shar and Zumurrud." She chooses 'Ali Shar from among the bystanders in the slave-market, gives him the money—he has just lost his fortune—to buy her, and when abducted first by a Christian and later by a robber, she rescues herself while he despairs.

Not all lovers are as lucky in the stories of unrequited love; the lovers usually suffer, fall ill physically, and eventually die of grief, much in the same fashion as the early Arabic stories of Qays and Layla (commonly know as Layla wa Majnun—*Majnun* means insane in Arabic), Qays and Lubna, and Jamil and Buthayna. In "Nur al-Din 'Ali and Anis al-Jalis," the protagonists fall in love, but are fated to be apart and to die from grief. The heroine of " 'Aziz and 'Aziza," (of Baghdadian origin), 'Aziza, though exhibiting endurance, dies of sorrow. Resigned to marry her cousin 'Aziz, as dictated by the customs and the wishes of her parents, she dedicates herself to the happiness of 'Aziz, sacrificing her own. Upon discovering his infatuation with another girl, she does everything she can to further the relationship while she herself withers away.

Crime Stories

The Arabian Nights also abounds with crime stories—factual and fictitious, exhibiting a curious fascination with crimes and a keen interest in their detection. These stories in some way reflect the low life in the urban centers of medieval Islam, specifically Baghdad and Cairo. Drugs, alcohol, begging, vandalism, charlatans, gambling, and cheating in cards are only some of the colorful aspects of low life depicted in the *Nights*.

Three types of criminals dominate the scene in the *Nights*; robbers, thieves, and rogues. Robbers, or highwaymen, are primarily Bedouins who operate alone or in bands in open road or desert, and who rely on brute force. Thieves, alone or in organized groups, operate in cities, towns and villages, and they rely on cunning as much as on violence. Rogues, usually city dwellers, but who sometimes travel from one city to another, specialize in turning tricks (*hiyal* in Arabic)—merry or cruel pranks—on innocent victims for gratuitous purposes. These characters form the basis of the underworld of the Middle East. The organization of criminals and rogues was not simply a fictional convention; brotherhood of crime with its own hierarchy and a code of honor flourished in medieval Cairo. The underworld, both the *futuwwa* organizations of the Middle Ages and the later organized guilds of thieves and beggars of the Ottoman period (sixteenth to eighteenth centuries), is well known and documented.

The Arabian Nights is full of long and short stories that deal with crimes in a matter-of-fact manner, even though they stress the sordid aspects of low life. This is especially true of the stories about rogues and their tricks. These stories, like the stories of the *Maqamat*, are varied, amusing, and at times convey admiration for the intelligence and street-smartness of these rogues, who are often portrayed as heroes. Thieves and rogues are not always portrayed as evil; in fact, some of the thieves may exhibit signs of social adjustment and, not unlike Robin Hood, are sometimes capable of prudence and generosity.

The three full-length rogue-stories about Ahmed al-Danaf and Hasan Shuman portray them as two reformed criminals turned policemen and amusingly recount their entanglements with Dalila, 'Ali Zaybaq (the Mercury), and 'Ala' al-Din al-

Shamat, including the gratuitous pranks played by these characters. Some stories, especially those about robbers, convey the hostility felt by city dwellers toward Bedouins.

The story of " 'Ali Baba," a story of criminals who meet their match, condemns robbery outright; its tone is distinctly moralizing, stressing that virtue will be rewarded and vice punished. The detection of crimes in some stories—"The Story of Three Apples" in the Harun al-Rashid cycle, and " 'Ali Khawaja"—requires some kind of deductive process that leads to crime solving, very similar to modern day mysteries. Some stories, such as "Baybars and the Sixteen Captains of the Watch," expose bureaucratic corruption, and yet others, such as "al-Malik Zahir and the Three Captains of the Watch," treat crime as just another way of life in the big city.

The uncontested heroes of *The Arabian Nights* are undoubtedly the travelers who embark on fantastic journeys. Many stories, which deal with travel wholly or partly, relate voyages by sea, by land, through air with the help of supernatural beings—a demon, a gigantic bird, or magical flying contraptions, and even underwater. Distant countries are described, as well as lands inhabited by demons and those of the merfolk. Positive and hopeful in tone, these stories, in conjunction with the extensive geographical literature of the ninth to fourteenth centuries, capture the excitement felt about the expansion of the horizon in the aftermath of the Muslim conquests into Byzantine, Persia, and Indian, and during the expansion of world trade, especially the maritime ventures into the Indian Ocean.

"The City of Brass," an ocean myth based on a well-known legend recorded in historical sources, is in fact an account of an expedition the Caliph 'Abd al-Malik b. Marwan (ruled 685–705) ordered to the coast of a western sea named al-Karkar for the purpose of fetching him some of the brass bottles King Solomon used to imprison demons. The expedition leads to the City of Brass, a dead city, and to the description of the journey from Damascus to Cairo, then across the desert to Maghreb (Algeria, Morocco, and Tunisia today), to the city on the coast (perhaps the Atlantic coast), and of the city, of both its material splendor and the starkness of its death. On the other hand, Sindbad—a man of action and courage—travels eastward in "The Seven Voyages of Sindbad," toward India and China, where he finds adventure and wealth.

As much as these stories are about adventure, they are about life and death, and God's omnipotence and omnipresence. While we are struck by the glamor of the City of Brass, we are also reminded that civilizations come and go, that life is transient but that death is omnipotent: While we learn from Sindbad that we can make no gain without pain, we also learn that God's world is so immense that all wonders have a place. It is even possible that there is a life alternative to, and perhaps better than, the one we know, as the story of " 'Abdallah the Fisherman and 'Abdallah the Merman" tells us. At the invitation of the Merman, the Fisherman visits the sea and the merfolk who inhabit it, and finds a society with its own rules and customs.

In addition, there are nearly one hundred short pieces of work that are purely for instructional purposes; they are in the form of anecdotes, designed to provide information about the expanding Islamic empire, about the conquest of Spain in "City of Lebta" and about the Pyramids of Egypt in "al-Ma'mun and the Pyramids"; or about the importance of knowledge, especially of the sciences considered essential to a Muslim, in "The Slave Girl Tawaddud"; or about virtues, such as generosity, piety, faith, justice, and love (as exemplified by historical characters from pre-Islamic or early Islamic times). There are also fables and other stories of obviously moral bent, about chastity ("The King and the Virtuous Woman"), about destiny and the vicissitudes of fortune (as in the story about the rich man who became poor and then rich again), and so forth.

A Universe of Marvels

The appeal of *The Thousand and One Nights*, however, lies not in its instruction, but in the power of its narrative to suggest a universe of marvels, a universe that provides an alternative to, and an escape from, the one we know. The universe of the *Nights* appeals to the young and the old, Easterners and Westerners, men and women, the illiterate and the intellectual alike, because it is both of and out of this world. Even though this body of stories was not highly regarded or considered literature by the educated Arabs for centuries, they have been immensely popular. The enthusiastic reception by the West to the *Nights* curiously provoked a keen interest among the Arabs themselves who in the past few decades, with increasing contact with the literature of the West, began to reconsider and redefine their literary tradition. As they incorporated the Western narrative genres—novels, short stories, and plays—into their writing, they also embarked on a journey in search for a unique identity. The discovery of *The Arabian Nights* as literature by the Arabs means the discovery of a prototype of Arabic literary narrative that legitimizes and authenticates Arabic novels and short stories, giving them a history of their own.

WEN-CHIN OUYANG

Further Reading

Translations

Lane, E. W., trans. *The Thousand and One Nights: The Arabian Nights' Entertainment*. 4 vols. London: C. Knight, 1839–41. New ed., E. Stanley Poole, ed. 3 vols. London: Bickers, 1877. Translation from the Arabic, with notes.

Payne, John, trans. *The Book of the Thousand Nights and One Night*. 9 vols. London, 1882–84; 4 supplementary vols., 1884–88. Literal translation from the Arabic.

———. trans. *Aladdin and the Enchanted Lamp: Zein ul Asnam and the King of the Jinn*. London, 1889. Two stories translated into English from a (then) newly discovered Arabic text.

Burton, Richard F., trans. *The Arabian Nights' Entertainments, or The Book of the Thousand Nights and a Night*. 10 vols. Benares: Stoke Newington, 1885.

———. trans. *Supplemental Nights to the Book of the Thousand Nights and a Night*. 6 vols. Benares: Stoke Newington, 1886–88. These two Burton translations have been the most popular. Other editions have been issued.

Related Studies

'Ali, Muhsin Jassim (known in the Arab world as Muhsin Jasim al-Musawi). *Scheherazade in England: A Study of Nineteenth-Century English Criticism of the Arabian Nights*. Washington, D.C.: Three Continents Press (with the assistance of Baghdad University), 1981. A study of the cultural and literary context of the reception of the translations of the *Arabian Nights* into English, beginning with the translation from Antoine Galland's French rendition at the beginning of the eighteenth century up to Burton's translation at the end of the nineteenth century. It traces and discusses the Romantic and Victorian responses to the *Arabian Nights*, both critically and aesthetically, which led to Lane and Burton's translations of the *Nights*.

Caracciolo, Peter L., ed. *The Arabian Nights in English Literature: Studies in the Reception of the Thousand and One Nights into British Culture*. New York: St. Martin's Press, 1988. A collection of articles dealing with the influence of the *Nights* on English literature. Each article addresses a specific genre in English literature, such as the *Nights'* influence on English Nursery, Coleridge, Dickens, Wilkie Collins, Thackeray, R. L. Stevenson, Elizabeth Gaskell, George Meredith, Joseph Conrad, Wells, Joyce, Yeats, and T. S. Eliot.

Gerhardt, Mia I. *The Art of Story-telling: A Literary Study of the Thousand and One Nights*. Leiden: E. J. Brill, 1963. The first literary study of the *Nights* in English focusing on the its storytelling techniques. It provides a history of the texts and translations of the *Nights*, classification of the *Nights* tales, literary analyses of the tales, and a study of the structure of the work, both as a whole and as independent tales. It remains the most readable literary study of the *Nights* to this date.

Ghazoul, Ferial J. *The Arabian Nights: A Structural Analysis*. Cairo: National Commission for UNESCO, 1980. A textual analysis of the text as object, providing a symbolic interpretation of the *Nights*: Scheherazade's narrative transforms Shahrayar.

Irwin, Robert. *The Arabian Nights: A Companion*. London: The Penguin Press, 1994. A carefully developed account of what is known of the genesis of *The Arabian Nights*, together with an accurate history of the many translations of the work, a description of the medieval Near East, and reflections on the stories—the whole serving as a guide to the understanding of the book's complex history and its unique charm.

Naddaf, Sandra. *Arabesque: Narrative Structure and the Aesthetics of Repetition in 1001 Nights*. Evanston: Northwestern University Press, 1991. A short study based on analysis of one specific story, "The Porter and the Three Ladies," of one specific feature in the techniques of the *Nights*—repetition—and its aesthetic effects.

Pinault, David. *Story-telling Techniques in the Arabian Nights*. Leiden: E. J. Brill, 1992. A study of the oral elements in a number of tales in the Nights (the tales included in the Enchanted Prince Cycle, and the City of Brass) primarily based on the theories proposed by Albert Lord in *The Singer of Tales*.

SHAHNAMEH

Title in Persian: *Shāhnāma* (The Book of Kings)
Author: Abo'l-Qāsem Ferdowsi (Firdawsi or Ferdausi: "The Paradisal")
Born: c. 934, Tus, in North-East Persia
Died: c. 1020
Literary Form: Epic poetry
Date of Composition: Completed in 1010

Major Themes

The work celebrates the heroic tradition of the feast, the hunt, and personal combat.
The world is the battleground between the forces of good and evil.
Despite the hostility of fate, man can possess the dignity to make a moral choice.
A good man can make a wrong decision for the right reason.
A value such as loyalty, good and admirable by itself, can sometime conflict with the higher value of truth, bringing tragic results.
The ideal ruler must embody the principle of goodness and guard against the corrupting nature of power.
Those filled with hubris are always struck down in the end.

The *Shahnameh* of Ferdowsi is the Iranian national epic. No other single work written in the Persian language has done more than the *Shanameh* to help preserve Iran's ancient cultural heritage which the epic celebrates. As a repository of myths, heroic lore, and pre-Islamic history of Iran, the poem is written in a monumental scale, consisting of 50,000 or more lines, depending on the manuscript. The great length of the poem befits its subject matter, which is nothing less than the entire history of the Iranian nation from the creation of the world to the defeat of the Sasanian dynasty by the rise of Islam.

Historical Background

Ferdowsi wrote his masterpiece more than three hundred years after the Islamic conquest of Iran. Under foreign domination, most Iranians converted to Islam and abandoned their ancient faith in Zoroastrianism. Along with the old faith, the Persian language itself faced the peril of obsolescence under the ascendence of Arabic as the common tongue of the new Islamic empire. There was a long period of silence in which the distinct Iranian cultural identity seemed all but lost. Then as the centralized control of the Caliphate over the extensive

Islamic lands began to wane, there began to emerge local Iranian dynasties who became the actual rulers of their regions with only a nominal allegiance to the Caliph in Baghdad.

The Samanids are the Iranian dynasty most closely associated with the tenth-century Persian renaissance. During the medieval period, Iran extended far beyond its present borders. Cites such as Bokhara, the Samanid capital, and Samarqand in the northeast, now largely a part of former Soviet Central Asia, were the centers of Iranian cultural revival. The Persian language, kept alive among the Iranian people, again became the court language and the medium of cultural productions.

The Samanids were an enthusiastic patron of the "new" Persian literature. It was under their rule that poets like Rudaki laid the foundation of the Persian poetic tradition which would continue to flourish for many centuries. The Samanids were also interested in preserving the history and the heritage of ancient Iran. Efforts were made to gather the scattered lore and traditions in order to reconstruct the history of Iran's past glory.

Ferdowsi also began working on his *Shahnameh* during this period of Persian cultural reawakening. In composing his epic poem, Ferdowsi drew from number of sources, including the prose version of the ancient history compiled under the Samanids. It was actually another poet, Daqiqi, who began to put the *Shahnameh* in verse. In his work, Ferdowsi acknowledges Daqiqi as his predecessor, and some one thousand lines of Daqiqi's are preserved in the finished work. Nevertheless, the credit for this monumental achievement in versification must be given almost entirely to Ferdowsi, who devoted over thirty years of his life to this work.

Ferdowsi

Despite Ferdowsi's lasting fame as the composer of the *Shahnameh*, the known facts about the poet's life are remarkably sparse. (Even his personal name is unknown.) The poet was a native of Tus, a city in the northeastern Iranian region of Khorasan. He belonged to the class of *dehqans*, the landed gentry. A conservative old Iranian class of gentlemen farmers, the *dehqans* were often the keepers of the old traditions.

Ferdowsi's predecessor, Daqiqi, is said to have been a Zoroastrian, although Ferdowsi himself was a Muslim. Ferdowsi began his work on the epic after Daqiqi's death in 980, when Ferdowsi was in his 40's. For the next thirty years or more, he devoted his life to its completion. According to a date found in the text, the *Shahnameh* was finished in 1010, when the poet was in his seventies. After finishing his poem, Ferdowsi dedicated his life-work to the ruler of the time, Mahmud of Ghazna, and sought his patronage.

Seeking the patronage of the powerful was customary for medieval poets and often the only means of their livlihood. Ferdowsi's independence from the court was more of an exception for his time. But reduced to poverty at the end of his long labor, Ferdowsi traveled to Mahmud's court, confident that the sultan would recognize the merit of his work. The result was nothing but disappointment for Ferdowsi. The sultan, known for generously rewarding his panegyrists, paid but scant attention to the aged poet's work.

Perhaps this was understandable, for the *Shahnameh* is a tribute to the Iranian national identity,

written in the spirit of Persian revival, promoted by the Samanids, the dynasty that the Ghaznavids had defeated and replaced. Moreover, one of the central motifs of the epic is the constant strife between Iranians and the Turanians, identified at that time with the Turks. Since Mahmud and the Ghaznavids were of Turkish extraction, *Shahnameh*'s treatment of the Turanians as the enemy of Iran must have been distasteful for the new rulers. As a result, the greatest poetic work of the time went unrewarded, and Ferdowsi died around 1020 in disappointment, without knowing the accolade the world would bestow upon his work.

The Iranian National History

As already noted, the great length of Ferdowsi's epic was dictated by the vastness of its subject matter, the Iranian national history from the creation of the world to the Islamic conquest in the seventh century. The scholars of the *Shahnameh* usually divide the epic into three parts, consisting of the mythological, legendary, and historical sections.

The Iranian national history covered by the epic greatly differs from what is known in the West through Greek historical writings. The pre-historic myths and legends that the Iranian people inherited from their tribal ancestors are not differentiated from factual accounts known to modern historians. The historical section of the epic deals with the Sasanians, an actual Iranian dynasty that ruled Iran until the seventh century. But the epic hardly mentions the Parthian or the Achaemenid empire that is so prominently featured in the Greco-Roman histories. The probable reason for this is that the Iranian sources that survived the Arab conquest and went into the making of Ferdowsi's tradition were of Sasanian provenance. The Sasanians were Zoroastrians, and despite their location in southwestern Iran, they inherited the Zoroastrian mytho-religious tradition of the northeast. In the epic, the mythic and legendary dynasties whose names are found among Zoroastrian writings are featured as the great predecessors of the Sasanians.

The Pishdadian Dynasty

The mythological section of the *Shahnameh* narrates the creation of the world and the deeds of its first sovereigns. Keyumars was not only the first man in the world, but also its first king. He began the dynasty of the Pishdadian, which ruled the world before its division into warring nations. The earliest Pishdadian rulers have the characteristics of culture heroes. For example Hushang, the second king, first taught people to use fire, and the third king, Tahmuras is associated with the discovery of writing. The first kings also battle and protect the world from the *divs*, the demonic minions of Ahriman, the embodiment of the evil principle. According to the Zoroastrian world view that infuses these myths, the world is the battleground between the forces of good and evil. The world was created by the all-good God, and it was the duty of the Pishdadian kings to protect it from the invading forces of evil.

During his reign, Keyumars battles the demon; he is folowed by Hushang and Tahmuras who continue the struggle. The fourth king, Jamshid, subdues the *divs* and reaches the height of glory. Eventually, however, he falls prey to hubris and begins to think himself equal to God. His vanity brings him destruction at the hands of Zahhak, a foreign invader who has gained power by contracting with the devil. The devil causes two snakes to grow out of Zahhak's shoulders that must be fed on human brains. The world suffers under Zahhak's tyranny, until finally a blacksmith named Kaveh finds the descendent of the royal family, Feridun, and starts a rebellion that defeats Zahhak. Feridun reigns justly and later decides to divide his kingdom among his three sons, Sam, Tur, and Iraj. Iraj inherits the best portion of the kingdom, the land of Iran. His two jealous brothers conspire together and kill Iraj treacherously, thus planting the seed of the perpetual enmity between the Iranians and the Turanians, the descendents of Tur. Manuchehr, Iraj's descendent, avenges Iraj's death and rules Iran. His rule is followed by a series of weak and incompetent kings, during whose reigns Iran is overrun by the invading Turanians.

Iran would not have survived the period of its weaknesss if it were not for the valors of Zal and his son Rostam. They belong to the line of the warrior kings of Sistan that had sworn allegiance to the ruling house of Iran. Rostam is often said to be the true hero of the entire epic, as written by Ferdowsi. He is the revered champion of the Iranians, and his exploits are much of the focus of the second, legendary section of the *Shahnameh.*

The Legendary Kayanian Kings

The second, and probably the most prominent section of the epic, deals with the reigns of the legendary kings of the Kayanian dynasty. In it, we find the narration of the more-or-less constant state of war between Iran and Turan, in which the exploits of Rostam and other Iranian heroes are colorfully featured. The most famous episodes, such as the stories of Sohrab and Rostam, Kavus and Seyavash, and Rostam and Esfandiyar, are all found here.

Qobad is the first Kayanian king to rule Iran. He was discovered and brought to the throne by Zal and Rostam. Qobad brings back prosperity to Iran and drives out the invading force of the Turanian king, Afrasiyab. Qobad is succeeded by his irascible son Kavus. Kavus turns out to be a petty, arrogant and incompetent ruler, yet he has one of the most complex characters among the numerous monarchs described by the epic.

The story of Rostam and his son Sohrab occurs during Kavus's long reign. Rostam sires a son, Sohrab, who grows up in the Turanian land. Sohrab becomes a Turanian champion and sets out to conquer Iran and to find his father, whom he has never met. In the course of the battle, Rostam kills his own son without knowing his true identity. As Sohrab lies dying, the father and son finally learn the bitter truth. The episode provides one of the finest tragic moments of the entire work.

The theme of a father destroying his own son is also repeated in the story of Seyavash. Kavus's wife Sudabeh tries to seduce her stepson, Seyavash, and then accuses him when refused. After proving his innocence through trial by fire, Seyavash sets out to fight the Turanians. When his enemies surrender, he promises them that he will save their lives. Hearing this news, Kavus flies into a rage and demands that Seyavash destroy the hostages in order to prove his loyalty to him. Seyavash chooses to go into exile rather than break his word, and he is treacherously murdered in the land of his exile.

Khosrow, the son of Seyavash, is secretly raised in Turan. Rostam finally finds him and bring him back to Iran. Khosrow becomes king, and under his reign the Iranian force finally triumphs over their archenemy, Afrasiyab of Turan. Khosrow proves to be a near-ideal king, but he abdicates out of the fear that his power might corrupt him. Khosrow leaves his kingdom to his distant relative, Lohrasp. After Lohrasp, his son Goshtasp becomes king. The prophet Zoroaster appears during his reign.

Out of jealousy, Goshtasp causes the death of his own son, Esfandiyar, by forcing him to fight Rostam. Rostam kills Esfandiyar against his will, but the shedding of the royal blood brings a curse upon him and his family. Rostam is later killed by the treachery of his own brother, and his family is destroyed by Bahman, the son of Esfandiyar.

Bahman marries his own daughter Homai. Their son, Darab, becomes king after them. Darab is followed by his son Dara, who becomes the last Kayanian king.

The Historical Section

At this point of the narrative, the legendary history joins that of fact. Dara, the last Kayanian ruler, can be identified with Darius, the last Achaemenid ruler, defeated by Alexander the Great. But according to the epic, Eskandar, or Alexander, is the stepbrother of Dara, and he is treated as essentially an Iranian ruler.

After recounting the exploits of Eskander, the epic virtually ignores the historic reigns of the Seleucids and the Parthians, dismissing them as periods of unrest and disunity in Iran. The historical narrative is resumed again with the rise of Ardavan, the last Parthian king, and his defeat by Ardeshir, the founder of the Sasanian dynasty.

With the rise of the Sasanians, the epic broadly follows the known historic outline, although many folkloric embellishments are added to the narrative. The Turanians of the legendary section are replaced by the Romans as the principal enemies of Iran.

The Evaluations of the Epic

Many contradictary statements can be made about a literary work with a scope as vast as the *Shahnameh*. Yet the epic is neither a simpleminded celebration of battles and of the heroic deeds of warriors, nor a uncritical paean to the institution of kingship, as some critics charge. Dick Davis points out in his book *Epic and Sedition* that Ferdowsi includes the point of view of those who suffered from monarchic abuses of power. Conflicting values of loyalty to the monarch and personal integrity torment a hero like Rostam. It is not just physical prowess that distinguishes the true heroes of the epic, but their ability to face moral dilemmas and make difficult choices. Certainly, there are more than enough battles and great feats of astonishing physical strengh in the *Shahnameh*, and Ferdowsi writes about them better than anyone else in Persian letters, but the true greatness of his work lies elsewhere. It is the unfailing humanism of Ferdowsi's poetic vision, and his understanding of the fragility of human existence that ensures the epic's lasting significance.

KATSUYO MOTOYOSHI

Further Reading

Translation

Clinton, Jerome. *The Tragedy of Sohrab and Rostam from the Persian National Epic, The Shahname of Abo'l-Qāsem Ferdowsi*. Seattle: University of Washington Press, 1987. A translation of one of the most famous episode of the epic. With the Persian text on facing pages, the translation is in modern English verse.

Davis, Dick. *The Legend of Seyavash*. London: Penguin Classics, 1992. A translation of the Seyavash episode. Together with Clinton's translation, a good introduction to Ferdowsi's epic.

Levy, Reuben. *The Epic of the Kings, Shāh-Nāma: the National Epic of Persia by Ferdowsi*. London: Routledge & Kegan Paul, 1967. A one-volume synoptic prose translation. An abridgement of the epic, with summaries of omitted parts.

Warner, Arthur George, and Edmond Warner. *The Shahnama of Firdausi*. 9 vols. London: K. Paul, Trench, Trubner, 1905–1925. The only complete English translation. Based on now superseded manuscript, the translation in Edwardian blank verse is antiquated but still readable.

Related Studies

Davis, Dick. *Epic and Sedition: the Case of Ferdowsi's Shahnameh*. Fayetteville: The University of Arkansas Press, 1992. An excellent thematic study of Ferdowsi's epic.

Davidson, Olga M. *Poet and Hero in the Persian Book of Kings*. Ithaca: Cornell University Press, 1994. Written from the perspective of comparative mythology and oral-poetic theory, Davidson's analysis contributes fresh insights about the epic's performative aspects.

Shahbazi, A. Shapur. *Ferdowsi: A Critical Biography*. Costa Mesa: Mazda Publishers, 1991. A detailed study of Ferdowsi's historical background and his sources for the *Shahnameh*.

Yarshater, Ehsan, ed. *The Cambridge History of Iran*. Vol. 3, part 1. Cambridge: Cambridge University Press, 1983. Yarshater's essays on the Iranian historical tradition are invaluable to those interested in the mythological dimension of the *Shahnameh*.

THE RING OF THE DOVE

Title in Arabic: *Tawq al-ḥamāmah* (The Neck-ring of the Dove)
Author: Abu Muhammad 'Ali ibn Ahmad ibn Ḥazm
Born: November 7, 994, Cordova, Spain
Died: August 15, 1064
Literary Form: Prose discourse, with occasional verses
Date of Composition: c. 1030

Major Themes

Love is the conjunction or fusion of souls.
The highest form of love is love in the spirit of God.
Love arises from family relationships, friendship, generosity and compassion, common interests, sexual attraction, accidental qualities, and the irresistible drawing together of souls.
When a soul is drawn to another, it is because of a likeness between them.
Love is often beset by misfortunes, but usually they can be overcome.
Love's greatest virtue is continence.

Ibn Hazm's *The Ring of the Dove* is an entertaining and informal treatise on the art of love, but it is fundamentally serious in its moral and spiritual themes. The author's concern for emphasizing spiritual values and ethical standards in the discussion of love partly derived from practical and even political considerations: an unadulterated celebration of sexual love would have gotten him into trouble (and he had already suffered from both political and religious persecution). Fortunately for his integrity, however, he was not interested in exploiting the sexual aspects of his subject; he was a fundamentally serious person (although he had a sense of humor); he was a devout Muslim, a theologian, and a distinguished author on religious and legal theories. When he declares that the highest love is spiritual and that souls come together in the most rewarding way when they are obedient to the highest principles of religion and morality, he speaks sincerely.

Ibn Hazm was also a careful observer of human beings, especially (in this case) of human beings who loved one another. He discusses the nature of love, ways of falling in love, ways of making love known, ways of recognizing love, the causes and solutions of problems that disrupt love, and the course of love, sometimes difficult, sometimes tragic, sometimes delightful, sometimes spiritually rewarding.

In a preliminary note, Ibn Hazm states that his book of thirty chapters deals with the following subject matter: Ten chapters (not necessarily in conjunction) are concerned with "the root-principles of Love"; twelve chapters discuss "the accidents of Love, and its praiseworthy and blameworthy attributes"; six chapters describe the misfortunes of love, while the remaining two are moral exhortations: "On the Vileness of Sinning," and "On the Virtue of Continence."

The Ring of the Dove is a psychologically acute, empirically based, realistic and idealistic discourse—both informative and entertaining—on the nature and art of love; it provides us with a perspective that is distinctively reflective of the culture and disposition of its author, yet is also of universal appeal and relevance. The gentle humor that shows itself frequently in the book keeps the tone humane and appealing, so that when the moral is drawn, it is not only tolerated but recognized as fundamentally true and worth remembering. Most of all, the book gives the reader a sense of the drama of life itself—of human beings with strengths and weaknesses, caught up in all kinds of love, and working through the adventures of souls drawn to

one another in various ways and with various results.

On Falling in Love

Ibn Hazm discussion of the "root-principles" of
love begins with an account of "the signs of love":
the brooding gaze, hanging on the beloved's every
word, following the loved one around, becoming
confused and excited when the beloved suddenly
and unexpectedly appears, doing everything one
can for the beloved, being on one's best behavior,
being cheerful while the beloved is around, sorrowful and depressed when the loved one is absent,
trying to get close and touch the beloved, moping
about and even weeping when the beloved is absent
or late, taking offense at what the lover interprets as
a sign of disdain or rejection.

The author then proceeds to discuss various
ways and occasions of falling in love: falling in
love while one is dreaming about someone who
exists only in the imagination (an entirely futile and
senseless way of falling in love); falling in love
through a description alone (also futile and senseless); falling in love at first sight (that is, falling in
love with "a mere form" while knowing nothing
substantial about the person—a kind of spontaneous passion that quickly fades); falling in love
after coming to know a person (giving rise to a love
that is likely to last).

Concerning the matter of falling in love after
long association as contrasted to falling in love at
first sight, Ibn Hazm writes:

> *True love is not a flower*
> *That springeth in an hour;*
> *Its flint will not strike fire*
> *At casual desire.*

(ARBERRY, TRANS., 1953)

Continuing his discussion of falling in love, Ibn
Hazm describes the imperiousness of love when it
springs from a stubborn attachment to a "certain
quality"—such as (Ibn Hazm's examples) a short
(or long) neck, blond (or dark) hair, a large (or

small) mouth, shortness (or tallness) of height.
Having fallen in love because of some such quality,
the lover is often doomed to be dissatisfied with
anyone who does not have it and may go to his or
her death longing for the reappearance of that quality.

The point here seems to be that love is often
irrational in giving priority to some quality that
may not appeal to others and, having done so,
"exercises ... a decisive sovereignty over the
soul. . . ."

The Communication of Love

The first device for expressing one's love, Ibn
Hazm declares, is the use of words: to quote poetry,
use "heightened" language, present a riddle, or in
some way to indicate one's feeling without having
to make a direct and simple statement. Such an
allusory use of language is often effective—and it
has the advantage of privacy: only the lovers know
what they are talking about.

Another way of expressing love is by "hinting
with the eyes." Ibn Hazm dwells on the power of
glances: "By means of a glance the lover can be
dismissed, admitted, promised, threatened, up-
braided, cheered, commanded, forbidden," but he
suggests that the significance of glances can be
appreciated only "by ocular demonstration."

Once lovers are aware of their love for each
other, they may communicate their love through
correspondence. Letters can be very important to
lovers, Ibn Hazm reminds us: letters are treasured,
handled, kissed, read and reread—and sometimes
wept over, thrown away, or burned (sometimes to
maintain secrecy, sometimes because of a change
of passion).

Glances and letters are "messengers," writes Ibn
Hazm, but sometimes no method of communication is more effective than employing a person as
messenger. The messenger must be "presentable,
quick-witted, able to take a hint," and, of course, be
a person of discretion and integrity. Ibn Hazm tells
us that he knew a pair of lovers for whom a dove
(presumably a ring-necked dove) was the messenger, and he inserts the following verses:

Old Noah chose a dove, to be
His faithful messenger, and he
Was not confounded so to choose:
She brought him back the best of news.

So I am trusting to this dove
My messages to thee, my love,
And so I send her forth, to bring
My letters safely in her wing.

(ARBERRY, TRANS., 1953)

The reference to the ring-necked dove in the title of the book is no doubt prompted by the long tradition, both in Asia and the West, of using the pigeon (dove) as a messenger; furthermore, the dove is both amorous and monogamous, and the soft cooing of the mourning dove (or turtledove) has often been regarded by poets as a love call. Noah's dove is a common symbol of peace and hope, and of the spirit. Finally, it is also possible that since love, as Ibn Hazm points out, is the conjunction of two complementary spirits, the "ring" (that circles the neck of love's messenger) is also a love symbol (as it is when rings are exchanged by lovers).

Some "Accidents" of Love

"But to admire beauty, and to be mastered by love—that is a natural thing," writes Ibn Hazm in "Concealing the Secret," after having indicated that some lovers, ashamed of how they might appear to others, attempt to hide their love. If the lover wishes to spare the beloved, then the attempt to conceal love is a sign of loyalty and is to be commended. Whatever the reason for concealment, however, after love has reached a certain stage of intensity, it cannot be concealed.

The opposite of concealment—namely, the *divulgence* of love—is another of love's accidents (circumstantial aspects, not essential to love). Whether prompted by an interest in being known as a lover, or by the desire for publicity, or by the lust for revenge when one has been abandoned, or at the entreaty of the beloved who, uncertain of herself, wants the love to become a matter of public knowledge, the divulgence of love is "deplorable . . . contemptible . . . disgusting" (and usually unnecessary).

Another of love's accidents is *compliance*: the lover seeks to comply with the beloved's every wish. Ibn Hazm suggests that this is generally self-defeating; the lover pursues love for the pleasure of its rewards, and to forego the rewards in order to please the beloved is irrational.

If, despite the *opposition* of the beloved, the lover insists on the fulfillment of his desire, "his cares will be at an end," Ibn Hazm writes. (The account here is brief, and it may be that the author is simply stressing the importance of persistence, but the text suggests that the lover who "follows his own lust . . . whether the beloved be angry or consent" will be rewarded and need not care about the "other.")

The Misfortunes of Love

The first of the misfortunes of love discussed briefly by Ibn Hazm is what he calls the "reproacher." The reproacher, who warns against destructive acts and engagements, may be a friend, who can indeed be helpful. But when the reproacher is a "thorough-going scolder," it is "a tough business, and a heavy burden to bear."

(The reproacher is then contrasted to "the helpful brother," a true friend who, without reproaching the lover, assists him by giving good advice. The helpful friend—who may be a woman, for Ibn Hazm says nothing can equal the helpfulness of women—is one of the "accidents" of love.)

The second of the misfortunes of love is the "spy." The spy delights in eavesdropping on lovers and thereby making a pest of himself. All one can do is conciliate him and win him over, ignore him, or avoid him.

The "slanderer" is the third of love's misfortunes. Slanders are "back-biters," Ibn Hazm claims, and he goes on to insist that all back-biters are liars; he then tells us that he has "never loved a liar."

Ibn Hazm now discourses on "union" as the

most rewarding of love's accidents. When lovers are attuned and free from spies and slanderers, they know the greatest happiness of this life. (This chapter, like the others in the book, is lightened by anecdotes and verses, most of them pertinent, lively, amusing, or instructive.)

Another of love's misfortunes, namely, "breaking off," is now contrasted to union. The breaking off may be temporary, a matter of prudence, as when a spy is present; it may be a matter of coquettishness; it may be the result of reproaches that are overcome by reconciliation—and there are other kinds of breaking off that eventually add to the delights of love, even though they are, at least at the time, misfortunes. When the breaking off is the result of hatred, however, it is catastrophic and final. it marks the death of love.

Ibn Hazm next discusses the pair of accidents consisting of "fidelity" and "betrayal," and then returns to the misfortune of "separation" (which has its positive aspects), with which the "accident" of "contentment" is paired.

The chapter "Contentment" is colorful and lively: it provides anecdotes and verses that describe ways of finding satisfaction when union is barred. Ibn Hazm calls attention to the exchange between lovers of objects of personal value, such as locks of hair "perfumed with ambergris and sprinkled with rosewater" and—surprisingly— "chewed toothpicks" (which appear to be especially delightful as personal souvenirs).

"Wasting away" is the accidental misfortune that comes from too-long separation; it is fatal when emaciation results; the lover takes to his bed, he goes mad, he loses consciousness, and he dies— the final unfortunate accident of love. (Ibn Hazm comments: "May Allah in His mighty power defend us from such a calamity!")

The last of the misfortunes of love is "forgetting," which results from various acts and circumstances, among which is "despair," attributed to God Almighty. "Every love," writes Ibn Hazm, "comes finally to one or other conclusion: either it is cut off by death, or ends in oblivion." Oblivion is provided by forgetting but is difficult to secure when the forgetting is something that, under the circumstances, one is constrained by the soul to do.

The Vileness of Sinning, the Virtue of Continence

The Ring of the Dove concludes with two chapters of moral exhortation. Human beings are capable of controlling their desires and following God's commandments, but if they fail to do, they sin in their amours and will suffer accordingly.

Continence—restraining oneself from "evil work" and "deadly lusts"—is a virtue; a love enhanced by continence is of great worth and yields not only pleasure but spiritual satisfaction and growth. Those who love God and love in His spirit will be eternally rewarded—and even if there were no "reckoning hereafter," Ibn Hazm writes, a love that is continent (free from sin and indecency) would be of immeasurable worth in this life alone.

IAN P. MCGREAL

Further Reading

Translation

Arberry A. J. *The Ring of the Dove by Ibn Hazm (994–1064): A Treatise on the Art and Practice of Arab Love.* London: Luzac, 1953. A clear and lively translation, with rhyming verses in meter and rhyme that reflect Ibn Hazm's enthusiasm and delight with the subject. Arberry's preface explains his approach to the problem of translation, and he suggests that although Ibn Hazm was not a great poet, his verses do lighten the text and succeed in conveying the feelings and lively imagination of the author.

MAQĀMĀT AL-HAMADHĀNĪ AND
MAQĀMĀT AL-ḤARĪRĪ

Title in Arabic: *Maqāmāt al-Hamadhānī*
Author: Abū al-Faḍl Aḥmad b. al-Ḥusayn (nicknamed Badi' al-Zamān al-Hamadhānī: Marvel or Wonder of the Age from Hamadhān)
Born: 969, Hamadhān, Western Iran
Died: 1008, Bushanj, a town near Herat in the modern day Afghanistan

Title in Arabic: *Maqāmāt al-Ḥarīrī*
Author: Abū Muḥammad al-Qāsim b. 'Alī b. Muhammad b. 'Uthmān (usually known as al-Ḥarīrī, an attribute derived from his or family profession, either the making or trading of silk [*ḥarīr* means silk in Arabic]).
Born: 1054, al-Mashan, a town near Basra in Iraq
Died: 1122, Basra.

Literary Form: Short tales (*ḥikāyāt*) usually in the form of anecdotes and written in highly ornate rhymed prose, commonly described as belonging to the genre of the anti-heroic or picaresque narratives

At the dawn of the modernization period in the Arab world, many writers chose the form of the *maqāmāt* to provide commentary on the period in which they lived, and on the changes that were taking place in their societies. Their experiments with this traditional literary form coincided with the massive movement to modernize the Arab culture in the wake of the colonial intrusion into the region. The colonial expedition brought to the Middle East, in addition to trauma, a new awareness of the necessity of a modern national identity, and an awakened sense of the need for cultural rejuvenation. The realization of the urgency of this matter triggered an all-encompassing cultural process that became known as the Arab Renaissance—*al-Nahḍa*. Looking at the early cultural projects of *al-Nahḍa* almost two hundred years later, one sees more clearly how they were all intricately related. These projects were all mosaics in a large canvas of cultural life, a life that was absorbed in a quest for an authentic, original identity. The search seemed to have pervaded all aspects of Arab culture, including literature—one of the expressions of this culture, and language—the medium of this expression. As well as unearthing and making available in print wonderful works of literature from the classi-

cal period to serve as representatives of Arabic culture "at its peak," writers and intellectuals were exploring ideas and sensibilities received from the West. The rediscovery of the *maqāmāt* genre is one manifestation of the cross-cultural fertilization of the frenetic *al-Nahḍa* period.

Arab intellectuals and writers of that period genuinely believed in and hoped for what seemed to be the shift of the power base in society from elitist to populist. They enthusiastically sought the appropriate language and literary forms to discuss their opinions, addressing a new audience that was unfamiliar with the traditional literary expressions, which had become ornate, manneristic and, more importantly, incomprehensible to those who were not trained in the traditional literary conventions. The *maqāmāt* seemed to be appropriate for the purposes of some Arab modernists. At the same time that the classical *maqāmāt* were put into print, they were also emulated, not only because of the beauty of their language and style, but also because they were the only genre in classical Arabic literature written in the *fuṣḥā* (which observes the standardized grammar and is usually contrasted to the colloquial which does not), in which fiction is an important component. They provide continuity in the Arabic literary tradition while paving the way for incorporating western narrative genres, especially those of fiction. When Nāṣif al-Yāzijī (1800–1871) from Levant and Muḥammad al-Muwayliḥī (1855–1930) from Egypt wrote in the *maqāmāt* genre, they were not merely imitating Badī' al-Zamān al-Hamadhānī and Abū Muḥammad al-Ḥarīrī; rather, they used the *maqāmāt* as a vehicles for displaying their linguistic dexterity—a sign of cultural rejuvenation, and expressing the changing sensibilities of their times.

The word *maqāmāt*, often translated as "assemblies," "sessions" or "séances," is the plural of either *maqām*, or *maqāma*. Both are derived from the root *q-w-m*, which implies the idea of "to rise, to stand in order to perform an action," or marks the beginning of an action when used as auxiliary verb. *Maqām* as used in the Qur'an can mean "abode," or "a meeting of important people." In poetry, it may convey the sense of "situation or state," which may be dramatic. In the later stages of the development of the use of the word, it came to mean "battle," which is also the sense conveyed by the word *maqāmā*. Used as a term designating the literary genre, the meaning of the words *maqām* and *maqāmā* may have evolved from "assembly," for in assemblies of important people, eloquence was a natural feature, and by extension *maqām* came to refer to the topics discussed in the course of these meetings, and the addresses delivered before a distinguished audience. *maqāmāt* may also mean "standings" in the Arabic language, perhaps an allusion to the conventional posture of the orator (*khaṭīb*) who spoke in rhymed prose (*saj'*) even though they are in fact anecdotes, which are traditionally in unadorned prose and were told at *majālis* (sing. *majlis*: sittings, sessions) where both narrator and audience were seated. In the ninth century, Ibn Qutayba (d. 889) gave the title *maqāmāt al-zuhhād 'ind al-khulafā' wa al-mulūk* to a chapter in his book *'Uyūn al-akhbār* in which he reproduced pious homilies designated, in the singular by the term *maqām*. Before him, the Mu'tazilite al-Iskāfī (d. 854) had written *Kitāb al-Maqāmāt fī tafḍīl 'Alī*, and in the following century, al-Mas'ūdī (d. 957)

spoke of homilies by 'Alī b. Abī Ṭālib and of a sermon by 'Umar b. 'Abd al-'Azīz, delivered on the occasion of their *maqāmāt*. By the tenth century, thanks to Badī'al-Zamān's *Maqāmāt*, this term came to designate a whole genre.

In the twentieth century al-Muwayliḥī consciously chose Badī'al-Zamān's *Maqāmāt* as a model for emulation, as the title of his book, *Ḥadīth 'Īsā Ibn Hishām*, indicates; for 'Īsā b. Hisham is the narrator of Badī'al-Zamān's *Maqāmāt* too. His choice is interesting; it signified the modern rediscovery of Badi'al-Zamān's *Maqāmāt* which had been obscured for centuries by al-Ḥarīrī's more elaborate imitations, even though al-Ḥarīrī openly acknowledged in the preface to his *Maqāmāt* that Badī'al-Zamān, who himself made the same claim, was the "inventor" of the genre, for even though some forms of *maqāmāt* were known before al-Hamadhānī, no one had written them in quite the same way as he who, nevertheless, was inspired by these prototypes.

The *maqāmāt* described by Ibn Qutayba often involve a Bedouin or a person of rather shabby appearance who addresses an aristocratic audience eloquently. Before an audience of common people, an analogous role was performed by the storyteller (*qāṣṣ*), who originally delivered edifying speeches but subsequently took on the dual function of storyteller and mountebank, whose activity was to a certain extent comparable to that of *mukaddī*, the wandering beggar or vagrant who went from town to town and easily gathered around him an audience who rewarded him financially for the fascinating stories he told. It seems probable that the first to introduce these colorful characters into Arabic literature was al-Jāḥiẓ (d. 869), who devoted a long treatment to them in the *Kitāb al-Bukhalā'* (Book of Misers) and wrote at least two other pieces on the stratagems of thieves (*ḥiyal al-lusus*) and of beggars (*ḥiyal al-mukaddīn*). The *Thousand and One Nights* contains a large number of stories about thieves, charlatans, beggars, and a specific type of mendicant, whose merchandise is their eloquence. Al-Hamadhānī's contemporary al-Tanūkhī (939–94) collected in his work *Al-Faraj ba'd al-shidda* anecdotes in which he presented persons of pitiable appearance who prove to be endowed with an exceptional talent for oratory.

While these stories seem obvious prototypes of al-Hamadhānī's *maqāmāt*, some scholars have also pondered the influence of the *aḥādīth* (sing. *ḥadīth*) of Ibn Durayd (d. 934). Prendergast, the translator of al-Hamadhānī, has drawn attention to and translated a subsequent well-known passage of *Zahr al-Adāb* by al-Ḥuṣri (d. 1022), who states that al-Hamadhānī imitated the forty *aḥādīth* of Ibn Durayd and composed four hundred "sessions" on the theme of *kudya*, the activity of the *mukaddūn*. Even though these *aḥādīth* are found in his student al-Qālī's (d. 967) book *al-Āmalī* (*Dictations*), it is uncertain whether they actually influenced al-Hamadhānī, and if they did to what extent. For one thing, Ibn Durayd was a grammarian and philologist, and the *aḥādīth* he composed were mainly for purposes of teaching the Arabic language. Furthermore, Ibn Sharaf (d. 1067), a contemporary of al-Ḥuṣrī, who at the beginning of *Masā'il al-Intiqād*, an epistle in the form of the *maqāmāt*, declares that he himself has been inspired by the *Kalīla wa Dimna* by Sahl Ibn Hārūn, and by Badī'al-Zamān al-Hamadhānī, but makes no mention of Ibn Durayd. Whatever the case may be, it seems that al-Hamadhānī was the first to have adopted the idea of the "session"—primarily the speeches, though retaining in the background the memory of the concept of feats of arms—for the creation of a new literary genre.

Scholars have also investigated whether Badī' al-Zamān owed anything to Greek or Byzantime models. C. E. Bosworth in *the Medieval Islamic Underworld, the Banū Sāsān in Arabic Society and Literature*, a lengthy study of the world of the mendicants, the Banū Sāsān, a study based on a long poem, "al-Qasīda al-Sāsāniyya," by Abū Dhulaf al-Khazrazī of the tenth-century and other relevant literature, including the *maqāmāt*, points to the possible influence of Greek mimes (*ḥikāya*), since the *maqāmā* contains an undeniable theatrical element, at least in the make-up of the hero and the posture of the narrator. Of course, Badī'al-Zamān was subject to various influences in the framework of Arabic literature and Arab-Islamic society in general, but he should be given credit for succeeding, through a commendable work of synthesis, in setting in motion two characters charged with precise roles, in particular a hero who symbolizes a whole social category. Indeed, for even though prototypes of the *maqāmāt* were known before Badī'al-Zamān, be they the stories composed by grammarians and philologists for the purpose of language instruction or the stories of the clever charlatans collected by the storytellers, Badī'al-Zamān's *maqāmāt*, though they share some stylistic features of their prototypes, are not only exhibition of his language skills and literary talents, or simply tales of smart mendicants—they are vehicles for him to exercise his sharp wit, insights, and his concern with certain moral and ideological issues; he made it a genre suitable for satire.

Badī'al-Zamān (al-Hamadhānī)

An Arab from the tribe of Taghlib, Badī'al-Zamān spent the first twenty-one years of his life in Hamadhan, a bilingual city (Arabic and Persian) in western Iran where he was born. He studied the various Arabic and Islamic sciences of his time (Qur'ān, the interpretation of Qur'ān, Ḥadīth, possibly also some law, poetry, prose, rhetoric, and history), especially the intricacies of language and philology, which he mastered under the guidance of the most famous linguist and philologist of his time and city, Aḥmad b. Fāris (d. 1004).

In 991 al-Hamadhānī left his hometown and his family, leaving his children in the custody of his father, for the city of ar-Rayy, the seat of one of the most powerful influential and learned patron-viziers of the time, al-Ṣāḥib Ibn 'Abbād (d. 995), where he became one of al-Ṣāḥib's courtiers. Al-Hamadhānī stood out among the illustrious scholars and men of letters with his literary and linguistic talents, his broad education, and his phenomenal memory. He often fascinated his audiences with his amazing ability to translate spontaneously Persian poems into Arabic verse. His stay at al-Ṣāḥib's court, however, was short, and within a few months he left this court abruptly, possibly after challenging the proud al-Ṣāḥib in his knowledge of Arabic poetry.

Al-Hamadhānī's sojourn at al-Ṣāḥib's court was typical of all al-Hamadhānī's stay at the various courts of medieval Islam. He traveled from one city to another, and one court to another, but never stayed for long. The list includes Jurjān, the capital of the Ziyarid dynasty, followed by Nishapur (in 993), Khurasān's major literary center, Sarakhs (also in 993), which he left in the wake of civil unrest; Sijistān, which he also left during civil strife, and finally Bushanj, near Herāt, where he spent the last ten or more years of his life. He died in 1008 in Herāt at the age of thirty-nine.

Of fiery disposition and hot temper, as al-Hamadhānī described himself in the large body of personal letters (*rasā'il*) that have come down to us, he was often proud and uncompromising. Even though his literary talents took him to high places, his nature often turned the world against him. In Nishapur he clashed with the elderly man of letters Abū Bakr al-Khwārizmī (d. 993), both being proud of their respective knowledge and literary achievement. They held a public debate and competed in various areas: memorization, verse, prose, spontaneous compilation of poetry and of literary epistles, and language and prosody, but not in rhymed prose (though al-Hamadhānī did challenge his opponent in this area too). Although al-Hamadhānī won a resounding victory in this debate, securing for himself a far-reaching fame which continued to serve him all his life, his arrogance usually made for him enemies, who spread malicious rumors about him, which led to a change in his patron's attitude toward him and forced him to leave. He eventually turned to commerce and became quite affluent.

The Maqāmāt of al-Hamadhānī

It was during his short stay in Nishapur that he composed the *Maqāmāt*, the only work known of al-Hamadhānī other than his letters. In his own account, he claimed that the *maqāmāt* he had composed were four hundred, a number taken by most scholars as a metaphor; it being a multiplication of

four, a number that means infinity in the Middle East.

The surviving *Maqāmāt* by al-Hamadhānī number only fifty-two. In fact, fifty may be reckoned the average number of the *Maqāmāt* of Badi'al-Zaman al-Hamadhānī in circulation in the Middle Ages, and the figure of fifty was subsequently considered (artificially) to be a traditional characteristic and was respected by numerous imitators of al-Hamadhānī, including al-Ḥarīrī who had himself adopted it.

In these anecdote-like short tales, we travel with the protagonist Abū al-Fath al-Iskandarī (from Alexandria), a free-loader, from one Islamic city to another and hear from his narrator 'Īsā Ibn Hishām about the pranks he plays on his victims for pure enjoyment or material gains. With his dazzling eloquence, Abū Al-Fath seems able to charm people into giving him things, money or food. The *Maqāmāt*, as well as being a showcase of Badi'al-Zamān's literary talents, served as a vehicle through which he satirized certain social mores and intellectual notions of his time.

Al-Ḥarīrī

Al-Ḥarīrī, a grammarian whose other writings are primarily of a grammatical nature, emulated al-Hamadhānī, and tried to exceed the literary accomplishments of his predecessor. Born in al-Mashān, a town near Basra in Iraq, al-Ḥarīrī moved to Basra where he studied the Arabic language and Islamic Law. He was later appointed chief of intelligence (*ṣāḥib al-khabar*) and occupied this position for the rest of his life, and passed it down to his children. He was wealthy; he reportedly possessed eighteen thousand palm trees, on the crops of which he relied for income. He became a well-known scholar, especially after he had composed the *Maqāmāt*, even though he had already authored many books. *Durrat al ghawwāṣ fi awhām al-khwāṣṣ*, a collection of critical notes on the incorrect use of certain expressions; a body of letters (*rasā'il*), which has been collected and published; a *Diwan*, which has not survived; and a didactic poem in the form of *urjūza* on grammar, accompanied by a commentary, *Mulhat al-i'rāb*, written at the prompting of Ibn Tilmīdh.

The Maqāmāt of al-Harīrī

Al-Harīrī, whose duties brought him into contact with various high dignitaries of Baghdad, might have been encouraged in his enterprise by the future vizier al-Mustarshid Ibn Sadaqa (1118–35), and composed and dedicated the *Maqāmāt* to him. Although we do not know for certain the date of their completion, we do know that they were already classics in the lifetime of the author, who died in 1122. Al-Harīrī's *Maqāmāt* appealed to the taste of readers to such an extent that, after having memorized the Qui'ān, children were made to memorize them. Eager students, albeit repelled at times by his ugly visage, came to his house from all over the Islamic world to study them with him. Yūsuf Ibn 'Ali al-Qudā'i, an Andalusian scholar, studied them under him, and later returned to Andalus to make them known in Spain. From the beginning of the twelfth century they were part of the curriculum of literary Andalusians. The popularity of the *Maqāmāt* in Spain, some scholars conjectured, may have been instrumental in the emergence of the Spanish picaresque tradition.

The success of al-Harīrī's *Maqāmāt* diverted attention from al-Hamadhānī's more easily intelligible pieces, and prompted many later writers to imitate the rhetorical artifices invented by al-Harīrī and to take little interest in the substance. For centuries, and until the twentieth century, the *Maqāmāt* of al-Harīrī eclipsed those of al-Hamadhānī, and they inspired many including the Judah ben Solomon Harīzī (a thirteenth-century Jew), who wrote a set of *Maqāmāt* in Hebrew. Between al-Harīrī and al-Muwaylihī, there are at least seventy authors who wrote in the *Maqāmāt* form, although most, like those by Spanish al-Ashtarkūwī (d. 1143) and Ibn al-Jawzī (d. 1201), are sermons, not stories. Even al-Yāzijī, a language scholar of modern sensibilities, could not escape the use of this form to show off his mastery of the Arabic language.

Al-Harīrī's *Maqāmāt*, similar to those of al-

Hamadhānī, consist of al-Harith Ibn Hammām's (the narrator's) accounts of his encounters with Abū Zayd a-Sarūjī, an eloquent mendicant from Sarūj, who travels from one Islamic city to another, alone or accompanied by his wife or son, and bamboozles audiences with his verbal virtuosity. Unlike al-Hamadhānī, al-Harīrī indulges in the demonstration of his genius in the Arabic language, leading most scholars to conclude that he gave the genre its classic form, freezing it, according only a secondary interest to the content, and placing his entire emphasis on the style which is often obscure, and that his ultimate aim was the preserving and teaching of the rarest vocabulary. The emphasis on language and its intricacies in the *Maqāmāt* of al-Harīrī prompted some twenty philologists to comment on them, and many of his imitators accompanied their own compositions with lexicographical commentaries.

The Maqāmāt

The *Maqāmāt*, written in the style very fashionable from the tenth century onward, are in general characterized by the almost invariable use of rhymed and rhythmic prose (*saj'*) sometimes blended with verse. The individual *maqāma* is usually constructed around a hero, in this case anti-hero, whose adventures and eloquent speeches are related by a narrator to the author who in turn conveys them the to readers. Abdelfattah Kilito observes that in the *maqāma*, a text is obtained through the research of *rāwī* (narrator) and transmitted through a second *rāwī* (the author) in such a way that the mode of transmission recalls that of ancient poetry, and still more precisely, that of *Hadīth*, with the difference that the text, the person who speaks it and the first *rāwī* are fictitious. In a typical *maqāma*, Kilito further notes, the order of events is as follows: arrival of the *rāwī* in town, encounter with the disguised *balīgh* (the eloquent man and the hero), speech, reward, recognition, reproach, justification, and parting. It need hardly be said that this general scheme does not apply without variation to all the *Maqāmāt* of al-Hamadhānī, still less to those of his successors. From the start, this literary form was employed to cover a great variety of subjects: criticism of ancient and modern poets, or prose writers like Ibn Muqaffaʿ and al-Jāḥiẓ, of the Mu'tazilites, exposure of the sexual slang and jargon of vagabonds, display of lexicographical knowledge, etc. For example, *six Maqāmāt* of Badīʿal-Zamān celebrate the author's benefactor Khalaf b. Aḥmad, the ruler of Sijistān, to whom the work may have been dedicated. More importantly, Badīʿal-Zamān seemed to have incorporated in his compositions numerous other genres such as the sermon, description, poetry in various forms, the letter, the travelogue, the dialogue, the debate, etc.. The diversity of the themes covered and the literary forms appropriated in al-Hamadhānī's *Maqāmāt* set the scene for the exploitation of the genre for the most varied of purposes. Later authors had no difficulty in obeying the exigencies of the form, namely rhymed prose, but it was not long before they indulged in verbal acrobatics. Al-Ḥarīrī retains the structure created by his predecessor and presents a hero and a narrator, but many of his imitators dispense with the former character, if not with both.

The *Maqāmāt* belongs to the broad category of *adab* in Arabic literature which, among other things, seeks to instruct through entertainment, by means of harmonious blending of the serious and the joking (*al-gad wa al-hazl*). This is especially true of al-Hamadhānī's compositions, but not of all *Maqāmāt*, many of which deviate from this purpose and in this respect follow the evolution of the *adab* which has a tendency either to neglect the *jidd* or to forget the *hazl*.

Two things must be taken into consideration when examining al-Hamadhānī's *Maqāmāt*: his experience as a courtier and his ideological framework. As a man of letters, he traveled far and wide in search for a patron whose gifts would provide him with a livelihood. Despite his talents, he was often frustrated. He was curiously aware of the power of the word, and paradoxically how meaningless it could be. His protagonist al-Iskandari is hauntingly similar to men of letters who rely on their language skills to make a living, but instead of receiving gifts from patrons, he swindles innocent people of their possessions. In other words, what a man of letters does at any particular court is no different from a mendicant turning tricks. Notwithstanding this sordid aspect of the life of men of letters, al-Hamadhānī was also of the opinion that literature as manifestation of knowledge must be functional and original; it must serve a purpose in society, and must not become stale. The *Maqāmāt* are indeed an invention that fulfills these two conditions: they provide social commentary, and constitute a new genre in Arabic literature. Most importantly, they became in al-Hamadhānī's skilful manipulations an instrument for satire. While the *Maqāmāt* aspire to the style and purpose of *adab*, they make fun of it as well; they constitute a new genre, or better, a counter-genre. Al-Muwaylihī's choice of al-Hamadhānī's *Maqāmāt* as a model for emulation in the *al-Nahḍa* period could not have been coincidental; he must have recognized these aspects of al-Hamadhānī's works.

Al-Muwaylihī *Maqāmāt*, which were published in a book form in 1906, are indeed a scathing satire on the social mores in the Cairo of the end of the nineteenth century; observations of a resurrected pasha of the age of Muḥammad ʿAli who toured Cairo in the company of the narrator. The similarities between the *Maqāmāt* of al-Muwaylihī and Badīʿal-Zamān are many. In addition to having a common narrator, ʿĪsā Ibn Hishām, al-Muwaylihī's *Maqāmāt* are structured around a protagonist and a narrator who have various adventures, or misadventures, as they travel from one place to another. Each adventure is recounted in one *maqāmā*, which functions like an episode, and all can be read independently or together, just like a novel. However, the similarities between the two authors separated by almost ten centuries are not limited to the formal aspects of their works, but exceed them to encompass their vision of the function of literature in society. Working under the pressure for cultural renewal, al-Muwaylihi, while commenting on social and cultural issues, was also subverting the literary tradition that had become lifeless. By reviving a subversive genre and adding a new dimension to it, he was leading the movement to revive Arabic literature. Al-Muwaylihī's *Maqāmāt* are understandably, and significantly, different from Badīʿ

al-Zamān's in some aspects; each of al-Muwayliḥī's episodes is presented in two sections, an introductory one of varying length in highly traditional rhymed prose, followed by another section in
unadorned prose. As the section in tradition
rhymed prose affirms the authenticity of his work,
the anti-traditional section in plain prose marks its
originality.

Al-Ḥarīrī's *Maqāmāt*, on the other hand, have
been regarded merely as exercises in language, and
have been dismissed as such by most Arab and
western scholars, except Abdelfattah Kilito, a Mo-
roccan scholar, and Jabir 'Asfour, an Egyptian literary critic. Given the complexity of al-Ḥarīrī's
language and style, much of which is lost in translation, this does not seem surprising, for one is easily
distracted from the more subtle connotations of the
Maqāmāt by their misleading appearance. Like al-
Hamadhānī, al-Ḥarīrī also conveys alienation experienced by a man of letters, as the latter travels
far and wide in a world plagued by chaos and destruction. His hero Abū Zayd al-Sarūjī, according to
al-Ḥarīrī, was a real person and may even on his
appearance in Basra have inspired the first *maqāmā*
by him, al-Ḥaramiyya—reference to Ḥaram district
of Basra where al-Ḥarīrī lived. According to Ibn
Tilmīdh and Yāqūt, two biographers of al-Ḥarīrī, the
Maqāmāt were begun in 1101, one year after the
Crusaders had taken Saruj, driving Abu Zayd al-
Saruji from Saruj to Basra for refuge. Al-Ḥarīrī's al-
Sarūjī, however, does not remain in Basra, but turns
into a nomad, or even a gypsy, whose vagabondage
becomes a metaphor for alienation.

Alienation is expressed at many levels in both al-
Hamadhānī and al-Ḥarīrī's *Maqāmāt*. The heroes'
homelessness, the heroes' and narrators' mobility
and instability, and circumstances that gave rise to
their situations, expose the insecurity of life, and of
the life of men of letters in particular in the Islamic
world; nothing is certain in life and the seemingly
united world of Islam is in reality fragmented. Paradoxically, the timelessness of the *Maqāmāt*, reflected in the agelessness of the main characters,
and their transcendence of place, reflected in the
occurrence of the events of each *maqāma* in a different place, make us even more acutely aware of

the sense of alienation conveyed by them. The
paradoxical use of language in the *Maqāmāt*, more
in al-Ḥarīrī's compositions than al-Hamadhānī's,
serves as yet another reminder of estrangement
from life; the glamorous facade of an intricately
woven speech is precisely what disguises the absence of its substance, just as the language and style
of the *Maqāmāt* distract us from exploring their
more profound meanings.

Today, thanks to over half a century of study, our
understanding and appreciation of the *Maqāmāt* of
al-Hamadhānī and al-Ḥarīrī have grown, even
though more studies are necessary for a more
meaningful interpretation of them. The language
and style, which were an obstacle, have seemingly
ceased to be so. It seems that better understanding
of the purpose, function and context of the *Maqāmāt*
can also help us to appreciate the works of the first
generation of the Arab modernists, such al-Yāzijī
and al-Muwaylihī, and the role they perceived literature should play in the Arab culture. These modernists had much in common with their two
predecessors; even as they operated in a culture and
"homeland" during periods of great turmoil, they
represented, deliberated, and resisted their conditions by participating in counter-narrative. Al-
Muwaylihī resurrected al-Hamadhānī's original
works of art, just as he brought his hero back to life
from death to provide a service. Al-Yāzijī, infusing
his work with nationalism, called to mind that hidden under the glittering garbs of al-Ḥarīrī's stories
were keen observations of the life and culture of his
times. As the twentieth century draws to a close, the
maqāmāt is still a source of wonder; their interpretation remains somewhat elusive, and their presence
continues to be felt in Arabic literary narratives,
whether they covertly or overtly appropriate partially or entirely this thousand-year-old genre.

WEN-CHIN OUYANG

Further Reading

Translations

Prendergast, W. J., trans. *The Maqamat of Badi'al-
Zamān al-Hamadhānī*. Madras, 1915; London

and Dublin: Curzon Press, 1973. The most complete translation, with an introduction.

Chenery, Thomas, and F. Stiengass, trans. *The Assemblies of al-Ḥarīrī*. London: Williams, 1867–98; reprint, 1969. The most complete and available translation. Chenery translated vol. 1; Stiengass, vol. 2. Includes introduction and notes.

Related Studies

Beeston, A. F. L. "The Genesis of the *Maqāmāt* Genre," *Journal of Arabic Literature*, (1971), pp. 1–12; and his chapter on al-Hamadhānī and al-Ḥarīrī in *'Abbasid Belles-Lettres*, in *Cambridge History of Arabic Literature*, Vol. II. Cambridge: Cambridge University Press, 1990 (pp. 125–135).

Blachere, R. "Al-Hamadhānī," *Encyclopaedia of Islam* (New Edition), Vol. III, Facsimile 41–42. Leiden: E. J. Brill, 1965 (pp. 106–07).

Brockelmann, C., and Charles Pellat. "Maqāma,"

Encyclopaedia of Islam (New Edition), Vol VI. Facsimile 99–100. Leiden: E. J. Brill, 1986 (pp. 107–115).

Hafez, Sabry. *The Genesis of Arabic Narrative Discourse: A Study in the Sociology of Modern Arabic Literature*. London: Saqi Books, 1993.

Kilito, Abdelfattah. *Les Séances: Récits et codes culturels chez Hamadhani et Hariri*. Paris: Sindbad, 1983.

Margoliouth, D. S., and Charles Pellat. "Al-Ḥarīrī," *Encyclopaedia of Islam* (New Edition), Vol. III, Facsimile 45–46. Leiden, E. J. Brill, 1966 (pp. 221–2).

Monroe, James. *The Art of Bad'al-Zaman al-Hamadhani as Picaresque Narrative*. Beirut: American University of Beirut, 1983.

Al-Qadi, Wadad. "Badi'al-Zaman al-Hamadhani and His Social and Political Vistion," *Literary Heritage of Classical Islam: Arabic and Islamic Studies in Honor of James Bellamy*, Musntansir Mir, ed. pp. 197–226. Princeton: The Darwin Press, Inc., 1993.

THE RUBAIYAT OF OMAR KHAYYAM

Author: Omar Khayyam
Born: 1048, Nayshapur, Iran
Died: 1131, Nayshapur, Iran
Major Work: *Rubaiyat* (Quatrains)

Major Themes

Since religious and philosophical certainty are impossible to come by, it is best to live for the day and not to let oneself be troubled by what cannot be known.

The world is very ancient; "There is no new thing under the sun," and any given individual's life in this world is short and insignificant.

The pleasures of friendship and shared conviviality are the best that our short, ignorant, and precarious life has to offer.

In Europe and the United States Omar Khayyam is the best known and most admired medieval Persian poet; in his homeland he is considered an interesting minor poet of—at best—the third rank, certainly not someone to rank with the literature's greatest authors (poets such as Ferdowsi, Sa'di or Hafez), or even with lesser but still major figures like Jami or Naser Khosrow. The reason for his popularity in the West is the extraordinary success of the translation of a selection of his quatrains made in the mid-nineteenth century by a British amateur linguist and man of letters, Edward FitzGerald. It is estimated that FitzGerald's *The Rubaiyat of Omar Khayyam* is the most widely sold and read book of verse ever to have appeared in English, and a large number of phrases from the translation have become virtual proverbial clichés of educated English. The first problem that faces a Western reader who wishes to form some idea of Khayyam's poetry is that of disentangling its substance from FitzGerald's immensely successful English version, a version that owes almost as much to FitzGerald's own concerns and to the conventions and expectations of Victorian British poetry as it does to his English quatrains' Persian originals.

Khayyam was born and lived most of his life in Khorasan, the northeastern province of Iran and one of its more prosperous areas. During Khayyam's lifetime the area had entered on a period of relative peace and security after the upheavals of the end of the tenth and the opening of the eleventh centuries, at which time Khorasan had born the brunt of two invasions, the first by the Ghaznavids, a relatively Persianized Turkish dynasty based in Afghanistan, and the second by the Seljuks, a Turkish tribe from central Asia who entered and conquered Iran largely ignorant of the culture upon which they were encroaching. The Seljuks were both brilliant soldiers and relatively recent converts to Islam; they imposed civil order and religious orthodoxy on what was still a very diverse and volatile alien culture. At the opening of the thirteenth century the area was to be devestated once again, even more thoroughly, by the invasion of Genghiz Khan's Mongols. Khayyam's life, then, was lived in an interval of relative peace and precarious security, imposed by an outside people, between two periods of conquest and devastation. Though he cannot have foreseen the Mongol invasion, the lessons of the recent past would have made him aware of the precariousness of the peace he enjoyed, as well as of the instability of ruling dynasties and the vanity of their pretensions. Further, Khorasan had been the area chiefly responsible for the emancipation of Persian culture from control of the Arab dominated caliphate (in the tenth century), and the region's consciously fostered links with the pre-Islamic past would have increased this sense of the vastness of historical process and the littleness of individual lives and hopes within it.

When we compare Khayyam's quatrains with medieval European verse we notice an immediate difference in emphasis, in that European verse of the period often insistently proclaims its newness, its sense of the youth and springtime of life, whereas Khayyam's verse shows a preternatural awareness of the immensity of human history that has existed beforehand and of the vanity of individual human effort when measured against this immensity. Khayyam's poetry is the expression of a very ancient culture that is profoundly conscious of its age; it is also the poetry of a sensibility that has internalized the meaning of defeat, that senses the nearness of chaos, and is all but convinced of the impotence of human efforts to keep this at bay.

But if for us the name "Khayyam" conjures up the epithet "poet," this was almost certainly not the case for his contemporaries. Not that he was an obscure man living far from centers of intellectual life; on the contrary, he was one of the better-known individuals of his time, but his fame had nothing to do with poetry. Khayyam's contemporary fame rested on his work in mathematics, astronomy, and philosophy. He wrote on these subjects in Arabic (the lingua franca of the educated throughout the lands of medieval Islam, much as Latin was for Christendom at the time), and some of his treatises survive, including one on Euclid's *Elements* and another, his most famous, on algebra. No prose in Persian by Khayyam has come down to us (the one Persian prose text that used to be attributed to him, the *Nowruz Nameh*, a treatise on the pre-Islamic Persian festival celebrating the spring equinox, is almost certainly not by him).

Khayyam's most impressive feat was his participation in the deliberations of a group of astronomers and mathematicians called together by the Seljuk king Sultan Malik Shah to reform the calendar. The reform, inaugurated in 1079, was a great success, resulting in a much more accurate system than had been used hitherto, and this established Khayyam's reputation.

During this period astronomy was conceived of by many as being all but identical with astrology (besides which, Persian savants had a particular reputation as astrologers in the medieval Islamic world), and Khayyam's success as an astronomer, whose calculations concerning the movements of heavenly bodies had facilitated the reform of the calendar, meant that he was often called on as an astrologer. Those who wrote on him in the years following his death, however, say that he did not believe there was any truth to astrology, and that he carried out astrological predictions for the court with reluctance and, as it were, with tongue in cheek.

This skepticism concerning a commonly credited system of belief also extended to other areas, and Khayyam acquired the reputation of being more interested in scientific proof and philosophical speculation than in the revealed truths of religion. In particular, his name was associated with the teachings and writings of Ibn Sina (Avicenna), the great Persian rationalist and neo-Aristotelian, who had died shortly before Khayyam's birth. Khayyam was said to have been reading a book of Ibn Sina's on his deathbed, and he was referred to as the philosopher's spiritual heir. In an earlier age this would not have mattered particularly, but the Seljuks had effectively put an end to the philosophical and religious speculation that had flourished in Iran for the previous century and a half, and under their rule suspicions of heresy or freethinking could result in persecution, and even execution.

A perhaps apocryphal story, occurring in a notice on Khayyam written some forty years after his death, tells of a meeting between one of the leading religious writers of the time, al-Ghazzali, and Khayyam. According to the tale the call to prayer interrupted Khayyam's description of an astronomical phenomenon, at which point al-Ghazzali unceremoniously rose to pray with the remark that "Truth has defeated falsehood," indicating the superiority of religious faith to scientific speculation. Even if the story was invented it indicates the atmosphere of the times in which Khayyam lived and the necessity for prudence in the expression of skeptical opinions; given such a situation it is not surprising that Khayyam was described as very unwilling to discuss matters with visitors or to accept students (and he made severe intellectual demands on those he did accept).

The first reference to Khayyam as a poet was made in a book written in the 1170's, but this cites only a few lines by him in Arabic, making no mention of *rubaiyat* in Persian. It was not until around the time of the Mongol invasion (the 1220's) that *rubaiyat* in Persian began to be attributed to Khayyam, by which time he had been dead for ninety years. Various reasons have been adduced for this gap in the record; the most compelling is that the skepticism frequently expressed in quatrains attributed to Khayyam might have proved dangerous to the author if the verses had been widely circulated in his own lifetime. Another is that the *rubai* was still conceived of in Khayyam's time largely as a popular folk form, somewhat beneath the diginity of a learned philosopher and mathematician like Khayyam (somewhat as if a present day Nobel laureate in physics were discovered to have written lyrics for a rock group), and that his early biographers had therefore thought the poems unworthy of mention. After the 1220's, however, the trickle of poems attributed to Khayyam gradually turned to a flood, and within a hundred years or so many hundreds, and later even thousands, of poems were recorded as being by him. If the Western reader's first difficulty lies in disentangling Khayyam from FitzGerald, the second—which is in many ways even more insuperable—lies in deciding just which of these hundreds of quatrains are actually by Khayyam.

The problem is compounded by the conventions that governed how medieval mansucripts of Persian poetry were produced. The notion that an author's intentions and the integrity of his oeuvre are somehow sacrosant is of course a relatively recent one (throughout much of the eighteenth century Shakespeare's plays were blithely rewritten for the British stage, and very few saw anything wrong with this), and had no place at all in medieval Persian manuscript production. Poems were often assigned on the basis of an author's reputation (a poet known for his skepticism, for example, would soon begin to "attract" skeptical poems by other poets—and this naturally had a snowball effect); a scribe might add or delete or "improve on" poems, according to personal preference; he might add

poems of his own or of more obscure poets whose works exhibited a similar style. Once a poet became known for a particular kind of poem, especially if it were written in a short form, his work would attract imitators, and the best of these imitations could well be added to the canon (this was especially true in a country like Persia where the ability to write tolerable verse was expected of everyone with a modicum of education). And many of the quatrains attributed to Khayyam turn up in the collected works of other poets; often it is impossible to decide to which of them the poem should be ascribed.

In general the *rubaiyat* attributed to Khayyam are concerned with four themes: (1) skepticism as to human knowledge of divine purposes; (2) a strong awareness of the immensity of historical time and the fleetingness of human life; (3) "*carpe diem*," admonitions to enjoy the beauty and sweetness of life while one can, as it will pass all too soon; (4) admonitions to look beyond the diversity of religious beliefs and to trust in an unknowable God.

Editors and scholars of Khayyam's work have pointed out that the first two themes—religious and philosophical skepticism and an awareness of the brevity of life—are the dominant themes in the earliest quatrains to be attributed to Khayyam. The mild hedonism of some quatrains seems linked to such themes: since we cannot know God's purposes or what if anything awaits us after death, it is prudent to enjoy life while we can. On the other hand few of the early poems are extravagantly or "shockingly" hedonistic, just as few of them are "mystical" in their implications. FitzGerald was convinced of Khayyam's religious skepticism and rejected mystical interpretations of the poems. In this he has usually been followed by later scholars; further, the Iranian scholar Ali Dashti has pointed out that it is often the obviously mystical quatrains which turn up in the works of other poets, and this too makes the "mystical" Khayyam a less convincing figure.

A further criterion for selection is that during the period in which *rubaiyat* began to be indiscriminately ascribed to Khayyam the prevalent style of Persian poetry became much more elusive and self-consciously rhetorical. On this basis it seems reasonable to suppose that poems written in the early simpler style of Khayyam's period are more likely to be by Khayyam. Using these thematic and stylistic criteria most editors have reduced the number of quatrains by Khayyam from the few thousand attributed to him to between 120 and 170. A pattern is discernible; the religious skepticism of the "core" quatrains is compatible with the "*carpe diem*" quality of similar works; the skepticism—popularly supposed to be blasphemous and therefore shocking—led to "shocking" poems of another kind being fathered on Khayyam, those that advocate a life of perpetual libertine licence. On the other hand, the mystical quatrains seem like an attempt to save the poet's reputation, which became associated with such libertine admonitions. But even when the canon has been reduced to the relatively small number of skeptical and melancholy "*carpe diem*" works it is virtually certain that many of these works are in fact not actually by Khayyam, but are exercises in his style by later admirers, the relative simplicity of the poems' form being a ready invitation for talented amateurs to try their skill.

The poems' force and popularity rest largely on the directness of this simple form. In Persian the form consists of two lines that rhyme with one another, and the same rhyme is present as an internal rhyme in the first line. The rhyme scheme is thus as follows:

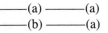

(Occasionally the same internal rhyme is present in the second line as well.) Persian meters can be very complex and demanding, but the meter of the *rubai* is, like the overall form, simple and straightforward. The form lends itself to epigrammatic and witty statements, and the concluding rhyme coming after the usual breathing space of the first half of the second line having no rhyme is, in the Persian phrase, "the knife that enters the (reader's) heart," the last underlining of the insight the poem offers. Much of the success of FitzGerald's versions of Khayyam comes from his retention of this

form, and his ability to reproduce the feeling of often despairing certainty that the returning last rhyme can give in Persian.

The reader of FitzGerald's versions, brilliant though they are, should however be aware that FitzGerald translates relatively freely at times and that he fundamentally changes the poems' formal status. In the Persian each poem is a separate entity, but FitzGerald strings the poems into a continuous narrative that tells the story of a day in the life of a disillusioned skeptic who seeks solace from philosophical uncertainty in wine drinking and convivial companionship. This narrative is entirely FitzGerald's own creation, his gloss as it were on Khayyam's life and interests as he perceived them through the poems, and there is no warrant at all for it in the quatrains' Persian originals. The historical Khayyam would seem to have been an altogether intellectually tougher individual than FitzGerald's at times rather maudlin, if still very attractive, reading of his character implies.

DICK DAVIS

Further Reading

Translations

FitzGerald, Edward, trans. *The Rubaiyat of Omar Khayyam*. (First edition) London: Bernard Quaritate, 1859. This is one of the most frequently printed books ever produced in English, and innumerable editions are available. The reader should be aware that FitzGerald takes considerable liberties with the Persian, expanding some quatrains and "mashing" (FitzGerald's word) others together; nevertheless, no translation from Persian verse into English rivals FitzGerald's versions, and they give more of the feeling of medieval Persian poetry than any other translations ever made.

Avery, Peter, and John Heath-Stubbs, trans. *The Ruba'iyat of Omar Khayyam*. London: Penguin, 1979. Frequently reprinted. This translates a selection of Khayyam's quatrains into free verse. It is far more accurate than FitzGerald, but as verse it is much less satisfactory. The book contains an excellent introduction on Khayyam and his poetry.

Related Studies

There have been many books in English on Khayyam but few of them are useful, as they tend to be based on FitzGerald's translation rather than on the original Persian poems. The best book on Khayyam in English is *In Search of Omar Khayyam* by Ali Dashti, translated by L. P. Elwell-Sutton, New York: Columbia University Press, 1971. The most useful book on FitzGerald's Khayyam is *FitzGerald's Rubaiyat of Omar Khayyam* by E. Heron Allen, London, Bernard Quaritch, 1899.

Dick Davis has edited the Penguin Poets edition of FitzGerald's *Rubaiyat of Omar Khayyam*, London, 1989, and the introduction to this edition examines the lives of Khayyam and FitzGerald, as well as the relationship between Khayyam's originals and FitzGerald's translations.

THE CONFERENCE OF THE BIRDS

Title in Persian: *Manteq at-Tair*
Author: Farīd ud-Dīn 'Aṭṭar
Born: Between 1120 and 1157 in Neishapour
Died: Probably between 1193 and 1235
Literary Form: Narrative verse
Date of Composition: 1177

Major Themes

To find truth and spiritual fulfillment one must set upon a long and arduous journey with the aid of a spiritual teacher.

To attain one's spiritual goal it is necessary to overcome one's self or ego, to become indifferent to one's infatuation with personal possessions, pride, and reputation.

Embracing an overwhelming, passionate, and unorthodox love is inevitable in this quest for fulfillment.

The ultimate realization of Truth and God is the recognition that all beings are one with God, each individual is Truth and God.

Farid ud-Din Attar is a twelfth-century Persian author whose writings center on Sufism, a particular expression of Islamic religion that stressed direct individual mystical experience of Allah. He was born in Neishapour (northeastern Iran) some time between 1119 and 1157, though an exact date is not possible. His name, "Attar," traditionally has been assumed to indicate his occupation as a seller of perfumes and medical drugs—the Persian word *attar* means perfume or essential oil derived from flowers. Attar is held to have written in his *daru-khane*, a store front that dispensed perfume oils and drugs for medicinal purposes.

His education had both a formal and informal dimension. He gained both his medical and theological knowledge at a school attached to the shrine of Imam Reza at Mashhad (northeastern Iran); additionally, he learned a great deal about Islamic saints (Sufis) and their doctrines while traveling extensively throughout the Middle East, going as far as Egypt to the west and India to the east.

Attar's encyclopedic knowledge of the Sufis is recorded principally in his work *Memorials of the Saints (Tadhkirat al-Auliya)* and to a lesser extent in *The Conference of the Birds.* Attar's writings often state and support Sufi doctrines, ideas that were generally attacked by the establishment as heretical.

Consequently, Attar was tried for heresy, convicted, and banished, much in the manner of some of the earlier Sufi saints he wrote about. Eventually, Attar made his way back to Neishapour, where he is reported to have died, some time between 1193 and 1235. According to tradition, Attar was butchered by the invading Mongols in 1230, though this date is quite late and unlikely, as it would make Attar well over a hundred years old at his death.

The Conference of the Birds

The Conference of the Birds is Attar's best-known work, and provides something of a Sufi guidebook on how to attain spiritual realization or *fana*. Scholars frequently speculate on whether Attar's work is but an elaboration on any one of several earlier works dealing with a similar theme of birds or animals seeking God and Truth; for example, Ghazzali's *Risalat al-Tayr*, Avicenna's *The Bird,* a section dealing with birds and God within Sama'i's *Divan,* or *The Fables of Bidpai (Kalila and Dimna),* which originated in India and was translated into Persian by Rudaki. Regardless of whether Attar "borrowed" the main theme of his work from one or more of these earlier works, *The Conference of the Birds* nevertheless stands out as a remarkable work exhibiting both poetic richness and theological insight. It is a significant Islamic work that gives the reader a rare and penetrating vista into the world of Sufi spiritual practices and aspirations.

The Conference of the Birds describes the adventure of a group of birds, led by a hoopoe, who seek out the king, Simorgh. Intended as an allegorical account of the Sufi's quest for spiritual liberation, Attar cleverly links each type of bird in the group with the assortment of obstacles (that is, excuses and attitudes) that frequently blocks one's ascent into spiritual fulfillment. What strikes one as most stunning in this work is the insight and sensitivity that Attar infuses into his description of the trials and tribulations that mark this road toward spiritual salvation. While this work is particularly relevant to the *ghalaba/sukr* (rapture and intoxication) school of Islamic Sufism, Attar's poetic descriptions penetrate deep into the human condition and allow the reader to identify with the inherent limitations and ignorance that each individual must come to terms with and overcome if spiritual advancement is to be gained. This is what makes this work so important and useful for anyone seeking spiritual elevation and purification.

The Conference of the Birds should be recognized as a complete theological treatise that begins with a statement of the human condition, then identifies the obstacles that limit human awareness of the Divine; it provides instructions on how one must overcome these shortcomings, and gives careful descriptions of levels of partial attainment and spiritually elevated attitudes that are developed on the path toward fulfillment; and finally, the work gives splendid, endearing portraits of spiritual liberation.

The choice of composing the text within an allegorical structure has the benefit of avoiding the often condescending connotation of similar spiritual writings, where easily taking offense, the reader strays from further reading of the text. This format also allows for the use of a host of literary devices to enliven the reading experience, playing on multiple word meanings and connotations that at once can be insightful, humorous, and clever. Hence, the text can be appreciated on many levels depending on the concerns and interests of the reader, appreciating it for either its literary, historical, theological, philosophical, and/or psychological aspects.

The Spiritual Guide

The Conference of the Birds is an allegorical text that describes a journey undertaken by the birds of the world. They are informed by the hoopoe that they have a king—the Simorgh—who should be sought out, but as he lives far away, they must undertake a hazardous journey to join him. The hoopoe takes on the role of the guide or teacher, and much of the text involves his listening to excuses the birds give for not agreeing to join him on the quest. For example, the nightingale cannot leave the one he loves, while the parrot seeks no more than to be set free from its cage; the peacock finds the Simorgh to be too unknown a goal, seeking instead the monarch's palace; the duck seeks no more than to dwell in the pure fresh water of his home; the partridge has but one desire, to pick through quarries for jewels; while the owl finds that the only worthy goal of life is to accumulate gold. Attar carefully catalogs all the potential excuses that might arise in one's mind for choosing not to seek out God and spiritual liberation, and methodically demonstrates the folly of each of these attitudes though the mouthpiece of the hoopoe.

Each of these rejoinders by the hoopoe is complemented in the text by the inclusion of several stories that illustrate and add support to the points developed in the responses. These narratives are delightful parables that involve saints, fools, kings, angels, infidels, and ordinary people, as well as famous individuals such as Moses, Abraham, Joseph, Jesus, Alexander the Great, King Solomon, and the Sufis, Hallaj and Junaid.

Throughout these exchanges between hoopoe and the other birds, it is repeatedly stressed that one must find a guide that will help one through the journey that we all must take if we hope to gain spiritual salvation. It is clear that not only would the other birds not have embarked on the journey had it not been suggested by the hoopoe, but none would have completed the journey without his step-by-step guidance along the way.

The narrative states, "You need a skillful guide ... You cannot guess what dangers you will find, you need a staff to guide you, like the blind. Your sight is failing and the road is long; [t]rust one who knows the journey and is strong." (Darbandi and Davis, trans., 1984).

Toward the end of the questioning, a bird asks how long is the journey? The hoopoe responds that the path is full of danger and despair, whereupon he identifies seven valleys that must be traversed, beginning with the Valley of the Quest, then through the Valley of Love, onward toward more developed and refined domains such as the Valleys of Insight, Mystery, Detachment, Serenity, Unity, Awe, and finally the Valleys of Poverty and Nothingness.

The hoopoe gives no definite answer as to how long it takes to travel across these areas, noting that none who have gone forth have returned. The point here seems to be that those who did not make it to the goal did not live to return and tell about their misadventure, while those who did make it would have no desire to retrace their way back to this world of ignorance and suffering.

Overcoming the Self and Its Desires

When the hoopoe first assembles the birds and tells them of the Simorgh, he sets forth the invitation, "Join me, and when at last we end our quest [o]ur king will greet you as His honored guest . . . Escape your self-hood's vicious tyranny—[whoever] can evade the Self transcends [t]his world and as a lover he ascends." (Darbandi and Davis, trans., 1984).

Throughout the text, Attar repeats this same reoccurring means for spiritual unfolding, namely, subduing the self. Without significant reduction in the influence of the worldly self or ego and its various forms of vanity, one cannot even begin to make progress on the path. Attar describes the self as "that whirlpool where our lives are wrecked." (Darbandi and Davis, trans., 1984).

The goal of the journey is to attain *total* spiritual absorption in God; thus, as long as one has *restric-*

tions in committing oneself to God and refuses to give up all personal concerns for personal welfare and property, this purified state of existence cannot be attained. The hoopoe (Attar) never tires of pointing out that worldly status, comfort, or wealth are insignificant in comparison to what is to be gained in union with God. In repeated brutal statements, the hoopoe continually draws the birds' attention to the meaningless nature of worldly life: "What are you here? Mere carrion, rotten flesh, [w]ithheld from Truth by this world's clumsy mesh." (Darbandi and Davis, trans., 1984) Contrast this summation with his description of the goal: "A hundred veils drew back, and there before the birds' incredulous, bewildered sight shone the unveiled, the inmost Light of Light. He [the herald] led them to a noble throne, a place [o]f intimacy, dignity and grace." (Darbandi and Davis, trans., 1984).

Love as Necessary to Fulfillment

In response to the question of how are we to detach ourselves from our association with the worldly, egoistic self, Attar is unequivocal in his response: the vehicle for salvation and liberation is love. Yet this is not the superficial love found in the world (as expressed by the nightingale); True Love is an unmitigated commitment directed exclusively toward God. This is a nonrational excursion, free from all conceptual limitations: "Give up the intellect for love and see [i]n one brief moment all eternity; [b]reak nature's frame, be resolute and brave, [t]hen rest at peace in Unity's black cave." (Darbandi and Davis, trans., 1984).

Salvation will occur only after one abandons all things that one owns and knows, for even the self (one's own egoistic self-identity) must give way to allow complete absorption in God. It is only when the aspirant is willing to sacrifice *everything* for God and projects one's total being into God, that one becomes free of the binding influence of the self and the world, and can for the first time join with the Divine. Even the traditional structures of morality and religion must be transcended through this intense expression of love. "Love will direct you to Dame Poverty, [a]nd she will show the way to Blasphemy. When neither Blasphemy nor Faith remain, [t]he body and the Self have both been slain; [t]hen the fierce fortitude the Way will as is yours and you are worthy of our task." (Darbandi and Davis, trans., 1984).

All Are One with God

The nature of the goal as finally portrayed in *The Conference of the Birds* is something quite distinct and different from the text's initial identification of a king or a God-like figure as the one to which the birds' love is to be directed. Consider this passage explaining the birds' final awakening: "There in the Simorgh's radiant face they saw themselves, the Simorgh of the world—with awe they gazed, and dared at last to comprehend [t]hey were the Simorgh and the journey's end." (Darbandi and Davis, trans., 1984).

Following the notorious statement by the martyred Sufi, Hallaj, "I am the Truth (or God)," Attar embraces a monistic metaphysical position, holding that ultimately there is but God, and all individuals are expressions of His Being. (The term "*haq*" used by Hallaj in this quotation can mean either God or Truth.) The ultimate object of the journey, Simorgh, is expressed in Attar's allegorical text by what is actually a play on words that literally means "thirty (*si*) birds (*morgh*)," so that when the thirty remaining birds finally see "Simorgh," in fact what they see is "thirty birds," meaning that they see

themselves as Truth and God. It is not surprising that Attar was tried and convicted for heresy, but he evidently was willing to pay the consequences for what he believed was the truth regarding reality and God, a realization given forth by such earlier Islamic mystics as Hallaj, whom Attar idealized and supported.

KIM SKOOG

Further Reading

Translation

Darbandi, Afkham, and Dick Davis, trans. *The Conference of the Birds*. New York: Penguin Books, 1984. This is the most complete and clearest translation of this work in English. It has a useful introduction that incorporates the most recent scholarship. As noted, all quotations in this article are taken from this translation.

Nott, C. S., trans. *The Conference of the Birds*. Boulder: Shambhala Publications, 1971. This translation is another economical and widely available translation that does an adequate job of presenting the basic ideas of Attar's work to the reader. However, Nott's translation is limited by the fact that it is based on a nineteenth-century French translation of the text by Garcin de Tassy. Besides some lack of clarity because of the multiple layers of translation, it is incomplete, as several of the stories are omitted from the original Persian text.

THE POETRY OF NEZAMI

Author: Elyas ebn Yusuf Nezami
Born: 1141, Ganjeh, Azerbaijan
Died: March 12, 1209, Ganjch, Azerbaijan
Major Works: *Khamzeh* ("Quintet"); *Makhzan al-Asrar* ("The Treasury of Secrets"); *Khosrow and Shirin*; *Leili and Majnun*; *Haft Paykar* ("The Seven Portraits"); *The Book of Alexander* (consisting of two parts: *Sharafnameh*, and *Eqbalnameh*)

Major Themes

The world is a "vale of soul-making."

Life is a series of tests and encounters which lead the soul on toward ethical purification and spiritual enlightenment.

The chief vehicle for this progression is the experience of love, which is a destructive sensual delusion when misunderstood, but the greatest force for spiritual ascent when apprehended correctly.

Elyas ebn Yusuf Nezami is considered to be one of the very greatest of Persian poets, and his five narrative poems (his *"Khamzeh"* or "Quintet") are by general consent the finest narrative poems of the Persian literary tradition after the *Shahnameh* of Ferdowsi. Very little is known of his life. He was born and died in Ganjeh, in what is now independent Azerbaijan, and he is only once known to have left his home town (at the express demand of a local ruler who was traveling nearby and wanted to see him). His mother was an Iranian Kurd and it is possible that his father had the same ethnic origin, though he is claimed also by Turkish Azerbaijanis as being of their stock. He is one of the first Persian poets who was not directly associated with a specific court (though all his poems were dedicated to local princes, in the hope of patronage), and how he supported himself is not clear.

After the success of his first poem, the *Makhzan al-Asrar* ("Treasury of Secrets"), a local prince rewarded him fairly munificently; and his gifts included a slave girl named Afaq, whom Nezami married, and whose death he laments in very affecting terms at the close of his second poem *Khosrow and Shirin*. Afaq left him a son, Mohammad, who is addressed in the poet's subsequent poems. The poet married twice more; both these wives also predeceased him and their deaths are recorded in his

works, though neither with the same intensity of feeling as is evident in the verses on Afaq.

It is clear from his works that Nezami was extremely well educated and well read. He had a very extensive knowledge of the literature in Persian that had been composed up to his time, and he shows in particular a thorough command of the works of the tenth- and eleventh-century epic poet Ferdowsi, of the eleventh-century mystical poet Sana'i, and of the eleventh-century poet Gorgani, whose one surviving narrative poem *Vis and Ramin* had a profound influence on Nezami's own poetry.

However, Nezami is not to be considered a merely derivative poet; in his hands the themes and techniques of his great predecessors are wholly absorbed and transmuted into a new unity that is at once personal to Nezami and expressive of the cumulative genius of medieval Persian poetry. His work unites a brilliance of secular rhetoric, a genius for storytelling, and an ethical and mystical seriousness in a way that was rarely if ever to be equaled in subsequent Persian verse. His achievement can in many ways be regarded as the crowning syncretic moment of a multivoiced tradition that had been developing within the literature since the mid tenth century; his poems integrate the secular and the mystical, the sensuous and the ascetic, the ludic and the didactic, the aristocratic and the "bourgeois," in a precarious and dazzling unity, which was to split into different schools after his death.

Makhzan al-Asrar

Nezami's first poem was the mystical work, the *Makhzan al-Asrar*, a collection of anecdotes interspersed with homilies, modeled fairly closely on the *Hadiqat al-Haqiqat* ("The Enclosed Garden of the Truth") of the eleventh-century poet Sana'i. Because it is unlike the three works which followed and for which he is most famous, which are—on the surface at least—secular love poems, this first mystical poem has often been regarded as a "false start" on Nezami's part. This is, however, to misread the nature of his talent and interests; the secular stories he retells in his later poems are given a highly allegorical and spiritualized treatment, and in his last work, on the life of Alexander the Great, he returns directly to the theme of the quest for spiritual truth. The *Makhzan al-Asrar* differs, however, from the rest of Nezami's work in some respects, in that it is episodic rather than a continuous narrative, and in that the integration of spiritual concerns with the realities of secular love and personal ethical growth, which is typical of his romances, is here largely absent. The work largely recommends renunciation of the world rather than growth within it, and breathes an atmosphere of *contemptu mundi*, mingled with strenuous asceticism and self-denial.

Khosrow and Shirin

His second work, *Khosrow and Shirin*, is in Iran the most popular of Nezami's narratives, and would seem to be the most personal. Nevertheless, he begins the work with a passage implying that he has turned from purely ascetic/religious exhortation to a love story somewhat against his will, saying, "Since I have the treasure of the *Makhzan al-Asrar*/ Why should I take the trouble to write a love story?/ But it seems that in these times there is no one/ Who is not attracted to love-stories. . . ."

Nezami's dissatisfaction with his own times, and with the spiritually unambitious instincts of most people, be they commoners or princes, is a common theme in his work. *Khosrow and Shirin* tells the story of the Sasanian king Khosrow Parviz's love for the Armenian princess Shirin; it also contains as an interlude the story of the lowly mason Farhad's love for Shirin. Farhad is instructed to hack a causeway out of a mountain to prove his love for her and, though he does this, he is then wrongly informed that Shirin is dead and he dies of grief. Both the king and Shirin also die.

The unhappy ending, as well as the very unsatisfactory nature of Khosrow's character—much of the poem is concerned with his attempts to become worthy of Shirin's love—remove the poem from the realm of the idyllic and relate it to a theme recurrent in all of Nezami's works, the necessity for ethical striving and for leaving the mundane world of ambition and personal desire behind. In this the poem is similar in its urgently ethical tone to Nezami's first poem, though in a less obviously hortatory way.

The source for Nezami's narrative is found in Ferdowsi's *Shahnameh*, but much of the manner of his treatment is that of a more intense elaboration of the rhetoric to be found in Gorgani's *Vis and Ramin* (which was either a verse translation of a pre-Islamic Sasanian work, or an original composition based on pre-Islamic sources). *Khosrow and Shirin* is in reality a long hymn to the potentially civilizing influence of love and to the benign effects of an allegorized feminine beauty; in this it is similar in tone and feeling to roughly contemporary European works like the *Roman de la Rose*, and the idealized figure of Shirin will frequently remind a Western reader of Dante's Beatrice. In an epilogue Nezami directly links the figure of Shirin to that of his dead wife, Afaq, and the poem is considered to be, in effect, an extended elegy on Afaq, as well as a hymn to her virtues and to the love the poet felt for her.

Leili and Majnun

The combination of didacticism and sensuality to be found in *Khosrow and Shirin* is also present in Nezami's next two works. His third poem was another love story; again he claims to have undertaken the work reluctantly, this time on the express orders of a local aristocrat, and to have completed the poem in less than four months. Here his narrative is based on the Arab legend of Leili and Majnun, in which two young people of enemy tribes fall in love. Since their love is forbidden, the young man, Majnun, becomes distracted by grief (his name means "crazy/maddened") and, as in *Khosrow and Shirin*, the story ends tragically and both lovers die. The similarity to Shakespeare's *Romeo and Juliet* is clear, but Nezami's usual insistence on an ethical dimension to the tale (Majnun is as much criticized as sympathized with) makes it very different in atmosphere from Shakespeare's play. The fact that the subject was suggested to him by a patron probably accounts for the fact that this is the only one of Nezami's four continuous narratives with a source not to be found at least in embryo in the works of Ferdowsi. Again the influence of Gorgani is apparent (for example, the opening scenes of *Leili and Majnun* and of Gorgani's *Vis and Ramin*, in both of which the affections of the young lovers are described as blossoming while they are at school together, are very similar). The verses describing the depth of Majnun's love-madness are among the most celebrated passages of love poetry in Persian literature, which abounds in treatments of the subject of hopeless love and its effects.

The Seven Portraits

Nezami's fourth work, the *Haft Paykar* ("Seven Portraits"), is normally considered to be his masterpiece. This too is, on the surface at least, largely taken up with erotic adventures; the hero is the Sasanian king Bahram Gur, and again the germ of the narrative is to be found in Ferdowsi's work. Ferdowsi presents Bahram as a somewhat brutal aristocractic hedonist; Nezami assiduously allegorizes the portrait and the narrative itself, in the process removing the poem even further from quotidian secular reality than is the case with either *Khosrow and Shirin* or *Leili and Majnun*. The poem becomes in effect an allegorized education of the questing soul, represented by Bahram, and the seven princesses he encounters and courts represent

stages on a journey of spiritual understanding and development. In its intensely spiritual treatment of the erotic—or intensely erotic treatment of the spiritual (it is sometimes difficult to say exactly which is being foregrounded at the other's expense)—combined with a simultaneous rich sensuousnes of description, it is unlike any major European poem, though the closest, in its leisurely but ardent neo-Platonism, in its fascination with an imaginary code of aristocratic chivalry, and in its complex allegorizing and schematizing of experience, is perhaps Spenser's *The Fairy Queen*.

The Sharafnameh *and the* Eqbalnameh

Nezami's last two poems, the *Sharafnameh* and the *Eqbalnameh*, form a unit dealing with the life of Alexander the Great. As is usual in the many Islamic treatments of the Alexander legend, he is regarded not so much as a world-conqueror as a searcher for spiritual enlightenment and truth. In these poems Nezami is able to return to the themes of his first work, the *Makhzan al-Asrar*, and to make the ethical understanding and ultimate renunciation of the world his central theme, unencumbered by a love narrative. However, the experience he had gained in writing three of the most famous love poems of Persian literature undoubtedly contributed to his mastery in this final work; if it is less passionate and beguiling than the narratives that immediately precede it, the poem has a measured wisdom that make it a fitting literary farewell. If *Leili and Majnun* is to be compared to *Romeo and Juliet*, as it frequently has been, the *Sharafnameh* and *Eqbalnameh* can be regarded as Nezami's equivalent of Shakespeare's last plays, in which a profound but still humanly troubled wisdom has replaced the more violent passions of earlier works.

Nezami also left a number of shorter poems, mostly lyrics (*ghazals*) which show considerable skill, though it seems that many of these shorter poems have been lost. The poet's immense reputation among Persian speakers, however, rests almost solely on his narrative works. The factors that have accorded him preeminence in the genre of Persian allegorical romance are (1) his brilliant narrative ability which combines great suaveness of rhetoric from moment to moment within a convincing overall structure; (2) the subtlety and complexity of his allegorization of the details of his narrative, and (3) the transparent integrity and seriousness of his ethical concerns which suffuse the texture of his verse, and which use character and incident as a constant admonition towards ideals of self-realization and spiritual growth. Nezami's work also provides an example of a paradox not uncommon in the work of medieval Persian mystical or quasi-mystical poets, in that admonitions to renounce the sensual life are presented by means of an extremely sensual and beguiling rhetorical mastery.

DICK DAVIS

Further Reading

Translation

Meisami, Julie Scott, trans. *The Haft Paykar*. Oxford: Oxford University Press, 1995. Dr. Mei-

sami is an excellent scholar and experienced translator from the Persian, and this version of *The Seven Portraits* has been enthusiastically received by the critics.

Gelpke, R. and E. Mattin and George Hill, trans. *The Story of Leili and Majnun*. London: Bruno Cassirer, 1966. A translation that is reasonably accurate, though sometimes sentimental.

Related Studies

Poeta Persiano Nizami e la leggenda Iranica di Alessandro Magno, Rome, 1977, has good essays in English, German, French, and Italian on Nezami's treatment of the Alexander legend.

There is no book in English devoted to a study of Nezami, but there is a great deal that is very useful on Nezami in *Medieval Persian Court Poetry*, by Julie Scott Meisami, Princeton: Princeton University Press, 1987.

THE POETRY OF JALĀL AL-DĪN RŪMĪ

Author: Jalāl al-Dīn Mohammad Balkhi
Born: 1207, Balkh, Aghanistan
Died: 1273, Konya, Turkey
Major Works: *Masnavi (Mathnavi), Divan-e Shams-e Tabrizi, Fihi ma Fihi (Prose Discourses)*

Major Themes

The soul is trapped within the physical world but when it becomes aware of this state it longs to return to God.
Emotion is a better guide on the journey to God than the intellect.
Existence is one beneath the superficial variety and glamor of the world.
The categories of the world are useful only for those who are content to live in the world and on its terms; for those who have set out on the search for divine unity, such categories fall into irrelevance.

Jalal al-Din Mohammad Balkhi is by common consent the greatest mystical poet to have written in Persian, and one of world literature's masters of the genre. The name by which he is commonly known, "Rumi," refers to his eventual home in "Rum" (Turkey); he is also known as "Mowlavi" and, especially in Iran, as "Mowlana" (meaning "Our Master").

Rumi was born in Balkh in present day Afghanistan (in Rumi's day an area considered as part of greater Persia); his father, Mohammad b. Hosayn Baha'ad-din Valad, was a noted theologian of the town. When Rumi was about eleven or twelve, the family left Balkh, perhaps in part because of hostility from the local ruler but probably mainly because of the growing threat to the town from the approaching Mongol hordes (in 1220 they besieged and subsequently razed the town, slaughtering most of its inhabitants). The family passed westwards through Iran, finally settling in the town of Konya in Anatolia, in Turkey. Konya was at this time the capital of Seljuk Turkey and the largest Muslim-ruled town in the area; it was also the reputed site of Plato's tomb, and the Greek philosopher's reputation in Islam as a kind of proto-mystic may have attracted Sufis (Muslim mystics) to the area. There is a story that on their journey westward Rumi's family visited the by then aged Persian mystical poet Attar (q.v.), who, recognizing the boy's precociousness, gave the young Rumi a copy of one his

works. Though the anecdote is probably apocryphal, it serves as a reminder of Rumi's later debt to Attar, both as poet and mystic, a debt he openly acknowledged in his writings.

Shortly afer arriving in Turkey, Rumi was married, and one of his sons born early in this marriage, Soltan Valad, was to become his father's most devoted disciple and disseminator of his teachings and works.

Rumi's father died in 1231, and Rumi took his place as one of Konya's leading Muslim theologians. At some time after his father's death Rumi became seriously interested in Sufism (Islamic mysticism) and either traveled to Syria to meet with mystical teachers (he may have met Ibn Arabi there, the most prominent Islamic philosopher/mystic of his time) or was visited by such teachers in Konya. Either way, the ground had been prepared for his meeting in Konya, in 1244, with the wandering dervish (religious mendicant) Shams-e Tabrizi. Virtually nothing is known for certain about this individual except that he was contemptuous of much orthodox theology, seeing it as a mere skating over the surface of religious truth, and clearly had a very strikingly charismatic personality which violently attracted or antagonized those with whom he came in contact. Rumi and he became inseparable companions for a while, to the extent that Rumi's friends and family complained that he was jeopardizing his position in the community by the association. Shams left Konya without warning, and Rumi made great efforts to find him again; when he finally heard his friend had been seen in Syria, he sent his son Soltan Valad there to bring him back to Konya. Shams became a member of Rumi's household until disappearing again, this time for good, in 1248. There is a story (most modern scholars doubt its veracity, though some still consider it possibly true) that one of Rumi's sons (Ala'al-din, not the more famous Soltan Valad) had Shams murdered, partly out of mere personal jealousy, but also partly because he feared that his father was falling into heresy by his association with someone who had scant regard for the outer forms of religious observance. Rumi's advocacy of music as an accompaniment to religious observances, which seems to have begun after his association with Shams, would have marked him as sufficiently unorthodox, this being a practice considered abhorrent by most Muslim clerics of the period.

After the disappearance of his mentor, Rumi devoted himself to mystical speculation and the composition of poetry; he also formed strong attachments, reminiscent of his relationship with Shams, to at least two other individuals whom he saw as having a particular spiritual charisma. The second of these, Chalabi, persuaded Rumi to write down his mystical speculations, and it is probably to his persuasive powers that we owe the existence of much of Rumi's poetry, particularly his major work the *Masnavi*. The very famous (it is perhaps the single best known passage in all Persian poetry) opening of the *Masnavi* is said to have been written independently; the rest of this immensely long poem (twice as long as Dante's *Divine Comedy*) was then dictated to Chalabi, at this disciple's request, as an extended commentary and compendium of illustrative anecdotes.

Rumi eventually became the center of a group of acolytes which evolved into the order of Mevlevi Dervishes; its members were (and still are) characterized by their devotion to Rumi's works and teachings and by their practice of "whirling," that is, dancing in rhythmical circular fashion to music dominated by the Middle Eastern flute (the "ney").

The purpose of the dance is to induce a state of mystical insight and a sense of proximity to, or oneness with, the Divine. After Rumi's death the group of acolytes was organized on a formal basis by Soltan Valad; it has stayed centered in Konya, where Rumi's very splendid tomb is still maintained as a place of pilgrimage for his followers.

Rumi's poetry is characterized by its often extreme emotionalism, energy, and enthusiasm, and by the seemingly endless interest the poet displays in anecdotal stories illustrative of the poems' main mystical doctrines. Despite its highly personal tone and flavor his work has deep roots in the writings of his predecessors and Rumi must have read omniverously in Persian poetry as well as in the theological and philosophical works in Arabic with which a prominent theologian of his time would be expected to be familiar. Anecdotes in his poems are drawn from the Qur'an and its commentaries, the *Hadith* (actions and, more especially, sayings of the prophet Mohammad), collections of fables like *Kalileh and Demneh*, prose romances like the *Marzban Nameh*, mirrors for princes like the *Qabus Nameh*, biographies of Sufi saints like the Tazkirat al-Auliya, and, especially, from the poems of the two great Persian mystical poets who preceeded him, Sanai and Attar. Over thirty-five passages in Rumi's writings are directly indebted to passages in Attar's works.

Masnavi

Rumi's major work the *Masnavi (Mathnavi)* is written in fluently prolific couplets and in this it resembles the works of Sanai and Attar, though Rumi seems to write much more effortlessly and with less visibly self-conscious artifice than either. The poem opens with a passage describing the lamentation of a reed flute which has been cut from a reed bed and longs to return to its original home. Both the philosopher Ghazali and the poet Sanai had previously used the plaintive sound of the flute as a metaphor for mystical longing, but Rumi's treatment of the topos is by far the best known.

The longing of the flute represents the longing of the human soul divorced from God by its sojourn in the world, and the whole poem is in essence a series of anecdotes illustrative of the force of this longing, the snares which keep the human soul trapped in the world, and the means by which it can ultimately return to its divine origin. The means of return lies in awakening and purification, by which the soul is purged of its desire for illusory benefits (the gaudy attractiveness of the physical world) and of its concern with its Self; as in Attar's work, the key to the soul's progress lies in its destruction of the animal Self and of all sense of self-importance or even self-identity. The illusory nature of the world's categories and attractions includes the worldly forms of religions, and the *Masnavi* contains numerous anecdotes illustrative of the essential unity of religious striving, despite superficial differences of creed (though naturally Rumi is convinced of the final superiority and truth of Islam). As Rumi puts it, when an Arab wants grapes he says a word in Arabic, when a Persian wants grapes he says a word in Persian, and when a Greek wants grapes he says a word in Greek, but they all desire the same thing; so it is with mankind and their various religions' outward observances. The nature of this illustration is not coincidental; Rumi's travels (he was born in what had been a Buddhist area and still contained Buddhist ruins, and he lived most of his life close to Islam's border with Christendom) would have made him aware of the literal proximity of other religions, and his voracious appetite for the quirks and subtleties of language—everywhere apparent in his voluminous writings—is appositely illustrated by his choosing an example to do with linguistic referents and translation to make a theological point. The cosmopolitan nature of his world and interests is also indicated by the fact that he not only has verses in Arabic (which is not unusual for a medieval Persian poet) but also brief moments in Turkish and even in Greek.

A particularly paradoxical quality of the *Masnavi* is that its insistently repeated mystical "message" often seems belied by the abundant, enthusiastically piled up detail of the poetry itself. If the message of the poem is that the physical world about us is a snare and a delusion, such a notion can rarely have been presented with such

descriptive relish for the very details from which the soul is supposed to be turning away. Like his contemporary Sa'di (q.v.), Rumi presents a panoramic view of medieval Moslem society, giving us rapid and psychologically persuasive thumbnail sketches of princes, beggars, maids, peasants, merchants, thieves, doctors, artisans, children, and so forth. Nothing and no one is too mean or insignificant to escape his attention. The life of the society—both in its public aspects as it is carried on in the streets, bazaars, law courts and countryside, and in its private existence in houses, harems, courts and sickrooms—is vividly set before the reader's eyes. Though the poem is prized primarily for its mystical doctrine, and the zeal with which this is presented, this brilliant anecdotal detail undoubtedly accounts for much of its popularity. Thus many passages are among the first that Persian schoolchildren read, because of their simple direct charm, and two successful volumes of translated "Tales From the Masnavi," which present the narratives almost purely as secular entertainment with little attention to their mystical meaning, have been published in English.

However, to read the anecdotes of the *Masnavi* primarily with this secular attractiveness in mind is not only to miss the point of the poem but frequently to be severely jolted in one's expectations. For example, the first anecdote concerns a young serving girl who falls in love with a goldsmith; she is then removed to the court of a king who has fallen in love with her, but she refuses the king's advances and falls ill pining for her goldsmith. A doctor informs the king of the reason for the girl's illness and the goldsmith is poisoned.

To a Western reader interested in the narrative as a secular love story, this is an extremely unsatisfactory and seemingly wantonly cruel outcome; in fact, the girl represents the human soul, while the goldsmith—the fabricator of glittering trinkets—is the physical world which the soul naturally and deluding loves even though all the while it could have the much more worthy love of God, and it is only with the destruction of the world in the soul's eyes that it is able to realize this. The impulse to read the stories for their "human interest—an impulse that often seems encouraged by Rumi's skill as a storyteller—rather than for their mystical doctrine can lead to many such puzzling disappointments.

Divan-e Shams-e Tabrizi

Rumi's very long (over 3,500 poems in the standard modern edition) collection of short lyrics is called the *Divan-e Shams-e Tabrizi*; this is because after Shams's second disappearance Rumi traveled to Damascus in search of him, and though he could not find him physically he claimed to to have discovered him within himself; his being had been "replaced" by that of Shams and it was "Shams" therefore who spoke in Rumi's lyric works.

Most typically, the poems are characterized by extreme longing for an enthusiastically and sometimes desperately apostrophized absent "beloved," who at times can be taken as Shams himself, at times as God, and at times as the one manifested through the other. The whirlwind of emotion presented in the poems, and their deliberate flouting of the conventions of normal social behavior, owe much to the "*malamati*" tradition of Sufi utterances and acts, by which Sufis deliberately indulged in socially unacceptable behavior, so drawing the wrath and scorn of the orthodox who were wedded to "outward" religion, while the Sufis considered themselves practitioners of an "inward" faith that had little to do with outward observances. Some of the poems of the *Divan-e Shams-e Tabrizi* have become so well known as to be virtual folk poems within Iranian culture, and they are still to this day set to catchy tunes and sung by popular singers, as well as being musically treated in a more classical and traditional style. Rumi's frequently expressed derision for hypocritical observers of outward religious observances has made his work especially liked by those who think of themselves as simultaneously religious and anti-clerical.

Rumi's literary style is very distinctive; though he has an extremely wide vocabulary the obvious meaning of his verses is not usually in doubt (though the mystical meaning may need exegesis), and he rarely indulges in the ornately obscure rhetoric typical of many medieval Persian poets. The superficial simplicity of his meaning, and its often relatively obscure "inner" meaning, have led to the *Masnavi*'s paradoxical reputation of being simultaneously both very simple and very difficult to understand properly. Rumi uses both colloquial words and idioms and the learnedly referential vocabulary of theology with equal ease; his rhetorical devices are usually straightforward (mainly grammatical parallelism between juxtaposed lines, verbal repetition, and puns, of which he is very fond). Particularly in his shorter poems his work has a driving rhythmic vitality which seems designed to induce in the audience a hypnotic suspension of rational processes, and this is also reflected in the excited emotionalism of the poems" content. Reflective passages, in which the language can be extremely moving in a more inward and contemplative manner than is usual in the short lyrics, are more common in the *Masnavi*. Besides the lyrics of the *Divan* and the *Masnavi*, almost 2,000 *rubaiyat* (quatrains) are attributed to Rumi, and there also exists a book of prose discourses *(Fihi ma Fihi)*, apparently taken down by a disciple while Rumi was addressing his circle of dervishes. Though less well known than his poetry, this work gives many insights into Rumi's manner of thinking, and some passages are directly useful for the interpretation of his meaning at various points in the *Masnavi*.

DICK DAVIS

Further Reading

Translations

Arberry, A. J., trans. *Tales from the Masnavi*. London, Allen and Unwin, 1961, and *More Tales from the Masnavi*. London, Allen and Unwin, 1963. These two volumes of prose selections from the *Masnavi* are much easier to read than the Nicholson translation.

———, trans. *Discourses of Rumi*. London, John Murray, 1961; reprinted New York, 1972. An accurate and very fluent translation of Rumi's "sermons," *Fihi ma Fihi*.

Nicholson, Reynold A. *The Mathnawi of Jalal-u'ddin Rumi*. 3 volumes. London, Luzac, 1926–

1940, reprinted, 1977. The only complete translation of the *Masnavi*. This (prose) translation is by one of the greatest of western scholars of Persian (all editions of the Persian text of the *Masnavi* are based on his work); it is therefore scrupulously accurate. It is also, however, very difficult to read for pleasure, other than in short passages, as its minute accuracy makes the English seem crabbed and unnatural. However, if a reader wishes to know what Rumi actually wrote and meant, this version cannot be bettered.

Note: The American poet Coleman Barks has published numerous free verse translations from the *Divan-e Shams-e Tabrizi*. These often have considerable charm but their ethos is more that of San Francisco in the 1960's and 70's than medieval Islam, and the reader should be aware that they often depart radically from the Persian originals.

Related Studies

Schimmel, Annemarie. *The Triumphal Sun: a Study of the Work of Jalaloddin Rumi*. Cambridge, MA: Harvard University Press, 1978. This and the following work by one of the leading western scholars of Islamic mystical literature present Rumi's writings and teachings in a very direct and unpretentious way, with a wealth of fascinating detail.

———. *I Am Wind You Are Fire: the Life and Work of Rumi*. London, 1992.

Also recommended:

Chittick, William C. *The Sufi Doctrine of Rumi*. Tehran, 1974.

Banani, Amin. "Rumi the Poet." In *Festshrift for Annemarie Schimmel*. Cambridge, MA: Harvard University Press, 1995.

THE POETRY AND PROSE OF SA'DI

Author: Sheikh Nuslih-uddin Sa'di Shirazi
Born: Between 1213 and 1219, Shiraz, Iran
Died: 1292, Shiraz, Iran
Major Works: *Golestan (The Rose Garden), Bustan (The Orchard), Ghazaliyat (Lyric Poems)*

Major Themes

Human life and its institutions are inherently unstable and untrustworthy.
Human life is both more various and more risky than most people want to believe.
A private life far from centers of power is preferable to the dangers of holding public office.
It is extremely necessary to be wary of powerful enemies.
Absolute moral judgments are elusive, so when judging others negatively do so only with caution and reluctance.
Our best guide when dealing with our fellow human beings is tolerance and a ready sympathy for the underdog.

Although compared with many Persian writers Sa'di was not a particularly voluminous writer. The two works for which he is best known in the West, the *Golestan (The Rose Garden)* and the *Bustan (The Orchard)*, were "published" within a year of each other, and the first impression we receive from his works is of the immense variety of human life which he has managed to observe and record, as well as his seemingly indiscriminate sympathy for any and every kind of person. This sympathy points to another important factor in his work, his repeated references to himself and to incidents from his own life, with the result that the reader has a stronger impression of being addressed by a specific author with a very special personality than is the case with almost any other Persian writer from the "classical" (eleventh century through fifteenth century) period. The reasons for both the variousness of his material and for the reader's strong sense of Sa'di's personality are twofold, arising on the one hand from the nature of Sa'di's life and the times in which he lived, and on the other from his often innovative use of the formal conventions of Persian classical literature.

Despite the fact that Sa'di talks about himself so much in his works we do not know a great deal about the details of his life, as it is virtually certain that many of the incidents he recounts are poetic inventions (for example his being captured by Christians and then ransomed), and this casts doubt on the literal truth of his other stories. He has anecdotes about his closeness to his father as a young boy, and he also claims that he was orphaned at a fairly young age. He says he was educated at the Nezamiyeh college in Baghdad (one of the most famous theological colleges of the medieval Islamic world) and also that he later taught there. He tells us stories about two different marriages, about a son who died, and about travels to as far away as Christendom (after he had been, supposedly, captured), as well as India. All or some or none of these stories may be true; that Sa'di loves to talk about himself as a traveler, and that one of the stories in the first chapter of the *Golestan* tells us not to trust travelers as they tell lies, seems to be his own oblique way of hinting that we should take the anecdotes about his life with a pinch of salt. Two of his claims though do seem wholly true; he was clearly very well educated (and an institution like the Nezamiyeh college would be an obvious place to have received such an education), and his works indicate that he must have traveled widely. The breadth of human sympathy which is almost everywhere evident in his writings clearly comes in part from his travels and observations of many different kinds and conditions of men.

Sa'di lived in particularly turbulent times, and the extremely violent and unstable political and social conditions prevalent in his lifetime had a strong effect on his writings. The work by which he is best known (in the West at least), the *Golestan* (sometimes *Gulistan*), was presented to its dedicatee (a member of the ruling family of Shiraz, Sa'di's hometown) in 1258; this was the year in which the Mongol invasion of South West Asia reached and conquered Baghdad, thus destroying the Abbasid caliphate which had ruled over much of the Islamic world virtually uninterruptedly since the mid eighth century. For almost forty years before this date (that is, for most of Sa'di's life up to this time) the Mongols had been gradually moving down into Iran and Iraq from central Asia, destroying cities, their inhabitants and the infrastructure of civilization (such as irrigation systems) with ferocious and apparently irresistable thoroughness. Shiraz itself was spared, largely due to the astute political maneuvering of the local rulers, but it is no surprise that in his writings Sa'di constantly emphasizes the instability of kingdoms, the violent unpredictability of politics, and the virtues and relative safety of retirement from public life. Much of the advice he freely dispenses in his work is concerned with sheer survival, and he most frequently implies that the best way to ensure this is to make do with a small establishment, out of the way of major historical events. His praise of dignified retirement and his suspicion of court life have led to his being compared by Western writers to the Roman author Horace, with whom he shares many sentiments. Though Sa'di is not a strongly religious writer (his works show a vigorous delight in the details and variety of secular life), he is said to have ended his life as a member of a Sufi (Islamic mystical) organization, and the religious tinge occasionally present in his writings is linked to ideas of retirement and dignified otherworldliness in the face of unstable and often sordid political conditions.

Sa'di has been criticized for the extent to which he did nevertheless compromise with the political realities around him. Like virtually all Persian writers of his period he dedicated works to local and national dignitaries and wrote poems in their praise. The list of dedicatees of his writings includes members of the ruling family in Shiraz as well as members of the Mongol dynasty that eventually destroyed many of this same family, and he wrote poems in praise of both the last Abbasid caliph and of the Mongol conqueror Hulagu who had the caliph murdered. In mitigation it must be said that not to have written poems in praise of, for example, Hulagu after he had written poems in praise of the rulers of Shiraz would have been extremely unwise, and also that some of his praise poems cannot have been written in the hope of gain or political favor (his poem on the last caliph is an elegy written after the caliph's murder and could have been construed as a politically subversive gesture).

In Iran itself, Sa'di is most famous as a lyric poet, but the many profound difficulties involved in translating Persian lyric poetry into Western languages have meant that in the West he is best known for his two collections of anecdotes, the *Bustan* (in verse—narrative verse tends to survive better in translation than lyrical work) and, especially, the *Golestan* (largely in prose but with verses interspersed throughout the text). The *Bustan* was written first, on Sa'di's return to his hometown Shiraz after the extensive travels of his youth. Up until this period long Persian poems had tended to tell one continuous narrative and to be examples of one of three genres: epic, secular romance, or mystical allegory (this last form often consisted of secondary stories contained within an overall frame story; sometimes the frame narrative was absent).

The *Bustan* fits none of these categories, and its form seems to be Sa'di's own modification of the conventions of Persian narrative verse. It represents a final loosening of the form of an anthology of mystical anecdotes, so that although many stories still retain a strong ethical and/or mystical implication they are bound together not by an overall religious dogma or goal but merely by the author's own implied predilections and sympathies. This is one of the main reasons for Sa'di's insistence on his own presence in his text; his poetic personality (which in all likelihood is a constructed fiction—we simply cannot know how similar to the "real" Sa'di is the Sa'di who appears in his works) becomes the chief unifying element of the poem. The work also owes something to the tradition of Mirrors for Princes, a relatively popular medieval Persian form, in that it adduces anecdotes from different cultural traditions for ostensibly moral purposes, but here too the breadth of reference and lack of an overall insistent didactic focus differentiates the *Bustan* from its models. An even more telling distinction, which entirely changes the atmosphere of the narrative, making it far more intimate in feeling, is that in both earlier mystical works and in the Mirrors for Princes, anecdotes are almost always about famous historical or mythological figures—mystics, kings or vizirs already canonized by literary, religious and historical tradition—whereas, although Sa'di does include some stories about such figures, many of his anecdotes are about obscure contemporary private individuals whom he claims to have met on his travels, or simply about himself.

The Bustan

The *Bustan* is a collection of verse anecdotes, divided into ten books. Each anecdote has an appended or implicit moral. The books are named: "On Justice, Prudence and Council"; "On Benevolence"; "On Love and Its Passions"; "On Humility"; "On Acquiescence"; "On Contentment"; "On the World of Education"; "On Gratitude for Health"; "On Repentance and the Right Path"; and "On Prayer, and the Conclusion of the Book."

The disparateness of subject matter implied by the books' headings indicates the breadth of Sa'di's interests, taking the work well beyond the confines of both the court and Sufi groups (the two normal audiences, and thus subject matter, of most Persian verse until Sa'di's time). The moral framework of the *Bustan* also implies an extension and a democratization of interest. Though the moral of a particular anecdote may be quite explicit, taken together the anecdotes and their appended axioms can be

ambiguous or even self-contradictory in their ethical implications (for example, at different moments Sa'di recommends both honesty and dissimulation when dealing with oppressors, as he also recommends both returning evil with mercy and exemplary punishment of evil doers). Though the individual "message" of any given anecdote may be quite clear-cut, the overall, cumulative "message" is that circumstances must modify behavior, that human life is so complex (and inherently interesting) that no absolutes are going to be always applicable.

The Golestan

The *Golestan*, which appeared hard on the heels of the *Bustan*, represents a further easing of the conventions of its apparent models. The mystical aura which still clings to some of the anecdotes of the *Bustan* (especially in book two) has largely disappeared, and the tendency toward a kind of ethical relativism has become even more noticeable. A long anecdote towards the end of the work has Sa'di arguing with a religious mendicant as to the relative merits of poverty and wealth—the argument is rancorously broken off with neither disputant getting the upper hand and a judge advising the two to respect each others' differing opinions; in the last book Sa'di discusses a problem to which he repeatedly returns (whether to kill or be merciful to enemies within your power) and simply says that some say one thing, and some the opposite. That the work is mostly in prose also contributes to its more relaxed atmosphere, as verse in Persian literature is strongly associated with ideal and hyperbolical states, whereas prose can deal more directly with quotidian and incidental matters.

The eight books of the *Golestan* are named: "On the Nature of Kings," "On the Ways of Dervishes," "On the Virtues of Contentment," "On the Advantages of Silence," "On Love and Youth," "On Weakness and Age," "On the Effects of Education," and "On Social Manners."

Many of the anecdotes of the *Golestan* are among the most famous passages of Persian literature, both for the apparently effortless elegance of their style and for the humanity of their sentiments.

Compared with the style of many of his predecessors, the characteristics of Sa'di's writing represent something of a simplification, and this seems on a par with his wider human sympathies, as if he were writing with a broader and less exclusive and highly trained audience in mind. However, this simplification does not by any means entail coarsening or loss of subtlety of nuance, and in fact his style, both in prose and in verse, is considered by Persians to represent a never surpassed perfection of limpid elegance and verbal sophistication. Compared with Western canons of good style Sa'di's works are still written in a highly florid and self-consciously rhetorical medium (for example, his prose in the *Golestan* uses emphatic rhythms, very frequent puns and alliteration, and a great deal of rhyme, so that to a Western ear it often sounds like verse) the incidental effects of which are largely untranslatable; (the closest equivalent to Sa'di's prose in English is perhaps Lyly's *Euphues*, or some of the excessively emotional passages in Burton's *Anatomy of Melancholy*).

The tolerant humanity of Sa'di's usual sentiments is best known by the anecdote (*Bustan*, book two) of Abraham being reproved by God because he has acted inhospitably to a non-Muslim (a Zoroastrian), and by the verses that conclude an anecdote in the first book of the *Golestan* which begin, "The sons of Adam are limbs of one another/ Having been created of one essence" (Rehatsek, trans., 1964). However, it should be noted that despite Sa'di's often expressed sympathy for life's outsiders and victims (he is particularly sensitive to the situation of children, and this concern is almost unique in the works of his time and culture) his sympathy is largely confined to those within the world of Islam (despite the above-mentioned anecdote about the Zoroastrian) and disparaging references to Jews, Christians, and Hindus can be found in his works, which also contain occasional anecdotes that imply contempt for both black slaves and women. It is, of course, pointless to judge him by late-twentieth-century Western standards of what is socially acceptable; nevertheless, given Sa'di's emphatic and often repeated insistence on tolerance, the unity of humanity, and the necessity for mutual respect, such moments in his writings can come as an undeniable shock to the modern reader.

Sa'di's influence on subsequent Persian literature was immense in that his works in prose and verse were almost immediately taken as models by succeeding generations. And this influence was not confined to Iran; his wide frame of reference and his ready sympthay with other Islamic cultures made his works extremely popular both in the Ottoman Empire and in India, and in both these areas he has had many imitators; in general, in countries that have considered Persian culture as a model for their own artistic productions Sa'di has been considered the archetypical Persian author. His widespread popularity in the Ottoman Empire and in India led to his name being known in the West relatively early, and he was one of the first Persian authors to be widely translated into Western languages, beginning with a Latin translation of the *Golestan* in the seventeenth century by Gentius. Sa'di was particularly admired by writers of the European Enlightenment (for example, Voltaire) and by the nineteenth-century American Transcendentalists (such as Emerson).

DICK DAVIS

Further Reading

Translations

Rehatsek, Edward, trans. *The Gulistan or Rose Garden of Sa'di*. Edited with a preface by W. G. Archer. Introduction by G. M. Wickens. London: Geroge Allen & Unwin, 1964. This translation was first published in 1888, but it is still the best translation available; it is in general very accurate, though it makes no attempt to reproduce the style of the original and its translation of the verses that occur in the text is pedestrian.

Wickens, G. M., trans. *Morals Pointed and Tales Adorned*. Leiden: E. J. Brill, 1974. The only available complete translation of the *Bustan*; it is extremely accurate, sometimes to the point that it is difficult to follow the meaning of the English. The translation follows the lineation of the verse in Persian, and the book includes an appendix of very useful notes. Though it is to be highly recommended for its accuracy, it does not, for this very reason, read easily or pleasantly as a narrative in English.

Related Studies

Yohannan, John D. *The Poet Sa'di.* New York: Caravan, 1987. There are many studies of the poet in Persian, but few in other languages; this is the only significant book in English to devote itself entirely to Sa'di.

THE *DIVAN OF HAFEZ*

Author: Hafez (Ḥāfiẓ of Shiraz) (Shams al-Din Mohammad Shirazi)
Born: c. 1325, Shiraz
Died: c. 1390, Shiraz
Literary Form: Poetry
Date of Composition: Probably compiled in late fourteenth century

Major Themes

Seek happiness while you can; fortune is fickle and inconstant.
Earthly glory is bound to fade; do not rely on its illusions.
Reason alone cannot solve the mysteries of existence.
Heed not the hypocrites" empty words, for truth already resides within the lover's heart.
Although the path of love is fraught with danger, the true lover ceaselessly seeks the annihilation of the self in union with the Beloved.

Shams al-Din Mohammad of Shiraz, known as Hafez (Hafiz), occupies a preeminent position in the patheon of Persian poets. The art of poetry was the lifeblood of the classical Persian culture, and the *Divan of Hafez*, his collected poems, is one of its greatest contributions to the world literature. Hafez's verse represents the distilled essence of Persian poetic vision. His words still resonate after centuries, retaining their vitality even today. Not confined to the literati's antiquarianism, the poetry of Hafez illuminates and resides within the hearts of the common men and women of Iran who still recite and find meanings in his words.

Hafez lived in the fourteenth century, one of the many tumultuous periods in the long and troubled history of Iran. As with a majority of Persian poets, there is an unfortunate paucity of historically verifiable information about his life. He was born around 1325 in the southwestern Iranian city of Shiraz, and he died there probably in 1389 or 1390.

According to traditional accounts, the poet's father or the grandfather brought the family to Shiraz, a thriving cultural center then and now. Hafez's father died early and left the family in relative poverty. Yet, Hafez must have received a solid education. His pen name, "Hafez," is the title given to those who have memorized the entire *Koran*, and his verse also gives ample evidence of his erudition in both Arabic and Persian litera-

tures, as well as in all areas of traditional Islamic sciences.

We know from tradition and directly from his verse that Hafez had ties with the ruling dynasties of Shiraz as a court poet. During the poet's lifetime, the city of Shiraz witnessed the rivalry of two local dynasties, bloody transferences of power, and the menace of Tamerlane's meteoric rise in the East.

The poet's relationship with the temporal powers ruling Shiraz must be seen in the context of the position of poets in the medieval Islamic world. Most medieval poets relied on the patronage of the powerful for their livelihood. Hafez served under several rulers, but his relationship with the court was not always favorable.

The dynasty under which the poet served intermittently but all together the longest was that of the Mozaffarids. Mobarez, the first Mozaffarid ruler of Shiraz, was a religious zealot who ordered the closing of taverns and prohibition against anything designed for pleasure. In his poems, Hafez makes references to this period, bemoaning the loss of freedom under religious hypocrisy and censorship. But Mobarez's ruthless rule did not last long; he was deposed, blinded, and replaced by his own son, Shah Shoja, whom Hafez celebrated as the liberator from oppression. It was during the reign of Shah Shoja that Hafez composed most of his mature works and that his fame spread throughout the

Persian-speaking world, as far as India and beyond. But curiously, despite all this, the poet had an uneasy relationship with the ruler and benefitted only sporadically from the court's favor.

Timur, known in the West as Tamerlane, conquered Shiraz and put an end to the Mozaffarids in 1393. Hafez did not live long enough to see this event, but a famous, if apocryphal, episode describes the encounter between the ferocious conqueror and the aged poet.

In one of his most famous poetic passages, Hafez had mentioned the two central Asian cities dear to Timur: "If that Shirazi Turk would take my heart into her hands/For her Hindu mole, I would bestow both Samerkand and Bukhara." According to the tale, Timur summoned Hafez to punish him for his temerity in treating Timur's prized cities in such a cavalier fashion. To this charge, Hafez answered that it was precisely such foolish generosity that led him to his present ruin. Delighted by this quick response, Timur is said to have richly rewarded the old poet instead of punishing him as he had first intended.

The Ghazal

Like many of his contemporaries, Hafez had to rely on patronage for his work. Thus, he was in part a court poet and a panegyrist, but what sets him apart and distinguishes his *Divan* is his mastery of the lyric form known as the *ghazal*. Sometimes translated as "sonnet," the ghazal is a relatively short poetic form, normally of five to twelve lines, though it could be longer. Each line, called the *beyt*, is composed of a couplet or two hemistich of equal length. Each beyt has an identical meter, and the same end-rhyme is repeated throughout, except for the first beyt, in which the rhyme also occurs at the end of the first hemistich. Thus the basic rhyme pattern of a ghazal follows the scheme, a-a, b-a, c-a, d-a, and so forth. Another conventional feature of a ghazal is the *takhallus*, the poet's pen name, woven into the final beyt of the poem.

By the time of Hafez, the ghazal was already established as the predominant poetic form, having superseded the longer form known as the *qasideh*

in which panegyric court poetry had typically been written. Hafez also wrote some qasideh and in other poetic forms, but their number is insignificant compared to his ghazals.

As the supreme practitioner of the lyric form, Hafez inherited from his predecessors at least two distinct but interrelated currents within the Persian poetic tradition. One was the secular poetic tradition, encompassing the court poetry and the lyrics of earthly love. The other was the tradition of religious poetry inspired by Sufi mysticism. The lyric ghazal was often the chosen medium for both kinds of poetry, since it was best suited for the expressions of a poet's inner passion, whether religious or secular.

What characterizes the ghazals by Hafez is the highly subtle synthesis of the mystical and the secular which results in the hermeneutic ambiguities of his works. Many of his verses cross over the genres of panyrgeric, lyric, and mystical poetry; and the beloved, longed for by the poet, can represent the monarch, the earthly lover, or the Divine, either simultaneously or separately, depending on one's interpretation.

Interpreting Hafez

The interpreters of Hafez often disagree among themselves whether a given poem is intended to be read mystically or not. The mystical content is undoubtedly there, as in the opening beyts of a well-known ghazal:

For years my heart has sought from me the cup of Jamshid;
it sought from a stranger that which it already possessed.

It sought for the pearl beyond the shell of time and space
from the lost ones stranded at the edge of the shore. . . .

The cup of Jamshid and the pearl symbolize mystical wisdom and truth. The object of the quest, the poet contends, already lies within the seeker, although one's blindness often prevents one from seeing this truth.

Yet, while much of his works provide fertile ground for mystical and allegorical readings, there are others that are unabashedly secular in nature. The shifts from the secular to the mystical and visa versa in his ghazals are often seamlessly fluid and can occur even within a single verse. Western critics confronted with this multivalence of the Hafezian verse have often pointed out the lack of unity in his works. Hafez's ghazal has been compared by such critics to a string of brilliant oriental pearls, with no apparent overall design connecting the individual beyts.

The concern for an overall unity seems to be a peculiarly Western preoccupation. It is true that in a ghazal a single motif is seldom sustained throughout the poem, but the apparent lack of discursive unity does not necessarily undermine the poem as an organic whole. A ghazal can achieve its unity through its sustained rhythm and mood. The musical paradigm for the ghazal's organicism has been suggested by Ehsan Yarshater in his essay on the affinities between Persian poetry and music. Various other scholars have shown that rhetorical devices, allegorical tropes, and the complex interweaving of related motifs and image-clusters provide the Hafezian ghazal with its underlying structural and thematic unity.

The Rend

There are number of themes to which Hafez returns again and again throughout his *Divan*. Whether as a nightingale in love with the perfect rose or as a moth enamored with the flame that will consume and destroy it, the poet extols the true path of love and longs for union with the beloved. Before the ultimate truth of love, worldly wealth and power are exposed as illusions:

Come! For the castle of desire rests on weak foundation!
Bring forth the wine! For the root of life rests upon the wind!

As in this opening beyt of one of his ghazals, Hafez constantly warns against the danger of clinging to false desires and the vanity of the world.

His attitude towards life is best represented by the concept of the *rend* that ran through his poetry. An adequate one-word translation of this term is difficult to find. Sometimes translated as "libertine" or "free spirit," a *rend* is above all a true lover, a path-seeker and a devotee whose devotion to the true path has liberated such a person from all worldly illusions and all forms of falsity. For Hafez, the union with the beloved is the final act of liberation. The spirit becomes truly liberated through the annihilation of the egoistic "self." His intoxication is with the spiritual, but to the eyes of the uninitiated his behavior can appear wild and sometimes even heretical.

Hafez celebrated the *rend* and the spirituality that leads to liberation and freedom, and he despised hypocrisy and oppression perpetrated in the name of religion. Hafez can also be a supreme satirist. Many lines mocking the sanctimonious ascetic, religious censor, and false mystic can be found throughout his *Divan*.

KATSUYO MOTOYOSHI

Further Reading

Translations

Translations in this article are by Katsuyo Motoyoshi.

Arberry, A. J., trans. *Fifty Poems of Hafiz.* Surrey: Curzon Press, 1993 (originally published in 1947). A collection of works by various translators. The introduction by Arberry is still very useful.

Bell, Gertrude, trans. *Teachings of Hafiz.* London: The Octagon Press, 1979 (originally published in 1897). Antiquated and impressionistic translations, but Bell succeeds in capturing some of Hafez's original mood.

Boylan, Michael, trans. *Hafez: Dance of Life.* Washington, D.C.: Magc Publishers, 1987. Charmingly illustrated translation of seven ghazals. The original Persian, transliterated in the back of the book, is helpful for those curious about the music of the original.

Clarke, Wilberforce, trans. *The Divan.* New York: Samuel Weiser, 1970 (originally published in 1891). Antiquated but still useful prose translation of the complete *Divan.*

Gray, Elizabeth, trans. *The Green Sea of Heaven.* Ashland, Oregon: White Cloud Press, 1995. Contemporary translation that does an admirable job preserving the compact brevity of the original beyts.

Related Studies

Browne, E. G. *A Literary History of Persia.* 4 vols. Cambridge: Cambridge University Press, 1969 (originally published in 1920). Still the standard reference, Browne's history will help readers locate Hafez's position in the context of his literary tradition.

Chittick, William. *The Sufi Path of Knowledge.* Albany: SUNY Press, 1989, and *The Sufi Path of Love.* Albany: SUNY Press, 1985. Chittick's works are excellent introductions to the Islamic mystical tradition.

Hillman, Michael. *Unity in the Ghazals of Hafiz. Studies in Middle Eastern Literatures*, No. 6. Minneapolis and Chicago: Bibiliotheca Islamica, 1976. A thorough treatment of the problem of unity in the Hafezean ghazals.

Meisami, Julie Scott. "Allegorical Techniques in the Ghazals of Hafiz." In *Edebiyat*, 4.1 (1979) : pp. 1–40.

———. "The World's Pleasance: Hafiz's Allegorical Gardens." In *Comparative Criticism*, 5 (1983): pp. 153–85. Julie Scott Meisami has written a series of innovative articles on Persian poetry using the critical tools of recent literary scholarship.

Yarshater, Ehsan. "Affinities Between Persian Poetry and Music." In *Studies in the Art and Literature of the Near East.* Edited by Peter Chelkowski. Pp. 59–78. Salt Lake City and New York: University of Utah and New York University, 1974. Insightful article, presenting a musical paradigm for the understanding of Persian poetry.

MUQADDIMAH

Title in Arabic: *Muqaddimah* (*Introduction* or *Prolegomena*)
Author: Ibn Khaldūn ('Abd ar-Rahman Abu Zayd ibn Muhammad ibn Muhammad ibn Khaldūn)
Born: 1332, Tunis
Died: 1406, Cairo, Egypt
Literary Form: Essay on the principles of history, and on the formation, rise, and fall of societies and civilizations
Date of Composition: Completed 1377

Major Ideas

The core of leadership, the state, and civilization is 'asabiya *(group solidarity).*
Geography, climate, and food source decide both the human body (color, stamina, intellect) and character.
The writing of history must include all the factors that influence whatever is under investigation; thus the historian must have wide and varied knowledge.
History is an eternal cycle.
History addresses the origin and operation of human culture.

Scholars have yet to decide whether Ibn Khaldun was a philosopher, political scientist, historian, historiographer, sociologist, or encyclopedic scholar generalizing about the rise and fall of civilizations—all or none of these. The scope of his *Muqaddimah* (*Introduction [to History]*) and his *Kitab al-'Ibar* (*Book of Examples*) is so wide and diverse that researchers have many choices of categories in which to place Ibn Khaldun's work, a multiplicity of ideas to emphasize, and innumerable assertions to critique. Remarkably, in the West very little attention is given to any aspect of Ibn Khaldun's thought. In Ibn Khaldun's era the social sciences and humanities had not been delineated as they are today. Therefore there are limits to the criteria of scholarship that we can hold him accountable for in these disciplines.

In the scholarship of his time, historical writing had a certain form, as did philosophy and science. Ibn Khaldun's discourse on civilization portrayed the human being as a product of nature rather than of nurture. He was concerned with discovering and elaborating the order that operates in society. The discussion of what he discovered also follows the path of philosophical inquiry as he seeks to provide answers to questions revolving around the connec-

tions between truth, knowledge, faith, and the nature of the universe.

Ibn Khaldun's elaboration of what he discovered about the order that operates in society also allowed the path of theoretical sociological concerns. He saw the individual, in contrast to the view held by Rousseau, as a product of the natural environment and, contrary to Kant's conception, as incapable of moral self-direction. Religion regulates humanity through obligation and law, while scientific or rational knowledge explains casualty. Ibn Khaldun considered himself a truth-teller of the facts of history, but this writing of history previsions the sciences of historiography, sociology, ethnology, and postmodern geography in both its focus and its scope.

Data are chosen from available historical sources and the author's personal experience of existing regimes and societies. There is a series of presumptions in place, the major assertion being that the sequences of stages through which societies, nations, and civilizations pass is similar. He proposes a methodology that proceeds in part from a number of generalizations which he attempts to support by numerous examples.

Theories on how societies are organized are, of

course, older than Ibn Khaldun. However, for him these approaches—especially those of Mulsim historians—are deficient in their presumptions of truth and accuracy. The history of individuals is important only in as much as the individuals contribute to the history of larger groups of which they are parts—prophets, diviners, magicians.

As a social scientist, Ibn Khaldun reported what particular events meant in their particular settings. He interpreted the meaning of data by reference to concepts he regarded as authoritative—the Qur'an, the law, his personal experiences, and related historical writings he could verify by cross-reference.

All of this and more is to be found in his *Muqaddimah* and his encyclopedic history *Kitab al-'Ibar* (*The Book of Examples*). For his effort to formulate a text of accurate accounts of nations and civilizations, Ibn Khaldun became known as "*the* historian" of his time and as the historiographer of medieval North African and Arab Islamic culture. The discussion of whether his ideas will maintain their status as the progenitors of modern social theory is only now beginning.

Ibn Khaldun

Ibn Khaldun was born on May 27, 1332, in Tunis, into an aristocratic, politically connected family. He was first tutored in the traditional manner in the Qur'an, the Hadith, jurisprudence, Arabic poetry, and Arabic grammar by scholars living in Tunis. The plague of the fourteenth century claimed the lives of his parents. By the age of twenty Ibn Khaldun was living in the midst of the chaotic politics of North Africa and serving as a recording secretary for the government. The fortunes of many families in North Africa arose and fell with the political tide, leaving most with status but few with means. It has been suggested that Ibn Khaldun left Tunis because he did not have the backing to move into a higher position, moving to Fez, Morocco, where he initially lived for eight years (1354–62). Having acquired a taste for political life, Ibn Khaldun joined the court of Abu 'Inan and then found himself imprisoned for either treachery or treason for two years until the king's

death. His political adventures resulted in a series of higher-level appointments in the government but ended in intrigue as his fate again was decided by the murder of the king.

Living the nomadic life as a self-styled diplomat to various tribes occupied Ibn Khaldun from about 1365 to 1374. It was apparently during these years that he gained his understanding of tribal life and the peace to increase the pace of his continuous education. Evidence of his scholarly endeavors is contained in several minor treatises he wrote during that time. In very much the same way as the cycles of history he described, the cycles of his own life are apparent, since once again political dispute caused him to take off for Cairo. His proven ability to ingratiate himself with the governing body was apparent in the court in Cairo, where he quickly obtained a position as a Maliki judge—an assignment to which he was reappointed four times. Cairo proved to be a ripe atmosphere for all of Ibn Khaldun's pursuits. Besides being occupied with his judgeship he taught a wide range of subjects and finished writing his "history."

To say that Cairo was Ibn Khaldun's last stand is probably accurate. Though his wife and five daughters died in a shipwreck while coming to join him in Cairo, his two sons (of whom we know little) survived. His life in Cairo was full of the political intrigue, discord, and personal upheaval he had known throughout his life. When he died he left behind him a considerable number of enemies, some students, and a few friends and family members.

The Muqaddimah

The Muqaddimah (*Prolegomena*), for which Ibn Khaldun is best known, is actually the introduction to his "history," the *Kitab al-'Ibar* (*Book of Examples*). In the *Prologomena* he formulates his basic theories of history. First, he registers his complaints against the past and contemporary writing of history. Next he outlines how an historical narrative should be undertaken: The historian must investigate (1) the conditions affecting the nature of civilization, (2) the factors that influence historical information, and (3) what is necessary and what are accidental occurrences in human social organization.

After Ibn Khaldun has carefully laid out the premises for historical examination, he proceeds to look at the evolution of various civilizations, their rise and demise, with a particular look at the North African Muslim states and their religious foundation and institutions.

While the aim of this work is enormous and almost impossible to achieve, Ibn Khaldun succeeded in inducing a wrinkle in the smooth fabric of the epistemology of his time by introducing ideas that continue to form some aspects of our understanding of human social organization.

Problems in the Writing of History

According to Ibn Khaldun, there are three categories of historical narrators—historians, Qur'an commentators, and transmitters. Careful critical examination of their texts reveals frequent errors, he argues. The causes of these errors are threefold: "negligence or ignorance of the legitimate process of historical writing," lack of comparative analysis, and an under-use of the critical tools of philosophy.

Ibn Khaldun points to several examples of defective narratives that would profit from critical inquiry. He refers to al-Mas'udi and many other historians who reported that Moses counted the army of the Israelites in the desert—and the number is said to have been 600,000 or more. In this connection, Ibn Khaldun writes, "al-Mas'udi forgets to take into consideration whether Egypt and Syria could possibly have held such a number of soldiers."

Ibn Khaldun asserts that when the historian writes in a vacuum the results are often filled with exaggerations, sensationalisms, and lies. In a direct attack on his contemporaries, he chastises them also for their lack of critical self-reflection. He exhorts them to an ethical standard that includes moderation and fairness in reporting. Beyond the fact that historians must be critical, comparative, and self-reflective, they must also be aware of the influences that affect the information they gather and of the contingencies that beset civilizations. Historians cannot blindly trust any source, nor can

they rely uncritically on the faithfulness of transmitters, who are often unaware of the contexts of events. Ibn Khaldun's conditions for the responsible study and recording of human social organizations are two: (1) knowledge of the nature of civilization, and (2) consideration of conformity with other known conditions.

Human Social Organization

History, Ibn Khaldun contends, is information about human social organization, about civilization. Human beings organize themselves into communities out of necessity. The necessity arises out of the qualities instilled in all persons by God. God created humankind and distinguished them from the other animals by their ability to think. In spite of their God-given qualities, solitary human beings are unable to defend themselves or to provide for their sustenance: social organization is necessary if these ends are to be secured. Whether a human community becomes a nation and then a dynasty depends on several factors, including geography, climate, and food source, and on whether these factors and others relate to the essence of civilization or are accidental.

Examining the world from available scientific data and confirmable historical narratives, Ibn Khaldun divides the world into zones. In very cold and very hot regions there is little civilization, but where the heat is temperate there is correspondingly an average degree of civilization, while where there is moderate coolness, there is the greatest degree of civilization. Communities develop forms of living and personality traits based on the zones they occupy. A community's ability to develop the degree of group solidarity necessary to become a power is based primarily upon these geographic factors.

Ibn Khaldun also argues that skin, eye, and hair color find their causes in the climate. The climate also determines the primary distinctions between races, as well as the general characteristics of their customs. The availability of food and seasonings determines whether the community develops the receptivity necessary for a prophet to emerge from among them. Ibn Khaldun's review of history leads him to affirm that prophecy occurs in communities where there is powerful group solidarity ('*asabiya*) and privation. The example Ibn Khaldun cites to illustrate these points is the Bedouin. The Bedouins are one of the primary groups in the history of peoples. Their mode of living is restricted to agriculture and animal husbandry, thus creating a life style that revolves around necessity. Their group solidarity is well formed, and their tempers are savage but amenable to royal authority and prophecy. Their nature encourages and even mandates courage, trust, and a well-developed sense of defense. Group solidarity is established over generations because of the homogeneity of these isolated communities and the emergence of strong leaders.

The Role of Prophecy in the Muslim State

Explanations of the role of prophecy and prophetic narrations on the rise of demise of various Muslim dynasties were of obvious concern to Ibn Khaldun. In contrast to most Muslim scholars, Ibn Khaldun asserts that prophecy is not necessary even though the messages of the prophets are "intrinsically and necessarily true." Prophecy is a link created by God between Himself and His Creation to "lead humanity to that which is correct." Prophecy is further differentiated from soothsaying and magic by its inspiration and the special qualities created in the constitutions of those who become prophets.

Prophets are special because they are specially chosen by God to know Him and thereby be obligated to model what is good for the community and to guide it. Confirmation of the particular nature of prophets has been observed in a continuous fashion throughout history through the presence of distinctive signs. These signs include remoteness from the present, prior reputations as good and trustworthy men, constancy in the methods used to spread religion, prestige in their communities, and the miracles they perform. The greatest of the miracles in the history of prophecy is the Qur'an revealed to Prophet Muhammad ibn Abdullah of Arabia. The proof of this is found in the inimitability of the Qur'anic recitation. The aim of the guidance to be

found there is to direct the human soul to spiritual perfection. There are three kinds of human souls: those that are very weak and limited in their knowledge, those who are drawn toward "spiritual intellection," and those of the prophets that are by nature "suited to exchange humanity altogether . . . for angelicality. . . ."

The Rise and Demise of States

The degree of group solidarity is pivotal to nation-building and the construction of civilizations, Ibn Khaldun maintains. Group solidarity undergirds leadership and dynasties. The state as an entity is the goal of group solidarity. In the Muslim world the first state was under the authority of Prophet Muhammad. As the ideal state, prophecy sat in its center, religion bound the supporters, and though the dynasty spread beyond the original group solidarity, the power was evident, and since the rule was just, it had loyal supporters. After the death of Prophet Muhammad, the authority was invested in a series of men whose collective rule is known as the caliphate. The caliphate drew its authority from its charge to act as a replacement for the Prophet in maintaining the tenets of religion and exercising political leadership.

Ibn Khaldun argues that those dynasties whose reaches are everywhere have their group solidarity in religion based on prophesy or "truthful propaganda." This accounts for the swift spread of Islam. Each state within the caliphate, though bound by religion, was subject to the cycles of history; the greatness of a dynasty, which is dependent on how far it spreads and the number of its supporters, does not alter its life span. The life span of a dynasty is three generations.

In the first generation there is the building of strong group solidarity. Community members of that generation are tough, savage, respectful of one another, used to privation, well-developed in strength and with enough power so that others submit to them.

Within the second generation natural competitiveness forces an authority to emerge. The resultant order, allows a life of relative ease to evolve, especially for the leadership. Ibn Khaldun says that as the rest of the community gets lazy, they simultaneously yearn for the group solidarity of the first generation.

By the time of the third generation, the characteristics of the group solidarity of the first generation are forgotten. The community can no longer defend itself and depends on the force of the authority to defend is. Group solidarity is no longer evident, and the dynasty begins a predicted demise. Ibn Khaldun implies that the homeogeneity characteristic of the first generation is lost in the spread of the dynasty and has something to do with its fall.

By the fourth generation, there are only narrations of past glory.

The *Muqaddimah* elaborates each of the previously mentioned claims in great detail and critiques even the methods of instruction to reveal deficiencies. The *'Ibar* provides even more detail on the order that operates in human social organization. The former book includes the discussion of civilization and its principles, while the latter book attempts to ferret out the order and fate of various races and nations. The history of the Berbers dominates the *'Ibar* along with a history of the courts of the Maghrib. Ibn Khaldun also attached to the *'Ibar* an autobiography that had only recently been compiled.

AMINAH BEVERLY MCCLOUD

Further Reading

Translation

Dawood, N. J., ed. *Ibn Khaldun: The Muqaddimah, an Introduction to History*. Franz Rosenthal, trans. Princeton, NJ: Princeton University Press, 1967. The best English translation of the *Muqaddimah*. Selections. (A three-volume edition of Rosenthal's complete translation was published in New York, Pantheon, 1958, and in London, Routledge and Kegan Paul, 1959.) An accurate translation that endeavors to illuminate the major portions of the work by providing careful translations of salient nuances that are usually lost in translations. Quotations in this article are from this edition.

Related Studies

Baali, Fuad. *Social Institutions: Ibn Khaldun's Social Thought*. Lanham, MD: University Press of America, 1992.

———. *Society, State, and Urbanism: Ibn Khaldun's Sociological Thought*. Albany, NY: State University of New York Pres, 1988.

Lascoste, Yves. *Ibn Khaldun: The Birth of History and the Past of the Third World*. London: Verso, 1984.

THE POETRY AND PROSE OF JĀMĪ

Author: Nur al-Din 'Abd al-Raḥmān Jami
Born: 1414, in the district of Jam, in Iran
Died: 1492, in Herat, in Afghanistan.
Major Works: *The Seven Thrones* (includes "Salaman and Absal" and "Joseph and Zuleikha"), *Baharistan (The Garden in Spring)*

Major Theme

One must purify the soul of attachment to the world in order that it be reunited with the Divine.

Jami is commonly referred to as the last of the great medieval Persian poets. Though his style remained immensely popular during subsequent centuries and was frequently imitated, the intellectual bases of his poetry—traditional Islamic (Sunni) and Naqshbandi Sufi lore—all but disappeared as potent forces in Persian life with the triumph of Shi'ism shortly after Jami's death (Shi'ism became the state religion of Iran in 1501 with the accession to power of the Safavid dynasty). The new intellectual and spiritual climate fostered by this dynasty proved much less conducive to the kind of poetic tradition in which Jami had grown up—one that had combined in a highly ambiguous fashion abstract mystical speculation with quasi-erotic narrative, and Jami is thus the last major representative of a poetic heritage which began in the twelfth century with the mystical poet Sanai.

Jami's name is taken from the area in which he was born, in Khorasan in northwestern Iran. As a child he displayed astonishing intellectual precocity as well as a formidably accurate memory. His early education was undertaken by his father, and though due to the great promise he showed he was sent to the best available teachers connected with the nearby court of Herat, he later said that he owed to his father all he had learned. Apart from a journey to the Hejaz and participation in the pilgrimage to Mecca he lived virtually all of his long life in Herat, where he was from an early age singled out for patronage and favor by the local aristocracy. As regards outward events, his story is a rare and happy one in the annals of Persian poets, and perhaps poets anywhere; for all his adult life he was regarded as one of the most brilliant men of his age; he was almost universally praised and never lived in want or had to search for patronage; when he finally died, peacefully and at a ripe old age, his funeral was attended by the most illustrious men of the area, including the local prince.

Jami was an extremely prolific author, producing a large number of works in both prose and verse. His learning is everywhere evident in these; there is hardly a significant Persian poet whose work was available to him on whom he does not draw for inspiration or as a model, and he also includes much theological, metaphysical, and speculative lore in his writings, as well as devoting whole works to the lives and writings of his predecessors. He was particularly drawn to Sufi (mystical) writers and teachers, and one of his books, the *Nafhat al Ons* ("The Breath of Intimacy") is a series of hagiographical sketches on the lives of dead Sufis; another is a commentary on the works of the mystical poet Eraqi, and he includes much literary criticism in other works (in the *Baharestan*, for example, one chapter is devoted to poets and their writings). His criticism is extremely valuable as indicating the literary criteria of his time, and can occasionally be quite harsh (for example, he takes the great poet Hafez to task for mistakes in versification). His very wide learning pervades his own poetry, which can be said at times to "smell of the lamp," in that his desire to demonstrate his encylopedic knowledge, as well as his mastery of poetic techniques, sometimes leads him to forget the matter supposedly in hand.

In many of his works there is evident a clear

desire to write with a particular literary model in mind (this is most frequently a work by Nezami, though he also utilizes works by Hafez, Sanai, Sa'di and others in this manner) and then to outdo the model in every possible way. His occasional choice of rare and difficult meters is another indication of his desire to demonstrate his special mastery. In the opinion of many critics, however, Jami's virtuosity can backfire against him; Sa'di's verse, for example, has been characterized as having a "difficult simplicity" (it appears simple but such simplicity is very hard to reproduce), whereas Jami's has been accused of having a "simple difficulty" (it looks extremely complex, but much of the complexity comes from the deployment of a few basic tropes, like exhaustively mining the possibilities of far-fetched puns, and these are not hard to imitate if a skillful poet puts his mind to it). This searching for rather outré linguistic effects was to be influential on the later *sabk-e hindi* (Indian style) poets writing in Persian, as was his occasional mention of "unpoetic" utilitarian objects in his verse. This latter habit sometimes gives his lines a sudden realism that can be very refreshing when surrounded by so much earnest but often nebulous mysticism (for example, it is in his works that the first mention of spectacles in Persian occurs, when Jami mentions himself as wearing them; he calls them "European glasses" (*shisheh-ye farangi*).

Jami's religious allegiances were pronounced and orthodox. He was a Sunni Muslim, of the Hanafi school, and regarded Shi'ism with a distaste that bordered at times on loathing (he would certainly have regretted the advent of the Shi'i Safavid dynasty had he lived to see it). His Sunni Islamic beliefs were supplemented by his membership of the Naqshbandi order of Sufis. The Naqshbandis particularly revered the memory and works of Ibn Arabi, and the strong strain of quasi neo-Platonism to be found in many of Jami's works (though this was in a diluted form part of the stock in trade of most Persian mystical poets) was probably reinforced by the poet's reading of Ibn Arabi. Despite his prominence in the order, Jami always refused formally to become a Sufi "sheikh" (a spritual

leader who accepts acolytes for instruction and guidance) saying "I could not bear the burden of being a sheikh."

Though he wrote poetry easily and fluently all his life (he claims in the introduction to his lyrical works that he found it extremely difficult not to write verse and that the urge to do so gave him no rest), the works on which his chief fame rests were all written relatively late in his career. These are the two narrative poems "Salaman and Absal" (written when the poet was in his sixties) and "Joseph and Zuleikha" (completed when he was sixty-nine)—repectively the second and fifth of his collection of such poems called *The Seven Thrones*— and the *Baharestan*, a prosimetrum (mixture of prose and verse), completed when he was seventy-three.

The story of Salaman and Absal had already been treated by Ibn Sina (Avicenna) and by the ethical philospher Nasr ad-Din Tusi, but Jami's treatment is a tour de force that goes far beyond anything his predecessors had done with the tale. It seems typical of Jami that he should be drawn to a story which to many might seemed to be flawed by an inherent lack of realism. His learned and theological interests, together perhaps with his uniformly comfortable and secure life, made him a poet who lived very far removed from the concerns of most people, and if any poet has ever deserved the description of an "ivory tower" writer, Jami is that poet.

"Salaman and Absal"

The plot of Salaman and Absal is as follows: A Greek king wishes for a son, but he has a horror of sexual relations. His minister tells him that he knows of a secret way in which the king's seed can be grown into a child without the benefit of a woman's womb (at this point a long diatribe against women is put in the mouth of the minister; this is the best known example of the topos in Persian poetry). Artificial conception is achieved and the boy Salaman is the result. He is given to a nurse called Absal who dotes on the boy, and as he grows to adolescence she falls in love with him. Finally, she seduces him. Fearing the king's wrath, the lovers flee to "The Island of Bliss," where they spend their time in amorous play. The king, however, possess a cup (the mythical "Goblet of Jamshid" which is mentioned in other Persian poems, including Ferdowsi's *Shahnameh*) which will show him anything that he wishes to see. By means of this cup he locates the lovers; he concentrates his will against them and by his mental power he is able to prevent Salaman from physically approaching Absal. Salaman and Absal decide to die together and fling themselves into a fire; the fire, however, consumes only Absal; Salaman emerges purified of all earthly attributes and desires. He grieves for his dead beloved but is gradually cured of this, and is crowned king.

The poem is clearly an allegory, and Jami concludes the work by explaining its symbolism; the king represents the intellect, the minister represents Divine Grace, Salaman is the soul, and Absal is the body. The difference from the allegories of Nezami, on which it is modeled, lies in the fact that it works only on the symbolic level (as a tale about real people it is obviously far too improbable to be taken seriously), whereas Nezami's allegories move with a wonderful ease between humanistic realism and symbolically presented mystical exhortation. The relentlessly symbolic nature of Jami's writing means that it almost entirely lacks human interest; strangely enough, what human interest there is centers on the figure of Absal, the nurse who is finally sacrificed in order that Salaman be purified of carnal needs. That is, the one figure Jami invites us to be interested in on the human level represents all that he wishes us to condemn according to the poem's allegorical scheme; this deliberate rejection of the fallible and human in favor of the metaphysical and—in the poem's terms—the perfect, is typical of his work.

"Joseph and Zuleikha"

The plot of Joseph and Zuleikha is taken from the Koran's story of Joseph, which is very similar to the story of Joseph and Potiphar's wife as re-counted in the Bible. The story is treated in explicitly allegorical fashion. Joseph represents the Divine Beauty, Zuleikha represents the human soul, while her love for Joseph represents that soul's longing for union with the Divine. The poem opens with Adam in love with Joseph before the latter descends into his corporeal form, and the love of his father Jacob is also represented as this individual's longing for the Divine rather than as simple paternal emotion. Zuleikha has dreamed of Joseph long before he arrives in Egypt, and has fallen in love with this dreamt image. However, she marries Pharaoh's minister, who is unable to consummate their marriage. The symbolism of her preexisting love for Joseph and her present marriage to the impotent minister is clear; the soul longs for the unseen Divine but is tied to the apparently splendid (her husband's position), but in reality useless (his impotence) world. When Joseph is sold into slavery by his brothers she buys him and makes one attempt after another to seduce him. Her blandishments are unsuccessful, though she almost succeeds after threatening to commit suicide. Joseph is about to succumb when he notices a curtain which Zuleikha says hides an idol; she has drawn the curtain so that it may not witness their lovemaking. Joseph shrinks back from her with the comment that she hides her sin from her idol but is shameless before the gaze of God. The pair go through many adventures, including that of the false accusation made against Joseph by Zuleikha as recounted in the Bible and the Koran. After this the two are separated; Joseph eventually becomes Pharaoh's minister (Zuleikha's husband has conveniently died), by which time Zuleikha is old and blind. They rediscover one another, marry, die, and are united in heaven.

Jami's version of this story, one of the most famous of Islamic narratives, has many similarities to his "Salaman and Absal." Both poems are love stories in which the central character, a chaste and supremely beautiful youth, is seduced by a persistent woman, and this leads to an apparent disaster that nevertheless ends in a happy conclusion. Both stories are allegories of the soul's relations with the world and with God; the difference lies in the fact that whereas the woman in "Salaman and Absal" represents the body, in "Joseph and Zuleikha" she represents the human soul, and whereas the beautiful Salaman represents the human soul, the beautiful Joseph represents the Divine for which the soul longs. Both poems are also characterized by a pronounced distaste for heterosexual sex (the Greek king's dislike of it, Salaman's and Joseph's chastity), which verges on outright misogyny, coupled with extremely sensual language at the appropriate moments (the scene of Zuleikha's almost successful seduction of Joseph is, given the time and culture in which it was written, extraordinarily explicit in its physical description).

The Baharistan

The *Baharistan* ("The Garden in Spring") was written in 1487 when Jami was seventy-three. The work is an imitation of Sa'di's *Golestan* ("The Rose Garden"), to which the author claimed it was superior. Both are collections of prose anecdotes gathered into books, each of which is concerned with a single theme; both are highly didactic, and both contain interspersed verses. Jami includes much more verse than Sa'di. The work has (for Jami) a relative simplicity and this is perhaps due to the fact that it was written as an instruction manual for the poet's young son. This paternal simplicity, and a certain mellowness which may perhaps be attributed to the poet's age when he wrote the book, has made it one of the most popular of his works. One of its most interesting features for the modern reader is the discussion of poetry and former poets in book seven.

DICK DAVIS

Further Reading

Translations

FitzGerald, Edward, trans. *Salaman and Absal*. London: Bernard Quaritch, 1879. This verse translation, like FitzGerald's versions of *The Rubaiyat of Omar Khayyam* and Attar's *The Bird Parliament*, takes considerable liberties with the original (as always, FitzGerald makes extensive cuts), but does succeed in conveying much of the atmosphere of Jami's poem. It is most successful in the philosophical passages. First published in 1856, and then published in a much revised form in 1879.

Arberry, A. J., trans. *FitzGerald's Salaman and Absal, a Study.* Cambridge, England: Cambridge University Press. 1959. This book also includes Arberry's own version of the poem, which is the best and most accurate available.

Rogers, Alexander, trans. *The Book of Joseph and Zuleikha, a Historical Romantic Persian Poem.* London, 1892. This verse translation (into heroic couplets, a form close to that of the original) occasionally rises above the competent though its rather fustian diction can make it hard going; it omits very little and is reasonably accurate.

Pendlebury, David, ed. and trans. *Yusuf and Zulaikha*. Abridged. London, 1980. This prose version reads easily and has considerable charm; however, it misses out a great deal of the poem and this renders the allegory of the poem even more obscure than it is in the original.

Rehatsek, Edward, trans. *The Beharistan*. London, 1887. The best translation in English of any work by Jami. It is an accurate and scrupulous translation of the whole text; it translates the verse interspersed at various points in the text as prose.

THE WORKS OF ṬĀHĀ-ḤUSAYN

Author: Ṭāhā-Ḥusayn
Born: 1889, ʿIzbat al-Kīlū, near Maghāgha, Upper Egypt
Died: 1973, Cairo, Egypt
Major Works: [Autobiography] (1927, 1932, 1955), *Recalling Abū al-ʿAlāʾ [al- Maʿarrī]* (1914), *On Pre-Islamic Poetry* (1925), *The Future of Culture in Egypt* (1938), *The Call of the Karawān* (1942)

Major Themes

Religion has no part to play in modern government.
In learning from the West, Muslims are following the example of their forefathers.
Egypt is not an Oriental, but rather a Mediterranean, country.
Classical Arabic literature offers rich material for modern study.

Taha-Husayn is often regarded as the most representative thinker and writer of a generation caught at a turning point of Arab cultural history. The Arabic-speaking countries have a rich heritage, at the heart of which is a holy book that offers a code of conduct affecting every aspect of life. The bedrock of their literature was a corpus of magnificent odes that antedates Islam by at least a hundred years, and pride in this poetry combined with the dogma that the Koran is the actual, and therefore untranslatable, word of God to give the language a sacrosanct status and an extremely conservative character. A large number of regional spoken forms soon branched out of it, but only compositions in the classical language earned recognition as literature.

In time, Arab/Islamic civilization lost a great deal of its intellectual impetus and actual power, and its territories attracted the expansionist aims of Western European nations. During the nineteenth century and the first quarter of the twentieth, virtually all were subjugated. Foreign ascendancy was resented by all, but the means by which this ascendancy was made possible roused envy and grudging admiration, and a growing number of educated Arabs saw in emulation of the West the best promise of reassertion. Egypt, first targeted by the Bonaparte expedition in 1798, then put under British tutelage in 1882, was at the forefront of this new direction, and Taha Husayn was to be one of its most energetic guides.

Taha-Husayn's Early Years

Taha-Husayn was born to a large provincial family of modest means, and at the age of two, as a result of ophthalmia and the crude treatment available, he lost his eyesight. He attended the local Koranic school, then in 1902 he was sent to the ancient University of al-Azhar in Cairo where an elder brother had preceded him. He had some contact with adherents of its great Reformist rector, Shaykh Muhammad ʿAbduh (1849–1905), but was loudly critical of the institution's conservatism, and in 1912 was denied its degree.

Taha had in fact gravitated towards the circles of more open-minded intellectuals, and attracted attention as a writer of pugnacious articles in their papers. He had also started attending classes at the first modern Arab University—now Cairo University—as soon as it was founded in 1908. There he was influenced by Orientalists such as Santillana and especially Carlo Nallino. And in 1914, he defended a doctoral thesis on the eleventh-century poet al-Maʿarrī and became the University's first graduate.

He also earned a scholarship to France, first to Montpellier, then to the Sorbonne. The doctorate he was awarded in 1918, followed by the Doctorat d'État in 1919, was for a dissertation on the fourteenth-century historian Ibn Khaldūn, but he had also studied literature with Gustave Lanson.

His exposure to Western culture had been such that he came to regard Paris as having not only inherited but also improved upon the status that Athens had in the ancient world. He had also married, in 1917, the Frenchwoman who had been engaged as his reader, and was to pay many tender tributes to her in his later writing.

Taha-Husayn's Public Career

On his return, Taha was appointed to the chair of Ancient History in his home university. This led him to stress the Hellenistic contribution to Islamic thought, and in 1925 he published a book entitled *Leaders of Thought*, which summed up human history in terms of the gradual ascendancy of the Greek mind, characterized as democratic and rational, over the Oriental mind, described as autocratic and religious.

He was no less controversial in his many articles on contemporary social and political issues. His stance was primarily that of a secularist, for without ever downplaying the value of a faith to the individual, he vehemently opposed the interference of religious authorities in State business. He was also a doughty proponent of democracy and of liberalism, although at a time when the majority of the population was illiterate, he shared with the educated élite to which he belonged the assumption that democracy would be realized by the enlightened few exercising power on behalf of the many. And on the cultural front, he fought a running battle with conservatives who contended that their heritage had no need of foreign transplants or even of neologisms.

The irony was that his own abiding love was for classical Arabic literature. For many years beginning in 1922, he ran a weekly column entitled *Wednesday Chats*—an echo of Sainte-Beuve's *Causeries du Lundi*—in most of which he cast a modernist's light on some great writing of the past.

Taha-Husayn's transfer to the Chair of Arabic in 1925 seemed auspicious, but within a year he precipitated a major crisis by publishing *On Pre-Islamic Poetry*. His thesis there—presented with all the trappings of a scholarly apparatus—was that

the corpus of magnificent ancient odes long esteemed as the spinal cord of all Arabic literature was almost entirely forged in early Islamic times. There was a furious reaction from many who felt that their forefathers had been traduced. He was most vulnerable in that he adduced religious motives among the reasons for the fabrications, one of which was the desire to substantiate such "Islamic myths" as that Abraham and Ishmael had resided in Mecca.

Taha was tried for apostasy but cleared. The book was banned, but he reissued it with some additions and some cosmetic changes as *On Pre-Islamic Literature*. He continued to advance in university service until 1932 when, having clashed with the government of the day over a matter of academic independence, the controversy was revived, he was dismissed from his post and banned from lecturing. He was reduced to severe straits for some two years, after which he was back in government service, as a high official in the Ministry of Education, until 1944.

By then Taha-Husayn was widely recognized as the leader of the modernist movement, a movement which he characterized as aiming at renovation rather than innovation, arguing that in learning from the West his contemporaries were following the example of their forefathers who had borrowed freely from Greek thought. And in a book that grew out of official reports on state education, *The Future of Culture in Egypt* (1938), he asserted that Egypt was not an Oriental country but a Mediterranean one.

This was also a time when a growing number of Arab modernists produced books that dealt sympathetically with Islamic themes. They may have been motivated by the realization that frontal attacks on religious sentiment were counterproductive, but the direction taken reflected not so much a retreat from secularism as confidence that their views now commanded a ready response from the reading public. Taha himself took to retelling stories of early Muslims in a series entitled *On the Margin of the [Prophet's] Life*, possibly imitating Jules Lemaître's *En Marge des Vieux Livres*. He explicitly stated, however, that his aim was to entertain and edify, but not to back the belief-system underlying these stories.

On the other hand, he was increasingly distressed to see that years of parliamentary government had brought little relief from the misery of the masses. In 1945 he founded a publishing concern called *The Egyptian Scribe*, which brought out a journal of the same name and a great many valuable books. It is probably because his own writing laid such stress on the plight of the poor that he was suspected of Communist sympathies, and he was forced to close the enterprise down in 1948. But all along— although not as loftily paternalistic as his friend Tawfīq al-Hakīm (q.v.)—he had based his hopes of social justice on the altruistic motivation of an enlightened élite. This was made even clearer in the 1950's when he conducted his last polemic against Marxist writers whose benevolent aims he shared, but whose doctrines conflicted with his liberalism.

In the meantime, the main nationalist party, the Wafd, had its last taste of power from January 1950 to January 1952. Although Taha-Husayn was not a member of it, he was appointed Minister of Education and he not only gave effect to his persistent call for a free pre-university education available to all, but also greatly extended higher education, and founded an Islamic Institute in Madrid and a chair of Arabic in Athens.

Although poor in health, he remained active mainly in journalism. After the monarchy had been swept away, he edited the newspaper *al-Jumhūriyya* (*The Republic*) until 1964.

Taha-Husayn's Literary Output

For all his involvement in public affairs, it is as a writer that Taha-Husayn is most highly rated. At a time when the literates were few but avid for new material, only the most prolific and versatile achieved a literary reputation. His output, including translations, amounted to more than 1,500 articles and some seventy books, several of these being reprinted articles. Their subjects ranged from histories of the first four Caliphs to summaries of French plays.

It is not profundity or even total consistency that one has a right to expect in all these works, but what does run through them is a lively curiosity, constant intellectual vigor, and a compelling style. The long-standing dichotomy of spoken and written Arabic made language a central issue for modern men of letters. In this respect, Taha-Husayn was an uncompromising traditionalist, tolerating no departure from the grammar of the classical language, but making full use of the plasticity of its morphology to adapt it to modern needs, and using it with unfailing elegance and power.

Taha-Husayn's Narratives

Taha-Husayn achieved a signal success with a lightly fictionalized account of his childhood entitled *The Days*, which he dictated in nine days and published serially in 1927. Suffused with the emotions of a blind village boy, adventurous and self-assertive but deeply vulnerable, the book was immediately hailed as a masterpiece, and was the first sample of modern Arabic literature to be translated into a number of world languages. This was followed in 1932 by a second volume covering his days at the Azhar. Much later, he wrote a record of his student days in France in a volume first published serially in 1955 and as a book in 1967. He called it simply *Reminiscences*, but critics and editors refer to it as the third volume of *The Days*, although it is of a different character.

The success of the first volume may well have given a fillip to the development of the Arabic novel. The genre had no roots in earlier Arabic literature. Its transplantation started with translations mainly from the French from the middle of the nineteenth century. Attempts at original novels were made now and then, but not until the early 1930's did the movement gather momentum, and the earliest practicioners drew heavily on autobiographical material.

Taha-Husayn himself was one of these pioneers, soon transcending the reliance on personal experience in six novels written between 1935 and 1944. His talent was not for inventing and sustaining a cohesive plot, but he was sufficiently innovative to make his mark on the history of the genre. His

Dreams of Shahrazad, for example, was the first use of the heroine of the *Arabian Nights* (which is a folk text despised by the establishment) to preach a modern message, here the duties of rulers towards their subjects. A curiosity is his *The Lost Love*, a rather hackneyed plot, but unique in that the setting and the characters are French and have no bearing on Arab social problems. On the contrary, *The Call of the* [mythical bird] *Karawān*, confronts as few others have dared the code of honor which demands the slaughter of any woman who defies sexual conventions. In the novel, the victim is a peasant girl who, because of her father's scandalous life, is reduced to working as a housemaid and is seduced by her employer, and so is killed by her uncle. Her sister then tries to avenge her by getting her seducer to fall in love with her, and then denying him; but the outcome is that they fall in love with each other, and find they must redeem the sin together. Social reality is ignored, but some poetry is achieved.

Taha-Husayn's Criticism of Literature

It is through his many studies of literature that Taha-Husayn proved most influential.

It is remarkable that not one of the writers who rose to prominence in the first half of the twentieth century produced a book on aesthetics or literary theory. The only systematic presentations were in translations of such books as Winchester's *Principles of Literary Criticism*, illustrated with samples of Arabic writing. The momentum was for trying out new ideas, not for taking them to pieces. Taha's literary creed therefore has to be extracted painstakingly from a succession of individual studies.

His earliest books trumpet the conviction that everything in literature is open to scientific analysis, but as he tackled one literary phenomenon after another, he found the theory applicable only to such limited areas as the study of a writer's background or the reconstruction and elucidation of a text. His ultimate stance seems to have been formed in 1936 when, having dictated a large book on the tenth-century poet al-Mutanabbi, he found himself recording different opinions from the ones he had started with. Criticism, he concluded, reflected nothing more than moments in one writer's life when he concerned himself with moments in another writer's consciousness.

This extreme subjectivity, however, does not negate the value of his applied criticism. His ventures into problems of literary history were not lacking in scholarly rigor, and the personal literary taste on which he ultimately relied in his aesthetic evaluations was always worthy of attention. His taste had taken shape at the height of a romantic wave given momentum by the West, and he never formulated a criterion for literary quality other than the capacity to stir the reader's emotions; but it was also a taste informed by wide and deep immersion in the Arab/Islamic heritage, and vitalized by an insatiable curiosity and a lively mind.

From his scattered writings one could compile, if not a complete and authoritative history of Arabic literature past and present, at least a vast survey in which each major issue in every age has received sharp scrutiny leading to a thought-provoking conclusion. One may instance his book on pre-Islamic literature, the scholarly value of which has been obscured by the debate on religious issues. Its conclusions are overstated and its argumentation is skewed by the fact that little was then known of oral composition; but it does present solid reasons for suspecting that the record has been tampered with, if only to eradicate traces of paganism.

It is unfortunate that the nature of the material and the diffusion of its presentation has made his most important contribution unattractive to translators, so that it is for his lesser works of fiction that he is known to the non-specialist reader.

Taha-Husayn's Standing

Taha-Husayn has not lacked honors, however. Under the monarchy, he earned the titles first of Bey then of Pasha, and under the Republic he was awarded, in 1965, the state's highest decoration. Internationally, too, he received honorary doctorates from several European universities, and the Légion d'Honneur from France. In 1949, he was nominated by André Gide for the Nobel prize. And one day before his death, he received the United Nations' Rights of Man prize.

In his time, he was a charismatic figure. Since then, his standing has suffered somewhat at the hands of intellectuals committed to a socialist ideology, accustomed to tighter theoretic thinking, and irritated by what seems to them excessive adulation of the West. They would do well to remember that he waged costly fights for the freedoms they now take for granted, that he helped to sweep away an attachment to superannuated values, and that he opened out the very paths along which they wish to advance further.

PIERRE CACHIA

Further Reading

Translations

as-Safi, A. B., trans. *The Call of the Curlew*. Leiden: Brill, 1980.

Cragg, Kenneth, trans. [Autobiography] III. *A Passage to France*. Leiden: Brill, 1976.

Glazer, S., trans. *The Future of Culture in Egypt*. Washington, D.C.: American Council of Learned Societies, 1954.

Magdi Wahba, trans. *The Dreams of Scheherezade*. Cairo: General Egyptian Book Organization, 1980.

Paxton, E. H., trans. [Taha-Husayn's autobiography] I. *An Egyptian Childhood*. London: Routledge, 1932; Heinemann, 1981.

Wayment, Hilary, trans. [Autobiography] II. *The Stream of Days*. Cairo: Anglo-Egyptian, 1943.

Related Studies

Cachia, Pierre. *Taha Husayn: His Place in the Egyptian Literary Renaissance*. London: Luzac, 1956. Written before any book on modern Arabic literature had appeared in English, this study stresses Taha-Husayn's representative quality in modernism.

Malti-Douglas, Fedwa. *Blindness and Autobiography*. Princeton: Princeton University Press, 1988. Limited almost entirely to material in the autobiography.

Semah, David. *Four Egyptian Literary Critics*. Leiden: Brill, 1974. Provides a useful basis for a comparison of Taha-Husayn with his contemporaries.

THE WORKS OF TAWFĪQ AL-ḤAKĪM

Author: Tawfīq al-Ḥakīm (also transliterated as Tewfik el-hakeem)
Born: ?1898, Alexandria, Egypt
Died: 1987, Cairo, Egypt
Major Works: *The Men of the Cave* (1933), *Shahrazad* (1934), *The Maze of Justice* (1937), *Pygmalion* (1942), *The Sultan's Dilemma* (1960), *The Tree Climber* (1962)

Major Themes

The function of the intellectual is that of an oracle.
Ideologies are best realized by well-intentioned individuals.

Various dates, some as late as 1903, have been given for Tawfiq al-Hakim's birth, and he admitted to having used different ones in different contexts; but in later years—perhaps glorying in his continued vigor—he opted for the earliest.

His father was a judge and a landowner and his mother shared in the widespread notion that her family, being of Turkish and perhaps ultimately of Persian extraction, was a cut above people of pure Egyptian stock. Initially, Tawfiq had only a scrappy education in Koranic schools, and he entered the regular state school system only when he was ten. His record there was undistinguished, and—already anonymously active in the theater—he barely scraped through the courses of the Faculty of Law of the Egyptian University. In 1925, his father sent him to Paris to study for a Doctorate of Law, but he devoted more of his energies to the theater and to music, and three years later he returned without the degree. He occupied a succession of governmental positions in the administration of justice and in the Ministries of Education and of Social Affairs. By 1943, however, he had made enough of a literary reputation to concentrate on writing, only intermittently holding state and honorific appointments between 1951 and 1960.

Al-Hakim's Guiding Principles

During the nineteenth and twentieth centuries, almost all the Arab countries came under the rule of one Western European power or another. The humiliation was resented, but especially as Arab/Islamic culture had been at a low ebb before, the intellectuals of al-Hakim's generation acquired an unmeasured admiration for the ways of their conquerors. They saw salvation in the emulation of a West that appeared to them uniformly dedicated to democracy, science, and rationalism, and they slipped easily into the role of guardians and apostles to the masses. Within this idealistic élite, al-Hakim was one of the most Olympian.

He professed what he called a philosophy of equilibrium between many forces, but mainly between humanism and spirituality and between idealism and pragmatism. He paid passing tribute to Islamic thinkers for having maintained such a balance, but the periods of human development that shaped his thinking were the Greek and the modern. His concept of spirituality was never elaborated into more than "a sense that we are not alone in the universe." His ultimate trust seems to have been in the perceptions of the intellectual (for whom he uses, seemingly interchangeably, the terms "artist," "thinker," or "man of knowledge"), for he pictured him as entirely devoted to liberty and to truth. He often spoke of the artist in monastic terms, at one time contending that he should not marry unless it be to an utterly self-denying woman who accepted the primordiality of art in his life—he himself did not marry until 1943. The social role he assigned to the artist/thinker was therefore that of an oracle.

Al-Hakim's Political Stance

It follows that, unlike most major writers of his generation, he kept aloof from practical politics. At one time he advised students given to noisy demonstrations to "leave politics to the politicians," and indeed entitled one collection of essays "From the Ivory Tower" (1941). Yet when attacked by Marxist critics he asserted that he was a "committed" writer.

The paradox can be resolved only by a close reading of his many creative works. In a novel entitled *The Return of the Spirit* (1933), he had drawn a parallel with the story of Osiris to celebrate the 1919 revolution against British rule as a manifestation of Egypt's eternal spirit. Yet he saw nationalism as a kind of collective selfishness. As early as 1941, he asserted that socialism had to be an element in any modern form of government. Yet he deemed it realizable only on an international scale. He trumpeted his attachment to democracy, strongly backing the Allies throughout the Second World War despite France's and Britain's imperialistic record. But in the mechanics of the parliamentary system he saw only a fit instrument for producing unfit rulers. He was deeply suspicious of politicians who courted the thinker not for his guidance but for his backing, so that even when the highest state honors were offered to him, he refused to meet President Nasser even socially. He said of democracy—as he might have said of the other ideologies he seemed to embrace—that he subscribed to it only as a principle dwelling in the heart of every being who values the Rights of Man, freedom, and human dignity. As for his "commitment," it consisted of his proclamation of the truths vouchsafed to him in the expectation that they would be heeded, for ultimately his hope was for a benevolent ruler, a king willing to be guided by the philosopher.

For a while after the 1952 revolution, he believed that Nasser was one such man of destiny, but by the 1960's he was expressing his disappointment in veiled terms, and in 1974 he published a sweeping denunciation in a document he entitled *The Return*

of Consciousness (as an echo to his earlier *The Return of the Spirit*), for he retained an attachment to the 1919 Revolution as a genuine spurt forward animating the whole of Egypt but let down by those who should have sustained it; whereas he saw its 1952 successor as flawed from the start, an attempt to create an Egypt molded by the state.

It is no doubt because of this that, whereas in 1955, in an epilogue to his play *Isis*, he forecast that by the end of the century well-intentioned men of learning would be asserting themselves against manipulating politicians, less than fifteen years later his pronouncements carried a note of such bitterness that he viewed the whole of his career as little more than "ink on paper."

It is clearly not in his theoretic thinking that his significance lies, but in this he was not alone. His entire generation was caught in a torrent of ready-made ideas and ideologies that had the momentum of Western prosperity and success behind them, and which threatened to sweep away all the edifices of the inherited culture. Survival seemed to call for open-mindedness and adaptability, and for courage, initiative, and vigor in carving new channels. These qualities al-Hakim had in abundance. His writings—which include journalistic articles, autobiographical and philosophic essays, criticism, fiction, and plays—have been estimated to run to 13,000 pages, his most lasting contributions being to the theater and to a lesser extent to the development of the Arabic novel.

Al-Hakim's Novels

Arabic literature remained strongly rooted in the Koranic language even after this had ceased to be the medium of everyday communication. For this and for other reasons, the Arab literary establishment was for many centuries elitist and conservative, ignoring or despising folk compositions couched in the regional vernaculars. Storytelling of the kind exemplified in the *Arabian Nights* was deemed frivolous, and although a handful of individuals wrote serious works in the form of a sustained narrative, only a kind of short, mannered tale providing a framework for displays of verbal agility gained acceptance as a genre within the canon.

Not until the middle of the nineteenth century did French and English fiction reach the small minority of literates in the Arab world. The journals that proliferated then easily accommodated translations, adaptations, and increasingly sophisticated imitations of short stories. The novel—more demanding of sustained invention and of space—followed a parallel but somewhat slower development. A few isolated attempts were made early in the twentieth century to root the genre in the realities of Arab life, but it is not until the 1930's that the movement gained breadth and continuity, mostly at the hands of men already well established as writers who tended to fictionalize their own experiences.

Tawfiq al-Hakim was one of these pioneers. His first novel, *The Return of the Spirit* (1933), justifies its title only in the last two chapters, which exalt in vibrant terms the 1919 Revolution in which the author played a minuscule part. The bulk of the book is a zestful, amusing, and convincing depiction of the chaotic household of Cairene relatives with whom he lodged during his secondary school days. *Bird from the East* (1938) is based on his student days in Paris, and gives him ample scope for comparisons of Eastern and Western cultures. But most impressive of all is *The Diary of a Rural Prosecutor* (1937), which drew on his early professional experience. Translated by the Israeli statesman Abba Eban as *The Maze of Justice*, it is a lifelike, compassionate (if paternalistic) series of vignettes of village life, of lasting value both as a social document and as a narrative.

It is, however, al-Hakim's contribution to dramatic literature—substantial, varied, lively, inventive, and boldly experimental—that has proved seminal.

Al-Hakim's Plays

Dramatic presentations, mainly in the form of puppet shows and shadow plays, had long been known to the Arabs but only at the folk level, and virtually no texts survived. In this as in other cultural activities, it was the example of Europe that led to new developments. A play loosely modeled on Molière's *L'Avare* is known to have been staged in Beirut in 1847, and thereafter several acting companies are known to have been active. The early start is deceptive, however, for the theater was viewed as mere entertainment, with singing one of the main ingredients. Even in the twentieth century, the only shows viable without state patronage were musicals, comedies, and melodramas. Plays were mostly the property of actors/managers. Their authorship was often unacknowledged, and the texts were hardly ever published. Certainly no one acquired a literary reputation mainly as a playwright.

Nevertheless, while still a schoolboy Tawfiq al-Hakim was enthralled by the theater and the cinema, and as soon as he could he mingled with actors, musicians, and producers. He joined the ranks of writers who transformed foreign plays to suit local mores and tastes and who often drew their material from synopses published in *La Petite Illustration*. He himself wrote several comedies which he sold outright to the 'Ukāsha Brothers' company, and at least one operetta. In his maturer years, he did not deem any of these worthy of publication, but the stagecraft he acquired in this period remained a live element in his art.

It was during his student days in Paris that he discovered the full potential of the theater, and on his return, with the express purpose of raising the writing of plays to a literary level, he published a series of works which he described as "cerebral," in that the dramatic tension in them was in a conflict of ideas, not of characters. The first, *The Men of the Cave* (1933), took its title from a brief Koranic reference to the seven sleepers of Ephesus and deals with the difficulties that men who have slept for three hundred years have in adjusting to a changed society. It was chosen as the inaugural production of the state-financed National Troupe in 1935, but it flopped. Al-Hakim nevertheless persisted with a string of plays which lent themselves to different interpretations, but in all of which one may detect some facet of the clash between what he often called the Real—this being the intellectual's perception of what is ultimately valid—and the Actual, as in his *Shahrazād* (1934) which portrays the Sultan as being diverted from his quest for perfection, or in *Pygmalion* (1942), in which Galatea, having come to life, has to cope with petty household chores. He asserted that these were to be read, not acted, in the same breath implying that this was mainly because the Egyptian public had too brief an acquaintance with the theater to savor such abstractions.

Yet no contemporary had a keener feeling for the stage. He brought to his writing not only immense energy and inventiveness, but also boldness in the choice of themes—he dared to review the life of the Prophet in *Muhammad* (1936)—and a readiness for experimentation.

Nowhere is the gulf between the literary language and the idiom of everyday speech more troublesome than in the theater, and he tried his hand at texts that can be read as either, but this entailed the avoidance of some functional constructions. Instead, in the bulk of his writing, although he did not object to producers translating him into the local vernacular, he remained faithful to the demands of classical grammar yet in a deceptively simple, flowing style in which his ever-present humor sat comfortably.

Most accessible to a wide public were his many social and political satires. A wry idea was developed in *The Anxiety Bank* (1967), a bank in which people are invited to trade in the commonest commodity of all, anxiety! Unfortunately, this was also a none too successful attempt to marry the novel and the play forms by having narrative passages alternating with dialogue. More impressive was the straight drama of *Song of Death* (1950), which dealt with the vendetta, still in honor in rural Egypt. Here a village woman is eagerly awaiting the day when her son would be old enough to avenge his father's murder, only to find herself in conflict with the lad who, blessed with a better education, has outgrown such a primitive impulse.

Of his political plays, *Soft Hands* (1954) was intended to glorify honest labor under the repub-

lican regime, and its premiere in 1957 was attended by President Nasser. It throws together two drones: a *ci-devant* prince who has never had to do anything useful, and a scholar too highly specialized for any job available. They are rescued by a successful young industrialist who considers his fortune a trust to be used for the benefit of his workers, and who finds outlets for their unsuspected abilities.

Except for such direct commentaries on society or politics, few of al-Hakim's plays have a realistic present-day setting. When they are not projected into the historical past or into a legendary realm, they take us—as in *The Fate of a Cockroach* (1966)—into the perceptions of insects who cannot conceive of higher beings than themselves and therefore interpret the world in terms of their needs, or—as in *Journey to the Future* (1958)—to outer space where a man who lands on a planet discovers that mere contact with the soil provides him with sufficient energy to maintain life, so he realizes that once our physical needs are met the only values remaining are the emotional ones that are satisfied by art.

As in *Soft Hands*, many of al-Hakim's plays begin with a piquant and intriguing situation, although the denouement is sometimes arbitrary. So it is with *The Sultan's Dilemma* (1960), where a mameluke, having inherited the throne from his master, discovers that he was not properly manumitted and is therefore not fit to rule. He arranges to be sold by auction on the understanding that his new master will then free him, only to be bought by a woman who is reputed to be a brothel-keeper and who insists that he spend a night in her establishment. It turns out, however, that she is a maligned patroness of the arts who does the honorable thing by him. This, al-Hakim said, was intended as a warning to President Nasser not to set power over the rule of law.

Belonging to the same period are experimental plays bearing some kinship with absurdism, such as *The Tree Climber* (1962). This takes its title from a piece of folk nonsense verse, and among its bewildering characters is a green lizard that lives under an orange tree, and a man whose first wife had a stillborn child and whose second wife he murders. Al-Hakim himself insisted that it was absurd in form only, being intended to waken the people to the lack of direction that had crept into their lives, and although it has caused much puzzlement it is capable of allegorical interpretation, the two marriages representing the revolutions of 1919 and 1952, and the lizard being Egypt's eternal spirit.

The sheer verve and competence of al-Hakim's many writings have made him one of the major figures of Arab modernism. Although his idealism may have been outgrown, it fired a generation (which included the young man who was to become President Nasser) whose greatest need was to cope with a wrenching change of cultural direction. The liveliness and originality of al-Hakim's plots have made him the most lavishly translated of modern Arab authors, and more than any other single force he has brought about the acceptance of drama into the Arabic literary canon, and his own admission to the Egyptian Academy in 1951.

PIERRE CACHIA

Further Reading

Translations

Cachia, Pierre, trans. *The Prison of Life*. Cairo: American University in Cairo Press, 1992.

Eban, A. S., trans. *The Maze of Justice*. London: Harvill Press, 1947; Austin: University of Texas Press, 1989.

Hassan El-Mougy, Ibraham, trans. *Muhammad.*

Cairo: Supreme Council for Islamic Affairs, [1964].

Hutchins, William, trans. *Plays, Prefaces and Postscripts of Tawfiq al-Hakim*. Vol. I: *Theater of the Mind*; Vol. II: *Theater of Society*. Washington, D.C.: Three Continents Press, 1981, 1984.

————. *The Return of the Spirit*. Washington, D.C.: Three Continents Press, 1990.

Johnson-Davies, Denys, trans. *The Fate of a Cockroach: Four Plays of Freedom*. London: Heinemann, 1973.

————. *The Tree Climber*. Oxford: Oxford University Press, 1966.

Winder, Bayly, trans. *Bird from the East*. Beirut: Khayat, 1967.

Winder, R. Bayly, trans. *The Return of Consciousness*. London: Macmillan, 1984.

Yousef, Riad Habib, trans. *Conversation with the Planet Earth; The World is a Comedy*. Cairo: General Egyptian Book Organization, 1985.

Related Studies

Cachia, Pierre. *An Overview of Modern Arabic Literature*. Edinburgh University Press, 1990. Chapter nine examines in detail al-Hakim's idealism and ideology.

Long, Richard. *Tawfiq al-Hakim: Playwright of Egypt*. London: Ithaca Press, 1979. Contains synopses of many plays.

Starkey, Paul. *From the Ivory Tower*. London: Ithaca Press, 1987. A largely negative evaluation of al-Hakim.

THE NOVELS AND STORIES OF SADEQ HEDAYAT

Author: Sadeq Hedayat
Born: February, 1903, Tehran, Iran
Died: April, 1951, Paris, France
Major Works: *Buried Alive* (short stories) (1930), *Three Drops of Blood* (short stories) (1932), *Chiaroscuro* (short stories) (1933), *Mrs. Alaviyyeh* (novel) (1933), *Mr. Bow Wow* (satirical sketches), *The Blind Owl* (novel) (1937), *The Stray Dog* (short stories) (1942), *Haji Aqa* (novel) (1945), *Parvin, Daughter of Sasan* (drama) (1930), *Maziyar* (drama) (1933)

Major Themes

Life is a prison where we are all alone; we should not be deceived.
Death is the final asylum from the pains, sorrows, troubles, and the injustices of life.
Faith, morals, and religion are the products of hypocrisy.

Sadeq Hedayat is considered to be the most significant writer of modern Persian prose fiction. He was born into an illustrious aristocratic family that had furnished the government with eminent officials for more than a century. He attended the Western-oriented Dar al-Fonun (Iran's first modern college) and was then educated at the French St. Louis High School where he became acquainted with French language and literature. In 1923 he published *Omar Khayyam's Quatrains*. Although this booklet is not stylistically representative of Hedayat's prose, it indicates his interest in Khayyam's religious skepticism even at this early age. In Khayyam, Hedayat found confirmation of his own cynicism, which remained with him all through his literary career.

In 1926, he went to Europe on a government scholarship to continue his studies. He began to study dentistry in Belgium but he shortly gave up, and he then went to France to pursue his studies in engineering, which he also abandoned to pursue his interests in literature. A vegetarian himself, he published *The Merits of Vegetarianism* in 1927. His compassion towards suffering animals was the reason for his predisposition to vegetarianism. Hedayat's remarkable humanity can readily be perceived from his works as early as 1924, when he wrote the schoolboy-like pamphlet *Man and Animal*, criticizing the cruel treatment of animals. In one of his best short stories, "The Stray Dog" (1942), Hedayat's description of the emotions of a dog who loses his owner and is driven to take his own life, clearly discloses his humaneness:

> There was a human soul in the depth of his eyes ... not only were his eyes similar to a human's but a kind of equality could be seen.... [I]n his new life of pain and torment, he needed endearment more than ever before.... He looked into every eye but saw nothing but spite and wickedness in them.

> (SAATI, TRANS.)

In 1927, he also wrote "Death," a two-page article praising the virtues of death. Hedayat's morbid interest in death pervades almost all of his future writings. Around the same time he attempted to drown himself in a river, from which he was rescued. He remained irresistibly attracted to suicide and death. "Buried Alive" (1930), the story of a Persian student abroad, succinctly reveals Hedayat's interpretation of the subject:

> All men fear death, but I fear my tenacious life.... No one simply makes up his mind to commit suicide. Suicide is only for certain people. It is in their nature and constitution, and they cannot shirk it off. It is destiny that directs, but, at the same time, it is I who have shaped my own destiny. I can no longer es-

cape from its grasp. I cannot flee from myself. At any rate, what can be done? Destiny is stronger than I.

(BRYANT, TRANS.; HILLMAN, 1978)

Fatalism is another dominant theme in Hedayat's writings. His typical stories have a pathetic end: if the characters do not die a natural death, they either commit suicide or are murdered. By making their fate seem inevitable, Hedayat validates his belief in predestination. In the short story "Dead End" (1942), the protagonist Sharif's otherwise uneventful life is marked by two episodes: his best friend drowns in the sea before his eyes, and the same friend's son drowns in the pool of Sharif's house some twenty years later. Sharif confronts both tragedies with the fateful words: "Had to happen."

In 1930, Hedayat returned to Iran without an academic degree. Instead he had spent his time in the literary and intellectual circles of Paris and had formed friendships with people such as Jean Paul Sartre. The value of his time in Europe is best judged by the extraordinary outburst of creativity upon his return to Iran. Between the years of 1930 and 1951, when he went back to Europe, he published some forty short stories, two short novels, a novelette, two historical dramas, a satirical puppet play, a travelogue, collections of satirical parodies and sketches, studies in Persian folklore, translations from Middle Persian and French, a number of articles on Persian literature, and two short stories in French.

Hedayat refused to take advantage of his aristocratic connections and chose low-level government employment throughout his life. His writing was in fact subordinate to his office job, as was the case for the majority of Persian writers. Soon Hedayat became a central figure in Tehran literary circles. Along with three other young Western-educated intellectuals, he formed the group known as "the Four." As Jennati Ataii has explained, the Four distinguished itself from the conservative literary circles in its attempt to discover what the Iranian people were actually saying and wanting and how

their language reflected these concerns, while the conservatives were becoming more and more incomprehensible.

The struggle against the traditional pompous style had begun in 1921 with Mohammad Ali Jamalzadeh's collection of short stories, *Once Upon a Time*. The book inaugurated a new era in Persian prose fiction in two respects: its use of colloquial language as a medium, and its use of fiction as a form. What began with Jamalzadeh, Hedayat perfected only a decade later and created, as Yarshater writes (see Further Reading), "almost singlehandedly a written dialect responsive to the rhythms and diction of spoken Persian."

One of Hedayat's most outstanding innovations was the use of the distinct style of speaking peculiar to his characters, whoever they were and wherever they came from. For the greater part his characters are the poor and the depraved. Hedayat had the remarkable ability to penetrate their lives and engage the reader in their pain and suffering.

"The Elder Sister" (1930) is the story of an unattractive sister who is enraged with jealousy when her younger sister, a housemaid, decides to get married to the servant in the house where she worked. On their wedding night, she drowns herself.

In "Davud, the Hunchback" (1930) Hedayat depicts a poor, lonely cripple who has been ridiculed and rejected by everyone. He finally seeks comfort in the companionship of a stray dog, but returns only to find that the dog has died.

When Hedayat depicts the middle class, he depicts persons in some way deformed, superficial, and confused in a period of rapid Westernization. The characters usually commit suicide or end up insane.

Persian Folklore

Hedayat's attention to the lower strata of society led to his interest in folklore. He is considered a major figure in the revival of interest in Persian folklore. He was the first to methodically collect and publish popular local songs, beliefs, tales, superstitions, and traditions of the Iranian people, thereby attaching great significance to ancient practices. His major work in this field was *Nayrangestan* (Persian Folklore) (1933). Folklore served him as a example of what he regarded as a purer Iranian culture. Love of ancient Persian culture is a key element in his works. However, his nationalism is peculiar in the sense that his extreme devotion to anything Persian is on the one hand nostalgic, and on the other hand focused on his hatred of Arabs and Islam, which he blamed for having uprooted the noble culture of ancient Persia.

Hedayat's contempt for present-day standards of morality is clearly evident throughout his works. In *Mrs. Alavtyyeh* (1933), a novelette in dialogue form, Hedayat exposes the moral depravity of a group of supposedly pious pilgrims whose language is imbued with obscenity and religious superstition. Religious hypocrisy is the theme of "Asking Absolution" (1932), in which three passengers of a caravan on their way to a pilgrimage make cynical confessions to each other. A woman who has murdered her husband's second wife and her two infants is comforted by a fellow traveler: "Did you not hear from the pulpit that as soon as the pilgrims specify their intention and set out, they become chaste and purified even if the number of their sins is as many as the leaves of a tree?" (Kamshad, trans., 1966).

Hedayat's nostalgia for the ancient Persian culture is manifest in his two historical dramas "Parvin, Daughter of Sasan" (1930) and "Maziyar" (1933), which concentrate on the theme of the defeat of the Persians by the Arabs.

The Blind Owl

Hedayat's romantic view of the past and his disgust with the present come together in a very unique manner in his masterpiece, *The Blind Owl* (1937). *The Blind Owl* is not only Hedayat's most important work, but is also regarded by many critics as the most remarkable piece of fiction in the Persian language.

In Hedayat's own words, the novel is "an historical fantasy." The narrator is a recluse who writes to introduce himself to his shadow; he calls himself a "blind owl." He gives two separate accounts of his life, one taking place in a fantasy world of the historical past, and one in the present day. The story has no proper sense of time or place. The reader is taken back and forth between two worlds with similar events and scenes. The characters seem like mirror images of three prototypes: the narrator, an ethereal woman, and an old man. In the first part, the "Blind Owl," the narrator, is a painter whose subject is always the same: an ethereal woman offering a lotus to an old man. One day the woman of his imagination appears at his doorway. She walks in, lies on his bed, and dies. The painter undresses and gets into bed:

> I wanted to warm her with the warmth of my own body, I wanted to give her the warmth of my body and take from her the coldness of death. . . . [H]er coldness penetrated the depth of my heart . . . I failed in all my attempts. No, it was not a lie. . . . She came here, in my bedroom, in my bed, and submitted her body to me. She gave me both her body and soul.
>
> (SAATI, TRANS.)

After painting her portrait, the painter cuts up the body and takes it to the graveyard.

In the second part of the novel, the Blind Owl is a convalescent who is desperately in love with his wife. Afraid of losing her, he takes her admirers to her. In the climactic scene, he makes love to her in the disguise of a grotesque old man whom he assumed to be her lover. He then kills her. Looking in the mirror he finds out that he has turned into the image of the grotesque man. He realizes that the life of ordinary people repels him: "Why should I think of them, the imbeciles who are healthy, eat well, sleep well, copulate well and have never felt a bit of my agonies?" (Kamshad, trans., 1966).

The philosophy of pessimism that this narrator expresses is very much like Hedayat's own, as can be seen in his personal letters and from many of his writings. It is for this reason that the book is considered to be a record of Hedayat's conversation with his inner self. This same sense of gloom, despair, and disgust pervades most of Hedayat's other stories—most prominently, his two surrealistic short stories: "Buried Alive" (1930) and "Three Drops of Blood" (1932).

Sexual frustration is a fundamental issue not only in *The Blind Owl* but in many other of Hedayat's stories. On the question of outside influences on *The Blind Owl*, the contemporary critic Michael C. Hillman writes: "To find Hedayat's source of inspiration in the East, we should familiarize ourselves with Khayyam and Buddha, who were always Hedayat's forerunners. On the other hand, to discover Western sources of his technique, we must turn to the simple realism of Chekhov, the inner vision of Rilke, and the fantasies of Edgar Allan Poe." (Hillman, 1978).

Haji Aqa

Hedayat's last works clearly reflect a change of mood. His childhood coincided with the turbulent years of the Constitutional Revolution of 1905–11 (during which a parliament and constitutional monarchy were established in Persia), which brought enduring social and cultural consequences. He witnessed the downfall of the Qajar dynasty and the accession of Reza Shah Pahlavi (1925), which marked an end to the liberal outbursts of the constitutional period and the beginning of a period of stern dictatorship.

Hedayat's writings of the period reflect the lost hopes of his generation, and he also criticizes the social and cultural conditions in his satirical works such as *Mr. Bow Wow* (1933). When nationalism became a tool for official propaganda, it disappeared from his works and is even disparaged by him.

With the abdication of Reza Shah in 1941, the rule of democracy was proclaimed. Hedayat's most representative work of this period, *Haji Aqa* (1945) is a masterpiece of sarcasm, showing glimpses of hope and even a renunciation of his fatalism.

Hedayat's last book, however, *The Message of Kafka* (1948) indicates that his depression and despair had set in again. In 1951, he went back to Paris, leaving a farewell note in which he had writ-

ten: "I left and broke your heart. See you on Doomsday. That's all." A Paris newspaper on April 10, 1951, read: "An Iranian called Sadeq Hedayat has committed suicide by opening the gas tap in his small flat. . . ."

Despite Hedayat's suicide, which symbolized his pervasive pessimism, he has survived as the most influential voice among present-day Persian writers.

PARGOL SAATI

Further Reading

Translations

Hedayat, Sadeq. *The Blind Owl.* D. P. Costello, trans. New York: Grove Weidenfeld, 1989.

———. *The Blind Owl and Other Hedayat Stories.* Iraj Bashiri, trans. Minneapolis, MN: Sorayya Publishers, 1984.

———. *Haji Agha: Portrait of an Iranian Confidence Man.* G. M. Wickens, trans. Austin, TX: University of Texas Press, 1979.

Yarshater, E. ed. *Sadeq Hedayat: An Anthology.* (*Modern Persian Literature Series, no. 2*), Boulder, CO: Westview, 1979. Includes "The Elder Sister" (translated as "The Spinster"), "Buried Alive," "Three Drops of Blood," and "Mrs. Alaviyyeh" (translated as "The Pilgrimage"), among others.

Related Studies

Beard, Michael. *Hedayat's "Blind Owl" as a Western Novel.* Princeton, NJ: Princeton University Press, 1990. Beard scrutinizes likely foreign literary sources of Hedayat's inspiration.

Hillman, Michael C. ed. *Hedayat's "The Blind Owl" Forty Years After.* Austin, TX: University of Texas Press, 1978. This volume contains essays interpreting *The Blind Owl* by reference to Hindu imagery, history, Khayyam, Buddha, a Jungian analysis, Oedipal features, and affinities with the Surrealists. The book also contains translations of "Three Drops of Blood" (translated by Guity Nashat and Marilyn Robinson

Waldman) and "Buried Alive" (translated by Carter Bryant), as well as of Al-e Ahmad's essay "The Hedayat of *The Blind Owl*."

Kamshad, Hassan. *Modern Persian Prose Literature*. Cambridge, England: Cambridge University Press, 1966. Pp. 135–208. Kamshad puts Hedayat into the context of modern Persian prose writing. He divides Hedayat's literary career into five stages: early years (1923–1930), creative period (1930–1937), barren period (1937–1941), period of high hopes (1941–1947), and the aftermath (1947–1951).

Katouzian, Homa. *Sadeq Hedayat: The Life and Literature of an Iranian Writer.* London: I.B. Tauris, 1991. The author offers a relatively detailed autobiographical sketch of the writer and relates *The Blind Owl* and other psycho-fictions of Hedayat to his personality.

Yarshater, E., ed. *Persian Literature. (Columbia Lectures on Iranian Studies*, no. 3.) Albany, NY: State University of New York Press, 1988. Pp. 318–335. An essay by Michael Beard puts Hedayat into the context of Persian prose fiction from 1921–1977. An essay by Ehsan Yarshater provides an appraisal of Hedayat's life and works.

THE NOVELS OF GHASSAN KANAFANI

Author: Ghassan Kanafani
Born: 1936, Acre
Died: 1972, Beirut
Major Novels: *Men in the Sun* (1962), *All That's Left to You* (1966), *Return to Haifa* (1969), *Umm Sa'ad* (1969)

Major Themes

Palestinian national liberation must be a democratic and secular struggle.
Cultural politics and the literature of resistance are part of the struggle for national liberation.
Exiles and refugees, like those Palestinians living under Israeli occupation, are crucial to an understanding of the contemporary Middle East.
A class analysis of the larger Arab world must be part of Palestinian liberation politics.

When Ghassan Kanafani was assassinated in a car bomb explosion in Beirut in July 1972, an explosion that also took the life of his young niece Lamees, an obituary in the *Daily Star* (a Beirut English-language newspaper) described him as the "commando who never fired a gun." The commemorative article went on, "His weapon was a ballpoint pen and his arena newspaper pages." In addition to his journalism and political writings, however, Kanafani was a major contributor to the development of the contemporary Arab and Palestinian narrative, as both a short story writer and a novelist.

As a journalist and critic, Kanafani played an important role in introducing new authors and their works to Arab readers. It was Kanafani as well who, in his study of the "literature of Resistance in Occupied Palestine" (1966), first employed the term "resistance" (*muqawama*) in speaking of Palestinian writing. His own fictional compositions, including both the short novel and the story as well as children's literature—the stories and poems composed for his niece Lamees—are widely recognized as a major contribution to modern Arabic literature. They offer, furthermore, an important critical perspective on contemporary literary criticism as practiced in the West. The stories, however, like Kanafani's other writings, address specifically the Palestinian situation. Kanafani described vividly the political, social and human realities which

continue still, more than two decades after his death, to characterize the lives of his people at a critical period in their history, at the acme of the struggle for decolonization and national liberation against a colonial regime, and when the traditional order and structures of Palestinian existence were being profoundly altered by these events on a regional and international scale. Kanafani's stories are stories of mothers in refugee camps who proudly send their sons to the *fedayeen* (or resistance fighters) and who visit them in the mountains with gifts of food from home, stories of fathers whose role of authority within the family is being threatened by the transformations in their social world, of children who learn early to fight for a place in that social order, of concern and love and fear among neighbors who feel threatened in their turn by strangers in their land.

Kanafani's own life, which is paralleled in his narratives, was not untypical of the lives of many Palestinians of his generation, the first generation to experience exile from their homeland. He lived his childhood in Palestine, in the seaside town of Acre, fleeing with his family in 1948 at the age of twelve, first to Lebanon and then to Syria, where he was educated in the refugee camps and the schools of UNRWA (United Nations Relief and Works Authority, established in 1950 to provide for the Palestinian refugees). From 1956 to 1960 he served his apprenticeship in the Gulf as an exiled Palestinian

547

teaching mathematics in the local schools of Kuwait. At the behest of George Habbash, a militant Palestinian leader in the Arab National Movement (ANM), he left Kuwait for Beirut where he spent the last eleven years of his life as a writer, editor, and participant in the activities of the Palestinian resistance movement. A member of the Popular Front for the Liberation of Palestine (PFLP) and founder and editor of its journal *Al-Hadaf* (*The Aim*), he was outspoken in policy debates and discussion of the goals and strategies of the resistance movement. After Kanafani was killed in 1972, the Ghassan Kanafani Cultural Foundation (GKCF) was established to administer his literary legacy. Kanafani's literary, political, and humanitarian concerns continue to influence Palestine's children in the kindergartens that the GKCF still operates in the Palestinian refugee camps in Lebanon.

Kanafani's stories present a Palestinian perspective, at once literary and politically informed, on a conflict that has anguished the Middle East and the Arab world for most of the twentieth century. While that conflict has had, and continues to have, many different and contested interpretations, readings that themselves often serve to reproduce the terms of the struggle, its chronology can be acknowledged in a sequence of key dates: 1917 and the Balfour Declaration, according to which the British government promised the Jews a home in the land of Palestine; 1936–39, the years of a major Palestinian revolt against both British occupation and Zionist settlement of that land; the creation of the state of Israel in 1948; the creation of the PLO in 1964; the June War of 1967 in which Israel defeated the Arab armies and occupied the West Bank and the Gaza Strip. Following Kanafani's death in 1972, the history would be punctuated by still further crises: the October War of 1973 in which Israel was again victorious; the Camp David Accords and Egypt's separate peace with Israel in 1978; the Israeli invasion of Lebanon in the summer of 1982; and the Palestinian intifada which began in December 1987. In September 1993, the Declaration of Principles was signed by Israel and the PLO, granting limited autonomy to a Palestinian authority in Jericho and the Gaza Strip.

Crucial to this Palestinian history also is a geography, the difference between the "inside" (*al-dakhil*) and the "outside" (*al-kharaj*), the distinction, that is, between exile (*manfa, ghurba*) and occupation (*ihtilal*), and the political imperatives and life experiences that characterize these two historic spaces. While Kanafani's stories and novels are radically determined by the pressures of exile, his three volumes of literary criticism were decisive in questioning this divide in the modern Palestinian narrative. *The Literature of Resistance in Occupied Palestine 1948–1966* (1966), *Palestinian Resistance Literature Under Occupation 1948–1968* (1968), and *On Zionist Literature* (1967) focussed unprecedented critical attention from the "outside" on the cultural practices that were evolving "inside," within Israel itself. But his stories took place, as they were written, in exile.

Men in the Sun

Men in the Sun was Kanafani's first novel. Published in 1962, it tells the story of three Palestinian refugees attempting to travel to Kuwait where they hope to find paid employment. Abu Qais, an elderly man with a family, Marwan, a young man whose brother is already in the Gulf but who has forgotten his mother and siblings at home, and Assad who is escaping an arranged marriage, all meet at a smuggler's office in the Iraqi capital of Baghdad. But the price demanded of them is too high for their meager resources, and eventually they arrange with Abul Khaizuran, a former Palestinian fighter who now drives a water truck for a Kuwaiti businessman, to transport them, desperately concealed in the truck's empty tank, across the Iraq-Kuwait border. At the first checkpoint, on the Iraqi side, they pass successfully, if nearly suffocated in the desert heat. The second checkpoint, however, proves fatal to the Palestinians' aspirations. Held up by the obscene banter of the border guards, Abul Khaizuran returns too late to his truck, only to find the three men dead. The story's final words, spoken by the truck driver as he disposes of the bodies on a rubbish heap, "Why didn't you knock on the sides of the tank? Why didn't you bang the sides of the tank? Why? Why? Why?" resonated loudly throughout the Arab world, and posed the urgent question of the historic and political fate of the Palestinan refugees. Made into a film, *Al Makhdu'un* (*The Duped*), ten years later by the Egyptian director Tawfiq Salih, the novel's controversial ending is just as controversially changed. The three men in the film do bang on the walls of the truck's water tank—but no one is there to hear them.

All That's Left to You

In 1966, Kanafani published a second novel, *All That's Left to You*. Hamid's family had been dispersed in the flight from Jaffa in 1948. His father dead, and his mother in Jordan, Hamid has been living with his sister Maryam, now pregnant and in an abusive marriage as second wife to Zakariyya, in a refugee camp in Gaza. Narrated in a self-consciously Faulkneresque stream of consciousness and presented in multiple typefaces, *All That's Left to You* tells the story of Hamid's conflicted struggle to cross the desert in the vain attempt to rediscover his mother in Amman. Alternating between Hamid's politically militant confrontation in the sands with an Israeli soldier encountered on his journey, and Maryam's resistance at home to her husband's faithlessness and brutality, the novel begins to engage both socially and symbolically the emergent issues of gender and sexuality and their place in a Palestinian ideology of national liberation.

Return to Haifa

Following the June 1967 war and Israel's occupation of the West Bank and the Gaza Strip, the border between Israel and the now Occupied Territories was opened. Palestinians who in 1948 had fled their homes in what was to become the state of Israel were allowed to visit their pasts. Such a visit is the occasion for Kanafani's novel *Return to Haifa*, published in 1969. Said S. and his wife Safiya, who have been living in Ramallah for the past twenty years, are seeing Haifa for the first time since they left in 1948. Their journey through the Mandelbaum Gate and across the borders takes place over a period of twenty-four hours, from 30 June to 1 July 1967. The history that they relive in the course of that day, however, is nearly two decades long. The husband and wife are returning to look for their son, Khaldun, left behind in the tumult of their flight, and the house they had once lived in. Said S. and Safiya find their house now inhabited by Miriam, the widow of Evrat Kushen, themselves both refugees from Nazi-occupied Poland. Their son, adopted by the Kushens when they were given the house by the Jewish Agency in Haifa, is now renamed Dov and is a recruit in the Israeli army. *Return to Haifa* is Kanafani's committed vision of a "democratic solution" for the future of Palestine, a vision that is suggested in the dramatic and painful encounter between father and son during that crucial visit to Haifa.

For Arabic literature, according to Edward Said, "the emphasis on scenes is intensified, is made more urgent, after 1948: a scene formally translated the critical issues at stake in the Arab world. This is not a matter of proving how literature or writing reflects life, nor is it confirmation of an allegorical interpretation of an Arab reality: for, unfortunately, these approaches to modern Arabic writing are endemic to most of the very scarce Western analyses of the literature. What is of greater interest is how the scene is itself the very problem of Arabic literature and writing after the disaster of 1948: the scene does not merely reflect the crisis, or historical duration, or the paradox of the present." Historically, the Palestinian scene in particular has been one of struggle, a struggle between two peoples for the possession of the scene, the space, the land and its past, present and future. Historical claims are offered in support of one side or the other, and the land itself is seen to be at stake in the storytelling competition: the desert, the city of Haifa, refugee camps. Although Kanafani's narratives are, on at least one level, politically motivated, they are neither tracts nor manifestos, but insist instead on the rigor of a socio-political analysis and the critically destabilizing possibilities inherent in stories and their telling for affecting the sense of an ending.

What the Story Meant

"To understand what the story meant from beginning to end" is the task the Palestinian child assigns himself in "The Land of Sad Oranges," an early story (1958) by Kanafani, in order to discover the answer to his dire question of "why we had become refugees." The Palestinian is himself, however, engaged in the historical project of writing that story. The narratives thus produced—like *Men in the Sun, All That's Left to You,* or *Return to Haifa,* as in Kanafani's other stories and unfinished novels—are seen to contribute to the historical record and to enter as well into the very events and significant moments of the life of the people: flight (*hurub*), exile (*ghurba, manfa*), resistance (*muqawama*), steadfastness (*sumud*), and ultimately the awaited return (*auda*) to Palestine. Kanafani not only describes the historical events and circumstances, but also provides a historical sense and identity for those who have lived them. *Um Sa'ad,* a collection of stories compiled in novel form, is based on his interviews and longtime friendship with an illiterate Palestinian woman from one of the Beirut camps. Told in her own language, *Um Sa'ad*'s narratives recount the struggles not only of a mother, but of a Palestinian living in the Lebanese capital, of women's waged work, and her sons' recruitment to the armed resistance. Kanafani, particularly during his years in Beirut, had spent much of his time receiving such visits from his compatriots living in the Palestinian refugee camps of Lebanon. Their stories, their memories, and their dreams, like those of *Um Sa'ad,* the "men

in the sun," Hamid and Said and Safiya, became part of his own literary and critical history of—and vision for—contemporary Palestine.

BARBARA HARLOW

Further Reading

Translations

Harlow, Barbara, trans. "Return to Haifa" in *Palestine's Children.* London: Heinemann; Cairo: Dar al-Fata al-Arabi; Washington D.C.: Three Continents Press, 1984.

Jayyusi, May, and Jeremy Reed, trans. *All That's Left to You: A Novella and Other Stories.* Austin, TX: University of Texas Press, 1990.

Kilpatrick, Hilary, trans. *Men in the Sun and Other Palestinian Stories.* London: Heinemann; and Washington D.C.: Three Continents Press, 1978.

"Um Sa'ad" and "Guns in the Camp." These stories from *Um Sa'ad* appear in *Men in the Sun and Other Palestinian Stories* and *Palestine's Children* (see above).

Further Reading

Kanafani, Anni. *Ghassan Kanafani.* Beirut: Near East Ecumenical Bureau, 1973.

Kilpatrick, Hilary. "Fiction and Tradition in the Fiction of Ghassan Kanafani," *Journal of Arabic Literature,* VII, 1976.

Said, Edward. "Introduction" to Halim Barakat, *Days of Dust.* Wilmette, IL: Medina University Press International, 1974.

Siddiq, Muhammad. *Man Is a Cause: Political Consciousness and the Fiction of Ghassan Kanafani.* Seattle: University of Washington Press, 1984.

Wild, Stefan. *Ghassan Kanafani: The Life of a Palestinian.* Wiesbaden: Otto Harrassowitz, 1975.

INDEX OF ARTICLES